INNOVATIVE CRYPTOGRAPHY

Second Edition

INNOVATIVE CRYPTOGRAPHY

Second Edition

NICK MOLDOVYAN

ALEX MOLDOVYAN

CHARLES RIVER MEDIA
Boston, Massachusetts

Cover Design: Tyler Creative

CHARLES RIVER MEDIA
25 Thomson Place
Boston, Massachusetts 02210
617-757-7900
617-757-7969 (FAX)
crm.info@thomson.com
www.charlesriver.com

This book is printed on acid-free paper.

Nick Moldovyan. *Innovative Cryptography.*
ISBN: 1-58450-467-6

Library of Congress Cataloging-in-Publication Data
Moldovyan, Alex.
Innovative cryptography / A. Moldovyan and N. Moldovyan. -- 2nd ed.
p. cm.
Includes bibliographical references and index.
ISBN 1-58450-467-6 (pbk. : alk. paper) 1. Data encryption (Computer science)
2. Telecommunication--Security measures. 3. Cryptography. I. Moldovyan, Nick. II. Title.
QA76.9.A25M665 2006
005.8'2--dc22
2006009839

06 7 6 5 4 3 2 First Edition

CHARLES RIVER MEDIA titles are available for site license or bulk purchase by institutions, user groups, corporations, etc. For additional information, please contact the Special Sales Department at 800-347-7707.

Requests for replacement of a defective CD-ROM must be accompanied by the original disc, your mailing address, telephone number, date of purchase and purchase price. Please state the nature of the problem, and send the information to CHARLES RIVER MEDIA, 25 Thomson Place, Boston, Massachusetts 02210. CRM's sole obligation to the purchaser is to replace the disc, based on defective materials or faulty workmanship, but not on the operation or functionality of the product.

Contents

Introduction

Currently, cryptographic transformations are widely used as an efficient and flexible method for solving various problems of information protection in computer networks and communications systems. Three main tasks of cryptography are the most important:

- Ensuring information confidentiality
- Authentication of the information and message source
- Ensuring user anonymity

For several thousand years, ensuring information confidentiality was considered the only task of cryptography, and many various approaches and methods have been suggested for doing so. The common feature of all these methods was the use of the secret key—certain information providing the key owner with the possibility of obtaining information from the cryptogram. Such systems of imposing secrecy are called *secret-key ciphers*, also known as *single-key* (or *symmetric*) *cryptosystems*. Tasks of the second and the third types emerged as a consequence of wide use of electric methods of information processing and transmission, and the development of computer technologies. They became especially urgent due to the necessity of validating electronic messages and ensuring anonymity in such applications as electronic commerce and secret electronic voting. Efficient methods of solving problems of this type are related to the use of public key cryptography, which was developed about 30 years ago. Starting from that moment, problems with public key ciphers became the most rapidly and intensely developing area of contemporary cryptography. Cryptographic systems of this type use the secret key, too, and are called *two-key* or *asymmetric cryptosystems*. However, despite the development of principally new cryptosystems, secret key ciphers have not lost their practical importance. They continue to attract considerable attention from developers of IT security tools and cryptanalysts, mainly because such ciphers ensure considerably higher performance and the possibility of secure transformation of relatively small data blocks (64- or 128-bit).

The first chapter of this book is a general discussion of cryptographic problems. It demonstrates the place and role of symmetric ciphers and issues of their practical application. Other chapters describe symmetric block ciphers. The practice has demonstrated the need for development of fast symmetric ciphers for the following applications:

- Hardware implementation (for example, DES)
- Software implementation (RC5, Blowfish)
- Universal (both software and hardware) implementation (AES, RC6, TwoFish, IDEA, GOST)

After completion of the AES contest, the number of newly suggested solutions in the field of symmetric cryptography has considerably reduced; however, some application still require further increase of the encryption speed both for software and hardware implementations. At the same time, in the case of hardware implementation, it is important to meet the requirements of reducing the cost and energy consumption (for example, when solving the problems of information security in mobile networks). The efficiency of ciphers being developed specially for such applications can be considerably improved by using innovative approaches to cipher design and abandoning the implementation universality; that is, orientation toward the highest performance either for hardware or software orientation. This book covers the issues of design and analysis of ciphers of this type based on the approach including data-dependent transformation operations characterized by exceedingly large numbers of potential modifications. Elements of this approach were earlier known in such ciphers as DES, RC5, and RC6. However, in the aforementioned ciphers, operations of this type had a small number of modifications possible to implement, which reduced the efficiency of such primitives. To make variable operations applicable as a basic cryptographic primitive, the authors have suggested the use of controlled substitution-permutation networks (CSPNs) and permutation networks (PNs) for implementing data-dependent operations. Substantiation of these primitives, and results of the research of several new hardware-oriented ciphers, are provided in a range of newly published articles. The obtained results are generalized in this book.

Also covered are the issues of development and design of software-oriented ciphers, including ciphers based on the algorithm formed depending on the secret key. The main primitive of these ciphers is the sample of subkeys depending on the data being transformed (data-dependent subkey selection). Some specific issues of evaluation of the cryptographic strength of ciphers with flexible algorithms of data transformation are considered, and a combinational-probabilistic model is suggested oriented toward obtaining minimal evaluations of the series of software ciphers being considered. The issue of introducing a new command into universal processors is discussed. The suggested command must execute controlled bit permutation. It is expected to sharply increase the performance of cryptographic algorithms, including bit permutations of an arbitrary type. This command is highly promising for various applications, including cryptographic problems and problems in many other areas. It is demonstrated that the presence of such a command in the standard command set of a commercial processor makes some of the suggested hardware ciphers universal and allows for ensuring higher transformation speeds in comparison to known universal ciphers.

This book is intended for a wide community of users, including students, teachers, engineers, researchers, and IT security professionals. The authors hope this book will attract the readers' attention to new interesting problems related to contemporary cryptography, which are described with orientation to the practical application.

1 Cryptography in the Information Age

1.1 INFORMATION PROTECTION PROBLEMS IN COMPUTER SYSTEMS

Historically, cryptography has emerged as a response to the requirement of transmitting secret information. For a long time, it was only concerned with designing special methods of information transformation to represent it in a form incomprehensible to a potential opponent. After electronic methods of information processing and transmitting had developed, cryptography's tasks became more varied. Nowadays, when computer information technologies have become widely applicable, cryptography includes an abundant number of tasks not directly related to making information secret, such as developing digital signature systems, computerized voting systems, coin-tossing protocols, remote user authentication protocols, and protection against creating false messages.

Many of software technology's actual problems are effectively solved using cryptographic methods. In cryptography, you must assume the existence of a potentially malicious person (an opponent, an enemy's cryptanalyst, an adversary, an unauthorized user) who is aware of the cryptographic algorithms, protocols and methods used, and tries to compromise them. Compromising a cryptosystem can involve, for example, unauthorized data reading, forging someone else's signature, modifying voting results, infringing on voting secrecy, or modifying data that won't be detected by the intended receiver. The opponent's actions are generally called a *cryptographic attack* (or simply an *attack*). One specific feature of cryptography is that it is aimed at developing methods that protect you against any opponent's actions, but when designing a cryptosystem, it is impossible to foresee the types of attacks that will be invented in the future, due to theoretical and technological advances. The main question is, how reliable is the solution of a certain cryptographic problem? The answer is directly related to estimating the effort required to attack the cryptosystem. As a rule, the solution to this problem is extremely complex and an individual research topic in itself, called *cryptanalysis*. *Cryptography* and *cryptanalysis* comprise a unified scientific area, called *cryptology*. Currently, new areas of mathematics has important applications in modern information technologies.

The wide use of computer technologies in data processing and control systems has aggravated the problem of protecting information from unauthorized access. Information protection in computer systems has certain specific features related to the fact that information isn't rigidly bound to a medium—it can be easily and quickly copied and transmitted over communication channels. There are many known threats to information, and they can be implemented both by inside and outside adversaries.

A radical solution to the problem of protecting information that flows in high-performance computer systems can be obtained using cryptographic methods. In this case, it is important to use fast enciphering algorithms that don't decrease the performance of the computer or telecommunication systems. Cryptographic data transformations are a flexible and effective tool for providing data privacy, integrity, and authenticity. Using cryptographic methods in combination with technological and organizational methods can protect against a wide range of potential threats.

The demands of modern software technologies have led to the emergence of nontraditional data protection tasks, one of which is information authentication in situations in which the parties exchanging information don't trust each other—a problem related to the design of digital signature systems. The theoretical foundation of the solution of this problem was the invention of two-key cryptography by American researchers Diffie and Hellman in the mid-1970s, which was a brilliant breakthrough in the centuries-old evolution of cryptography. The revolutionary idea of two-key cryptography led to a drastic growth in public research in this area, and revealed new directions for the development of cryptography and its unique worth in the present context of rapidly developing electronic information technologies.

The technological basis of the transition to an information society is modern microelectronic technology, which provides for a continuous growth in the quality of computers, and in turn is the basis for their main design tendencies:

- Decreasing the size and power consumption of the hardware
- Increasing the capacity of the random-access memory and built-in and removable disks
- Increasing the performance and reliability of computer systems
- Expanding the areas for and increasing the intensity of computer use

These trends in computer development have led to a situation in which modern protection of computer systems against unauthorized access requires using *software cryptographic protection tools.*

As recent practice shows, the use of *hardware ciphers* has gained popularity. One of the currently central problems in applied cryptography is designing algorithms that will provide a speed of 1500 MBits/sec or more when implemented as inexpensive microcircuits (*cryptochips*). First, this is related to the wide use of enciphering in commercial TV. Another popular area using cryptochips is mobile telephony. Recently, information security specialists and users have become aware of the need to cryptographically protect information transmitted from video security cameras and other security devices. This area of using cryptography requires that enciphering devices with a low hardware complexity be designed.

One of the important social and ethical problems that arose due to the expanding use of cryptographic data protection methods was the conflict between the users' desire to protect their information and messages transmitted and the desire of government intelligence services to access companies' and individuals' information to prevent illegal activities. In industrial countries, there is a wide range of opinions concerning regulations on the use of enciphering algorithms. The suggestions vary from total prohibition of using cryptographic methods on a large scale, to unlimited freedom in using them. Some proposals only give permission to use weak algorithms, or require the mandatory registration of encryption keys.

It is extremely difficult to solve this problem. How can one estimate the relationship between the losses of law-abiding citizens due to the illegal use of their private information and the losses of the government due to the impossibility of accessing the cryptographically protected information of certain groups trying to conceal criminal activities? How can one ensure that cryptalgorithms will not be used illegally by people who violate other laws? Besides that, there are various other ways to secretly store and transmit information. The answers to these questions have yet to be found by sociologists, psychologists, lawyers, and politicians.

As for research in the area of cryptography that can result in convenient and practically secure algorithms, hindering it doesn't seem to be reasonable. Law-abiding citizens and organizations should be provided an equal opportunity to protect their information, because criminals who use cryptographic advances would thus be in a much better position if this were not the case.

Furthermore, limiting research in the field of cryptography would most likely slow the development of cryptography, but it will by no means prevent criminals from using modern cryptographic methods obtained, for example, from other countries. As a result, law-abiding citizens' and organizations' rights will be most seriously infringed upon. In many countries, this problem is fully understood, which has increased the number of industrial countries in which rigid limits on using encryption have been removed.

Regardless of the progress in developing cryptographic methods of data protection, the government can always require by law that all users of ciphers must register their keys (or a necessary portion of key data) with specially organized institutions. In this case, information is controlled, no matter how secure the algorithms used are. This and other issues demonstrate that hindering research in the area of cryptography is not objectively justified. As far back as the early 1970s, the demands of practice in Western industrial countries aroused an interest in cryptography in many researchers in different areas, and gave the impetus to public research in this area, which was previously considered exclusive and was a matter of concern only to intelligence services.

There are a number of examples in which secrecy in the field of cryptography has led to significant failures in producing enciphering devices, and even to falling behind scientific and technological progress. Intensive activities in such a "hot" domain of science created conditions ripe for increasing the quality of cryptographic research, which thus allowed Diffie and Hellman to discover *two-key cryptography*. Their ideas brought into existence new, nontraditional divisions of cryptography, and made it one of the most rapidly developing trends in modern mathematics. The discovery of two-key cryptography is a vivid example of the interaction between theory and practice, and an example of how politics influences theoretical advances.

Hindering research in the realm of cryptography simplifies some problems for intelligence services. However, the nation as a whole strongly suffers from it, and the negative effect is related to falling behind in designing modern data protection systems, spreading computer crimes, and so forth. Examples are found in global computer networks, such as the Internet, which are revolutionary achievements of computer technologies, but also are playgrounds for a great number of crimes and infringements.

As a result of working in the Internet, the vulnerabilities and shortcomings of traditional administrative and system mechanisms of data protection became clearer. Cryptography presents fundamentally new possibilities in providing information security in computer systems, and nowadays its methods have been widely introduced into global network technologies. It is not the refusal of progress in informatization, but rather the use of modern cryptography advances that has turned out to be the strategically correct decision, verified in practice. The possibility of widely using cryptography in computer networks is a great achievement and a sign of a democratic society.

Knowing the basics of cryptography in an information society cannot objectively be a privilege of individual government services, but is a vital necessity for scientists and engineers who use computer data processing or develop information systems, employees of security departments, and upper management in various organizations and companies. Only this approach can be a basis for introducing and operating high-quality tools for information protection.

A single organization cannot provide sufficient control over information streams within a whole country, and it cannot provide proper protection for national distributed information resources. However, certain government organizations can create conditions that allow a market of high-quality protection tools to emerge, a sufficient number of specialists to be trained, and "common users" to be taught the basics of data protection and cryptography.

In the early 1990s, in Russia and the countries of the former Soviet Union, there was a distinct trend in which the intensity and propagation of the use of information technologies was getting ahead of the development of data protection systems. This situation, to some extent, is typical for certain industrial countries. This is a natural order: first, practical problems must emerge, and then their solutions will be found. The turning point in the situation of the late 1980s, when the countries of the former Soviet Union were falling behind in the domain of informatization, created fertile ground for overcoming the aforementioned trend. The example of the industrial countries and the possibility of purchasing system software and computers encouraged Russian users. A wide range of users concerned with online data processing and other advantages of modern computer systems were involved in solving the problem of expanding computer technologies, which led to a very high rate of development in this area in Russia and the other countries of the former Soviet Union. However, the natural joint development of information processing tools and information protecting tools was broken, which was the cause of abundant computer crimes. It's no secret that these crimes have now become an urgent problem.

Using foreign protection tools can't correct this imbalance. Because software products of this type available in the Russian market don't satisfy modern requirements due to the export limitations adopted in the U.S., the main vendor of data protection tools. Another issue of prime importance is that software products of this type are subject to an established certification procedure in authorized organizations. Checking encryption algorithms, software, and hardware for various bugs and viruses is an extremely labor-consuming task. Recent investigations of cryptographers revealed that it is possible to design trapdoor encryption algorithms, these trapdoors being practically impossible to detect in a reasonable time, even by high-class specialists.

Certificates given by foreign companies and organizations cannot be a substitute for national ones. Just the fact of using foreign system and application software in crucial areas creates a threat for information resources. Using foreign protection tools without proper analysis of their correspondence to the functions performed and the security level provided can drastically complicate the situation.

Speeding up the informatization process requires that users be adequately provided with protection tools. An insufficient supply of tools that protect the information in computer systems in the internal market hampers top-quality data protection on the necessary scale for a long time. The situation is aggravated by the lack of a sufficient number of data protection specialists, because such professionals are usually only trained to work in intelligence services. The restructuring of these intelligence organizations caused by the processes taking place in Russia has led to independent firms that specialize in data protection absorbing the available staff. As a result, there arose competition, which produced a sufficiently large number of certified Russian-produced data protection tools.

One of the important features of the wide use of information technologies is that an effective solution of the problem of protecting national information resources requires distributing data protection measures to all users. Information must first be protected where it is created, gathered, and processed, and by the organizations that would suffer from unauthorized access to their data. This principle is both reasonable and effective: protecting individual organizations' interests is the basis of protecting national interests as a whole.

1.2 PROBLEMS IN CRYPTOGRAPHY

The word *cryptography*, taken from Greek, means "secret writing," which well reflects its original purpose. Cryptographic methods that seem primitive from the modern viewpoint have been known since antiquity, and have long been treated as puzzles rather than as a strict branch of science. The classical cryptographic task is to provide for a reversible transformation of an understandable *plaintext* (*original text*) to a seemingly random character sequence called a *ciphertext* or a *cryptogram*. The ciphertext can contain both new characters and those present in the original message. Generally, the number of characters in a cryptogram and the number in the plaintext may differ. A mandatory requirement is the possibility of uniquely and fully restoring the plaintext by simply performing some logical operations with the characters of the ciphertext. In old times, the security of the information was determined by how well the transformation method was kept secret.

However, a secret algorithm alone cannot provide *absolute security*, the impossibility of reading a cryptogram by an opponent possessing infinite computing resources. Because secret algorithms aren't available for large-scale cryptanalytical research, there is a much higher probability, as compared to public algorithms, that the vulnerabilities of secret algorithms will be found, and thus so will effective ways of breaking them. In addition, public algorithms that have undergone long-term testing and discussions in public cryptographic literature are more widely used nowadays.

1.2.1 Traditional Cryptography Issues

The security of modern cryptosystems is not based on the secrecy of the algorithm, but on the secrecy of a relatively small amount of information, called a *secret key*. The key is used to control the process of cryptographic transformation (ciphering), and it is an easily changeable element of a cryptosystem. Users can change the key at any time, whereas the ciphering algorithm itself is a constant element of the cryptosystem, and it is the result of long-term research and testing.

Other things being equal, the lack of comprehensive information on the ciphering algorithm (provided it is implemented properly) significantly hampers any cryptanalytical attack. This is why modern ciphers with a ciphering algorithm directly being a pseudo-random changeable element were proposed. The information about the overall structure of such cryptosystems is available, thus making it possible to estimate its security as a whole. Such ciphers are implemented as flexible cryptosystems in which an algorithm used in a ciphering session is created according to a special *initializing algorithm*. This latter algorithm is public, and the algorithm used is unknown and depends on the user's secret key.

Many ages have passed, during which cryptography was mostly the occupation of the elite—priests, kings, military leaders, and diplomats. Although uncommon, cryptographic methods of breaking the opponent's ciphers had a significant influence on the results of important historical events. There are many examples where overestimating ciphering methods led to military and diplomatic losses. Despite using cryptographic methods in important areas, the occasional usage of cryptography didn't have anywhere near the importance it now has in modern society. Cryptography owes the fact that it has turned into a scientific discipline to practical demands and the development of electronic information technologies.

In the 19th century, a significant interest in cryptography led to further development in connection with emerging electrical means of communication. In the

20th century, the intelligence services of most industrial countries began to regard it as an essential tool for their activities.

When speaking about the historic aspects of scientific research in cryptography, we must mention the fact that the whole period from ancient times to 1949 can be called pre-scientific, since methods of making written information private had no strict mathematical grounds. The turning point that made cryptography scientific and set it off as an individual branch of mathematics was the publication of C. E. Shannon's article "Communication Theory of Secrecy Systems" in 1949. This work was the basis for the emergence of *one-key symmetric cryptosystems*, in which it was necessary to exchange secret keys between the correspondents. Later, due to some peculiarities of their design, symmetrical ciphers were divided into two cryptosystems: *stream ciphers* and *block ciphers*. A distinguishing feature of the former is that individual characters in the input data stream are converted, whereas the latter converts whole blocks of data.

A fundamental conclusion in Shannon's work was that the reliability of an algorithm depends on the size and quality of the secret key, and on the *informational redundancy* of the original text. Shannon introduced the formal definition of information and a key's unreliability as a function of the number of known bits in cipher text. Furthermore, he introduced the important notion of *unicity distance* as the minimum text size for which only one decryption of an original text is possible. He showed that the unicity distance is in direct proportion to the key length and in inverse proportion to the redundancy of the original text. One result of Shannon's work was proof of the possibility of perfectly secure ciphers, such as Vernam's cryptosystem.

Another fundamental impetus in the development of cryptography was the publication of Diffie and Hellman's article "New Directions in Cryptography" in 1976. In this work, it was shown for the first time that information secrecy can be provided without exchanging secret keys. This was the beginning of the epoch of *two-key asymmetric cryptosystems*, which are manifest in digital signature systems, online secret voting, protection against false messages creation, computerized coin-tossing, remote user identification and authentication, and other systems.

Over the past few years, due to the progress in electronic technologies, a number of theoretical works have appeared in the area of *quantum cryptography*, based on Heisenberg's uncertainty principle.

In parallel with the development of cryptographic systems, methods have been developed that make it possible to restore an original message based on the ciphertext and other known information. These methods are collectively known as *cryptanalysis*. Advances in cryptanalysis have led to tightening the requirements on cryptographic algorithms. The reliability of cryptosystems has always been of fundamental importance. This problem has been treated differently throughout the history of cryptography.

The Dutch cryptographer Kerkhoff (1835–1903) was the first to formulate the *cipher security rule*, according to which the complete transformation mechanism is assumed to be known by the opponent, and the security of an algorithm can only be determined by the unknown value of a secret key. This means that an opponent has no way of unlocking the protection, or of finding the true key in a time significantly shorter than the time it would take to *try every possible secret key*.

Apparently, one of the tasks for estimating a cipher's security, according to Kerkhoff, is testing cryptosystems under conditions more favorable for attacks than the conditions under which a potential violator usually acts. Kerkhoff's principle stimulated the emergence of higher-quality ciphering algorithms. One could say that here we have the first element of cryptography standardization, since it assumes the development of public methods of transformation. At present, this rule is more widely interpreted: it is assumed that all persistent elements of a security system are known to the potential opponent. This last definition of a cryptosystem includes security systems as a special case. The extended interpretation of Kerkhoff's principle assumes that all elements of a cryptosystem are divided into two categories—constant and easily changeable. Constant elements are those related to the cryptosystem structure, and can only be changed by specialists. Easily changeable elements of a cryptosystem are those intended for frequent modification in accordance with a specified procedure. For example, the easily changeable elements of a cipher are the secret key, the password, the identifier, and so forth. Kerkhoff's principle reflects the fact that the required secrecy level must be achieved only by using the secret easily changeable elements of the cipher.

According to modern requirements posed on cryptosystems with a secret key of a limited size (128–256 bits), such ciphers must be secure when facing a cryptanalysis based on a known algorithm, a great amount of plaintext, and its corresponding ciphertext. Despite these general requirements, ciphers used by intelligence organizations are usually kept secret. This is due to the necessity of having an additional safety margin to protect secret information, since creating cryptosystems with provable security is nowadays a developing theory, and a rather complex problem. To avoid any possible weaknesses, a ciphering algorithm can be built on the basis of much-studied and approved principles and methods of transformation. Currently, no serious user will rely on simply keeping his algorithm secret, since it is extremely difficult to guarantee that information about the algorithm will remain unknown to a potential attacker.

Proving the reliability of systems being used is done both theoretically and experimentally, by modeling cryptattacks with the help of a team of experienced specialists to whom much more favorable conditions are given than the conditions under which the cryptalgorithm will actually be used. For example, the cryptanalysts are provided not only with a ciphertext and a transformation algorithm, but also with an original text or some part of it, several independent ciphertexts obtained using the same key, or ciphertexts obtained from the given plaintext using different keys. The security of the tested cryptosystem is estimated against all known cryptanalytical methods, and ways of breaking the system are invented if possible. If the cryptosystem appears secure, it is recommended for actual use.

Modern cryptanalysis considers attacks on encrypting systems based on the following known data:

- Ciphertext
- Plaintext and its corresponding ciphertext
- Chosen plaintext
- Chosen ciphertext
- Adapted plaintext
- Adapted ciphertext

Additionally, some attacks use:

- Hardware faults
- Power consumption measurements
- Calculation time measurements

We detailed the types of attacks on cryptosystems designed to cipher data for protecting against unauthorized reading. As for other kinds of cryptosystems, there are a number of other attacks that will be discussed later. In the case of *known ciphertext cryptanalysis*, it is assumed that the opponent knows the ciphering mechanism, and that only the ciphertext is available to him. This assumption corresponds to the model of an external interceptor who has physical access to the communication line, but doesn't access the enciphering/deciphering device.

With *known plaintext cryptanalysis*, it is assumed that the cryptanalyst knows the ciphertext and a portion of the original text, and in special cases knows the correspondence between the ciphertext and the original text. The possibility of such an attack appears when enciphering standard documents are prepared according to standard forms under conditions in which certain data blocks are known and repeated. In some modern tools intended for protecting information circulating over computer systems, the total ciphering mode is used, in which all information on the hard disk is written down as a ciphertext, including the main boot record, the boot sector, system programs, and so forth. If this hard disk (or the computer) is stolen, it will be easy to determine which part of the cryptogram corresponds to the standard system information, and obtain the bulk of a known original text to perform a cryptanalysis.

In *chosen plaintext cryptanalysis*, it is assumed that the cryptanalyst can enter a specially chosen text into the enciphering device and get a cryptogram created under the control of the secret key. This corresponds to the inside adversary model. In practice, this situation emerges when an attack on the cipher involves people who don't know the secret key, but, according to their given rights, can use the enciphering device to encrypt transmitted messages. To perform such an attack, lower-level employees can also be involved, who can prepare document forms, electronic spreadsheets, and so forth.

Chosen ciphertext cryptanalysis assumes that the opponent can use ciphertexts created by him or her for deciphering. The texts were specially chosen to most easily compute the secret key from texts obtained at the output of the deciphering device.

Adapted text cryptanalysis corresponds to a case in which the attacker repeatedly submits texts for encryption (or decryption), with each new portion being chosen depending on previously obtained cryptanalysis results. This kind of attack is the one most favorable for the opponent.

Currently, the most powerful kinds of attacks based on chosen or adapted texts are *differential cryptanalysis* (DCA) and *linear cryptanalysis* (LCA), along with some methods derived from them.

When testing new cryptosystems, of special interest are attacks based on a known secret key, or an *extended (working) key*. We'll make a distinction between a secret key and a working key because the secret key isn't necessarily used in transforming a text being encrypted, but is often just used to create an extended key, which is what is actually used in enciphering. There are ciphers (such as the GOST block cipher) in which the secret key is used directly when enciphering data; in other words, the secret key is also the working key. Obviously, the extended key is a secret element. When carrying out a cryptanalysis based on known elements of the key (whether it is secret or extended), it is assumed that the cryptanalyst possesses some information about a part of the working key. The larger the known portion of the key that still doesn't provide enough information to uniquely determine the plaintext using which the cipher remains secure, the less concern there will be over the cipher in actual attack conditions, where the attacker doesn't know the key, but attempts to restore its elements. When comparing two ciphers, the cipher that better meets the aforementioned criteria should be chosen.

One of the current trends in designing fast software-oriented ciphers is to have the ciphering algorithm depend on the secret key. In such cryptosystems, a certain ciphering algorithm is known to the attacker, and it is changed simultaneously when the secret key is changed. Such ciphers are called *non-deterministic* or *flexible ciphers*. When testing flexible ciphers, it seems reasonable to analyze their secureness against attacks based on a chosen modification of the enciphering algorithm. In this kind of cryptanalysis, the attacker has the possibility of choosing the weakest (in his opinion) modification of the cryptalgorithm among those that can be implemented. Cryptanalysis is then carried out for the chosen algorithm modification based on specially selected texts, with a variant of the attack where there is a partially known ciphering key also conceivable. If the cryptanalyst fails to find the weakest modification of the cryptalgorithm, the flexible cipher in question can be called secure.

1.2.2 Modern Applications

The importance of cryptography goes far beyond providing data secrecy. As data transmission and processing become more automated, and the information flow becomes more intense, cryptographic methods gain greater importance. New information technologies are founded on two-key cryptography, which makes it possible to implement protocols that assume the secret key is only known to a single user—in other words, protocols oriented toward the mutual distrust of the interacting parties. Here are the main applications of modern cryptography:

- Protection against unauthorized reading (or providing information privacy)
- Protection against creating false messages (both intentional and unpremeditated)
- Valid user authentication
- Information integrity control
- Information authentication
- Digital signatures
- Computerized secret voting
- Digital cash
- Computerized coin-tossing
- Protection against the repudiation of the receipt of a message
- Simultaneous contract signing
- Protection against document forgery

The first application was discussed previously. We'll now briefly explain the other uses for cryptography. Data ciphering itself isn't sufficient to protect against creating false messages, but in many cases a valid receiver can easily detect that a cryptogram has been modified or substituted; for example, while being transmitted over the communication line. This can be done by analyzing the semantics of the message. However, when digital data are distorted, and in some other cases, it is extremely difficult to detect the fact that the data has been distorted judging by just semantics. One of the methods of protection against creating false messages by intentional or accidental ciphertext tainting is a message integrity check. *Message integrity check* is a notion related to protecting against creating false messages by generating some special additional information, depending on the secret key. This information is called the *message integrity detection code*, and is transmitted with the cryptogram. To compute the message integrity detection code, an algorithm is used that specifies how the message integrity detection code depends on each bit of the message. Here, two variants are possible: computing the message integrity detection code from the plaintext, and computing the message integrity detection code from the ciphertext. The longer the message integrity detection code, the higher the probability that ciphertext distortion will be detected by the authorized (valid) receiver. An opponent can modify the ciphertext, but since he doesn't know the secret key, the new value of the message integrity detection code that corresponds to the modified message can't be computed. The opponent either doesn't change the message integrity detection code, or replaces it with a random value. If the algorithm used for the message integrity detection code computation has good cryptographic properties, the probability that the modification won't be detected by the valid user is $P = 2^{-n}$, where n is the length of the message integrity detection code in bits.

Valid user authentication involves user recognition, after which the users are provided with certain access permissions to the resources of computational and automated information systems. Authentication is based on the fact that valid users possess some information unknown to outsiders. A special case of the authentication procedure is password protection of logging in to a computer system. For example, the user generates some random information and uses it as a password, while keeping it secret. The password isn't explicitly stored in the memory of a computer or other device used to perform authentication. This requirement is aimed at preventing a possible inside adversary from reading a user's password and misappropriating the user's authorization. For a security system to be able to identify valid (authorized) users, the images of their passwords, which were computed according to a special cryptographic algorithm that implements a so-called one-way function—$y = F(x)$—are stored in the computer's memory. The main requirement to this function is that the complexity of computing its value from an argument be low, but the complexity of computing the argument from a function value be high (for example, it should be impossible to do in 10 years, provided all the computational resources of humanity are used).

User authentication on a workstation can be carried out in the following way:

1. The security system asks for an identifier.
2. The user enters his or her identifier (username) NAME.
3. The security system asks for a password.
4. The user enters his or her password P.
5. The system computes the value of the one-way function y corresponding to the argument value $x = P$.
6. The security system compares the $F(P)$ value with the password image value (S) that relates the user to the NAME identifier.

If $F(P) = S$, the security system gives the user the access rights (authorization) corresponding to the NAME identifier. Otherwise, an attempt at unauthorized access is registered in the user log. To pretend to be an authorized user, an intruder has to enter a valid password. It is computationally impossible to find the P password from the S image. If the security system is provided with mechanisms preventing the interception of a password by introducing software viruses or hardware bugs, or with induced electromagnetic radiation, or through an acoustic or optic channel, this user authentication method provides high-level protection against the misappropriation of someone else's access rights.

This example concerns user authentication on a workstation; in other words, logging in to a computer. For mutual authentication of remote workstations, it is important to assume that an eavesdropper is listening in on the communication line, and, therefore, the described authentication method is unsuitable, because password transmission via an unsecure channel is unacceptable. Remote workstation authentication can be done according to the following procedure, using the ***E*** enciphering algorithm and the ***K*** secret key shared by remote stations **A** and **B**:

1. The **A** workstation sends a request for connection to the **B** workstation.
2. The **B** workstation sends **A** a random number R.
3. The **A** workstation encrypts R with the ***K*** secret key, thus obtaining the $C_a = \boldsymbol{E}_K(R)$ ciphertext, and sends **B** the value C_a.
4. The **B** workstation computes $C_b = \boldsymbol{E}_K(R)$ and compares C_b with C_a. If $C_b = C_a$, it concludes that the request for connection was sent by the **A** workstation; otherwise, it hangs up.

Only one who knows the secret key can correctly encrypt a random text. If a violator intercepts correct cryptograms of random numbers with a key length of no less than 64 bits, he won't encounter two equal numbers in any reasonable amount of time. Therefore, he won't be able to replace a previously intercepted correct cryptogram. In this scheme, a LAN server can take on the **B** workstation's role. We'd like to note that this scheme allows the **B** workstation to make sure the connection is established to the **A** workstation. However, the **A** workstation can face a similar problem authenticating the **B** workstation. In this case, a similar authentication procedure is carried out to let **A** authenticate **B**. Such a scheme of mutual recognition by two remote parties (workstations) is called a *handshake protocol.*

Information integrity control means detecting any unauthorized modification of information stored in a computer, such as data or programs. In fact, a message integrity check is an important special case of the integrity control of information transmitted as a ciphertext. In practice, you often need to make sure that some programs, initial data, or databases haven't been modified by some unauthorized method when the data themselves aren't secret and are stored in public. Information integrity control is founded on using a cryptographic scheme to build a modification detecting code (MDC) that has a much smaller size than the information being protected against modifications. The basic requirement of the MDC computing algorithm is to specify how the MDC's value will depend on each binary representation bit of all the characters in the original text.

Checking that the information corresponds to its reference state (information integrity control) is done as follows. When freezing a reference state, say, of the FILE.EXE program, the MDC value that corresponds to this file is computed. The value obtained is written in a table that will be used for every check of information integrity. Suppose that the FILE.EXE program controls a complex and important technological process, and its failure can lead to downtimes that result in financial losses. If this is the case, it makes sense to check its integrity before every start. To do so, we compute the MDC and compare it to the corresponding value stored in the code table. This method is effective for detecting occasional data distortions.

This scheme of data integrity control isn't suitable when information is modified intentionally, since a violator can get around it. He can change the data at will, compute the new MDC value for the modified data, and substitute this value in the code table for the reference one (which corresponds to the reference state of the data). To prevent such an attack, you'll have to use one of the following additional techniques:

- Use a secret algorithm to compute the MDC.
- Use an MDC computing algorithm with a secret key that determines the MDC value.
- Keep the code table in a protected memory area or on portable media, access to which is controlled by organizational arrangements.

In the first case, it is difficult to keep the algorithm secret, since it is a constant element of the cryptosystem. The third case requires significant effort in order to provide organizational arrangements. The second variant is probably the best. However, all three cases still require protection against spy programs.

Methods used for integrity control must ensure that the probability of intentional or occasional data modification that will not affect the code's representation is extremely small. Here, the task of cryptanalysis is to study the weaknesses of the MDC generating algorithm and modify the original information so that the control code doesn't change. MDC computing algorithms are called *checksumming algorithms*, and the generated value is called a *checksum*. In modern cryptographic protocols and systems, *hash functions*, which are a special case of checksumming algorithms, are of great importance.

Information authentication is an action performed by an authorized receiver to establish the fact that a received message was sent by an authorized sender. Following a previously agreed protocol (a set of rules and procedures) should provide the maximum probability of this. Obviously, this also includes integrity checks to avoid replacement or distortion of the message. The accepted protocol must provide for counteractions against an opponent using previously sent messages. In symmetric cryptosystems, authentication is performed using one or more secret keys and checksums. In asymmetric cryptosystems, authentication is performed using public keys. For this to be possible, when public keys are distributed, they are authenticated using organizational arrangements.

The problem of open key authentication explicitly appeared as a fundamental cryptographic problem as soon as *public-key cryptography* (two-key asymmetrical cryptography) was invented in the mid-1970s. Public-key cryptography provided a very convenient solution to the secret key distribution problem, but using it requires performing a public key authentication procedure. It should be mentioned that the key authentication problem wasn't caused by two-key cryptography; it has always implicitly existed in secret key cryptography. Indeed, when distributing secret keys via a secure channel, their authentication is done at the same time. For example, when receiving a sealed package with a secret key inside, the receiver checks to make sure the package and the seal aren't damaged.

While Shannon's work "Communication Theory of Secrecy Systems" laid the foundation for cryptology to become a science, the invention of two-key cryptography marked the shift to a radically new stage of its development. This became the basis for the exhaustive solution to such problems as information authentication and creating digital signature systems that were to legalize documents and other messages transmitted in electronic form.

Digital signature (DS) is based on two-key cryptographic algorithms that involve using two keys—one *public* and one *private.* The idea of using a public key (i.e., a key known to all users of a cryptosystem, including a potential attacker) is fundamental, and so two-key cryptosystems are also called *public ciphers*, and the transformations performed are called *public ciphering*. Two-key cryptalgorithms make it possible to provide strict proof as to whether a certain message has been composed by certain subscribers (users) of the cryptosystem. The proof is based on the fact that two-key cryptosystems operate under conditions in which the user doesn't have to tell his private key to anyone else. The fact of using a private key when generating a digital signature on a particular electronic document is verified with a *public key*. Knowledge of the public key doesn't make it possible to generate the correct digital signature. Thus, the responsibility for keeping the *private key* and for observing the rules of using it is wholly on the owner of this key. The private key makes it possible to compose a message with a special internal structure related to the document being signed and the public key. The fact that the message structure was built with the private key is verified with the public key, a procedure called *digital signature verification*. The probability that a message composed by an intruder could be mistaken for a message signed by a subscriber to the DS system is extremely low—say, 10^{-30}.

Thus, the DS verification procedure using a public key makes it possible to state with a high degree of assurance that a received message was composed by the owner of the private key. The public key is derived from the private key, or both are simultaneously generated according to special procedures, computing the private key from the public key being a computationally complex mathematical problem.

Computationally complex (hard-to-solve) problems definitely have a solution, but finding it requires an extremely large number of computational operations (performed by a computer or other device). The number must be large enough so that using all the computational resources that might be involved in the process won't make it possible to find the solution with a significant probability (say, 0.001) in a reasonable time (decades, centuries, millennia, etc.). The average number of operations required to find the solution with the help of the best algorithm is used as a quantitative measure of the complexity of a hard problem. The problem of estimating the complexity is itself difficult because the complexity depends on the algorithm used to solve the problem. In general, different complexity values are obtained for different algorithms. Given a particular hard problem, it is difficult to prove that the minimum-effort algorithm has been found (in other words, the best algorithm). Using two-key ciphers is based on the assumption that hard problems do exist—problems for which no solution can be achieved with comparatively little effort.

Based on two-key cryptographic algorithms, *computerized secret voting* systems use a blind signature mechanism, which makes it possible to sign a message without knowing its contents. Various methods of computerized secret voting are very promising when it comes to improving political systems in modern societies with an advanced information infrastructure.

A blind signature protocol makes it possible to build various digital cash systems. The difference between digital cash and payments using DS is that the former ensures the purchaser's secrecy. Also of social interest are computerized coin-tossing systems, a variant of which is playing poker by telephone. In a broader approach, computerized gambling houses can be opened, in which protection against cheating will be guaranteed on a higher level than in conventional gambling houses.

Let's consider the simplest variant of *computerized coin tossing*. Suppose **A** and **B** are telephone subscribers who wish to play chess by telephone. They want to fairly decide who gets to be white; in other words, to provide an equal probability of the white color being selected for either player. Cryptography allows them to implement such coin tossing according to the following procedure, in which the

$y = F(x)$ one-way function is used. It is stipulated that the player who guesses the result of an experiment with two equally probable results will move first.

1. Player **A** chooses a random value—x_a—whose binary representation is, say, 80 bits long, computes the $y_a = F(x_a)$ value, and tells **B** the y_a value (**B** must guess whether x_a is odd or even).
2. Because the function used is one-way, **B** cannot compute x_a from y_a, so he has to guess whether x_a is even or odd. Let's say that **B** guesses that it is even and tells **A** this.
3. **A** tells **B** the number x_a.
4. Player **B** computes the value of $y = F(x_a)$. If $y = y_a$, he is convinced that his partner actually did provide the initially chosen number for verification.

If the result of the coin tossing is not to decide the color selection in an amateur chess game, but to deal cards when playing poker for money by telephone (dealing cards by telephone is only technically more complex), a DS system can be additionally provided to sign all messages concerning dealing cards and making bets by telephone.

As an example of how computerized coin tossing can be economically justified, consider it being used in world (European, etc.) soccer (basketball, volleyball, etc.) championships. To make traditional lot-casting decisions, representatives of participant teams and international sport organizations periodically come together at the same place, spending a lot of time and money. If this procedure is replaced with computerized coin tossing, time will be saved, and expenses will be kept to a minimum. Other examples of using coin tossing are organizing lotteries and fairly distributing limited resources.

Cryptographic protection against document forgery is the most reliable modern method of preventing the forgery of documents, and so forth. It is based on the microstructural uniqueness of a particular physical medium. Given the appropriate equipment (such as a high-resolution scanner to analyze the paper), it is possible to reveal unique structural peculiarities of every piece from the same "factory lot." Cryptographic protection against forgery is done as follows. The unique peculiarities of the particular medium are scanned, and a digital passport is created, which includes the document's contents and information about the paper's (etc.) microstructure. Then, the legitimate document issuer uses his (or its) private key to generate a digital signature for the passport, and writes the passport and the corresponding digital signature to the medium.

Validation of the document is done by scanning the microstructure of the medium on which the document is issued, reading the information it contains, and verifying the digital signature of the issuer using a public key that was published, say, in a number of official publications, or distributed through official channels. Forgery of the document on another physical medium, or modification of the document's contents (or its digital passport), is impossible without knowing the private key used to generate the digital signature. Any forgery will be detected by reading the digital passport and digital signature, comparing the passport with the document's contents, and verifying the digital signature with the public key (assuming this method of protection against document forgery uses a cryptographically secure digital signature system).

1.2.3 Information Protection Technology

When developing a computer security system for general use, the topic of protecting information technologically becomes imperative. One peculiarity of this problem is that it is necessary to build a security system that allows the user to configure it according to specific operational conditions.

The best opportunities to launch an attack on a computer system (CS) are available to valid users who are technically involved in the operational process, and who can abuse their access rights. Generally, the complex part of technological information protection is that it is necessary to provide operators with certain access rights, and at the same time prevent them from abusing these access rights. Strongly limiting access rights results in the users' performance decreasing, and therefore the performance of the CS itself decreasing. To keep performance high, CS's security mechanisms must work in real time, which will minimize nonproductive delays related to data protection transformations or to control any analytical functions of the security system.

One of the most effective and flexible security mechanisms is cryptographic transformations. In connection with this, the problem of creating fast software-oriented ciphering algorithms is an obvious one. The solution to this problem is a major stage in the development of a computer security system that can be widely used.

Thus, using data encryption in computer security systems that are widely used is mostly technological, and requires maximum speed for the cryptographic transformation methods used, provided they are secure enough. This is only one of the problems confronting developers of computer security systems. Another specific problem is creating various types of computer-oriented transformation algorithms.

From the technological point of view, it is important to solve the following problems:

- Creating real-time algorithms for file encryption (transparent file encryption algorithms)
- Creating algorithms to encrypt the information in the hard drive boot sector (so-called mini-algorithms)

- Creating fast algorithms to encrypt data before writing them to the built-in hard disk (transparent disk encryption algorithms)

Each of these algorithm types must satisfy particular requirements related to its specific role in the security systems. The disk encryption procedure is very important, due to how intensely it is used. Obviously, it must operate automatically and in real time; that is, in transparent mode.

It is possible to give some requirements to computer security systems that would correspond to the viewpoints of the various parties participating in creating and using security systems. From an operator's (user's) point of view, a computer security system should satisfy the following requirements:

- It shouldn't alter the regular way of working with the computer.
- It shouldn't demand excessive action from users.
- It should allow users to use the applications they need.
- It shouldn't result in additional delays.

From the point of view of economic efficiency, the following requirements could be placed on a security system:

- Low cost
- Ease of maintenance and operation that would allow you to decrease the technical staff
- Full-scale functionality that would allow you to decrease the number of security tools used to provide overall security
- The possibility of enabling security tools without having to stop data processing
- Operating in real-time mode

To develop a security system that complies with these requirements, it seems reasonable to observe the following design principles:

- Total disk encryption
- Multilevel encryption (disk encryption, transparent file encryption, encryption on demand)
- Keeping the basic operating system untouched
- Controlling information integrity in real-time mode

The types of common computer security threats are shown in Figure 1.1. External, internal, and combined threats are the reasons for the three main types of potential losses: information privacy violation, information integrity violation, and

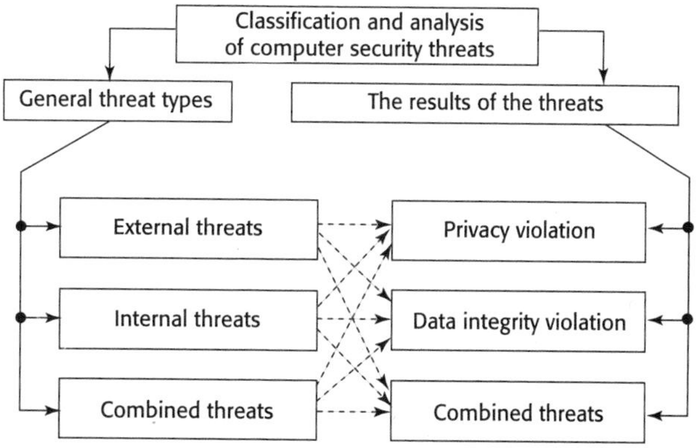

FIGURE 1.1 The types of common computer security threats and the analysis of potential losses.

CS operation violation. In Figure 1.2, various types of external threats and their goals are shown. Internal threats are oriented toward the same goals as external ones, but are implemented in other ways, using other kinds of attacks (Figure 1.3).

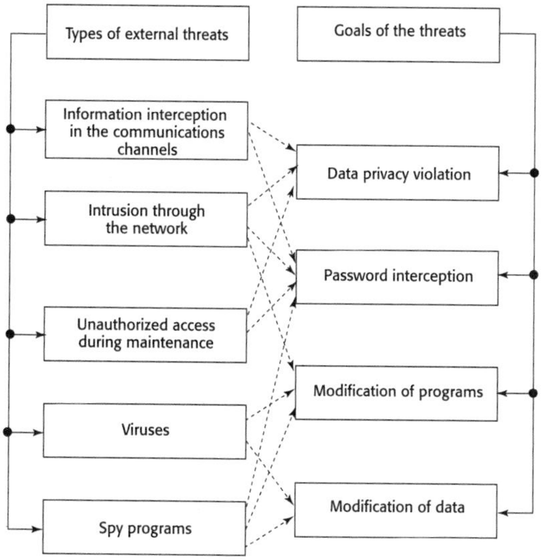

FIGURE 1.2 The classification of external threats and the analysis of their goals.

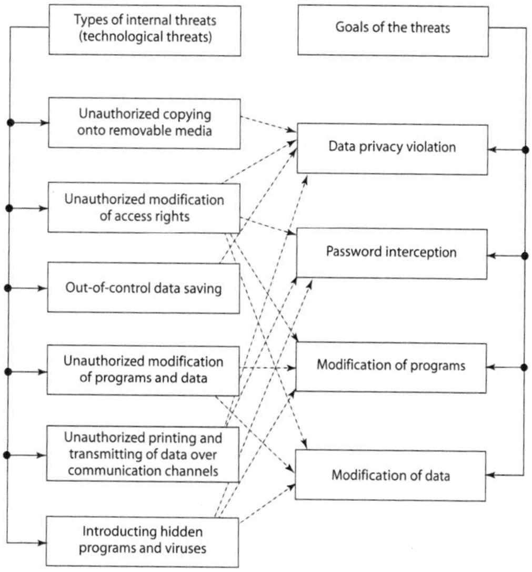

FIGURE 1.3 The classification of internal threats and the analysis of their goals.

In general, computer security mechanisms must provide data privacy and integrity, and failure protection. The three main security mechanisms (Figure 1.4) are data enciphering, controlling the bootstrap procedure, and using cryptographic

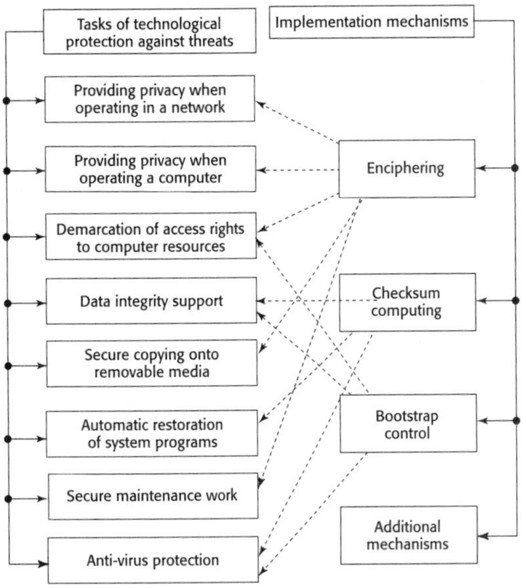

FIGURE 1.4 Security tasks and mechanisms of their implementation.

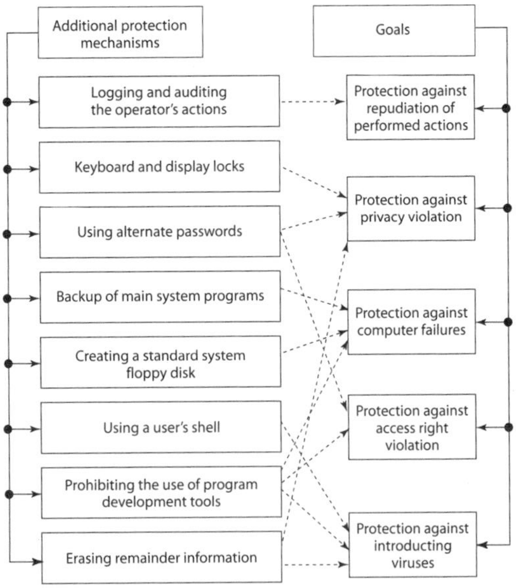

FIGURE 1.5 Additional protection mechanisms and their goals.

checksums. These mechanisms must be built into the security system in various forms, depending on the peculiarities of its development for particular operating conditions. The main mechanisms must be combined with additional ones (Figure 1.5), which will provide for the completeness of the security system and its efficiency in technological data protection.

1.3 THE FUNDAMENTALS OF ONE-KEY CRYPTOGRAPHY

In this section, our main attention is on symmetric-key cryptography, which refers to encryption methods in which either both the sender and the recipient use the same key, or in which their keys are different, but interrelated in an easily predictable way. Other terms designating one-key cryptography are *secret-key*, *private-key*, *one-key* and *single-key* cryptography.

1.3.1 Conditional and Unconditional Security

Claude Shannon published a remarkable theoretical paper on cryptography in the late 1940s. This fundamental work devoted to the theoretical analysis of secret systems (ciphers) triggered the development of modern cryptology and became the basis for creating new cryptosystems. Shannon looked at enciphering as mapping an original message into a ciphered one (a cryptogram): $C = F_i(M)$, where C is a cryptogram, F_i is the mapping, M is an original message, and the i index is to the particular key used. For the message to be deciphered uniquely, the F_i mapping must have a unique reverse mapping, so that $F_iF_i^{-1} = I$, where I is the identity mapping: $M = F_i^{-1}(C)$.

It is assumed that the source of keys is a statistical process or a device that creates mappings $F_1, F_2, \ldots, F_{N_1}$ with probabilities $p_1, p_2, \ldots, p_{N_1}$, the number of possible messages N_2 is finite, and messages $M_1, M_2, \ldots, M_{N_2}$ have a priori probabilities $q_1, q_2, \ldots, q_{N_2}$ (q_i is the probability that can be assigned to the fact that an intercepted cryptogram contains the M_i message, without performing a cryptanalysis).

Let's look at a simple cipher, in which the initial character set of the message is the same as that of the key and of the cryptogram, and encryption is done using a sequential substitution of the characters of the original message with the characters of the cryptogram according to the next character of the key. In this case, the message, the key, and the cryptogram look like a series of characters from the same character set: $M = (m_1, m_2, \ldots, m_n), K = (k_1, k_2, \ldots, k_n), C = (c_1, c_2, \ldots, c_n)$.

This step of encryption is described by the equation $c_i = f(m_i, k_i)$. In actual cryptosystems, the length of the key is usually much smaller than the length of a message being encrypted, so the series $k_1, k_2, \ldots, k_n$ (called a *keystream*) is computed based on a primary key, or can even be periodical.

The task of cryptanalysis is to compute the original message from a cryptogram, provided the set of mappings $F_1, F_2, \ldots, F_{N_1}$ is known. There are cryptosystems, for which any amount of intercepted information isn't sufficient to find the encrypting mappings, and this doesn't depend on the computational resources available to a cryptanalyst. This type of cipher is called *unconditionally secure*. Strictly speaking, ciphers are unconditionally secure if a cryptanalyst (even one possessing infinite computational resources) cannot improve the evaluation of the original message M based on his knowledge of the C cryptogram, as compared to an evaluation when the cryptogram is unknown. This is possible only when M and C are statistically independent; in other words, the condition $P(M = M_i / C = C_i) = P(M = M_i)$ is true for all possible messages M. This condition means that the probability that the M message is contained in the cryptogram being analyzed doesn't depend on the cryptogram's look, or rather, on the sequence of characters in the ciphertext.

There are unconditionally secure systems that can be easily proved. In the simple cipher discussed earlier, let a character set of L characters be used, and the next character of the cryptogram be computed according to the $c_i = f(m_i, k_i) = (m_i + k_i) \bmod L$ formula, where each character c_i, m_i, and k_i is matched with its ordinal number in the character set. For a keystream, let's take the sequence of n random characters $k_1, k_2, \ldots, k_n$; in other words, we take a random key whose length is equal to the message length. To generate the key, let's use a physical random number generator that provides an equal probability for each element from the $\{1, 2, ..., L\}$ number set at its output. A number generated by this generator will be taken as the index of the chosen key character. This source will provide equal probability for any key having the n length. In this case, the probability of choosing a given random key having a length of n is $P(K = K_i) = L^{-n}$.

The ciphering method used can transform any message M_i into the cryptogram C_i by using a K_i key whose value depends on M and C_i. Since $P(K = K_i) =$ const for every i, an arbitrary message M_i can be transformed into any cryptogram M_i and C_i with equal probability; in other words, the $P(M = M_i \ / \ C = C_i) = L^{-n}$ condition is true.

This last statement means that a given cryptogram with the length n can correspond to any original message with the n length with the L^{-n} probability. When encrypting a new message, we'll take a new random key. The described encryption procedures provide unconditional security. Cryptosystems that use an equally probable random key having a length equal to the length of the message are called ciphers with a *one-time tape*, or ciphers with an *infinite keystream*. In practice, such cryptosystems are of limited use, since they require transmitting very long keys.

It can be clearly proven that, to achieve unconditional security, it is necessary to use an equally probable random key having a length equal to the length of the message, regardless of the encryption procedure used. This means that these cryptographic transformation procedures play a secondary role for these types of ciphers, while it is principally important to use an infinite random key.

Cryptosystems of the second type have a feature that states that as the amount of the cryptogram available to the cryptanalyst increases when $n = n_0$, there is only one solution to the cryptanalytic problem. The minimum amount of a cryptogram for which only one solution exists is called the *unicity distance*. With a one-time tape, n_0 tends to infinity: $n_0 \rightarrow \infty$. When the length of a private key is finite, the n_0 value is also finite. We know that for a given cryptogram having a length greater than the unicity distance, it is possible to find the only solution to the cryptanalytic problem. However, for a cryptanalyst possessing limited computational resources, the probability of finding this solution (in the time for which the information remains valuable) is extremely small (10^{-30} or less).

These type of ciphers are called *conditionally secure*. Their security is based on the high computational complexity of the cryptanalytic problem.

The goal of a developer of secure cryptosystems is to decrease the costs of encrypting/decrypting procedures, and at the same time set such a level of complexity for the cryptanalytic problem that finding its solution becomes economically inexpedient. Problems that require such an amount of computations are called *hard* or *computationally complex*, and their solutions are called *computationally unfeasible*. Ciphers based on problems for which finding the solution is computationally unfeasible are also called *computationally secure*. Computationally secure cryptosystems are most commonly used.

By the security of cryptosystems of this type, we mean the complexity of solving the cryptanalytic problem under certain conditions. Shannon introduced the notion of the *work factor* $W(n)$ as the average amount of work required to compute the key from n known characters of a cryptogram, provided the best cryptanalytic algorithm is used. The amount of work can be measured, say, by the number of operations needed to compute the key. This parameter is directly related to the key-computing algorithm. The difficulty of determining $W(n)$ is related to that of finding the best algorithm. Of special interest is the limiting $W(n)$ value, when $n \rightarrow \infty$. At present, no computationally secure cryptosystems are known for which the lower boundary $W(\infty)$ has been definitely found. In light of the complexity of such estimations, actual ciphers are characterized by an estimation of the $W'(\infty)$ work factor, which is obtained for the best of the known key computing methods.

Shannon suggested a model for estimating the unicity distance, from which the equation $n_0 = H(K)/D$ is obtained, where $H(K)$ is the *entropy of the key* (for a random key, this is the key length in bits), and D is the *redundancy of the language* in bits per character. This relation can be rewritten as $H(K) \leq nD$, where $H(K)$ is the number of unknowns in the binary representation of the key, and nD is the number of equations available for computing the key. If the number of equations is less than the number of unknowns, there is no one solution to the system of equations, and therefore the cryptosystem is unconditionally secure. If the number of equations is greater than the number of unknowns, there is only one solution, and the cryptosystem isn't unconditionally secure. However, it can remain conditionally secure when $n >> n_0$. The security level of conditionally secure cryptosystems heavily depends on the particular type of encrypting procedure (here we don't consider the case in which a very small private key is selected, where the complexity of trying every possible key is low). Certain transformation procedures also determine the profile of the work factor; in other words, the specific type of the $W(n)$ dependency. In the following sections, we'll look at two-key ciphers, which are determining modern trend in the development of cryptography. By their nature, they are computationally, but not unconditionally, secure cryptosystems. The assumption that computationally complex problems exist is fundamental in modern cryptography.

1.3.2 General Issues of Cipher Design

In the last section, we showed that an unconditionally secure cipher can be built only by using an equally probable random key having a length equal to the length of the message, a new key being used for each new message. Since the key is used once and chosen at random, one might speak about an infinite random key. We'd like to note that, when using an infinite key, there is no need for any complex procedures that transform the characters of the original text into the characters of the ciphertext, since it will suffice to use the simple operation of applying key characters to the corresponding plaintext characters (for example, the operation of bitwise addition modulo 2).

Practical secrecy most often means the work effort needed to solve the cryptanalytic problem for ciphers with finite keys. This concerns a theoretical model of a cryptosystem that is disassociated from specific conditions of cipher usage; in other words, it has to do with a theoretical estimation of the computational complexity of the cryptanalytic problem. It seems best to describe ciphers having finite keys as computationally secure cryptosystems. This is because by practical secrecy we can also mean secrecy that depends on a theoretical security level and on the organizational and technical conditions of the cipher's use. For example, when using ciphers with infinite keys, practical secrecy is determined by various leakage channels related to processing the original message in the cryptosystem. These tapping channels can be used to intercept a part of the message or key. Actually, even when these ciphers are used, there is some probability that the transmitted information will become known to an interceptor.

In a broad sense, we can also understand practical security to mean the cipher's security, taking into account a great number of things that happen under the actual operating conditions of a cryptosystem, and that are related to the integrity control of all components of the actual cryptosystem. These are things like the cryptographic protocol, the enciphering device, the secure channel used to transmit the secret key, the key controlling procedures, and the environmental elements (such as a protected premises, staff, physical and technical means of protection, etc.). In the theoretical model of a cryptosystem, only security that is related to solving the cryptanalytic problem and that determines the maximum achievable secrecy level is considered. (Under the actual operating conditions of cryptosystems, their secrecy may be much lower than this limiting value.)

Since actual practical secrecy cannot guarantee complete security of information, even when ciphers with an infinite keystream are used, using practically convenient cryptosystems with finite keys based on the high computational complexity of the cryptanalytic problem is completely justified. The fact that computationally secure ciphers can be decoded doesn't indicate the work effort such disclosure would take. When decoding a cipher in practice, the effort the cryptanalytic task takes is the most important feature, because an attacker's resources are limited in practice.

When using ciphers with keys that have a finite length, the specific choice of enciphering algorithm is crucial to ensure practical security. The transformation procedures determine the complexity of the cryptanalysis. It is also important to keep in mind that the key length must be large enough to prevent completely the exhaustive search (i.e., to make it computationally impossible to try every possible key when using modern computing systems). With a key length of 128 bits or more, this requirement is satisfied.

If a computationally secure cipher doesn't allow key disclosure with a probability greater than the probability of information leakage through the channels connected to the actual operating conditions of a cryptosystem, using this cipher is preferable. Besides which, there are a number of applications in which ciphers with infinite keys cannot be used (for example, when protecting information that flows in a computer system where all data stored on the hard drive is encrypted). In such cases, it is better to use ciphers with finite keys (provided the computational security of such cryptosystems is high enough).

When developing computationally secure ciphers, two general techniques are used: confusion and diffusion.

Confusion is the extension of the influence of one character of a plaintext over several characters of a ciphertext. This begins an avalanche effect (in the case of block ciphers, it is necessary to extend the effect of every bit of an input text over all bits of the output text). *Diffusion* is a ciphering transformation that destroys the relationships between the statistical characteristics of the input and output texts; in other words, obscures the statistical characteristics of the input message. An example of a procedure that performs diffusion is a transposition of plaintext characters that leads to an equal redundancy distribution over the entire text. (Note that the redundancy of an original text plays a significant role in a cryptanalysis based on a ciphertext. However, when performing a cryptanalysis based on a known or chosen text, there is no point in considering this.)

To prevent the possibility of computing the key in parts, it is also commonplace to implement a principle of extending the effect of one key character over many characters of the cryptogram. In cryptosystems in which several successive simple ciphering procedures are carried out, this principle is automatically implemented during diffusion.

1.3.3 Product and Iterated Block Ciphers

In modern automated information processing systems, it is often preferable to use block ciphers. *Block ciphers* are cryptosystems that encrypt information in blocks of a fixed length; for example, n bits. This type of cryptographic transformation is called *block ciphering*. For block ciphering, data are represented as a series of n-bit blocks. In actual practice, files, certain fields in spreadsheets, and other types of computer messages have an arbitrary length, which usually isn't a multiple of the block length. This is why a method of complementing the last data block is used.

The last data block is often complemented with a binary vector (1, 0, 0, ..., 0), in which the number of zeroes can be anywhere from 0 to $(n - 2)$. If the length of the last block is n, an additional n-bit block, having the (1, 0, 0, ..., 0) structure, is appended to the message. This method makes it possible to unambiguously determine the appended binary vector and drop it if necessary. Using such a way of complementing a message up to a length that is a multiple of n, one can represent any message M as a series (concatenation) of n-bit subblocks M_i: $M = M_1||M_2|| \ldots ||M_i|| \ldots ||M_m$. Each block of the original message can be transformed independent of the other blocks, and so, when using block ciphers, direct access to encrypted data is possible. The most general mechanism of block enciphering is one that makes it possible to transform any input block into any output block, the size of the output block being greater than or equal to the size of the input block. A block of a ciphertext cannot be less than a plaintext block, because in that case several different plaintext blocks would correspond to the same ciphertext block. This would mean ambiguous decryption. If the length of the output block is greater than n, several different ciphertext blocks will correspond to the same plaintext block. In that case, deciphering is possible and unique. (Examples of such cryptosystems are probabilistic ciphers.) Since an increased length of encrypted data places certain limitations on the areas in which it can be applied, the most commonly used ciphers have the size of output blocks equal to that of input blocks. Block ciphers specify a one-to-one correspondence between possible input and output blocks. Since input and output block sets coincide, encryption makes a substitution on the $0, 1, \ldots, 2^n - 1$ set of numbers, which can be presented as:

$$\begin{pmatrix} 0 & 1 & 2 & \ldots & 2^n - 1 \\ \mathbf{E}_K(0) & \mathbf{E}_K(1) & \mathbf{E}_K(2) & \ldots & \mathbf{E}_K(2^n - 1) \end{pmatrix},$$

where $\boldsymbol{E}_K(M)$ is a function of enciphering with the K key; in other words, a function specified by enciphering procedures using the K enciphering key.

The enciphering function sets the correspondence between a plaintext block M and a cryptogram block C, which is written as $C = \boldsymbol{E}_K(M)$. For a given key, one substitution is implemented. In general, different substitutions correspond to different keys. If a cipher uses a key that is k bits long, this cipher specifies no more than 2^k different substitutions, which is usually an extremely small portion of the number of all possible substitutions, equal to $2^n!$. To implement all possible substitutions, you need to use a key with the length of $k = \log_2(2^n!) \approx n2^n$ bits.

One of the statistical methods of breaking ciphers is a *frequency cryptanalysis*. This method is based on the examination of the frequency of characters in the cryptogram, and then making a correlation with the frequency of characters in the original text. The frequency method makes it possible to break mono-alphabetic substitution ciphers that correspond to block ciphering when small input blocks are used (for example, when $n = 8$). As the input block size increases, the frequency properties of the language of the plaintext become less pronounced, but even with

$n = 16$, the unevenness of the frequency properties of the original text can be effectively used to break the cipher. With $n = 32$, frequency cryptanalysis becomes extremely complex, and a block cipher with such an input size can be used in some cases. The minimum secure block length is considered to be $n = 64$. The greater the input block size, the higher the security that can be achieved. However, for large block sizes, manufacturing ciphering devices becomes more complex. When developing the American DES standard, the choice of the $n = 64$ value was a certain compromise between security and implementation convenience. This size was commonly used for over 25 years. Currently, the potentialities of microelectronics have dramatically increased, and the $n = 128$ input block size is now standard.

A large input block size itself is simply a necessary condition for the high security of the algorithm being developed. Designing secure block ciphers is associated with using nonlinear transformations that have good diffusion and confusion properties, or with combining linear and nonlinear transformations. The advantages of linear transformations are ease of implementation, small operating time, and the convenience of using the secret key as the transformation parameter. However, using only linear transformations isn't sufficient to design secure ciphers.

One method of achieving good diffusion and confusion is building a compound (*product*) cipher that includes a number of sequentially used simple ciphers, each of which makes a small contribution to diffusion and confusion. The idea of building product ciphers was suggested and justified by Shannon. In product ciphers, ciphering procedures of one type alternate with those of another type. For simple ciphers, substitutions (S), transpositions (T), and linear transformations (L) can be used. In such a case, the resulting cipher can be presented as $F = S_n T_n L_n \ldots S_2 T_2 L_2 S_1 T_1 L_1$.

A secret key can be used with procedures of any one type (T, L, or S). The key can be also used with procedures of all (or some) types.

The simplest product cipher is shown in Figure 1.6, where the S boxes denote a substitution operation on 4-bit subblocks of the input message, T means a transposition on a $4k$-bit data block being transformed, and L is a linear transformation operation, using which the mixing of encrypted data is performed with a secret key represented as the $K_1, K_2, \ldots, K_r$ subkey set. In this r-cascade cryptoscheme, the encrypting procedure consists of r successive rounds of transformation using different round keys. A substitution operation involves replacing a 4-bit input binary vector with a 4-bit output binary vector according to a *substitution table.* If we represent 4-bit binary vectors with their numeric values (i.e., interpret a binary vector as a binary number), we can write the substitution table as

$$\begin{pmatrix} 0 & 1 & 2 & \ldots & 15 \\ \alpha_0 & \alpha_1 & \alpha_2 & \ldots & \alpha_{15} \end{pmatrix},$$

where $\forall i$, $\alpha_i \in \{0, 1, \ldots, 15\}$, and the columns set up a correspondence between the 4-bit input value (the upper row) and the 4-bit output value (the lower row).

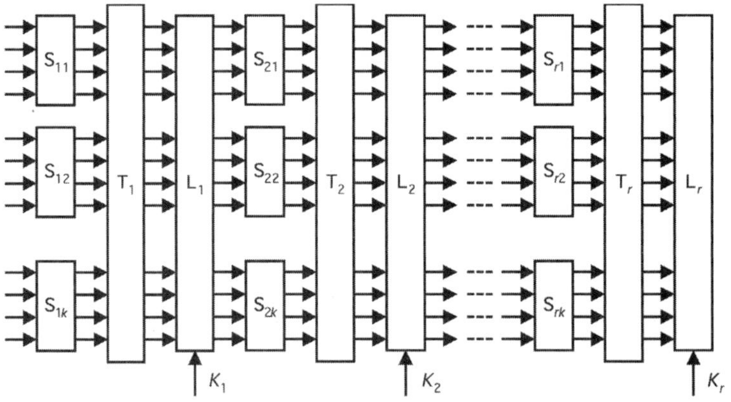

FIGURE 1.6 The structure of a product cipher based on substitutions and transpositions.

For an arbitrary substitution table, it is easy to write a table that specifies the inverse substitution. Similarly, the bit transposition operation T and the corresponding inverse transposition T^{-1} can be specified. For the linear transformation L, it is also easy to specify the corresponding inverse transposition L^{-1}. The deciphering procedure is performed according to the scheme shown in Figure 1.7.

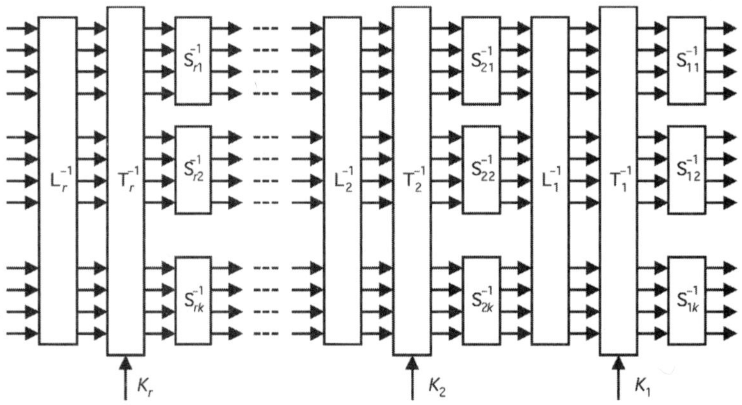

FIGURE 1.7 The deciphering procedure scheme in a product cipher.

The discussed cipher belongs to the so-called *iterated ciphers*, in which ciphering is done in the form of repeatedly performing a standard transformation procedure (called a *ciphering round*, or a *round ciphering function*), which is a composition of three simple transformations of different types. In the process, different keys called *round keys* are used in different rounds.

When implemented as a high-speed device, the enciphering/deciphering procedure for a product cipher will be performed using various electronic circuits. Later in this book, we look at special cryptoschemes that make it possible to use the same electronic circuit for both encrypting and decrypting, thus making the hardware implementation more cost-effective. In such ciphers, changing the ciphering mode is done by changing the order of round keys.

Feistel's Cryptoscheme

Feistel's cryptoscheme (Figure 1.8) is a general scheme for designing an n-bit block cipher based on an arbitrary function F with the $n/2$ input block size. An important advantage of this structure is that it specifies the same algorithm for both encrypting and decrypting. Specifying a particular enciphering mode is determined by the order of using the round keys. Changing the ciphering mode is done by inverting the order of the round keys.

The security of ciphers designed using this scheme is determined by the properties of the F round function. A great many various ciphers are known that are designed according to this scheme, and only differ in the number of rounds and the structure of the round function.

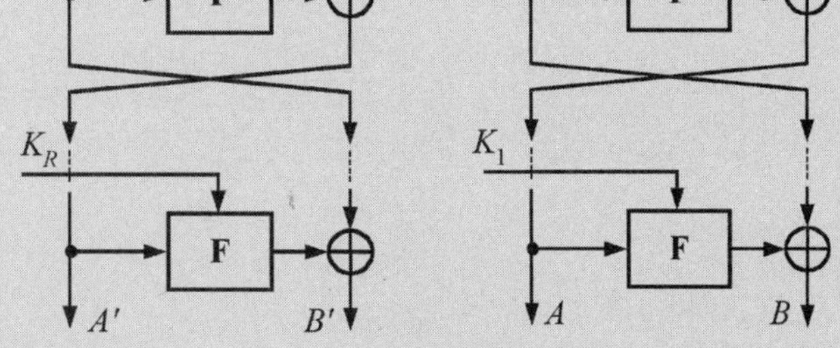

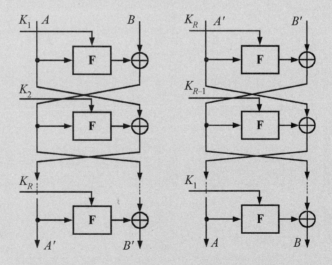

FIGURE 1.8 Feistel's cryptoscheme: *a*—enciphering, *b*—deciphering.

1.3.4 Controlled Operations—a New Cryptographic Primitive

Controlled operations are essential to the entire concept of contemporary cryptography. In general, a controlled operation is an operation on one data block that is carried out conditionally on the state of another data block. This section covers the use of controlled operations as a cryptographic primitive.

General Characteristics of Controlled Operations

Modern applied cryptography increasingly tends to take into account requirements related to the peculiarities of electronic information technologies. At present, using encryption to protect information is becoming increasingly technological. The technological nature of using encryption manifests itself in:

- Common use
- The variety of tasks fulfilled
- The variety of operational conditions
- Specialization to solve specific problems

This has led to increasing requirements imposed on:

- Security (in various operating conditions, new kinds of cryptanalytic attacks, such as a so-called differential fault analysis, become relevant)
- Encryption speed (this follows from the need to keep a high performance of the computer system and telecommunications after placing the security system in operation)
- Cost-effectiveness of the hardware implementation (this is related to the wide use of enciphering devices)

The fact that contests for designing new ciphers take place in the United States (the AES contest), Europe (the NESSIE contest), and Japan indicates the recognition of encryption's technological role. The technological areas of application are so varied that designing new specialized encryption algorithms will still be an urgent topic for a long time. In modern cryptography, there is significant interest in looking for new cryptographic primitives to build block ciphers that may prove promising for technological applications, and that will provide:

- High speed
- High security
- A low complexity of implementation

The cryptographic primitives traditionally used when designing one-key cryptosystems are *substitutions*, *transpositions (permutations)*, *arithmetic and algebraic operations*, and some other auxiliary operations. The most frequently used operation is substitution, which is also the most general. This operation is the cryptographic primitive on which the security of most block ciphers is based. The following ways of implementing substitutions are known:

- In software and software-hardware ciphers, substitutions are implemented as substitution tables stored in the computer memory. In this case, it is easy to implement substitution over binary vectors that are 13-bits long (the required memory is about 10 KB). Despite the large memory size of modern computers, implementing substitution operations over vectors longer than 16 bits is problematic.
- In hardware ciphers, substitutions are implemented as complex electronic circuits. General substitutions over binary vectors longer than 13 bits are very hard to implement.

An advantage of general substitution operations is that the best substitutions that comply with certain cryptographic criteria can be found. In the case of substitutions with a small size (say, 6×4), many effective substitutions can be found. However, for substitutions having a size of 8×8 or larger, choosing the best variants is problematic. In connection with this, choosing substitutions with big sizes is done in some ciphers by using certain known operations with certain properties. A typical example is the SAFER cipher, in which substitutions are defined by raising to a discrete power and performing a discrete logarithm operation on a modulo 257 residue field.

Because of some problems that emerge when designing fast block ciphers based on substitutions, alternative solutions were suggested. One such solution is the RC5 cipher, in which the only nonlinear operation is rotation (end-around shift), which depends on the data being transformed, and is easily implemented on modern widely used processors. Despite its extreme simplicity, the RC5 cipher has proven to be very secure against linear and differential cryptanalysis. Theoretical investigations have revealed that having the selection of the rotation operation depend on the transformed data is an effective way to protect against these two important types of attacks. Due to its effectiveness, data-dependent rotation has found a use in such new ciphers as RC5 and MARS.

If a fixed rotation operation that is a special case of a substitution operation is linear, *making it dependent on the transformed data leads to the creation of a new nonlinear operation with good cryptographic properties*. Apparently, besides the data-dependent rotation operation, there are other types of controlled operations. Their important features are their type, and the number of different variants from which the current modification used to transform a data subblock is chosen. The second parameter determines how many additional data bits can be used when performing a controlled operation on the current n-bit data subblock. For a controlled rotation operation, there are n modifications. Despite such a small number of modifications, this controlled operation appears to be an effective cryptographic primitive. One can expect that operations with an essentially greater number of modifications—say, from 2^n to 2^{3n} or more—will prove to be more effective. An example of such a controlled operation is a bit permutation operation that depends on data being transformed, and is a generalized case of controlled rotation.

A different important direction is the design of special *controlled operational substitutions* for cryptographic applications—in particular, controlled binary operations. The simplest way to implement such operations is by using a controlled adder (Figure 1.9), which makes it possible to specify 2^n different modifications of the $Y = X *_V A$ addition operation, including the bitwise addition modulo two ("$*_V$" = XOR) for $V = (0, 0, 0, ..., 0)$, and the addition modulo 2^n ("$*_V$" = "+") for $V = (1, 1, 1, ..., 1)$ as a special case.

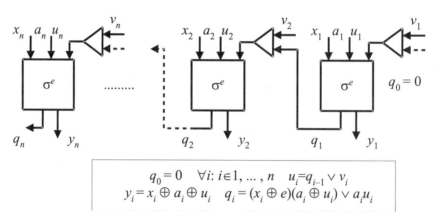

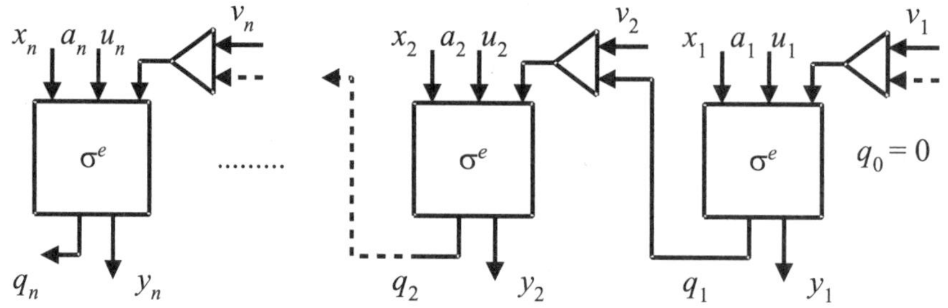

$$q_0 = 0 \quad \forall i: i \in 1, \ldots, n \quad u_i = q_{i-1} \vee v_i$$
$$y_i = x_i \oplus a_i \oplus u_i \quad q_i = (x_i \oplus e)(a_i \oplus u_i) \vee a_i u_i$$

FIGURE 1.9 A controlled adder (e = 0–"addition," e = 1–"subtraction").

As opposed to table substitutions, it is possible to create a great many different types of controlled transformation operations with a sufficiently large input block size (32, 64, or 128 bits) that can be easily implemented as hardware. In this case, the operations actually implement a special substitution subclass. However, this substitution subclass belongs to substitutions of a much greater size, which creates prerequisites for designing secure fast ciphers with a low hardware implementation complexity.

Traditionally used table substitutions, and arithmetic and other operations that were initially used to solve other problems, aren't oriented toward cryptographic applications. From a cryptographic point of view, they have both advantages (for example, the bitwise addition modulo 2 is easy to implement and very fast) and disadvantages (for example, linearity). For cryptographic usage, it is best to develop operations that are adjusted for cryptographic applications and possess the special properties necessary for high security encryption algorithms. As a prototype for such operations, we can use the data-dependent rotation operation that was used as a basic cryptographic primitive in such ciphers as RC5, RC6, and MARS. Specifying the current modification of such an operation depending on the data being transformed determines its nonlinear properties. Despite the fact that the choice can only be made from n different modifications (n is the length of the binary vector on which the rotation is performed), this cryptographic primitive appears to be quite effective. Its merits are the simplicity of program implementation, nonlinearity, and increasing the effective input size to log2n bits (this is the number of data bits that specify the choice of the current modification; in other words, of control bits).

In general, *controlled permutations* (CP) and *controlled binary operations* (CBO) seem to be more effective for cryptographic applications, since they include a very large number of possible modifications, which makes it possible to implement a control input with a size from n to $3n$ (and in some cases even more). Preliminary investigations of algebraic and probability-statistical properties of CP and CBO showed their usability for developing secure fast ciphers.

The structure and working principles of controlled permutations and controlled adders are quite descriptive, so these variants of controlled operations are thought of as an individual class of cryptographic primitives. Controlled operational substitutions (COS) are an even wider class of controlled operations. However, this type of operation isn't so clearly perceived as an individual class of cryptographic operations. In connection with this, it is worth stressing how controlled operations differ from substitution operations of an $m \times n$ size, where $m > n$.

In essence, controlled operational substitutions are specially designed cryptography-oriented operations performed over two or more binary vectors. They are built according to a special rule that allows you to design operations for transforming binary vectors of arbitrary size. These operations have a structure that makes the complexity of their hardware implementation increase approximately according to a linear law, while increasing the size of binary vectors being transformed. COSs have the following features:

- Use standard boolean functions that specify the relationship between the input and output bits
- The possibility of designing COSs to transform binary vectors that are from 32 to 256 bits
- A low complexity of hardware implementation
- High performance
- The possibility of a theoretical justification for choosing a COS of a certain type for an arbitrary input size

Figure 1.10 illustrates the possible types of controlled operational substitutions.

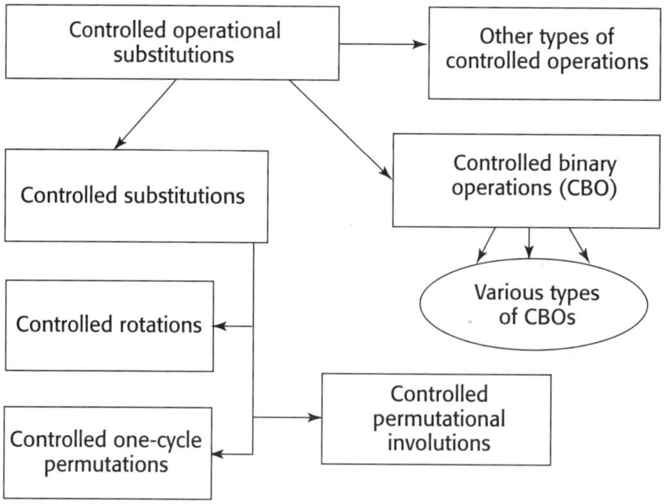

FIGURE 1.10 Types of controlled operational substitutions.

Controlled operations have the following advantages:

- They make it possible to use all the bits of the data block being transformed when a unified nonlinear operation is performed. They also make it possible to reverse a direct operation by inverting a special bit that specifies the encryption or decryption mode.
- They make it possible to design new types of cryptoschemes that allow you to change the transformation mode by changing the order of the subkeys used.
- They make it possible to design effective mechanisms of internal key extension, which provides a high encryption speed in applications with frequent changes of secret keys.

Despite the initial hardware orientation, designing effective controlled operations can potentially lead to a significant leap in the performance of software-oriented ciphers. This is related to the fact that some types of controlled operations, such as controlled substitutions, are extremely effective as cryptographic primitives, and the cost of their hardware implementation is very low. This cost/effectiveness ratio makes it very attractive for processor vendors to include a new command—controlled permutation—among the standard processor commands. The possibility of providing a high software encryption speed, from 800 to 2000 Mbit/sec, significantly increases the competitiveness of such processors, with minimum hardware costs. For example, implementing an operational controlled permutation box (CPB) with a 64-bit transformed data input and a 192-bit control input requires less than 1200 transistors, and implementing a CPB with a 32-bit transformed data input and an 80-bit control input requires less than 1000 transistors.

1.4 TWO-KEY CRYPTOSYSTEMS

Symmetric-key cryptosystems considered earlier in this chapter either use the same key for encryption and decryption, or the key used for decryption is easily computed on the basis of the encryption key. The main drawback of such ciphers is that the two parties that exchange data must share a secret key, which results in difficulties in initially establishing secret communications. *Two-key cryptosystems* (also known as *asymmetric key* or *public key* cryptosystems) considered in this section are free from this drawback

1.4.1 The Public Key Distribution System

In 1976, Diffie and Hellman published a paper that marked the birth of two-key cryptography and led to increasing the number of public investigations in the area of cryptography. This work contained a stunning conclusion: *it is possible to design practically secure secret systems that don't require secret key sending.* Diffie and Hellman introduced the notion of a trapdoor one-way function. A one-way function f means that the $f(x)$ function is easily computable for any argument x from the area of definition, but for a randomly chosen y from the area of values, it is computationally difficult to find a value of the x argument so that $f(x) = y$. Using such functions to protect login using a one-way password transformation is common. However, how can you use a one-way function in cryptographic systems if even the valid receiver cannot perform the decryption procedure? For encryption, a *trapdoor one-way function* was suggested.

A trapdoor one-way function is a family of invertible functions f_z with the z parameter such that for a given z it is possible to find the $\mathbf{E}_z$ and $\mathbf{D}_z$ algorithms that make it easy to compute the $f_z(x)$ value for all x from the area of definition, and also to compute the $f_z^{-1}(y)$ value for all y from the area of values. However, for essentially all values of the z parameter and essentially all values of y from the area of values of f_z, finding $f_z^{-1}(y)$ is computationally impossible, even when $\mathbf{E}_z$ is known. As a one-way function, Diffie and Hellman suggested the discrete exponentiation function

$$f(x) = \alpha^{x} (\bmod p),$$

where x is an integer, $1 \le x \le p-1$, and p is a k-bit prime number. The $\alpha < p$ number is chosen so that its power modulo p is an ordered set of numbers $\{\alpha^1, \alpha^2, ..., \alpha^{p-1}\}$

that is a permutation of the {1, 2, ..., $p-1$} number set. (Such a number α is called the primitive element modulo p.)

Even for a very large modulo p (for example, when $k = 1024$ bits), it is easy to compute the value of this function from a given x. The procedure of computing the function is called *discrete exponentiation*. To perform this procedure, it would suffice to perform about $2\log_2 p$ multiplications of k-bit numbers (or $\log_2 p$ multiplications and $\log_2 p$ divisions of $2k$-bit numbers by k-bit numbers). The procedure of discrete exponentiation is based on the preliminary computation of the α^1, α^2, α^4, α^8, ..., $\alpha^{2^{k-1}}$ values (modulo p).

The inverse function for the discrete exponentiation is the $f^{-1}(y)$ function, which sets the correspondence between the given value y and a value x for which the $\alpha^x = y \pmod p$ condition is true. The problem of finding such an x is called the *discrete logarithm problem* (finding the discrete logarithm). Discrete logarithms are hard to compute when the $p-1$ number includes one large prime factor—for example, when it can be presented as $p-1 = 2p'$, where p' is a prime number. Under this condition, the complexity of the discrete logarithm problem is approximately equal to performing $p^{1/2}$ multiplied by modulo p. The solution to this problem is computationally impossible for large k values (for example, when $k \geq 512$), and therefore, for the conditions posed on the choice of the p and α numbers, the discrete exponentiation function is one-way.

The Diffie-Hellman method of *public key distribution* is the following method of using discrete exponentiation to exchange private keys between network users, using only public messages. A large prime number p is chosen, as well as the corresponding primitive element $\alpha < p$. (To provide for the security of the public encryption system being discussed, the following requirement is posed on the p number: the expansion of this number into factors must include at least one large prime factor; the size of the p number must be no less than 512 bits.)

The mechanism of private key distribution over a public channel is as follows. Every subscriber chooses a random private key x and computes the corresponding public key y according to the formula $y = \alpha^x \pmod p$.

It is easy to compute y from any value of x. However, when the size of the p number is 512 bits or more, it is computationally impossible to find the discrete logarithm, and therefore to find the number x for which $\alpha^x \bmod p$ is equal to the given y value. All subscribers place their public keys in a commonly available directory. This directory must be certified by a specially founded certification center, in order to exclude possible attacks involving public key substitution or using false public keys. If two subscribers, **A** and **B**, want to establish a secret connection, they act in the following way. Subscriber **A** takes **B**'s public key from the directory, and computes the shared private key using his (i.e., **A**'s) private key:

$$Z_{AB} = (y_B)^{x_A} = \left(\alpha^{x_B}\right)^{x_A} = \alpha^{x_B x_A} \pmod p$$

where y_A and y_B are **A** and **B**'s public keys, and x_A and x_B are the corresponding private keys. There is no need to transmit the shared private key Z_{AB} over a communication network because subscriber **B** computes its value in a similar fashion from **A**'s public key taken from the directory

$$Z_{AB} = (y_A)^{x_B} = (\alpha^{x_A})^{x_B} = \alpha^{x_B x_A} (\text{mod } p).$$

An opponent (a possible intruder) knows the $y_B = \alpha^{x_B} (\text{mod } p)$ and $y_A = \alpha^{x_A} (\text{mod } p)$ values, but, to compute Z_{AB}, he must solve a complex discrete logarithm problem. The shared private key can be used by the subscribers to encrypt session secret keys, and those can be used to encrypt messages using symmetric encryption methods. The solution to the discrete logarithm problem exists, but it is computationally impossible. Thus, the security of the Diffie-Hellman method is based on the complexity of finding the discrete logarithm.

There are two basic problems in one-key cryptosystems:

- Secret key distribution over a secure channel
- Secret key authentication

By authentication, we mean a procedure that allows the receiver to become convinced that the secret key belongs to a valid sender (for example, a key distribution center).

The public key distribution system solves the first problem; in other words, it makes it possible to do without a secure channel when distributing secret keys. However, it doesn't eliminate the necessity of authentication. It should be noted that in two-key cryptography, the authentication problem doesn't arise, but rather moves to the foreground, since the key distribution problem is solved using its methods.

1.4.2 The Notion of a Cryptographic Protocol

The terms *algorithm* and *protocol* are often used in cryptography. Intuitively, their meaning is clear enough. They are widely used in other areas of science and technology. An algorithm is one of the main notions in programming and applied mathematics, just as a protocol is in communications. From now on in this book, by an *algorithm* we will mean a set of commands, actions, instructions, or computations that must be performed to obtain some result. In the process, new data can appear as the result of source data transformation, a random choice at some step of the algorithm, or the computer taking some measurements of the environmental parameters (the parameters of external objects). The algorithm is performed by a subject (computer).

By a *protocol*, we mean a collection of actions (instructions, commands, computations, algorithms) performed in a specified order by two or more subjects to obtain a certain result. The correctness of performing a protocol depends on the actions performed by each subject (user, subscriber) of the cryptosystem. A subject can be a workstation, a computer program, a radio transmitter, an artificial satellite, an operator, a server, an authority, and so forth. Subjects participating in protocols of a system usually act according to specified algorithms; in other words, an algorithm appears as an internal element of the protocol. For a protocol to lead to a desired goal, it is necessary to satisfy the following requirements:

- The protocol must be correct—the set of actions specified by the protocol must allow you to obtain the required result under all possible conditions.
- Completeness and unambiguity—the protocol must specify the actions of each participant for every possible situation.
- Consistency—the results obtained by different participants mustn't contradict each other.
- Awareness and agreement of all the participants—each subject must know the protocol and all the steps he or she (or it) must perform; all the subjects must agree to play their roles.

Cryptographic protocols are protocols in which cryptographic data transformations are used. Even though cryptographic protocols often use some encryption algorithm, secrecy isn't always their goal. For example, the parties of a cryptographic protocol may wish to simultaneously sign a contract, carry out computerized coin tossing, authenticate the participants of a conference, and so forth.

Enciphering data and computing one-way functions constitute the execution of corresponding algorithms. The schemes of user or remote workstation authentication and computerized coin tossing we discussed previously are examples of protocols. If a protocol uses a cryptographic function, the function must be secure. Even if encryption algorithms used are secure, this doesn't ensure the protocol's security. For a cryptographic protocol to be secure, it is necessary that the cryptographic algorithms used are secure under the conditions of this particular application.

In cryptosystems, the existence of a probable adversary is assumed (in practice, this theoretic notion is quite real). Developers of cryptographic algorithms and protocols take precautions, as far as possible, against an adversary's (or adversaries') possible actions, and try to ensure that the protocol's goal is achieved with regard to all possible attacks. An attack on an algorithm, protocol, or cryptosystem is made up of the adversary's actions, using which he or she tries to read a cryptogram, break a one-way function (i.e., compute the argument value by a function value), pretend to be another subject, create false messages, widen his authorization, and in general, create conditions under which the correctness of using the algorithms and protocols of the cryptosystem will be violated. If such actions are possible, it is said that the cryptosystem is vulnerable with respect to such-and-such an attack. Two types of adversaries can be distinguished by their actions: active and passive.

A *passive adversary* doesn't take any action that causes the disorganization of a cryptographic protocol. His goal is to intercept messages that pass over the cryptosystem in order to read their contents, compute distributed keys, or discover the results of a vote or a coin tossing. Using radio communication to transfer messages creates conditions favorable for a passive adversary, under which an attack on the cryptosystem can be detected only indirectly. When using a wired means of communication, unauthorized connections reveal a passive adversary. However, it must be taken into account that he can use induced electromagnetic radiation.

An *active adversary* tries to create false messages, intercept and modify messages, get access to databases, widen his or her authorization, make a false public key, forge a signature, and so forth. When using a wired telephone communication, conditions are ripe for an active adversary, whereas, when using radio communication, the adversary's actions can be easily detected. You will also need to foresee cases in which an active adversary is a valid user of the system.

According to their relationships with the organization using the cryptosystems (or other protection tools), adversaries can be divided into two types: internal and external.

An internal adversary is a person with certain valid authorization inside the organization he attacks, or a participant in a cryptographic protocol who tries to do harm to other participants of the protocol. Both internal and external adversaries can be active or passive. An attack by an internal adversary is called an *internal* attack.

An attack in which only external adversaries are involved is called an *external* attack. It is possible for external and internal adversaries to unite, thus creating the most serious threat to the secure operation of the cryptosystem. If there is an adversary among the developers, attacks that use trapdoors built into the algorithms that compute the key parameters or hard-to-detect harmful software viruses will also be possible.

1.4.3 Digital Signatures

Based on the aforementioned idea of using a trapdoor one-way function, Diffie and Hellman suggested a public-key cryptosystem structure for a multisubscriber network. Each subscriber—say, the *i*th—chooses a random value of the z_i parameter and keeps it secret. Next, he designs the $\mathbf{E}_{z_i}$ algorithm and publishes it in a commonly available directory. He also designs the $\mathbf{D}_{z_i}$ algorithm and keeps it secret. Any other subscriber—say, the *j*th—uses the public encrypting algorithm $\mathbf{E}_{z_i}$ and computes the $C = f_{z_i}(M)$ cryptogram, which he then sends to the *i*th subscriber. Using the $\mathbf{D}_{z_i}$ private algorithm, the *i*th subscriber computes the original plaintext: $f_{z_i}^{-1}(C) = M$.

The authors of this generalized scheme of public-key encryption proved that it can be used to obtain *digital signatures.* In general, a digital signature is a number with a specific structure that makes it possible to use a public key to verify that this number was created for some message with the help of a private key. To implement a digital signature, you have to choose a trapdoor one-way function f_z so that for every value of the z parameter, the area of the definition of the f_z function coincides with its area of values. With this requirement, for every message that can be represented as a number from the area of definition of the $f_z(x)$ function, the subscriber i can use the private algorithm to compute the $S = f_{z_i}^{-1}(M)$ number. (If the message is too long, it can be divided into parts of the necessary sizes, and each can be signed independently.)

Each user of the cryptosystem can restore the M message from the S value. If M is an understandable message, or if it can be correlated with such a message according to a pre-specified rule, the S value can be considered the i subscriber's digital signature of the M message. Indeed, only the owner of the $\mathbf{D}_{z_i}$ private algorithm can generate a "plaintext" text S that is encrypted to the understandable cryptogram M with the help of the $\mathbf{E}_{z_i}$ algorithm, since only the i subscriber knows how to compute $f_{z_i}^{-1}$.

The i subscriber can also send the j subscriber a signed secret message. To do this, he encrypts S using the private algorithm $\mathbf{E}_{z_j}$, thus obtaining the $C = \mathbf{E}_{z_i}(S)$ cryptogram. Having received the encrypted message, the *j*th subscriber decrypts it with his secret algorithm $\mathbf{D}_{z_j}(C) = S$ and then decrypts the S number with the *i*th subscriber's public algorithm $\mathbf{E}_{z_i}(S) = M$. Therefore, the *j*th subscriber restores *i*'s signature and the original message with the received cryptogram C.

Using protocols based on symmetric cryptographic methods assumes that the two parties *trust each other.* Public-key cryptosystems (asymmetric cryptosystems) make it possible to implement interaction protocols for parties that *don't trust each other.* Digital signature systems are one of the most important examples of these. To effectively use a digital signature in actual business relationships, it is necessary to legalize it. For this, it is necessary to adopt corresponding national (or international) laws, and support public key exchanging with a regular legal procedure that will provide protection against public key repudiation.

1.4.4 The RSA Cryptosystem

The RSA cryptosystem is the most widely known digital signature system, and is the simplest one to understand. It was invented by R. Rivest, A. Shamir, and L. Adleman. Let's examine this cryptosystem. According to Euler's theorem that comes from number theory, for each relatively prime number M and n, where $M < n$, the $M^{\varphi(n)} = 1 \pmod{n}$ equation is true.

For M, we're going to take the original message that needs to be signed or encrypted. The requirement of relative primeness of the M and n numbers will be satisfied by choosing an n equal to the product of two large prime factors. In this case, the probability that a random message won't be relatively prime with the modulus is negligibly small. For a one-way transformation, we're going to take the modular exponentiation. With an e value of the power, we have the **E** encryption function, which transforms the original message M into the cryptogram $C = \mathbf{E}(M) = M^e \pmod{n}$.

The e parameter is considered public. It is computationally difficult to find M from a known value S with a known n and e. As the trapdoor of the corresponding one-way enciphering function $M^e \pmod{n}$, we're also going to use exponentiation, but with another value for the power. The new power value d must be chosen so that the deciphering function $\mathbf{D}(C) = C^d \pmod{n}$ is the inverse of $\mathbf{E}(M) = M^e (\bmod\ n)$; in other words, the condition $M = \mathbf{D}[\mathbf{E}(M)] = (M^e)^d = M^{ed} \pmod{n}$ must be true.

From this equation, it follows that $ed = 1 \pmod{\varphi(n)}$. Thus, two exponentiations of modulo n will be mutually inverse if the product of the powers equal one modulo of the Euler function of the n number. The d parameter is the key to the trapdoor, and therefore it is private. Now the problem is choosing the necessary values for the e and d powers. Obviously, it is first necessary to find the value of the Euler function of the n number. You can see that, for every prime number p, we have $\varphi(p) = p - 1$. Since we choose $n = pq$ where both factors are prime numbers, then, using the multiplicative property of Euler's function, we obtain: $\varphi(n) = \varphi(pq) = \varphi(p)\varphi(q) = (p-1)(q-1)$.

Even as far back as Euclid's time, it was known that if integer numbers e and m fit the conditions $0 < e < m$ and $\gcd(m, e) = 1$, then there is only one d that meets the conditions $0 < d < m$ and $de = 1 \pmod{m}$. Besides which, d can be computed using an extended Euclidean algorithm.

Let's turn to the following operating scheme of the RSA cryptosystem.

(1) Each user chooses two large, unequal numbers p and q, finds their product $n = pq$, and computes $\varphi(n) = (p-1)(q-1)$.

One of the requirements for choosing p and q is that at least one of the numbers $(p-1)$ or $(q-1)$ must have one large prime factor. The size of the n value modulus must be no less than 512 bits. For important applications of an RSA system, the recommended size of a modulus is 1,024 bits.

(2) Then, an integer e is chosen such that $e < \varphi(n)$ and $\gcd(e, \varphi(n)) = 1$, and a d is calculated that complies to the $ed = 1 \pmod{\varphi(n)}$ condition.

(3) A *private key* is a triplet of numbers—p, q, and d—that is kept secret. (Actually, it will suffice to keep d secret, since the prime numbers p and q are only

necessary at the stage when the n modulo is chosen and the d number is computed. After that, the p and q numbers can be destroyed.)

(4) The n and e pair of numbers is a *public key* that is available to all subscribers of the RSA cryptosystem.

(5) The *signing procedure* for the M message is raising the M number to the d power modulo n: $S = M^d \pmod{n}$.

(6) The *verification procedure* for the S signature corresponding to the M message is raising the S number to the e integer power modulo n: $M' = S^e \pmod{n}$.

If $M' = M$, then the M message is recognized as signed by the user who previously provided the e public key. Obviously,

$S^e = (M^d)^e = M^{de} = M^{Q\varphi(n)+1} = M^{Q\varphi(n)}M = (M^{\varphi(n)})^Q M = 1^Q M \pmod{n}$, that is, it is possible to generate a cryptogram corresponding to a given public key and a given message with only a known private key d.

The security of an RSA cryptosystem is based on the complexity of factoring a modulus into two large prime factors. If the problem of such factoring were solved, it would be easy to compute Euler's function of the modulus and then compute the private key from the public key, using Euclid's algorithm.

Up to the present, no practical feasible general ways to solve this problem for a modulus 512 bits long or greater have been found. However, for special cases of prime numbers p and q, the complexity of this problem decreases drastically, and so when generating a private key in an RSA cryptosystem, it is necessary to perform a number of special tests. Another peculiarity of the RSA cryptosystem is its multiplicativity—$\mathbf{E}(M_1, M_2) = \mathbf{E}(M_1)\mathbf{E}(M_2) \pmod{n}$—which makes it possible for an adversary to use two signed messages to generate the signature of a third message $M_3 = M_1M_2 \pmod{n}$. Since M_3 in the great majority of cases won't be a comprehensible text, this peculiarity isn't a disadvantage. In the RSA system, it is also necessary to take into account the following possibility. Having chosen an arbitrary value S, it is possible to compute the $M' = S^e$ value; in other words, an arbitrary value can be presented as the signature of a message. Of course, such forged messages are random. However, in some applications, it is sometimes required that you sign random messages. In such cases, the following scheme is used:

1. A prearranged binary vector V with a length of $v = 64$ bits is appended to the T message, which you must sign and transmit over a public channel:

$$\mathrm{M} \rightarrow \mathrm{T} \,||\, \mathrm{V}.$$

2. The signature for the M message is generated:

$$S = M^d \pmod{n}.$$

3. The S value is sent to the receiving party.
4. The receiver computes the values from the S value:

$$M' = S^e \pmod n,\ V' = M' \pmod{2^v} \text{ and } T' = M' \operatorname{div} 2^v.$$

5. If V' is equal to the prearranged value V (i.e., if the $V' = V$ condition is true), the receiving party decides that the T' message is signed by the owner of the public key used to verify the signature. (The probability that a random message can be mistaken for a signed one is 2^{-v}.)

One useful feature of the public-key encryption system being discussed is that, when encrypting a message with two or more users, the encryption procedures can have any order. For example, let $C = \mathbf{E}_1[\mathbf{E}_2(M)]$; then $\mathbf{D}_1[\mathbf{D}_2(C)] = \mathbf{D}_2[\mathbf{D}_1(C)] = M$. This feature can be used in blind signature protocols or in computerized ballot systems.

Thus, the private key is used to sign messages, and the public key is used to verify the signature. To send subscriber **A** a secret message, any user can use **A**'s public key to generate the $C = \mathbf{E}_A(M)$ cryptogram. Only subscriber **A** can restore the M message with the C value, because only he knows the private key corresponding to the public key used to create the cryptogram. In the RSA cryptosystem, signature generation is the same as the decryption procedure, and signature verification is the same as the encryption procedure.

The speed of encryption provided by two-key (asymmetric) ciphers is much lower than the speed of one-key (symmetric) cryptosystems. This is why hybrid cryptosystems, in which information is encrypted using one-key ciphers and distribution of session keys is performed via a public channel with the help of two-key ciphers are most effective. For example, using the RSA cryptosystem, it is easy to exchange a session key with any subscriber, having encrypted the session key with his public key. The encrypted session key can be easily transmitted over a nonsecure communication channel, since the private key necessary for decryption belongs only to the subscriber whose public key was used for encryption. To directly encrypt information, two-key ciphers are of limited usefulness.

1.4.5 The El Gamal Digital Signature

Let's now look at a digital signature system named after its inventor, Tahir El Gamal, and based on the public and private key generating scheme used in the Diffie-Hellman method. Let's say that there is a large prime number p such that factoring the number $p-1$ includes at least one large prime factor and the primitive element α modulo p.

The procedure of signing is as follows. A subscriber **A** chooses a private key x_A, with which he generates the public key $y_A = \alpha^{x_A}$. **A**'s signature under the M document (the signed message must have a length less than the p prime modulus; $M < p$) is the (r, s) pair of numbers (where $0 \le r < p - 1$ and $0 \le s < p - 1$) that fits the $(\alpha^M) = y_A{}^r r^s \pmod p$ equation.

This equation is used to verify the fact that the document was signed by subscriber **A**. (The $y_A = \alpha^{x_A}$ value is **A**'s public key, and it is available to all users, which makes it possible for anyone to verify that a given message was indeed signed by subscriber **A**.)

This digital signature system is based on the fact that only the true owner of the x_A private key can generate the (r, s) pair of numbers that fits the signature verification equation. Using the x_A value, subscriber A generates a digital signature according to the following algorithm:

- Generate a *random* number k that fits the conditions: $0 < k < p-1$ and $\mathrm{GCD}(k, p-1) = 1$.
- Compute $r = \alpha^k \pmod p$.
- Compute s from the $M = x_A r + ks \pmod{(p-1)}$ equation.

From number theory, it is known that the last equation has a solution for s if $\mathrm{GCD}(k, p-1) = 1$. This equation is easily obtained by substituting the $r = \alpha^k \pmod p$ value into the signature verification equation: $\alpha^M = \alpha^{x_A r} \alpha^{ks} = y_A{}^r r^s \pmod p$.

From the two last formulas, it is obvious that the owner of the private key can sign the document, and his signature can be verified using the public key. Finding the (r, s) pair of numbers without knowing the private key is computationally complex. There can be many extremely different signatures corresponding to a given document (note that k can have different values), but only the owner of the private key can generate the correct signature. Possible signatures differ in their r value, but it is practically impossible to find the corresponding s value for a given r without knowing the private key. To compute the private key from the public one, you need to solve a computationally complex discrete logarithm problem.

One peculiarity of the El Gamal digital signature is generating a random number k. In this cryptosystem, you aren't allowed to use the same k value to generate signatures for two different messages. This is connected with the fact that it is possible to compute the private key from two different signatures generated using the same k values. In addition, the k values used during generation are to be destroyed. If an adversary gets the k value, he will be able to compute the private key. Systems that are actually used generate a random k number with a large size, and implement a mechanism for destroying the number after generating the signature. In a program implementation, a scheme of digital signing is provided in which the number k only appears in the processor registers and the random-access memory, and the destroying mechanism involves writing a random value at the memory location that just held the *k* value.

Earlier in this chapter, we looked at two-key cryptography schemes that make it possible to sign messages that have a limited length (about 10^3 bits). If a message has a large size, the straightforward use of such schemes requires that you split the original message into a large number of smaller blocks and generate as many signatures as there are message blocks. This significantly complicates the task of storing the signatures and the signed messages in a database containing many signed documents. To simplify this problem, it is not the document itself that is signed, but its small digital image obtained according to special cryptographic procedures called *hashing*.

The hashing algorithm must be one that provides for the computational impossibility of finding two messages with the same value for the digital image (the hash function value of the message). Currently, there are algorithms that comply with this requirement and make it possible to compute the hash function value of a given document. Rather than create many separate parts of a document, actual digital signature systems compute the hash function of a document and sign the hash function value. If the hash function is signed, the document is considered signed.

1.4.6 The Chaum Blind Signature

The notion of the blind signature was first introduced by David Chaum, who also suggested the first variants of its implementation. By a *blind signature*, we mean a two-key cryptosystem that makes it possible to sign electronic messages so that the signing party has no access to the information contained in the message being signed. This requirement, far-fetched and absurd at first glance, is very important for a number of cryptographic protocols. For example, blind signatures are used in computerized voting systems and for digital cash; in other words, in cryptographic protocols where it is necessary to provide untraceability. The blind signature procedure itself requires that one of the participants agree that he may be subject to a certain penalty consisting of obligations that he or she would likely prefer not to undertake.

In actual protocols where blind signatures are used, there are also procedures that assure the signing party that he won't be cheated. This assurance is based on certain additional procedures and conventions that put limitations and responsibility on the party that is submitting a document for a blind signature. Naturally, either party must agree to a certain risk and have a certain assurance; otherwise, it would be impossible to solve the problem both parties want to solve. For example, when using a DS system, users take the risk that someone may compute their private keys. The assurance of their interests lies in the high complexity of private key computation. Another type of assurance used in cryptographic protocols is the low probability of replicating random numbers if they are long enough. With the blind signature protocol, it is possible to solve some important practical problems (such as building a computerized voting system, using digital cash, etc.).

Let's examine the Chaum digital signature protocol based on the RSA cryptosystem with which you are already familiar. Suppose subject **A** wants subject **B** to sign message M. To do this, it is necessary to perform the following steps.

1. User **A** (the subjects are users of this cryptosystem) generates a random prime number k, such that GCD(k, N) = 1, where N is a part of **B**'s public key; in other words, the modulus used for computations. Then, he computes the $M' = k^eM \pmod N$ value, and submits it for signing. The signer cannot read the M message because it is encrypted with a one-time key, k^e, and by performing the modular multiplication operation.
2. The **B** user signs the M' message according to the procedure of signing a message in the RSA system:

$$S' = (k^eM)^d = kM^d \pmod N.$$

3. Having generated the S' signature, the signer cannot read the M^d value, since it was encrypted by applying the k one-time key to it. If the signer could find out the M^d value, he could easily compute M: $(M^d)^e = M \pmod N$. This means that, having obtained the $M^d \pmod N$ value (which is the goal of the blind signature protocol), user **A** must keep it secret from the signer.
4. Now, using the extended Euclidean algorithm, user **A** takes k and computes its multiplicative inverse element (k^{-1}) in the residue field modulo N, and restores the signature for the M message:

$$S' = k^{-1}S' = k^{-1}kM^d = M^d \pmod N.$$

Thus the goal is achieved—user **A** has generated **B**'s correct signature corresponding to the M message, and he is sure the signer doesn't know the contents of the M message.

1.4.7 Types of Attacks on a Digital Signature

In the digital signature system, three cryptographic algorithms are used: the algorithm of generating a signature with the private key, the algorithm of verifying a signature with the public key, and the algorithm of computing the hash function of the message being signed. The algorithms of generating the private and public keys can also be said to have a mathematical foundation. Operating actual systems also requires a legal, organizational, software, and hardware basis. The legal basis includes adopting laws that legalize digital signatures. The organizational basis includes user registration in a trust center and the signing of documents between the user and the trust center (or between two users) that states their responsibility for the public keys exchanged. The software and hardware basis includes a set of software and hardware tools that make it possible to perform complex computations and provide for the security of a database containing signed documents and signature samples for them.

The possible types of attacks against a digital signature can be divided into several groups:

- Attacks on cryptographic algorithms
- Attacks related to protocol violations
- Attacks related to violations of the integrity of a digital signature system

An attacker can be an external subject, or the signing party (signature repudiation), or the signature verifying party (creating a false signature).

Attacks on cryptographic algorithms involve solving complex mathematical problems, such as finding a discrete logarithm modulo of some large prime number. An attacker has very little hope of success. Such an attack can be launched against a two-key cryptographic algorithm or a hash function. In the case of the former, the signature is forged, while in the latter case the document is forged. Attacks related to protocol violations include, for example, the replication of signed messages, or delaying messages. To prevent such actions, the document includes special fields in which the data and the number of the document are specified. It is also necessary to use mechanisms that protect against the repudiation of message reception.

Attacks related to violations of the digital signature system's integrity are the most diversified ones. They include deleting a signed message from the database, private key interception using software or hardware tools, using a false public key, and replacing a public key in the database. These examples illustrate that many attacks are related to unauthorized access to the data in the digital signature system. The safe operation of a digital signature system requires a secure environment.

Attacks on a cryptosystem can also be based on assigning the system user a false digital signature or by taking advantage of hidden vulnerabilities of facilities meant to protect against unauthorized access, or on forced use of some system software or an application that has built-in undocumented viruses. To prevent this, cryptographic tools and facilities that protect against unauthorized access must be certified by special organizations.

1.5 PROBABILISTIC CIPHERS

One promising method of increasing the security of known ciphers is making the enciphering process nondeterministic. This idea can be implemented by introducing random data into the message being transformed. If data-dependent operations or procedures are used in an enciphering mechanism (as in the RC5 cipher), the operations themselves will change randomly. The idea of introducing probabilistic elements in the enciphering process pursues the goal of hampering the use of the general principle of block cipher cryptanalysis that is based on attempts to reveal the statistical properties of the encryption algorithm; for example, by choosing special original texts or cryptograms.

1.5.1 Homophonic Ciphers

Cryptograms obtained by using monoalphabetic or polyalphabetic substitution are easily disclosed by a frequency cryptanalysis. To hide the frequency properties of the message source, and thus hamper the cryptanalysis, a homophonic (or monophonic) encryption method can be used, which involves equalizing the frequencies of the cryptogram characters; in other words, using cryptographic transformations that will produce cryptograms using each character used to write down the ciphertext an equal number of times. The simplest homophonic encryption method is the following. Let's say there is a message source with known statistical properties. We denote the frequency of the occurrence of every letter of the original alphabet by an integer number f_i, where i is the number of the letter in the alphabet—$f_1, f_2, ..., f_L$, where L is the number of letters in the original alphabet. We'll match each letter T_i of the original alphabet, where $i = 1, 2, ..., L$, with the Ψ_i subset of the output alphabet (i.e., the alphabet used to write down the cryptogram). We specify these subsets with two requirements: no pair of subsets can include the same elements, and the number of different characters in a Ψ_i subset is equal to f_i.

We're going to perform encryption by substituting each letter T_i of the original text with a randomly chosen character from the Ψ_i subset. Then, when a given letter T_i of the original text is repeatedly substituted with characters of the Ψ_i subset, the characters of the output alphabet will be used, on average, an equal number of times. This number is inversely proportional to the number of elements in the Ψ_i subset; in other words, it is directly proportional to $1/f_i$. The frequency of accessing the Ψ_i subset is equal to the frequency of the occurrence of the letter T_i in the original text; in other words, it is directly proportional to f_i. From these ratios, we conclude that the average frequencies of all the characters of the output alphabet in a cryptogram are equal. Decryption isn't difficult: using a character of the cryptogram, we determine its corresponding subset, and from the subset, we determine the letter of the original alphabet. The described encryption method requires using $f_1 + f_2 + ... + f_L$ characters in the output alphabet. The most important feature of this method is that the transformation includes a probabilistic process—choosing a random element from the given subset.

The described method isn't of great interest for practice now, but the basic idea of introducing randomness into the encryption process can be used when designing modern probabilistic block ciphers.

1.5.2 Ciphers with a Simple Probabilistic Mechanism

In the previous sections, we examined a number of ciphers in which data-dependent transformation operations are used. Such operations aren't predefined, and vary from one input block to another. If such encryption mechanisms are used to transform random data, the operations will vary randomly. "Mixing up" random data with the message being encrypted makes it possible to impart random features to the transformation operations, thus enhancing the computational security of the system. Let **E** be a b-bit encryption function, P be a p-bit block of plaintext, and R an r-bit random block where $b = r + p$. Give the $B = R||P$ block at the input of the encryption function, where the "||" character denotes the concatenation of two binary vectors, R and P: $P \rightarrow B = R||P \rightarrow C = \mathbf{E}(B, K)$, where K is the encryption key. Since the size of the input block increases during encryption, this encryption maps the given block of the P plaintext on a large set of ciphertext blocks $\{C_1, C_2, ... , C_n\}$, where $n = 2^r$. The general scheme of a probabilistic cipher with a simple mechanism of appending random data is shown in Figure 1.11. The random number generator (RNG), and the encryption algorithm implementing the **E** encryption function, are internal components of the enciphering device. It is assumed that the RNG is located in a protected part of the enciphering device, and that an adversary cannot replace it (i.e., the adversary has no access to the R value). This assumption is acceptable, since enciphering devices are designed to provide protection against encryption algorithm substitution, as well as against reading and copying the key. When decrypting a block of ciphertext, the valid user who owns the private key restores the $B = R||P$ block, after which the R value is discarded and the original message P is separated.

When choosing various values of the b/p ratio, it is possible to control the encryption strength. The greater this ratio, the greater the strength. The difference between probabilistic encryption and a cryptoscheme with frequently changing session keys is that it doesn't significantly decrease the encryption speed when using ciphers with a precalculation stage, during which the encryption key is generated using the session key. The probabilistic encryption scheme makes it possible to control decreasing the transformation speed. If the **E** function has the s_0 initial value of the transformation speed, the speed of the probabilistic encryption is $s = s_0(b - r)/b$.

There were a number of successful attacks on the DES, RC5, and Blowfish cryptosystems when a small number of enciphering rounds was used. Obviously, one can choose a size of a random block R that will make reduced versions of these ciphers secure against known attacks. For this purpose, the $r = b - 1$ value will do. Ciphers with a simple probabilistic mechanism have the following advantages:

- The security of the known block ciphers can be significantly increased.
- In a sense, it is possible to control the cipher's security by choosing various values for the r/b ratio.
- The probabilistic cryptoscheme makes it possible to use new mechanisms of specifying the dependence between ciphering procedures and the private key. The cost of these advantages is in the following drawbacks:
- The speed decreases by a factor of r/b.
- Ciphertext blocks are longer than plaintext blocks.

The latter disadvantage puts significant limitations on using probabilistic ciphers in computer systems. To compensate for the expansion effect, it is possible to compress the original message beforehand. In some cases, this method makes it possible to design probabilistic ciphers in which the ciphertext length is equal to the length of the original message. (It is interesting to note that the compression of data before their encryption significantly increases the encryption's security against ciphertext attacks. However, pre-compressing information doesn't increase the encryption's security against known plaintext or chosen-text attacks, since, according to Kerkhoff's principle, we must assume that the cryptanalyst knows the compression algorithm used.)

1.5.3 Probabilistic Combination of Data Bits and Random Bits

The aforementioned simple probabilistic encryption mechanism, based on generating a ciphered data block by combining random and data bits, can be used to increase encryption security when using many of the known block cryptoalgorithms. In regard to many types of attacks, this problem is solved with a relatively small ratio of random bits to data bits. However, for some known ciphers vulnerable to differential (DCA) and linear (LCA) cryptanalysis, strengthening on the basis of this probabilistic encryption method (including the patented variant of random and data bit combination depending on the private key) requires that you significantly increase the portion of random bits—up to 80 percent or more. This results in noticeably decreasing the effective encryption speed, and significantly increasing the ciphertext size.

In this section, we'll look at variants of making this probabilistic encryption method more effective for a small portion of random bits when using encryption procedures with good diffusion properties, but possibly, with unexpected vulnerabilities to DCA and LCA. These variants can be also used to protect against possible attacks using trapdoors in cryptoalgorithms.

The probabilistic enciphering scheme, is shown in Figure 1.11, where the random number generator (RNG) is assumed to be an internal component of a ciphering device unavailable to an attacker. Let **E** be a b-bit encryption function, T a t-bit block of a plaintext, and R an r-bit random block where $t < b$ and $r = b - t$. Supply the $B = R||T$ data block at the input of the **E** encryption function. The original text T can be written as

$$\mathrm{T} \rightarrow \mathrm{B} = \mathrm{R}||\mathrm{T} \rightarrow \mathrm{C} = \mathrm{E}(\mathrm{B}, \mathrm{K}),$$

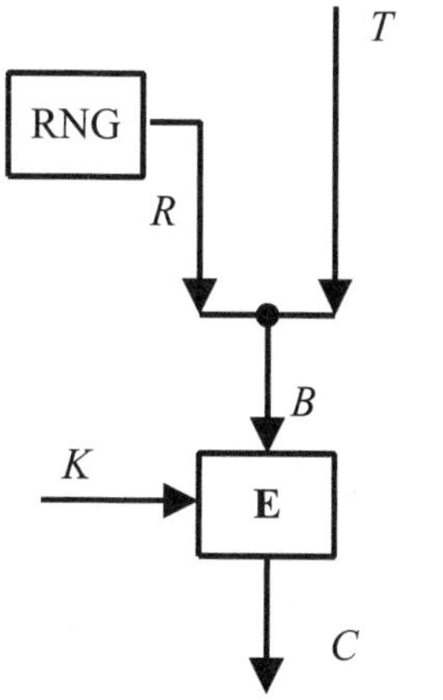

FIGURE 1.11 The basic scheme of probabilistic encryption.

where K is the encryption key. Since the size of the input block increases during encryption, such encryption maps a given text T to a large set of ciphertext blocks $\{C_1, C_2, \ldots, C_n\}$, where $n = 2^r$. When decrypting the block of the ciphertext, the valid user who owns the private key restores the $B = R||T$ block, after which the R value is discarded, and the original message T is separated. When choosing various values of the b/t ratio, it is possible to control the encryption strength. The greater this ratio, the greater the strength.

Obviously, the encryption speed decreases by a factor of $b/t = 1 + r/t$, and the size of the C ciphertext increases by the same factor.

In the first variant of enhancing the probabilistic encryption, the decrease in the r/t ratio, with a significant growth in security, can be achieved by using a non-deterministic mix of random and data bits. To implement this idea, a random binary vector is divided into two parts with a pre-specified length: $R = R_1||R_2$. Then, prior to carrying out encryption transformations over the $R_2||T$ binary vector, a bit permutation is done, which depends on the R_1 random value that specifies randomly mixing the bits of the T message and those of the R_2 random value. For bit mixing, it is possible to use controlled operational permutation boxes **P**, used earlier as a basic cryptographic primitive to design secure fast ciphers. The permutation performed by a **P** box depends on the value of the control vector V that is generated depending on R_1. The sequence of transformations in a variant with a random combination of data and random bits (Figure 1.12) is:

$$T \rightarrow R_2||T \rightarrow \mathbf{P}_V(R_2||T) \rightarrow R_1||\mathbf{P}_V(R_2||T) \rightarrow \mathbf{E}_K(R_1||\mathbf{P}_V(R_2||T)).$$

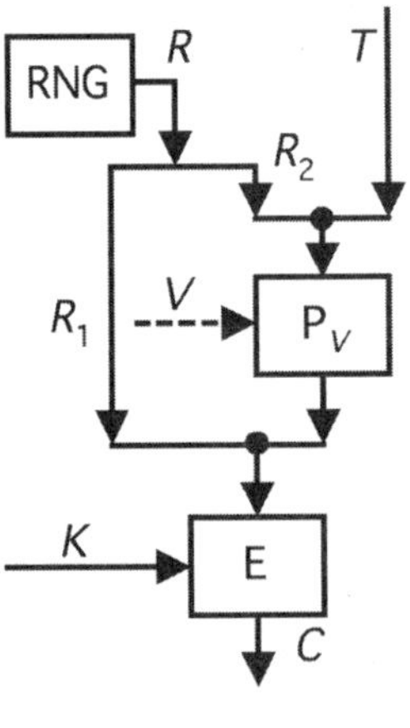

FIGURE 1.12 A scheme with a probabilistic mix of random and data bits.

In typical **P** boxes, the length v of the V control vector is at least twice the length of the $R_2||T$ $(r_2 + t)$ vector being transformed. In this case, it is assumed that the $r_1 < r_2 + t < v$ condition is true, so the control vector can be created, for example, by repeatedly replicating the R_1 vector ($V = R_1||...||R_1||R_1$), or by alternating R_1 and the K_1 fragment of the private key ($V = R_1||K_1||R_1||K_1$). In the latter case, mixing the bits of R_2 and T is done probabilistically, depending on the private key.

Increasing the security against DCA and LCA is connected with the probabilistic distribution of the data bits over the bit positions of the data block being encrypted. For example, when performing a chosen-plaintext DCA, the probability of getting two data blocks with a given difference is significantly small for r_1, $r_2 = 8$. When $b = 64$ and 128, this corresponds to a rather small portion of random bits (25% and 12%, respectively).

The second way to make a simple probabilistic encryption scheme more secure is related to the idea of pre-encrypting an original text T using a randomly generated value R as a one-time pre-encryption key (Figure 1.13). The transformation sequence is:

$$T \rightarrow \mathbf{E}'_R(T) \rightarrow \mathrm{E}''_K(R||\mathbf{E}'_R(T)).$$

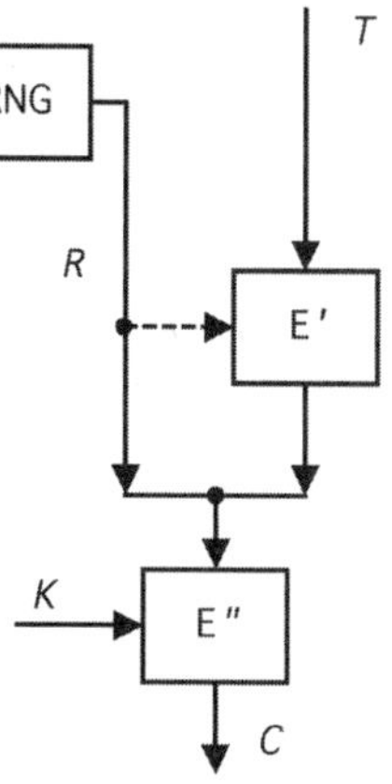

FIGURE 1.13 A pre-encryption scheme with a random vector.

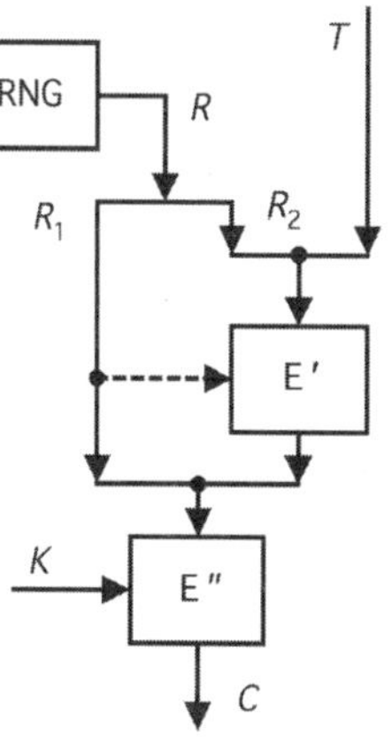

FIGURE 1.14 Two-stage probabilistic encryption.

Strengthening is done using additional transformations with a one-time key whose duplication probability is about 2^{-r} during attacks based on the chosen T and C values (due to good diffusion properties of $\mathbf{E}''$ encryption procedures). When doing the pre-encryption, the basic scheme of probabilistic encryption can be used, which will lead to the following transformation sequence (Figure 1.14):

$$T \rightarrow R_2||T \rightarrow \mathbf{E}'_{R1}(R_2||T) \rightarrow \mathbf{E}''_K(R_1||\mathbf{E}'_{R1}(R_2||T)).$$

This case relates to the third variant of increasing security, and it is a generalization of the first variant, in which mixing up random and data bits can be considered a special case of encrypting transformation.

For a hardware implementation, the first variant is the most cost-effective, while the second and third variants are the most cost-effective for a software implementation. From the standpoint of increasing security, the third variant is best. In general, the increase in security in the variants discussed is related to the fact that the ratios that connect the T and C pairs of values also include a random (pseudo-random) value R during chosen-plaintext T attacks (chosen-plaintext C attacks).

These probabilistic encryption methods seem to be quite effective for insuring against unexpected weaknesses of the encryption algorithm used, and against built-in trapdoors. Expanding the ciphertext block puts significant limitations on using probabilistic ciphers in computer systems. To compensate for the expansion effect, it is possible to compress the original message beforehand. In some cases, this method makes it possible to design probabilistic ciphers in which the ciphertext length is equal to the length of the original message. Besides which, compressing data before they are encrypted significantly increases the security of the encryption. For many applications in telecommunication systems, this variant of probabilistic encryption can be used without significant limitations.

1.5.4 Probabilistic Mechanisms in Two-Key Ciphers

In two-key cryptosystems, enciphering is done according to a widely known enciphering algorithm $\mathbf{E}_z$ (a public key), and so the following attack is possible in principle. Having an $\mathbf{E}_z$ ciphertext, in order to find the original text T, a cryptanalyst can randomly choose different variants of possible plaintexts T_i' and compute his corresponding cryptograms $C_1' = \mathbf{E}_z(T_1')$, $C_2 = \mathbf{E}_z(T_2)$, ... , $C_m' = \mathbf{E}_z(T_m')$. If he guesses the true original text, it will be clear from the $C' = C$ equation. In such a cryptanalytic scheme, each unsuccessful attempt gives the cryptanalyst certain information, since it decreases the number of remaining variants of possible original texts.

Naturally, the probability of choosing the correct original text is extremely low for typical original message sizes, so this attack will not likely be successful in actual practice, if this probability is relatively large. Right now, we are only concerned with the fact that some information about the original message might be leaked. However, one might imagine the following situation, in which such an attack could be highly effective. Suppose an administrative center sends its subordinates instructions (plaintexts) as documents that have a certain format and style. In this case, various plaintexts differ only in certain fields of a spreadsheet. Besides which, a standard style of instructions will lead in some cases to a situation in which only a small part of an original message is unknown to the cryptanalyst (for example, the date, the amount of money paid, the name of a contractor, etc).

Probabilistic mechanisms make it possible to prevent an information leakage in the foregoing cryptanalytic method. As with one-key cryptosystems, when probabilistic encryption mechanisms are used in two-key ciphers, a given original text is mapped to a set of possible cryptograms $\{C_1, C_2, ..., C_N\}$, each of which is decrypted with a secret decryption algorithm $\mathbf{D}_z$ (a private key) to the same original text T: $T = \mathbf{D}_z(C_1) = \mathbf{D}_z(C_2) = ... = \mathbf{D}_z(C_N)$. This is only possible if the length of the ciphertext is greater than that of the original text. If the length of the ciphertext is r bits greater than the length of the original text, it is possible to design a probabilistic mechanism, such that the number of ciphertexts corresponding to a given plaintext is $N = 2^r$. During probabilistic encryption, for the given text T, we generate one of the possible cryptogram—for example, C_i, chosen from the $\{C_1, C_2, ..., C_N\}$ set according to the probabilistic law.

A cryptanalyst can correctly choose the original text, but he cannot verify this fact, since, when encrypting, he will generally obtain another cryptogram from the set of possible variants. Having encrypted T, the cryptanalyst will get $C_j = \mathbf{E}_z(T)$. The probability that $C_j = C_i$ is $1/N$. The cryptanalyst has to guess the original text, and the value of a randomly selected parameter that controls the probabilistic encryption process.

1.5.5 The El Gamal Public Cipher

Let's now look at the El Gamal enciphering algorithm. This method is based on discrete exponentiation procedures, and is outlined here. As in the Diffie-Hellman public key distribution method, a large prime number p and its corresponding primitive element α are chosen. Each user of the secure network chooses a private key, computes his public key $y = \alpha^x (\text{mod } p)$, and puts y into a certified directory. To send the ith user a secret message T, the sender must perform the following steps:

1. Choose a random number R that is reciprocally prime with the p–1 number.
2. Compute the $C' = \alpha^R \ (\text{mod } p)$ value.
3. Compute $C'' = y^R T \ (\text{mod } p)$ from the ith user's public key.
4. Send the ith user the (C', C'') cryptogram.

In this method, the length of the ciphertext is approximately twice the length of the original text, and a given plaintext is matched by no less than 2^k different cryptograms (k is the length of the p modulus in bits). Having received the (C', C'') cryptogram, the user i can easily compute the $T = C''/(C')^x \ (\text{mod } p)$ original text. Indeed,

$$(C')^x = (\alpha^R)^x = \alpha^{Rx} \ (\text{mod } p)$$
$$C''/(C')^x = y^R T/\alpha^{Rx} = (\alpha^x)^R T/\alpha^{Rx} = \alpha^{xR} T/\alpha^{Rx} = T \ (\text{mod } p).$$

With two-key ciphers, for a general method of introducing randomness into the enciphering process, one can use a simple mechanism of adding random data to the message being enciphered. In this case, a size t for the original text block is stipulated, and a random binary vector is appended to the most significant bit side, for example. The structure of the B block being encrypted can be the following: $B = R||T$, where R is a random number and T is a block of the original text. Obviously, the numeric value of the B block mustn't exceed the maximum valid value for the cryptosystem used. This is why the b size of the B block must be such that its maximum value doesn't go beyond the range of valid values. For example, in the RSA cipher, the B value must be less than the $n = pq$ modulus. Therefore, we obtain the $2^b < n$ or $b < \log_2 n$ condition.

If these requirements are met, the steps of enciphering an original text are described in such way:

$$T \to B = R||T \to C = \mathbf{E}_z(R||T),$$

and deciphering the cryptogram is done as follows:

$$C \to B = \mathbf{D}_z(C) \to R||T \to T.$$

Any message can be divided into texts of the required size, and each can be encrypted using probabilistic encryption.

1.6 USING ENCRYPTION IN PRACTICE

Modern microelectronic technologies support the continuous growth of computer quality, and are the basis of maintaining the main trends in computer development—minimizing their sizes, decreasing power consumption, increasing the capacity of random-access memory and built-in and removable disks, enhancing the performance and reliability of computers, and expanding the area and increasing the intensity of use.

1.6.1 Encryption Algorithms in Protection Tools

These trends led to a situation in which, in the present circumstances, the protection of computer systems against unauthorized access (UA) is leaning more and more toward software protection tools than hardware tools. We should mention that the role of physical and hardware protection tools aimed, for example, at protecting against side-effect electromagnetic radiation, induced current, acoustic eavesdropping, and so forth, is considered traditional, and using computers and specialized software in these areas is auxiliary. The increasing importance of software protection tools should be understood in the sense that newly emerging problems in the area of protecting computer systems (CSs) against UA requires using mechanisms and protocols with a comparatively high computational complexity and can be effectively solved by using computer resources.

Using “pure” software mechanisms in data protection tools (DPTs) makes it possible to effectively solve important practical problems. Among these problems, one might mention reducing the cost of DPTs, minimizing the time it takes to develop secure information processing technologies, speeding up the spread of DPTs, and providing a high degree of portability to other platforms and compatibility with system and application software.

When designing data protection tools, it makes sense to use encryption techniques on various levels of computer data processing. This will make it possible to effectively solve the following problems by using only software tools:

- Protecting CSs against intentional bugs
- Protecting information in case of the theft of a hard drive or a whole computer
- Detecting unauthorized modifications in the data or software
- Protecting against viruses
- Establishing demarcation between the users’ authorizations
- Retaining high performance and routine operation procedures for the users
- Providing data protection when maintenance or other services are performed

CSs are subject to a many potential threats to information, which makes it necessary to provide a comprehensive range of possible protection tools and functions. It makes the most sense to first protect the most informative channels of data leakage, such as the possibility of quickly and easily copying data onto removable high-capacity media, unsecure communication channels, and the theft of a hard drive or a whole computer. The problem of barring these leakage channels is complicated by the requirement that data protection procedures shouldn’t lead to a noticeable decrease in the performance of the CS.

This places high requirements on ciphers oriented toward use in systems that protect against UA and that operate in real time:

- High security against known-text or chosen-text cryptanalysis, based on a large amount of text encrypted with the same key.
- A high encryption speed of a software implementation.
- Retaining the possibility of random access to the data. This issue makes it necessary to use block ciphers in DPT against UA.

A modern computer security system oriented toward extensive use must be secure, technologically effective, and ergonomic. Here are a number of basic properties that make such a system attractive to a wide circle of users:

Universality: The possibility of installing various modes of secure data processing, depending on the needs of different users.

Compatibility: The system must be compatible with all applications written for the particular operating system, and must provide for the secure network operation of the computer.

Portability: The possibility of installing the system on various types of computers, including laptops.

Operating convenience: The system must be easy to operate, and shouldn't change the working procedures users are accustomed to.

Real-time operating mode: Data processing (including encryption) must be fast.

Data protection: The system should have a high level of data protection.

Cost: The cost of the system should be minimal.

As an ideological basis of designing DPTs intended for wide use, we suggest that you extensively use fast software enciphering methods using new types of block ciphers. When designing effective real-time DPTs, the following principles should be observed:

- Pertaining to global encryption, all information on the hard disk, including the boot sector, the system and application software, and so forth, must be transformed with a fast software cipher.
- The platform operating system must be kept unchanged to provide high portability and compatibility.
- A special cryptographic module should be used for the startup initialization to provide complete control over the startup procedure.

The mechanisms listed are just the main ones. They should be supplemented with a number of additional modules in order to perform standard tasks of securely operating the CS, such as program and data integrity control, guaranteed destruction of the remaining information, locking the keyboard and display, protecting information transmitted through network communication lines, and so forth.

In modern software systems of computer security, a technology called *transparent protection* is used. According to it, the user's everyday working environment doesn't change, and he or she doesn't feel uncomfortable as a consequence of the protection tools being enabled. In other words, the security system, when working, is invisible to the user. The basic technology of transparent protection is the method of dynamic encryption of the private information with which the user is working. Private information written on external media is automatically encrypted using a key that depends on the user's password. When being read by an authorized user, this information is automatically decrypted. Since this dynamic encryption isn't noticed by the user, it is called *transparent encryption*, or *transparent cryptographic transformation*.

In integrated computer security systems (such as the COBRA system that protects against UA), one can note the subsystems shown in Figure 1.15. Among these are:

- An erasing subsystem, to destroy the remaining data in the external memory

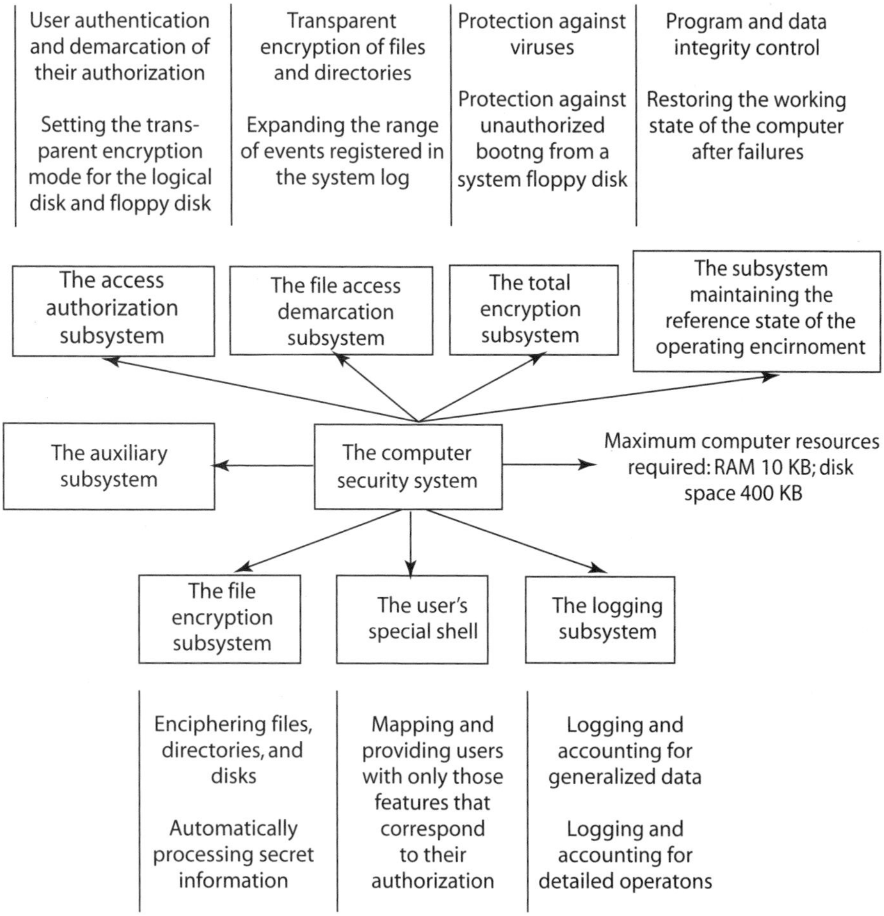

FIGURE 1.15 The structure of the COBRA system and the purpose of its main components.

- A keyboard and display locking subsystem, providing time-out locking of these access devices when left unattended
- A shutdown subsystem, to correctly finish the user session by checking whether the state of the operational environment matches the reference state and writing the appropriate record into the work log
- A system creating an additional logical disk on the hard disk, which makes it possible to save information without repeatedly partitioning it

The information protection level provided depends both on the design quality and completeness of the computer security system and the setup of its operating modes, taking into account the opponent model. The security administrator must set up the necessary protection scheme. By a *protection scheme*, we mean a set of activated components of the security system, and their setup parameters and enabled operating modes. To configure a particular scheme, the security administrator must perform the following steps:

1. Determine and understand security requirements by finding and analyzing threats to information in the computer system.
2. Determine the required security levels by analyzing the potentialities of the information protecting system.
3. Generalize the acquired information and perform the final configuration of the protection scheme.

When performing the preceding steps, you need to take into account the fact that effective protection should satisfy two mutually contradictory requirements:

- Provide secure information protection in the computer system.
- Provide comfortable working conditions for computer users (the protection system shouldn't be troublesome; it also should not have any other demerits that interfere with users' normal work).

Taking these requirements into account results in a more effective use of computer security systems. After having determined the protection scheme, the security administrator can proceed with the installation and setup of all the necessary components of the protection scheme.

Typical features demarcating the users' access to the computer resources that are provided by security systems are:

- Demarcation at the logical disk and I/O port level implemented by the authorized access subsystem
- Demarcation at the file and directory level implemented by the file access demarcation subsystem

Many computer security systems support multilevel encryption—disk encryption, file encryption, and boot sector encryption.

1.6.2 Some Features of Applications

Although some important characteristics might not be quantifiable, it seems logical to identify some cryptographic algorithm characteristics that can be expressed either in objective, numeric values or subjective, adjectival values. Metrics might be used for evaluating and comparing cryptographic algorithms and the confidentiality protection value of products containing cryptographic algorithms.

The Key Length and Security

The length of the key determines the upper boundary of the cryptosystem's security. An attacker can always launch a brute-force attack, which consists of trying every possible key from the keyspace. However, the size of the keyspace increases exponentially with the increase of the key length. If the length of a key in bits is equal to $l = 64$, the number of possible keys is more than 10^{19}. When $l = 128$, there are $>10^{38}$. Currently, computational technologies are approaching a solution to the problem of trying 10^{20} variants in a reasonable time interval. Trying 10^{38} variants is considered unfeasible for up-to-date technologies, and in the foreseeable future. At present, there is a general shift from 56-bit keys in the DES cryptosystem to 80-bit or 128-bit keys in modern symmetric ciphers.

Among the provably secure block cryptosystems are ciphers, for which it was theoretically proven that even the best method of cryptanalyzing them requires a work effort that is no less than a value that guarantees this method will remain computationally unfeasible in the near future. At present, various cryptographic methods have been proposed for many ciphers, and an estimation of the work effort needed to solve the cryptanalytic problem has been given for each. However, there is the fundamental theoretical complexity of finding the best cryptanalytic algorithm, and this determines the complexity of the general proof of security.

For a new cipher to be adopted, it must conform to the following conditions:

- It must be designed in accordance with the requirements of a specific application, and it must include mechanisms that implement modern principles of providing cryptographic security.
- It must have been tested by experienced experts for a long time, and its security against all known methods of cryptanalysis must be proven.

Cipher testing is the most complex and expensive stage of cryptosystem development. To increase confidence in the security of new ciphers, they are tested in conditions favorable for solving the cryptanalytic problem. For example, versions with a decreased number of enciphering rounds are investigated; the possibility of generating hardware failures in the enciphering device is considered; an assumption is made that a portion of the encryption key is known to an opponent, and so forth. When testing nondeterministic ciphers, testers consider attacks based on a known version of the encryption algorithm, or on its weakest version. Other types of attacks can be used, such as attacks on cipher versions with decreased sizes of the encryption key and input data block. The stricter the testing procedure, the greater the assurance that no new specific types of attacks will be found. Theoretical guarantees of security can only be provided by ciphers that have infinite random keys. However, these are extremely inconvenient for computer information protection. Besides which, in such applications, there is the problem of protecting a key whose length is equal to the length of the message.

The notion of a password is close to the notion of a secret key. A password is also a secret component. By the term *key*, we mean a component that controls the encryption process, while a *password* is a component used to authenticate a subject (such as a user or a workstation). In many cases, a password is used to control enciphering, and a secret key is used to authenticate subjects. A random key or password is difficult to remember, so it is often stored in removable media that, in turn, are kept protected against unauthorized access. Choosing a password that is easy to remember significantly diminishes the number of possible variants, so in this case, longer passwords or even pass-phrases are required.

In two-key ciphers, private keys whose length is significantly greater than the lengths of keys used in one-key cryptosystems are used. This is due to certain peculiarities of the cryptanalytic problem for asymmetric ciphers. In some two-key cryptosystems, private keys are chosen at random, and then the corresponding public keys are generated (for example, in the Diffie-Hellman method and the El Gamal digital signature). In other cryptosystems, private keys that satisfy special requirements are generated (such as p and q factors in the RSA digital signature system). In the latter case, private keys are also chosen at random, but, after the random choice of a private key, the key is checked to see whether it satisfies certain requirements (for example, prime numbers are required, or numbers that are relatively prime to some previously chosen parameter).

It is convenient to store random private keys in removable electronic devices (such as electronic keys or smart cards). You can also use combinations of passwords stored in the memory and keys stored in removable media.

Enciphering and Archiving

When creating secret archives, it is assumed that the data is stored in encrypted form. As a rule, archives contain a great amount of information; this is why it is good to compress data when archiving to eliminate excessive information. This procedure decreases the archive's size and simplifies creating work and backup copies. It also makes sense to previously compress data when transmitting large amounts of data over low-speed communication channels. Encryption transforms an original text into a pseudo-random sequence that won't compress, and so the data compressing procedure must be performed prior to encryption. (One of the tests used to qualitatively estimate cipher security is a test for cryptogram compression. If a cryptogram compresses poorly, the cipher passes the test.)

Thus, when archiving secret data (or transmitting them over a telecommunication channel), the following sequence of transformations takes place:

1. Data compression
2. Enciphering
3. Writing on a medium (or sending over a communication channel)

To extract data from an archive or receive them from a communication channel, the reverse sequence is done:

1. Reading the ciphertext from a medium (or receiving encrypted data over a communication channel)
2. Deciphering
3. Restoring (decompressing) the data

Eliminating the redundancy of an initial message significantly increases the encryption's security against ciphertext attacks. However, the encryption security against known-text attacks doesn't change if a known compression algorithm is used. Since we assume that the opponent knows the encryption algorithm, we must assume that he also knows the data compression algorithm.

Of special interest is using the data compression procedure in combination with probabilistic encryption with a simple mechanism of inserting random data into the cryptogram. Each of these two additional transformations increases the encryption security. When used, one of them decreases the initial size of the message, while the other increases it. Probabilistic ciphers based on the concatenation of blocks of encrypted data with random binary vectors make it possible to easily control increasing the size of the cryptogram, and therefore parameters of the probabilistic encryption can be chosen so that the generated ciphertext will have a size approximately equal to the size of the message before the redundancy was eliminated.

Encrypting and Coding

When transmitting private information over telecommunication channels with noise, you need to perform enciphering, and interference-tolerant coding of the data being transmitted. For block cryptosystems, the enciphering and deciphering procedures exhibit a pronounced diffusion of the influence of input characters over many output characters, this influence being pseudo-random. In connection with this, when using block cryptosystems, the interference-tolerant coding procedure must be performed after enciphering on the sending side. As for the receiving side, you must first decode and then decipher the message.

Error propagation during deciphering doesn't take place when you use stream enciphering, which involves the generation of a keystream by a secret key and synchronous bitwise XORing of the keystream and transmitted message. In this case, regardless of the order of the ciphering and coding procedures, deciphering and decoding on the receiving side can be successfully carried out. For example, when sending and receiving, you can use the following sequence of data transmission: coding-enciphering-deciphering-decoding.

1.6.3 Standardization of Encryption Algorithms

The significant role of enciphering algorithms when solving the data protection problem on a broad scale is the reason for the adoption of enciphering standards. Of these, among which the most known and widely used was the American Federal Standard DES, adopted in the mid-1970s; it was a predecessor of the Russian Standard GOST. Today, both standards seem obsolete, and neither conforms to modern requirements of data transformation speed. Besides which, DES uses a 56-bit private key that nowadays cannot provide sufficient security against an attack of trying every possible key value, and the Russian Standard is difficult for hardware implementation. A significant disadvantage of GOST is that it uses persistent secret components, such as substitution tables, that are supplied in a set order. According to widely adopted cryptographic requirements, the security of an algorithm must be based only on the secrecy of an easily changeable element—a key. Neither of the ciphers is secure against attacks based on a differential fault analysis. Such an attack is relevant for ciphers used in smart cards. (In this type of attack, it is assumed that the opponent can physically influence the enciphering device from outside and cause occasional random failures in the registers containing data when the enciphering procedure is being carried out.)

The fact that the world's first public official standard was adopted in the United States played an important role in strengthening the leadership of American vendors of data protection systems. The influence of the American DES standard on public cryptography trends all over the world appeared to be so significant that, for many years, developers of block enciphering algorithms were "hypnotized" by the approaches used in DES development. The general design scheme of the DES cryptosystem became a common pattern. This fact became the reason for a certain restraint in trying new approaches to the design of block cryptosystems, which vividly showed itself in the early 1990s, when there was a boom in the need for using fast software-oriented encryption methods.

The leading industrial countries pay much attention to developing new encryption algorithms that satisfy modern technological requirements. In 1998–2000, the United States, while retaining their leadership in this area, held a worldwide contest (visit *http://www.nist.gov/aes*) for the adoption of their new standard—Advanced Encryption Standard (AES). A number of conferences were devoted to this contest, in which the proposed ciphers were discussed. The leading world cryptographers were involved in this competition, and 15 AES candidates were presented. The contest is now over. A Belgian cipher, Rijndael, was the winner. The RC6 and TwoFish ciphers were also among the better competitors. Soon after, a similar European contest was announced, which is currently in full swing. When distributing encryption algorithms and data protection tools, the leading countries strengthen their positions in the information security market by offering their products and services; they increase their influence and, to some extent, acquire the possibility of controlling the information resource security of other countries.

In Russia, the problem of developing fast ciphers satisfying modern requirements and trends has also been officially declared. One of these trends is the increasing technological requirements for encryption algorithms. While the requirements of providing guaranteed security remains urgent, there is also the problem of providing a high encryption speed, both with a software implementation (more than 100 Mbit/sec) and a hardware one (more than 1000 Mbit/sec). At the same time, the cost of enciphering devices should be affordable enough for the average buyer. There is also the need to provide algorithm security against a number of nontraditional attacks, such as differential fault analysis.

The needs of software technology formed the public cryptographic school of thought outside Russia in the mid-1970s. In Russia, public cryptography began to actively develop in the mid-1990s. Currently, applied cryptography topics are common in many Russian scientific magazines. Russian cryptographers took out more than 30 patents for enciphering. Enciphering issues are usually discussed at conferences devoted to information security. At the end of 1999, a nonprofit organization was founded in Russia—the "RusCrypto" association—which intends to propagate cryptographic knowledge, increase the quality of the data protection tools developed in Russia, and expand Russian public research in the field of cryptography.

Russian approaches to the design of fast ciphers and certain particular ciphers include important new elements. For example, some suggested encryption methods based on data-dependent permutations (Russian patents Nos. 2140710, 2140714, 2140716, 2141729) are advantageous for hardware implementation. This approach has sufficient theoretical and experimental justification, and it has led to the rise of a new direction in applied cryptography related to the use of specially designed cryptographic operations—controlled cryptographic primitives.

The prime requirement for encryption algorithms is high security; when this isn't satisfied, the other features are of no concern. A specialist familiar with the basics of cryptography and having sufficient skills in this area can design a secure algorithm relatively quickly. However, there are other requirements on algorithms intended for wide use. Here are some of them:

- It is necessary to convince experts and consumers that a suggested algorithm is secure. To do this, design criteria are specified, and theoretical investigations of the operations and transformation mechanisms used are carried out. Statistical properties of the cipher are also explored.
- It is necessary to convince users that the proposed algorithm doesn't include trapdoors that make it possible to compute the key or read ciphertexts without knowing the private key.
- The algorithm must possess necessary properties that make hardware implementation inexpensive (and/or software implementation convenient).
- The algorithm must provide a high encryption speed.
- The algorithm must provide high security against traditional cryptanalytic attacks (such as known-plaintext attacks and chosen-plaintext or chosen-ciphertext attacks), and attacks related to special applications. These are, for example, differential fault analysis, power consumption measurements, computing time measurements, and others.

AES candidates had to meet the requirement of a high-speed hardware and software implementation (provided the hardware implementation is inexpensive). This seems reasonable because a widely used algorithm whose aim is first to provide information privacy should be able to be implemented in various ways. The maximum speed of encryption is difficult to achieve. Obviously, an algorithm oriented toward only a software or only a hardware implementation can provide a higher performance in the corresponding area. This is very important when designing ciphers with high technological requirements. Now, when information technologies are advanced, even minor losses in performance result in significant economic damage when they are multiplied. In crucial application areas, even a small delay can lead to a disaster. These considerations show that even the adoption of a common encryption standard can't cope with all the problems of applied cryptography. The cryptanalysis of already designed algorithms is continuously developing, and the design of new ciphers is as well.

1.6.4 Built-in Trapdoor Issues

By a *trapdoor*, we mean the presence of a secret that, if known, it is possible to disclose the cipher; in other words, to read a ciphertext without knowing the key, or to compute the encryption key. One of the major issues of the wide usage of encryption methods is gaining users' confidence. In the DES algorithm, no trapdoors have been found in more than 20 years, but many users still have doubts about this point. Using secret substitutions in GOST complicates comprehensive trapdoor investigations, which increases the distrust of independent users. How important for users is the threat that trapdoor ciphers can be imposed on them? The discussion of trapdoor issues in public cryptographic papers has been one-sided for a long time. In particular, it was directed toward looking for trapdoors in ciphers that had already been designed. Belgian scientists V. Rijmen and B. Preneel formulated the trapdoor topic in another way: is it possible in principle to design ciphers for which it would be computationally impossible to detect the presence of trapdoors? (Even if the encryption algorithm is published and thoroughly explored by users and cryptographers.) The Belgians' research gave a positive answer. They revealed ways of designing block DES-like ciphers containing trapdoors that nowadays would be computationally impossible to detect. This result is rather disappointing for users. If the risk of trapdoor presence in ciphers must be taken into account, is it possible to avoid attacks based on trapdoors? It is difficult to guarantee protection against such an attack. However, the following approaches that significantly diminish the risks can be suggested:

- The users or their proxies should take part in designing substitution boxes or the whole cipher (this approach requires professional training; it also has another disadvantage related to the confidence of other users in a cryptoscheme designed in such a way).
- The user can reject using a cryptosystem with predefined substitutions, and choose ciphers in which substitutions (for example, substitution tables) are generated from the user's private key (such as Blowfish or TwoFish).
- The user can reject using substitutions as a basic cryptographic primitive (for example, the RC6 and SPECTR-H64 ciphers); this variant is also connected with the trapdoor issue: will it be possible some day to build trapdoors in ciphers without substitutions as well?
- It is possible to use cryptosystems in which controlled operations are used; in other words, cryptographic primitives that specify transformations depending on variable parameters of the encryption process—on the user's private key and/or on the message being encrypted. Using data-dependent operations as cryptographic primitives gives a relatively secure guarantee that there aren't trapdoors in the ciphers used. Examples of such ciphers are RC5, RC6, MARS, and SPECTR-H64 with data-dependent operations.
- To neutralize trapdoors, it is possible to use simple probabilistic encryption schemes, which are comprehensively described in Section 1.5 and Chapter 5. To retain the original data size, you can compress the data beforehand (note

that this method significantly increases the encryption security at the same time).

- It is possible to use double encryption using two different algorithms, whose developers are unlikely to be in collusion with each other. For example, you can encrypt data first using DES and then using GOST (one cipher will neutralize the trapdoor of the other cipher, and vice versa).

1.6.5 Cryptography and Steganography

Steganography is a technique used for secret transmission or secret storage of information, the goal of which is to conceal the very fact of the message's transmission. To do this, one can use invisible ink, acrostics, microphotography, hiding places, and so forth. Electronic data processing devices make it possible to use new steganographic methods. These methods use the pseudorandom distribution of information over time or space (or both), adding noise, and masking information in a container message or in auxiliary information. In multimedia, they can be based, for example, on hiding a message inside video frames.

The basic distinction between cryptography and steganography is that the former doesn't conceal the fact of sending messages, but only conceals their content. Using steganography to transmit important messages is very risky. Cryptography is a much more secure tool for data protection. Steganographic methods can provide a high level of information protection only if they are supplemented with a preliminary cryptographic transformation of messages. The transformation will actually determine the security of such a combined secret scheme.

Currently, developers of steganographic methods use secret keys, and this actually means developing steganographic methods that include cryptographic subsystems. The fact that steganography needs to use secret keys means accepting the fact that the development of secure methods of concealing message transmission involves cryptography. The ideas of one-key and two-key cryptography can significantly enrich steganography.

Steganography doesn't include the versatile internal possibilities that are inherent to cryptography, and which have defined the very important role of cryptography in this society with its advanced information infrastructure.

2 Flexible Software Ciphers

2.1 THE SECRECY AND CRYPTOGRAPHIC STRENGTH OF THE ALGORITHM

In the most general sense, any block cryptosystem is a method of specifying a kind of substitution. The essence of encryption is the replacement of the block of the plaintext by the block of ciphertext. Obviously, for ensuring strong encryption, it is necessary to use sophisticated transformation procedures that, according to the Kerckhoff's principle, are assumed known to the attacker. In practice, ciphers with 64-bit and 128-bit input blocks are used most often. Although rarely, it is also possible to encounter 32-bit block ciphers and 512-byte block ciphers. Every block cipher can formally be represented in the form of the set of substitution tables. Each of these tables corresponds to one of the possible secret keys and specifies (for the given key) the mapping of all possible input messages and their corresponding cryptograms. However, the size of each of these tables is excessive ($n2^n$ bits), which makes this method of specifying ciphers practically unusable.

Table description of ciphers is the most general. Ciphers specified in the form of an algorithm are only a small part of possible substitutions; however, these substitutions are exactly the ones that can be used in practice because they are described using a compact method. Thus, the block cipher represented in the form of a certain transformation algorithm implements the method of choosing a specific table for substituting the input block by the output block depending on the secret key. Replacement of the secret key means replacement of the substitution table, which must not be rebuilt completely. Working with the substitution table is computing the output block by the specified input block if the encryption key is known.

The encryption algorithm characterized by high cryptographic strength specifies a "pseudorandom" transformation; that is, a transformation that is practically undistinguishable from a random one. For a good block algorithm, without knowing the secret key it is computationally difficult to choose such input texts for which observing the corresponding ciphertexts would allow you to predict any relationship between the result of transformation of the next specially chosen text with the known output texts. In reality, such dependence has already been specified by the encryption algorithm as such. However, for cryptographically strong transformation, this relation is pseudorandom. The first stage of cryptanalysis consists of determining certain conditions under which the encrypting transformation can be distinguished from a random transformation. If such conditions have been discovered, this means that prerequisites for the cipher disclosure have been created. However, it is necessary to bear in mind that the task of computing the secret key might happen to be much more labor-intensive than the task of detecting the encryption transformation and distinguishing it from a random transformation.

Knowing the transformation algorithm is a considerable help for the attacker, because it allows the cryptanalyst to investigate statistical properties of the cipher. If you discover specific statistical relationships between input and output texts, you'll create the prerequisites for disclosing (computing) the secret key. A natural theoretical question arises: Is it possible to build cryptosystems with secret algorithms that ensure unconditional security if the key of finite size is used? In this chapter, it will be shown that ensuring unconditional security of ciphers with secret algorithm is possible only under conditions of infinite complexity of encrypting procedures. In this case, the encryption time of any text is infinite, which makes the practical use of such ciphers meaningless.

Consider the issue of unconditional security of the cryptosystem with the secret algorithm and finite encryption time. It is assumed that a potential intruder is human, has access to many contemporary computers, and knows the language in which the original message was written. Assume that the attacker wants to read a cryptogram corresponding to the original text of the size that exceeds the key size multiple times. Because unconditional security is considered in this case, it must be assumed that the attacker's computational resources are infinite.

The size of the text describing any algorithm with finite encryption time is finite; therefore, the attacker can try all possible algorithms. Actually, for the given level of computing technology, each finite text can be interpreted as an algorithm written using machine language commands. With all this being so, the number of variants of interpreting an arbitrary finite sequence of bytes is finite. Consequently, if the attacker has infinite computing resources, by means of brute-force attack it is possible to determine both the finite secret key and the encryption algorithms.

Thus, from the unconditional security point of view, the uncertainty of the dynamically formed algorithm is not a serious issue. Only a random key valid for one occasion only, the length of which is equal to the length of the message being encrypted, allows for achieving unconditional security. The latter concept has more theoretical than practical value. Actually, the practice is not closed. All possible occurrences of the attacker's actions under real-world conditions of the cryptosystem's operations cannot be predicted beforehand by the closed theoretical model.

The use of long keys generates the problem of further complication of the procedures of the secure key management, which can make unconditionally strong ciphers less reliable than conditionally strong cryptosystems with 512-, 256-, or even 128-bit keys. For conditionally strong cryptosystems (that is, computationally strong ones), the secrecy of the algorithm is the issue of principal importance. In reality, the labor intensity required to compromise the cryptosystem is evaluated in relation to specific cryptanalysis algorithms. The cryptographic strength of the cipher is adopted to be equal to the labor intensity required to disclose it using the best-known method of cryptanalysis.

The best method of cryptanalysis depends on the encryption algorithm. In addition, the most efficient methods of cryptanalysis are based on the knowledge of the encryption algorithm and preliminary investigation of its mathematical and probabilistic properties. This gives grounds to the assumption that keeping the encryption algorithm secret will considerably complicate the cryptanalysis. This method of improving the encryption strength is not widely used in practice mainly because it is very hard to practically ensure the secrecy of the cryptosystem elements that are used for a long time, thus becoming known to wide user community (which initially was limited). In addition, the secrecy of the algorithm must also be ensured at the stage of designing and testing of the algorithm.

Thus, in case of computationally complex cryptosystems, the secrecy of the encryption algorithm can be principally used as one of the mechanisms of considerable increase of the strength. However, to use this circumstance in practice, it is necessary to build such a cryptosystem where the encryption algorithm would be easily changeable. This can be achieved using precomputations, with which it would be possible to generate the encryption algorithms depending on the user's secret key. Such cryptosystems can be called *nondeterministic* or *flexible*. The first term emphasizes the fact that the encryption algorithm is not known to the cryptanalyst, while the second term stresses the fact that the encryption algorithm is modified depending on the secret key.

In nondeterministic cryptosystems, the precomputations algorithm is a form of specifying a large number of possible encryption algorithms. Because it is assumed that the precomputation algorithm is known (this is a long-term cipher element), then the description of possible modifications of encrypting functions is known to the cryptanalyst. It is assumed that the cryptanalyst knows everything, except for the choice of specific modification. In this chapter, we cover the practical schemes of building nondeterministic ciphers, allowing for specifying a large number of different modifications of the encryption algorithm.

The encryption algorithm can be considered secret (in the sense of the uncertainty of the choice of the encrypting procedures modification), despite that such cryptosystems are investigated and discussed in detail in the open publications. The secrecy of the algorithm is a specific form of improving the strength of the cryptosystem, and can be successfully used for building new strong ciphers. The presence of the precomputations stage is a factor that introduces several limitations to the use in specific areas; for example, in cases when it is necessary to change the key often (for example, once per second or fraction of second). In most applications, the use of the precomputations stage is allowable, therefore nondeterministic software ciphers are potentially promising for the wide areas of application.

2.2 THE PRINCIPLES OF DESIGNING SOFTWARE CIPHERS

In using the term *software* ciphers, we mean those that use operations with computer words and take into account the features of data processing in computer systems, making it possible to obtain high encryption speeds when using common microprocessors. Considering the huge problem of protecting electronic information, software ciphers have quite good possibilities when it comes to practical use. Let's look at the peculiarities of designing software ciphers. Ensuring the most reliable secure data processing mode in computer systems is connected with the enciphering of all data stored in the nonvolatile memory. In general, data processing involves random requests for data reading and writing, so it is necessary to encrypt individual data blocks independently.

Modern computers typically have a large volume of persistent memory, and provide high speeds of reading and writing. These two features make serious demands on ciphers oriented toward use in real-time systems that protect data from unauthorized access:

- A high security against cryptanalysis based on a large volume of known or chosen texts encrypted using the same key
- A high enciphering speed in a software implementation

To design fast software ciphers, it is suggested that you use pseudorandom subkey selection. For cryptoschemes with such a nondeterministic selection of subkeys, elements of the cryptographic key used to transform input data blocks are typically selected in accordance with the structure of the data block being transformed and the structure of the encryption key. For ciphers based on such a cryptoscheme, subkey scheduling isn't predetermined, which significantly increases the security of the encryption. Due to this, the number of enciphering rounds can be decreased, thus increasing the encryption speed. Ciphers with a data-dependent subkey selection can be called pseudorandom thanks to this type of key selection.

Data-dependent subkey selection is generally just a formal mapping operation (substitution) performed according to the table specified by the encryption key. The encryption key consists of a set of numbered subkeys. An input block specifies the number of the selected subkey, and the subkey specifies the value obtained as a result of the mapping operation. The array of elements that implements the mapping operation is called an **S**-box (or a substitution box). We're going to use the term *data-dependent subkey selection*, since the transformed data subblock that determines the currently selected subkey isn't replaced by the selected subkey, but rather *both of them* are used in subsequent transformations. In such cases, the encryption process is easier to understand when it is described in terms close to the procedures actually performed. The term *substitution operation* is best used in cases in which the transformation procedure is limited to replacing an input block with a value from the substitution table.

For software ciphers, the basic principle of diffusion and confusion is supplemented with the following mechanisms:

- The dependence of **S**-boxes on the secret key
- An increase in the size of **S**-boxes
- An increase in the size of the transformed data block, up to 512 bytes
- The dependence of the encryption algorithm on the secret key (for example, adjusting the transformation operations by the secret key)
- Data-dependence of the transformation operations (i.e., controlling the selection of a modification of the current operation depending on the input message)
- Data-dependence of the subkey selection
- Various combinations of the mechanisms listed in the first five items (for example, specifying the dependence of the subsets of possible modifications of the controlled operation on the secret key; in other words, a combination of the third and fourth items)

Despite the large number of various encryption mechanisms and their actual implementations, in general, a block cipher can be considered a subset of substitutions assigned to the set of possible input data blocks. The number of substitutions does not exceed the number of different possible secret keys in the cipher. The choice of a secret key corresponds to the choice of a particular substitution. Thus, a block cipher is a way of specifying a simple substitution in a very large alphabet. Due to the large size of the input alphabet (for n-bit input blocks, the number of possible input blocks is 2^n, and the number of possible permutations is $2^n!$), substitutions cannot be specified in tabular form, and the only practical, convenient way to specify them is algorithmically—in other words, by specifying a rule for computing output blocks using input blocks.

The method of specifying substitutions in the form of procedures controlled by the secret key determines that substitutions are randomly selected not from the (2^n) subset of all possible substitutions, but from the subset of 2^k substitutions, where k is the maximum length of the secret key in bits. Since it is assumed that the cryptanalyst knows the encryption algorithm, this means that he also knows the subset of substitutions implemented by this algorithm. The complexity of cryptanalysis results from the fact that the number of possible substitutions is extremely large, and each can be only considered an algorithm describing it when the secret key has a certain value.

The specific kind of the algorithm determines the rule for building the subset of possible substitutions, and therefore, the block cipher has certain algebraic and statistical properties that can be used when performing a cryptanalysis. The question is only how complex a certain cryptanalytic method is for a particular encryption algorithm. While the encryption algorithm plays a secondary role in ensuring the security of ciphers with infinite keys, for block ciphers with fixed secret keys, the characteristics of the encryption mechanism are the most important. The principles of cipher design and the specific kinds of the mechanisms used are oriented toward specifying a pseudorandom substitution that is hard to distinguish from a random one, provided the cryptanalyst has a large (but reasonable) amount of initial data to launch an attack.

The complexity of the cryptanalysis is related to two different factors. When encryption algorithms with good diffusion and confusion properties are used, the work effort needed for a successful cryptanalysis depends on *the complexity of analyzing the enciphering procedures themselves*. When the encryption algorithm depends on the secret key, the complexity of the cryptanalytic problem significantly increases due to the *ambiguity of the interpretation of the statistical connections between the original texts and their corresponding cryptograms*. Ciphers in which the encryption algorithm is built depending on the secret key are called *flexible* or *non-deterministic*. In flexible ciphers, a given key corresponds to only one implemented modification of the encryption algorithm. A limited set of keys means that a flexible cipher is a set of encryption algorithms described using an algorithm that specifies a rule for building an encryption algorithm depending on the secret key. Building secret substitution tables or an encryption algorithm assumes that software ciphers use a precomputation stage, which is executed only once after entering the secret key. This is the stage in which is initialized a cryptosystem that will later repeatedly perform the data encryption and decryption procedures.

2.3 INITIALIZING SOFTWARE CIPHERS

As a rule, iterated ciphers use keys with a length of 56 to 256 bits. Currently, if you have a key of 80 bits or more, an attack based on trying every possible key cannot be launched by any organization, even one with many computational resources. To ensure security against all the other known cryptanalytic methods, a large number of transformation rounds are used, with transformation procedures that have good diffusion and confusion properties being executed in each.

Obviously, when longer encryption keys are used, there are more possibilities for designing fast encryption procedures. However, when using longer keys, it is more difficult to control (generate, transfer, and store) them. In cryptosystems intended for a software implementation, the possibility of using and storing long encryption keys can be provided by special procedures of one-way transformation of a relatively small initial secret key into an extended cryptographic key, whose size can be anywhere from 1 to 64 KB. In this case, it would suffice to control the secret keys because the encryption key can be generated from the secret key when needed according to the known procedures. The stage of generating the encryption key is a precomputation stage, executed only once when the enciphering device or computer is switched on. When such a scheme of cipher design is used, the cryptanalyst must choose between the two main variants of an attack:

- He may assume that the extended key is chosen at random, and analyze relatively simple encryption procedures with the aim of revealing their vulnerabilities.
- He may investigate significantly more complicated procedures of generating the encryption key and try to solve the encryption equations for the secret keys.

Obviously, the procedures of generating the encryption key must be complex enough so it would be impossible to compute any portion of the secret key from individual fragments of the extended encryption key. The basic algorithm requirements for generating the encryption key are:

- An approximately equal influence of each bit of the secret key on all the bits of the extended key being generated
- A high computational complexity of finding the secret key using the known extended key

A high cipher security based on the key extension mechanism is achievable in principle, since in the precomputation stage you can use algorithms belonging to a wider class of transformations than encryption algorithms. We know that a basic limitation of the latter is the necessity of performing an inverse transformation controlled by key parameters and restoring the original message from the ciphers. Such a limitation isn't put on an algorithm generating the encryption key, and a wider class of algorithms suggests that there are even more secure ones from the cryptographic point of view.

Because the setup procedure is supposed to be performed only during the initialization (switching on) of the cryptosystem, there are no substantial restrictions on how long it takes to execute the setup algorithm or on the computational resources used (the precomputation subprogram isn't a resident program). This means that it is acceptable to use multistage one-way procedures, including nondeterministic algorithms: in the first precomputation stage, a one-way transformation algorithm is generated, and executed in the second stage, in which the final transformation of the secret key into the extended encryption key is carried out.

When performing setup procedures, you can also make the generation of the encrypting algorithm modification unique for each user. In fact, the algorithm for generating the encryption procedures is just a form of specifying the choice of a certain modification of the encryption algorithm from a very large number of possible modifications according to the user's secret key. The practical implementation of cryptosystems with nondeterministic encryption algorithms is a special feature of software tools, which follows from the idea of using precomputations.

Thus, a software cipher can be implemented as one of two subroutines—an initialization module intended for a single run, and a resident enciphering module servicing requests from other programs to encrypt and decrypt data.

One of the requirements put on the algorithm generating the encryption key is that the number of output sequences mustn't be significantly less than the number of the possible secret keys. The length of the extended output key is greater than that of the secret key, but for certain precomputation procedures, it may appear that different secret keys correspond to the same encryption key. When one-way transformations are used in the encryption key generating stage, narrowing the encryption keyspace seems unlikely. However, it is best to ensure that the capacity of a set of encryption keys is equal to that of the set of secret keys of the specified length. This can be easily achieved by using encryption procedures for the extended key algorithm generation. Indeed, by repeating the secret key the necessary number of times, we can easily obtain a unique extended text for every secret key. After encrypting this extended text, we obtain a ciphertext that can be used as an extended key. When a nondeterministic cipher is required, build an input extended text whose size is greater than the necessary length of the extended key. A portion of the transformed text will be used as an extended encryption key, and the other portion will be used to build the encryption algorithm.

2.4 NON-DETERMINISTIC SOFTWARE CIPHERS

In the traditional approach, a cryptosystem is built based on a fixed set of transformation operations. A key is used to control the encryption process by specifying the parameters used in the encryption transformations. These parameters can be either key elements selected according to a certain rule, or characters of a pseudorandom sequence generated based on the key. The most favorable conditions to launch cryptanalytic attacks are the availability of:

- Complete information about the data encryption procedures used
- A sufficient amount of a known plaintext, including a specially chosen one, and the corresponding ciphertext

Testing the cryptosystem under such conditions is a general rule.

Using cryptalgorithms in software tools for computer protection requires that all the encryption procedures be stored on the computer's magnetic carrier if we don't want to burden users with having to repeatedly perform additional actions. Thus, in a user-friendly computer security system, the algorithm of the cryptomodule is basically available to a malefactor. Obviously, the absence of information or partial information about the cryptographic procedures used makes it much more difficult for a potential adversary to solve the task of breaking the protection system. This goal is achieved by implementing so-called *flexible (non-deterministic) ciphers*, in which the encryption algorithm is automatically changed when the secret key changes.

2.4.1 The Principles of Designing Flexible Ciphers

Using software tools to carry out cryptographic transformations and the precomputation stage, in which the encryption mechanism is initialized, makes it possible to design cryptosystems in which the encryption algorithm for a particular user isn't known to an attacker beforehand. This is achieved thanks to the fact that, in the precomputation stage, the procedures generating the encryption algorithm are executed depending on the secret key. Thus, when using a computer to complicate cryptanalytic attacks, the encryption algorithm can be built according to a generating algorithm, which must be assumed to be known to an attacker. The set of possible encryption algorithms is finite, and the rule that determines the generating algorithm is considered known to the cryptanalyst. However, the cryptanalyst doesn't know which particular modification of the encryption algorithm will be implemented, since its choice is determined by the secret key.

If the number of implementable modifications is 10^9 or more, the nondeterminism of the transformation procedures can be an effective tool for counteracting cryptanalytic attacks. Moreover, reducing the cryptanalytic problem to trying every possible variant doesn't seem realizable, since it requires that you first consider the majority of the algorithms of this class, and then find an individual approach to each. This is unlikely. It is possible to execute a cryptanalytic attack that looks for any general regularities over the entire set of possible modifications of the cryptalgorithm, or over a sufficiently large subsets. Building such a generalized cryptanalytic algorithm is a much more complicated task than designing a method to analyze a cipher with a fixed encryption algorithm.

A universal method of cryptanalysis is keyless reading, based on known input texts and corresponding blocks of ciphertext. However, it is easy to design a flexible algorithm, each modification of which will be secure against such a generalized type of cryptanalysis. In the following sections, we describe flexible algorithms that meet this requirement. In addition, these flexible ciphers are secure against attacks based on a known modification of the cryptoalgorithm and attacks based on a chosen modification (in the latter case, the attacker can choose the weakest cryptoalgorithm from the set of potentially implementable modifications).

The following theoretical question is directly related to the problem of creating cryptosystems with nondeterministic transformation algorithms: can the system generate a weak second-stage algorithm during the initialization stage? It is difficult to formally describe such an object as a cryptoscheme with a nondeterministic transformation algorithm, and it is even more difficult to provide a strict theoretical proof of the security of all its modifications. However, the following points in favor of using these new systems can be listed:

- The probability of generating a weak algorithm is very small, and drastically decreases when using diversified methods of specifying nondeterministic procedures.
- The generating algorithm can be made responsible for controlling the quality of the encryption algorithm generated (for example, you can have a control encryption in this stage and then analyze the cipher as to whether it passes a special spectral test).

- In systems with a multipass encryption mode, you can use cryptoschemes with fixed encryption procedures as one or more of the component algorithms. The security of these cryptoschemes can be estimated according to approved methods.
- It is possible to design cryptoschemes that will allow for arbitrary modification of a certain set of operations or transformation procedures; in other words, cryptoschemes whose security is not sensitive to the modification of the set of operations and procedures used.

The latter approach seems the most promising in designing practical, nondeterministic ciphers.

Non-deterministic ciphers pose a basically new logical problem for the cryptanalyst—algorithmic uncertainty, which can be quantitatively described with a number of different potentially implementable modifications of the encryption algorithm. In ciphers with a fixed algorithm, the uncertainty of the encryption process for a cryptanalyst is related to the fact that he doesn't know the secret key, whose components (subkeys) are used as parameters in the transformation procedures.

From the standpoint of the uncertainty of the encrypting transformations, flexible ciphers can be presented as a form of specifying key components as adjustable operations and encrypting transformation procedures. Obviously, it is possible to design nondeterministic ciphers that use only such "functional" key components. However, it is more reasonable to design flexible ciphers in which all modifications of the encryption algorithm also use a regular encryption key that contains "parametric" key components. One feature of using "functional" key components is specifying the uncertainty of the encryption procedures, which strongly hampers giving a general analytic description of even elementary transformation steps.

With a high level of algorithmic uncertainty, the transformation of a given block (or a number of blocks) can be described by the subset of all the possible modifications of the encryption algorithm. From the point of view of quantitative uncertainty characteristics, parametric and functional components are equivalent, since the number of variants that can direct the encryption process depends only on the number of key bits. However, algorithmic uncertainty introduces an important qualitative feature—the difficulty of using analytic expressions when carrying out a cryptanalysis. The uncertainty specified by parametric key elements is often removed when mathematical formulas are used, whereas the uncertainty specified by functional key elements is very difficult to generalize, and it is by no means obvious as to how to write down the transformation equations. This significantly complicates building a cryptanalytic algorithm that would make it possible to eliminate a trial-and-error method of finding key elements.

It is especially advantageous to use combinations of functional and parametric key components. The former give us logical complexity, while the latter give us quantitative complexity. The major reason for such a combination is overcoming the difficulties of providing a high level of algorithmic uncertainty.

We should mention that a strict discussion of the security of non-deterministic cryptosystems is related to a number of formalized issues that are difficult to consider, such as how to take into account the differences in the security properties of individual modifications. Minimum estimations can be considered acceptable, but excessive assumption in favor of the cryptanalyst can result in the rejection of promising cryptoschemes. Other important problems that require solutions when designing non-deterministic software ciphers are:

- Ensuring high security for all possible modifications of the encrypting algorithm against the keyless reading method
- Specifying a large number of nonequivalent modifications
- Providing an approximately equal probability of choosing a modification from each subset of equivalent modifications
- Providing for security against attacks based on a known and chosen modification of the cryptalgorithm

Let's consider a number of ideas that can be used as the basis for creating non-deterministic ciphers.

2.4.2 A Cryptoscheme with Permutations of Fixed Procedures

Let's assume that the encryption of each input message consists of sequentially performing a number of elementary operations on it—$\mathbf{F}_1$, $\mathbf{F}_2$, ..., $\mathbf{F}_n$. In this case, a specific encryption algorithm can be created by specifying the dependence of the sequence of elementary transformations on the secret key. In practice, this can be easily implemented as the creation of an encrypting program basing on subroutines. The number of various possible algorithms is $S \doteq n!$, and for $n = 16$ we have $S > 10^{13}$.

2.4.3 Multipass Cryptoschemes with Flexible Algorithms

When using fast ciphers, it is possible to repeatedly encrypt the original text. Let's say we have a library of encrypting programs $\mathbf{E}_1$, $\mathbf{E}_2$, ..., $\mathbf{E}_n$, and their corresponding deciphering programs $\mathbf{D}_1$, $\mathbf{D}_2$, ..., $\mathbf{D}_n$. To specify nondeterminism for the encryption algorithm, we can provide an implementation of variants of the encryption procedure that consist of m sequential procedures selected from the $\{\mathbf{E}_1, \mathbf{E}_2, ..., \mathbf{E}_n, \mathbf{D}_1, \mathbf{D}_2, ..., \mathbf{D}_n\}$ set; in other words, the resulting encryption will take the form of the superposition of m procedures: $\mathbf{E} = \mathbf{F}_{i_m} \circ ... \circ \mathbf{F}_{i_2} \circ \mathbf{F}_{i_1}$, where $\mathbf{F} \in \{\mathbf{E}_1, \mathbf{E}_2, ..., \mathbf{E}_n, \mathbf{D}_1, \mathbf{D}_2, ..., \mathbf{D}_n\}$ and $i \in \{1, 2, ..., n\}$.

Since sequential execution of the **E** and **D** procedures with the same indices doesn't change the message being encrypted, we'll prohibit modifications of the resulting function that corresponds to such cases. For $\mathbf{F}_{i_1}$, any of $2n$ elements of the $\{\mathbf{E}_1, \mathbf{E}_2, ..., \mathbf{E}_n, \mathbf{D}_1, \mathbf{D}_2, ..., \mathbf{D}_n\}$ set can be chosen, while for $\mathbf{F}_{i_2}, \mathbf{F}_{i_3}, ..., \mathbf{F}_{i_{2m}}$, you can choose one of the $2n-1$ elements. Taking this into account, it is easy to calculate the number of all possible modifications S of the resulting encryption function: $S = 2n(2n-1)^{m-1}$.

If the encryption function has the form $\mathbf{E} = \mathbf{F}_{i_m} \circ ... \circ \mathbf{F}_{i_2} \circ \mathbf{F}_{i_1}$, its corresponding decryption function will be

$$\mathbf{D} = \mathbf{F}^{-1}_{i_1} \circ \mathbf{F}^{-1}_{i_2} \circ ... \circ \mathbf{F}^{-1}_{i_m},$$

where $\mathbf{F}^{-1}_i = \mathbf{E}_j$ if $\mathbf{F}_i = \mathbf{D}_j$, and $\mathbf{F}^{-1}_i = \mathbf{D}_j$ if $\mathbf{F}_i = \mathbf{E}_j$, $(j = 1, 2, ..., n)$.

Of special interest are ciphers based on procedures and transformation operations that depend on the data being transformed. In these ciphers, the particular form of the operation (or procedure) performed at a given step depends on the value of the text being transformed. When describing an encryption algorithm based on standard operations, the set of these operations changes from one input text to another. Unlike the nondeterministic ciphers discussed earlier, the transformation algorithm in ciphers with data-dependent operations is fixed, since the rule for choosing a particular type of operation depending on the current value of the data being transformed is known. The use of encryption procedures with operations that depend on the input message is rather promising when building fast ciphers that have a high security.

2.4.4 A Cryptosystem Adjusting of Transformation Operations

The idea of using transformation operations as key elements consists of the following. A template for the procedure of transformation of a current data subblock is set. The template contains a set of numbered transformation operations. The particular values of the operations are adjusted in the precomputation stage depending on the secret key. This can be done according to the following scheme. A pseudorandom number sequence is generated under the control of the secret key. Depending on the value of the number that corresponds to the number of the operation, a specific variant of that operation is adjusted. For example, a procedure for transforming the current 32-bit data subblock T can include computations according to the following formulas:

$$G := \{[(T *_{n_1} K_1)^{>>>x_1} *_{n_2} K_2)]^{>>>x_2} *_{n_3} K_3\}^{>>>x_3} *_{n_4} G$$

$$C := [(G^{>>>x_4} *_{n_5} K_4)^{>>>x_5} *_{n_6} K_5]^{>>>x_6} *_{n_7} K_6,$$

where C is the transformed value of the data subblock; $K_1, K_2, \ldots, K_6$ are 32-bit subkeys that are constants in the encryption program or variables selected depending on the data being transformed; G is a binary vector that determines the influence of the previous data subblocks on the transformation of the current subblock; the $^{>>>x}$ operator denotes a reserved unary operation (i.e., an operation performed on one number—for example, $W^{>>>x}$ denotes a right circular shift by x bits), the $*_n$ symbol denotes a binary operation such as modulo 2^{32} addition (+), modulo 2^{32} subtraction (−), or bitwise addition modulo 2 (⊕), and $n_1, n_2, \ldots, n_7$ are the numbers of the reserved binary operations. It is suggested that you establish a specific set of reserved operations in the precomputation stage depending on the secret key.

2.4.5 A Pseudo-Probabilistic Non-deterministic Cipher

There is a definite interest in creating ciphers in which a non-deterministic transformation mechanism is directly combined with data-dependent subkey selection. With such a combination, the creation of weak algorithm modifications is prevented because the security of encryption procedures with pseudorandom subkey selection is not terribly important when it comes to choosing the particular set of binary and unary transformation operations used. (Moreover, if the subkey selection is dependent on every bit of the input message for any modification, it is impossible to create a weak modification, even if you specially choose the operation sets.)

An example of implementing such an approach is the following algorithm, in which an encryption key including 2051 8-bit words is used: $\{q_j\}$, where $j = 0, 1, 2, \ldots, 2050$. The 32-bit subkeys are specified by the relationship $Q(x) = q_{x+3} \,||\, q_{x+2} \,||\, q_{x+1} \,||\, q_x$, where $x = 0, 1, 2, \ldots, 2^{11} - 1$. The encryption key should be created at the precalculation stage. The right circular shift of the W word to $x(f)$ bits serves as a reserved unary $W^{>>>x}$ operation, where $f = 1,2,3\ldots$, is the ordinal number of the reserved operation. The input message is a 512-byte data block that is represented as a sequence of 32-bit words $\{T_w\}$, $w = 0, 1, \ldots, 127$.

INPUT: The 512-byte data block $\{T_w\}$, $w = 0, 1, \ldots, 127$.

1. Set $r = 1$, $R = 2k$ (k is a natural number) and define $L_w = T_w$, $w = 0, 1, \ldots, 127$.
2. Set the counter $i := 1$ and the initial values of the variables U, V, Y, G and n: $U := Q(1)$, $V := Q(2)$, $Y := Q(3)$, $G := Q(4)$, $n := Q(5) \bmod 2^{11}$.
3. Compute:
   - $n := \{[n \oplus (G \bmod 2^{11})] - U\} \bmod 2^{11}$
   - $V := \{[V *_{n_{7r-6}} Q(n)]^{>>>x(5r-4)} + G\}^{>>>11}$

- $n := (n *_{n_{7r-5}} V) \bmod 2^{11}$
- $U := [U *_{n_{7r-4}} Q(n)]^{>>>x(5r-3)} - (G^{>>>22})$
- $n := (n + U) \bmod 2^{11}$
- $Y := [Y *_{n_{7r-3}} Q(n)]^{>>>x(5r-2)}$

4. Compute the index of the subblock currently being transformed: $w = 120 - i$ if $r = 2, 4, ..., 2k$ or $w = i - 1$ if $r = 1, 3, \ldots, 2k - 1$.
5. Perform the current encryption step:
   - $G := (Lw *_{n_{7r-2}} V)^{>>>x(5r-1)} *_{n_{7r-1}} Y$
   - $Cw = G^{>>>x(5r)} *_{n_{7r}} U$
6. Save the C_w value.
7. If $i < 128$, increase i and go to step 3.
8. If $i < R$, increase r, define $L_w = C_w$, $w = 0, 1, ..., 127$, and go to step 2. If not, **STOP**.

OUTPUT: The 512-byte ciphertext block $\{C_w\}$, $w = 0, 1, ..., 127$.

This algorithm describes the encryption procedures. Their corresponding decryption procedures are easy to create, since they differ only in steps 3 and 4. The number of possible modifications (different variants of setting the reserved operations) of this nondeterministic algorithm is $S \approx 10^{10R}$. The size of the resident part of the encryption program for these algorithms does not exceed 5 KB. The number of encryption cycles of the given input block is determined by the R parameter, whose valid values are $R \geq 3$. The encryption speed is about $300/R$ Mbits/sec (for Pentium processors), and the number of implementable nonequivalent modifications of the cryptalgorithm is greater than 10^{10R}. This algorithm is secure, assuming that an attacker knows all the transformation operations and 90 percent of the subkeys. A variant of an attack based on a known part of the extended key will be discussed later.

In general, the security of specific modifications of pseudorandom ciphers isn't critically sensitive to the operation sets used or their specific types, so using a subkey selection mechanism depending on the data being transformed presents many opportunities of varying and combining various types of binary and unary transformation operations. The main advantage of this feature of pseudorandom ciphers is not so much in the ease of creating a wide range of fast cryptalgorithms for software implementation as in the possibility of developing a great number of fast, nondeterministic cryptosystems, in which the transformation algorithm and the encryption key are unknown to the cryptanalyst. To build ciphers with a modifiable cryptalgorithm, you must additionally provide an initialization function for the encryption algorithm, this function being executed under the control of the user's secret key (or password). If the number of possibly implementable modifications of a cryptalgorithm is very large (for example, 10^{20}), this method of providing for the transformation's security will be quite effective.

Even though the modification being implemented is assumed unknown in nondeterministic ciphers, this doesn't contradict Kerkhoff's principle, according to which the data encryption algorithm must be considered known to an attacker. This principle is one of the most important ones when creating new single-key cryptosystems. It can be stated more generally: all constant elements of data protection mechanisms must be considered known to an attacker. For example, in the Russian encryption standard GOST 28147-89, "filling in the tables of the substitution box," which is a "constant key element common for the computer network," must be considered known to an attacker, even though, according to the documentation, it is "a secret element supplied in compliance with the established procedure." Using such permanent (although changeable) secret parts of encryption schemes provokes some other comments. In nondeterministic ciphers, the setup procedures for the encryption algorithm are constant elements, and its particular modification and the encryption key are changeable elements of the cryptosystem, which are automatically changed simultaneously when changing the passwords, and are unique for every user (or every pair of subscribers to the protected communication network).

Ciphers with pseudorandom key selection are secure against known cryptanalytic methods. However, new methods may be invented in the future based on the analysis of the statistical properties of the transformation procedures and operations or some other features of the encryption algorithm. The development of nondeterministic ciphers is aimed at minimizing the risk of compromising the cryptosystem for a long time to come.

2.4.6 Flexible Ciphers with a Provable Non-equivalence of Cryptalgorithm Modifications

A key selection mechanism depending on the transformed data seems to be the basis that can provide high transformation security over the entire set of implementable modifications of the cryptalgorithm. This is ensured by the fact that every possible modification determines the uniqueness of the subkey selection for every input message. For non-deterministic ciphers, one important issue is the following: could it be possible to select such modifications of a multiround encryption function so that several subsequent rounds are equivalent to a decryption function that specifies inverse transformations relative to several previous enciphering rounds? This question is urgent for ciphers that generate a transformation algorithm using a randomly selected secret key. One can assume that for the class of encryption functions based on the subkey selection depending on the transformed data, such situations are impossible.

The proof of this statement generally seems to be quite complex. However, it can be true for specific types of flexible ciphers. An example is the flexible cipher discussed in Section 5.6.7. No modifications of direct encrypting transformations can lead to inverse modifications for this flexible 64-bit block cipher. It is possible to demonstrate that, for a number of rounds from among all possible modifications of the algorithm, it is impossible to find such a modification to which one could specify round groups that determine mutually inverse transformation functions. In other words, no modification of the algorithm includes two mutually inverse transformation stages.

This proof makes sense as one of the properties supporting the conclusion that security increases as you increase the number of encryption rounds. It was proved earlier for the aforementioned 64-bit cipher that, in a certain sense, all possible modifications of the cryptalgorithm are unique. This assertion is very useful when estimating the effectiveness of the dependence of the encryption algorithm on the secret key, in the sense that the set of modifications will not break up into subsets of equivalent cryptalgorithms, which in principle could significantly simplify the cryptanalysis. Another example of flexible cryptosystems for which the properties of uniqueness and irreducibility can be proved is the 128-bit cipher discussed in "Cipher and Hash Function Design," Ph. D. thesis by J. Daemen.

We should mention that the aforementioned issues, specific to flexible ciphers, only indirectly indicate the security of this type of cryptosystem. If the cryptosystem didn't satisfy the requirements of the irreducibility of the direct and inverse transformations and the uniqueness of all enciphering transformations, it would be possible to speak about the insufficient effectiveness of the mechanism for specifying the dependence of the encryption algorithm on the secret key. However, just because these requirements are satisfied, the issue of estimating the security of a flexible cipher doesn't become less urgent. This means that the security estimation must be performed with the assumption that the cryptalgorithm modification is known.

The possibility of using the subkey selection mechanism depending on the transformed data as a basis for designing flexible cryptosystems that possess uniqueness and irreducibility is an important general feature. For practical use, fast ciphers are more interesting, but it is more difficult to prove these properties for them, due to their more complex subkey selection controlling mechanism. Building flexible ciphers in which both common operations and data-dependent ones are adjusted according to the key also seems promising. It is also difficult to present a formal proof that these flexible ciphers possess the properties of uniqueness and irreducibility, but the presence of these properties in simpler constructions based on key selection depending on the transformed data is one of the elements for justifying the practical use of more complex constructions.

2.5 THE COMBINATIONAL-PROBABILISTIC MODEL

The security of the cipher described in the preceding section is mainly based on the following points:

- The subkey selection is unique for every input block.
- The number of possibly implementable modifications of the cryptalgorithm is extremely large.
- The subkeys aren't directly used when transforming the words of an input message.

The nature of the transformations is such that the numbers of the subkeys selected during encryption make up a pseudorandom sequence—in other words, the subkey selection depending on data seems random. For a general estimation of the security of this type of cipher, we can use a combinational-probabilistic model (CPM), which is expressed in the following assumptions:

- A cryptosystem is considered cracked if an attacker finds a pair of words that were transformed using the same set of values of the *U*, *V*, and *Y* variables.
- The effort it takes to find such a pair of words in the set of known or chosen texts determines the value of the security of the cryptosystem.
- In the case of a known-plaintext attack (CPM-1) or a chosen-plaintext attack (CPM-2), in the rounds with the numbers $r \geq 2$ (CPM-1) or $r \geq 3$ (CPM-2), the *U*, *V*, and *Y* variables take random values.

The probability that the values of the used variables coincide for two transformed words is $P = M^{-3(R-1)}$ (CPM-1) and $P = M^{-3(R-2)}$ (CPM-2), where $M \approx 2^{32}$ is the number of different possible values taken by the *U*, *V*, and *Y* variables. Taking into account the "birthday paradox," the $N \approx P^{-1/2}$ value specifies the number of input words for which, with a probability approximately equal to 0.5, there are two input words transformed using the same values of the *U*, *V*, and *Y* variables in the rounds with the numbers $r \geq 2$ (CPM-1) or $r \geq 3$ (CPM-2). The *N* value determines the volume of texts necessary to launch a cryptanalytic attack. The minimum effort the attack takes, S_{min}, is determined by trying half of the possible combinations of 2 out of *N* elements. It is easy to obtain $S_{min} \approx s_r M^{3(R-1)}/4$ (for CPM-1), $S_{min} \approx s_r M^{3(R-2)}/4$ (for CPM-2), where s_r is equal to the complexity of some criterion of repetition detection ($s_r \geq 1$ operations). Here we assume the algorithm modification is known to the attacker. The secrecy of the algorithm is considered an additional guarantee of security. To test the factor related to the secrecy of the set of transformation operations, it is possible to suggest an attack based on a specially chosen modification of the cryptalgorithm that would allow a cryptanalyst to select the most convenient of the implementable modifications.

Pseudorandom ciphers similar to those described earlier are secure against attacks based on a known part of the extended key, even if the modification is known.

Let's consider the issue of estimating security when an attacker knows a portion of the extended key equal to Δ.

When the value of Δ is large enough, in a chosen-text attack (we are referring to CMP-2) an attacker can choose an input text for which the subkeys will be selected only from the known part of the extended key in the first round. This is why the input text for the second round can be computed, but in the second and subsequent rounds, the subkeys will be selected according to a pseudorandom law. Therefore, in each selecting step, addressing an unknown part of the key will take place with a probability of $1 - \Delta$. If this happens before completing the transformation of several words in the next to last round, the problem of computing the subkey values will seem complicated, since, in this situation, the numbers of the selected subkeys are unknown. The probability that, when transforming the current word in the second and subsequent rounds, only subkeys from the known part of the extended key will be selected is $P_1 = \Delta^3$. The probability of selecting known subkeys in all the steps in rounds $r = 2, 4, \ldots, R - 1$ is $P_2 = \Delta^{3e(R-2)}$, where e is the number of words being transformed. If P_2 is a small value P_a, say, $P_a = 10^{-30}$, *we can consider the cipher secure against this attack variant.* From the P_a value, it is possible to compute a secure known portion of the extended key Δ_a. For e = 120, we can easily obtain from the previous formula that

$$\Delta_a = \exp \frac{\ln P_a}{360(R-2)}.$$

For CPM-1, the following estimation can be obtained in a similar fashion:

$$\Delta_a = \exp \frac{\ln P_a}{360(R-1)}.$$

For the algorithm described in Section 2.3.5, CPM-2 gives the following estimate: Δ_a is about 0.82 (for $R = 3$) and 0.91 (for $R = 4$). Obviously, for the same R value, the secure portion of the known key for CPM-1 is greater than Δ_a for CPM-2.

2.6 FAST SOFTWARE CIPHERS—DESIGNATIONS AND TERMINOLOGY

When considering fast software algorithms of cryptographic transformations, the following designations and terms will be used.

- The term *word* should be interpreted as a 32-bit number designated by uppercase Latin characters; bytes will be designated by lowercase Latin letters.
- "||" stands for the concatenation operation. Concatenation of two bytes, a_1 and a_2, is designated as $a_2||a_1$, where a_2 corresponds to most significant bits. Concatenation of four sequential bytes $\{a_1, a_2, a_3, a_4\}$ is represented as $A = a_4||a_3||a_2||a_1$.
- The sequence of bytes $\overline{\mathbf{L}} = \{l_0, l_1, \ldots, l_n\}$ will also be interpreted as sequences of 32-bit words $\overline{\mathbf{L}} = \{L_0, L_1, \ldots, L_s\}$, where $L_j = \{l_{4j+3}, l_{4j+2}, l_{4j+1}, l_{4j+2}\}$ and $j = 0, 1, \ldots, s$. When interpreting several sequential bytes as a binary number, the rightmost byte relates to most significant bits of the number. For example, the sequence $\overline{\mathbf{L}}$ is interpreted as the number $l_n||\ldots||l_1||l_0$; in some cases, the L_i designation will be interpreted as equivalent designation $L[i]$: $\overline{\mathbf{L}} = \{l_0, l_1, \ldots, l_n\} = \{l[0], l[1], \ldots, l[n]\}$.
- ":=" stands for the assignment operation.
- "$+_f$" stands for the modulo 2^f addition (i.e., the $j := Z \bmod 2^{11}$ expression is equivalent to $j := Z +_{11} 0$).
- "$-_f$" designates modulo 2^f subtraction.
- "$\oplus$" designates the modulo 2 bitwise summation.
- "$\otimes$" designates bitwise logical multiplication.
- ">>>" ("<<<") stands for cyclic right (left) shift. For example, cyclic right shift of the word X by Y bits is designated in the following form: "$X^{>>>Y}$" (note that only $\log_2 32 = 5$ least significant bits of Y are used for specifying the shift value). The ">>>" operation has higher priority (">>>" > "$*$", where "$*$" $\in$ {"$\otimes$", "$\oplus$", "$+_f$", "$-_f$"}).
- "$W \leftrightarrow V$" designates the operation of exchanging values between words W and V.
- Hexadecimal constants used: F = FFFF07FF, a = 0D, P = B25D28A7 1A62D775, R = 98915E7E C8265EDF CDA31E88 F24809DD B064BDC7 285DD50D 7289F0AC 6F49DD2D.

2.7 CIPHERS BASED ON SUBKEY SELECTION DEPENDING ON THE DATA

One of the promising areas of applied cryptography is development of fast software-oriented ciphers. Several approaches have been suggested for building such ciphers. One of the promising approaches consists of using a sample of subkeys depending on the data being transformed as the basic cryptographic primitives. A range of 512-byte block encryption algorithms based on such mechanisms was suggested. It is interesting that until now, no one has suggested practically implementable approaches to compromising these ciphers. To obtain a generalized evaluation of the lower level of cryptographic strength of ciphers of this type, a combinatorial-probabilistic cryptanalysis model was suggested. Evaluations obtained using this model have not been lowered until now, despite the model's heuristic nature. These facts serve as evidence in favor of the efficiency of the mechanism based on subkey sampling on the basis of transformed data for development of fast software-oriented ciphers.

In a first approximation, the mechanism of subkeys sampling depending on the transformed data is the classical large substitution operation (ranging from 8×16 in first algorithms to 11×32 in newer ones), carried out according to the secret table, the role of which is played by the encryption key. For example, the 64-bit BLOWFISH cipher, built based on the Feistel cipher, implements round function as a 32×32 substitution using four 8×32 S-boxes and three binary operations. The fact that this cipher has been acknowledged strong after many years of its public discussion also provides a general confirmation of the mechanism of data-dependent subkeys sampling.

When considering the subkeys sampling mechanism depending on the data, it is possible to discover that its main implementation makes provision for subkey sampling depending on the current data subblock, and on the other data subgroups transformed in the previous steps. Although this difference from the table substitution at first glance seems insignificant, it is principally important. Thanks to the prolonged influence of the data being transformed, the subkey sampling mechanism under consideration cannot be described not only by simple table substitution of a reasonable size (such as 32×32, for example), but it also cannot be described as a data-dependent table substitution (for example, a 32×32 substitution carried out from the current value of one of 32-bit data subblocks). Because data-dependent key sampling cannot be described as a table substitution of a reasonable size, this cryptographic primitive has enormous internal potential.

One of the most interesting implementations of ciphers based on data-dependent subkeys selection is the "SPECTR-Z" software-oriented block algorithm. In contrast to earlier 512-byte block software algorithms, this algorithm is faster thanks to the use of special transformation of the initial and final 32-bit subblocks of the input 512-byte data block. A specific feature of the block ciphers characterized by the large size of the input text is that they allow you to build such an encryption algorithm, in which powerful avalanche effect evolves within a single encryption round, when sequentially encrypting data subblocks, the number of which can be large enough. For example, in the case of 512-byte ciphers, the input data block is split into 256 16-bit subblocks or into 128 32-bit subblocks. The bottleneck of the software-oriented ciphers of this type is that encryption of the first data subblock in each round is carried out using fixed values of variables participating in the encryption procedure. This circumstance makes it necessary to carry out additional transformation of the initial and final data subblocks. In earlier versions of this method, one or two additional rounds of transformations were carried out. In the SPECTR-Z cipher, additional transformation is carried out only over eight 32-bit data subblocks (four initial and four final) in the form of a reduced round made up of 40 steps (five loops with eight iterations each) converting individual data subblocks. The reduced round is intended for efficient and fast amplification of the avalanche effect initiated by inversions of bits in extreme data subblocks. Actually, a reduced round is executed three times faster than a complete round. Thanks to the use of a reduced round of such a structure, the encryption procedure can be limited only by two complete rounds. This allowed the SPECTR-Z algorithm to reach the encryption speed exceeding 140 Mbps for the Pentium-II 266 microprocessor.

2.8 ENCRYPTION ALGORITHMS IN CONTEMPORARY COMPUTER SECURITY SYSTEMS

Contemporary information security products for protection against unauthorized access are based on the global encryption technology. The requirement of ensuring security of the information circulating within computer systems in relation to multiple potential threats makes it necessary to employ multiple cryptographic mechanisms in complex information security products for protecting computer systems against unauthorized access. Cryptographic mechanisms are classified into three basic groups: cryptographic mechanisms for supporting the global encryption in real-time mode, cryptographic mechanisms for file encryption in real-time mode, and cryptographic mechanisms for encryption of the operating system loader.

The example of contemporary computer security systems is the software-oriented information protection complex based on the SPECTR-Z algorithm, generally recognized and widely used in Russia. The SPECTR-Z system (Russian Federation State Technical Committee certificate #251) is intended for protecting PCs running Windows 95/98 and is a new version of the COBRA information security product for protecting information against unauthorized access (Certificate #20), which is widely used for protecting PCs running MS DOS.

2.8.1 Fast Encryption of Disk Data

In computer security systems operating in real-time mode, it is necessary to use fast encryption algorithms for encrypting information processed by computer systems; namely, for supporting automatic encryption of all data stored on the fixed storage devices in the real-time mode. In real-world implementations, the algorithm must ensure the possibility of dynamic encryption (encryption in the course of writing the data and decryption when reading the data from the fixed storage devices). The encryption speed must be considerably higher than the data reading speed. Contemporary built-in magnetic storage media ensure the read/write speed of about several tens Mbps, which makes it necessary to ensure the encryption speed higher than 100 Mbps when using commercial Pentium-compatible processors.

Criteria of Definition

An example of the fast encryption algorithm is SPECTR-Z used in the information security product for protection against unauthorized access of the same name for transforming the data stored on hard disks. When the SPECTR-Z algorithm was initially designed, it was assumed that its main field of application would be ensuring internal encryption in computer systems and used as part of security products intended for protection against unauthorized access retaining high performance of computer systems.

NOTE

Information protection in communications links often requires ciphers to be implemented as cryptochips. Development of universal algorithms that are oriented both toward software and hardware implementations doesn't allow for reaching the fastest encryption speed for narrower application areas.

The technological nature of application of this cipher makes it urgent to achieve the maximum possible performance and high strength against attacks based on known and specially chosen texts. The need to maintain the initially high performance of the computer systems being protected also results in the need to preserve the possibility of arbitrary access to the data stored on fixed storage media.

The value of 512 bytes was chosen as the value of the input data block for the SPECTR-Z algorithm. This corresponds to the minimal discrete data block in the course of information exchange between RAM and fixed storage memory. In addition, this size is large enough to ensure high cryptographic strength along with relative simplicity of the block encryption procedures. To achieve this strategic goal, developers used the following criteria:

- The procedure of encrypting the input 512-byte data block must be carried out as a sequential transformation of 128 4-byte (in other words, 32-bit) words using operations that require a minimum number of clocks ("$+_{32}$," "$-_{32}$," "$\oplus$"," ">>>," "<<<," swapping data between registers, sampling data from RAM).
- Every bit of all words transformed at previous stages of the encryption process must have a significant influence on the process of conversion of all further words. In other words, sequential transformation of words must be executed in the concatenation mode. This will ensure a strong avalanche effect when passing from initial to the final words of the input block. Because it is assumed to carry out 128 elementary steps for conversion of 32-bit words within one round, this mechanism will play a considerable role in ensuring high cryptographic strength with low number of encryption rounds.
- To ensure efficient concatenation mode, the encryption algorithm must make provision for at least two variables, the current values of which will be formed depending on their previous values and on the value of the currently transformed word.
- As a basic mechanism of transformation, it is expedient to use the approved sample of subkeys depending on the data being converted. This mechanism is a variant of the table substitution using secret tables.
- To strengthen the influence of the bits of the words being transformed on the encryption process, it is expedient to execute some cyclic-shift operations depending on the data being transformed. Contemporary commercial processors execute these operations fast; furthermore, such operations were found highly efficient as the basic cryptographic primitive in such ciphers as RC5, RC6, and MARS.
- To obtain the possibility of building an efficient subkey sampling mechanism depending on the data being converted, the size of the encryption key was chosen to be equal to 2051 bytes. This allows for specifying the influence of 11 bits of the word currently being transformed per one key access operation.
- To form an extended encryption key, it is necessary to provide the procedures of transforming the user's secret key implemented as precomputations. In this case, precomputations must ensure strong influence of each bit of the secret key on the value of the extended key. Modification of any bit of the secret key must result in the inversion of each bit of the extended key with the probability of 50 percent.

General Scheme of Transformations

In the SPECTR-Z cryptographic system, and in other extended-key ciphers, it is assumed that the extended key is built depending on the secret key of comparatively small length using special procedures carried out as precomputations. In ciphers oriented toward the use in computer systems in the form of software modules, the precomputations procedure might be complicated enough, because it is assumed this procedure will be executed only when the cryptographic system is initialized (powered on). It is expedient that such a procedure be executed at the phase of the bootstrap loading of the PC. Thus, in the variant under consideration, the cryptographic algorithm doesn't imply any considerable limitations on the duration of the precomputations procedure. Consequently, no considerable limitations are implied on the computer resources, because the precomputations subroutine is nonresident. This means that it is possible to use multistep procedures that cause a strong avalanche effect. In particular, this means that multiple use of the direct encryption algorithms of the SPECTR-Z cryptographic system described in the next section is also possible.

The use of precomputations forces the intruder to choose between two main variants of the attack implementation:

- The intruder can assume that the secret key is chosen arbitrarily and can consider relatively simple encryption procedures to detect some kind of vulnerabilities.
- The intruder can consider more sophisticated procedures of forming the encryption key to discover the secret key by solving the encryption equation.

Obviously, procedures of forming the encryption key must be sophisticated enough to ensure that computation of any part of the secret key is impossible based on individual fragments of the encryption key. The main requirements to the algorithm of building the encryption key are:

- Approximately equiprobable influence of each bit of the secret key on all bits of the extended key being formed
- High computational complexity of discovering the secret key on the basis of partially (for example, by 50 percent) disclosed extended key.

These conditions are satisfied for the precomputations algorithm implemented in the SPECTR-Z system. Thus, the SPECTR-Z software cipher can be implemented in the form of two subroutines: initialization module intended to run once, and resident encryption module that serves requests of other programs for data encryption and decryption. The structure of the software encryption module with precomputations is shown in Figure 2.1.

In computer applications, the presence of precomputations plays an additional role. The use of sophisticated computational procedures considerably complicates implementation of password attacks. In this case, the check of each password variant will require the attacker to carry out precomputations.

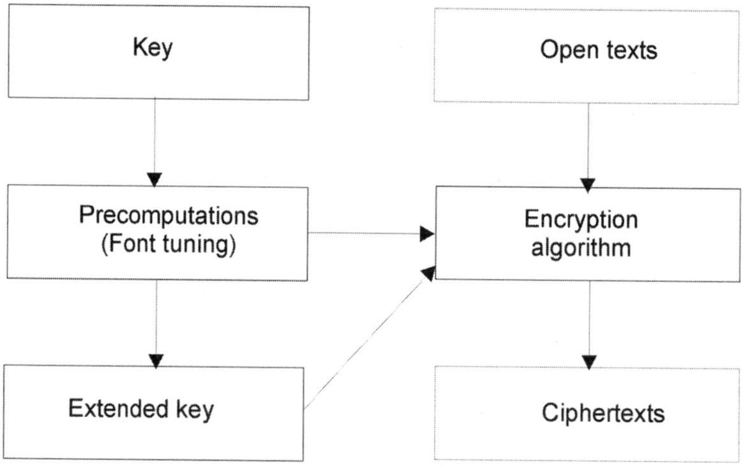

FIGURE 2.1 Scheme of a software cipher with precomputations.

2.8.2 Precomputations

The SPECTR-Z algorithm uses the 2051-byte encryption key **Q**, which is formed at the precomputations stage based on the user's secret key. The extended key is an ordered byte sequence $q[i]$: $\mathbf{Q} = \{q[i]\}$, where $i = 0, 1, \ldots, 2050$. When forming the encryption key, the ***Encrypt_Z*** procedure and specified table **Z** are interpreted as the sequence $\overline{\mathbf{Z}} = \{z[i]\}$, where $i = 0, 1, \ldots, 2050$ are used. Both the ***Encrypt_Z*** procedure and the **Z** table are described here. The algorithm for generation of the extended key consists in execution of the ***Form_Q*** procedure, which accepts the user's secret key as the input parameter. The length of the user's secret key ranges from 64 to 512 bits.

The $\overline{\mathbf{Z}}$ table is a 2051-byte sequence:

$$\{\mathbf{Z}', z[1024], z[1025], z[1026], z[1027], \mathbf{Z}''\},$$

where z[1024] = 9A, z[1025] = 05, z[1026] = 3C, z[1027] = 29, and the $\overline{\mathbf{Z}}'$ and $\overline{\mathbf{Z}}''$ sequences ($\overline{\mathbf{Z}}''$ differs from $\overline{\mathbf{Z}}'$ only in that the last five bytes are missing from $\overline{\mathbf{Z}}''$) are represented by the $\overline{\mathbf{G}} = \{G_0, G_1, \ldots, G_{512}\}$ sequence made up of 32-bit words written in the form of hexadecimal numbers $G_k = g_{4k+3}||g_{4k+2}||g_{4k+1}||g_{4k}$, where $k = 0, 1, \ldots, 256$:

59CD4F6D,	90873546,	F408639D,	B3B33D0D,
A226970F,	DD6C55E9,	4EE9E996,	E0BBD6B2,
ED569ED7,	422895FD,	F5A08568,	F260AA2E,
97CEFB13,	06D4837F,	B51D92BF,	1F1C2D64,

```
97F7A7CB,    7ED14440,    93DC3AE2,    3CC5A6C1,
E8CF40AB,    A75CEBD4,    F741D801,    852E14E2,
FC386A79,    136DD74A,    22E25EA8,    0E4F18E4,
2D96801C,    3C80C89C,    2587EBA7,    D5DA001D,
7C897B55,    76E1023E,    7329EC2A,    D8DF68AB,
04C87FF6,    B6249125,    B63EF3D8,    3DAE29FB,
BE73CD22,    DE96E603,    FA4A8E95,    8D5F76CA,
A69F48A7,    3AFBB8CE,    2CE563DA,    D9994EC9,
6B7DFA9F,    5A6B2CEB,    0A0B7E78,    0A4E2064,
EF964255,    D0C8F360,    55266FBB,    3A166B3E,
1FEFDEE8,    76CEB1B8,    35480947,    25704556,
70026E20,    67B492E3,    B91D054D,    1D850806,
125163DC,    D4177C68,    2BA29D5E,    E857ABCD,
69BF02D5,    7EDC842D,    6114C2C7,    2DB5A9F1,
983E70A3,    71B68CDD,    2DB7B8D9,    CF4E94B2,
0E4B408B,    E79E14A4,    FCD8328C,    0CB4816E,
A1277953,    C05BD4FE,    E28C3697,    0552C004,
D692E406,    D1ADBB1A,    5E66E661,    DF4C1388,
11905A1C,    7625AB81,    E46165AD,    F0D8FAD0,
804A9589,    A7A71158,    523A80A7,    1DD95546,
A7588D94,    960BDFD4,    152F1BE7,    1C3123BB,
EA88761F,    62ABD13A,    04A8986B,    73EC0AE6,
F78A987B,    8B34DB2F,    0C5152A3,    AC2B2612,
360320D2,    562DC9BC,    349C5922,    1D021BF7,
6155500B,    AB28C8B7,    1889F88C,    2A35806C,
D7DA49E7,    F218B83B,    39FCEE19,    FFD5F4AF,
3C81278E,    6FB41F54,    67EBC971,    6019F1F0,
D315E4C6,    91E47276,    F73D93E4,    C240B75A,
33F14370,    D2457429,    A32A5CCF,    40DDF94E,
80E47D16,    B2C7BD8E,    90BA4275,    6C7922AB,
B2A51B55,    E6250E32,    D9971E0F,    D70EF0DB,
685779AA,    05674EC3,    393D6C1B,    5A3CCDEA,
2374D804,    F3659EDD,    5BF178CD,    04AE819B,
F984DD85,    81FCA05D,    8548F8D7,    FCF546F9,
F7CC93BE,    EFC9298C,    8F8C98D0,    756C4F45,
F14223E1,    86FEF671,    2B112DA4,    331C975E,
1BBCA16D,    8D695847,    CC6097F7,    E914DF4F,
1B97C93D,    DB12475D,    57BBFFFC,    4D7A5833,
AECFB8B9,    8C8CB213,    F7A9E9D9,    C4AADB49,
950D7683,    C68375EA,    9E4A232C,    2EF4700E,
27B2A314,    A01D80B1,    5161633B,    2954D4C4,
B494D1AF,    1420879E,    EEAE1361,    0F183EB0,
4973279C,    E7A80D21,    E5671416,    86D8CE7A,
D247FA63,    D7AF44C2,    87443304,    BBBE9F57,
```

202C07FD,	875FF05A,	43CC216C,	06350407,	
9FA206BB,	95319458,	AC8F2486,	E822D6DB,	
0DC11C62,	B5479520,	45C446D7,	85938591,	
948F0F43,	839F1C97,	D407CB1A,	A3537935,	
E7DB9374,	3925653F,	D15A2D07,	97530098,	
7FD905D0,	7CCCDFBC,	77AAF70E,	833676F2,	
BEDF2436,	F6C26720,	D866E30C,	DFB940E9,	
785E5336,	1C42407B,	0FCE38E6,	28E21B1A,	
5D7DEB36,	FB3C8B16,	24B5C173,	28BC5727,	
6ED16186,	BDDC35F7,	3B715F42,	C1A60EEA,	
1B6D0DC3,	A43393D5,	59D046BA,	2799B4B6,	
206DAD0A,	A37D7588,	17F4653D,	E98EDD7F,	
DC941394,	6F81AD8E,	7611F662,	CA191B6C,	
BDD491CF,	C6910F8F,	C94137C2,	40D5E6D5,	
D0C4D719,	5760AA69,	6F819234,	F8E83558,	
A5A482C9,	520DCAB6,	92E24E59,	8D1B7005,	9A053C29

The elements of the sequence $\overline{\mathbf{Z}}$ are expressed through elements of the sequence $\overline{\mathbf{Z}}'$ as follows: $z[j] = z[1028+j] = z'[j]$ having $0 \leq j \leq 1023$. Elements of the sequence $\overline{\mathbf{Z}}'$, in turn, are expressed through elements of the sequence $\overline{\mathbf{G}}$ as follows: $z'[j] = g_j$.

The *Form_Q* Procedure

The ***Form_Q*** procedure includes the following steps:

1. Repeat the user's secret key the required number of times until the $\{p[i]\}$ 2051-byte sequence is obtained, where $i = 0, 1, \ldots, 2050$. Repeated records must be separated by the bytes with the value 0.
2. Form a new sequence $\overline{\mathbf{H}} = \{h_0, h_1, \ldots, h_{2050}\}$, where $h_i = z_i \oplus p_i$ for $i = 0, 1, \ldots, 2050$, and z_i are elements of the previously described $\overline{Z}$ sequence.
3. Form the $\overline{\mathbf{R}} = \{r_0, r_1, \ldots, r_{511}\}$ sequence, where $r_i = p_i$ for $i = 0, 1, \ldots, 511$.
4. Using the byte sequence $\overline{\mathbf{H}}$ as a key, call the ***Encrypt_Z*** procedure to carry out the following transformations: $\mathbf{R}^{(0)}$:= ***Encrypt_Z*** ($\overline{\mathbf{R}}$); $\overline{\mathbf{R}}^{(1)}$:= ***Encrypt_Z*** ($\overline{\mathbf{R}}^{(0)}$); $\mathbf{R}^{(2)}$:= ***Encrypt_Z*** ($\overline{\mathbf{R}}^{(1)}$); $\overline{\mathbf{R}}^{(3)}$:= ***Encrypt_Z*** ($\overline{\mathbf{R}}^{(2)}$).
5. Form the following 2051-byte sequence: $\mathbf{L} = \{ \overline{\mathbf{R}}^{(0)}, \overline{\mathbf{R}}^{(1)}, \overline{\mathbf{R}}^{(2)}, \overline{\mathbf{R}}^{(3)}, r[0], r[1], r[2]\}$.
6. Using the byte sequence $\overline{\mathbf{L}}$ as a key, call the ***Encrypt_Z*** procedure to carry out the following transformations: $\mathbf{C}^{(0)}$:= ***Encrypt_Z*** ($\overline{\mathbf{R}}$); $\overline{\mathbf{C}}^{(1)}$:= ***Encrypt_Z*** ($\overline{\mathbf{C}}^{(0)}$); $\mathbf{C}^{(2)}$:= ***Encrypt_Z*** ($\overline{\mathbf{C}}^{(1)}$); $\mathbf{C}^{(3)}$:= ***Encrypt_Z*** ($\overline{\mathbf{C}}^{(2)}$).

7. Form a 2051-byte extended key $\overline{\mathbf{Q}}$: $\mathbf{Q} = \{ \overline{\mathbf{C}}^{(0)}, \overline{\mathbf{C}}^{(1)}, \overline{\mathbf{C}}^{(2)}, \overline{\mathbf{C}}^{(3)}, c[0], c[1], c[2]\}$, where $c[0]$, $c[1]$, $c[2]$ are the first three bytes of the sequence $\overline{\mathbf{C}}^{(0)}$.
8. STOP

Execution of the transformations procedure produces the key $\overline{\mathbf{Q}}$, which further will be used for encryption of 512-byte blocks of data (for example, these might be hard disk sectors of a PC). The encryption key $\overline{\mathbf{Q}}$ is considered an ordered byte sequence $q[i]$: $\overline{\mathbf{Q}} = \{q[i]\}$, where $i = 0, 1, \ldots, 2050$. The encryption procedure uses subkeys $Q[j]$, where $j = 0, 1, \ldots, 2047$ and $Q[j] = q[j+3]||q[j+2]||q[j+1]||q[j]$.

2.8.3 Disk Encryption Algorithms

The SPECTR-Z encryption algorithm includes three rounds. The first and the third rounds are complete and correspond to sequential transformation of all 128 words of the initial block, starting from the first word. The second round is reduced. It corresponds to the transformation of the reduced data block formed by joining up four initial and four final 32-bit words of a 512-byte data block (Figure 2.2).

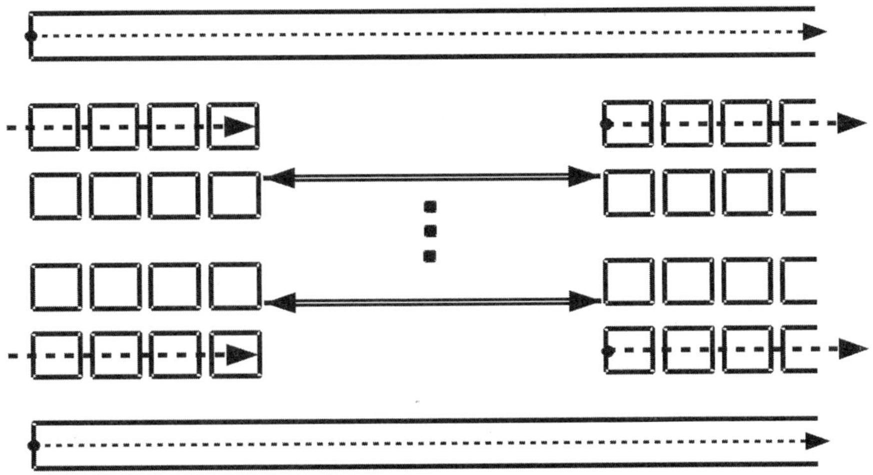

FIGURE 2.2 The sequence of word transformation.

The reduced round is executed in the form of five encryption loops for encrypting the 256-bit reduced data block. Each of the loops includes eight iterations for transforming 32-bit words. These iterations are executed similarly to the transformation iterations in the complete round. The second round consists in sequential transformation of the following words: T_{124}, T_{125}, T_{126}, T_{127}, T_0, T_1, T_2, T_3. Each loop of encryption of the Each loop of the preceding eight words, except for the last, is followed by exchanging values of the following pairs of words: $T_0 \leftrightarrow T_{127}$, $T_1 \leftrightarrow T_{126}$, $T_2 \leftrightarrow T_{125}$, $T_3 \leftrightarrow T_{124}$. The complete encryption round consists of the following. The block of plaintext $\overline{\mathbf{T}}$ is split into 128 32-bit words T_i: $T = \{T_i\}$, $i = 0, 1, \ldots, 127$. The words of the data block being transformed are converted according to the following sequence: $T_0, T_1, \ldots, T_{127}$. The procedure for encrypting the data block ***Encrypt_Z*** is provided next.

The *Encrypt_Z* Procedure (Encryption of a 512-Byte Data Block)

The ***Encrypt_Z*** procedure includes the following steps:

1. Carry out the complete round of encryption.
2. Carry out the reduced round of encryption.
3. Carry out the complete round of encryption.

Complete Round of Encryption

To carry out the complete round of encryption, it is necessary to execute the following steps:

1. Set the counter value $i := 0$ and compute the initial value of internal variables $R := Q[9]$, $V := Q[7]$, $Y := Q[3]$, $U := Q[9]$, $N := Q[5]$, $n := N +_{11} 0$.
2. Carry out the following transformations:
   - $N := n \oplus R;\ V := V +_{32} N;$
   - $n := N +_{11} 0;\ V := (V +_{32} Q[n])^{>11>};$
   - $N := n \oplus V;\ Y := Y +_{32} N;$
   - $n := N +_{11} 0;\ Y := (Y +_{32} Q[n])^{>11>};$
   - $N := n +_{32} Y;\ n := N +_{11} 0;$
   - $U := ((U \oplus Q[n]) +_{32} R)^{>>>V};\ R := 0T_i.$
3. Carry out the transformation of the next word of the text: $T_i := ((T_i -_{32} V) \oplus U)^{<<<V} -_{32} Y$.
4. Increment the counter $i := i + 1$. If $i \neq 128$, then go to step 2, else **STOP**.

Reduced Round of Encryption

To carry out the reduced round of encryption, it is necessary to execute the following steps:

1. Set the value of the external counter $j := 5$.

2. Set the value of the internal counter i:=124 and compute the initial values of internal variables $R := Q[9]$, $V := Q[7]$, $Y := Q[3]$, $U := Q[9]$, $N := Q[5]$, $n := N +_{11} 0$.
3. Carry out the following transformations:
   - $N := n \oplus R;\ V := V +_{32} N;$
   - $n := N +_{11} 0;\ V := (V +_{32} Q[n])^{>>>11};$
   - $N := n \oplus V;\ Y := Y +_{32} N;$
   - $n := N +_{11} 0;\ Y := (Y +_{32} Q[n])^{>>>11};$
   - $N := n +_{32} Y;\ n := N +_{11} 0;$
   - $U := ((U \oplus Q[n]) +_{32} R)^{>>>V};\quad R := T_i.$
4. Carry out the transformation of the next word of the text: $T_i := ((T_i -_{32} Y)^{>>>V} \oplus U) -_{32} V$.
5. Increment the counter $i := i + 1 \bmod 128$. If $i \neq 4$, then go to step 3.
6. Decrement the external counter $j := j - 1$. If $j = 0$, then **STOP.**
7. Exchange the values of initial and final words of the text: $T_0 \leftrightarrow T_{127}$, $T_1 \leftrightarrow T_{126}$, $T_2 \leftrightarrow T_{125}$, $T_3 \leftrightarrow T_{124}$.
8. Return to step 2.

Decryption of the encrypted text is carried out using the ***Decrypt_Z*** procedure.

The *Decrypt_Z* Procedure

The ***Decrypt_Z*** procedure includes the following steps:

1. Carry out the complete round of decryption.
2. Carry out the reduced round of decryption.
3. Carry out the complete round of decryption.

The Complete Round of Decryption

To carry out the complete round of decryption, it is necessary to accomplish the following steps:

1. Set the counter value $i := 0$ and compute the initial values of internal variables $R := Q[9]$, $V := Q[7]$, $Y := Q[3]$, $U := Q[9]$, $N := Q[5]$, $n := N +_{11} 0$.
2. Carry out the following transformations:
   - $N := n \oplus R;\ V := V + N;$
   - $n := N +_{11} 0;\ V := (V +_{32} Q[n])^{>11>};$
   - $N := n \oplus V;\ Y := Y +_{32} N;$
   - $n := N +_{11} 0;\ Y := (Y +_{32} Q[n])^{>11>};$
   - $N := n +_{32} Y;\ n := N +_{11} 0;$
   - $U := ((U \oplus Q[n]) +_{32} R)^{>>>V}.$

3. Transform the next word of the text: $T_i := ((T_i +_{32} Y)^{>>>V} \oplus U) +_{32} V$.
4. Assign the value $R := T_i$ and increment the counter $i := i + 1$. If $i \neq 128$, then go to step 2, else **STOP**.

Reduced Encryption Round

To carry out the reduced encryption round, it is necessary to accomplish the following steps:

1. Set the value of external counter $j := 5$.
2. Set the value of internal counter $i := 124$ and compute the initial values of internal variables $R := Q[9]$, $V := Q[7]$, $Y := Q[3]$, $U := Q[9]$, $N := Q[5]$, $n := N +_{11} 0$.
3. Carry out the following transformations:
   - $N := n \oplus R;\ V := V +_{32} N;$
   - $n := N +_{11} 0;\ V := (V +_{32} Q[n])^{>>>11};$
   - $N := n \oplus V;\ Y := Y +_{32} N;$
   - $n := N +_{11} 0;\ Y := (Y +_{32} Q[n])^{>>>11};$
   - $N := n +_{32} Y;\ n := N +_{11} 0;$
   - $U := ((U \oplus Q[n]) +_{32} R)^{>>>V}$.
4. Transform the next word of the text: $T_i := ((T_i +_{32} V) \oplus U)^{<<<V} +_{32} Y$.
5. Assign the value $R := T_i$ and increment the counter $i := i + 1 \bmod 128$. If $i \neq 4$, then go to step 3.
6. Decrement the counter $j := j - 1$. If $j = 0$, then **STOP**.
7. Exchange the values of initial and final words of the text. $T_0 \leftrightarrow T_{127}$, $T_1 \leftrightarrow T_{126}$, $T_2 \leftrightarrow T_{125}$, $T_3 \leftrightarrow T_{124}$.
8. Go to step 2.

Note that the structures of the encryption and decryption procedures are identical. In both cases, transformation of words in complete rounds starts with the word T_0, and proceeds in the order $T_0, T_1, T_2, \ldots, T_{127}$. By analogy to the subkeys of the extended key, which are related to the elements of the secret key by a sophisticated functional dependency, the values of accumulating variables are functions of the extended key and subblocks transformed at the previous steps. Such a mechanism is due to the fact that subkeys $Q[j]$ are not used in the equation of the direct transformation of the input block (step 3 of the complete round algorithm and step 3 of the reduced round algorithm). In addition, three accumulating variables that take pseudorandom values participate in the direct transformation of the words of the input block in each round. These factors influence the efficiency of transformations of the SPECTR-Z cipher, which combines high cryptographic strength and high performance.

If you consider encryption of two texts differing only by the word T_i, where $i < 127$, you'd easily note that when transforming the word T_{i+1} as early as in the first round, the value of at least one of the variables U, V, or Y is changed, which results in an avalanche-like change of parameters U, V, Y at further n elementary steps of the transformation.

If two input blocks differ in the last word T_{127} of the input block, the avalanche-like increase of the influence of this difference starts from the step corresponding to the encryption of the word T_0 in the first loop of the second round.

Thus, a specific feature of the SPECTR-Z cipher is that the strong avalanche effect takes place when passing from one word being transformed to another word within the same encryption round. The encryption round as such represents a sequential repetition of some iterative encryption function over all words in the input message. The reduced encryption round is used to ensure strong dissipating influence of the bits of the last 32-bit word on the ciphertext.

The scheme of the software-oriented cipher shown in Figure 2.1 in relation to the SPECTR-Z algorithm can be represented in more detail as shown in Figure 2.3.

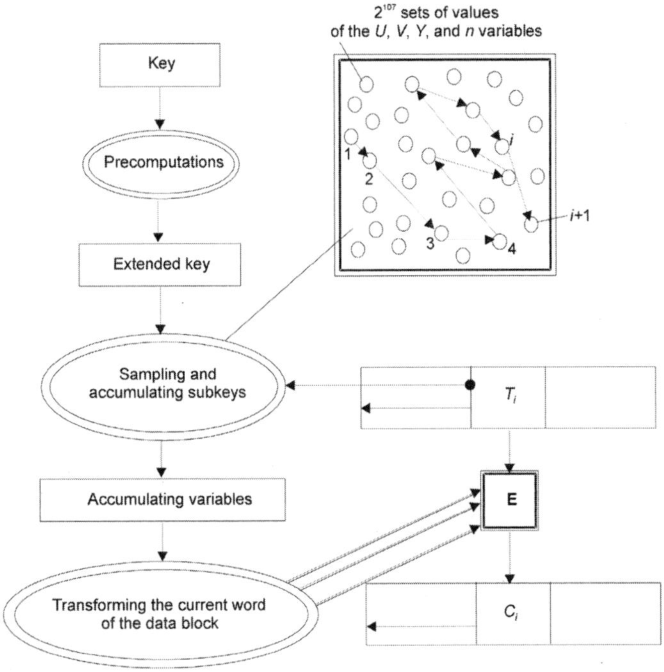

FIGURE 2.3 Generalized structure of transformations of the SPECTR-Z cipher.

In this illustration, the mechanism of forming the accumulating variables is shown. This mechanism can be interpreted as an automat having at least 2^{107} different states defined by sets of four values of the *U*, *V*, *Y*, and *n* variables.

The first three variables directly participate in the transformation of the words of the input text, and the last variable is the internal parameter that indirectly influences the process of encryption. Thanks to the large number of internal states of this automat, the use of several rounds of encryption and dependence of the transition from state to state on the words being transformed, the unique sequence of transitions for each input message is ensured. Note that the complete round of encryption is a certain mechanism of bit-stream encryption using the influence of the previous words on the procedure of encryption of the further words.

An important feature of the used concatenation mechanism is that it is implemented using four parallel mechanisms; namely, through the *U*, *V*, *Y*, and *n* variables. The *n* variable determines the influence of the concatenation mode and practical impossibility of disclosing the sequences of words being transformed (without knowing the key), which would switch the automat from the specified initial conditions to the specified final condition within several steps of transformation.

2.8.4 Evaluating the Cryptographic Strength

The SPECTR-Z cryptographic algorithm is strong against known analytical attacks, including linear and differential cryptanalysis. The strength of the algorithm is ensured not by the number of founds, but by the structure of the transformation procedures as such and by the large number of words transformed within the two main encryption rounds. When developing the SPECTR-Z cipher for comparative analysis of the strength of different variants of cryptographic schemes with pseudorandom subkey sampling, the attack based on hardware errors was used. The random errors variant was considered; in other words, it was assumed that the intruder cannot reproduce the error that has the required value (which means the attacker cannot invert bits in the predefined positions). In addition, it was assumed that the protection against introduction of an error into the value of the encryption procedure completion parameter must be ensured by additional mechanisms complementing specific implementation of the algorithm. This assumption is common for all known algorithms of block encryption.

The SPECTR-Z algorithm is also strong against attacks based on generation of random hardware errors that are intentionally introduced by the attacker into registers containing the values of the data subblocks being transformed by means of external physical influence on the encrypting device. According to our evaluations, its strength against such an attack is no less than 10^{30} operations. At the same time, most other widely used ciphers, including RC5, DES, GOST 28147-89 (Russian ГОСТ, GOsudarstvennyi STandard, Russian for "Government Standard"), ensure the computational strength against this attack that doesn't exceed 10^9 operations. High strength against this kind of cryptanalysis is achieved thanks to the following factors:

- The values of numbers of the chosen subkeys are never present in the ciphertext. The numbers are formed as values of the internal variable of the encryption mechanism.
- The error introduced at the last round into some word propagates using the mechanism of forming the U, V, Y, and n variables. This error is introduced into all these variables, and, at the same time, modifications of n result in the change of the subkey sample. These changes are difficult to differentiate according to their integral effect on the next word.
- Variable U formed using the last subkey sample doesn't participate in the transformation of the words of the input text as an operand of the last operation, which considerably distorts the statistics of subkey differences, because of the superposition of variables Y (during encryption) and V (during decryption), which are not known beforehand.
- Disclosing nonuniformities in the subkey differences statistics is further complicated. Because after superposition of a subkey on the initial value of variable U, the value R is superimposed on it, after which the cyclic shift operation takes place. This shift is carried out by the number of bits, which is not known to the attacker beforehand.

To obtain a generalized evaluation of the minimal level of cryptographic strength of the SPECTR-Z cipher, the combinational-probabilistic model used earlier for block ciphers with the similar structure of transformations will be used. In the SPECTR-Z algorithm, variables U, V, Y, and n change in the course of transition from word to word, taking sequential values that form a pseudorandom sequence. The values of variables U, V, and Y at the step of conversion of the i-th word are formed depending on the combinations of i subkeys ($i = 1, 2, \dots, 128$). At the same time, the number of different possible values M_i of these variables depends on i (for a given i, the values of U, V, and Y depend on the input block). It can be easily shown that $M_0 = 1 = 2^0$, $M_1 \approx 2^{11}$, $M_2 \approx 2^{22}$ and $M_i \approx 2^{32}$ for $i = 3, 4, \dots, 128$. Thus, at steps with number $i = 3, 4, \dots, 128$, approximately 2^{96} different sets of $\{Y, U, V\}$ are possible. Implementation of a specific set depends on the input block and the encryption key. The algorithm under consideration is composed in accordance to the following criterion: *transformation procedures must be designed so that the change of any bit of the input message would result in the change of the subkeys sample.* This criterion guarantees that for all different input messages, unique sequences of $\{Y_{(i)}, U_{(i)}, V_{(i)}\}$ parameters will be generated, where the variables' values at the steps corresponding to the transformation of the i-th word are marked with index (i).

Procedures of a single encryption round can schematically be represented as follows: depending on the values of the current input words being transformed, the subkeys that will be used for forming the U, V, and Y variables are sampled. These variables are used for transforming further words. The algorithm is designed so that the change of any bit in an arbitrary input data block results in the modification of the subkeys sample and the change of the key variables. This means that each input message is transformed using unique sequences of the U, V, and Y variable values. At the same time, during the first, and, partially, the second rounds (during the first loop of the second round) at certain steps of the transformation, the values of U, V, and Y might be predetermined to match for specially selected input messages. To achieve this, it is necessary to choose two input messages differing only in the T_{127} word. As relates to the four last loops of the second round and all steps of the third round, the values of internal variables for each pair of input messages might match only occasionally.

Although conversion of 32-bit words is carried out in accordance with relatively simple equations, the set of variable values is pseudorandom.

Determination of the values of subkeys $Q[j]$ is related to finding the values of U, V, and Y at certain steps of the transformation (for example, at the two nearest sequential steps of the word transformation). Therefore, fixing the values of U, V, and Y at specific steps is the prior condition for computation of subkeys $Q[j]$. *Fixing* in this case must be interpreted as finding such words within the same input message or in different input messages that were transformed using the values of U, V, and Y, related by a certain condition. For example, for two different words, T and T', the corresponding pairs of values of each of the accumulating variables might be equal ($U = U'$, $V = V'$, and $Y = Y'$), differ by a specified value ($U \oplus U' = \text{const1}$, $V \oplus V' = \text{const2}$ and $Y \oplus Y' = \text{const3}$), or be related by a linear relationship. Note that the concept of fixing includes any predefined dependencies between the values of accumulating variables corresponding to the chosen pair of words, which means that employment of differential and linear cryptanalysis is covered by the combinatorial-probabilistic model as a particular case.

The equation describing the encryption of an individual word T (belonging to the middle of the input data block; that is, excluding four starting and four final words) in the general case is formulated by the expression $C = f(T, U_1, V_1, Y_1, U_3, V_3, Y_3)$, where index corresponds to the encryption round. Analysis of the experimental statistics of the sequence of values taken by the U, V, and Y variables confirms that these variables take pseudo-random values.

To obtain generalized minimum evaluations, it is necessary to adopt a set of assumptions, which the attacker cannot suggest under real-world conditions. Assume that the solution of the system of equations corresponding to transformation of two different words is a problem with a low level of complexity, provided that these words were transformed using fixed sets of accumulating variables U_1, V_1, Y_1, U_3, V_3, Y_3. Assume that the complexity of cryptanalysis depends only on the detection of the pair of words that correspond to the fixing condition.

This corresponds to the general principles of attacking ciphers—recognition (in case of known-plaintext attack) or specification (in case of chosen-plaintext attack) of certain expectable relations between unknown parameters. In this case, the search for pairs of words satisfying the fixing condition can be characterized according to several generalized criteria:

- The attacker must develop a certain criterion for recognizing words that satisfy the fixing condition. Such a criterion can be related to the use of statistics of certain computations carried out using a certain assumption. Assume that the attacker has a simple and efficient criterion that for two specified words allows the attacker to discover whether these words satisfy the fixing condition with minimal labor expenses (within a single conventional operation).
- The attacker cannot know beforehand the numbers of words that with a high level of probability correspond to the adopted fixing condition; however, the attacker can choose for testing words with specific numbers, for which the fixing condition can be satisfied with higher probability.
- To find the pair of words corresponding to the fixing condition, the attacker tries pairs of words corresponding to increased probability of the fixing condition occurrence.

In case of known-plaintext attack for the tested pairs of words T and T', the values of U_1, V_1, Y_1, U_3, V_3, Y_3 are different in general case. In the case of a chosen plaintext attack, it is possible to choose such pairs of the input blocks, for which at each specified step of the first round the same values of the U_1, V_1, Y_1 variables are formed (these variables will change from word to word; however, in the first round for such pairs of input blocks this change will take place synchronously). Such pairs of input messages can be easily obtained by means of modifying the T_i word in the $\overline{\mathbf{T}}$ input block, where $0 < i < 127$. In the pair of texts $\overline{\mathbf{T}}$ and $\overline{\mathbf{T}}'$ obtained in this way, the T_j words, where $0 \le j \le i$, in the first round will be transformed using the same values U_1, V_1, Y_1. However, after execution of the reduced round, any change in $\overline{\mathbf{T}}'$ will result in the modification of all bits of words T_0, T_1, T_2, T_3, T_{124}, T_{125}, T_{126}, T_{127} with the probability equal to 0.5. The process of encryption in the third round will be related to the pseudorandom values of the differences $U_{3(i)} - U_{3(i)}'$, $V_{3(i)} - V_{3(i)}'$, and $Y_{3(i)} - Y_{3(i)}'$. In the pair of texts $\overline{\mathbf{T}}$ and $\overline{\mathbf{T}}'$, the attacker can exploit the fact of repetition in the first round the values U_1, V_1, Y_1 for words T_j and T'_j, where $5 \le j \le 123$. (Analysis of the four starting and four final words is less efficient because the starting and ending words are additionally transformed in the second round.)

With the account of these facts, two variants of the generalized combinational-probabilistic model (CPM) were suggested:

- Combinational-probabilistic model for known-plaintext attack (CPM-1)
- Combinational-probabilistic model for chosen text attack (plaintext or ciphertext) (CPM-2).

Note that in the second case, the complexity of the cryptanalysis in case of chosen ciphertext has approximately the same value as in case of chosen plaintext, because encryption and decryption algorithms are practically identical. CPM-1 and CPM-2 differ by the probability of the event in which two arbitrarily taken words were transformed using the same values of accumulating variables. Such a pair of words is called the target pair. The required probability for CPM-1 is $p_1 = M^{-6}$, and for CPM-2 it is $p_2 = M^{-3}$, where $M = 2^{-32}$ is the number of different values that variables U, V, and Y can take.

If there is a certain amount of known or chosen texts, in which there are L words (related to words with indexes $i = 4, 5, \ldots, 123$), it is possible to distinguish C_L^2 different pairs, which in a first approximation can be considered independent. With the account of the latter fact it is possible to evaluate the probability that among given L words, there will be the target pair of words as $P = 1 - A_M^L M^{-L}$. For the case $P<0.6$, it is possible to use the approximate formulae $P_1 \approx p_1 C_L^2$ for CPM-1 and $P_2 \approx p_2 C_L^2$ for CPM-2. For $P_1 = P_2 = 0.5$, it is easy to obtain the values L_1 and L_2, which can be considered minimal numbers of known or chosen words, among which the target pair of words can be found with the probability of 0.5: $L_1 \approx p_1^{-0.5}$ and $L_2 \approx p_2^{-0.5}$. These values correspond to the numbers of different encrypted input data blocks: $L_1' > 2^{-7}L_1$ for CPM-1 and $L_2' > 2^{-7}L_2$ for CPM-2. If such information is available for the cryptanalyst, the attacker can find the target pair, using the criterion for recognizing repetitions.

The complexity of finding this pair W is taken for the complexity of cryptanalysis; that is, for the cryptographic strength of the algorithm. In reality, considering individual pairs of words cannot ensure identification of a repetition; however, with the model under consideration, this assumption is taken in favor of the attacker because the goal of this evaluation is determining the lower limit of the algorithm strength. Assume that the attacker has some additional condition that needs to be checked for different pairs of arbitrarily chosen words. To find the target pair with the probability of 0.5, it is necessary to check half of the total number of possible combinations C_L^2. Assuming that the attacker carries out one check within a single operation, the cryptanalysis complexity can be evaluated as $W_1 = 0.5p_1^{-1}$ and $W_2 = 0.5p_2^{-1}$.

Numeric values of generalized evaluations are provided in Table 2.1. The obtained results make it clear that in the best case, the cryptanalyst can disclose the encryption key, provided that he has no less than 2^{18} GB of chosen plaintexts and corresponding ciphertexts. In this case, cryptanalysis will require no less than 2^{95} operations. These evaluations demonstrate that the SPECTR-Z algorithms can be used for safe encryption of all data on contemporary storage media or greater size.

TABLE 2.1 Numeric Values of Generalized Evaluations of the Cryptanalysis Complexity

Attack variant	P	L, words	L', blocks	W, operations
CPM-1	2^{-192}	2^{96}	$>2^{89}$	2^{191}
CPM-2	2^{-96}	2^{48}	$>2^{41}$	2^{95}

From the developer's point of view, CPM provides a good generalized evaluation, because it doesn't overestimate the cryptographic strength. Comparison of the results obtained using CPM-1 to the results of specialized cryptanalytical research carried out for the COBRA system confirms these results. Actually, expert analysis using known methods of cryptanalysis has produced the values $L \approx 6{\cdot}10^{13}$ bytes and $W \approx 4{\cdot}10^{15}$ operations, while CPM-1 produces considerably smaller values: $L \approx 10^{7}$ bytes and $W \approx 10^{14}$ operations. This, along with the fact that no cryptanalysis variants producing smaller value than the one determined according to CPM have been found for the SPECTR-Z cipher, allows us to adopt the evaluation obtained according to CPM.

2.8.5 File Encryption Algorithm

File encryption in the SPECTR-Z cryptographic system is carried out using the transformation mechanism that satisfies the following requirements:

- Execution of encrypting procedures implemented at the software level in real-time mode.
- Forming of the temporary unique key for file encryption by the secret key and arbitrarily formed file label.
- Ensuring the possibility of arbitrary access to all bytes of the encrypted file (independent encryption of each byte).
- Execution of file encryption at each file write operation.
- Invariability of the file lengths and system attributes.

The file encryption key is some extended key formed based on the secret key. With this being so, the procedure uses the precomputations algorithm that doesn't allow for computation of the secret key even if the extended key is known. The secret key is common for encryption of all files of a given user. The user's secret key is formed at the PC bootstrap phase at the precomputation stage. The key is 1024-bytes long, and represents a set of 256 32-bit subkeys $Q[j], j = 0, 1, \ldots, 255$.

The general scheme of file encryption consists of the generation of 8-bit elements of the key range depending on the ordinal number of specific bytes in the file and on the additional local key with subsequent superposition of the range elements over corresponding bytes of the file. The local key is 64-bits long. It is formed when opening the file depending on the secret file encryption key and a 64-bit label, presumably known to the intruder. Local labels are generated arbitrarily and are assigned as attributes to each file, for which encryption mode is specified. The probability of forming the matching labels for different files is negligibly small (about 2^{-64}).

Assume that $M = U||V$ is a 64-bit label represented as a concatenation of two 32-bit words $U = u_4||u_3||u_2||u_1$ and $V = v_4||v_3||v_2||v_1$. In the further few sections, the algorithm used for generation of the local key will be considered in more detail.

Forming the Local Key

The algorithm used for generation of the local key is made up of the following steps:

1. Set the counter $i = 1$.
2. Carry out the following transformations:
   - $U := U + Q[v_1]; V := V + Q[u_1];$
   - $U := U \oplus Q[v_2]; V := V \oplus Q[u_2];$
   - $U := (U + V)^{<16<}; V := V + Q[u_1];$
   - $V := V^{<16<}; U := U + Q[v_1];$
   - $V := V \oplus Q[u_2]; U := (U \oplus Q[v_2])^{<13<};$
   - $V := (V + U)^{<13<}$.
3. If $i < 5$, then increment the counter $i := i + 1$ and go to step 2.
4. STOP.

The value $R = U||V$ after executing five rounds of the transformation will represent the local key. File encryption is carried out according to the algorithm described in the next section, where the following designations are used: $N = n_4||n_3||n_2||n_1$ is the number of the currently transformed byte represented in the form of concatenation of an 8-bit number, $R = r_8||r_7||r_6||r_5||r_4||r_3||r_2||r_1$ is the local key represented in the form of concatenation of eight-bit subkeys, $F = f_4||f_3||f_2||f_1$ is a 32-bit variable, and j is the 8-bit number of the chosen subkey.

Encryption of the Current Byte

The algorithm for encryption of the current byte of the file being encrypted includes the following steps:

1. Carry out the following transformations:
   - $j := n_1 + r_5;\ F := Q[j] \oplus (r_4 \| r_3 \| r_2 \| r_1);$
   - $j := (j \oplus n_2) + (f_1 \oplus r_6);\ F := \{(F + Q[j]) \oplus (r_8 \| r_7 \| r_6 \| r_5)\}^{>5>};$
   - $j := (j + r_7) \oplus (f_1 + n_3);\ F := (F + Q[j])^{>6>};$
   - $j := (j + n_4) \oplus (f_1 + r_8);\ F := (F \oplus Q[j])^{>7>};$
   - $j := j + r_2;\quad F := F + Q[j];$
   - $j := j + r_3;\quad F := F \oplus Q[j];$
   - $(f_2 \| f_1) := (f_4 \| f_3) \oplus (f_2 \| f_1).$
2. Form the current 8-bit element of the key range: $g := f_1 + f_2$.
3. Transform the current byte t_N: $t_N := t_N \oplus g$.
4. STOP.

This algorithm is used for both encrypting and decrypting files. It ensures the transformation rate of about 80 Mbps for the Pentium-II 266 microprocessor. Obviously, this algorithm ensures independent encryption of each byte of the file being encrypted. This ensures high flexibility when working with large files such as database files, for example. The key range being generated $g(N)$ is practically unique for every file, because it is generated depending on the local key, which is formed on the basis of an arbitrary label.

Note some specific features of the file encryption algorithm under consideration. If some file is known to the cryptanalyst in the plaintext form and in the encrypted form, he will easily compute the key range corresponding to this file. However, disclosing the file encryption key by the key range is complicated, even if the chosen plaintext is available. Because of this, disclosure of some files doesn't compromise the confidentiality of the others, and an attack based on the encryption of the specially chosen files doesn't provide the cryptanalyst with any additional possibilities of computing the secret key. If storage media are stolen, the cryptanalyst can easily discover the label value; however, it will be impossible to compute the local key, because this requires the attacker to know the file encryption key. The file encryption algorithm is strong against known methods of cryptanalysis, including attacks based on generating arbitrary hardware errors.

2.8.6 Transformation of the Boot Sector Data

To decrypt or encrypt the operating system loader in the SPECTR-Z cryptosystem, a special mini-algorithm has been developed. This algorithm is implemented in the form of the software cryptographic module smaller than 100 bytes, which allows for placing it within the protection system loader (which is only 512 bytes in size).

The general cryptoscheme of the mini-algorithms includes two stages:

1. Precomputations carried out to form the 1024-byte extended key $K[j]$.
2. Decryption procedure **D** using the extended key. The extended key is represented in the form of the sequence of 32-bit subkeys $\{K[j]\}$, where $j = 0, 1, 2, \dots, 255$.

To carry out precomputations, the 1024-byte auxiliary key L is formed by means of repetition of the password required number of times and simultaneously modifying the bytes of the password. The subkey is formed as follows: $K:=L$. After that, the following transformations are carried out 35 times: $L := \mathbf{D}_K(L)$, $K := L$, where $\mathbf{D}_K(L)$ is interpreted as the result of applying procedure **D** with key K to block L. As the result, the extended key is obtained: $K = \{K[j]\}$, $j = 0, 1, \dots, 255$, which is further used as a key in procedure **D** to decrypt the boot sector. Procedure **D** is implemented by splitting the message being encrypted into 64-bit blocks and sequentially transforming these blocks. Data blocks are presented as $T = A||B$, where $A=a_4||a_3||a_2||a_1$, $B = b_4||b_3||b_2||b_1$, a_i and b_i are 8-bit subblocks, and the "||" operator means concatenation. The procedure of decrypting 64-bit data blocks uses the algorithm described in the next section.

Procedure *D* (Decryption Mini-Algorithm)

The decryption mini-algorithm comprises the following steps:

1. Set the counter $r = 1$.
2. Carry out the following transformations:
   - $A := A + K[b_1]; B := B \oplus K[a_1];$
   - $A := A \oplus B; A := A^{>3>};$
   - $B := B^{>3>}; B := B + A.$
3. If $r < 35$, increment the counter $r := r + 1$ and return to step 2.
4. STOP.

After 35 rounds of encryption, the value $A||B$ is the output value of the mini-algorithm. The procedure of encrypting the operating system loader is carried out when installing the protection system or changing the secret key. This procedure can be easily built by the decryption algorithm.

Mini-algorithm ensures high strength against attacks based on known and chosen text several KBs in size. This mechanism ensures an excellent balance between the module size and cryptographic strength. It should be mentioned that a potential cryptanalyst does not have a sufficient amount of corresponding pairs of the plaintext and ciphertext blocks for implementing statistical cryptanalysis methods. In addition, it will be very difficult for the attacker to input any chosen text for encryption or decryption because of specific features of the way in which the protection system uses the mini-algorithm. The use of the operating system loader encryption allows for ensuring a high level of protection against built-in trapdoors. Because the code size rather than the encryption speed is important for the minicipher algorithm, the strength of the minicipher can be increased if you use multiplication as one of the basic operations and/or increase the number of transformation rounds.

Thus, in the SPECTR-Z system, the disk encryption algorithm is optimally complemented by the system of fast file encryption and by miniciphers allowing for controlling the PC bootstrap phase. This combination ensures a strong system of multilevel encryption of this fully functional information security product.

2.9 SOFTWARE CIPHER WITH FLEXIBLE INPUT

Building a software cipher with flexible input is an issue of practical interest. This task can be accomplished based on the algorithm of the SPECTR-Z system, and, at the same time, the variable block length must relate to that part of the block that is transformed in two rounds. This will allow for obtaining high speeds for smaller blocks. If the block size is small, the speed will be several times lower, because for starting and terminating words of the input block the number of rounds cannot be smaller than six because of security considerations.

The software block algorithm SPECTR-F considered in this section is a modified version of the SPECTR-Z algorithm, which differs from the original in that the size of the input block is not fixed. Instead, the size of the input block in the modified algorithm can have the size from 128 bits or higher; however, this value must be a multiple of 32 bits. Thanks to this, SPECTR-F provides the flexibility required to optimize the selected block lengths for specific applications. This allows for obtaining considerable improvement of the encryption speed when encrypting large data blocks (up to 300 Mbps for contemporary commercial processors). For encryption speeds about 100 Mbps, this algorithm ensures the possibility of encrypting data in 128-bit blocks, if necessary.

The SPECTR-F cryptosystem was developed based on the same criteria as the ones used for the SPECTR-Z cryptosystem. Variable length of the input block ensures better flexibility of the SPECTR-F algorithm. The parameterized value $32m$ (bits), where m is a natural number satisfying the inequality $m \geq 4$, was chosen as the input block size for the SPECTR-F algorithm.

Similar to other ciphers with extended key, in the SPECTR-F cryptosystem it is assumed that the extended key is generated depending on the secret key of relatively small length using special procedures executed as precomputations. The SPECTR-F cipher is implemented in the form of two software modules: initialization module intended to run once, and resident encryption module intended to serve requests of other programs for data encryption and decryption.

Precomputations

To carry out precomputations, the secret key (input parameter) is repeated the required number of times to obtain a 2051-byte sequence designated as $\overline{\mathbf{Q}}' = \{q_0', q_1', \ldots, q'_{2050}\}$. After that, the auxiliary key $\overline{\mathbf{H}} = \overline{\mathbf{Q}}' \oplus \overline{\mathbf{Z}}$ is formed, where $\overline{\mathbf{Z}}$ is a sequence formed using the ***Table_Z*** procedure. The $\mathbf{Q}'$ key is then transformed several times using the ***Encrypt512*** procedure and the **H** key. The extended key $\overline{\mathbf{Q}}$ is formed according to the ***FormKey*** procedure described here. In this procedure, $\overline{\mathbf{Q}}'$ is interpreted as a sequence of four 512-byte blocks $\overline{\mathbf{Q}}^{(1)}, \overline{\mathbf{Q}}^{(2)}, \overline{\mathbf{Q}}^{(3)}, \overline{\mathbf{Q}}^{(4)}$ and three bytes; that is, $\overline{\mathbf{Q}}'=\{ \overline{\mathbf{Q}}^{(1)}, \overline{\mathbf{Q}}^{(2)}, \overline{\mathbf{Q}}^{(3)}, \overline{\mathbf{Q}}^{(4)}, q^{(0)}, q^{(1)}, q^{(2)}\}$, where $q^{(0)}=q'_{2048}$, $q^{(1)}=q'_{2049}$ and $q^{(2)}=q'_{2050}$. The encryption key $\overline{\mathbf{Q}}$ is a sequence of bytes q_i: $\overline{\mathbf{Q}} = \{q_i\}$, where i=0,1,…,2050. In the course of data encryption the subkeys $Q_j = q_{j+3}||q_{j+2}||q_{j+1}||q_j$, where $j = 0, 1, \ldots, 2047$, are used.

The *Table_Z* Procedure

The ***Table_Z*** procedure algorithm includes the following steps:

1. Set the counter $i = 0$.
2. Compute the 32-byte number $Z_i' = (a^{23+i} \bmod P)^{17} \bmod R$.
3. Increment the counter $i := i + 1$. If $i \neq 64$, go to step 2.
4. Form a 2051-byte number $S = z_2'||z_1'||z_0'||Z_{63}'||\ldots||Z_0'$, where $z_2'||z_1'||z_0' = Z_0' +_{24} 0$.
5. Represent S in the form of the sequence of bytes: $\overline{\mathbf{Z}} = \{z_0, z_1, \ldots, z_{2050}\}$.

The *FormKey* Procedure

The ***FormKey*** procedure includes the following steps:

1. Set the parameter $m = 128$ and accept $\overline{\mathbf{H}}$ as the encryption key.
2. Transform $\overline{\mathbf{Q}}^{(1)}$: $\mathbf{Q}^{(1)} :=$ ***Encrypt512***$_{\mathrm{H}}(\overline{\mathbf{Q}}^{(1)})$.
3. Transform $\overline{\mathbf{Q}}^{(2)}$: $\mathbf{Q}^{(2)} :=$ ***Encrypt512***$_{\mathrm{H}}(\overline{\mathbf{Q}}^{(2)} \oplus \overline{\mathbf{Q}}^{(1)})$.
4. Transform $\overline{\mathbf{Q}}^{(3)}$: $\mathbf{Q}^{(3)} :=$ ***Encrypt512***$_{\mathrm{H}}(\overline{\mathbf{Q}}^{(3)} \oplus \overline{\mathbf{Q}}^{(2)})$.
5. Transform $\overline{\mathbf{Q}}^{(4)}$: $\mathbf{Q}^{(4)} :=$ ***Encrypt512***$_{\mathrm{H}}(\overline{\mathbf{Q}}^{(4)} \oplus \overline{\mathbf{Q}}^{(3)})$.

Generate the extended key: $\overline{\mathbf{Q}} = \{ \overline{\mathbf{Q}}^{(1)}, \overline{\mathbf{Q}}^{(2)}, \overline{\mathbf{Q}}^{(3)}, \overline{\mathbf{Q}}^{(4)}, q^{(0)}, q^{(1)}, q^{(2)}\}$.

Transformation Algorithms

The SPECTR-F encryption algorithm includes two complete and four reduced encryption rounds. The block of plaintext $\overline{\mathbf{T}}$ is split into four 32-bit words T_i: $T = \{T_i\}$, where $i = 0, 1, \ldots, m - 1$ ($m \geq 4$). The value of the natural number m is set depending on the application area. In each encryption round, the input 32-bit words $T_0, T_1, T_2, \ldots, T_{m-1}$ are transformed. Note that when $m = 4$, complete and reduced rounds are identical. After each round, except for the last, the values are exchanged in the pairs of words $T_0 \leftrightarrow T_3$ and $T_1 \leftrightarrow T_2$. Transformation algorithms include the following two standard procedures: ***Initialize*** and ***Change_NVYU***.

The Initialize Procedure

The ***Initialize*** procedure includes the following steps:

1. Set the value of the internal counter $i := 0$ and initial values of variables $R := Q[9], V := Q[7], Y := Q[3], U := Q[9], N := Q[5]$.
2. END.

The Change_NVYU Procedure

The algorithm of the ***Change_NVYU*** procedure includes the following steps:

1. $N := N \oplus R;\ V := V +_{32} N;$
2. $N := N \otimes F;\ n := N +_{11} 0;\ V := (V +_{32} Q[n])^{>>>11};$
3. $N := N \oplus V;\ Y := Y +_{32} N;$
4. $N := N \otimes F;\ n := N +_{11} 0;\ Y := (Y +_{32} Q[n])^{>>>11};$
5. $N := N +_{32} Y;\ N := N \otimes F;\ n := N +_{11} 0;$
6. $U := ((U \oplus Q[n]) +_{32} R)^{>>>V}.$
7. END.

The SPECTR-F cipher is described by the following algorithms.

Procedure of Encryption in Four Reduced Rounds

The algorithm of the encryption procedure in four reduced rounds includes the following steps:

1. Increment the external counter value $j := 0$.
2. Execute the ***Initialize*** procedure.
3. Execute the ***Change_NVYU*** procedure.
4. Transform the next word of the text: $T_i := (T_i -_{32} V) \oplus U$.
5. Transform the variable R: $R := R +_{32} T_i$.

6. Complete the transformation of the word T_i: $T_i := T_i^{<<<V} -_{32} Y$.
7. Increment $i := i + 1$. If $i \neq 4$, go to step 3.
8. Exchange values of the following pairs of words: $T_0 \leftrightarrow T_3$ and $T_1 \leftrightarrow T_2$.
9. Increment $j := j + 1$. If $j \neq 4$, go to step 2.
10. STOP.

Decryption Procedure in Reduced Rounds

The algorithm of the decryption procedure in reduced rounds includes the following steps:

1. Set the value of the external counter $j := 0$.
2. Execute the ***Initialize*** procedure.
3. Execute the ***Change_NVYU*** procedure.
4. Transform the next word of the text: $T_i := (T_i +_{32} Y)^{>>>V}$.
5. Transform the variable R: $R := R +_{32} T_i$.
6. Complete the transformation of the word T_i: $T_i := (T_i \oplus U) +_{32} V$.
7. Increment $i := i + 1$. If $i \neq 4$, go to step 3.
8. Exchange the values of the following pairs of words: $T_0 \leftrightarrow T_3$ and $T_1 \leftrightarrow T_2$.
9. Increment $j := j + 1$. If $j \neq 4$, go to step 2.
10. STOP.

The *Encrypt_512* Procedure: The First (Complete) Encryption Round

The algorithm of the ***Encrypt_512*** procedure includes the following steps:

1. Execute the ***Initialize*** procedure.
2. Execute the ***Change_NVYU*** procedure.
3. Transform the next word of the text: $T_i := (T_i -_{32} V) \oplus U$.
4. Transform the variable R: $R := R +_{32} T_i$.
5. Complete the transformation of the word T_i: $T_i := T_i^{<<<V} -_{32} Y$.
6. Increment $i := i + 1$. If $i \neq m$, go to step 2.
7. If $m > 4$, transform words T_2 and T_3 in the following order: $T_2 := T_2 \oplus T_{m\text{-}2}$ and $T_3 := T_3 \oplus T_{m-1}$.
8. Exchange the values of the following word pairs: $T_0 \leftrightarrow T_3$ and $T_1 \leftrightarrow T_2$.
9. STOP.

The Procedure of the Sixths (Complete) Round (Encryption)

The algorithm of the procedure of the sixths (complete) round (encryption) includes the following steps:

1. Execute the ***Initialize*** procedure.

2. If $m > 4$, transform words T_3 and T_2 in the following order: $T_3 := T_3 \oplus T_{m-1}$ and $T_2 := T_2 \oplus T_{m-2}$.
3. Execute the ***Change_NVYU*** procedure.
4. Transform the next word of the text: $T_i := (T_i -_{32} V) \oplus U$.
5. Transform the variable R: $R := R +_{32} T_i$.
6. Complete transformation of the word T_i: $T_i := T_i^{<<<V} -_{32} Y$.
7. Increment $i := i + 1$. If $i \neq m$, go to step 2.
8. STOP.

The Procedure of the First (Complete) Round (Decryption)

The procedure of the first (complete) round (decryption) comprises the following steps:

1. Execute the ***Initialize*** procedure.
2. Execute the ***Change_NVYU*** procedure.
3. Transform the next word of the text: $T_i := (T_i +_{32} Y)^{>>>V}$.
4. Transform the variable R: $R := R +_{32} T_i$.
5. Complete transformation of the word T_i: $T_i := (T_i \oplus U) +_{32} V$.
6. Increment $i := i + 1$. If $i \neq m$, go to step 2.
7. If $m > 4$, transform words T_2 and T_3 in the following order: $T_2 := T_2 \oplus T_{m-2}$ and $T_3 := T_3 \oplus T_{m-1}$.
8. Exchange the values of words: $T_0 \leftrightarrow T_3$ and $T_1 \leftrightarrow T_2$.
9. STOP.

The Procedure of the Sixths (Complete) Round (Decryption)

The algorithm of the sixths (complete) round (decryption) is made up of the following steps:

1. Execute the ***Initialize*** procedure.
2. If $m > 4$, transform words T_3 and T_2 in the following order: $T_3 := T_3 \oplus T_{m-1}$ and $T_2 := T_2 \oplus T_{m-2}$.
3. Execute the ***Change_NVYU*** procedure.
4. Transform the next word of the text: $T_i := (T_i +_{32} Y)^{>>>V}$.
5. Transform the variable R: $R := R +_{32} T_i$.
6. Complete transformation of the word T_i: $T_i := (T_i \oplus U) +_{32} V$.
7. Increment $i := i + 1$. If $i \neq m$, go to step 2.
8. STOP.

The scheme of transformation of the plaintext into ciphertext is shown in Figure 2.4.

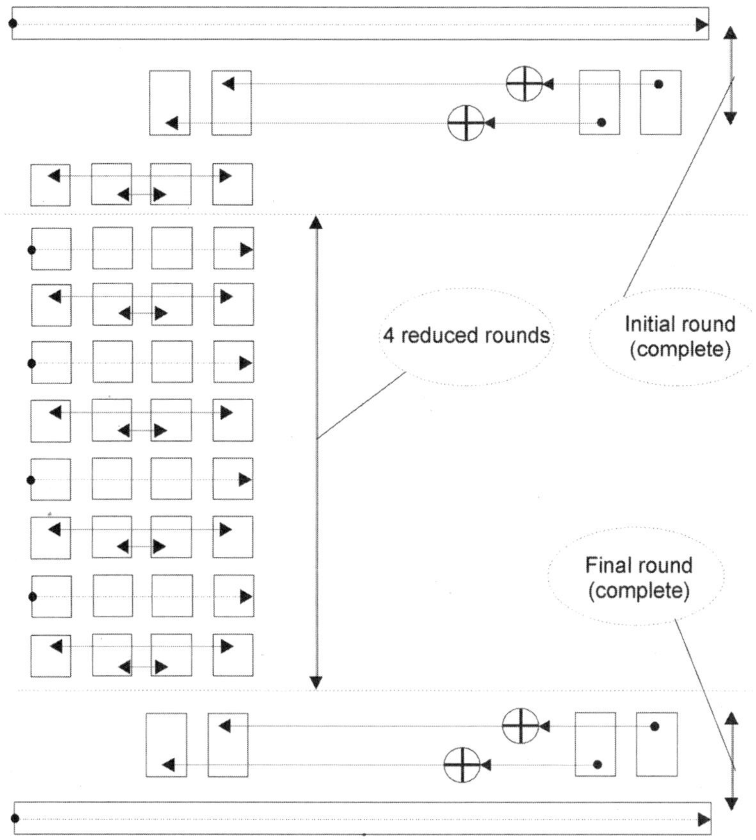

FIGURE 2.4 The scheme illustrating the order of transformation of 32-bit words into ciphertext in the SPECTR-F cipher.

The SPECTR-F cryptoalgorithm is oriented toward software implementation. The encryption speed depends on the size of the input block. When $m = 4$ the encryption speed is at a minimum and makes about 50 Mbps (for Pentium 266). With the increase in the block size, the encryption speed grows. For example, it makes about 140 Mbps for $m \geq 32$.

Thanks to the use of the value exchange operation, each of the words T_0, T_1, T_2, and T_3 during four reduced rounds is converted using a set of 27 variable subkeys chosen depending on the data being transformed. Output values of the extreme words T_0 and T_3 depend on three additional subkeys that are introduced three times into the procedures of the words transformation. However, this set of three subkeys is fixed for all data blocks and its contribution to the overall cryptographic strength. The main factor of the improvement of the cryptographic strength is specifying a dynamic sample of 27 subkeys for each transformed word. The procedure of transforming words with indexes $i = 4, 5, \dots, m - 1$ includes $6i$ "variable" subkeys (at the same time, more than 50 percent of these keys are included multiple times).

By choosing a special subset of texts, the attacker can specify the process of conversion to be identical for any text of such a subset. However, using this fact for analyzing the transformed values of words T_0, T_1, T_2 and T_3 for disclosing subkeys is considerably more problematic in comparison to the analysis of words $T_4, T_5, \dots, T_{m-1}$, because the first are transformed when carrying out all six rounds, and the latter only in the first and the last rounds. This feature was introduced for achieving high-encryption speed when encrypting large data blocks. Attacks related to the analysis of $T_4, T_5, \dots, T_{m-1}$ can be used as a foundation of the combinational-probabilistic model that accounts for specific features of the SPECTR-F cipher.

The SPECTR–F cryptoalgorithm is strong against all known methods of cryptanalysis, including linear and differential cryptanalysis. Despite the small number of complete rounds of transformation, this algorithm ensures high strength thanks to specific features of transformation typical for cryptosystems with a large size of the input text and based on data-dependent subkey sampling. When developing the SPECTR-F cipher, comparative analysis of different variants of cryptoschemes based on pseudorandom subkey sampling was carried out using attack, which accounted for the possibility of external physical influence on the encrypting devices on the part of the attacker. As a variant of attack, this analysis of the cryptographic strength considered the forming of *random* errors in registers containing data being encrypted. The SPECTR-F cryptoalgorithm is strong against such attacks, which is ensured by the same mechanisms as the ones used in the SPECTR-Z cipher (this is due to the similarity of the transformation mechanisms used in these two ciphers).

For the generalized evaluation of the minimal level of cryptographic strength of the SPECTR-F cipher in the case when $m \geq 5$ (that is, when the input block size makes 20 bytes or more), it is possible to use the combinational-probabilistic model (CPM), which earlier in this chapter was used for evaluating the strength of the SPECTR-Z cryptographic algorithm. The values of variables U, V, and Y at the step when the i-th word is transformed are generated depending on the combinations of i replaceable subkeys ($i = 0, 1, 2, \dots, m - 1$), and, with all that being so, the power of the set of values M_i, which can be taken by these variables, depends on i (for the given i the values of U, V, and Y depend on the input block). It can be easily shown that $M_0 = 1\ 2^0$, $M_1 \approx 2^{11}$, $M_2 \approx 2^{21}$, $M_3 \approx 2^{30}$, and $M_i \approx 2^{32}$ for $i \geq 4$. Thus, words with numbers $i \geq 4$ are transformed using one of the possible $\approx 2^{96}$ different sets $\{Y, U, V\}$, which depend on the input block and the encryption key. The algorithm is built so that *transformation procedures ensure the influence of any bit of the input message on the subkeys sample.* This criterion guarantees that for all different input messages, unique sequences of sets $\{Y_{(i)}, U_{(i)}, V_{(i)}\}$ will be generated, where index (i) marks the values of variables at the i-th step of the transformation.

The values of variables U, V, and Y might match by predefinition only in the first, and, partially, at the second round (during the first loop) at certain steps of the transformation for specially chosen input messages. The cryptanalyst can easily specify this condition; however, specific variable values will not be known beforehand. To achieve this goal, the cryptanalyst can choose two input messages that differ only in the word T_{m-1}. As relates to the last four rounds, the values of variables for any pair of input messages might match only by chance.

Although transformation of 32-bit words is carried out according to relatively simple equations, the set of variable values is pseudorandom. Determination of values of subkeys $Q[j]$ relates only to finding values of the U, V, and Y variables at certain steps of the transformation (for example, at two nearest sequential steps of the word transformation); therefore, fixing values U, V, and Y at certain steps is a preliminary condition for computing subkeys $Q[j]$. Fixing must be interpreted as finding such words within the same input message or within different input messages that were transformed using values U, V, and Y, related by a certain condition. For example, for two different words T and T', the pairs of values of each of the accumulating variables corresponding to them, which were used for their transformation, are equal (that is, $U = U'$, $V = V'$, and $Y = Y'$), or differ by a predefined value (that is, $U \oplus U' = \text{const}_1$, $V \oplus V' = \text{const}_2$, and $Y \oplus Y' = \text{const}_3$) or are related by a linear relationship. Note that the concept of fixing includes any specified dependencies between the values of accumulating variables corresponding to the chosen pair of words; that is, the use of differential and linear cryptanalysis is covered by the combinational-probabilistic model as a particular case.

The equation describing encryption of words T that have numbers $i \geq 4$ at the input (these words are transformed only in the first and in the sixth rounds, while all the other words are transformed during all six rounds) in the general form is specified by the expression $C = f(T, U_1, V_1, Y_1, U_6, V_6, Y_6)$, where the index corresponds to the number of the encryption round. Analysis of the experimental statistics of the sequence of values taken by the U, V, and Y variables confirms that these variables take pseudorandom values.

For obtaining generalized minimal evaluations, consider the weakest link in the chain of transformation; namely, the words with numbers $i \geq 4$, which are subject to the minimal transformation. Make a range of assumptions, which under real-world conditions the attacker cannot make. Assume that the solution of the system of equations corresponding to two individual words is a problem with low complexity level, if these words are transformed using fixed sets of values of the accumulating variables U_1, V_1, Y_1, U_6, V_6, Y_6. To obtain numeric evaluations of the cryptographic strength, the combinational-probabilistic model will be used. The complexity of solution of the equations corresponding to the fixing condition will be neglected, assuming the complexity of cryptanalysis depends only on the detection of the pair of words that correspond to the fixing condition. This corresponds to a general principle of attacking ciphers—recognition (known-plaintext attack) or specification (chosen-texts attack) of some expectable relations between unknown parameters.

In case of known-text attack for the pairs of words T and T' under consideration, the values U_1, V_1, Y_1, U_6, V_6, Y_6 are in general case different. In case of the chosen-text attack, it is possible to choose such pairs of input blocks for which at each step of the first round the matching values of variables U_1, V_1, Y_1 are formed (these variables will be measured when changing from word to word; however, in the first round of encryption such switching will take place synchronously for such pairs of input blocks). Such pairs of input messages can be easily obtained by means of modifying the word T_i, where $0 < i < m - 1$ in the text $\overline{\mathbf{T}}$. Denote the modified text as $\mathbf{T}'$. In the pair of texts $\mathbf{T}$ and $\mathbf{T}'$ obtained this way, words T_j, where $0 \leq j \leq i$, in the first round will be transformed using the matching values U_1, V_1, Y_1.

However, after execution of the next four rounds, any change in $\overline{\mathbf{T}}'$ will result in the change of all bits of words T_0, T_1, T_2, T_3 with the probability of 0. The process of encryption in the third round will be related to the pseudorandom values of the differences $U_6 - U_6'$, $V_6 - V_6'$, and $Y_6 - Y_6'$. In the pair of texts $\overline{\mathbf{T}}$ and $\overline{\mathbf{T}}'$, the most promising for the attacker is exploiting the fact of repetition of the values U_1, V_1, Y_1 for words T_j and T'_j, where $5 \leq j \leq m - 1$ in the first round of encryption. (Analysis of the four starting words is more complex, because they are additionally transformed in the second, third, fourth, and fifth rounds.) As can be easily seen, evaluation of the cryptographic strength of the SPECTR-F algorithm is the same as for SPECTR-Z (see Table 2.1).

The difference of two values of each of the U, V, Y variables used for transformation of two neighboring words in the sequence T_4, T_5, …, T_{m-1} is, probably, "least pseudorandom"; however, the use of this fact for cryptanalysis is considerably complicated because the values of these words after the first encryption round are unknown. For example, by fixing the text $\overline{\mathbf{T}}$ and choosing the set of corresponding texts $\mathbf{T}'$, it is possible to try to accumulate the statistics of the changes of the pair of neighboring words in the sequence T_4, T_5, … , T_i. However, the values of these words after the first round of encryption are unknown because the values of the U_1, V_1, Y_1 sets of variables used at the first round of encryption and subject to change when changing from word to word are unknown. At the same time, thanks to forming these variables using concatenation mechanisms, the value of the current word influences the transformation of all further words.

Increments of the values of variables U, V, Y when executing the sixths round of encryption (that is, incrementing U_6, V_6, Y_6, which take place when changing from word to word) depend on the three chosen subkeys, and on the earlier chosen subkeys. With this being so, this dependence is specified through two 32-bit variables N and R, which are part of the expression used for transforming these variables. The values of $N_{(4)}$ and $R_{(4)}$ used when transforming the word T_4, are pseudorandom, because they are formed in the course of execution of the starting five rounds.

On all the other steps of transformation of the words $T_5, \ldots, T_{m-1}$ the values of variables N and R are mutually dependent on $N_{(4)}$ and $R_{(4)}$, which together specify 64 independent bits. Taking into account that when changing from word to word three new subkeys are used (the power of the set of implemented values of each being equal to 2^{11}), it is possible to assume that for such a system of analysis an exceeding amount of statistical data will be required. This is because the process of encryption is influenced by some pseudorandom "generalized" 97-bit parameter. Thus, this variant of attack corresponds well enough to CPM-2 under consideration, which can be characterized by a 96-bit pseudorandom parameter represented by a set of three variables (U_6, V_6, Y_6).

3 Substitution–Permutation Networks with Minimal Controlled Element

3.1 CONTROLLED BIT PERMUTATIONS AS CRYPTOGRAPHIC PRIMITIVE

The main cryptographic application of the controlled permutations (CP) operation is related to the execution of the data-dependent bitwise permutations. This approach was first suggested in the publications "A cipher based on data-dependent permutations" by A. A. Moldovyan and N. A. Moldovyan, and "Fast block ciphers based on controlled permutations" by A. A. Moldovyan. Earlier research aimed at building cryptographic mechanisms based on controlled permutations related to the use of CP as operations dependent on the encryption key. Such a type of operation requires the use of controlled permutations networks (CP-networks, CPNs), which are well known by the publications of different authors. Although the possibility of building strong cryptosystems based on the use of key-dependent CPs, the suggested ciphers could not compete with other symmetric cryptosystems by the speed of operation and simplicity of the schematic implementation. This is mainly because key-dependent bit permutation remains a purely linear operation, because it is fixed after the key input. The situation becomes principally different when the permutation is a variable operation; that is, in cases when the result of its execution depends on the value of the data block being transformed, which is a variable value by its nature.

To execute variable permutations, the most suitable are CPNs with the layered structure shown in Figure 3.1, where the main building block is a permutation element $\mathbf{P}_{2/1}$, which can be called the elementary block of controlled permutations (controlled permutations block, CPB), because it implements two different permutations of two input bits x_1 and x_2 depending on one control bit v. An elementary block $\mathbf{P}_{2/1}$ is controlled by a single bit v and forms a two-bit output (y_1, y_2), where $y_1 = x_{1+v}$ and $y_2 = x_{2-v}$. Since there are only two permutations of this type, elementary CPM implements all possible permutations. With the increase of the CPB input size, implementation of all permutations becomes problematic, for

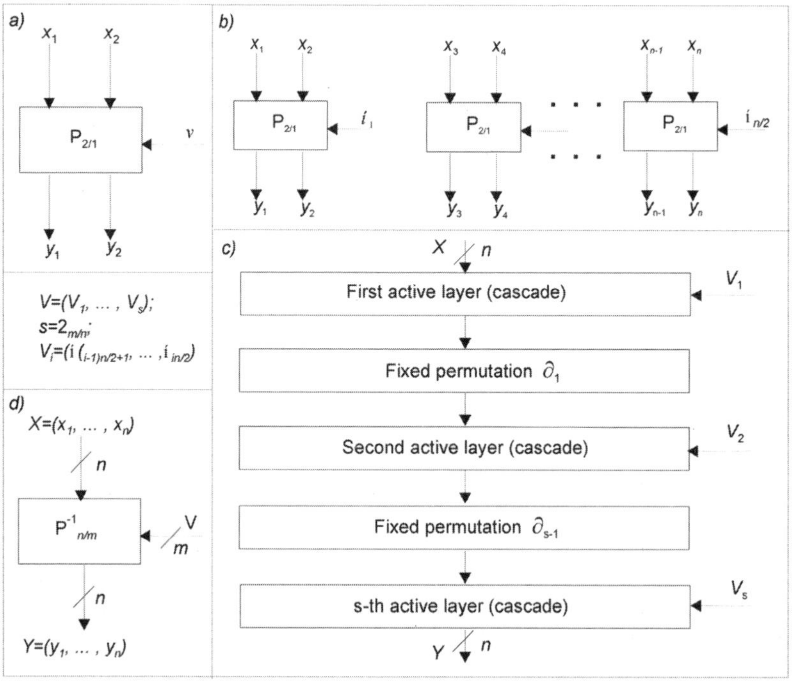

FIGURE 3.1 The structure of a CPB: a)—elementary $\mathbf{P}_{2/1}$ block; b)—structure of an active layer, c)—general structure of multilayered CPBs, d) —inverse $\mathbf{P}^{-1}{}_{n/m}$ block.

mostly all practically significant values of the input size n CPBs implementing all possible $n!$ permutations can be built. At the same time, such operating blocks are fast enough to ensure high encryption speed based on variable permutations. In layered CPBs, the number of active layers s is related to parameters m and n as follows: $s = 2m/n$.

Assume that some CPB implements a set of different permutations corresponding to different values of the controlling vector V. According to the number of layers, vector V can be represented as a union of s vectors $V_1, V_2, ..., V_s \in GF(2)^{n/2}$; that is, $V = (V_1, V_2, \ldots, V_s)$. When the value of the controlling vector is fixed, a certain permutation $\prod_V$ is implemented. The block of controlled permutations $\mathbf{P}_{m/n}$ can be described using an ordered set of modifications $\{\prod_0, \prod_1, \ldots, \prod_{2^m-1}\}$, where each modification $\prod_V$, $V = 0, 1, \ldots, 2^m-1$ is a fixed permutation of n bits. Permutations $\prod_V$ will be called *modifications of controlled permutation*. Execution of the controlled permutation $\mathbf{P}_{m/n(V)}(X)$ consists of the execution of the permutation $\prod_V$ over $X: Y = \mathbf{P}_{m/n(V)}(X) = \prod_V(X)$. For cryptographic applications, the most interesting are values of n, which are natural powers of two. The most promising is development of CPBs of different orders, because the number of active layers in a CPB decreases with the decrease of the order, which results in the improvement of CPB the operating speed.

Definition 3.1

Assume that for a given $d \leq n$ of arbitrary sets of indexes $\alpha_1, \alpha_2, \ldots, \alpha_h$ and $\beta_1, \beta_2, \ldots, \beta_h$ there exists at least one value of the controlling vector V such that input bits $x_{\alpha_1}, x_{\alpha_2}, \ldots, x_{\alpha_h}$ are transformed into output bits $y_{\beta_1}, y_{\beta_2}, \ldots, y_{\beta_h}$, respectively. The maximum possible value of d is called the order of the $\mathbf{P}_{m/n}$ CPB and is denoted as h.

The possibility of constructing CPBs of different orders, uniform enough, which are of greatest interest ($h = 1, 2, 4, \ldots, n/4$), is the most important issue of the cipher developer's toolset. It allows for finding the required compromise between the const of implementation and performance of the cipher being designed. Another important issue is the simplicity of designing inverse CPBs.

Definition 3.2

Blocks of controlled permutations $\mathbf{P}_{m/n}$ and $\mathbf{P}^{-1}_{m/n}$ are called mutually inverse, if for all possible values of vector V modifications of bit permutations $\prod_V$ and $\prod^{-1}_V$ implemented by blocks $\mathbf{P}_{m/n}$ and $\mathbf{P}^{-1}_{m/n}$, respectively, are mutually inverse.

The general scheme of constructing direct and inverse layered blocks of controlled permutations is shown in Figure 3.2. The characteristic issue of such a design is that the components of the controlling vector $V = (V_1, V_2, \ldots, V_s)$ are

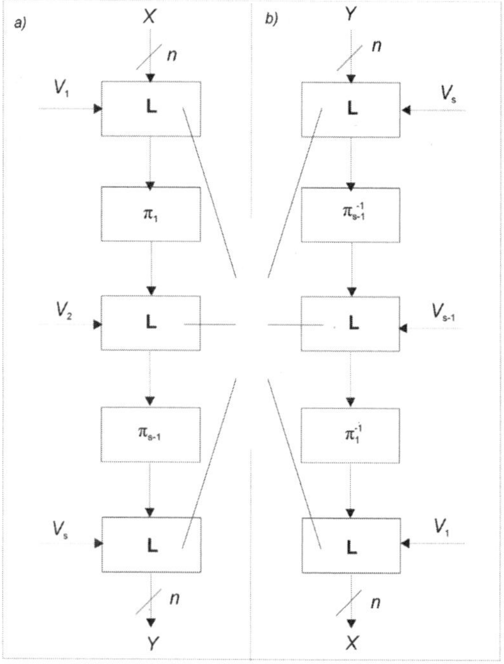

FIGURE 3.2 Structures of direct (a) and inverse (b) blocks of controlled permutations.

distributed by active layers in different orders. In the case of a direct block, they are distributed from top to bottom, starting from input to output, and in the case of an inverse block, they are distributed from bottom to top (from output to input). At the same time, the numbering of active cascades in both blocks goes similarly—from input to output. Thus, according to the adopted agreement, the component V_l controls the l-th active layer in the direct block, and $(s - l + 1)$-th active layer in the inverse block. Layered P-box can be considered a matrix of elementary switching elements that are sequentially numbered from left to right and from top to bottom in the direct P-box, and from left to right and from top to bottom in the inverse P-box. The i-th bit of vector V controls i-th switching element of $\mathbf{P}_{2/1}$.

One active cascade can be considered a single-layered P-box $\mathbf{L}_n$. Obviously, $\mathbf{P}_{2/1} = \mathbf{P}^{-1}_{2/1}$; therefore, the conversion carried out using an active cascade is an involution. Thus, it is possible to obtain the result $\mathbf{L}_n = \mathbf{L}^{-1}_n$. The multilayered block of controlled permutations $\mathbf{P}_{m/n}$ can be represented as a superposition:

$$\mathbf{P}_{m/n} = \mathrm{L}_{V_1} \circ \pi_1 \circ \mathrm{L}_{V_2} \circ \pi_2 \circ \ldots \circ \pi_{s-1} \circ \mathrm{L}_{V_s}.$$

The corresponding block $\mathbf{P}^{-1}{}_{m/n}$ has the following structure:

$$\mathbf{P}^{-1}{}_{m/n} = \mathrm{L}_{V_s} \circ \pi^{-1}{}_{s-1} \circ \mathrm{L}_{V_{s-1}} \circ \pi^{-1}{}_{s-2} \circ \ldots \circ \pi_1{}^{-1} \circ \mathrm{L}_{V_1}.$$

Thus, to build a block of controlled permutations that is an inverse of the $\mathbf{P}_{m/n}$ block, it is enough to renumber $\mathbf{P}_{2/1}$ blocks from left to right and from bottom to top, and replace π_i by $\pi^{-1}{}_{s-i}$. Blocks of controlled permutations are used in a range of ciphers covered in Chapter 5, "Designing Fast Ciphers Based on Controlled Operations," and publications (for example, "Fast Encryption algorithm SPECTR-H64" by N. D. Goots, A. A. Moldovyan, and N. A. Moldovyan) for carrying out data-dependent bit permutations. Although controlled permutations allow for considerably improving the operating speed of block ciphers while decreasing the cost of implementation, as a cryptographic primitive, they are not free from drawbacks. The most important drawback is that they are linear cryptographic primitives, although the only linear combination of outputs, which is a linear boolean function, includes all output bits $y_1, y_2, \ldots, y_n$. Such a linear combination is the sum $\Sigma = y_1 \oplus y_2 \oplus \ldots \oplus y_n$, which is equal to the sum of input bits due to the nature of permutations.

Because linear combinations with smaller numbers of outputs are nonlinear boolean functions, variable bit permutations ensure the possibility of efficiently building block ciphers while using additional nonlinear cryptographic primitives playing an auxiliary role; namely, preventing linear cryptanalysis using masks with maximum possible weight. The use of additional primitives masks the contribution of variable permutations into the strength of the ciphers developed according to the scheme being considered, because the high strength of such ciphers is ensured by the two main primitives. Data-dependent bit permutations are efficient, because they are used only in combination with the XOR operation, fixed permutations and extension blocks implemented as simple branching of conductors. Such a formulation of the problem in practice means the necessity of preliminary design of the permutation operation, representing a nonlinear cryptographic primitive.

For solving this problem, the DDP-64 cipher described in the next section uses the idea of truncation of the output bits of the controlled permutations block used for implementation of variable permutations. This approach can be used while preserving the possibility of correctly executing the decryption procedure, if the aforementioned permutation is used as an element included into the function **F** of the Feistel network. This is exactly how additional primitives are used in known ciphers based on data-dependent permutations (for example, nonlinear operation **G** in ciphers such as SPECTR-H64, SPECTR-128, and CIKS-128). Thus, the DDP-64 cryptosystem uses controlled permutations blocks implementing variable permutations of two types: normal and with truncated output. Controlled permutations blocks with truncated output represent a nonlinear primitive according to the cryptographic definition.

3.2 Block Cipher Based on Variable Permutations

When developing the DDP-64 cryptosystem (DDP stands for Data-Dependent Permutations), the main idea was to build a cryptographically strong cipher, in which variable bit permutations are the only nonlinear cryptographic primitive. Fixed permutations, extension operations, and modulo-e bitwise summing are used as auxiliary primitives. The following criteria were used when designing the DDP-64 cryptoscheme:

- The cryptosystem must be a block iterative 64-bit cipher ensuring high rate of the data transformation combined with relatively low cost of the hardware implementation.
- The same algorithm must be used for encryption and decryption. The change of the transformation mode must be ensured by quick change of the subkey use schedule.
- The cipher must ensure high performance with applications requiring frequent change of the key. To achieve this, the key schedule must be easy enough. The key schedule must not require any precomputations for building an extended key (set of round subkeys).
- The procedure of round encryption must be characterized by relatively high parallelism of computations to ensure fast encryption speed.
- Only variable permutations must be used as the main cryptographic primitive. In addition to bit permutations and extension nodes implemented as simple branching of wires, only one auxiliary operation can be used—modulo-2 bit by bit summation (XOR).

As the prototype of the round transformation, the DDP-64 cipher uses the round transformation procedure of the SPECTR-H64 cryptosystem, which is well suited for implementation of the adopted design criteria. Nonlinear variable permutations are carried out by the operating block **F**, the synthesis of which is based on the use of "truncated" variable bit permutations carried out over the left data subgroup. Another example of the use of variable bit permutations is represented by permutations carried out using second-order controlled permutations blocks $\mathbf{P}_{32/96(V)}$ and $\mathbf{P}^{-1}_{32/96(V')}$ shown in Figure 3.3. The $\mathbf{P}_{32/96(V)}$ and $\mathbf{P}^{-1}_{32/96(V')}$ blocks are built on the basis of the $\mathbf{P}_{8/12}$ and $\mathbf{P}^{-1}_{8/12}$ blocks of controlled permutations shown in Figure 3.3 (a, b). The cascade of $\mathbf{P}_{8/12}$ blocks is connected to the cascade of $\mathbf{P}^{-1}_{8/12}$ block using switching that specifies the following bit permutations representing an involution:

$$(1)(2,9)(3,17)(4,25)(5)(6,13)(7,21)(8,29)(10)(11,18)(12,26)$$
$$(14)(15,22)(16,30)(19)(20,27)(23)(24,31)(28)(32).$$

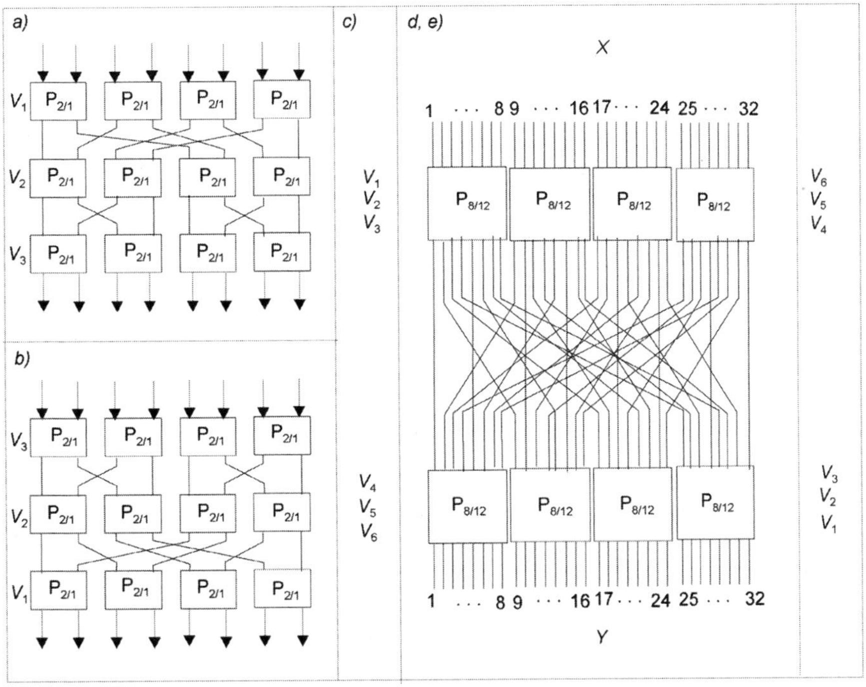

FIGURE 3.3 The structure of controlled permutations blocks $\mathbf{P}_{8/12}$ (a), $\mathbf{P}^{-1}_{8/12}$ (b), $\mathbf{P}_{32/96}$ (c), and $\mathbf{P}^{-1}_{8/12}$ (d).

Thanks to the symmetric structure of the $\mathbf{P}_{32/96}$ and $\mathbf{P}^{-1}_{32/96}$ blocks, they differ only by the distribution of the controlling bits of vector V. Because these blocks use the 96-bit controlling vector, and the left subgroup of the controlling data is 32 bits in length, it is necessary to use the extension block **E**, for the synthesis of which the following criteria were used:

- For all values of the controlling vector, the permutation of each input bit of the CPB must be defined by six different bits of L.
- Exactly three bits of the controlling vector must depend on each bit of the controlling data subgroup.

Assume that a 96-bit vector $V = (V_1, V_2, V_3, V_4, V_5, V_6)$ is the output of the block **E**, and a 32-bit vector $X = (X_l, X_h)$, where $X_l, X_h \in GF(2)^{16}$ is its input. The DDP-64 cipher uses the extension block **E″** that satisfies the previously provided criteria. It is described by the following relationships:

$$V_1 = X_l,\ V_2 = (X_l)^{<<<6},\ V_3 = (X_l)^{<<<12},$$
$$V_4 = X_h,\ V_5 = (X_h)^{<<<6},\ V_6 = (X_h)^{<<<12}.$$

Obviously, because the provided criteria have been met, each bit of the left data subgroup L controls exactly six bits of the right data subgroup R (independently on the value of the vector supplied to the input of the CPB) in each of the $\mathbf{P}_{32/96}$ and $\mathbf{P}^{-1}_{32/96}$ blocks. It is also obvious that an arbitrarily specified input bit of the blocks in each of the $\mathbf{P}_{32/96}$ and $\mathbf{P}^{-1}_{32/96}$ blocks moves to each of the output positions with equal probability, provided that L is a uniformly distributed random value.

Operating blocks **F** represent a specific variant of specifying variable permutations. The design of each of the two **F** blocks used ensures the randomnicity of the change of the output value parity. It should be mentioned that the $\mathbf{P}_{32/96(V)}$ and $\mathbf{P}^{-1}_{32/96(V')}$ CPBs are not characterized by such a property. To form an 80-bit controlling vector of the **F** blocks, the extension block **E′** is used, which is specified as follows. Let the 80-bit vector $W = (W_1, W_2, W_3, W_4, W_5)$ be the output of the block **E**, and the 32-bit vector $X = (X_l, X_h)$, where $X_l, X_h \in GF(2)^{16}$ be its output. Then, 16-bit components W_1, W_2, W_3, W_4, W_5 are defined by the following relations:

$$V_1 = X_l,\ V_2 = (X_l)^{<<<5},\ V_3 = (X_l)^{<<<10},\ V_4 = X_h,\ V_5 = (X_h)^{<<<5}.$$

The general scheme of the encrypting transformation implemented in DDP-64 is shown in Figure 3.4a, and the structure of the its round transformation Crypt$^{(e)}$ is presented in Figure 3.4b. Bit e is the bit that specifies the transformation mode: $e = 0$ corresponds to encryption, and $e = 1$ stands for decryption.

The use of the superscript index of the Crypt$^{(e)}$ procedure means that this procedure used switched permutation $\Pi^{(e')}$: when $e = 0$, the procedure executes the direct bit permutation over the current value of the left subgroup; and when $e = 1$, the procedure carries out an appropriate inverse bit permutation. Two different mechanisms determine the change of the transformation mode—change of the key schedule and switching of the permutation $\Pi^{(e')}$.

The DDP-64 block cryptosystem includes a simple initial transformation of a 64-bit block of input data, ten rounds of transformation using the Crypt$^{(e)}$ procedure, and a simple final transformation. The transformation of the data block can be represented in the following form:

$$C = \mathbf{CRYPT}^{(e=0)}(M, K) \text{ and } M = \mathbf{CRYPT}^{(e=1)}(C, K),$$

where M is the plaintext, C is the ciphertext ($M, C \in GF(2)^{64}$), and K is the secret key ($K \in GF(2)^{128}$). The DDP-64 cipher uses a 128-bit secret key considered as a set

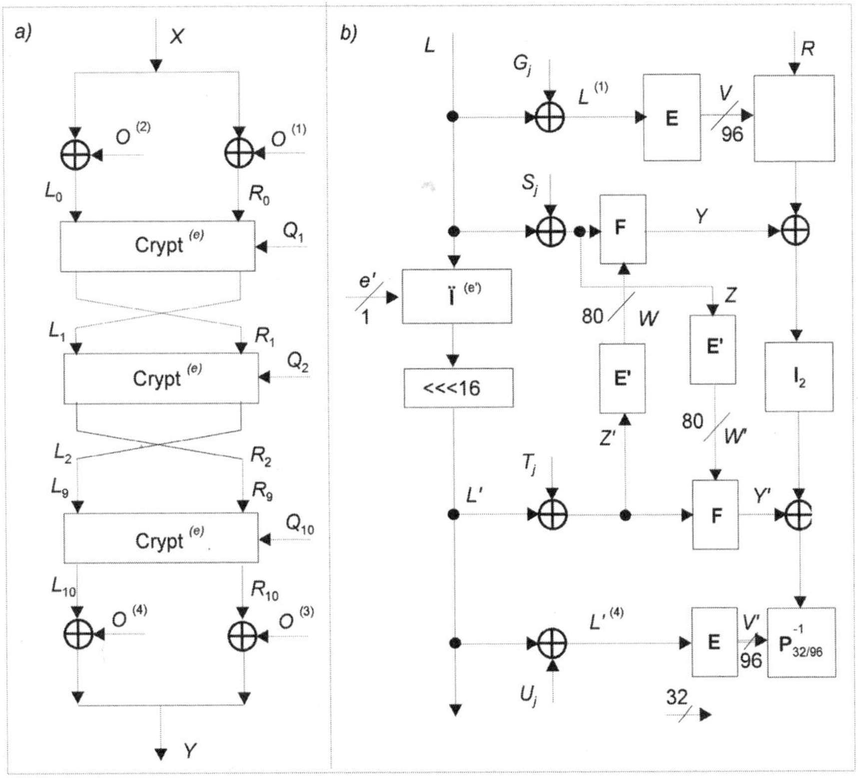

FIGURE 3.4 The general scheme of the DDP-64 cipher (a) and the procedure of its round transformation ***Crypt***$^{(e)}$ (b).

of four 32-bit subkeys K_i, $i = 1, 2, 3, 4$: $K = (K_1, K_2, K_3, K_4)$. Each round key Q_j is made up of four independent round subkeys $G_j, S_j, T_j, U_j \in GF(2)^{32}$, which means that $Q_j = (G_j, S_j, T_j, U_j)$. Table 3.1 describes the key schedule using subkeys O_1, O_2, O_3, and O_4, which are outputs of the subkeys permutation block shown in Figure 3.5a. The subkeys permutations block is made up of two $\mathbf{P}^{(e)}_{2\times32/1}$ CPBs. The first $\mathbf{P}^{(e)}_{2\times32/1}$ is supplied with the pair of subkeys K_1 and K_3, and the second block accepts the pair of subkeys K_2 and K_4. The output subkeys O_i depend on the value e. When $e = 0$, $O_i = K_i$ for $i = 1, 2, 3, 4$. If $e = 0$, then $O_1 = K_3$, $O_3 = K_1$, $O_2 = K_4$, and $O_4 = K_2$.

TABLE 3.1 Key Schedule and Specification of the Value of Bit E′ in the Encryption (E = 0) and Decryption (E = 1) Modes

j =	1	2	3	4	5	6	7	8	9	10
G_j =	O_3	O_2	O_1	O_4	O_3	O_3	O_4	O_1	O_2	O_3
S_j =	O_2	O_1	O_4	O_3	O_4	O_4	O_3	O_4	O_1	O_2
T_j =	O_4	O_3	O_2	O_1	O_2	O_2	O_1	O_2	O_3	O_4
U_j =	O_1	O_4	O_3	O_2	O_1	O_1	O_2	O_3	O_4	O_1
e′ (e = 0)	1	0	1	1	0	1	1	1	0	1
e′ (e = 1)	0	1	0	0	0	1	0	0	1	0

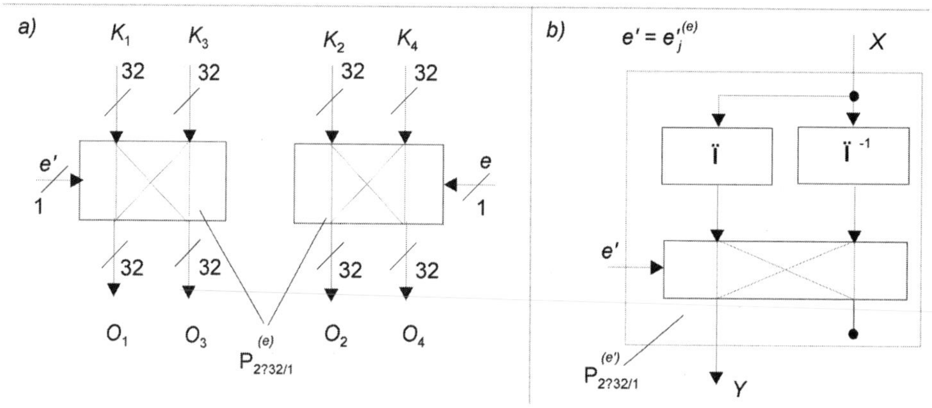

FIGURE 3.5 Transposition of subkeys (a) and the structure of the switched permutation (b).

The encryption procedure is carried out as follows. The input data block X is divided into two 32-bit subgroups L and R. Then, the data encryption is carried out according to the following algorithm:

1. Carry out the initial transformation.
2. Sequentially increasing the value j by one, from $j = 1$ to $j = 9$, carry out the following transformations:
   a. Transform (L_j, R_j): $(L_j, R_j) := \mathbf{Crypt}(L_{j-1}, R_{j-1}, Q_j)$.
   b. Swap data subgroups: $(L_j, R_j) := (R_j, L_j)$.

3. Transform (L_9, R_9): $(L_{10}, R_{10}) :=$ **Crypt**(L_9, R_9, Q_{10}).
4. Carry out the final transformation.

Switched permutations $\Pi^{(e')}$ is implemented using the $\mathbf{P}^{(e')}_{2\times32/1}$ CPB and two fixed mutually inverse permutations Π and Π^{-1}, as shown in Figure 3.5b. From the scheme provided in this illustration, it is clear that the following relationships take place: $\Pi^{(0)}= \Pi$ and $\Pi^{(1)}= \Pi^{-1}$. The permutation Π being used is described as follows:

$$(1,4,7,2,5,8,3,6)(9,12,15,10,13,16,11,14)$$
$$(17,20,23,18,21,24,19,22)(25,28,31,26,29,32,27,30).$$

As can be seen from the algorithm description, subkeys K_i $(i = 1, 2, 3, 4)$ are directly used in each round without carrying out any precomputations over them. After addition to the left data subgroup, keys G and U are used for forming controlling vectors V and V', which determine implementation of the current modifications of the permutations implemented using blocks $\mathbf{P}_{32/96}$ and $\mathbf{P}^{-1}_{32/96}$, respectively. Subkeys S and T are also added to the left data subgroup; however, after completion of this operation the result is transformed using block **F**. Note that the round transformation doesn't represent an involution for two reasons: the execution of the $\Pi^{(e')}$ operation over the left data subgroup, and the use of mutually inverse CPBs controlled by binary vectors having different values in the right branch of the round transformation. The difference between the values of controlling vectors V and V' is due to the transformation of the left data subgroup and to the use of different subkeys when forming the input values of the extension blocks corresponding to the $\mathbf{P}_{32/96}$ and $\mathbf{P}^{-1}_{32/96}$ operations (see Figure 3.4b). To invert a certain j-th round of encryption, appropriate subkeys must be exchanged, and bit e' must be inverted. That is, at the $(11-j)$-th round of decryption, the following transformation must be carried out:

$$X' = \boldsymbol{Crypt}^{(1)}(Y, Q_{11-j}),$$

where $Q_{11-j} = (U_j, T_j, S_j, G_j)$, and the value was obtained using the $Y = \boldsymbol{Crypt}^{(0)}(X, Q_j)$ transformation, where $Q_j = (G_j, S_j, T_j, U_j)$. Table 3.1 specifies the values of bit e' for encryption $(e = 0)$ and for decryption $(e = 1)$.

The use of fixed permutations representing involutions is typical for the round transformation of the DDP-64 cipher. The cyclic-shift operation $<<< 16$, carried out over the left data subgroups is used for specifying the "symmetric" use of the most significant (L_h) and the least significant (L_l) parts of the data subgroup L when executing two variable bit permutations carried out using operational blocks **F**. Permutation involution $\mathbf{I}_2$, carried out over the right data subgroup is used for specifying the influence of each input bit of the block $\mathbf{P}_{32/96}$ on 31 output bits of block $\mathbf{P}^{-1}{}_{32/96}$ in the case when $V = V'$. In this case, every i-th input bit doesn't affect only the i-th output bit. Note that if the $\mathbf{I}_2$ permutation is not used, then in the aforementioned case, every input bit of $\mathbf{P}_{32/96}$ has the effect only to one output bit of $\mathbf{P}^{-1}{}_{32/96}$. The $\mathbf{I}_2$ permutation has a simple structure and can be described by two cyclic shifts by 8 bits:

$$Y = \mathbf{I}_2(X_1,X_2) = (X_1{}^{<<<8}, X_2{}^{<<<8}).$$

This permutation improves the resulting controlled permutation, corresponding to sequential execution of the $\mathbf{P}_{32/96(V)}$ and $\mathbf{P}^{-1}{}_{32/96(V'}$. operations. Actually, even if $V = V'$, the superposition $\mathbf{P}_{32/96(V)} \circ \mathbf{P}^{-1}{}_{32/96(V)}$ forms an efficient controlled permutation, all modifications of which are permutation involutions. In the general case, we obtain that $V \neq V'$, because the data are combined with different subkeys when forming controlling vectors that correspond to operations $\mathbf{P}_{32/96(V)}$ and $\mathbf{P}^{-1}{}_{32/96(V)}$. Therefore, the influence of each input bit of block $\mathbf{P}_{32/96}$ is extended to all output bits of block $\mathbf{P}^{-1}{}_{32/96}$. To study the role of the fixed permutation between two mutually inverse CP operations, many statistical experiments were conducted previously (for example, see "Fast DDP-Based Ciphers: Design and Differential Analysis of Cobra-H64" by Moldovyan N. A). These experiments have shown that the use of such permutation considerably improves the properties of the transformation carried out by two mutually inverse blocks of controlled permutations.

The structure of block **F** is shown in Figure 3.6. To ensure nonlinearity of all linear combinations of output bits of this block, internal extending and compressing mapping were used. Block **F** includes two three-layered CP blocks $\mathbf{P}_{32/48}$ and one $\mathbf{P}^{-1}{}_{32/48}$ block separated by a fixed permutation Π', which is described as follows:

$$\Pi' = (1,33)(2,9)(3,17)(4,25)(5)(6,13)(7,21)(8,34,29,40)$$
$$(10,35)(11,18)(12,26)(14)(15,36,22,38)$$
$$(16,30)(19,37)(20,27)(23)(24,31)(28,39)(32).$$

The structure of three-layered $\mathbf{P}_{32/48}$ CP blocks and $\mathbf{P}^{-1}{}_{32/48}$ blocks made up of the $\mathbf{P}_{8/12}$ and $\mathbf{P}^{-1}{}_{8/12}$ blocks is shown in Figure 3.6b. The input value $Z = (Z_1, Z_2, Z_3, Z_4)$ of block **F** is simultaneously the input value of block $\mathbf{P}_{32/48}$. The binary vector $D = (D_1, D_2, D_3, D_4)$ generated at the output of block $\mathbf{P}_{32/48}$ is extended by connecting a constant binary vector $C = (10101010)$ to the size of 40 bits. The extended vector (D_1, D_2, D_3, D_4, C) obtained using the method is supplied to the input of the Π′ permutation. At the output of this permutation, the $(H_1, H_2, H_3, H_4, H_5)$ vector is formed, which is divided into two vectors: (H_1, H_2, H_3, H_4) and H_5. The first of these vectors is supplied to the input of the second internal $\mathbf{P}^{-1}{}_{32/48}$ CPB, and the

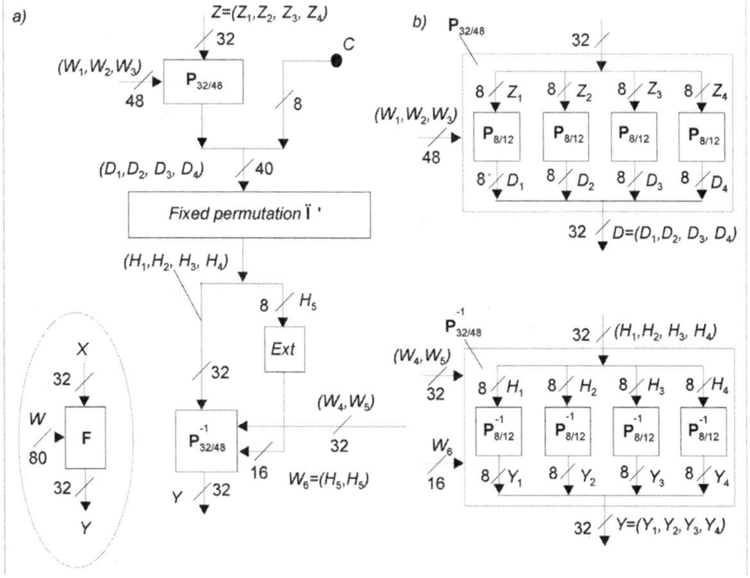

FIGURE 3.6 The structure of block **F**, implementing nonlinear cryptographic transformation using variable permutations.

second vector is used as part of the controlling vector when carrying out the $\mathbf{P}^{-1}_{32/48}$ operation. The output value of block $\mathbf{P}^{-1}_{32/48}$ is simultaneously the output of block **F**.

The controlling vector $W = (W_1, W_2, W_3, W_4, W_5)$ of the block **F**, where $W_1, W_2, W_3, W_4, W_5 \in GF(2)^{16}$, is used as follows. Binary vectors W_1, W_2, and W_3 control the first, second, and third active layers of block $\mathbf{P}_{32/48}$, respectively, and vectors W_4 and W_3 control the first and second active layers of block $\mathbf{P}^{-1}_{32/48}$, respectively. Vector W_6, controlling the third layer of block $\mathbf{P}^{-1}_{32/48}$, is formed using an 8-bit vector H_5 according to the expression $W_6 = (H_5, H_5)$.

As can be easily seen, having a fixed key, the left data subgroup defines the value of vector (D_1, D_2, D_3, D_4); and two bits with arbitrary numbers from each of vectors D_1, D_2, D_3, D_4 are moved to vector H_5, being replaced by one 1 and one 0 bit of the constant C. Each of the bits of vector (Z_1, Z_2, Z_3, Z_4) with the probability of 1/4 can be replaced. The probability of the bit's being replaced by zero bits is equal to 1/8, and the probability of the bit's being replaced by 1 bit is the same. As a result of such a replacement, the permutation carried out by block **F** arbitrarily changes the parity of the weight of its output value.

3.3 EXTENDING THE CLASS OF CONTROLLED OPERATIONS USING ELEMENTARY CONTROLLED INVOLUTIONS

In the previous section, the efficiency of variable permutations as a cryptographic primitive was demonstrated. At the same time, the most important issue was the control over the choice of different modifications of data-dependent bit permutations. For this reason, the issue of searching for new types of data-dependent operations that could be easily implemented in the form of fast electronic circuits gains urgency. With this goal in mind, it was suggested to replace all elementary $\mathbf{P}_{2/1}$ blocks by some other controlled elements (CEs) of minimal size (that is, having 20-bit input and output and 1-bit controlling input) while preserving the general topology of controlled permutations blocks. Such controlled elements were suggested to be used as a standard design unit. To achieve this goal, it is necessary to formulate several criteria for choosing specific variants of CEs.

Because $\mathbf{P}_{2/1}$ blocks ensure building cryptographically efficient controlled operations, they can serve as a prototype for choosing CEs; that is, for formulating the criteria for choosing specific CEs from all possible variants. Provided that the required criteria have been formulated, this task can be easily solved by exhaustive search because of the small CE size. Denote the general form of CE as $\mathbf{F}_{2/1}$. In general, the CE can be described as a pair of boolean functions (Figure 3.7).

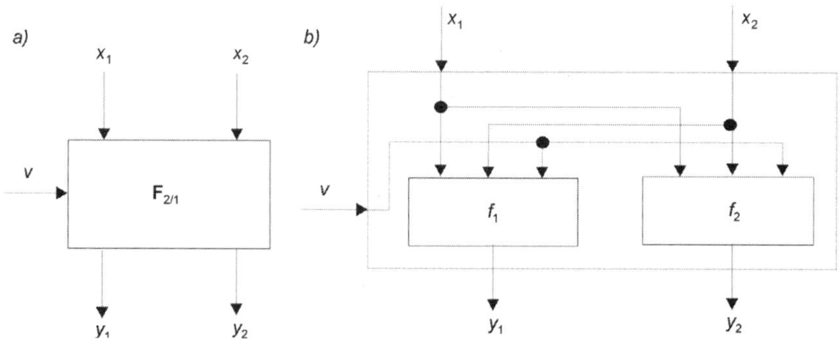

FIGURE 3.7 Controlled element (a) and its representation in the form of a pair of boolean functions (b).

Another representation of a CE is a pair of permutations of the size 2×2, where one of the permutations is carried out over a 2-bit vector (x_1, x_2) having $v = 0$, and the second having $v = 1$. A pair of such permutations can be represented as a pair of tables in the form of the pair of elementary transformation schemes. In particular, the schematic representation of the $\mathbf{P}_{2/1}$ block appears as shown in Figure 3.8.

An elementary switch can be characterized as follows. Each of the two modifications of the elementary transformations is an involution; that is, $\mathbf{P}_{2/1}$ represents

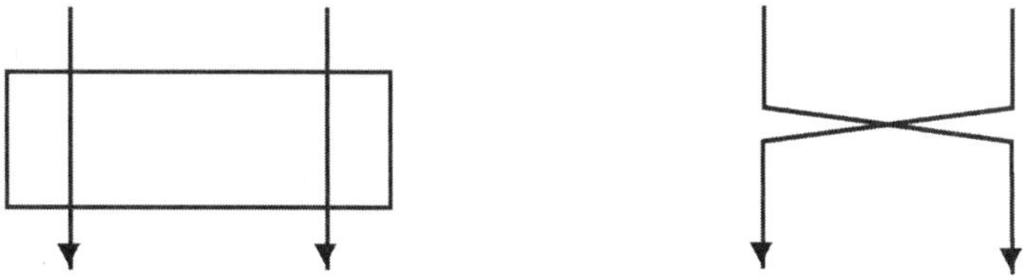

FIGURE 3.8 Schematic representation of the $P_{2/1}$ block in the form of two elementary bijective transformations carried out over a 2-bit vector (x_1, x_2) provided that $v = 0$ (a) and $v = 1$ (b).

an elementary controlled involution. Obviously, both elementary modifications are bijective; consequently, each pair of boolean functions describing the $\mathbf{P}_{2/1}$ CE is balanced. boolean functions f_1 and f_2 are nonlinear:

$$y_1 = f_1(x_1,x_2,v) = x_1v \oplus x_2v \oplus x_1; y_2 = f_2(x_1,x_2,v) = x_1v \oplus x_2v \oplus x_2.$$

Nonlinear boolean functions of three variables have the same value of nonlinearity in the sense of the minimal distance to the set of affine boolean functions of three variables. With the account of the aforementioned, it is possible to suggest the following basic criteria for choosing CEs:

C1: Boolean functions $y_1 = f_1(x_1, x_2, v)$ and $y_2 = f_2(x_1, x_2, v)$ must have the maximum nonlinearity.

C2: Modifications of elementary transformations formed by $\mathbf{F}^{(v)}{}_{2/1}$ controlled elements—namely, $\mathbf{F}^{(0)}{}_{2/1}$ and $\mathbf{F}^{(1)}{}_{2/1}$—must be different and represent an elementary bijective transformation of the form (x_1, x_2) Æ (y_1, y_2).

C3: Each of the two modifications of the $\mathbf{F}^{(v)}{}_{2/1}$ controlled element must be an involution.

Although among 2×2 permutations there are only linear permutations, nonlinearity of each of the CE outputs is implemented because of the dependency of the elementary modification on the controlling bit. Two variants of searching for CEs might be used. The first method consists of exhaustive search of all possible pairs of boolean functions $y_1 = f_1(x_1, x_2, v)$ and $y_2 = f_2(x_1, x_2, v)$, while the second consists of exhaustive search of all possible pairs of $\mathbf{F}^{(0)}{}_{2/1}$ and $\mathbf{F}^{(1)}{}_{2/1}$ modifications, which can be specified as substitution tables or schematically.

The latter representation is more illustrative and simple, because the search is limited to trying 90 pairs of modifications out of 10 existing elementary involutions, shown in Figure 3.9.

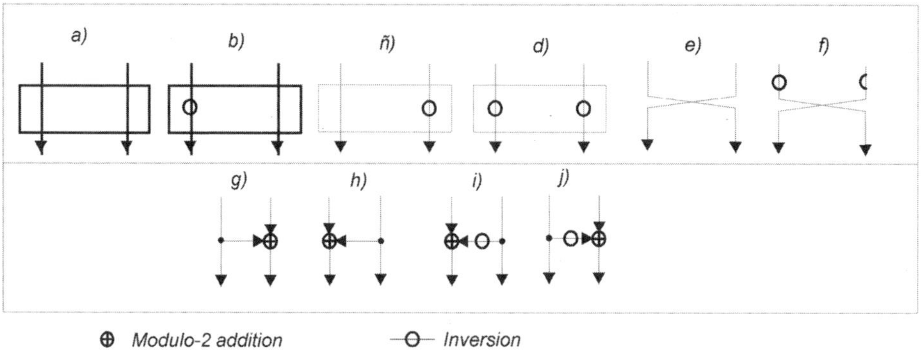

FIGURE 3.9 Schematic representation of all existing $(x_1, x_2) \rightarrow (y_1, y_2)$ transformations representing involutions.

There are 256 possible different boolean functions (BFs) of three variables. To limit the exhaustive search range, it is necessary to exploit the fact that from Criterion 2 (C2), which requires the bijectivity of each of modifications of $\mathbf{F}^{(0)}{}_{2/1}$ and $\mathbf{F}^{(1)}{}_{2/1}$, it follows that boolean functions must be balanced. This considerably limits the possible variants for exhaustive search from the very beginning. Thus, when trying the pairs of different boolean functions it is necessary to initially select the complete set of balanced boolean functions, the number of which is 70, and then choose all nonlinear ones, which limits the number of boolean functions that are of any interest down to 56. After that, it only remains to carry out an exhaustive search among 56×55 variants of pairs of nonlinear balanced boolean functions of three variables. This number of variants, equal to 3080, is considerably greater than the number of variants for exhaustive search by pairs of elementary involutions. When using the first approach, the CE representation will be obtained in algebraic form, while the second approach produces an illustrative schematic form. However, as the result, the same CEs will be chosen, satisfying criteria C1–C3.

After choosing the required controlled elements using the second approach, the algebraic representation can be easily derived using the following approach. For any of the two possible modifications of the chosen CE, it is possible to write boolean functions of two variables describing the outputs y_1 and y_2. For example, assume that modification of $\mathbf{F}^{(0)}{}_{2/1}$ is described by a pair of boolean functions $y_1 = f'_1(x_1, x_2)$ and $y_2 = f'_2(x_1, x_2)$, and modification of $\mathbf{F}^{(1)}{}_{2/1}$ is described by the pair $y_1 = f''_1(x_1, x_2)$ and $y_2 = f''_2(x_1, x_2)$. Then, the pair of boolean functions of three variables describing CE can easily be written in the form of the following two formulae:

$$y_1 = (v \oplus 1)f'_1(x_1, x_2) \oplus vf''_1(x_1, x_2)\,;$$
$$y_2 = (v \oplus 1)f'_2(x_1, x_2) \oplus vf''_2(x_1, x_2)\,.$$

Using the second approach, the complete set of CEs satisfying the C1–C3 criteria was found. This set of criteria is represented in Table 3.2, the rows and columns of which are labeled with lowercase Latin characters denoting 10 elementary involutions shown in Figure 3.9. The "+" or "⊕" sign at the intersection of rows and columns specifies that modifications corresponding to the given row and column make a pair that satisfies criteria C1–C3. The row identifies modification $\mathbf{F}^{(1)}{}_{2/1}$, and the column corresponds to modification $\mathbf{F}^{(0)}{}_{2/1}$. From the provided set of CEs, two variants denoted by the "⊕" sign correspond to switching elements. In particular, the pair e/a corresponds to the elementary block $\mathbf{P}_{2/1}$, which initially was chosen as a prototype. Let CE described as the pair a/e be denoted by $\mathbf{P'}_{2/1}$. These two switched elements are related by the equations $\mathbf{P}^{(0)}{}_{2/1} = \mathbf{P'}^{(1)}{}_{2/1}$ and $\mathbf{P}^{(1)}{}_{2/1} = \mathbf{P'}^{(0)}{}_{2/1}$.

TABLE 3.2 Complete Set of CEs Satisfying Criteria C1–C3

$F^{(1)}\backslash F^{(0)}$	a	b	c	d	e	f	g	h	i	j
a					⊕	+				
b					+	+				
c					+	+				
d					+	+				
e	⊕	+	+	+			+	+	+	+
f	+	+	+	+			+	+	+	+
g					+	+		+	+	
h					+	+	+			+
i					+	+	+			+
j					+	+		+	+	

Thus, 40 variants of different CEs have been obtained, which can be used for synthesis of data-dependent operations. Differential characteristics of cryptographic primitives are among the most important.

Because differential characteristics of controlled operations depend on the size of the input and the topology, describing such characteristics for practically important variants of controlled operations built using each of the discovered CEs is an unrealistic job. However, this task can be solved for each individual CE. This is an interesting task, because differential characteristics of the first standard design element define differential characteristics for the given topology of the operational block. Figure 3.10 shows the variants of all possible differences related to a controlled element.

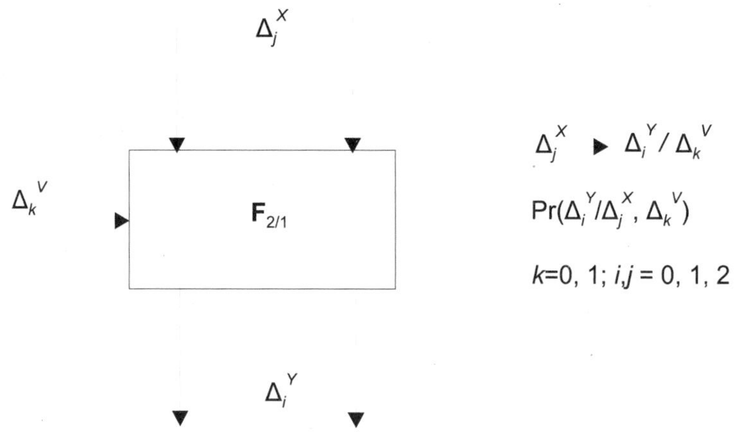

FIGURE 3.10 Possible variants of differences related to a CE.

The results of investigation of probabilities of all nontrivial differential characteristics of all 40 variants of controlled elements are presented in Table 3.3. The notable fact is that characteristics turned out to be identical for four subsets of CEs, among which two subsets are distinguished by considerably smaller predictability of the output difference. Because of this, these subsets are preferred for building controlled operations. When considering circuit representations of CE modifications belonging to the subset related to the first column in Table 3.3, it can be noticed that neither of them includes the transposition operation. Denote CEs from this subset as $\mathbf{S}_{2/1}$. The subset of controlled elements related to the second column is characterized by the fact that its elements include bit transposition (with or without inversion of both bits) as one of the elementary modifications; at the same time, the second elementary modification is one of modifications typical for $\mathbf{S}_{2/1}$ elements. Elements of the second subset are denoted as $\mathbf{R}_{2/1}$, which appear the most promising for building controlled operating blocks. Subsets of CEs related to the third and fourth columns are classified as elements of types $\mathbf{Z}''_{2/1}$ and $\mathbf{Z}'_{2/1}$, respectively. Element $\mathbf{P}_{2/1}$ relates to $\mathbf{Z}'_{2/1}$ controlled elements.

When considering circuit representations of CEs belonging to each subset, it is possible to discover that CEs shown in Figure 3.11 are typical for the $\{\mathbf{S}_{2/1}\}$ subset, CEs shown in Figure 3.12 are typical for the $\{\mathbf{R}_{2/1}\}$ subset, and CEs presented in Figure 3.13 are typical for the $\{\mathbf{Z}_{2/1}\} = \{\mathbf{Z}'_{2/1}, \mathbf{Z}''_{2/1}\}$ subset.

For all 40 controlled elementary involutions, based on their circuit representations, pairs of boolean functions were composed as follows: $y_1 = f_1(x_1, x_2, v)$ and $y_2 = f_2(x_1, x_2, v)$. Based on their analysis it was discovered that each output of CEs belonging to the $\{\mathbf{Z}_{2/1}\}$ subset is described by a boolean function containing the terms

TABLE 3.3 Differential Characteristics of 40 Controlled Involutions of Minimal Size (divided into four subsets)

CE types i j k	g/h, g/i, h/g, h/j, i/g, i/j, j/h, j/i	e/g, e/h, e/i, e/j, f/g, f/h, f/i, f/j, g/e, g/f, h/e, h/f, i/e, i/f, j/e, j/f	b/e, b/f, c/e, c/f, e/b, e/c, f/b, f/c	a/e, a/f, d/e, d/f, e/a, e/d, f/d, f/a
0 0 1	1/4	1/4	0	1/2
1 0 1	1/2	1/2	1	0
2 0 1	1/4	1/4	0	1/2
0 1 1	1/4	1/4	1/2	0
1 1 1	1/2	1/2	0	1
2 1 1	1/4	1/4	1/2	0
1 1 0	1/2	3/4	1	1
2 1 0	1/2	1/4	0	0
1 2 0	1	1/2	0	0
2 2 0	0	1/2	1	1
0 2 1	1/4	1/4	0	1/2
1 2 1	1/2	1/2	1	0
2 2 1	1/4	1/4	0	1/2

x_1v and x_2v, because their sum is a linear Boolean function and, consequently, such CEs are linear cryptographic primitives. For CEs related to subset $\{\mathbf{S}_{2/1}\}$, boolean functions $y_1 = f_1(x_1, x_2, v)$ and $y_2 = f_2(x_1, x_2, v)$ contain only one quadratic term; therefore, quadratic terms in these functions are different. Because of this, the sum $y_1 \oplus y_2$ represents a nonlinear boolean function, and CEs as such are nonlinear primitives. For CEs related to subset $\{\mathbf{R}_{2/1}\}$, one of the $y_1 = f_1(x_1, x_2, v)$ and $y_2 = f_2(x_1, x_2, v)$ boolean functions contains only one quadratic term, while another function contains two such terms, one of which matches the quadratic term of the first Boolean function. The sum $y_1 \oplus y_2$ is a nonlinear boolean function with one quadratic term; that is, CEs of the $\mathbf{R}_{2/1}$ type are nonlinear cryptographic primitives. Thus, CEs belonging to subsets $\{\mathbf{S}_{2/1}\}$ and $\{\mathbf{R}_{2/1}\}$ satisfy another important criterion:

> **C4**: The sum of boolean functions of a CE, $y_1 = f_1(x_1, x_2, v)$ and $y_2 = f_2(x_1, x_2, v)$ must represent a nonlinear boolean function with maximum possible nonlinearity.

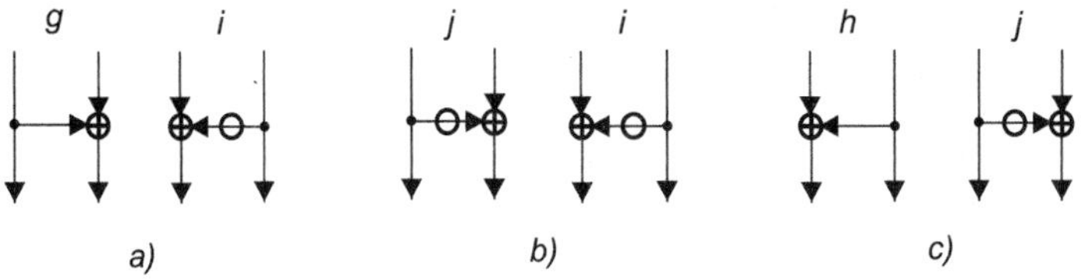

FIGURE 3.11 Typical $\mathbf{S}_{2/1}$ CEs represented by pairs of elementary modifications: g/i (a), j/i (b), and h/j (c).

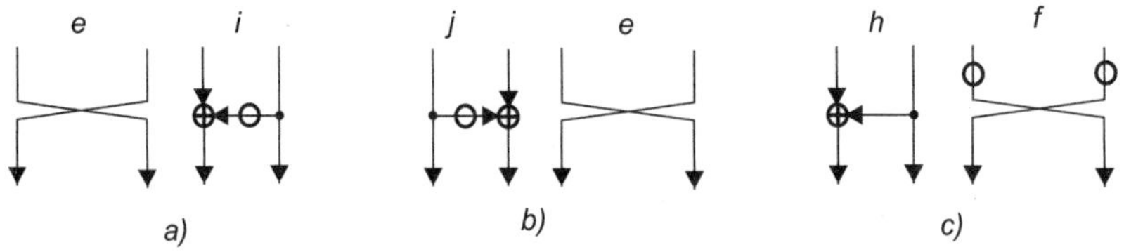

FIGURE 3.12 Typical $\mathbf{R}_{2/1}$ CEs represented by pairs of elementary modifications: e/i (a), j/e (b), and h/f (c).

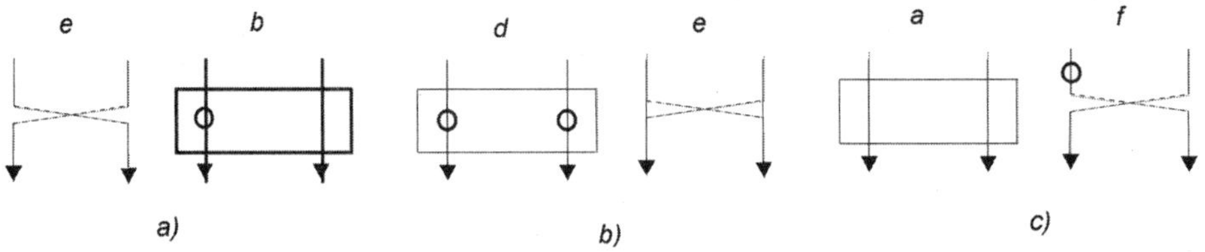

FIGURE 3.13 Typical $\mathbf{Z}_{2/1}$ CEs represented by pairs of elementary modifications: e/b (a), d/e (b), and a/f (c).

In all cases, quadratic terms are products of the controlling bit v and one of the input bits. This circumstance definitely shows that using only the key for forming the controlling vector in CPBs or other operational blocks built based on $\mathbf{S}_{2/1}$ and $\mathbf{R}_{2/1}$ CEs will result in the controlled operation carrying out linear transformation. Only by specifying the control on the part of the data being transformed ensures nonlinear mode for controlled operations built on the basis of substitution-permutation networks with CEs of minimal size. In addition, it is obvious that $\mathbf{S}_{2/1}$ and $\mathbf{R}_{2/1}$ elements are preferred in comparison to $\mathbf{Z}_{2/1}$ CEs, including $\mathbf{P}_{2/1}$ elements, both by the nonlinearity properties and by differential characteristics. This allows for drawing a conclusion that elements of the $\mathbf{S}_{2/1}$ and $\mathbf{R}_{2/1}$ types can be used for building promising controlled operational blocks for development of fast hardware cryptosystems. Complete characteristics of CEs belonging to $\{\mathbf{S}_{2/1}\}$ and $\{\mathbf{R}_{2/1}\}$ subsets are presented in Table 3.4. Evaluation of the hardware implementation of nonlinear CEs using standard 0.33-mkm technology is presented in Table 3.5.

TABLE 3.4 The Complete Set of CEs that Are Controlled Nonlinear Involution

CE	CE type	$f_1(x_1,x_2,v)$		$f_2(x_1,x_2,v)$	
		ANF	TT	ANF	TT
g/e	R	$x_1v\oplus x_2v\oplus x_1$	00011011	$x_2v\oplus x_1\oplus x_2$	00101101
g/h	S	$x_2v\oplus x_1$	00011110	$x_1v\oplus x_1\oplus x_2$	00111001
e/g	R	$x_1v\oplus x_2v\oplus x_2$	00100111	$x_2v\oplus x_1$	00011110
e/h	R	$x_1v\oplus x_2$	00110110	$x_1v\oplus x_2v\oplus x_1$	00011011
h/g	S	$x_2v\oplus x_1\oplus x_2$	00101101	$x_1v\oplus x_2$	00110110
h/e	R	$x_1v\oplus x_1\oplus x_2$	00111001	$x_1v\oplus x_2v\oplus x_2$	00100111
g/i	S	$x_2v\oplus x_1\oplus v$	01001011	$x_1v\oplus x_1\oplus x_2$	00111001
g/f	R	$x_1v\oplus x_2v\oplus x_1\oplus v$	01001110	$x_2v\oplus x_2\oplus x_1\oplus v$	01111000
i/g	S	$x_2v\oplus x_2\oplus x_1\oplus v\oplus 1$	10000111	$x_1v\oplus x_2$	00110110
f/g	R	$x_1v\oplus x_2v\oplus x_2\oplus v\oplus 1$	10001101	$x_2v\oplus x_1\oplus v\oplus 1$	10110100
i/f	R	$x_1v\oplus x_2\oplus x_1\oplus 1$	11000110	$x_1v\oplus x_2v\oplus x_2\oplus v$	01110010
f/i	R	$x_1v\oplus x_2\oplus 1$	11001001	$x_1v\oplus x_2v\oplus x_1\oplus v\oplus 1$	10110001
h/j	S	$x_2v\oplus x_1\oplus x_2$	00101101	$x_1v\oplus x_2\oplus v$	01100011
j/h	S	$x_2v\oplus x_1$	00011110	$x_1v\oplus x_2\oplus x_1\oplus v\oplus 1$	10010011
j/f	R	$x_1v\oplus x_2v\oplus x_1\oplus v$	01001110	$x_2v\oplus x_2\oplus x_1\oplus 1$	11010010
f/h	R	$x_1v\oplus x_2\oplus v\oplus 1$	10011100	$x_1v\oplus x_2v\oplus x_1\oplus v\oplus 1$	10110001
f/j	R	$x_1v\oplus x_2v\oplus x_2\oplus v\oplus 1$	10001101	$x_2v\oplus x_1\oplus 1$	11100001

→

CE	CE type	$f_1(x_1,x_2,v)$		$f_2(x_1,x_2,v)$	
		ANF	TT	ANF	TT
e/j	R	$x_1v\oplus x_2v\oplus x_2$	00100111	$x_2v\oplus x_1\oplus v$	01001011
j/e	R	$x_1v\oplus x_2v\oplus x_1$	00011011	$x_2v\oplus x_2\oplus x_1\oplus v\oplus 1$	10000111
j/i	S	$x_2v\oplus x_1\oplus v$	01001011	$x_1v\oplus x_2\oplus x_1\oplus v\oplus 1$	10010011
i/e	R	$x_1v\oplus x_2\oplus x_1\oplus v\oplus 1$	10010011	$x_1v\oplus x_2v\oplus x_2$	00100111
i/j	S	$x_2v\oplus x_2\oplus x_1\oplus v\oplus 1$	10000111	$x_1v\oplus x_2\oplus v$	01100011
h/f	R	$x_1v\oplus x_1\oplus x_2\oplus v$	01101100	$x_1v\oplus x_2v\oplus x_2\oplus u$	01110010
e/i	R	$x_1v\oplus x_2\oplus v$	01100011	$x_1v\oplus x_2v\oplus x_1$	00011011

In the aforementioned technology, $\mathbf{P}_{2/1}$ CEs are implemented using the area of 3 sqmil and operate at frequencies up to 2.12 GHz. The comparison demonstrates that among nonlinear CEs are elements that are close to $\mathbf{P}_{2/1}$ switching elements by their operating speed, but at the same time more economical by their implementation. This allows us to conclude that with the account of the comparison of nonlinearity properties and differential characteristics, it can be expected that characteristics of hardware ciphers based on variable operations and built on the basis of nonlinear CEs will considerably exceed the implementation characteristics of the DDP-64, CIKS-1, and SPECTR-H64 ciphers.

3.4 FULL CLASSIFICATION OF $F_{2/1}$ NONLINEAR ELEMENTS

In the previous section, the complete class of CEs that represent elementary controlled involutions was built. However, there arises the problem of enumerating all CEs of minimal size that can be used for building controlled operations similar to CPBs by their cryptographic properties. That CEs are involutions is a useful property that simplifies building of controlled operational blocks. However, the most important topologies of CPBs can also be implemented using mutually inverse CEs. For example, it is possible to use $\mathbf{P}_{32/96}$ blocks as the prototype. Therefore, the promising strategy consists in searching for all possible variants of CEs that meet the requirements of the C1 and C2 criteria, and then separating from this class a subset of CEs that would satisfy the additional nonlinearity criterion (C4). Solving this problem allows us to get the full pattern of all possible variants and provides the possibility of choosing the most suitable elements for solving the problem of synthesizing controlled operations.

The analysis of all possible combinations of two nonlinear balanced boolean functions presented in Table 3.5 allowed for discovering 288 variants of CEs satisfying C1 and C2 criteria, and 192 variants of CEs meeting the requirements of the C1, C2, and C3 criteria (Table 3.6).

TABLE 3.5 Main Characteristics of the Hardware Implementation of the $\mathbf{S}_{2/1}$ and $\mathbf{R}_{2/1}$

CE	CE type	ASIC 0.33 mkm		CE	CE type	ASIC 0.33 mkm	
		Area, sqmil	Frequency, GHz			Area, sqmil**	Frequency, GHz
g/e	R	3	0.95	h/j	S	3	1.35
g/h	S	3	1.37	j/h	S	3	0.59
e/g	R	2	1.92	j/f	R	3	1.28
e/h	R	2	1.92	f/h	R	3	0.89
h/g	S	3	1.35	f/j	R	2	1.72
h/e	R	3	0.95	e/j	R	4	0.95
g/i	S	3	1.37	j/e	R	4	0.60
g/f	R	4	0.83	j/i	S	4	0.74
i/g	S	4	0.74	i/e	R	4	0.60
f/g	R	3	0.89	i/j	S	4	0.63
i/f	R	3	0.89	h/f	R	4	0.83
f/i	R	2	1.72	e/i	R		

* These evaluations were obtained at the University of Patras (Greece).

** The area of the used area of a semiconductor chip is provided in technological units sqmil; 1 sqmil = 7.45×10^{-4} mm².

TABLE 3.6 Complete Class of Nonlinear CEs (the $\{\mathbf{S}_{2/1}, \mathbf{R}_{2/1}\}$ subset)

No.	TT		No.	TT		No.	TT		No.	TT	
	10	16		10	16		10	16		10	16
			73	00100111	4B	145	10000111	87	217	11000110	C6
				00100111	27		00011011	1B		00011110	1E
2	00011011	1B							218	11000110	C6
	00101101	2D								00100111	27
3	00011011	1B	75	01001011	4B	147	10000111	87			
	00110110	36		00111001	39		00110110	36			
4	00011011	1B	76	01001011	4B				220	11000110	C6
	01100011	63		01101100	6C					01001011	4B
			77	01001011	4B	149	10000111	87			
				01110010	72		01001110	4E			
6	00011011	1B				150	10000111	87	222	11000110	C6
	01111000	78					01100011	63		01110010	72
7	00011011	1B				151	10000111	87	223	11000110	C6
	10000111	87					10011100	9C		10001101	8D
			80	01001011	4B	152	10000111	87			
				10001101	8D		10110001	B1			
9	00011011	1B	81	01001011	4B				225	11000110	C6
	10011100	9C		10010011	93					10110100	B4
10	00011011	1B	82	01001011	4B	154	10000111	87			
	11001001	C9		11000110	C6		11001001	C9			
11	00011011	1B							227	11000110	C6
	11010010	D2								11011000	D8
			84	01001011	4B	156	10000111	87	228	11000110	C6
				11011000	D8		11100100	E4		11100001	E1
13	00011110	1E							229	11001001	C9
	00100111	27								00011011	1B
			86	01001110	4E	158	10001101	8D	230	11001001	C9
				00101101	2D		00011110	1E		00101101	2D
15	00011110	1E	87	01001110	4E	159	10001101	8D			
	00111001	39		00110110	36		00111001	39			
16	00011110	1E	88	01001110	4E	160	10001101	8D	232	11001001	C9
	01101100	6C		01100011	63		01001011	4B		01001110	4E
17	00011110	1E									
	01110010	72									
			90	01001110	4E	162	10001101	8D	234	11001001	C9
				01111000	78		01101100	6C		01111000	78
			91	01001110	4E	163	10001101	8D	235	11001001	C9
				10000111	87		10010011	93		10000111	87
20	00011110	1E									
	10001101	8D									
21	00011110	1E	93	01001110	4E	165	10001101	8D	237	11001001	C9
	10010011	93		10011100	9C		10110100	B4		10110001	B1
22	00011110	1E	94	01001110	4E	166	10001101	8D			
	11000110	C6		11001001	C9		11000110	C6			
			95	01001110	4E	167	10001101	8D	239	11001001	C9
				11010010	D2		11100001	E1		11010010	D2
24	00011110	1E							240	11001001	C9
	11011000	D8								11100100	E4
			97	01100011	63	169	10010011	93	241	11010010	D2
				00011011	1B		00011110	1E		00011011	1B
26	00100111	27	98	01100011	63	170	10010011	93			
	00011110	1E		00101101	2D		00100111	27			
27	00100111	27							243	11010010	D2
	00111001	39								00110110	36
28	00100111	27	100	01100011	63	172	10010011	93			
	01001011	4B		01001110	4E		01001011	4B			
									245	11010010	D2
										01001110	4E
30	00100111	27	102	01100011	63	174	10010011	93	246	11010010	D2
	01101100	6C		01111000	78		01110010	72		01100011	63
31	00100111	27	103	01100011	63	175	10010011	93	247	11010010	D2
	10010011	93		10000111	87		10001101	8D		10011100	9C
									248	11010010	D2
										10110001	B1
33	00100111	27	105	01100011	63	177	10010011	93			
	10110100	B4		10110001	B1		10110100	B4			
34	00100111	27							250	11010010	D2
	11000110	C6								11001001	C9
35	00100111	27	107	01100011	63	179	10010011	93			
	11100001	E1		11010010	D2		11011000	D8			
			108	01100011	63	180	10010011	93	252	11010010	D2
				11100100	E4		11100001	E1		11100100	E4

No.	TT		No.	TT		No.	TT		No.	TT	
	10	16		10	16		10	16		10	16
37	00101101	2D	109	01101100	6C	181	10011100	9C			
	00011011	1B		00011110	1E		00011011	1B			
			110	01101100	6C	182	10011100	9C	254	11011000	D8
				00100111	27		00101101	2D		00011110	1E
39	00101101	2D							255	11011000	D8
	00110110	36								00111001	39
			112	01101100	6C	184	10011100	9C	256	11011000	D8
				01001011	4B		01001110	4E		01001011	4B
41	00101101	2D									
	01001110	4E									
42	00101101	2D	114	01101100	6C	186	10011100	9C	258	11011000	D8
	01100011	63		01110010	72		01111000	78		01101100	6C
43	00101101	2D	115	01101100	6C	187	10011100	9C	259	11011000	D8
	10011100	9C		10001101	8D		10000111	87		10010011	93
44	00101101	2D									
	10110001	B1									
			117	01101100	6C	189	10011100	9C	261	11011000	D8
				10110100	B4		10110001	B1		10110100	B4
46	00101101	2D							262	11011000	D8
	11001001	C9								11000110	C6
			119	01101100	6C	191	10011100	9C	263	11011000	D8
				11011000	D8		11010010	D2		11100001	E1
48	00101101	2D	120	01101100	6C	192	10011100	9C			
	11100100	E4		11100001	E1		11100100	E4			
49	00110110	36							265	11100001	E1
	00011011	1B								00100111	27
50	00110110	36	122	01110010	72	194	10110001	B1			
	00101101	2D		00011110	1E		00101101	2D			
			123	01110010	72	195	10110001	B1	267	11100001	E1
				00111001	39		00110110	36		00111001	39
52	00110110	36	124	01110010	72	196	10110001	B1	268	11100001	E1
	01001110	4E		01001011	4B		01100011	63		01101100	6C
									269	11100001	E1
										01110010	72
54	00110110	36	126	01110010	72	198	10110001	B1			
	01111000	78		01101100	6C		01111000	78			
55	00110110	36	127	01110010	72	199	10110001	B1			
	10000111	87		10010011	93		10000111	87			
									272	11100001	E1
										10001101	8D
57	00110110	36	129	01110010	72	201	10110001	B1	273	11100001	E1
	10110001	B1		10110100	B4		10011100	9C		10010011	93
			130	01110010	72	202	10110001	B1	274	11100001	E1
				11000110	C6		11001001	C9		11000110	C6
59	00110110	36	131	01110010	72	203	10110001	B1			
	11010010	D2		11100001	E1		11010010	D2			
60	00110110	36							276	11100001	E1
	11100100	E4								11011000	D8
61	00111001	39	133	01111000	78	205	10110100	B4			
	00011110	1E		00011011	1B		00100111	27			
62	00111001	39							278	11100100	E4
	00100111	27								00101101	2D
			135	01111000	78	207	10110100	B4	279	11100100	E4
				00110110	36		00111001	39		00110110	36
64	00111001	39				208	10110100	B4	280	11100100	E4
	01001011	4B					01101100	6C		01100011	63
			137	01111000	78	209	10110100	B4			
				01001110	4E		01110010	72			
66	00111001	39	138	01111000	78				282	11100100	E4
	01110010	72		01100011	63					01111000	78
67	00111001	39	139	01111000	78				283	11100100	E4
	10001101	8D		10011100	9C					10000111	87
			140	01111000	78	212	10110100	B4			
				10110001	B1		10001101	8D			
69	00111001	39				213	10110100	B4	285	11100100	E4
	10110100	B4					10010011	93		10011100	9C
			142	01111000	78	214	10110100	B4	286	11100100	E4
				11001001	C9		11000110	C6		11001001	C9
71	00111001	39							287	11100100	E4
	11011000	D8								11010010	D2
72	00111001	39	144	01111000	78	216	10110100	B4			
	11100001	E1		11100100	E4		11011000	D8			

For further classification and determining pairs of boolean functions describing the selected CEs, it is convenient to represent CEs using circuit representation; that is, in the form of pairs of $\mathbf{F}^{(0)}{}_{2/1}$ and $\mathbf{F}^{(1)}{}_{2/1}$, which represent elementary bijective transformations of the type $(x_1, x_2) \rightarrow (y_1, y_2)$. All possible variants of such transformations are presented in Figure 3.14.

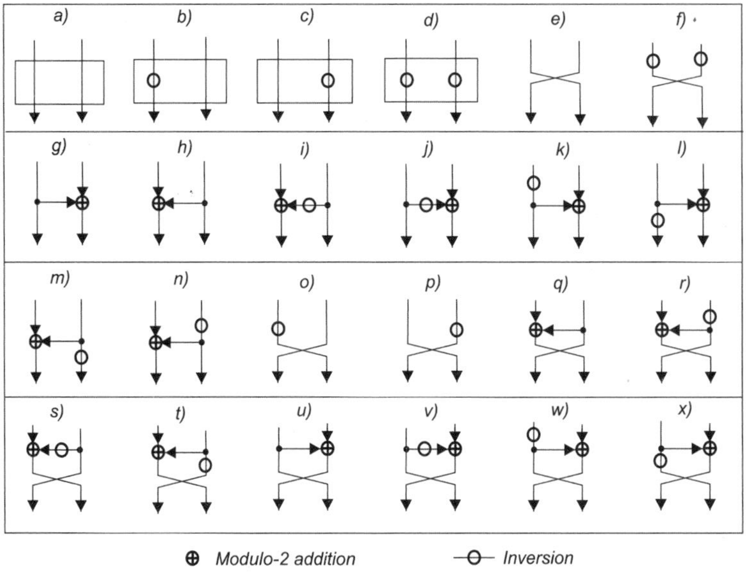

FIGURE 3.14 All existing variants of bijective transformations of the $(x_1, x_2) \rightarrow (y_1, y_2)$ type.

The investigation of differential characteristics of 248 variants of CEs that have nonlinear outputs but do not represent involutions has shown that they all can be divided into four subsets, among which two subsets relate to the subset of 168 nonlinear CEs that have differential characteristics identical to differential characteristics of controlled involutions $\mathbf{S}_{2/1}$ and $\mathbf{R}_{2/1}$ (see Table 3.7).

The study of circuit representations of CEs in the first and the second subsets allowed us to discover that the subset that is similar by its differential characteristics to the elements of the $\mathbf{S}_{2/1}$ type (and, accordingly, to the elements of the $\mathbf{R}_{2/1}$ type) is similar to $\{\mathbf{S}_{2/1}\}$ (and, accordingly, to $\{\mathbf{R}_{2/1}\}$) by the characteristic elementary modifications $\mathbf{F}^{(0)}{}_{2/1}$ and $\mathbf{F}^{(1)}{}_{2/1}$. Consequently, it is expedient to join these subsets of CEs to their corresponding subsets of involutions of the types $\mathbf{S}_{2/1}$ and $\mathbf{R}_{2/1}$ into two subclasses, $\{\mathbf{S}_{2/1}\}$ and $\{\mathbf{R}_{2/1}\}$, respectively (see Figures 3.15 and 3.16).

TABLE 3.7 Differential Characteristics of 248 CEs that Do Not Represent Involutions and Are Selected from the Class of CEs with Two Nonlinear Outputs

CE examples and type *i j k*	l/h, l/i, l/m, l/n, m/g, m/j, m/k, u/q, v/s, w/t ($S_{2/1}$)	g/o, h/p, o/l, o/m, p/k, m/p, a/r, b/t, a/x, d/w, t/c, u/b, w/d, p/n ($R_{2/1}$)	q/i, q/m, r/i, r/m, t/h, t/n, k/v, k/x, h/t ($Z^*_{2/1}$)	f/u, f/w, j/v, j/x, n/q, n/r, u/k, v/l, x/l ($Z^{**}_{2/1}$)
0 0 1	1/4	1/4	0	1/2
1 0 1	1/2	1/2	1	0
2 0 1	1/4	1/4	0	1/2
0 1 1	1/4	1/4	1/4	1/4
1 1 1	1/2	1/2	1/2	1/2
2 1 1	1/4	1/4	1/4	1/4
1 1 0	1/2	3/4	1/2	1/2
2 1 0	1/2	1/4	1/2	1/2
1 2 0	1	1/2	1	1
2 2 0	0	1/2	0	0
0 2 1	1/4	1/4	1/2	0
1 2 1	1/2	1/2	0	1
2 2 1	1/4	1/4	1/2	0

Subsets of CEs related to the fifths and sixths columns presented in Table 3.7 are related to subsets $\{\mathbf{Z}^*_{2/1}\}$ and $\{\mathbf{Z}^{**}_{2/1}\}$, respectively. Now it is natural to extend the $\{\mathbf{Z}_{2/1}\}$ subclass as follows: $\{\mathbf{Z}_{2/1}\} = \{\mathbf{Z}'_{2/1}, \mathbf{Z}''_{2/1}, \mathbf{Z}^*_{2/1}, \mathbf{Z}^{**}_{2/1}\}$. This extension is natural, because for all CEs from $\{\mathbf{Z}_{2/1}\}$, the sum of outputs represents a linear boolean function. Characteristic circuit representations of CEs related to subsets $\{\mathbf{Z}^*_{2/1}\}$ and $\{\mathbf{Z}^{**}_{2/1}\}$ are shown in Figures 3.17 and 3.18.

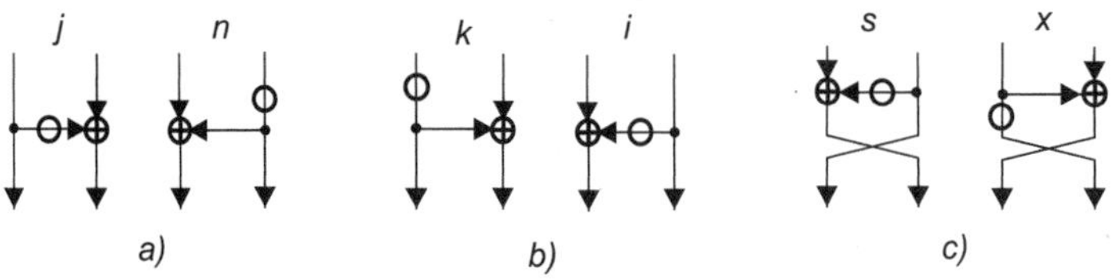

FIGURE 3.15 Typical CEs of the $\mathbf{S}_{2/1}$ type represented by pairs of elementary modifications j/n (a), k/i (b), and s/x (c).

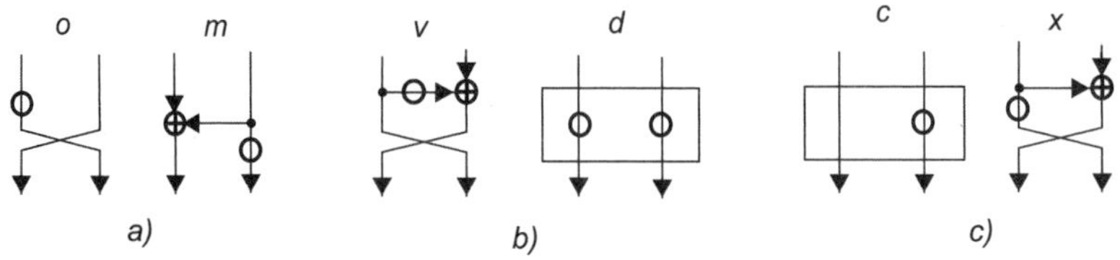

FIGURE 3.16 Typical CEs of the $\mathbf{R}_{2/1}$ type represented by pairs of elementary modifications o/m (a), v/d (b), and c/x (c).

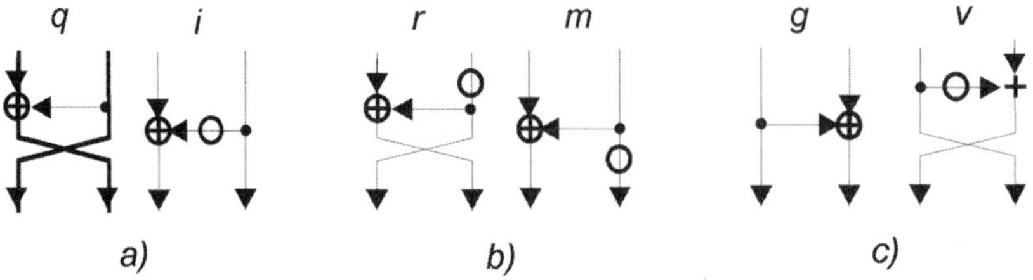

FIGURE 3.17 Typical CEs of the $\mathbf{Z}^{*}_{2/1}$ type represented by pairs of elementary modifications q/i (a), r/m (b), and g/v (c).

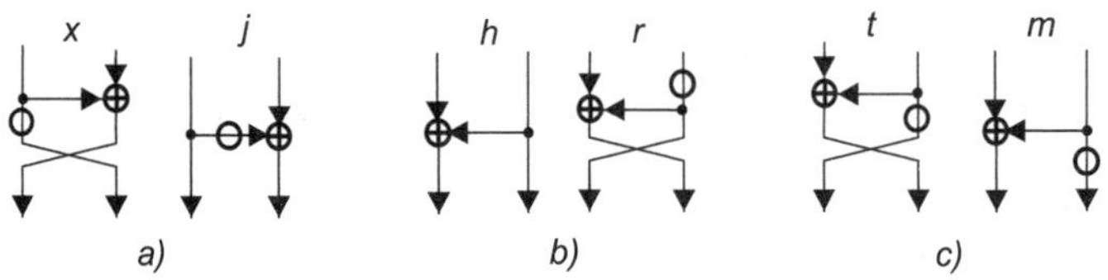

FIGURE 3.18 Typical CEs of the $\mathbf{Z}^{**}_{2/1}$ type represented by pairs of elementary modifications x/j (a), h/r (b), and t/m (c).

The following assumptions have been used in the suggested classification:

- If $\mathbf{F}_{2/1} \in \{\mathbf{S}_{2/1}\}$, then $\mathbf{F}^{-1}_{2/1} \in \{\mathbf{S}_{2/1}\}$.
- If $\mathbf{F}_{2/1} \in \{\mathbf{R}_{2/1}\}$, then $\mathbf{F}^{-1}_{2/1} \in \{\mathbf{R}_{2/1}\}$.
- Assuming that $\mathbf{Z}'_{2/1}$ and $\mathbf{Z}''_{2/1}$ CEs are not involutions, if $\mathbf{F}_{2/1} \in \{\mathbf{Z}'_{2/1}\} \cup \{\mathbf{Z}''_{2/1}\}$, then $\mathbf{F}^{-1}_{2/1} \in \{\mathbf{Z}'_{2/1}\} \cup \{\mathbf{Z}''_{2/1}\}$.
- If $\mathbf{F}_{2/1} \in \{\mathbf{Z}^{*}_{2/1}\} \cup \{\mathbf{Z}^{**}_{2/1}\}$, then $\mathbf{F}^{-1}_{2/1} \notin \{\mathbf{Z}_{2/1}\} \cup \{\mathbf{R}_{2/1}\} \cup \{\mathbf{S}_{2/1}\}$, because one of the two outputs of such $\mathbf{F}^{-1}_{2/1}$ blocks is a linear boolean function.

The first two assumptions are important for the design, because they demonstrate that mutually inverse CEs of the $\mathbf{S}_{2/1}$ and $\mathbf{R}_{2/1}$ relate to the same subclass. Because of this, when building easily invertible operating blocks, if necessary, it is possible to use pairs $\mathbf{S}_{2/1}$ and $\mathbf{S}^{-1}_{2/1}$ ($\mathbf{R}_{2/1}$ and $\mathbf{R}^{-1}_{2/1}$) without detriment to nonlinearity of the operating block being designed.

3.5 SYNTHESIS OF CONTROLLED OPERATIONAL SUBSTITUTIONS BASED ON $\mathbf{F}_{2/1}$ ELEMENTS

Controlled substitutions based on $\mathbf{F}_{2/1}$ elements represent one of the most efficient cryptographic algorithms, because they can be easily implemented in custom and programmable integrated circuits. Therefore, the issues of building controlled substitution-permutation networks based on such elements are of special importance. This section concentrates on the principles of building controlled operational substitutions, and provides evaluations of their probabilistic characteristics. Also covered are the issues of hardware implementation complexity of such elements.

3.5.1 Principles of Building Controlled Operational Substitutions

With the account of the goals of using the use of controlled operational substitutions (COS) in cryptographic algorithms and quality parameters, they must be built according to the following principles:

- The transformation carried out by a controlled operational substitution $Y=\mathbf{F}_{n/m}(X, V)$, where $X, Y \in GF(2)^n$, $V \in GF(2)^m$ is bijective in relation to X for a fixed value of V.
- The mechanism of controlling $\mathbf{F}_{n/m}$ controlled operational substitutions ensures forming of the wide range of different modifications of substitution operations.
- Transformation carried out by $\mathbf{F}_{n/m}$ COS is characterized by high nonlinearity.
- Boolean functions implementing $\mathbf{F}_{n/m}$ COS have good correlation characteristics.

- Hardware or hardware and software implementation of an $\mathbf{F}_{n/m}$ COS is characterized by relatively low computational complexity and ensures high performance of the information transformation.

As shown earlier in this chapter, replacing an elementary switch $\mathbf{P}_{2/1}$ in a CPB by more general elementary transformation $\mathbf{F}_{2/1}$ while preserving the layered structure of a CPB, it is possible to synthesize efficient controlled operational substitutions blocks (COSBs) over long vectors.

An elementary substitution block $\mathbf{F}_{2/}$ is used as a base element of COSB (Figure 3.19), which carries out the mapping of the form $GF(2)^3 \rightarrow GF(2)^2$ on the basis of two boolean functions of three arguments: $y_i = f(x_1, x_2, v)$, i=1, 2, where $y_i \in GF(2)$, x_1, $x_2 \in GF(2)$ are the values of input bits, and $v \in GF(2)$ is the value of the controlling bit. The set of controlling bit will further be interpreted as controlling vector V.

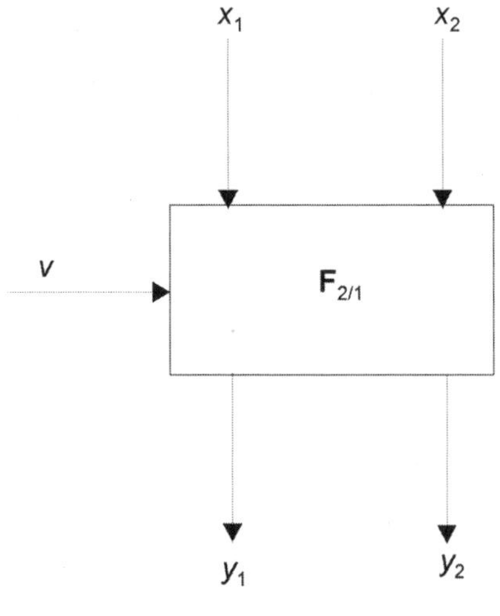

FIGURE 3.19 An elementary controlled substitution element.

The use of such elements results in the increase of the number of possible variants of building blocks of controlled operating dependent on the value of the controlling vector and including blocks of controlled substitutions as a particular case, because the aggregate of boolean functions that carry out controlled permutation of two bits is a variant of an elementary controlled substitution $\mathbf{F}_{2/1}$.

By combining the basic substitution blocks $\mathbf{F}_{2/1,}$ it is possible to synthesize $\mathbf{F}_{n/m}$ blocks, where n is the number of input (output) bits, and m is the number of controlling bits. Such blocks specify the mapping of the type $GF(2)^{n+m} \rightarrow GF(2)^n$. The use of a layered building scheme, each layer of which is made up of $\frac{n}{2}$ $\mathbf{F}_{2/1}$ elements connected in parallel appears the most promising. Between the layers are fixed permutations $\{\mathbf{P}_1, \mathbf{P}_2, \ldots, \mathbf{P}_{k-1}\}$, as shown in Figure 3.20. In this case, the $\mathbf{F}_{n/m}$ COSB can be represented as a superposition of k substitution layers and k–1 fixed permutations, namely:

$$\mathbf{F}_{n/m} = \sigma_1 \circ \mathbf{P}_1 \circ \sigma_2 \circ \mathbf{P}_2 \circ \ldots \circ \mathbf{P}_{k-1} \circ \sigma_k,$$

where σ_j is the j-th layer of $\frac{n}{2}$ $\mathbf{F}_{2/1}$ blocks, and $\mathbf{P}_j$ is the j-th layer of fixed permutations.

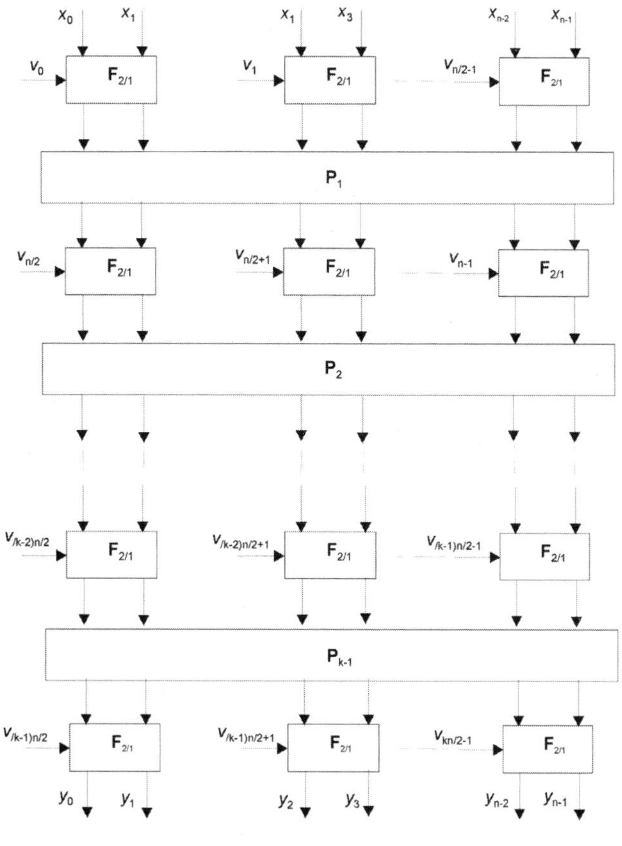

FIGURE 3.20 Layered structure of the COSB.

Basic element $\mathbf{F}_{2/1}$ has been used for synthesis of COSBs carrying out the mappings $GF(2)^{112} \to GF(2)^{32}$, $GF(2)^{256} \to GF(2)^{64}$, $GF(2)^{576} \to GF(2)^{128}$. The layered structure of COSB with $n = 2^k$–bit output of data has the controlled vector $m = \frac{kn}{2}$ bits long, where k is the number of base substitutions.

3.5.2 Probabilistic Characteristics of Controlled Operational Substitutions

When investigating the strength of encryption algorithms against a differential method of analysis, probabilistic properties of the algorithms and cryptographic primitives implementing those algorithms are used. In particular, an important parameter characterizing the algorithm property against differential cryptanalysis is the diffusion of the cryptographic primitive. Because of this, it is necessary to cover probabilistic properties of controlled operation substitutions of the $\mathbf{S}_{n/m}$ type.

For COSs of different dimensions, it is necessary to determine the probabilities of the event when differences with different Hamming weight appear at the output provided that the input difference was equal to one.

The probability that the event Ω in n independent trials will appear exactly m times is equal to the coefficient of the formal variable z^m in the expression of the generating function:

$$\varphi_n(z) = \prod_{i=1}^{n} (q_i + p_i z),$$

where p_i is the probability of the occurrence of the event Ω in the i-th trial, and q_i=1−p_i is the probability of nonoccurrence of the even Ω in the i-th trial. Expression above is equivalent to the following equality:

$$\prod_{i=1}^{n} (q_i + p_i z) = \sum_{m=0}^{n} P_{m,n} z^m,$$

where left and right parts represent the same generating function $\varphi_n(z)$. The left part represents this function as a mononomial, and the right part as a polynomial. If you open the brackets in the left part and then collect the terms, you'll get all probabilities $P_{0,n}$, $P_{1,n}$, ..., $P_{n,n}$ in the form of coefficients at the power of 0, 1, ... of the formal variable z.

For the $\mathbf{S}_{2/1}$ block, obtaining the generating function of the probability of the occurrence of the difference with weights $\boldsymbol{wt}(\Delta y)$=2 and $\boldsymbol{wt}(\Delta y)$=1 at the output provided that the difference $\boldsymbol{wt}(\Delta x)$=1 is supplied to the input is a trivial task. If these blocks correspond to blocks of the **S** type (see, for example, Table 3.4), then, with the account of differential characteristics provided in Table 3.4, the generating function will appear as follows:

$$\varphi_2^{\mathbf{S}_{2/1}}(z) = \frac{1}{2} z + \frac{1}{2} z^2.$$

This means that the probabilities of the occurrence of the differences with weights $\boldsymbol{wt}(\Delta y)$ = 1 and 2 are equal to $P_{1,2} = P_{2,2} = 0.5$. With the account of the cascading structure of a large COS, it is possible to obtain the generating probability functions $\varphi_n^{sn/m}(z)$ by means of iteratively substituting the expressions for generating functions from the previous layer of COS into expressions of the generating function of the next layer. Thus, for n=4 $\varphi_4^{\mathbf{S}_{4/4}}(z) = \frac{1}{2}\varphi_4^{\mathbf{S}_{4/4}}(z) = 0.2z + 0.4z^2 + 0.2z^3 + 0.2z^4$ and, having substituted previous expression into it, after collecting the terms, you'll get the expression for the generating function in the following form:

$$\varphi_4^{\mathbf{S}_{4/4}}(z) = 0.2z + 0.4z^2 + 0.2z^3 + 0.2z^4,$$

Proceeding the similar way, it is possible to obtain the following: $\varphi_{64}^{\mathbf{S}_{64/192}}(z) = 0.016z + 0.031z^2 + 0.04z^3 + 0.049z^4 + 0.054z^5 + 0.059z^6 + 0.061z^7 + 0.062z^8 + 0.062z^9 + 0.061z^{10} + 0.059z^{11} + 0.056z^{12} + 0.052z^{13} + 0.048z^{14} + 0.044z^{15} + 0.04z^{16} + 0.035z^{17} + 0.031z^{18} + 0.027z^{19} + 0.023z^{20} + 0.019z^{21} + 0.016z^{22} + 0.013z^{23} + 0.011z^{24} + 0.084z^{25} + 0.065z^{26} + 0.05z^{27} + 0.038z^{28} + 0.028z^{29} + 0.02z^{30} + 1.4\ 10^{-3}z^{31} + 9.8\ 10^{-4}z^{32} + 6.6\ 10^{-4}z^{33} + 4.4\ 10^{-4}z^{33} + 2.8\ 10^{-4}z^{35} + 1.8\ 10^{-4}z^{36} + 1.1\ 10^{-4}z^{37} + 6.6\ 10^{-5}z^{38} + 3.8\ 10^{-5}z^{39} + 2.1\ 10^{-5}z^{40} + 1.2\ 10^{-5}z^{41} + 6.2\ 10^{-6}z^{42} + 3.1\ 10^{-6}z^{43} + 1.5\ 10^{-6}z^{44} + 7.2\ 10^{-7}z^{45} + 3.3\ 10^{-7}z^{46} + 1.4\ 10^{-7}z^{47} + 5.9\ 10^{-8}z^{48} + 2.3\ 10^{-8}z^{49} + 8.6\ 10^{-9}z^{50} + 3\ 10^{-9}z^{51} + 10^{-9}z^{52} + 3.1\ 10^{-10}z^{53} + 8.8\ 10^{-11}z^{54} + 2.3\ 10^{-11}z^{55} + 5.6\ 10^{-12}z^{56} + 1.2\ 10^{-12}z^{57} + 2.3\ 10^{-13}z^{58} + 3.9\ 10^{-14}z^{59} + 5.6\ 10^{-15}z^{60} + 6.5\ 10^{-16}z^{61} + 5.7\ 10^{-17}z^{62} + 3.5\ 10^{-18}z^{63} + 1.1\ 10^{-19}z^{64}$. Discrete probabilities distributions and discrete functions of probabilities distributions are shown in Figures 3.21 and 3.22, respectively. These distributions were obtained by using generating functions and simulation for $\mathbf{S}_{64/192}$ COS in cases when all bits of the controlling vector are independent and equiprobable, and the difference Δx with the weight $\boldsymbol{wt}(\Delta x) = 1$ is supplied to the input of the controlled operational substitution block.

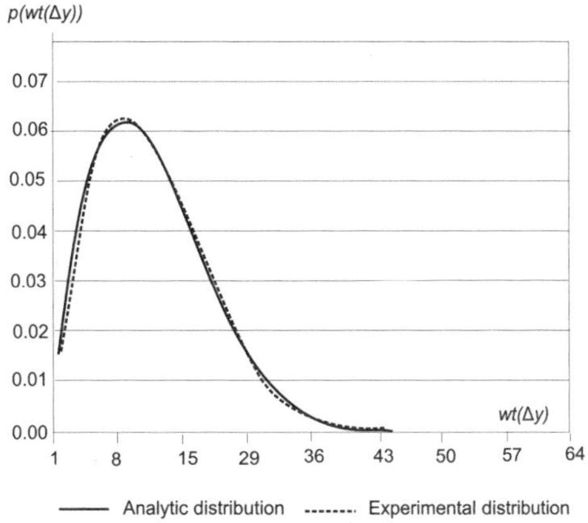

FIGURE 3.21 Discrete distributions of probabilities.

Tables 3.8 through 3.12 provides distributions of the probabilities of occurrence of the weight differences $\boldsymbol{wt}$ at the output of $\mathbf{S}_{n/m}$ blocks of different dimensions in cases when the difference with the weight $\boldsymbol{wt}(\Delta x)$=1 is supplied to the input.

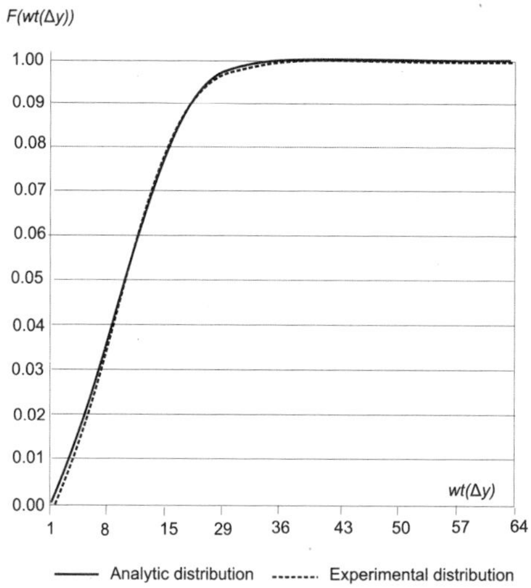

FIGURE 3.22 Discrete functions of probability distributions.

TABLE 3.8 Distribution of the probabilities of occurrence of the weight differences wt at the output of the $\mathbf{S}_{4/4}$ block provided that the difference with the weight wt(Δx)=1 is supplied to the input.

wt	p
1	0.25
2	0.375
3	0.25
4	0.125

TABLE 3.9 Distribution of the probabilities of occurrence of the weight differences wt at the output of the $\mathbf{S}_{8/12}$ block provided that the difference with the weight wt(Δx)=1 is supplied to the input.

wt	p	wt	p
1	0.125	5	0.125
2	0.219	6	0.078
3	0.219	7	0.038
4	0.195	8	0.008

TABLE 3.10 Distribution of the probabilities of occurrence of the weight differences wt at the output of the $\mathbf{S}_{16/32}$ block provided that the difference with the weight wt(Δx)=1 is supplied to the input.

wt	*p*	*wt*	*p*	*wt*	*p*	*wt*	*p*
1	0.063	5	0.13	9	0.049	13	$3.4\ 10^{-3}$
2	0.12	6	0.12	10	0.032	14	$1.1\ 10^{-3}$
3	0.14	7	0.095	11	0.018	15	$2.4\ 10^{-4}$
4	0.15	8	0.071	12	$8.5\ 10^{-3}$	16	$3.1\ 10^{-5}$

TABLE 3.11 Distribution of the probabilities of occurrence of the weight differences wt at the output of the $\mathbf{S}_{32/80}$ block provided that the difference with the weight wt(Δx)=1 is supplied to the input.

wt	*p*	*wt*	*p*	*wt*	*p*	*wt*	*p*
1	0.031	9	0.077	17	0.011	25	$5.8\ 10^{-5}$
2	0.061	10	0.067	18	$6.8\ 10^{-3}$	26	$2.0\ 10^{-5}$
3	0.076	11	0.057	19	$4.2\ 10^{-3}$	27	$6.4\ 10^{-6}$
4	0.090	12	0.041	20	$2.5\ 10^{-5}$	28	$1.7\ 10^{-6}$
5	0.093	13	0.037	21	$1.4\ 10^{-3}$	29	$3.7\ 10^{-6}$
6	0.096	14	0.029	22	$7.0\ 10^{-4}$	30	$6.3\ 10^{-8}$
7	0.091	15	0.021	23	$3.3\ 10^{-4}$	31	$7.5\ 10^{-9}$
8	0.085	16	0.015	24	$1.5\ 10^{-4}$	32	$4.7\ 10^{-10}$

Such characteristics can also be obtained for controlled operational substitutions of the **R** type. To achieve this, it is necessary to find the expression for the generating probabilities function:

$$\varphi_2^{\mathbf{R}_{2/1}}(z) = \frac{3}{4}z + \frac{1}{4}z^2;$$

TABLE 3.12 Distribution of the probabilities of occurrence of the weight differences wt at the output of the $\mathbf{S}_{64/192}$ block provided that the difference with the weight wt(Δx)=1 is supplied to the input.

wt	*p*	*wt*	*p*	*wt*	*p*	*wt*	*p*
1	0.016	17	0.035	33	$6.6\ 10^{-4}$	49	$2.3\ 10^{-8}$
2	0.031	18	0.031	34	$4.4\ 10^{-4}$	50	$8.6\ 10^{-9}$
3	0.040	19	0.027	35	$2.8\ 10^{-4}$	51	$3.0\ 10^{-9}$
4	0.049	20	0.023	36	$1.8\ 10^{-4}$	52	10^{-9}
5	0.054	21	0.019	37	$1.1\ 10^{-4}$	53	$3.1\ 10^{-10}$
6	0.059	22	0.016	38	$6.6\ 10^{-5}$	54	$8.8\ 10^{-11}$
7	0.061	23	0.013	39	$3.8\ 10^{-5}$	55	$2.3\ 10^{-11}$
8	0.062	24	0.011	40	$2.1\ 10^{-5}$	56	$5.6\ 10^{-12}$
9	0.062	25	0.084	41	$1.2\ 10^{-5}$	57	$1.2\ 10^{-12}$
10	0.061	26	0.065	42	$6.2\ 10^{-6}$	58	$2.3\ 10^{-13}$
11	0.059	27	0.05	43	$3.1\ 10^{-6}$	59	$3.9\ 10^{-14}$
12	0.056	28	0.038	44	$1.5\ 10^{-6}$	60	$5.6\ 10^{-15}$
13	0.052	29	0.028	45	$7.2\ 10^{-7}$	61	$6.5\ 10^{-16}$
14	0.048	30	0.02	46	$3.3\ 10^{-7}$	62	$5.7\ 10^{-17}$
15	0.044	31	$1.4\ 10^{-3}$	47	$1.4\ 10^{-7}$	63	$3.5\ 10^{-18}$
16	0.040	32	$9.8\ 10^{-4}$	48	$5.9\ 10^{-8}$	64	$1.1\ 10^{-19}$

that is, the probability of the occurrence of the differences with weight $\boldsymbol{wt}(\Delta y) = 1$ $P_{1,2} = 0.75$, and $\boldsymbol{wt}(\Delta y) = 2$ $P_{2,2} = 0.25$. Using an iterative procedure, on the basis of the expression above, it is possible to obtain several distributions of the probabilities of occurrence of differences with different weights at the output of R blocks of different dimensions provided that the difference with weight $\boldsymbol{wt}(\Delta x)=1$ was supplied to the block input (Tables 3.13 through 3.17).

TABLE 3.13 Distribution of the probabilities of occurrence of the weight differences wt at the output of the $\mathbf{R}_{4/4}$ block provided that the difference with the weight wt(Δx)=1 is supplied to the input.

wt	p
1	0.56
2	0.33
3	0.094
4	0.016

TABLE 3.14 Distribution of the probabilities of occurrence of the weight differences wt at the output of the $\mathbf{R}_{8/12}$ block provided that the difference with the weight wt(Δx)=1 is supplied to the input.

wt	p	wt	p
1	0.42	5	0.02
2	0.33	6	$4.8\ 10^{-3}$
3	0.16	7	$7.3\ 10^{-4}$
4	0.065	8	$6.1\ 10^{-5}$

TABLE 3.15 Distribution of the probabilities of occurrence of the weight differences wt at the output of the $\mathbf{R}_{16/32}$ block provided that the difference with the weight wt(Δx)=1 is supplied to the input.

wt	*p*	*wt*	*p*	*wt*	*p*	*wt*	*p*
1	0.32	5	0.055	9	$1.2\ 10^{-3}$	13	$2.3\ 10^{-6}$
2	0.29	6	0.025	10	$3.2\ 10^{-4}$	14	$2.8\ 10^{-7}$
3	0.19	7	0.01	11	$7.6\ 10^{-5}$	15	$2.2\ 10^{-8}$
4	0.11	8	$3.6\ 10^{-3}$	12	$1.5\ 10^{-5}$	16	$9.3\ 10^{-10}$

For comparison, Figure 3.23 provides distributions of the probabilities of occurrence of the differences with different weights at the output of COS of S- and R-types provided that the difference with weight $wt(\Delta x) = 1$ has been supplied to

TABLE 3.16 Distribution of the probabilities of occurrence of the weight differences wt at the output of the $\mathbf{R}_{32/80}$ block provided that the difference with the weight wt(Δx)=1 is supplied to the input.

wt	p	wt	p	wt	p	wt	p
1	0.24	9	$8.3\ 10^{-3}$	17	$5.2\ 10^{-6}$	25	$3.2\ 10^{-11}$
2	0.24	10	$4.0\ 10^{-3}$	18	$1.6\ 10^{-6}$	26	$4.5\ 10^{-12}$
3	0.19	11	$1.9\ 10^{-3}$	19	$4.4\ 10^{-7}$	27	$5.3\ 10^{-13}$
4	0.13	12	$8.1\ 10^{-4}$	20	$1.1\ 10^{-7}$	28	$5.3\ 10^{-14}$
5	0.086	13	$3.3\ 10^{-4}$	21	$2.1\ 10^{-8}$	29	$4.2\ 10^{-15}$
6	0.052	14	$1.3\ 10^{-4}$	22	$5.8\ 10^{-9}$	30	$2.6\ 10^{-16}$
7	0.03	15	$4.8\ 10^{-5}$	23	$1.2\ 10^{-9}$	31	$1.0\ 10^{-17}$
8	0.016	16	$1.6\ 10^{-5}$	24	$2.0\ 10^{-10}$	32	$2.2\ 10^{-19}$

the input. Analysis of the obtained histograms allows us to conclude that S-type COSs are preferred when designing block cryptographic algorithms, because they have better difference properties.

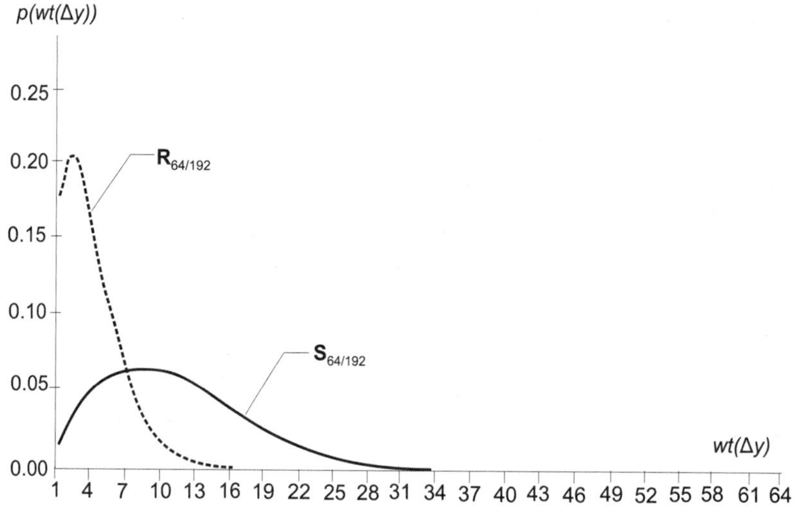

FIGURE 3.23 Distributions of the probabilities of the occurrence of the differences with different weights at the output of S- and R-type COS provided that the difference with weight ***wt***(Δx) = 1 has been supplied to the input.

TABLE 3.17 Distribution of the probabilities of occurrence of the weight differences wt at the output of the $\mathbf{R}_{64/192}$ block provided that the difference with the weight wt(Δx)=1 is supplied to the input.

wt	*p*	*wt*	*p*	*wt*	*p*	*wt*	*p*
1	0.18	17	2.6 10^{-4}	33	1.5 10^{-10}	49	8.4 10^{-21}
2	0.2	18	1.3 10^{-4}	34	4.6 10^{-11}	50	1.2 10^{-21}
3	0.17	19	6.4 10^{-5}	35	1.4 10^{-11}	51	1.7 10^{-22}
4	0.14	20	3.1 10^{-5}	36	4.0 10^{-12}	52	2.2 10^{-23}
5	0.1	21	1.4 10^{-5}	37	1.1 10^{-12}	53	2.6 10^{-24}
6	0.074	22	$6.5^{6}10$	38	3.0 10^{-13}	54	2.9 10^{-25}
7	0.052	23	2.8 10^{-6}	39	7.8 10^{-14}	55	2.9 10^{-26}
8	0.034	24	1.2 10^{-6}	40	2.0 10^{-14}	56	2.6 10^{-27}
9	0.022	25	5.0 10^{-7}	41	4.6 10^{-15}	57	2.1 10^{-28}
10	0.014	26	2.0 10^{-7}	42	1.1 10^{-15}	58	1.4 10^{-29}
11	8.6 10^{-3}	27	8.0 10^{-8}	43	2.3 10^{-16}	59	8.7 10^{-31}
12	5.1 10^{-3}	28	3.0 10^{-8}	44	4.8 10^{-17}	60	4.4 10^{-32}
13	3.0 10^{-3}	29	1.1 10^{-8}	45	9.5 10^{-18}	61	1.8 10^{-33}
14	1.7 10^{-3}	30	4.0 10^{-9}	46	1.8 10^{-18}	62	5.5 10^{-35}
15	9.2 10^{-4}	31	1.4 10^{-9}	47	3.2 10^{-19}	63	1.1 10^{-36}
16	4.9 10^{-4}	32	4.6 10^{-10}	48	5.3 10^{-20}	64	1.2 10^{-38}

3.5.3 Evaluation of the Complexity of Circuit Design when Implementing Controlled Operational Substitutions

In contrast to table substitutions with the output data block length n ($\log_2 n \geq 5$), various types of controlled permutations and controlled operational substitutions can be easily implemented in the form of easy electronic circuits with the delay time comparable to the time required for sequential execution of several XOR operations.

Synthesized blocks of controlled operational substitutions are characterized by low complexity of circuit implementation $C_{\Omega}(\mathbf{F}_{n/m})$, which is interpreted as the number of gates implementing the $\mathbf{F}_{n/m}$ circuit. Here, $\Omega = \{\&, \vee, ^{-}\}$ is the complete basis of simplest logical operations in use. One-bit boolean functions in the elementary $\mathbf{F}_{2/1}$ block in this basis have the complexity $C_\Omega(\mathbf{F}_{2/1}) = 9$. When evaluating the speed parameters of a block of controlled operational substitutions, consider the time required to execute the slowest operation called the *delay clock* τ_Ω. In the preceding complete basis $\tau_\Omega = \tau_\&$, for existing blocks of controlled operational permutations, the time required to carry out the transformation is $t(\mathbf{F}_{n/m}) = k\tau_\&$, and implementation complexity appears as $C_\Omega(\mathbf{F}_{n/m}) = mC_\Omega(\mathbf{F}_{2/1}) = 6m$. Based on contemporary electronics technologies, this allows us to produce cryptochips implementing block cryptoalgorithms, including blocks of controlled operational substitutions with the large input size (n = 32, 64, 128, 256). Thanks to this, it is possible to reach the encryption speed considerably exceeding 1 Gbps.

Despite initial orientation toward hardware implementation, efficient use of controlled operations can result in considerable advances in the operating performance of software-oriented ciphers. This is because some types of controlled operations, such as controlled permutations, are highly efficient as cryptographic primitives and are at the same time characterized by exceedingly low cost of circuit implementation. Such a relationship between cost and efficiency makes the idea of including new commands in the standard set of the processor command exceedingly attractive for the manufacturers of commercial processors. The possibility of ensuring the speed of software encryption up to 800–2000 Mbps considerably increases the competitive capability of such processors while minimizing implementation costs. Implementation of a command of controlled bit permutation, the practical application of which considerably exceeds the range of purely cryptographic applications (data encryption and hashing algorithms), appears to be the most promising. Variants of implementation of such a command will be considered in Chapter 4, "Switched Controlled Operations."

3.6 VARIANTS OF REPRESENTATION AND CRITERIA FOR SELECTION OF $\mathbf{F}_{2/2}$ CONTROLLED ELEMENTS

In previous sections of this chapter, controlled SP-networks (controlled operational substitutions) based on the $\mathbf{F}_{2/1}$ controlled element were considered. However, building efficient CSPNs based on other blocks, such as elementary $\mathbf{F}_{2/2}$ controlled elements, is also of great interest. The schematic representation of an elementary $\mathbf{F}_{2/2}$ block is shown in Figure 3.24. Such blocks also can be easily implemented as fast electronic circuits. In this case, while preserving the general topology of controlled SP-networks, it is possible to replace all elementary $\mathbf{F}_{2/1}$ CEs by another standard CE with 2-bit input and output, and a 2-bit controlling input.

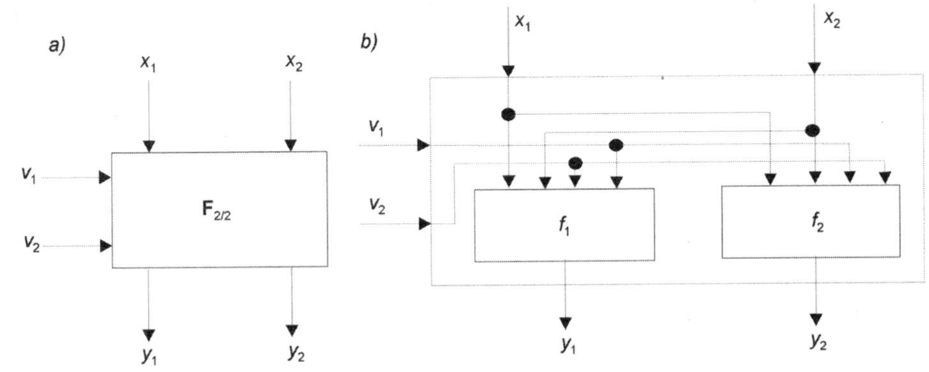

FIGURE 3.24 Controlled element $\mathbf{F}_{2/2}$ (a) and its implementation using two boolean functions (b).

Practical expediency of migration to the use of CEs with 2-bit controlling input is related to their hardware implementation on the basis of programmable logical matrices, where standard logical blocks usually have two logical cells representing 16-bit memory cells. Each of such memory cells allows for implementing an arbitrary boolean function of four variables. When implementing any CE of the $\mathbf{F}_{2/1}$ type, two cells are used, each of which implements specific boolean functions of three variables. This means that only half of the resource of the memory cell is used (in other words, only 50 percent of the cell size), because for implementing a boolean function of three variables, 8-bit memory is enough. Apparently, it is impossible to efficiently use the remaining part of the memory.

Migration to CEs of the $\mathbf{F}_{2/2}$ type ensures the complete use of the cell's potential. In addition, using extended controlling input creates the prerequisites for specifying stronger influence of the controlling data subgroup on the data being transformed. In particular, this allows for increasing the nonlinearity of each of the CE outputs, and increase of its algebraic degree of nonlinearity and intensification of the avalanche effect in case of modification of single bits of the controlling data subgroup. It is reasonable to assume that an appropriate choice of the $\mathbf{F}_{2/2}$-type CE will allow for considerable increase of the cryptographic characteristics of the operational block being synthesized. This will provide the possibility of reducing the number of the transformation rounds while preserving high cryptographic strength of the algorithms based on controlled operations. This, in turn, ensures the possibility of reducing the complexity of the hardware implementation (in case of pipelined architectures) and an increase in the encryption speed (in case of iterative implementation architecture).

For synthesizing efficient multilayered controlled SP networks, it is necessary to formulate several criteria for choosing specific variants of $\mathbf{F}_{2/2}$ controlled elements.

In general, an $\mathbf{F}_{2/2}$ controlled element can be represented as:

- Two boolean functions of four variables.
- Four 2×2 substitutions, each of which is carried out over the 2-bit input binary vector (x_1, x_2) having $v = (0, 0)$, $(0, 1)$, $(1, 0)$, and $(1, 1)$, respectively.

Boolean functions of four variables have different values of nonlinearity in the sense of the minimal distance to the set of affine boolean functions of four variables, different values of the algebraic degree of nonlinearity, and greater variety of differential characteristics in comparison to boolean functions of three variables. These circumstances must be taken into account when formulating criteria for choosing CEs of the $\mathbf{F}_{2/2}$ type and their classification.

Criteria for Building $F_{2/2}$ Blocks

Based on the considerations in the preceding section and the results obtained in previous sections of this chapter, the basic criteria for designing and choosing $\mathbf{F}_{2/2}$ blocks appear as follows:

- Any of the two outputs of an $\mathbf{F}_{2/2}$ block must represent a nonlinear Boolean function of four variables: $y_1 = f_1(x_1, x_2, v_1, v_2)$ and $y_2 = f_2(x_1, x_2, v_1, v_2)$, each of which must satisfy the degree of nonlinearity close to maximum.
- Each of four elementary modifications of the $\mathbf{F}_{2/2}$ block—namely, $\mathbf{F}^{(0)}$, $\mathbf{F}^{(1)}$, $\mathbf{F}^{(2)}$, $\mathbf{F}^{(3)}$—must carry out a bijective transformation $(x_1, x_2) \rightarrow (y_1, y_2)$.
- Each of the four modifications $\mathbf{F}^{(v)}$ of the controlled element must represent an involution.

It is possible to use two variants of searching for efficient $\mathbf{F}_{2/2}$ controlled elements satisfying the preceding criteria:

- Exhaustive search of all possible pairs of boolean functions $y_1 = f_1(x_1, x_2, v_1, v_2)$ and $y_2 = f_2(x_1, x_2, v_1, v_2)$.
- Exhaustive search of all possible sets of modifications $\mathbf{F}^{(0)}$, $\mathbf{F}^{(1)}$, $\mathbf{F}^{(2)}$, $\mathbf{F}^{(3)}$, carrying out the 2×2 transformation.

For the first variant, the number of computations required for choosing elementary controlled elements of the $\mathbf{F}_{2/2}$ type satisfying the formulated criteria is large enough. Obviously, there exist 2^{16} various boolean functions of four variables. Consequently, in the general case it is necessary to try $2^{16} \cdot (2^{16}-1) \approx 4{,}3 \cdot 10^9$

sets of different boolean functions. To limit the number of variants to try, it is possible to use the requirement that the boolean function be balanced, which is the con-sequence of the second criterion of choice. The number of balanced boolean functions of n variables is $\#\{f(x_1, ..., x_n)\}_{Bal} = \binom{2^n}{2^{n-1}}$, consequently, for $n = 4$ $\#\{f(x_1, ..., x_4)\}_{Bal} = 12{,}870$, determining this value for balanced functions with even even n, the number of Boolean function will be 10,920. Consequently, in this case it will be necessary to try H $1{,}2 \cdot 10^8$ sets of boolean functions, which also requires considerable computational overhead.

TABLE 3.18 The Set of Boolean Functions $f(x_1, x_2, x_3, x_4) : GF(2)^4 \rightarrow GF(2)$

Nonlinearity of a Boolean function NL (f)	6	5	4	3	2	1	0
Number of Boolean functions	896	14,336	28,000	17,920	3,840	512	32
Number of balanced Boolean functions	0	0	10,920	0	1,920	0	30

It is possible to slightly reduce the amount of computations, if you take into account the requirement to the linear combination of boolean functions implementing an $\mathbf{F}_{2/2}$ block to be balanced (this requirement also follows from the second criterion). Obviously, distribution of the Hamming weights in a linear combination of boolean functions will be determined by the following expression:

$$\#\{\mathbf{F}_{2/m} : wt(f_1 \oplus f_2) = l\} = \#\{\mathbf{F}_{2/m} : wt(f_1 \oplus f_2) = 2^h - l\} =$$

$$\#\{f\}_{Bal} \binom{2^{h-1}}{2^{h-1} - \frac{l}{2}}^2 = \binom{2^h}{2^{h-1}} \binom{2^{h-1}}{2^{h-1} - \frac{l}{2}}^2,$$

where $h = 2 + m$; $m = 1, 2$; $l\{0, 2, ..., 2h{-}2, 2h\}$. Hence, for the case $h = 3$, the following result is obtained: $\#\{\mathbf{F}_{2/1} : wt(f_1 \oplus f_2) = 4\} = 2{,}520$ balanced linear combinations of boolean functions at the output of the $\mathbf{F}_{2/1}$ element, and for the case $h = 4$ the result will be $\#\ \{\mathbf{F}_{2/2} : wt(f_1 \oplus f_2) = 8\} = 63{,}063{,}000$ balanced linear combinations determining the number of variants to try.

Visual Design of $F_{2/2}$ Blocks

When using the second approach to building efficient $\mathbf{F}_{2/2}$ controlled elements, the choice of pairs of boolean functions can be reduced to the formal choice of controlled elements with the predefined properties. In this case, $\mathbf{F}_{2/2}$ blocks are formed by four different modifications depending on the controlling vector $v = (v_1, v_2)$, $v_1, v_2 \in GF(2)$ and carrying out the mapping $(x_1, x_2) \rightarrow (y_1, y_2)$:

- $\mathbf{F}^{(0)}$, if $v = (0, 0)$
- $\mathbf{F}^{(1)}$, if $v = (0, 1)$
- $\mathbf{F}^{(2)}$, if $v = (1, 0)$
- $\mathbf{F}^{(3)}$, if $v = (1, 1)$

To carry out a bijective transformation as a whole, the transformation carried out by modifications $\mathbf{F}^{(0)} \div \mathbf{F}^{(3)}$ must be bijective. There are 24 variants of bijective modifications (see Figure 3.14). Visual design is reduced to the choice of the quartets of modifications from the set of bijective variants. It is necessary to note that every elementary modification carries out a linear transformation. Nonlinear properties of $\mathbf{F}_{2/2}$ blocks depend on specific features of the choice of elementary modifications depending on the value $v = (v_1, v_2)$. Among the entire variety of $24^4 = 331{,}776$ variants of sets of quartets of 2×2 substitution transformations carrying out bijective mapping, only 126,720 define nonlinear $\mathbf{F}_{2/2}$ blocks satisfying criteria 1-2. With the account of the third criterion of choice, 104 variants of building $\mathbf{F}_{2/2}$ blocks satisfying criteria 1-3 are obtained. At the same time, the most important issue is that such a considerable reduction of the number of the variants worth trying is ensured at the initial stage. When using the first approach, the third criterion works less efficiently.

Given the specified modifications $\mathbf{F}^{(0)} \div \mathbf{F}^{(3)}$, it is easy to obtain the algebraic normal form of boolean functions f_1 and f_2 implementing the $\mathbf{F}_{2/2}$ block. Let $\{f_1^1(x_1, x_2), f_2^1(x_1, x_2)\}$ be the boolean function implementing modification F(0) for $v = (0, 0)$, and $\{f_1^2(x_1, x_2), f_2^2(x_1, x_2)\}$, $\{f_1^3(x_1, x_2), f_2^3(x_1, x_2)\}$, $\{f_1^4(x_1, x_2), f_2^4(x_1, x_2)\}$-boolean functions implementing modifications $\mathbf{F}^{(1)}$, $\mathbf{F}^{(2)}$, and $\mathbf{F}^{(3)}$ for $v = (0, 1)$, $v = (1, 0)$, $v = (1, 1)$, respectively. Then, specific boolean functions implementing the required $\mathbf{F}_{2/2}$ block can be obtained as follows:

$$y_1 = (v_1 \oplus 1)(v_2 \oplus 1) f_1^1(x_1, x_2) \oplus (v_1 \oplus 1) v_2 f_1^2(x_1, x_2) \oplus v_1 (v_2 \oplus 1) f_1^3(x_1, x_2) \oplus v_1 v_2 f_1^4(x_1, x_2),$$

$$y_2 = (v_1 \oplus 1)(v_2 \oplus 1) f_2^1(x_1, x_2) \oplus (v_1 \oplus 1) v_2 f_2^2(x_1, x_2) \oplus v_1 (v_2 \oplus 1) f_2^3(x_1, x_2) \oplus v_1 v_2 f_2^4(x_1, x_2).$$

For example, for the elementary $\mathbf{F}_{2/2}$ block presented in Figure 3.25, the obtained result appears as follows:

$$f_1^1(x_1, x_2) = x_2; f_2^1(x_1, x_2) = x_1;$$
$$f_1^2(x_1, x_2) = x_1 \oplus x_2 \oplus 1; f_2^2(x_1, x_2) = x_2;$$
$$f_1^3(x_1, x_2) = x_1; f_2^3(x_1, x_2) = x_1 \oplus x_2 \oplus 1;$$
$$f_1^4(x_1, x_2) = x_1 \oplus x_2; f_2^4(x_1, x_2) = x_2.$$

Consequently,

$$y_1 = v_1 v_2 x_1 \oplus v_1 v_2 x_2 \oplus v_1 x_1 \oplus v_1 x_2 \oplus v_1 v_2 \oplus v_2 x_1 \oplus v_2 \oplus x_2;$$
$$y_2 = v_1 v_2 x_2 \oplus v_1 x_2 \oplus v_2 x_1 \oplus v_2 x_2 \oplus v_1 v_2 \oplus v_1 \oplus x_1;$$
$$y_1 \oplus y_2 = v_1 v_2 x_1 \oplus v_1 x_1 \oplus v_2 x_2 \oplus v_2 \oplus v_1 \oplus x_2 \oplus x_1.$$

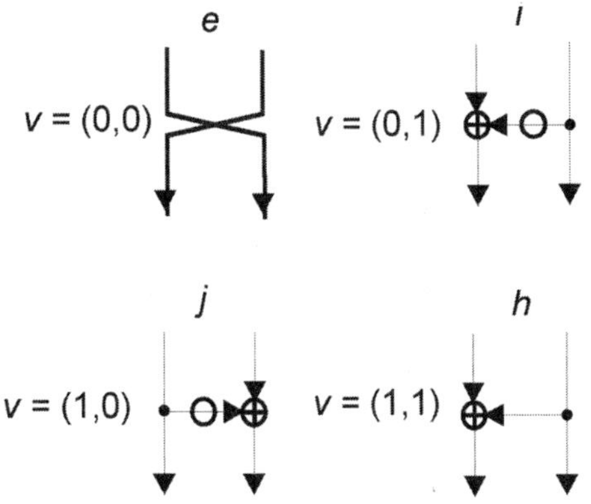

FIGURE 3.25 A variant of the $\mathbf{F}_{2/2}$ block implementation.

4 Switched Controlled Operations

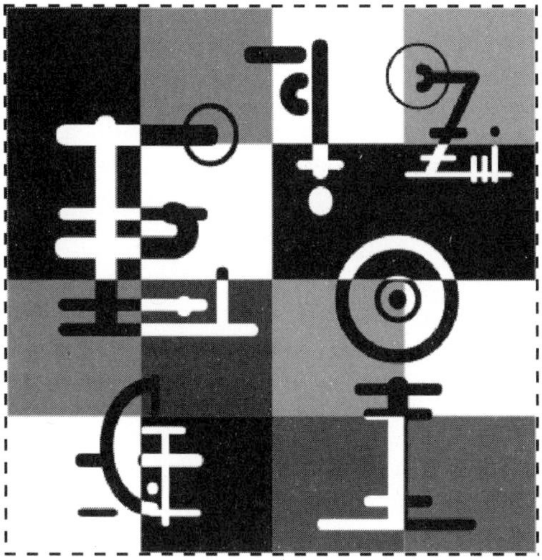

4.1 BUILDING CONTROLLED SUBSTITUTION-PERMUTATION NETWORKS OF DIFFERENT ORDERS

Properties of controlled operations built based on controlled substitution-permutation networks (CSPNs) can be characterized both with and without association to the use of cryptographic primitives. In the first case, which is of the greatest interest to the goals of this book, they depend on the following issues:

- Properties of controlled elements used for building the network
- Network homogeneity
- Network topology describing relations between controlled elements and with the controlling input

- Dimensions of the information and controlling inputs of the operational block
- The size of the controlling data subgroup

It is expedient to carry out synthesis of operational blocks intended for use in encryption algorithms considering these issues. When they are implemented, it is possible to use the predefined influence of each input bit to each output bit as the initial criterion. In case of controlled permutations, this can be implemented for controlled operational substitutions of the first order. As shown in the previous chapter, replacement of each elementary switch in the $\mathbf{P}_{n/m}$ block of the first order by any controlled element (CE) from the set $\{\mathbf{R}_{2/1}, \mathbf{S}_{2/1}, \mathbf{Z}_{2/1}\}$ ensures the possibility of building controlled SP-networks $\mathbf{R}_{n/m}$, $\mathbf{S}_{n/m}$, and $\mathbf{Z}_{n/m}$ satisfying the initial criterion. This example demonstrates that topological structure of controlled substitutions blocks of different types can be taken as prototypes when building controlled substitution-permutation networks $\mathbf{F}_{n/m}$ of different types.

When building controlled permutations a block for cryptographic applications, the order of controlled permutation is of special interest. Therefore, it is expedient to further extend this concept to controlled substitution-permutation networks of the $\mathbf{F}_{n/m}$ type build based on $\mathbf{F}_{2/1}$ and $\mathbf{F}_{2/2}$ controlled elements with 2-bit input. In case of bit permutation, the concept of order is defined with the account of the variants of placement of the specified number of input bits into the specified number of output bits of the controlled permutations block. In case when networks are built based on controlled elements other than elementary switches, such a direct physical interpretation of the order concept is blurred by the presence of the modulo-2 bit-by-bit addition and inversion within the CE. Because of this, for $\mathbf{F}_{n/m}$ blocks the concept of order must be provided in the more general form, using the concept of influence propagation instead of the physical bit permutation. Propagation of the influence of one input bit for a certain fixed value of the controlling vector V, in turn, can be interpreted as passing of the single-bit difference through controlled substitution-permutation networks; in the course of which difference propagation can take place. In the latter case it is possible to state that for the specified value V, the input bit (or simply input) under consideration influences specific output bits (or simply outputs). This influence can be shown as the propagation of single-bit differences Δ_1 and δ_1. A typical scheme of propagation of the influence of one (left and right) input in $\mathbf{R}_{2/1}$ and $\mathbf{S}_{2/1}$ elementary blocks is shown in Figure 4.1. In these schemes, typical features are clearly visible: in $\mathbf{R}_{2/1}$ controlled elements, the influence of the right (propagation of the difference Δ_1) and left (propagation of difference δ_1) inputs is asymmetric, and in elementary $\mathbf{S}_{2/1}$ blocks, this propagation is symmetric.

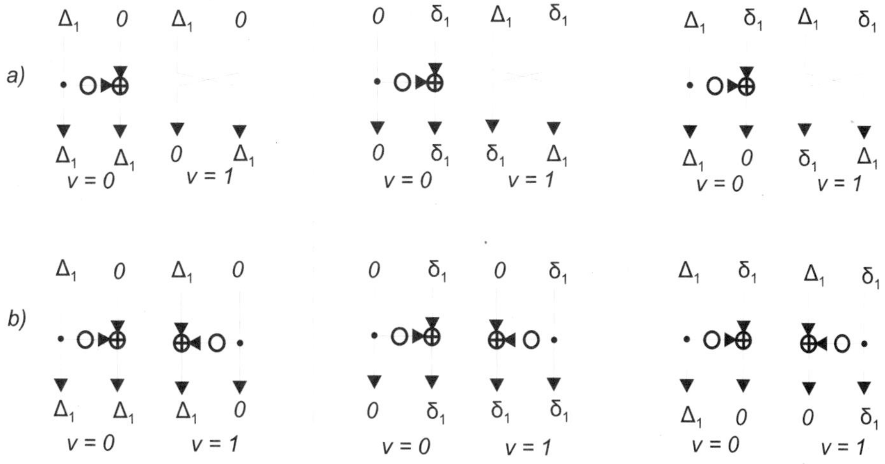

FIGURE 4.1 Typical scheme of the propagation of the input bits influence in $\mathbf{R}_{2/1}$ (a) and $\mathbf{S}_{2/1}$ (b) controlled elements.

From the scheme illustrating the propagation of the influence on two outputs in elementary blocks $\mathbf{R}_{2/1}$ and $\mathbf{S}_{2/1}$ (Figure 4.1), it is clear that in $\mathbf{R}_{2/1}$ blocks, the influence of each input can propagate in cross directions depending on the value of the control bit. In $\mathbf{S}_{2/1}$ elements, the left (right) input influences only the left (right) output. This shows that $\mathbf{R}_{2/1}$ elements have more in common with $\mathbf{P}_{2/1}$, than with $\mathbf{S}_{2/1}$. In the case of $\mathbf{R}_{2/1}$, similar to similar to $\mathbf{P}_{2/1}$, the influence of the left and the right inputs can propagate in cross directions depending on the value of the control bit, which allows for drawing a conclusion on the expediency of introducing the concept of order for $\mathbf{R}_{2/1}$ elementary blocks.

The order for $\mathbf{R}_{n/m}$ controlled substitution-permutation networks has the following meaning. Assume that an arbitrary mapping of k inputs $x_{\alpha_1}, x_{\alpha_2}, \ldots, x_{\alpha_k}$ and k outputs $y_{\alpha_1}, y_{\alpha_2}, \ldots, y_{\alpha_k}$ is specified as follows:

$$x_{\alpha_1} \leftrightarrow y_{\beta_1}, \ldots, x_{\alpha_i} \leftrightarrow y_{\beta_i}, \ldots, x_{\alpha_k} \leftrightarrow y_{\beta_k}$$

(here the "$\leftrightarrow$" sign stands for switching (mapping) of the pair of inputs and outputs). Assume that there exists such a value of control vector, that for each $i = 1, 2, \ldots, k$, inversion of x_{α_i} results in inversion of y_{β_i} provided that all inputs except for x_{α_i} are fixed. At the same time, inversion of outer outputs, including outputs from the set $y_{\alpha_1}, y_{\alpha_2}, \ldots, y_{\alpha_k}$, might or might not be inverted. The maximum value of k, for which this condition has been satisfied, can be adopted as the value of order h. Having adopted such interpretation of the order of a controlled substitution-permutation network of the **R** type, then replacement of all $\mathbf{P}_{2/1}$ controlled elements in a certain $\mathbf{P}_{n/m}$ block of order h by $\mathbf{R}_{2/1}$ elements results in forming an $\mathbf{R}_{n/m}$ controlled substitution-permutation network of order h. In case of the aforementioned replacement, it can be stated that a controlled permutations block and a controlled substitution-permutation network of the **R** type have the same topology. The analogy between controlled substitution-permutation networks of the $\mathbf{S}_{n/m}$ type and controlled permutations block is less obvious; however, to unify the approach to different types of substitution-permutation networks, the following definition of the order of $\mathbf{F}_{n/m}$-type controlled substitution-permutation network will be adopted:

Definition 4.1

Assume that $\mathbf{F}_{n/m}$ controlled substitution-permutation network has been specified. The $\mathbf{F}_{n/m}$ block has the order h, if it has the same topology as a certain controlled permutations block of order h.

In the course of the propagation of the influence of inputs on the outputs, the important property is the existence of the value V ensuring the influence of a given input to the specified number of arbitrarily chosen outputs. The larger the number of such output, the more pronounced the avalanche effect.

In most cryptoschemes based on controlled operations, mutually inverse operational blocks are used. Similarly to the case of building controlled permutations block, for every controlled substitution-permutation network of the $\mathbf{F}_{n/m}$ type, it is easy to synthesize the corresponding inverse block $\mathbf{F}^{-1}{}_{n/m}$. In contrast to building inverse controlled permutations blocks, where only inverse fixed permutations were required, building $\mathbf{F}^{-1}{}_{n/m}$ blocks in general case requires the use of inverse active layers; that is, active layers made up of inverse controlled elements. The general scheme of mutually inverse F-blocks is shown in Figure 4.2.

The most interesting subclasses of controlled elements—namely, $\{\mathbf{R}_{2/1}\}$ and $\{\mathbf{S}_{2/1}\}$—for each specific type of controlled element also include its inverse element. This means that direct and inverse blocks will be equivalent in a certain sense. In case of controlled substitution-permutation network built based on $\mathbf{Z}_{2/1}$ controlled elements, switching to inverse blocks is in general related to the change of differential and nonlinear properties. At the same time, depending on the $\mathbf{Z}_{2/1}$ element, properties of $\mathbf{Z}^{-1}{}_{2/1}$ elements turn out to be different even with the limits of $\{\mathbf{Z}'_{2/1}\}$, $\{\mathbf{Z}''_{2/1}\}$, $\{\mathbf{Z}^{*}{}_{2/1}\}$, and $\{\mathbf{Z}^{**}{}_{2/1}\}$ subclasses. Further on, the main attention will be drawn to controlled substitution-permutation networks based on nonlinear controlled elements.

All the aforementioned demonstrates that topological structures developed for controlled permutations blocks can be used also for controlled substitution-permutation networks of the $\mathbf{R}_{n/m}$ and $\mathbf{S}_{n/m}$ types. Because of this, building controlled substitution-permutation networks of the first order based on the recursive scheme shown in Figure 4.3a, and inverse first-order controlled substitution-permutation networks based on the recursive scheme of the second type.

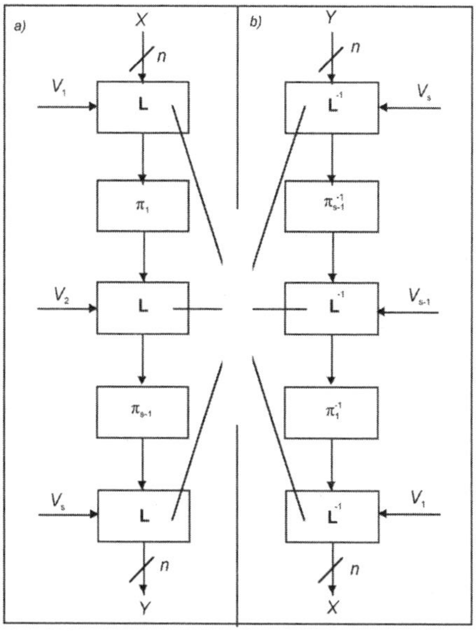

FIGURE 4.2 Structure of mutually inverse blocks $\mathbf{F}_{n/m}$ (a) and $\mathbf{F}^{-1}{}_{n/m}$ (b).

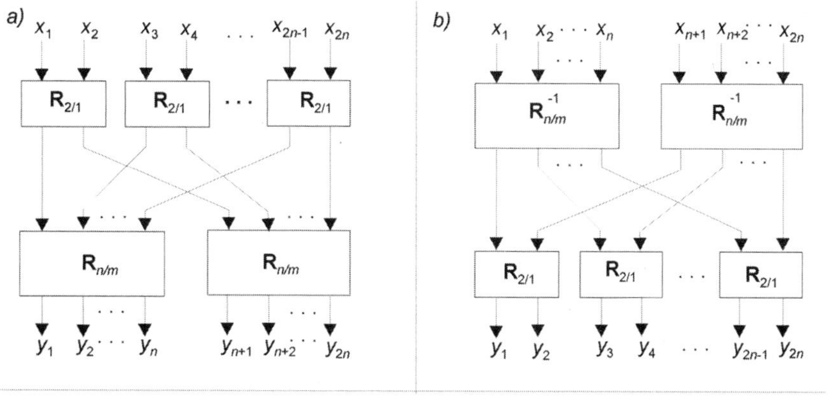

FIGURE 4.3 Building a first-order controlled substitution-permutation network $\mathbf{R}_{2n/2m+n}$ (a) and its inverse network $\mathbf{R}^{-1}{}_{2n/2m+n}$ (b) using first-order blocks $\mathbf{R}_{n/m}$ (a) and $\mathbf{R}^{-1}{}_{n/m}$ (b).

When considering the given pair of recursive design schemes, it is easy to show that the minimum number of layers required to implement a first-order controlled substitution-permutation network $\mathbf{F}_{n/m}$ makes

$$s' = \log 2n.$$

It is also possible to build controlled substitution-permutation networks $\mathbf{F}_{n/m}$ of orders 2, 4, ..., $n/4$, and n on the basis of the scheme of recursive design with order duplication (recursive scheme of the third type) shown in Figure 4.4 for the case of **R**-blocks. The latter scheme of recursive design was used for building controlled permutations blocks of different orders for the case when $n = 32$. By analogy, this scheme can be applied for the arbitrary value $n = 2^k$, where k is a positive integer number. However, this has not been proven in a formal way. Consider the procedure of building an R-type controlled substitution-permutations network for the case of an arbitrary k (obviously, this design also covers building appropriate controlled permutations blocks).

Assume it is necessary to build a block with the input size $n = 2^k$ and order $h = 2^q$, where $q < k$. Take the first-order block $\mathbf{R}_{2^{k-q}/m/1}$, where the $\mathbf{R}_{n/m/h}$ designation has been adopted, for which index h denotes the order of the controlled substitution-permutation network. Executing q sequential steps of the recursive procedure of building a controlled substitution-permutation network with duplication of the order according to the scheme shown in Figure 4.4 will produce the following result:

$$\mathbf{R}_{2^{k-q}/m_0/1} \rightarrow \mathbf{R}_{2^{k-q+1}/m_1/2} \rightarrow \mathbf{R}_{2^{k-q+2}/m_2/2^2} \rightarrow \dots$$
$$\rightarrow \mathbf{R}_{2^{k-q+i}/m_i/2^i} \rightarrow \dots \rightarrow \mathbf{R}_{2^k/m_q/2^q}.$$

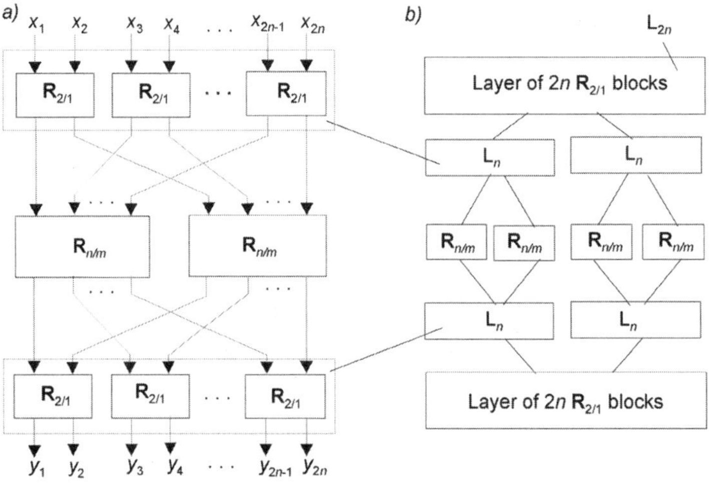

FIGURE 4.4 Structure of the $\mathbf{R}_{2n/2m+2n}$ (a) and $\mathbf{R}_{4n/4m+8n}$ (b) controlled substitution-permutation networks.

Thus, the required controlled substitution-permutation network has been built. The values m_i after each step of the recursive procedure can be easily defined. The number of layers in the resulting controlled substitution-permutation network is equal to the number of layers in the source first-order substitution-permutation network $\mathbf{R}_{2^{k-q}/m/1}$ ($s' = k - q$) plus the duplicated number of steps of the recursive procedure ($2q$), which makes:

$$s = k + q = \log_2 n + \log_2 h = \log_2 nh.$$

The latter formula allows for determining the number of layers for arbitrary values of n and $h \leq n/4$. The case $h = n/2$ doesn't present any practical interest, because it requires the use of the same number of active layers as in the case of the controlled substitution-permutation network of order $h = n$, for which $S = 2\log_2 n - 1$. This specific feature can be easily explained, because in case of order $h = n/2$ in the previously considered method of formal procedure of building a CSPN, it is necessary to use the original CSPN with a 2-bit input, which has the order $h = 2$, because according to the controllability definition it must implement at least two different permutations of the input bits, and there are only two of them. With the use of such an initial block (for example, $\mathbf{F}_{2/1}$ controlled element) at each step of the recursive procedure, the block of minimum order is implemented.

Figure 4.5 shows examples of controlled substitution-permutation networks $\mathbf{F}_{n/m}$ of orders $h = 1, 2, \ldots, n/4, n$ for the case when $n = 32$. The initial block of the recursive building procedure with the duplication of order is enclosed by the dashed frame. The design schemes considered here are universal for the input size equal to natural powers of two. However, in certain particular cases other variants of CSPN topology are preferred, which are characterized by bilateral symmetry and higher structuredness, which simplifies their circuit implementation. In addition, for symmetric blocks the mechanism of forming control vectors satisfying several predefined criteria is simplified. The use of symmetric structure results in the most significant simplification in case of building a switched controlled substitution-permutation network.

Definition 4.2

A controlled substitution-permutation network is called switched, if it can implement both direct controlled operation and its inverse operation depending on the value of some additional control bit.

Several reasons for which the use of controlled operation is the most promising for the synthesis of block ciphers will be covered later. Also covered will be different variants of building them based on controlled elements of different standard sizes.

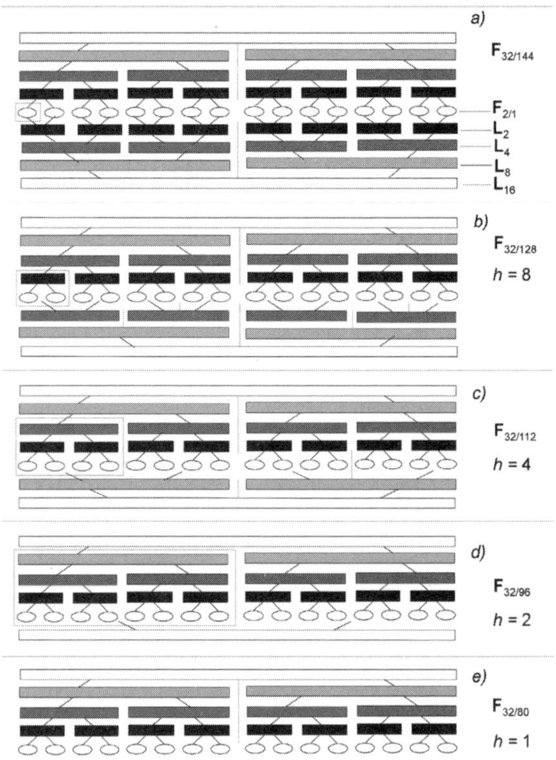

FIGURE 4.5 Controlled operational blocks $\mathbf{F}_{32/m}$ of different orders: **a**) $h = 32$, b) $h = 8$, c) $h = 4$, d) $h = 2$, e) $h = 1$.

At the same time, the important role of symmetric CSPN topologies and several differences of this concept for the cases of use of different mechanisms for specifying the switching property (which also can be called the *invertibility property*) will be traced. For example, when using the invertibility mechanism at the cost of inversion of the control bits, operational blocks are built using controlled elements, most elementary modification of which is divided into pairs of mutually inverse modification. Symmetric (or bilaterally symmetric) CSPNs are defined as follows.

Definition 4.3

A controlled substitution-permutation network is called symmetric, if for each $i = 1, 2, \ldots, s - 1,$ *the following relationships are true:* $\mathbf{L}_i = \mathbf{L}_{s-i+1}$ *and* $\pi_i = (\pi_{s-i})^{-1}$.

In other variants of building the invertible controlled substitution-permutation network, switching is ensured by means of permutation of control vectors corresponding to specific pairs of active cascades. In this case, a symmetric controlled substitution-permutation network is the one, the structure of which satisfies the following definition.

Definition 4.4

Controlled substitution-permutation network is symmetric, if in this network for each $i = 1, 2, \ldots, s - 1$*, the following relationships are true:* $\mathbf{L}_i = \mathbf{L}^{-1}_{s-i+1}$ *and* $\pi_i = (\pi_{s-i})^{-1}$.

Other, asymmetric topologies of switched controlled substitution-permutation networks will also be covered. However, the most economic solutions in terms of hardware expenses are ensured using controlled substitution-permutation networks with symmetric topology. The most interesting is the fact that some controlled substitution-permutation networks can be implemented both using symmetric and asymmetric structure. At the same time, both variants of the network structure require an equal number of active layers and ensure similar differential and nonlinear properties, such as the same algebraic degree of nonlinearity. This demonstrates that implementation of additional symmetry property is achieved without detriment to the cryptographic properties of the controlled substitution-permutation networks in cases when the symmetry is optimally combined with the input size of the block being synthesized.

In the "Cryptography: Fast Ciphers" publication by A. A. Moldovyan, N. A. Moldovyan, N.D. Goots, and B. V. Izotov, it was shown that for arbitrary k first-order controlled permutations blocks synthesized according to the first scheme of recursive synthesis, implement such a set of permutations modifications that can be split into pairs of mutually inverse modifications. This means that there exists the principal possibility of building switched controlled permutation blocks of the first order for arbitrary input sizes $n=2^k$. If a controlled substitution-permutation network of the first order is built according to the first recursive scheme using standard controlled element $\mathbf{F}_{2/1}$ representing an involution, then for arbitrary k this CSPN implements the set of modifications of controlled operation that can be split into pairs of mutually inverse modifications. This statement can be easily proven using topological transformations applicable for the case $\mathbf{F}_{2/1} = \mathbf{P}_{2/1}$.

Statement 4.1

One step of the recursive procedure of building controlled substitution-permutation networks of the third type preserves the property of splitting modifications of the original controlled substitution-permutation network into pairs of mutually inverse modifications provided that the original CSPN is characterized by such a property.

Proof

Consider an $F_{2n/2m+2n}$ block built according to the recursive scheme of the third type of using the $F_{n/m}$ original block (Figure 4.6). The block built this way can be represented as a superposition of single-layer L_1 CPSP, $F_{2n/2m}$ CSPN representing a cascade of two $F_{n/m}$ blocks and single-layer CSPN L_S. The $F_{2n/2m}$ block will be designated as $(F^{(W_1)}{}_{n/m}|F^{(W_2)}{}_{n/m})$, where W_1 and W_2 are control vectors corresponding to the left and right $F_{n/m}$ blocks. Control vectors of blocks L_1 and L_S are designated as V_1 and V_S, respectively. Let original blocks $F_{n/m}$ have the splitting property under consideration. Then, for arbitrary W_1 and W_2 there exist values W'_1 and W'_2, such that the following condition is satisfied:

$$(\mathbf{F}^{(W'_1)}{}_{n/m}|\mathbf{F}^{(W'_2)}{}_{n/m}) = ((\mathbf{F}^{(W_1)}{}_{n/m})^{-1}|(\mathbf{F}^{(W_2)}{}_{n/m})^{-1}) = (\mathbf{F}^{(W_1)}{}_{n/m}|\mathbf{F}^{(W_2)}{}_{n/m})^{-1}.$$

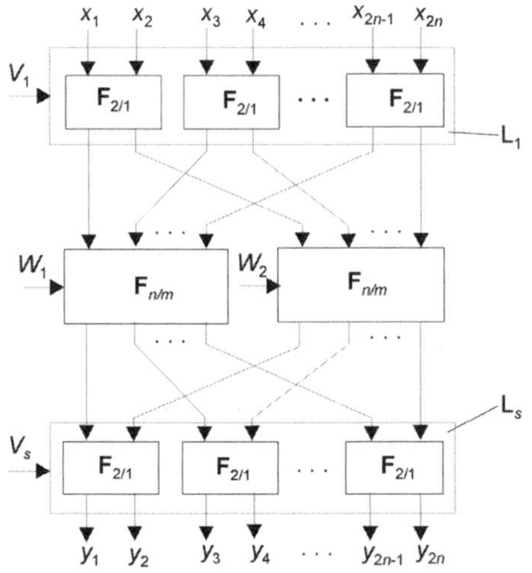

FIGURE 4.6 The structure of the $\mathbf{F}_{2n/2m+2n}$ blocks.

Now it is easy to prove that the CSPN $\mathbf{F}_{2n/2m+2n}$ controlled substitution-permutation network with control vectors $V'_1 = V_S$, $V'_S = V_1$, W'_1, and W'_2 implement modification inverse in relation to the one that is implemented with control vectors V_1, V_S, W_1 and W_2. Actually, taking into account that $\mathbf{F}_{2/1}$ controlled elements are involutions, and, consequently, the same CSPNs $\mathbf{L}_1$ and $\mathbf{L}_S$ also are controlled involutions, for transformation of the input vector X the result will appear as follows:

$$Y = (X)\,\mathbf{L}_1^{(V_1)} \bullet (\mathbf{F}^{(W_1)}{}_{n/m}|\mathbf{F}^{(W_2)}{}_{n/m}) \bullet \mathbf{L}_S^{(V_S)};$$

$$\begin{aligned}
Y' &= (Y)\,\mathbf{L}_1^{(V'_1)} \bullet (\mathbf{F}^{(W'_1)}{}_{n/m}|\mathbf{F}^{(W'_2)}{}_{n/m}) \bullet \mathbf{L}_S^{(V'_S)} \\
&= ((X)\,\mathbf{L}_1^{(V_1)} \bullet (\mathbf{F}^{(W_1)}{}_{n/m}|\mathbf{F}^{(W_2)}{}_{n/m}) \bullet \mathbf{L}_S^{(V_S)})\,\mathbf{L}_1^{(V_S)} \bullet (\mathbf{F}^{(W'_1)}{}_{n/m}|\mathbf{F}^{(W'_2)}{}_{n/m}) \bullet \mathbf{L}_S^{(V_1)} \\
&= (X)\,\mathbf{L}_1^{(V_1)} \bullet (\mathbf{F}^{(W_1)}{}_{n/m}|\mathbf{F}^{(W_2)}{}_{n/m}) \bullet \mathbf{L}_S^{(V_S)} \bullet \mathbf{L}_1^{(V_S)} \bullet (\mathbf{F}^{(W'_1)}{}_{n/m}|\mathbf{F}^{(W'_2)}{}_{n/m}) \bullet \mathbf{L}_S^{(V_1)} \\
&= (X)\,\mathbf{L}_1^{(V_1)} \bullet (\mathbf{F}^{(W_1)}{}_{n/m}|\mathbf{F}^{(W_2)}{}_{n/m}) \bullet (\mathbf{F}^{(W'_1)}{}_{n/m}|\mathbf{F}^{(W'_2)}{}_{n/m}) \bullet \mathbf{L}_S^{(V_1)} \\
&= (X)\,\mathbf{L}_1^{(V_1)} \bullet (\mathbf{F}^{(W_1)}{}_{n/m}|\mathbf{F}^{(W_2)}{}_{n/m}) \bullet (\mathbf{F}^{(W_1)}{}_{n/m}|\mathbf{F}^{(W_2)}{}_{n/m})^{-1} \bullet \mathbf{L}_S^{(V_1)} \\
&= (X)\,\mathbf{L}_1^{(V_1)} \bullet \mathbf{L}_S^{(V_1)} = X.
\end{aligned}$$

This is exactly what was required to prove.

Using Statement 4.1, it is easy to prove the following theorem that is of practical importance for applied issues, because it demonstrates the principal possibility of building switched controlled permutations blocks and controlled substitution-permutation networks of orders $h = 1, 2, \ldots, n/4, n$.

Theorem 4.1

For orders $h = 1, 2, \ldots, n/4, n$ and $n = 2k$, where k is a positive integer number, controlled substitution-permutation networks build according to the recursive scheme of the third type using a typical $\mathbf{F}_{2/1}$ controlled element representing an involution, implement the set of modifications of the controlled operation $\mathbf{F}_{n/m}$, which can be split into pairs of mutually inverse modifications.

Proof

In the case of $h = n$, the statement follows directly from the bilateral symmetry of the controlled substation-permutation network of the maximum order. In case of $h = 1$, the proof can be easily carried out using the topological conversion for the case $\mathbf{F}_{2/1} = \mathbf{P}_{2/1}$, described in "Cryptography: Fast Ciphers" by A. A. Moldovyan, N. A. Moldovyan, N. D. Goots, and B. V. Izotov. Because in controlled substitution-permutation networks of orders $h = 2, \ldots, n/4$ a first-order controlled operational substitution is used, for which the splitting property takes place, then, according to Statement 4.1, this property takes place for $h = 2$. By sequentially applying Statement 4.1, it is easy to prove that the same property takes place also for $h = 4, \ldots, n/4$.

The proven fact allows for building switched controlled substitution-permutation networks of different orders. However, to obtain more illustrative structuredness of such a design, it is necessary to use symmetric controlled substitution-permutation networks in particular cases or other design mechanism in the general case.

When evaluating hardware resources required for implementing $\mathbf{F}_{n/m}$ controlled substitution-permutation networks of different orders, it is possible to use the formula $N_{CE} = (n \log_2 nh)/2$ for computing the number of controlled elements N_{CE} in a CSPN. Tables 4.1 and 4.2 provide assessments of the required resources in case of custom VLSI circuits manufactured using 0.33-mkm technology.

TABLE 4.1 Chip Area Required for Implementing $\mathbf{F}_{32/M}$ Substitution-Permutation Networks of Different Orders (in sqmil units)

CE	$h = 1$	$h = 2$	$h = 4$	$h = 8$	$h = 32$
e/g, e/h, f/i, f/j	160	192	224	256	288
g/e, g/h, h/g, h/e, g/i, f/g, i/f, h/j, j/h, j/f, f/h	240	288	336	384	432
g/f, i/g, e/j, j/e, j/i, i/e, i/j, h/f	320	384	448	512	576

TABLE 4.2 Chip Area Required for Implementing $\mathbf{F}_{64/M}$ Substitution-Permutation Networks of Different Orders (in sqmil units)

CE	$h = 1$	$h = 2$	$h = 4$	$h = 8$	$h = 16$	$h = 64$
e/g, e/h, f/i, f/j	384	448	512	576	640	704
g/e, g/h, h/g, h/e, g/i, f/g, i/f, h/j, j/h, j/f, f/h	576	672	768	864	960	1056
g/f, i/g, e/j, j/e, j/i, i/e, i/j, h/f	768	896	1024	1152	1280	1408

From the data provided in Tables 4.1 and 4.2, it is obvious that all considered controlled substitution-permutation networks require reasonable hardware resources, and, therefore can be used for implementing ciphers of different types. 32-bit $\mathbf{F}_{32/96}$ CSPNs and 64-bit $\mathbf{F}_{64/192}$ CSPNs characterized by low-circuit implementation complexity appear the most promising for this purpose. Evaluations provided in Tables 4.1 and 4.2 demonstrate that ciphers based on controlled substitution-permutation networks can be implemented economically enough. The complexity of their implementation is approximately equal to, and, in some cases (for certain types of controlled elements) considerably lower than implementation of ciphers based on data-dependent permutations.

This book provides detailed coverage of controlled elements of the $\mathbf{F}_{2/1}$ and $\mathbf{F}_{2/2}$ types. However, similar ciphers based on controlled substitution-permutation networks of other size can be built; for example, $\mathbf{F}_{3/2}$, $\mathbf{F}_{4/1}$, $\mathbf{F}_{3/3}$, and $\mathbf{F}_{4/2}$. In the latter case, the 6×4 S-boxes are practically used. For this purpose, it is possible to use S-boxes employed in the DES cipher. They are covered in detail in many publications on cryptography, and therefore won't be considered here. It is only necessary to point out that the criteria of choice of $\mathbf{F}_{4/2}$ controlled elements must not necessarily match the criteria of choice for 6×4 substitutions discussed earlier when substantiating their choice for cryptographic applications.

This is because $\mathbf{F}_{4/2}$ elements are assumed to be used in cryptosystems of other type; namely, in cases when control data subgroup and data subgroup being transformed remain independent in the course of executing a controlled operation built on their basis. In case of the DES algorithm 6×4, substitutions are used differently: a cascade of eight such substitutions actually implements a fixed substitution carried out over a 32-bit data subgroup by means of executing controlled operations over 4-bit data subgroups (the choice of one of the four substitutions of the 4×4 type depending on the values of two bits belonging to other subgroups). Because of the sharp growth of the number of controlled elements satisfying the criteria of applicability of synthesis of controlled substitution-permutation networks, when migrating from $\mathbf{F}_{2/1}$ to $\mathbf{F}_{2/2}$ and $\mathbf{F}_{3/1}$ elements it is possible to assume that there will be many $\mathbf{F}_{4/2}$ elements suitable for synthesis of controlled substitution-permutation networks, and their number would considerably exceed the number of 6×4 substitutions considered satisfying criteria of applicability in classical substitution-permutation ciphers.

Thus, cryptoschemes based on the use of variable operations implemented using substitution-permutation networks provide the following possibilities:

- Efficiently use controlled elements of comparatively low size, including minimal CEs.
- Considerably extend the number of variants of $\mathbf{F}_{4/2}$ elements and larger CEs that are of interest for cryptographic applications.

Controlled elements with minimal input size ($\mathbf{F}_{2/1}$ and $\mathbf{F}_{2/2}$) are minimal building blocks for the synthesis of cryptographic operations. Their application is expedient because of the following reasons:

- They have been tried and tested in multiple ciphers; in particular, in the ciphers based on variable bit permutations.
- The complete classification of $\mathbf{F}_{2/1}$ controlled elements has been built, and two best subclasses of such elements have been found.
- Criteria of the choice of $\mathbf{F}_{2/2}$ elements have been defined and their detailed classification has been developed.
- The use of such elements ensures considerably more economic hardware implementation in comparison to building controlled substitution-permutation networks with the input size of 4 bits or more.

The use of $\mathbf{F}_{3/1}$ elements also is interesting and promising and ensures building of economic ciphers. Although 3-bit input introduces some limitations on the use of such elements, they can be employed, for example, for synthesis of controlled substitution-permutation networks oriented toward the following applications:

- In cryptographic systems with splitting into unequal data subgroups (for instance, when a 128-bit data block is split into one 32-bit and one 96-bit subgroup, and the latter is transformed using a controlled substitution-permutation network, while the first subgroup is used for specifying the control vector).
- In hash functions, where there is no need to ensure reversibility of transformation, and, therefore, it is possible to use the operation of extension of the binary vector being transformed.
- In the round function of the generalized Feistel cryptoscheme.

4.2 PROBLEMS WITH BUILDING BLOCK CIPHERS WITH SIMPLE KEY USE SCHEDULE

The use of data-dependent operations as a basic cryptographic primitive—that is, the use of variable transformation operations—creates prerequisites for building fast ciphers characterized by low complexity of circuit implementation. Based on primitives of this type, it is possible to build transformation cryptoschemes, which strengthen the computations parallelism, and make it possible to transform round subkeys simultaneously with data subgroup transformation. The latter is the prerequisite for the application of the simple key use schedule, consisting in that instead of round keys fragments of the secret key (subkeys) or some of their combinations are used.

Simple key use schedule ensures the following possibilities:

- Considerable additional economy of the circuit resources in case of hardware implementation of ciphers.
- Improvement of the performance of encrypting devices in case of frequent key change, which is important for most network applications.

Examples of ciphers based on data-dependent operations and using simple schedule of key use are SPECTR-H64, SPECTR-128, CIKS-128, COBRA-F64a, COBRA-F64b, etc. However, no matter how complex transformations might be used in one round of iterative cryptoschemes where the encryption mode switches to the decryption mode by means of changing the order of using round keys to the inverse one, simple schedule of key use results in that for certain classes of keys (even if their share in the complete keyspace is negligible) the encryption procedure will coincide the decryption procedure. Such keys are considered weak. In case of the aforementioned cryptoschemes, the simple key use schedule results in the existence of weak keys of this type because in both encryption mode the same transformation procedures are used. Furthermore, for certain key subclasses the use of simple key use schedule results in that all round key turn out identical, and, consequently, all rounds of encryption represent the same transformation (this take place even in some practically used ciphers, for example, in GOST 28147–89 cryptosystem). The latter circumstance represents a prerequisite for implementation of the slide attack suggested in "New Types of Cryptanalytic Attacks Using Related keys" by E. Biham. Although the probability of choosing a weak key is very low ($2^{-192} - 2^{-128}$) for the aforementioned ciphers, it is highly desirable to eliminate this feature. When building round hash functions based on the use of block ciphers, the presence of even a very small share of weak keys is undesirable. For example, for iterative hash functions, where blocks of hashed data take part in the transformation instead of the key, the presence of weak keys provides the possibility of easily forming large number of different messages, the hash function of which equals the same value, which cannot be tolerated.

The following approaches can be suggested to eliminate weak keys in iterative block ciphers using simple key use schedule:

- The use of different transformation procedures for encryption and decryption. A considerable drawback of this approach is that in case of hardware implementation it actually requires you to implement two algorithms. In addition, a class of keys is preserved, for which all rounds of encryption represent the same transformation, although that transformation differs from the decryption round. Because of this, prerequisites for slide attack still remain.

- Including constants the values of which depend on the round number and encryption mode into the round transformation. This method allows for eliminating both weak keys and similarity of all encryption rounds. A certain drawback of this approach is that at least one additional operation must be included into each round, and, in addition, it is necessary to implement the mechanism of appropriate change of the order of using constants when changing the encryption mode.
- The use of switched operations controlled by a bit specifying direct or inverse order of the use of round keys (thanks to which the choice of the encryption or decryption mode is ensured). This approach requires minimum additional expenses for implementation of circuit resources and eliminates the need in switching constant values in each round when changing the encryption mode. Furthermore, it creates prerequisites for substantiating ciphers, in which the change of the order of the round keys use is not required. The latter circumstance even allows for reducing the general cost of hardware implementation.

The comparison of all the previous approaches shows that the use of switched controlled operation is of greatest interest. The main issue here consists in development of switched operations satisfying the following requirements:

- Low cost of circuit implementation
- Efficiency of the use of the scheme as cryptographic primitive
- High performance

The switching property of the operation is in essence a special variant of the implementation of the controllability property. This inspires the idea of implementing switched controlled operations by means of appropriate modification of the schemes used for building controlled operations. In addition, there are prerequisites for efficient implementation of switched controlled operations, in which the entire set of modifications that can potentially be implemented is split into pairs of mutually inverse modifications. Assume that in some hypothetic controlled operation there is an additional 1-bit control input, to which bit e is supplied, specifying the mode of operation. Assume that when $e = 0$ the direct controlled operation is executed, and when $e = 1$ the inverse operation corresponding to it takes place. This means that for each fixed value of the control vector the direct modification will take place in the course of encryption ($e = 0$), and the corresponding inverse operation will take place in the course of decryption ($e = 1$), which means that a certain switched controlled operation is implemented. The idea of building a switched controlled operation can be efficiently implemented based on symmetric topologies of controlled permutation networks and controlled substitution-permutation networks. Subsequent few sections of this chapter will cover building of switched controlled operations of different types.

4.3. THE NOTION OF SWITCHED OPERATION

In general, the concept of controlled operation can be defined as follows.

Definition 4.5
Let $\{F_1, F_2, \ldots, F_{2^m}\}$ be a set of operations defined by the formula $Y = F_i = F_i(X_1, X_2, \ldots, X_q)$, where $i = 1, 2, \ldots, 2^m$, $X_1, X_2, \ldots, X_q$ are input n-bit binary vectors (operands), and Y is the output n-bit vector. Then, the operation $F^{(V)}$ dependent of V and defined by the formula $Y = F^{(V)}(X_1, X_2, \ldots, X_q) = F_V(X_1, X_2, \ldots, X_q)$, where V is m-bit control vector is called controlled q-bit operation. Operations $F_1, F_2, \ldots, F_{2^m}$ will be called modifications of controlled operation $F^{(V)}$.

Examples of controlled operations are controlled permutations and controlled 2-bit operations. The concept of inverse controlled operation is of the greatest interest for further consideration.

Definition 4.6
Let $\{F_1, F_2, \ldots, F_{2^m}\}$ be a set of modifications of the controlled operation $F^{(V)}$. Operation $(F^{(V)})^{-1}$ containing modifications $F_1^{-1}, F_2^{-1}, \ldots, F_{2^m}^{-1}$ is called inverse in relation to the controlled operation $F^{(V)}$, if for all V modifications F_V^{-1} and F_V are mutually inverse.

In general, switched operation can be defined as follows.

Definition 4.7
Let $F'^{(e)}$, where $e \in \{0,1\}$ be some operation depending on e, and containing two modifications: $F'^{(0)} = F'_1$ and $F'^{(1)} = F'_2$, where $F'_2 = F'^{-1}_1$. Then operation $F'^{(e)}$ is called switched operation.

Further on, various kinds of controlled operations will be considered. However, the switched controlled operation determined as follows is the most important and presenting the greatest interest.

Definition 4.8
Let two modifications of the switched operation $F'^{(e)}$ represent a pair of mutually inverse controlled operations $F'^{(0)} = F^{(V)}$ and $F'^{(1)} = (F^{(V)})^{-1}$. Then $F'^{(e)}$ is called switched controlled operation $F^{(V,e)}$.

For the first time, a particular case of switched controlled operations, namely, switched controlled permutations were built based on permutation networks with symmetric structure. Building controlled operations based on controlled substitution-permutation networks considerably extends the class of switched controlled operations and provides new possibilities of designing fast block ciphers oriented toward efficient hardware implementation. It is possible to suggest several approaches to implementation of switched controlled operations based on substitution-permutation networks. The main approaches among them are based on the use of:

- Elements of the network topology symmetry
- Symmetry of the bit distribution of the control vector

In the first case, the internal node of switched controlled operation is implemented as some switching block that changes the distribution of control bits so that for the specified control vector the modification being implemented switches from direct to inverse one. This case ensures the possibility of using the control vector, in which every bit is independent. In the second case, internal nodes of switched controlled operations are implemented as 1) the switching block of smaller size and implemented with lower overhead for circuit resources and 2) the extension block implemented as simple branching of wires and introducing practically no additional expenses for the hardware. In the first variant, the extension block is not required, although in particular cases of the use of switched controlled operations it can be used, for example, for forming the control vector of large size based on a data subgroup of small size. The symmetry of the topological structure of a certain switched controlled operation assumes that controlled elements located in symmetric positions are either involutions of mutually inverse controlled elements of a generally type.

When using special types of controlled elements, the switching mechanism consists of inversion of all bits of the control vector instead of stepwise redistribution of control bits over controlled elements of the controlled substitution-permutation network. To implement this switching mechanism, the controlled element is designed so all its modifications are split into pairs of mutually inverse modifications. If such controlled elements are included into symmetric topology, switching of the direct controlled operation to the inverse operation is carried out by means of inverting each bit of the control vector.

4.4 CONTROLLED OPERATIONAL SUBSTITUTIONS AS A CLASS OF PAIRWISE MUTUALLY INVERSE MODIFICATIONS

Recursive schemes of building permutation networks are of practical importance and can be used for designing controlled operational substitutions. For building switched controlled operational substitutions, it is interesting to prove that the recursive building procedure forms controlled permutation network and substitution-permutation networks, the set of implemented modifications of which is split into pairs of mutually inverse modifications. This result has been proven in "Cryptography: Fast Ciphers" by A. A. Moldovyan, N. A. Moldovyan, N. D. Goots, and B. V. Izotov for recursive first-order blocks of controlled permutations. The scheme of recursive procedure of building a first-order block of controlled permutation can be extended to controlled operational substitutions by means of replacing an elementary controlled switch with the controlled substitution element $\mathbf{F}_{2/1}$. This results in a recursive scheme of the procedure of building switched controlled operational substitutions, shown in Figure 4.7 and related to the first type. This procedure consists of the use of two identical parallel $\mathbf{F}_{n/m}$ blocks, the inputs of which are connected to the outputs of the active cascade $\mathbf{L}_n$ made up of n parallel $\mathbf{F}_{2/1}$ elements according to the following rule. The left (right) 1-bit output of each i-th $\mathbf{F}_{2/1}$ element of the active cascade $\mathbf{L}_n$ is connected to the i-th 1-bit input of the left (right) $\mathbf{F}_{n/m}$ block. As a result, the $\mathbf{F}_{2n/2m+n}$ block is formed. At the first step of the recursive building procedure of the first type uses controlled $\mathbf{F}_{2/1}$ elements as $\mathbf{F}_{n/m}$ blocks, and active $\mathbf{L}_2$ cascaded made up of two $\mathbf{F}_{2/1}$ elements as $\mathbf{L}_n$ (Figure 4.7c).

The proof of splitting of all modifications of the controlled permutations blocks into pairs of mutually inverse modifications is based on the use of specific features of the topology of recursive procedure of the first type, and that the switched element is an elementary controlled involution. Considering this, it is easy to show that this proof also can be extended to controlled permutation blocks with similar topology, if elementary controlled operational substitution (that is, $\mathbf{F}_{2/1}$ controlled element) represents an elementary controlled involution. Because of availability of many different variants of $\mathbf{F}_{2/1}$ elements characterized by nonlinear properties, it is possible to build many different switched controlled operational substitutions.

The specified type of splitting also takes place in cases with switched controlled operational substitutions obtained according to the recursive building procedure of the second type, which is analogous to the similar recursive building procedure of the first type. This recursive procedure consists of the following. Outputs of two parallel $\mathbf{F}'_{n/m}$ blocks are connected to the input of the active $\mathbf{L}_n$ cascade according to the following rule. The left (right) 1-bit input of each i-th $\mathbf{F}_{2/1}$ element of the active $\mathbf{L}_n$ cascade is connected to the i-th 1-bit output of the left (right) $\mathbf{F}'_{n/m}$ block. As a

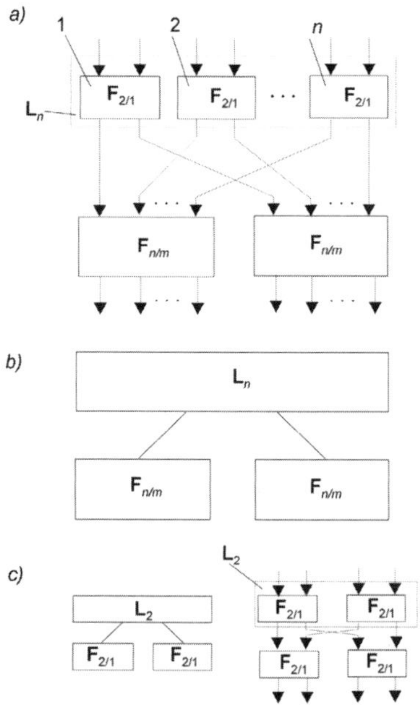

FIGURE 4.7 The first variant of the recursive procedure of building controlled substitution-permutation network: a) block size duplication step, b) schematic representation of the duplication step, c) the first step of the building procedure.

result, the $\mathbf{F}'_{2n/2m+n}$ block is formed. At the first step of the recursive building procedure of the second type, $\mathbf{F}_{2/1}$ controlled elements are used as $\mathbf{F}'_{n/m}$ blocks. The $\mathbf{F}'_{2n/2m+n}$. block is bilaterally symmetric in relation to the $\mathbf{F}_{2n/2m+n}$ block obtained using the recursive scheme of the first type (Figure 4.8).

This means that if in the bits of the control vectors in $\mathbf{F}'_{2n/2m+n}$ blocks are distributed by controlled elements according to the rule corresponding to inverse controlled substitution-permutation networks, the result will be $\mathbf{F}'_{2n/2m+n} = (\mathbf{F}'_{2n/2m+n})^{-1}$. Because modifications of $\mathbf{F}_{2n/2m+n}$ blocks are split into pairs of mutually inverse modifications, from the latter relationship it follows that this property also takes place for $\mathbf{F}'_{2n/2m+n}$ controlled substitution permutation networks. The first and the second types of the recursive building procedure at each step result in the synthesis of first-order substitution-permutation networks.

Two previously considered variants of the building procedure can be used for building mutually inverse blocks when using $\mathbf{F}_{2/1}$ controlled elements of the general

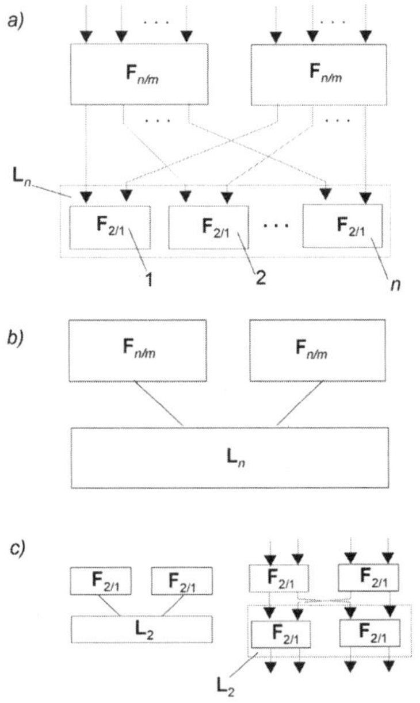

FIGURE 4.8 The second variant of recursive procedure of building controlled substitution-permutation networks: a) block duplication size step, b) schematic representation of the duplication step, c) the first step of the building procedure.

type. In this case, the first-type recursive procedure is carried out using direct $\mathbf{F}_{2/1}$ elements, and the recursive procedure of the second type is carried out using corresponding inverse $(\mathbf{F}_{2/1})^{-1}$ elements as shown in Figure 4.9.

The use of the third type of recursive procedure of building controlled permutation blocks ensuring synthesis of networks of maximum order is also of interest for synthesis of controlled substitution-permutation networks. This variant can be represented as a combination of the first two. Within a single step, the $\mathbf{F}_{2n/2m+2n}$ block is formed on the basis of two $\mathbf{F}_{n/m}$ blocks and two active $\mathbf{L}_n$ cascades (Figure 4.10). In this case, both the input size of the CSPN input and its order are duplicated. At the first step of the building procedure, two controlled $\mathbf{F}_{2/1}$ elements and two active cascades of the $\mathbf{L}_2$ type are used. Because $\mathbf{F}_{2/1}$ elements have the maximum order, each step of recursion results in the synthesis of a CSPN of maximum order with the duplicated input size. In all three types of recursive building procedures, the use of controlled elementary involutions $\mathbf{F}_{2/1}$ is assumed to ensure that

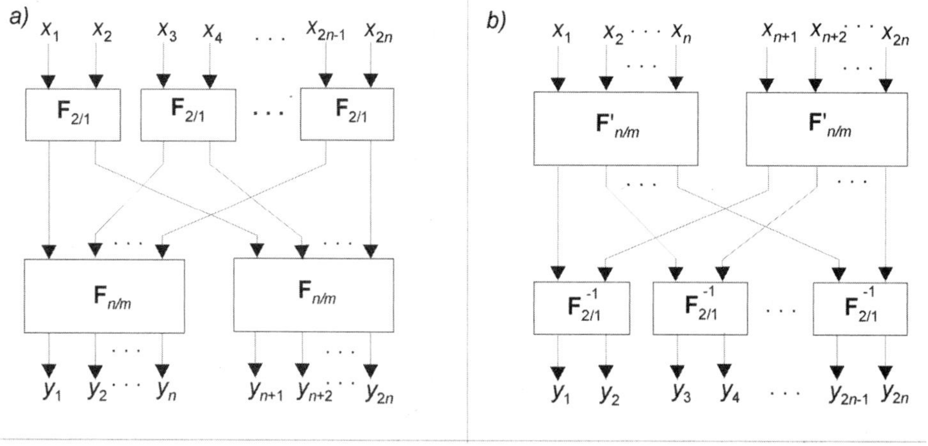

FIGURE 4.9 Schemes of recursive building of controlled substitution-permutation networks with mutually symmetric topologies.

implemented modifications are split into the pairs of mutually inverse modifications (in case of the general building procedure, this condition is not mandatory). Such a splitting serves as evidence of the principal possibility of building switched controlled operations, although the issue of the complexity of this synthesis deserves to be considered separately.

Because of the internal bilateral symmetry of $\mathbf{F}_{2n/2m+2n}$ blocks, the existence of the aforementioned splitting for them is obvious. Actually, for each value of the control vector $V = (V_1, V_2, ..., V_s)$, a modification is implemented, which is inverse in relation to the modification corresponding to the control vector $V' = (V_s, V_{s-1}, ..., V_1)$ obtained on the basis of V by writing $V_1, V_2, ..., V_s$ components in the inverse order. Similarly, it is possible to show that the aforementioned splitting can be implemented for every symmetric substitution-permutation network. Symmetric controlled substitution-permutation networks (and controlled permutations blocks as a particular case) are convenient for synthesis of switched controlled operations of different types. That being so, in symmetric controlled substitution-permutation networks it is possible to use controlled elementary involutions, and pairs of mutually inverse $\mathbf{F}_{2/1}$ elements of the general type, located in symmetric positions. For example, if at the first step of the third-type recursive building procedure two controlled elementary involutions $\mathbf{F}^*_{2/1}$ are used, and at each step of the recursive procedure cascades built on the basis of direct $\mathbf{F}_{2/1}$ elements and corresponding inverse $(\mathbf{F}_{2/1})^{-1}$ elements are employed as upper $\mathbf{L}_n$ and lower $\mathbf{L}^{-1}{}_n$ active cascades, a new wide class of symmetric controlled substitution-permutation networks will be obtained. This scheme is presented in Figure 4.11.

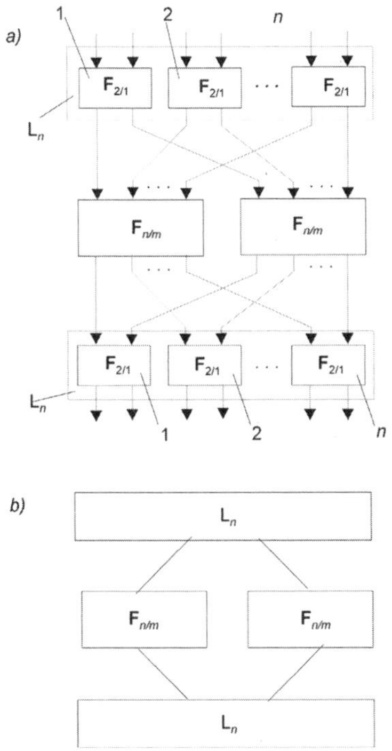

FIGURE 4.10 The third variant of recursive procedure of building controlled substitution-permutation networks: a) block size duplication step, b) schematic representation of the duplication step.

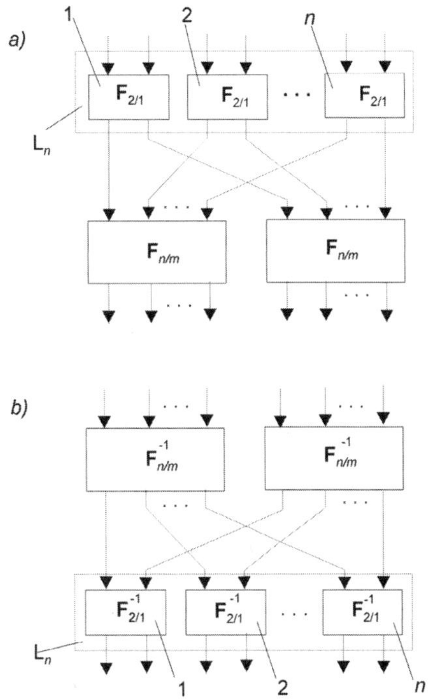

FIGURE 4.11 Recursive procedure of building mutually inverse controlled substitution-permutation networks based on mutually inverse controlled elements: a) direct block, b) inverse block.

Using the property of the order duplication implemented in the third type of the recursive building procedure, it is possible to build controlled substitution-permutation networks of orders 2, 4, …, $n/4$. This operation is carried out by analogy to the synthesis of controlled permutations blocks of the same orders, described earlier in the "Cryptography: Fast Ciphers" publication by A. A. Moldovyan, N. A. Moldovyan, N. D. Goots, and B. V. Izotov. The minimal number of active cascades required for implementation of a first-order controlled substitution-permutation network makes $s_{\min} = \log_2 n$. This can be easily discovered by considering the first or the second variants of the recursive building procedure. By carrying out the recursion step of the third type when using two $\mathbf{F}_{n/m}$ blocks of the first order, you'll obtain the $\mathbf{F}_{2n/2m+2n}$ block of the second order with the following number of layers:

$$s_{\min} = 2 + \log_2 n = 1 + \log_2 2n,$$

where $2n$ is the size of the synthesized block of the second order; that is, for this input size the minimum number of active cascades required for implementation of the second-order controlled substitution-permutation network is greater by one than the s_{min} value for the first-order controlled substitution-permutation network. If the initial $\mathbf{F}_{n/m}$ block has the order h, the third-type recursion step ensures building of the $\mathbf{F}_{2n/2m+2n}$ block of order $2h$. It can be easily shown that for the given values n and $h \leq n/4$ the s_{min} value makes $s_{min} = \log_2 nh$. The case $h = n/2$ can be implemented; however, it is of no practical interest, because its implementation requires you to use $s_{min} = 2\log_2 n - 1$ active cascades, which is equal to the number of active cascades in a controlled substitution-permutation network of order n.

Now it is necessary to prove that the controlled substitution-permutation networks of orders 2, 4, ..., $n/4$ have the property of modifications splitting into two subsets of mutually inverse modifications. Figure 4.12 illustrates the structure of the **F** block of order $2h$, where internal blocks **F′** and **F″** have the order h and are characterized by this property. At the first step of recursion, it is possible, for example, to take mutually inverse first-order controlled substitution-permutation networks built using elementary controlled involutions according to the first and the second

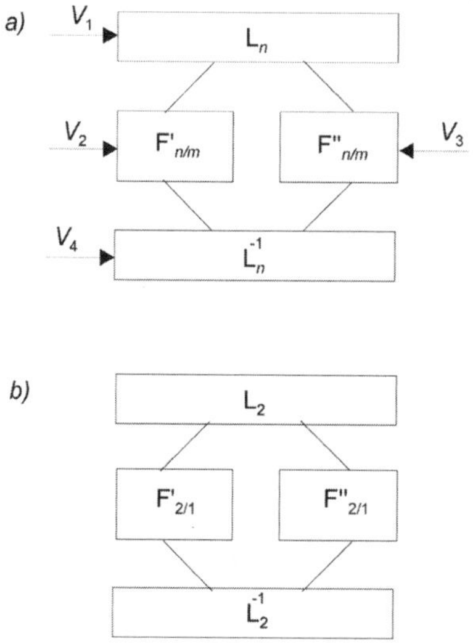

FIGURE 4.12 The third variant of recursive building of symmetric substitution-permutation networks using different blocks: a) general scheme, b) the first step of the building procedure.

recursive building schemes. In the particular case, it is possible to take the pair of $\mathbf{F}'_{2/1}$ and $\mathbf{F}''_{2/1}$ controlled elements as original blocks $\mathbf{F}'$ and $\mathbf{F}''$. For $\mathbf{F}'_{2/1}$ and $\mathbf{F}''_{2/1}$ controlled elements, the following relations are true: $\mathbf{F}'^{(0)}_{2/1} = (\mathbf{F}'^{(1)}_{2/1})^{-1}$ and $\mathbf{F}''^{(0)}_{2/1} = (\mathbf{F}''^{(1)}_{2/1})^{-1}$, which means that the recursive procedure uses controlled elements with the set of modifications that can be split into two subsets of mutually inverse modifications. For such controlled elements, it is possible to take CEs described as the following pairs of elementary modifications: q/u, v/s, u/q, x/r, w/t, r/x, s/v, and t/v.

The control vector V corresponding to block $\mathbf{F}$ can be represented in the form of concatenation of elements V_1, V_2, V_3, V_4, which are control vectors of the upper cascade $\mathbf{L}_n$, block $\mathbf{F}'$, block $\mathbf{F}''$ and lower cascade $\mathbf{L}_n$, respectively: $V = (V_1, V_2, V_3, V_4)$. For an arbitrary control vector V, because of the assumed properties of blocks $\mathbf{F}'$ and $\mathbf{F}''$, it is possible to specify another control vector $V' = (V_4, V'_2, V'_3, V_1)$, where V'_2 is such a control vector of block $\mathbf{F}'$, for which the latter implements the modification inverse in relation to the modification implemented at V_2; and V'_3 is such a control vector of block $\mathbf{F}''$, for which the latter implements the modification that is inverse in relation to the modification implemented with V_3. Because of the bilateral symmetry of the inclusion of the upper and lower cascades $\mathbf{L}_n$, block $\mathbf{F}$ with $V' = (V_4, V'_2, V'_3, V_1)$ implements the modification that is inverse in relation to the modification, which it implements having $V = (V_1, V_2, V_3, V_4)$. Actually, it is possible to represent the $\mathbf{F}_{2n/2m+2n}$ controlled substitution-permutation network as a superposition of a single-layered $\mathbf{L}_n$ controlled substitution-permutation network, $\mathbf{F}'_{2n/2m}$ controlled substitution-permutation network representing a cascade of two blocks, $\mathbf{F}'_{n/m}$ and $\mathbf{F}''_{n/m}$, and a single-layered controlled substitution-permutation network $\mathbf{L}_n^{-1}$. Denote block $\mathbf{F}'_{2n/2m}$ as $(\mathbf{F}'^{(V_2)}_{n/m}|\mathbf{F}''^{(V_3)}_{n/m})$, where V_2 and V_3 are control vectors corresponding to the left and right internal blocks.

Now, convert the input vector X according to the following scheme:

$$Y = (X)\,\mathbf{L}_n^{(V_1)} \bullet (\mathbf{F}'^{(V_2)}_{n/m}|\mathbf{F}''^{(V_3)}_{n/m}) \bullet (\mathbf{L}_n^{-1})^{(V_4)};$$

$$\begin{aligned}
Y' = (Y)\,\mathbf{L}_n^{(V_4)} \bullet (\mathbf{F}'^{(V'_2)}_{n/m}|\mathbf{F}''^{(V'_3)}_{n/m}) \bullet (\mathbf{L}_n^{-1})^{(V_1)} &= \\
= ((X)\,\mathbf{L}_n^{(V_1)}\bullet(\mathbf{F}'^{(V_2)}_{n/m}|\mathbf{F}''^{(V_3)}_{n/m})\bullet(\mathbf{L}_n^{-1})^{(V_4)})\,\mathbf{L}_n^{(V_4)}\bullet(\mathbf{F}'^{(V'_2)}_{n/m}|\mathbf{F}''^{(V'_3)}_{n/m})\bullet(\mathbf{L}_n^{-1})^{(V_1)} \\
= (X)\,\mathbf{L}_n^{(V_1)}\bullet(\mathbf{F}'^{(V_2)}_{n/m}|\mathbf{F}''^{(V_3)}_{n/m})\bullet(\mathbf{L}_n^{-1})^{(V_4)}\bullet\mathbf{L}_n^{(V_4)}\bullet(\mathbf{F}'^{(V'_2)}_{n/m}|\mathbf{F}''^{(V'_3)}_{n/m})\bullet(\mathbf{L}_n^{-1})^{(V_1)} \\
= (X)\,\mathbf{L}_n^{(V_1)}\bullet(\mathbf{F}'^{(V_2)}_{n/m}|\mathbf{F}''^{(V_3)}_{n/m}) \bullet (\mathbf{F}'^{(V_2)}_{n/m}|\mathbf{F}''^{(V_3)}_{n/m})^{-1} \bullet (\mathbf{L}_n^{-1})^{(V_1)} \\
= (X)\,\mathbf{L}_n^{(V_1)} \bullet (\mathbf{L}_n^{-1})^{(V_1)} = X.
\end{aligned}$$

Thus, for an arbitrary value of the control vector V, it is possible to specify the value V', such that the following relationship is true $\mathbf{F}^{(V')}_{2n/2m+2n} = (\mathbf{F}^{(V)}_{2n/2m+2n})^{-1}$, which is exactly what was required to prove.

If internal blocks **F**′ and **F**″ are built according to the recursive scheme of the first or second type, they are characterized by the splitting property being considered. Consequently, this property has been proven for second-order **F** blocks. Using such second-order blocks, according to the scheme under consideration, it is possible to build blocks of order 4, characterized by this splitting property. Further, it is possible to consider blocks of orders 8, 16, and higher orders.

Thus, in the example of three types of a recursive procedure of building $\mathbf{F}_{n/m}$ blocks, it is principally possible to build switched controlled operational substitution of orders 1, 2, …, n; however, symmetric topology providing a convenient implementation of the mechanism of inverting a controlled operation is implemented only in the case of maximum order. In case of orders 2, 4, …, $n/4$ the development of the switching mechanisms for distribution of control bits requires detailed elaboration considering each step of the recursive building procedures used in the course of synthesizing $\mathbf{F}_{n/m}$ blocks. In further sections, particular cases of building symmetric switched controlled operations of the first and second orders will be used, along with another scheme of order duplication allowing for simplification of the synthesis of switched controlled operations of orders 1, 2, 4, …, $n/4$ for an arbitrary value of n representing a natural power of two.

4.5 SWITCHED CONTROLLED OPERATIONAL SUBSTITUTIONS WITH SYMMETRIC TOPOLOGICAL STRUCTURE

When developing ciphers using controlled permutations, symmetric controlled permutations blocks $\mathbf{P}_{32/96}$ and $\mathbf{P}_{64/192}$ have found a wide application. These blocks have the second and the first orders, respectively. Using topologies of these blocks, it is possible to build switched controlled operational substitutions $\mathbf{F}^{(V,e)}{}_{32/96}$ and $\mathbf{F}^{(V,e)}{}_{64/192}$, characterized by different properties that are determined by the choice of controlled elements of a specific type. In contrast to synthesis of controlled permutations block, which is carried out using a single variant of a controlled element—namely, elementary controlled permutation $\mathbf{P}_{2/1}$ representing an involution—in case of a controlled substitution-permutation network, there are considerably more different types of controlled elements available. Some of these elements are involutions, while most other elements are not. Consider the procedure of building a controlled substitution-permutation network with symmetric topology. First, it is necessary to build first-order blocks $\mathbf{F}_{8/12}$ and $\mathbf{F}^{-1}{}_{8/12}$, which contain three active cascades (Figure 4.13). In this case, the $\mathbf{F}_{8/12}$ block will be built using $\mathbf{F}_{2/1}$ elements of arbitrary type, and $\mathbf{F}^{-1}{}_{8/12}$ blocks will be built using $\mathbf{F}^{-1}{}_{2/1}$ elements, which are inverted $\mathbf{F}_{2/1}$ elements.

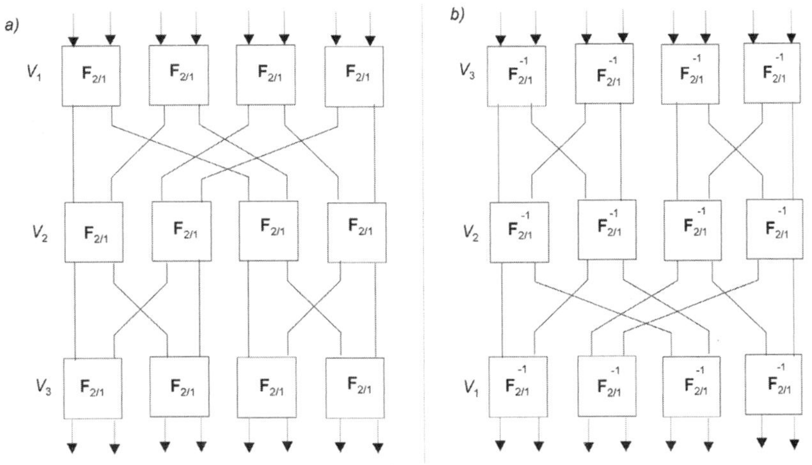

FIGURE 4.13 The structure of operational blocks $\mathbf{F}_{8/12}$ and $\mathbf{F}^{-1}_{8/12}$.

If the standard element is an elementary controlled involution, the following relationship is true: $\mathbf{F}^{-1}_{2/1} = \mathbf{F}_{2/1}$. In this case, active cascades in blocks $\mathbf{F}_{8/12}$ and $\mathbf{F}^{-1}_{8/12}$ are identical and represent single-layer controlled substitution-permutation networks representing involutions.

Having built $\mathbf{F}_{8/12}$ and $\mathbf{F}^{-1}_{8/12}$ blocks, it is possible to proceed with building six-layer blocks $\mathbf{F}_{32/96}$ and $\mathbf{F}_{64/192}$. The $\mathbf{F}_{32/96}$ block is implemented using four $\mathbf{F}_{8/12}$ blocks that make up the input cascade, and four $\mathbf{F}^{-1}_{8/12}$ blocks that form the output cascade (Figure 4.14a).

Outputs of the first cascade are connected to the inputs of the second cascade according to the fixed permutation $\mathbf{I}_1$, which represents an involution and is described by the following cyclic structure:

$$(1)(2,9)(3,17)(4,25)(5)(6,13)(7,21)(8,29)(10)$$
$$(11,18)(12,26)(14)(15,22)(16,30)(19)(20,27)(23)(24,31)(28)(32).$$

The controlled operational block $\mathbf{F}^{-1}_{32/96}$ (Figure 4.14b) is an inverted block $\mathbf{F}_{32/96}$. It has the similar structure, differing only in that the components of control vector V_1, V_2, V_3, V_4, V_5, and V_6 are distributed by active layers from bottom to top, while in the direct block they are distributed from top to bottom.

Block $\mathbf{F}_{64/192}$ is implemented using eight $\mathbf{F}_{8/12}$ blocks that make up the input cascade, and eight $\mathbf{F}^{-1}_{8/12}$ blocks that make up the output cascade (Figure 4.14c). The outputs of the first cascade are connected to the inputs of the second cascade according to the fixed permutation $\mathbf{I}_2$, which represents an involution and is described by the following cyclic structure:

(1)(2,9,3,17,4,25,5,33,6,41,7,49,8,57)(10)
(11,18,12,26,13,34,14,42,15,50,16,58)(19)
(20,27,21,35,22,43,23,51,24,59)(28)(29,36,30,44,31,52,32,60)(37)
(38,45,39,53,40,61)(46)(47,54,48,62)(55)(56,63)(64).

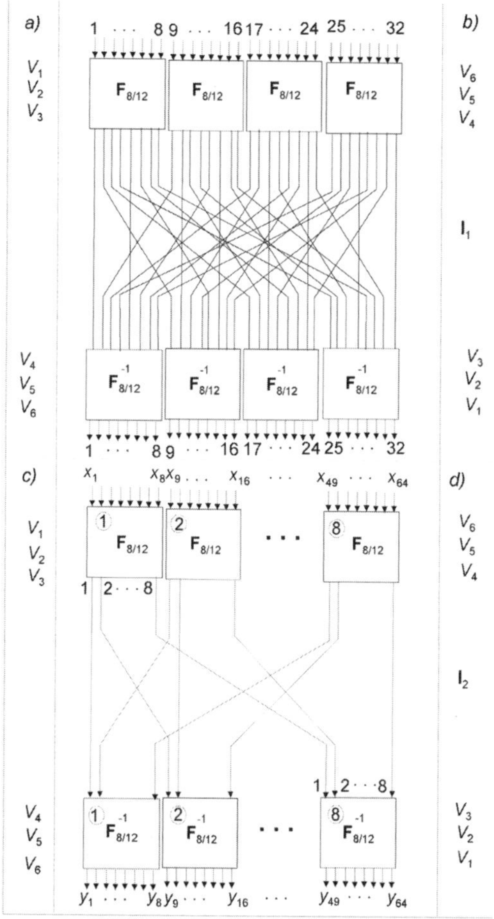

FIGURE 4.14 The structure of operational blocks: $\mathbf{F}_{32/96}$ (a), $\mathbf{F}^{-1}_{32/96}$ (b), $\mathbf{F}_{64/192}$ (c), $\mathbf{F}^{-1}_{64/192}$ (d).

Because of bilateral symmetry of blocks $\mathbf{F}_{32/96}$ and $\mathbf{F}_{64/192}$, inverse blocks $\mathbf{F}^{-1}_{32/96}$ and $\mathbf{F}^{-1}_{64/192}$ corresponding to them are different only in that the components of the control vector $V = (V_1, V_2, ..., V_6)$ are distributed over active cascade in the inverse order. In the case of direct controlled substitution-permutation networks, they are distributed from top to bottom, and in the case of inverse controlled substitution-permutation networks, they are distributed from bottom to top. Because of the symmetry of the $\mathbf{F}_{32/96}$ and $\mathbf{F}_{64/192}$ blocks, modifications implemented by them with control vector $V = (V_1, V_2, ..., V_6)$ are inverse in relation to modifications implemented with control vector $V' = (V_6, V_5, ..., V_1)$, where for $i = 1, 2, \ldots, 6$ components V_i are 16 bits in length for $\mathbf{F}_{32/96}$ and 32 bits in length for $\mathbf{F}_{64/192}$. This property is true also for the pair of blocks $\mathbf{F}^{-1}{}_{32/96}$ and $\mathbf{F}^{-1}{}_{64/192}$. This is because the V_i component controls the i-th active layer in case of $\mathbf{F}_{32/96}$ and $\mathbf{F}_{64/192}$ and $(7 - i)$-th active layer in case of $\mathbf{F}^{-1}{}_{32/96}$ and $\mathbf{F}^{-1}{}_{64/192}$. This, in turn, means that by changing the order in which the components of control vector are used, it is possible to specify the switching from direct controlled substitution-permutation network to the inverse one. Obviously, this method of building switched controlled operational substitutions is suitable for an arbitrary symmetric structure of a controlled substitution-permutation network. In other words, the problem of building switched controlled operational substitution can be solved by previously building a controlled substitution-permutation network with symmetric topology.

If every value V_i, where $i = 1, 2, \ldots, s$, is formed before the data bits pass the i-th layer, the delay time of the controlled substitution-permutation network will be defined by the number of active layers. The delay time of one active layer fits within the limits between τ and 2τ depending on the variant of circuit implementation of controlled elements. Here, τ is the delay time of the XOR operation denoted as $\oplus$, which approximately corresponds to the delay of the signal passing through one gate. The delay time of switched controlled operational substitution is practically equal to the delay of controlled substitution-permutation network of normal type.

For building a switched block $\mathbf{F}^{(V,e)}{}_{32/96}$, it is possible to supply the components of the control vector to active cascades of block $\mathbf{F}^{(V)}{}_{32/96}$ through the $\mathbf{P}^{(e)}{}_{96/1}$ block of permutation of 16-bit components V_i, as shown in Figure 4.15. The $\mathbf{P}^{(e)}{}_{96/1}$ block is implemented as a single-cascade controlled permutation block made up of three parallel single-layer $\mathbf{P}^{(e)}{}_{2\times16/1}$ blocks (Figure 4.15a). Each of the $\mathbf{P}^{(e)}{}_{2\times16/1}$ blocks has 16-bit left and 16-bit right inputs and outputs. The $\mathbf{P}^{(e)}{}_{2\times16/1}$ block represents 16 parallel blocks $\mathbf{P}^{(e)}{}_{2/1}$, controlled by the same bit e. The right (left) input (output) bit of each of 16 parallel $\mathbf{P}^{(e)}{}_{2/1}$ blocks forms the right (left) 16-bit input (output) of the $\mathbf{P}^{(e)}{}_{2\times16/1}$ block. The control vector $V = (V_1, V_2, ..., V_6)$ is supplied to the input of block $\mathbf{P}^{(e)}{}_{96/1}$. Each of the $\mathbf{P}^{(e)}{}_{2\times16/1}$ blocks, depending on e, carries out a permutation of some pair of 16-bit components of the control vector V, so that when $e = 0$, components $V_1, V_2, ..., V_6$ are distributed from top to bottom, and when $e = 1$, these components are distributed from bottom to top. This mechanism ensures implementation of the direct $\mathbf{F}_{32/96}$ operation having $e = 0$, and inverse operation $\mathbf{F}^{-1}{}_{32/96}$ having $e = 1$. The structure of the switched block $\mathbf{F}^{(e)}{}_{32/96}$ is shown in Figure 4.15b.

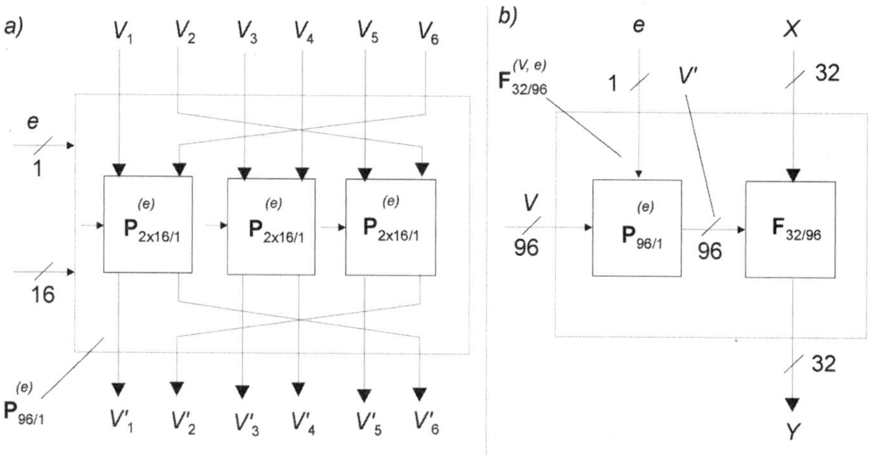

FIGURE 4.15 Building of the switched block $\mathbf{F}^{(V,e)}_{32/96}$: a) mechanism of redistribution of the control vector components, b) structure of the switched controlled operational substitution $\mathbf{F}^{(V,e)}_{32/96}$.

Proceeding in a similar way, it is possible to build a switched controlled substitution-permutation network $\mathbf{F}^{(V,e)}_{64/192}$ using a single-cascade permutation block $\mathbf{P}^{(e)}_{192/1}$, representing three parallel single-layered $\mathbf{P}^{(e)}_{2\times32/1}$ blocks (Figure 4.16a). Each $\mathbf{P}^{(e)}_{2\times32/1}$ block is a set of 32 parallel blocks $\mathbf{P}^{(e)}_{2/1}$, each of which is controlled by bit e. The structure of the $\mathbf{F}^{(e)}_{64/192}$ block is shown in Figure 4.16b.

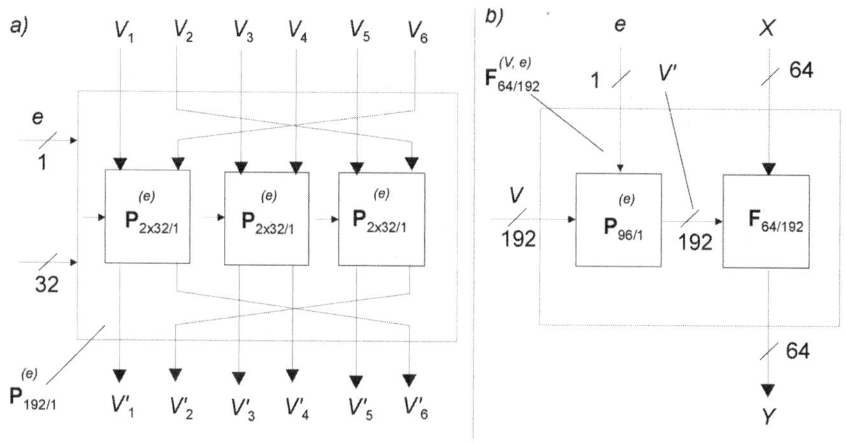

FIGURE 4.16 Building a switched $\mathbf{F}^{(V,e)}_{64/192}$ block: a) mechanism of redistribution of the control vector components, b) structure of the switched controlled operational substitution $\mathbf{F}^{(V,e)}_{64/192}$.

4.6 SWITCHED CONTROLLED SUBSTITUTION-PERMUTATION NETWORKS OF DIFFERENT ORDERS

The use of symmetric topology when designing switched controlled substitution-permutation networks is a particular case. In the general case, building a controlled permutation block with symmetric structure characterized by predefined values of order and input size is a difficult task. Because of this, methods of synthesizing switched controlled operational substitutions of different orders are the issue of great interest. The most important is synthesis of blocks of orders 2, 4, 8, ..., $n/4$ (switched blocks of order n with symmetric topology can be easily synthesized using the recursive procedure of the third type considered in Section 4.4). A universal method of building switched controlled substitution-permutation networks can be obtained on the basis of using two mutually inverse blocks $\mathbf{F}_{n/m}$ and $\mathbf{F}^{-1}{}_{n/m}$ of the order of half of the required, and two mutually inverse cascades $\mathbf{L}_n$ (input) and $\mathbf{L}^{-1}{}_n$ (output), connected to blocks $\mathbf{F}_{n/m}$ and $\mathbf{F}^{-1}{}_{n/m}$ according to the scheme shown in Figure 4.17. In this case, the following typical rule of recursive building procedure is implemented: each controlled element of the top (input) and bottom (output) cascades is connected to each of the $\mathbf{F}_{n/m}$ and $\mathbf{F}^{-1}{}_{n/m}$ blocks.

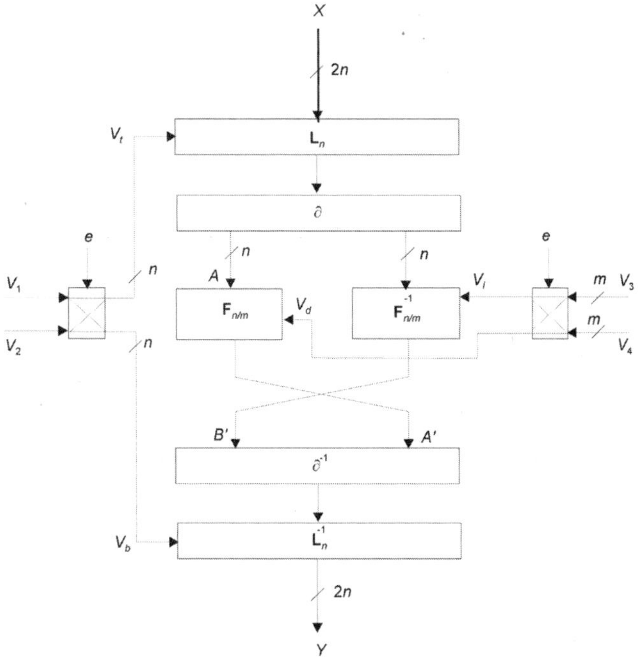

FIGURE 4.17 Building a switched controlled operation on the basis of two mutually inverse controlled substitution-permutation networks.

This scheme of building a switched controlled operation is similar to one step of a recursive building procedure of the third type. However, in this case, the use of two mutually inverse internal substitution-permutation networks ensures implementation of the pairs of mutually inverse modifications for each fixed bit permutation π (permutation π^{-1} is determined by the choice of π). However, for this scheme to duplicate the order of the controlled substitution-permutation network being synthesized, permutation π must correspond to the typical rule of the recursive building procedure (obviously, permutation π^{-1} also will correspond to this rule). The number of permutation π satisfying this rule is exceedingly large; however, it is expedient to choose the permutation that is used in the course of the recursive building procedure, because this simplifies the description of the operational block structure.

Using mechanisms of recursive building of controlled substitution-permutation networks, it is easy to build $\mathbf{F}_{n/m}$ substitution-permutation networks of orders 1, 2, 4, ..., $n/4$. If this procedure is carried out using elementary controlled involutions $\mathbf{F}^{*}_{2/1}$ or $\mathbf{F}_{2/1}$ elements of arbitrary type, in both cases it will be easy to build a controlled substitution-permutation network $\mathbf{F}^{-1}_{n/m}$ inverse in relation to the specified s-cascades block:

$$\mathbf{F}_{n/m} = \mathbf{L}^{\circ}\boldsymbol{\pi}_1{}^{\circ}\mathbf{L}^{\circ}\boldsymbol{\pi}_2{}^{\circ}\ldots{}^{\circ}\boldsymbol{\pi}_{s-1}{}^{\circ}\mathbf{L}:$$
$$\mathbf{F}^{-1}{}_{n/m} = \mathbf{L}^{-1}{}^{\circ}\boldsymbol{\pi}^{-1}{}_{s-1}{}^{\circ}\mathbf{L}^{-1}{}^{\circ}\boldsymbol{\pi}^{-1}{}_{s-2}{}^{\circ}\ldots{}^{\circ}\boldsymbol{\pi}^{-1}{}_1{}^{\circ}\mathbf{L}^{-1}.$$

If the $\mathbf{F}_{n/m}$ block has order h, then the $\mathbf{F}^{-1}{}_{n/m}$ block also has order h, and, with all this being so, implementation of controlled permutations blocks $\mathbf{F}_{n/m}$ and $\mathbf{F}^{-1}{}_{n/m}$ of the same order requires the use of the same minimum number of active layers. Thus, the method represented in Figure 4.17 allows for creating a switched controlled substitution-permutation network $\mathbf{F}^{(V,e)}{}_{2n/2(m+n)}$ of order $2h$ using two mutually inverse controlled substitution-permutation networks $\mathbf{F}_{n/m}$ and $\mathbf{F}^{-1}{}_{n/m}$ of the same order h. Here, $V = (V_1, V_2, V_3, V_4)$ is the control vector of the newly-built controlled substitution-permutation network. It can be easily shown that for all values of V the following relationships are true:

$$X = \mathbf{F}^{(V,1)}{}_{2n/2(m+n)}(Y), \text{ if } Y = \mathbf{F}^{(V,0)}{}_{2n/2(m+n)}(X),$$
$$X = \mathbf{F}^{(V,0)}{}_{2n/2(m+n)}(Y), \text{ if } Y = \mathbf{F}^{(V,1)}{}_{2n/2(m+n)}(X).$$

If $n = 2^k$, where k is some natural number, the minimum number of active layers in block $\mathbf{F}_{n/m}$ (or $\mathbf{F}^{-1}{}_{n/m}$) of order $h = 1, 2,\ldots, n/4$ makes

$$s_{min} = \log_2 hn.$$

For the case of minimum order $h = n$ the result is as follows:

$$s_{min} = \log_2 hn–1.$$

To build a switched block $\mathbf{F}^{(V,e)}{}_{n'/m'}$ of order $h' = 2, 4, \ldots, n'/4$, where $n' = 2n$ and $m' = 2(n+m)$ using the previously described method, it is necessary to use blocks $\mathbf{F}_{n/m}$ and $\mathbf{F}^{-1}{}_{n/m}$ of order $h = h'/2$ and add two extra active layers.

Thus, the minimum number of required active layers is

$$s'_{min} = \log_2 hn + 2 = \log_2 4hn = \log_2 h'n'.$$

In the case when $h' = n'$ corresponds to switched controlled substitution-permutation networks of maximum order, which can be built using blocks $\mathbf{F}_{n/m}$ and $\mathbf{F}^{-1}{}_{n/m}$ of order $h = n$, it is possible to prove that in this case

$$s'_{min} = \log_2 h'n' - 1.$$

If $n = 2^k$, it is easy to create a block $\mathbf{F}^{(V)}{}_{n/m}$ of maximum order with the symmetric structure. Consequently, a switched block $\mathbf{F}^{(V,e)}{}_{n/m}$ of maximum order can also be built using the method described in Section 4.4.

4.7 SIMPLIFICATION OF THE HARDWARE IMPLEMENTATION OF SWITCHED CONTROLLED OPERATIONAL SUBSTITUTIONS

Variants of synthesis of switched controlled operational substitutions considered earlier use the stepwise change of the distribution of all control bits of the m-bit vector V. The switching property in this case is ensured for an arbitrary distribution of dependent or independent control bits. However, implementation of these schemes of building switched controlled operational substitutions requires that $m/2$ switching elements $\mathbf{P}_{2/1}$ be used (each of which changes the distribution of two control bits). When developing ciphers, the size of the control data subgroup, depending on which the control vector V is formed, in most cases is considerably smaller than the value m and is equal to the value n (that is, to the size of the controlled substitution-permutation network input). Controlled substitution-permutation networks in which the m/n ratio is equal to a natural number are the most convenient to use, because this allows us to ensure a certain uniformity of the influence of all bits of the controlling data subgroup on the choice of the current modification of the controlled operational substitution. For $n = 32$, the aforementioned ratio in second-order blocks is 3. The same value takes place in first-order controlled substitution-permutation blocks with the 64-bit input. In these cases, it is expedient to specify the dependence of "nonintersecting" triads of bits of the control vector V on each bit of the controlling data subgroup. This is achieved by extending the controlling data subgroup (for example, by increasing its length three times). The extended data subgroup can be used directly as the control vector. The control vector can also be formed by superposition (usually carried out with the XOR operation) over the extended controlling data subgroup of one or more subkeys. In this case, the currently implemented CSPN modification is dependent on the data subgroup and the secret key.

If the control vector is an equiprobable random value, it is possible to use arbitrary distribution of control bits over controlled elements of the controlled substitution-permutation network. If there is a dependency between control bits, the distribution is chosen based on specific criteria ensuring the uniformity of the influence of all bits of the controlling subgroup on the choice of the current modification of the controlled operation. Distribution of control bits satisfying specific criteria can most easily be built for certain specific topological structures of controlled substitution-permutation networks. For example, symmetric structures of the $\mathbf{F}_{32/96}$ and $\mathbf{F}_{64/192}$ blocks described in the previous section can serve as examples. In case of 64- and 128-bit ciphers, achieving independence of the bits in control vector is related to splitting the input data block into subgroups of different size. At the same time, the controlling subgroup must have the size two or three times greater than the data subgroup being transformed. Such splitting is not typical, and requires specialized cryptoschemes to be developed. In addition, in this case a larger number of rounds are required to ensure the influence of each input data bit on each output bit.

Because dependence of control bits in vector V cannot be eliminated in a reasonable way, it is expedient to try to find more economic mechanisms of switching the distribution of control bits resulting in inversion of controlled substitution-permutation networks; that is, in change of the direct operation to the inverse one. Actually, it is possible to assume that it is enough to carry out a certain permutation of n bits in the controlling data subgroup that will result in redistribution of m bits of vector V depending on the operation mode bit e. It is also possible to assume that the implementation of such a method of inverting the controlled operation must be based on the use of the symmetry of the CSPN topological structure, and on the corresponding symmetry of the bit distribution in the controlling data subgroup. Now it is time to consider the method of inverting controlled substitution-permutation networks demonstrating practical applicability of this approach. The most considerable advantage of the discussed methods of switching bit distribution in the controlling data subgroup is that their implementation requires using only $n/2$ $\mathbf{P}_{2/1}$ switching elements instead of $m/2$ elements, as was the case of switching arbitrary distribution of bits in control vector V. In case of implementation of switched controlled substitution-permutation networks $\mathbf{F}^{(e)}{}_{32/96}$ and $\mathbf{F}^{(e)}{}_{64/192}$, the number of required $\mathbf{P}_{2/1}$ blocks will be smaller by 32 and 64 elements, respectively. This will allow us to reduce the cost of circuit implementation down to the values of 1.03–1.17 of the implementation complexity of $\mathbf{F}_{32/96}$ and $\mathbf{F}_{64/192}$ controlled substitution-permutation networks that do not have the switching property. The previously specified dispersion of values relates to different complexity of implementation different types of $\mathbf{F}_{2/1}$ control elements and to the possibility of different values of their circuit implementation (circuit resources required for implementing the switching mechanism remain fixed).

Switched controlled substitution-permutation networks $\mathbf{F}^{(e)}_{32/96}$ and $\mathbf{F}^{(e)}_{64/192}$ of this type have the same size of the control and information inputs, and the extension block represents an internal component. If it is supposed to superimpose keys over the extended control vector being formed, it is necessary to make a provision of additional input for supplying keys, and additional circuits for the operation that will carry out this superposition. In most cryptoschemes based on controlled operation, the element for superimposing subkeys over extended control vector is not used. In these cryptoschemes, it is possible to use simpler switched controlled operational substitutions.

Figure 4.18 schematically shows the $\mathbf{F}_{n/m}$ controlled substitution-permutation network with a bilaterally symmetric structure as a superposition of two mutually

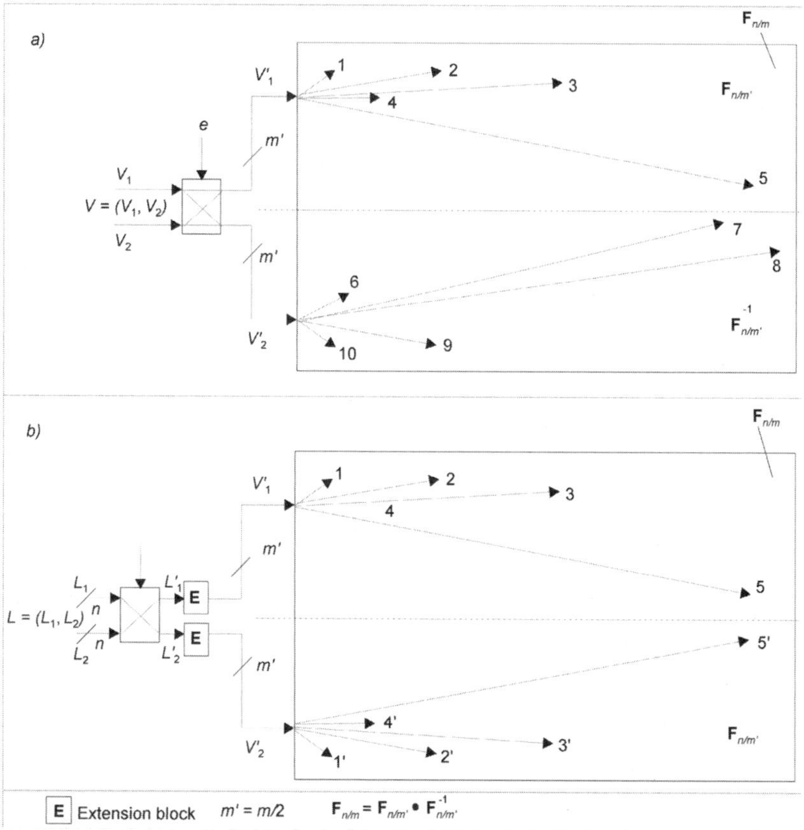

FIGURE 4.18 Comparison of two variants of implementing switched controlled operational substitutions: a) with arbitrary control vector, b) using extension of the control data subblock.

inverse blocks $\mathbf{F}_{n/m'}$ and $\mathbf{F}^{-1}_{n/m'}$. This scheme illustrates the procedure of building switched operational blocks in the case when all control bits are independent (a), and in case of extension of the controlling data subgroup for forming the control vector (b). In the latter case, control bits of vectors V'_1 and V'_2 are distributed over blocks $\mathbf{F}_{n/m'}$ and $\mathbf{F}^{-1}_{n/m'}$ according to the bilateral symmetry, thanks to which in the case of permutation of vectors L_1 and L_2, correct switching of the controlled substitution-permutation network from direct controlled operation to inverse control operation is ensured.

Switched controlled substitution-permutation networks $\mathbf{F}^{(e)}_{32/96}$ and $\mathbf{F}^{(e)}_{64/192}$ can be easily built according to the design scheme oriented toward economical hardware implementation (Figure 4.18b). In comparison to normal controlled substitution-permutation networks $\mathbf{F}_{32/96}$ and $\mathbf{F}_{64/192}$, the $\mathbf{F}^{(e)}_{32/96}$ and $\mathbf{F}^{(e)}_{64/192}$ blocks used in the previously described variant of implementation require 16 and 32 additional $\mathbf{P}_{2/1}$ elementary switches, respectively.

4.8 SWITCHED CONTROLLED SUBSTITUTION-PERMUTATION NETWORKS WITH CONTROLLED ELEMENTS INCLUDING PAIRS OF MUTUALLY INVERSE MODIFICATIONS

A promising area of investigation is implementation of switched controlled operational substitutions, in which the mechanism of inverting the controlled operation being executed is based on that the controlled substitution-permutation network is built based on controlled elements $\mathbf{F}_{2/1}$, $\mathbf{F}_{2/2}$ or $\mathbf{F}_{3/1}$, modifications of which are split into pairs of mutually inverse modifications. Such controlled elements can be inverted by means of inverting control bits. In case of the $\mathbf{F}_{2/2}$ element, this is implemented if all of the two pairs of modifications corresponding to the pairs of control vectors, such as (00) and (11), and to the (01) and (10) pair, includes two mutually inverse modifications.

The method of inverting controlled substitution-permutation networks based on inverting all control bits also requires the use of symmetric CSPN topology and symmetric distribution of control bits. Because of the latter circumstance, this method is applicable only in cases when no more than half of the control bits are independent (the same bit must be supplied to the control input of two controlled elements placed in bilaterally symmetric positions). If the control vector of the $\mathbf{F}_{n/m}$ block is formed based on a data subgroup that is n bits in size, then, as a rule, bits of the control data subgroup can be easily distributed symmetrically. However, if the m/n ratio is an odd number, then bits from one-half of this data subblock must be used for controlling more elementary substitution elements in comparison to the bits from the second half. This nonuniformity is not critical; however, it must be taken into account when developing switched controlled operational substitutions intended for use in specific ciphers. A certain drawback of the method of inverting controlled substitution-permutation network by means of inverting control bits is that the aforementioned symmetric distribution of control bits makes it impossible to implement one of the useful criteria of forming control vectors. This criterion can be formulated as follows: control bits must be distributed so that neither of the bits of the data subgroup being transformed is exposed to the influence of the same bit of the control data subgroup twice.

Despite the aforementioned specific features, the CSPN inversion method under consideration is of practical importance, because it provides another way of economic implementation of the mechanism of switching between direct and inverse operations. Consider the variants of building switched controlled operational substitutions of this type using different types of controlled elements.

4.8.1 Switched Controlled Substitution-Permutation Networks on the Basis of $F_{2/1}$ Elements

Having considered the existing types of nonlinear controlled elements $\mathbf{F}_{2/1}$, described in Chapter 3, it can be easily discovered that elements specified by pairs of modifications q/u, r/x, s/v, t/w, u/q, x/r, v/s, and w/t (Figure 4.19) are controlled elementary substitutions implementing pairs of mutually inverse modifications.

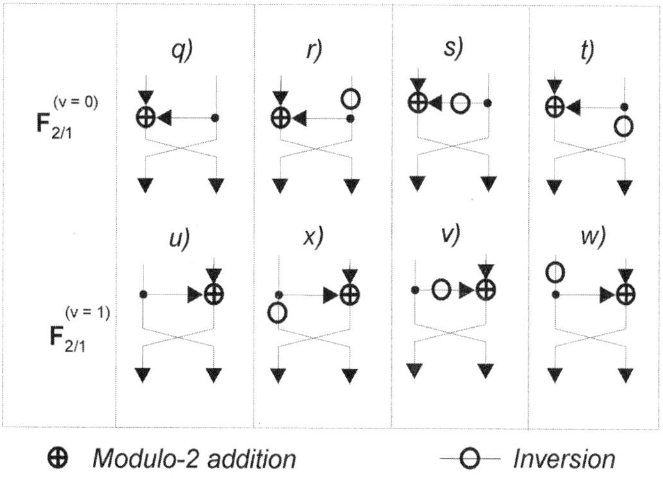

FIGURE 4.19 Pairs of mutually inverse elementary transformation of the $(x_1,x_2) \rightarrow (y_1,y_2)$ type.

The use of other pairs of elementary modifications of 2×2 substitutions doesn't result in building of the variants of $\mathbf{F}_{2/1}$ elements satisfying the criterion of nonlinearity of both outputs. The previously listed eight variants are the only ones. Actually, there are four pairs of modifications of 2×2 substitutions, each specifying two variants of $\mathbf{S}_{2/1}$ controlled elements differing by the choice of modification implemented at zero (or one) value of the control bit. The most favorable is the circumstance that each output of these elements is a nonlinear boolean function, the arguments of which are two input bits and a control bit, and the sum of outputs represents a nonlinear boolean function of the aforementioned variables. This means that these are elements of the $\mathbf{S}_{2/1}$ type. Table 4.3 describes the aforementioned four variants of elements characterized by the $\mathbf{S}^{(1)} = (\mathbf{S}^{(0)})^{-1}$ property as pairs of boolean functions of three variables.

TABLE 4.3 Boolean Functions Describing $\mathbf{S}_{2/1}$, Controlled Elements Implementing Pairs of Mutually Inverse Modifications

	$y_1 = f_1(x_1, x_2, v)$	$y_2 = f_2(x_1, x_2, v)$	$y_1 \oplus y_2$
q/u	$vx_1 \oplus x_2$	$vx_2 \oplus x_1 \oplus x_2$	$vx_1 \oplus vx_2 \oplus x_1$
s/v	$vx_1 \oplus v \oplus x_2$	$vx_2 \oplus v \oplus x_1 \oplus x_2 \oplus 1$	$vx_1 \oplus vx_2 \oplus x_1 \oplus 1$
t/w	$vx_1 \oplus x_2 \oplus 1$	$vx_2 \oplus v \oplus x_1 \oplus x_2$	$vx_1 \oplus vx_2 \oplus v \oplus x_1 \oplus 1$
r/x	$vx_1 \oplus v \oplus x_2 \oplus 1$	$vx_2 \oplus x_1 \oplus x_2 \oplus 1$	$vx_1 \oplus vx_2 \oplus v \oplus x_1$
u/q	$vx_1 \oplus x_1 \oplus x_2$	$vx_2 \oplus x_1$	$vx_1 \oplus vx_2 \oplus x_2$
v/s	$vx_1 \oplus v \oplus x_1 \oplus x_2 \oplus 1$	$vx_2 \oplus v \oplus x_1$	$vx_1 \oplus vx_2 \oplus x_2 \oplus 1$
w/t	$vx_1 \oplus x_1 \oplus x_2 \oplus 1$	$vx_2 \oplus v \oplus x_1 \oplus 1$	$vx_1 \oplus vx_2 \oplus v \oplus x_2$
x/r	$vx_1 \oplus v \oplus x_1 \oplus x_2$	$vx_2 \oplus x_1 \oplus 1$	$vx_1 \oplus vx_2 \oplus v \oplus x_2 \oplus 1$

4.8.2 Switched Controlled Substitution-Permutation Networks on the Basis of $F_{2/2}$ Elements

In comparison to the synthesis of $\mathbf{F}_{2/1}$ elements forming of elementary controlled substitutions of the $\mathbf{F}_{2/2}$ type is related to consideration of significantly larger number of variants. However, the requirement of mutual reversibility of two pairs of the $\mathbf{F}_{2/2}$ element's modification considerably narrows the range of choice. Furthermore, in contrast to the case of $\mathbf{F}_{2/1}$ elements, for which this requirement didn't result in discarding the most efficient nonlinear elements of this type, in the case of $\mathbf{F}_{2/2}$ elements the most efficient variants (in terms of the nonlinearity criteria) do not satisfy the condition. This requires us to ensure the possibility of splitting four implemented modifications into two pairs of mutually inverse modifications. Nevertheless, the remaining types of $\mathbf{F}_{2/2}$ elements are characterized by good nonlinear properties and by the modifications propagation characteristics. This allows us to use them for building switched controlled operation substitutions suitable for applying in cryptosystems. At least, boolean functions describing each of their two outputs and their sum have higher values of nonlinearity and algebraic degree of nonlinearity in comparison to $\mathbf{F}_{2/1}$ elements.

At the same time, despite considerable limitations implied by the $\mathbf{F}^{(11)} = (\mathbf{F}^{(00)})^{-1}$ and $\mathbf{F}^{(10)} = (\mathbf{F}^{(01)})^{-1}$ conditions, the number of $\mathbf{F}_{2/2}$ elements of this type, implementing four different modifications is large enough. In addition, variants of $\mathbf{F}_{2/2}$ elements implementing the same modification at two different values of the control vector (v_1, v_2) are also possible. For example, both outputs of the m/e/e/n elements (where the latter notation lists modifications of 2×2 substitutions implemented at the values of the control vector equal to (0, 0), (0, 1), (1, 0), and (1, 1), respectively), and their sum, are nonlinear boolean functions of four variables:

$$y_1 = v_1v_2x_1 \oplus v_1v_2x_2 \oplus v_1v_2 \oplus v_1x_2 \oplus v_2x_2;$$
$$y_2 = v_1x_1 \oplus v_1x_2 \oplus v_2x_2 \oplus v_1 \oplus v_2 \oplus x_2 \oplus 1;$$
$$y_1 \oplus y_2 = v_1v_2x_1 \oplus v_1v_2x_2 \oplus v_1v_2 \oplus v_1x_1 \oplus v_2x_1 \oplus v_1 \oplus v_2 \oplus x_2 \oplus 1.$$

It is necessary to mention that when fixing one control bit (v_1 or v_2) in the m/e/e/n element, it turns into an element of the $\mathbf{S}_{2/1}$ type. Consider several examples of controlled elements with four different modifications. Element q/k/l/u is described by the following boolean functions (Figure 4.20a):

$$y_1 = v_1v_2x_1 \oplus v_1x_2 \oplus v_2x_2 \oplus v_2x_1 \oplus v_1x_1 \oplus v_1 \oplus v_2 \oplus x_2;$$
$$y_2 = v_1v_2x_2 \oplus v_1v_2 \oplus x_1 \oplus x_2 \oplus v_2;$$
$$y_1 \oplus y_2 = v_1v_2x_1 \oplus v_1v_2x_2 \oplus v_1v_2 \oplus v_1x_1 \oplus v_1x_2 \oplus v_2x_1 \oplus v_2x_2 \oplus v_1 \oplus x_1.$$

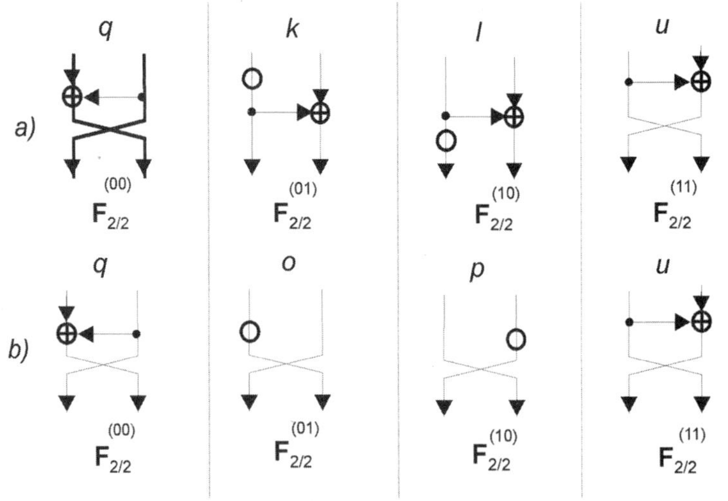

FIGURE 4.20 Switched controlled elements: a) q/k/l/u, b) q/o/p/u.

Element q/o/p/u is described by the following boolean functions (Figure 4.20b):

$$y_1 = v_1v_2x_1 \oplus v_1v_2 \oplus v_1 \oplus x_2;$$
$$y_2 = v_1v_2x_2 \oplus v_1v_2 \oplus v_1x_2 \oplus v_2x_2 \oplus v_2 \oplus x_1 \oplus x_2;$$
$$y_1 \oplus y_2 = v_1v_2x_1 \oplus v_1v_2x_2 \oplus v_1x_2 \oplus v_2x_2 \oplus v_1 \oplus v_2 \oplus x_1.$$

The variants of implementation of $\mathbf{F}_{2/2}$ controlled elements switched by means of inverting control bits can be used for the synthesis of switched controlled operational substitutions.

Note that in switched controlled operational substitutions on the basis of $\mathbf{F}_{2/2}$ elements, the symmetric distribution of control bits assumes that the same control vector (v_1v_2) is supplied to the control input of the elements located in symmetric positions; that is, these elements implement the same modification of the 2×2 substitution.

4.9 EXTENSION OF THE SWITCHING PROPERTY OF CONTROLLED OPERATIONAL SUBSTITUTIONS

One of the most important goals of using switched controlled operational substitutions is elimination of the homogeneity of iterative encryption when using relatively short keys in case of a simple key use schedule. To achieve this goal of having only one switched operation in the procedure of a single encryption round, it is possible to set different values of the operation mode switching bit in sequential rounds, so that they form a periodic sequence of one and zero values. A more efficient variant is using several switched controlled operational substitutions in the same round. This allows for ensuring more significant difference in the procedures of sequential rounds. Recurrence of the encryption rounds takes place only when bits on the switching input of all switched controlled operational substitutions are repeated. It is possible to develop a cryptoscheme with a larger number of switched operations carried out in parallel over reduced data subgroups. This will ensure the possibility of using a large number of independent switching bits; however, the efficiency of controlled operations grows considerably when such operations are used for transforming large data subgroups. Consequently, the use of large number of switched operations within one round is not proposed.

Nevertheless, the idea of introducing more considerable differences into the neighboring rounds and into the rounds separated by several steps from each other also deserves attention. This task can be solved by means of developing switched controlled operational substitutions with an extended switching range, where switching is carried out using switching vector E with the length equal; for example, to $k = 4 - 8$ bits instead of a single switching bit. It is possible to assume that for a given value $E = (e_1, e_1, \ldots, e_k)$, some controlled operation will be executed, and that $E = (e_1 \oplus 1,\ e_1 \oplus 1,\ \ldots,\ e_k \oplus 1)$ will correspond to the inverse controlled operation. This produces $2^{k/2}$ pairs of mutually inverse controlled operations.

Implementation of switched controlled operational substitution with an extended switching range is also based on the stepwise modifications of the distribution of control bits over elementary controlled substitution blocks $\mathbf{F}_{2/1}$ for a certain fixed topology. The type of controlled substitution-permutation network is determined by the topology of interrelations between controlled elements and distribution of the control bits. Earlier, switched controlled operational substitutions with two-variant distribution were covered, which were switched by a single bit e. By analogy, it is possible to build switched controlled operational substitutions with multivariant distribution of control bits. Evaluation of the maximum length of the switching vector E is not a difficult task. To achieve this, it is necessary to account for the following specific features characteristic of switched controlled operational substitutions based on redistribution of control bits:

- The original controlled substitution-permutation network $\mathbf{F}_{n/m}$ must have symmetric topology.

- Two bits supplied to the input of the same elementary switch $\mathbf{P}_{2/1}$, which is a part of a certain switching block of control bits $\mathbf{P}^{(E)}{}_{m/g}$ (in case of all independent bits in control vector) or $\mathbf{P}^{(E)}{}_{n/g}$ (in case of economic implementation of a switched controlled operational substitution when using permutation of the bits of controlling data subgroup), where g is the length of vector E, must be supplied to the input of one or more pairs of symmetrically placed controlled elements $\mathbf{F}_{2/1}$ in the $\mathbf{F}_{n/m}$ block.

If these conditions have been satisfied, then inversion of all bits of an arbitrary vector E will result in forming of a new controlled operation that is an inverse of the original one; that is, the following relationship will take place: $\mathbf{F}^{(V,E)}{}_{n/m} = (\mathbf{F}^{(V,E')}{}_{n/m})^{-1}$. This means that the number of pairs of mutually inverse modifications of the controlled operation $\mathbf{F}^{(V,E)}{}_{n/m}$ is equal to 2^{g-1}. The greatest value of g corresponds to the case $g = m/2$ (implementation of a switched controlled operational substitution with m independent control bits) and $g = n/2$ (economic implementation of a switched controlled operational substitution). For blocks of the $\mathbf{F}^{(V,E)}{}_{32/96}$ type, it is possible to have up to 2^{47} or 2^{15} different variants of distribution of control bits depending on the method of implementation of a switched controlled operational substitution (general or economic).

Even in the case of the economical type of implementation of a switched controlled operational substitution, the switching range is wide enough. In practice, it is sufficient to use vectors E up to six bytes in length, which ensures availability of 32 different pairs of mutually inverse controlled operations implemented using a single switched controlled operational substitution. This means that every bit of vector E will control many elementary switches in $\mathbf{P}^{(E)}{}_{m/g}$ or $\mathbf{P}^{(E)}{}_{n/g}$ blocks.

When building switched controlled operational substitutions in practice, it is convenient to structure $\mathbf{F}_{2/1}$ controlled elements so that they form pairs of active cascades or pairs of some internal CSPNs within the original $\mathbf{F}_{n/m}$ controlled substitution-permutation network. These pairs must be switched by one of the bits of vector E. This simplifies the design and analysis of switched controlled operational substitutions with an extended switching range. The most important circumstance is that the properties of the original controlled substitution-permutation network (such as nonlinearity, avalanche effect, etc.) in a certain sense remain intact for each variant of a controlled operational substitution belonging to the switching range. Therefore, substantiation of a controlled substitution-permutation network is at the same time substantiation of the switched controlled operational substitution as a cryptographic primitive. Figure 4.21 presents the scheme of building a switched

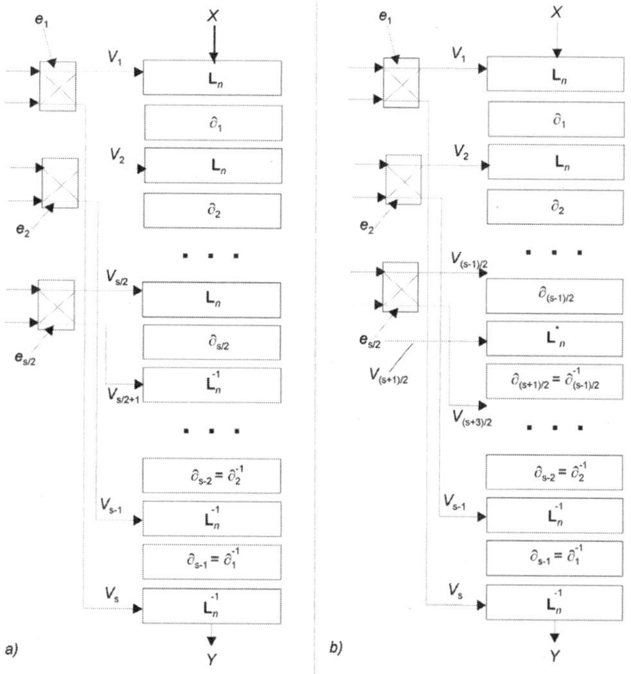

FIGURE 4.21 Building a switched controlled operational substitution based on controlled substitution-permutation network with bilaterally symmetric topology: a) with an even number of active cascades, b) with odd number of active cascades (**L*** stands for involution).

controlled operational substitution inverted by means of permutation of control vectors corresponding to symmetrically placed active layers in cases when the number of such layers is even (a) and odd (b). Different combinations of initial values of bits e_1, e_1, …, $e_{s/2}$ correspond to different direct controlled operational substitution. Simultaneous inversion of all switching bits transforms each block into the corresponding inverse controlled operational substitution. Similar schemes of building controlled operational substitutions with an extended switching range can also be used in cases when controlled operational substitutions are built based on controlled elements with mutually inverse modifications (Figure 4.22).

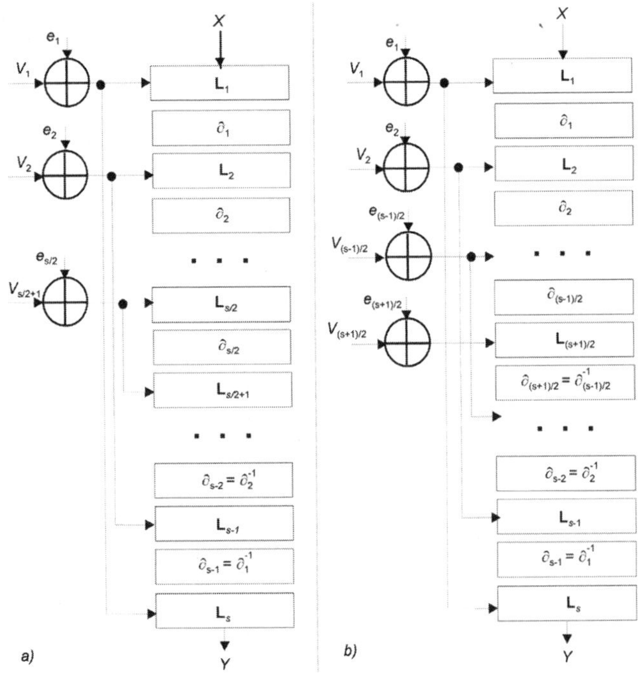

FIGURE 4.22 Building of a switched controlled operational substitution with extended switching range on the basis of controlled substitution-permutation networks with bilaterally symmetric topology: a) with an even number of active cascades, b) with an odd number of active cascades.

SUMMARY

One of the most important problems related to designing ciphers with simple key use schedule is preventing the occurrence of weak keys. In this chapter, it was shown that the use of data-dependent operations is a prerequisite for the development of inexpensive hardware-oriented ciphers. This chapter also suggested an approach for solving the problem of weak keys based on using switched controlled operations. Several variants of methods of building switched controlled operations have been suggested. Being a particular case of the controllability property, the switching property can be easily and seamlessly built into various types of controlled operations.

Another problem is related to so-called slide attacks covered in "Advanced Slide Attacks" by A. Biryukov and D. Wagner. This type of attack is based on the periodicity of the recurrent subkeys use, which results in occurrence of the same round transformations. The potential possibility of implementing such attacks must be taken into account when designing ciphers of the type under consideration. The use of long secret key (128...256 bits) allows us to easily build the schedule of key use, free from any periodicity, thus eliminating the prerequisite to implementation of slide attacks. However, when using short keys, a situation frequently encountered in practical application, simple key schedule actually represents the use of the same subkeys in each round. This case is the most favorable for slide attacks. Thus, the need for ensuring the possibility of eliminating repetitions of round transformations by means of using some other mechanisms irrelevant to the key length is obvious.

The switching property allows for suggesting three variants of such mechanisms:

- Using mixed iterative transformation, including the combination of encrypting ($e = 0$) and decrypting ($e = 1$) rounds. Such a mixed transformation can be represented in the form of a certain sequence of values of bit e; for example, 0, 0, 1, 0, 1, 1, 0, 0, 1, 0 (10 encryption rounds) and 1, 1, 0, 1, 0, 0, 1, 1, 0, 1 (10 decryption rounds). This method is the simplest one that can be used for introducing aperiodicity. However, it is necessary to avoid the cases when two sequential rounds are mutually inverse (in some cryptoschemes, such cases are possible).
- Development of a special variant of switched operations that can be called extended switched operations. These are some $\mathbf{F}^{(E,V)}$ operations dependent on parameter E, where E is some k-bit vector ($k \geq 2$) dependent on e and on the number of encryption round. At the same time, for all V modifications $\mathbf{F}^{(E,V)}$ and $\mathbf{F}^{(E',V)}$ are mutually inverse having $E \oplus E' = \{1\}^k$. Thus, $\mathbf{F}^{(E,V)}$ contains 2^{k-1} pairs of mutually inverse modifications of controlled operation $\mathbf{F}^{(V)}$, which allows for easily building 2^k unique round transformation for each round subkey. The use of a large number of round transformations of different types allows for easy elimination of the periodicity when using the same round subkey in all encryption rounds; that is, in the case of the simplest key use schedule. For example, an improved switched controlled permutations block $\mathbf{P}^{(E,V)}_{32/96}$, where $E = (e_1, e_2, e_3)$, can be easily built using independent switching bits e_1, e_2, and e_3 for each $\mathbf{P}^{(e)}_{2\times16/1}$ block (see Figure 4.15). Proceeding in a similar way, it is possible to transform block $\mathbf{P}^{(V,e)}_{64/192}$ (see Figure 4.16) into $\mathbf{P}^{(V,E)}_{64/192}$, where $E = (e_1, e_2, e_3)$.
- Development of the round transformation containing several (for example, k) switched controlled operations controlled by independent switching bits e_1, $e_2,\ldots, e_k$, each of which is assigned a value dependent on the round number.

Thus, the following conclusions can be drawn:

- The use of switched controlled operations allows us to avoid the occurrence of weak keys in ciphers using the simplest key schedule.
- The use of extended switched controlled operations allows us to prevent repetitions of the same round transformations when using the same round key in all encryption rounds.
- The use of switched controlled operations allows us to eliminate the vulnerability to slide attacks based on the possibility of choosing the same round keys for all encryption rounds in ciphers with simple key schedule.
- The use of controlled operations and switched controlled operations ensures development of fast and inexpensive hardware-oriented ciphers.
- Switched controlled operations in combination with controlled operations allows for efficient use of new types of cryptoschemes combining Feistel networks with substitution-permutation networks.
- There are diverse mechanisms for defining the switching property for controlled substitution-permutation networks.
- There exist efficient cryptoschemes for building switched controlled operations of orders 1, 2, 4,..., $n/4$, n, where n is the bit width of the switched controlled operation input.
- In terms of a variety of solutions for building switched controlled substitution-permutation networks, the use of controlled elements of the $\mathbf{F}_{3/1}$ type provides the best possibilities in comparison to $\mathbf{F}_{2/1}$ and $\mathbf{F}_{2/2}$ elements. Migration to switched controlled operations on the basis of $\mathbf{F}_{3/2}$ and $\mathbf{F}_{4/1}$, 1 elements will provide even greater possibilities for designing efficient switched controlled operations. However, full classification of controlled elements of the latter type is considerably more complex task in comparison to classification of $\mathbf{F}_{2/1}$, $\mathbf{F}_{2/2}$, and $\mathbf{F}_{3/1}$ controlled elements.
- Switched controlled substitution-permutation networks by their properties are identical to normal controlled substitution-permutation networks, because they have similar topologies. Evaluations of probabilistic properties, nonlinearity, and other characteristics obtained for normal controlled substitution-permutation networks can be extended to switched controlled substitution-permutation networks.
- Provided that a correct cryptoscheme has been chosen, switched controlled operations and controlled operations introduce the same delay into the encryption procedure having the same number of active layers.
- Switched controlled operations allow for using cryptoschemes free from inversion of the key use schedule when changing the encryption mode, thus providing further possibilities of reducing the complexity of circuit implementation for block ciphers.

5 Designing Fast Ciphers Based on Controlled Operations

This chapter deals only with the block cipher algorithms developed by the authors of the book. All terms and designations used here correspond to those in the two previous chapters, unless otherwise specified.

5.1 THE SPECTR-H64 BLOCK CIPHER

This algorithm is a practical implementation of the main ideas—of block cipher synthesis based on controlled operations and aimed at high-speed information handling with a 32-bit data exchange bus considered in the previous chapters.

5.1.1 The General Scheme of Block Encryption

For the SPECTR-H64 algorithm, the general encryption scheme (encryption and decryption) is determined by the formula:

$$Y = \mathbf{F}(X, Q^{(e)}),$$

where $Q^{(e)} = \mathbf{H}(K, e)$ is the *extended key*, a function of the 256-bit secret key K and the encryption mode e (e = 0—encryption, e = 1—decryption). In encryption mode, X is the initial block of binary data (plaintext), and in decryption mode, it is the transformed block of binary data (ciphertext). In encryption mode, the resulting value Y is ciphertext, and in decryption mode, it is plaintext.

The secret key K is represented as a combination of eight 32-bit subkeys; namely, $K = K_1||K_2||\ldots||K_8$, where $K_1, K_2, \ldots, K_8 \in GF(2)^{32}$.

The encryption algorithm (the **F** function) is described in Section. 5.1.2, and the procedure for building the $Q^{(e)} = \mathbf{H}(K, e)$ working key is in Section 5.1.3.

5.1.2 The Encryption Algorithm

The **F** function (Figure 5.1) is implemented with the following procedures:

- Initial transformation—***IT***.
- 12 rounds (loops) of *transformations* using the ***Crypt*** procedure.
- Final transformation—***FT***.

First, the ***IT*** procedure is performed: $Y = \boldsymbol{IT}(X, Q_{IT}^{(e)})$.

The Y block is divided into two subblocks of the same length—L_0 and R_0; in other words, $(L_0, R_0) = Y$, where $L_0, R_0 \in GF(2)^{32}$. Then, 12 rounds of transformation are performed with the ***Crypt*** procedure according to the formulas:

$$L_j = \boldsymbol{Crypt}(R_{j-1}, L_{j-1}, Q_j^{(e)});$$

$$R_j = L_{j-1}\ (j = 1, 2, \ldots, 12).$$

After the 12th round over the $X = (R_{12}, L_{12})$ block, the final transformation, ***FT***, is performed according to the formula:

$$Y = \boldsymbol{FT}(X, Q_{FT}^{(e)}).$$

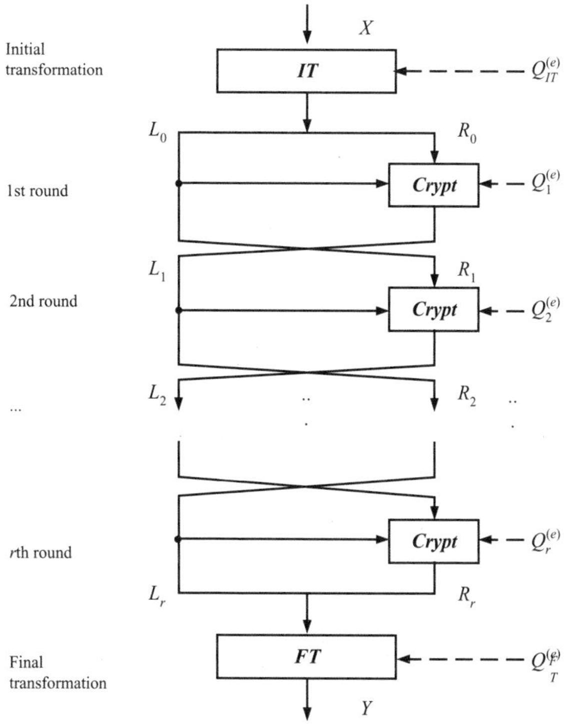

FIGURE 5.1 A basic model of an iterative block cipher algorithm.

Initial Transformation

The initial transformation ***IT*** is as follows:

$$Y = \boldsymbol{IT}(X, A),$$

where $X, Y \in \mathrm{GF}(2)^{64}$, $A \in \mathrm{GF}(2)^{32}$.

The implementation scheme of this transformation is shown in Figure 5.2, where each pair of bits of the input block X with the indices $2j$–1 and $2j$ ($j = 1, 2, ..., 32$) is either permuted ($a_j = 1$) or not permuted ($a_j = 0$), after which each even bit is inverted. The bit values of the Y vector are calculated with the following formulas:

$$y_{2j-1} = (x_{2j-1} \oplus x_{2j})a_j \oplus x_{2j-1} \text{ and } y_{2j} = (x_{2j-1} \oplus x_{2j})a_j \oplus x_{2j} \oplus 1.$$

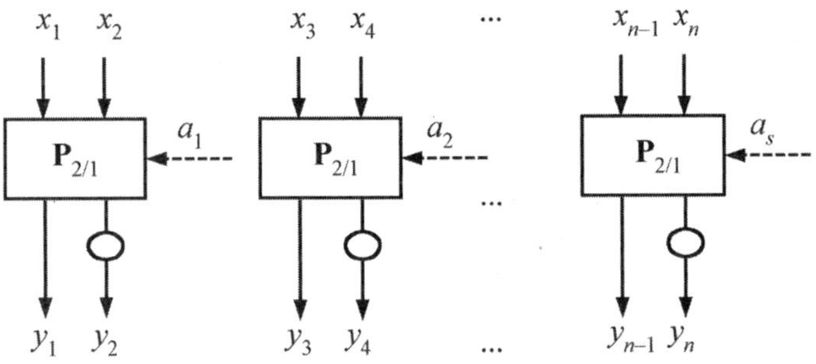

FIGURE 5.2 Initial transformation ($s = n/2$).

The *Crypt* Procedure

A formal record of the ***Crypt*** procedure looks as follows:

$$R = \boldsymbol{Crypt}(R, L, (A^{(1)}, A^{(2)}, A^{(3)}, A^{(4)}, A^{(5)}, A^{(6)})),$$

where $L, R \in \mathrm{GF}(2)^{32}$ and $A^{(1)}, A^{(2)}, \ldots, A^{(6)} \in \mathrm{GF}(2)^{32}$.

The elements $A^{(1)}, A^{(2)}, \ldots, A^{(6)}$ are the formal parameters of key information; in other words, $Q_j^{(i,e)}$ is an element of round key $Q_j^{(e)} = (Q_j^{(1,e)}, Q_j^{(2,e)}, \ldots, Q_j^{(6,e)})$, and corresponds to the $A^{(i)}$ parameter. Accordingly, R and L are formal parameters for the left and right parts of the input data block.

One feature of such an implementation of the ***Crypt*** procedure is the use of six subkeys with a length of 32 in one round.

The procedure uses:

- The rotation operation ">>>" by a fixed number of bits
- *Bit-wise addition modulo 2* "$\oplus$"
- A nonlinear vector boolean function **G**
- *Controlled permutation boxes* $\mathbf{P}_{32/80}$ and $\mathbf{P}^{-1}_{32/80}$ of the first order
- A procedure for expanding control vector **E** (expansion box)

Two-stage Clos networks $\mathbf{C}_{<8,\,4>}$ and $\mathbf{C}_{<4,\,8>}$ are used as $\mathbf{P}_{32/80}$ and $\mathbf{P}^{-1}_{32/80}$ boxes, respectively, when for the $\mathbf{C}_{<8,\,4>}$ box the smaller boxes are $\mathbf{R}_3$ and $\mathbf{R}_2$ boxes, and for $\mathbf{C}_{<4,8>} = \mathbf{C}^{-1}_{<4,8>}$ they are the $\mathbf{R}_2^{-1}$ and $\mathbf{R}_3^{-1}$ boxes. This differs from the classical structure of the $\mathbf{C}_{<8,\,4>}$ Clos network in that the order of $\mathbf{R}_2$ boxes is changed (see the box numeration in Figure 5.3). A commutation between the third and fourth layers in box $\mathbf{P}_{32/80}$ has this involution:

$$\pi = (1)(2, 9)(3, 17)(4, 25)(5)(6, 13)(7, 21)(8, 29)(10)(11, 18)(12, 26)$$
$$(14)(15, 22)(16, 30)(19)(20, 27)(23)(24, 31)(28)(32).$$

The sequence of transformations and their interaction is shown in Figure 5.4.

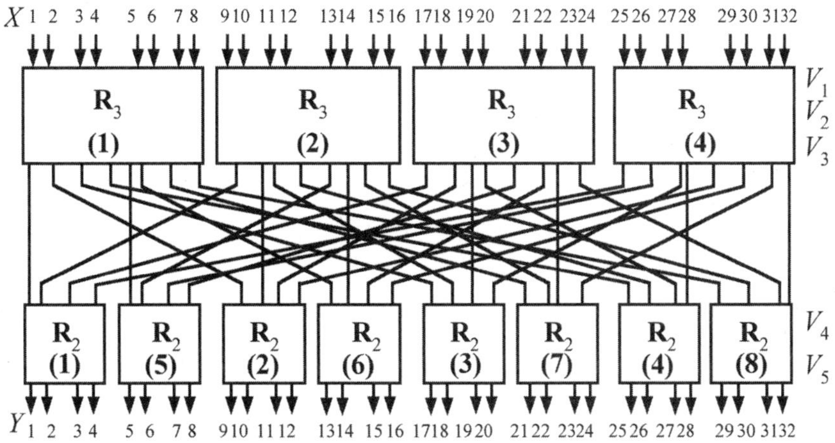

FIGURE 5.3 The controlled permutations box $\mathbf{P}_{32/80}$.

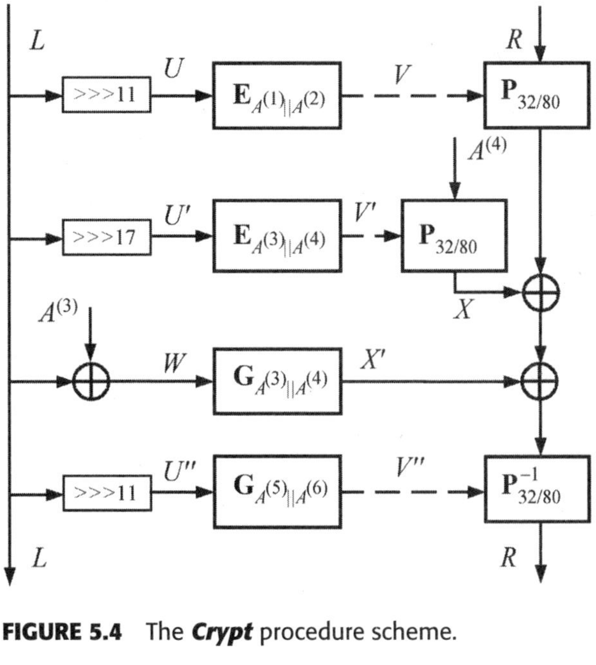

FIGURE 5.4 The ***Crypt*** procedure scheme.

The time base of operations in ***Crypt*** procedure is presented in Table 5.1.

TABLE 5.1 The Time Base for Performing an Operation in the ***Crypt*** Procedure

No.	Time base ($\tau_\oplus$)	Operations
1	0	$U = L^{>>>11}$ $U' = L^{>>>17}$ $U'' = L^{>>>11}$
2	0 ÷ 1	$V = \mathbf{E}_{A(1)\|A(2)}(U)$ $V' = \mathbf{E}_{A(3)\|A(4)}(U')$ $V'' = \mathbf{E}_{A(5)\|A(6)}(U'')$ $W = L \oplus A^{(3)}$
3	0 ÷ 5	$R = \mathbf{P}_{32/80(V)}(R)$ $X = \mathbf{P}_{32/80(V')}(A^{(4)})$
4	1 ÷ 5	$X' = \mathbf{G}_{A(3)\|A(4)}(W)$
5	5 ÷ 6	$R = R \oplus X$
6	6 ÷ 7	$R = R \oplus X'$
7	7 ÷ 12	$R = \mathbf{P}^{-1}_{32/80(V'')}(R)$

As it follows from Table 5.1, most operations are performed concurrently, and the total time required for the performance of the procedure is equal to the consecutive performance of 12 operations of the XOR type.

This index can be improved if a matrix structure of implementing $\mathbf{R}_2$ *boxes in boxes* $\mathbf{P}_{32/80}$ *and* $\mathbf{P}^{-1}_{32/80}$ *is used. In this case, the time for the* ***Crypt*** *procedure's implementation will not exceed the time it takes to consecutively perform nine operations of the XOR type.*

Vector Boolean Function *G*

A controlled substitution operation is used as the vector boolean function **G**, one of the implementations of a sequential bijective model Formally, the **G** function looks like this:

$$X' = \mathbf{G}(W, A, B), \text{ where } X', W, A, B \in \mathrm{GF}(2)^{32}.$$

The formal parameters A and B correspond to the formal parameters $A^{(3)}$ and $A^{(4)}$ of the ***Crypt*** procedure. In vector form, the **G** function is determined by the formula:

$$X' = M^{(0)} \oplus M^{(1)} \oplus (M^{(2)} \otimes A) \oplus (M^{(2)} \otimes M^{(5)} \otimes B) \oplus (M^{(3)} \otimes M^{(5)}) \oplus (M^{(4)} \otimes B).$$

The binary vectors $M^{(0)}, M^{(1)}, \ldots, M^{(5)}$ are expressed recursively via W; namely,

$$M^{(0)} = (m_1^{(0)}, m_2^{(0)}, m_3^{(0)}, \ldots, m_{31}^{(0)}, m_{32}^{(0)}) = (w_1, w_2, w_3, \ldots, w_{31}, w_{32})$$

and $\forall j = 1, 2, \ldots, 5$,

$$M^{(j)} = (m_1^{(j)}, m_2^{(j)}, m_3^{(j)}, \ldots, m_{31}^{(j)}, m_{32}^{(j)}) = (1, m_1^{(j-1)}, m_2^{(j-1)}, \ldots, m_{31}^{(j)}).$$

Taking into account the option of concurrent performance of some operations, it is easy to establish that the **G** function is implemented during four delay time units ($4\tau_\oplus$) instead of the allowable five time units—in other words, there is a reserve kept for its meshing.

Grounds for Choosing a Nonlinear *G* Function

Let's define the mapping **G**: $GF(2)^{32} \times GF(2)^{32} \times GF(2)^{32} \rightarrow GF(2)^{32}$ as a boolean vector function $Y = \mathbf{G}(X, A, B)$ of the following appearance:

$$(y_1, y_2, \ldots, y_{32}) = (\mathbf{g}_1(X, A, B), \mathbf{g}_2(X, A, B), \ldots, \mathbf{g}_{32}(X, A, B)),$$

where $\mathbf{g}_i$ are certain generator boolean functions.

If, for each i, the condition $\mathbf{g}_i(X, A, B) = \mathbf{g}_i(x_1, x_2, \ldots, x_i, A, B)$ is true, then such a mapping is a sequential model of a controlled substitution operation. If the functions $\mathbf{g}_i(X, A, B) = x_i \oplus \mathbf{g}'_i(x_1, x_2, \ldots, x_{i-1}, A, B)$ are selected as generator functions in the considered model, then the vector boolean function **G** implements bijective mapping by X. A single unified boolean function of eight variables is used as a *generator functions prototype* in the **G** function. It looks as follows:

$$\mathbf{g} = \mathbf{g}(z_1, z_2, \ldots, z_8) = z_7 \oplus z_8 \oplus \varphi(z_1, z_2, \ldots, z_6),$$

where $\varphi(z_1, z_2, \ldots, z_6) = z_1z_2z_3 \oplus z_1z_4 \oplus z_2z_5 \oplus z_3z_6$ is a bent function, defined as follows.

> ***Definition 5.1***
> *A boolean function f(X) (X ∈ GF(2)n) is called perfect nonlinear, or a bent function [76], if for* $\forall\, \alpha \in GF(2)^n$, *the following equality is true:* $\mathbf{U}^*_{\alpha}(f) = \pm 2^{n/2}$.

In differential, linear, and other types of cryptanalysis, the leading role belongs to the notion of the *Walsh-Hadamard transformation*, which is a modification of the *discrete Fourier transform*.

> ***Definition 5.2***
> *A Walsh-Hadamard transformation (WHT) of a real function* $f(X) \in GF(2)$ *over an* $\boldsymbol{\alpha}$ *vector* ($X, \alpha \in GF(2)^n$) *is a linear transformation, which takes its values from the set of real numbers, and has the following form:*

$$\mathbf{U}_{\alpha}(f) = \sum_{X \in GF(2)^n} f(X)(-1)^{\alpha \bullet X}$$

A Walsh-Hadamard transformation of the **g** function consists of 64 elements having the value $|\mathbf{U}^*_{\alpha}(g)| = 32$ for all vectors $\boldsymbol{\alpha} = (\alpha_1, \alpha_2, \ldots, \alpha_6, 0, 0)$, and for the rest of the 192 elements, they have a value of $\mathbf{U}^*_{\alpha}(g) = 0$. With respect to the selected structure and properties of bent functions, we have the following characteristics of the **g** function:

- The nonlinearity of the **g** function is equal to $\mathbf{N}(\mathbf{g}) = 2^{m-1} - 2^{((m+2)/2)-1} = 112$ (with $m = 8$), which is quite close to the maximally possible nonlinearity of boolean functions of 8 variables ($\mathbf{N}_{\max} = 2^{m-1} - 2^{(m/2)-1} = 120$).
- **g** is a correlation immune function on a set of vectors $\{(z_1, z_2, \ldots, z_8)\} \subset GF(2)^8$, where $z_7 \neq 0$ or $z_8 \neq 0$, which makes up 75% of the whole $GF(2)^8$ set.
- **g** possesses good autocorrelation properties, because for all nonvanishing avalanche vectors $(\Delta z_1, \Delta z_2, \ldots, \Delta z_8) \in GF(2)^8$ except for three—((0, …, 0, 0, 1), (0, …, 0, 1, 0), and (0, …, 0, 1, 1))—*the 8th order propagation* criterion is fulfilled; that is, the function $\Delta\mathbf{g} = \mathbf{g}(z_1, z_2, \ldots, z_8) \oplus \mathbf{g}(z_1 \oplus \Delta z_1, z_2 \oplus \Delta z_2, \ldots, z_8 \oplus \Delta z_8)$ is balanced (see Section 4.2.6).
- The degree of the algebraic normal form of function **g** is equal to 3 (**deg**(**g**) = 3).

A transition from the general form of the **g** function to certain generator functions of a controlled substitution operation sequential model is performed by the following substitution of variables:

$$\begin{pmatrix} z_1 & z_2 & z_3 & z_4 & z_5 & z_6 & z_7 & z_8 \\ x_{i-2} & x_{i-5} & b_i & a_i & x_{i-3} & x_{i-4} & x_{i-1} & x_i \end{pmatrix},$$

where $\forall i \in \{1, 2, \ldots, n\}$ and $n = 32$.

Thus, generator functions look as follows:

$$y_i = \mathbf{g}_i(X, A, B) = x_i \oplus x_{i-1} \oplus x_{i-2}a_i \oplus x_{i-2}x_{i-5}\, b_i \oplus x_{i-3}x_{i-5} \oplus x_{i-4}b_i,$$

where x_i, a_i, and b_i are the components of vectors $X, A, B \in GF(2)^{32}$, and the initial conditions correspond to the vector $(x_{-4}, x_{-3}, x_{-2}, x_{-1}, x_0) = (1, 1, 1, 1, 1)$.

In cryptographic primitives, linear transformations of original vectors are often used as intermediate transformations. In connection with this, to increase the effectiveness of estimating such primitives, the following properties of transformations should be taken into account:

Statement 5.1

*If **B** is a nonsingular matrix of the order n over the GF(2) field, and the g(X) = f(X**B**) relationship is true for a boolean function f(X), f(X) and g(X) have the same algebraic degree (**deg**(f) = **deg**(g)) and nonlinearity (**N**(f) = **N**(g), **N***(f) = **N***(g)), and they also have the same dimension.*

Statement 5.2

If a boolean function has the form $f(X) = h_{aff}(X_1) \oplus h_{bent}(X_2)$, where $h_{aff}(X_1)$ ($X_1 \in GF(2)^l$) and $h_{bent}(X_2)(X_2 \in GF(2)^{n-l}$, $n - l$ is even) are affine and bent functions, respectively, the original function has the linear dimension l and a nonlinearity value of $\mathbf{N}(f) = 2^{n-1} - 2^{1/2(n+l)-1}$.

According to the scheme of the ***Crypt*** procedure (Figure 5.4), the **G** function is preceded by a linear transformation $X = L \oplus A$ that does not change either the initial values of nonlinearity or the degree of the algebraic normal form of generator functions (see Statement 5.1), but does complicate the resulting appearance of the generator functions. The function $\mathbf{G}' = \mathbf{G}(L \oplus A)$ is bijective by L at various fixed values of the A and B parameters.

The Extension Procedure for Control Vector *E* (Extension Box)

This procedure is intended for building an 80-bit control vector from a 32-bit one. It formally looks as follows:

$$V = (V_1||V_2||V_3||V_4||V_5) = \mathbf{E}(U, A, B) = \mathbf{E}_{A||B}(U),$$

where $V \in GF(2)^{80}$, $V_1, V_2, V_3, V_4, V_5 \in GF(2)^{16}$, $U, A, B \in GF(2)^{32}$.

Actually, the V vector is calculated according to the formulas:

$$V_1 = U_{hi};\ V_2 = \mathbf{P}_{\pi(1)}((U \oplus A)_{hi});\ V_5 = \mathbf{P}_{\pi(1)}((U \oplus A)_{lo}),$$
$$V_3 = \mathbf{P}_{\pi(5)}((U \oplus B)_{hi});\ V_4 = \mathbf{P}_{\pi(5)}((U \oplus B)_{lo}),$$

where the transformation $\mathbf{P}_{\pi(s)}$ looks as follows: $\mathbf{P}_{\pi(s)}(Z) = (Z_{hi})^{>>>s}||(Z_{lo})^{>>>s}$.

For the $\mathbf{P}_{32/80}$ box, there is a correspondence of the V and U vector bit-numbers shown in Table 5.2. For example, 17 in the first line means that the $\mathbf{P}_{2/1}$ box control input $v_1^{(1)}$ is fed the value u_{17}, 22_1 corresponds to a value of $v_{13}^{(2)} = u_{22} \oplus a_{22}$, and 7_2 corresponds to a value of $v_{10}^{(4)} = u_7 \oplus b_7$. The extension procedure **E** is created in such a way that the 16 lower order bits of the U vector participate in controlling only $\mathbf{R}_2$ boxes, whereas higher order bits control only $\mathbf{R}_3$ boxes, with all the bit numbers of vector U being different in each $\mathbf{R}_2$ and $\mathbf{R}_3$ box.

TABLE 5.2 Control Bit Values for the $P_{32/80}$ Box

V_1	17	18	19	20	21	22	23	24	25	26	27	28	29	30	31	32	U_{hi}
V_2	26_1	27_1	28_1	29_1	30_1	31_1	32_1	25_1	18_1	19_1	20_1	21_1	22_1	23_1	24_1	17_1	$(U \oplus A)_{hi}$ and $(U \oplus B)_{hi}$
V_3	30_2	31_2	32_2	25_2	26_2	27_2	28_2	29_2	22_2	23_2	24_2	17_2	18_2	19_2	20_2	21_2	
V_4	14_2	15_2	16_2	9_2	10_2	11_2	12_2	13_2	6_2	7_2	8_2	1_2	2_2	3_2	4_2	5_2	$(U \oplus B)_{lo}$ and $(U \oplus A)_{lo}$
V_5	10_1	11_1	12_1	13_1	14_1	15_1	16_1	9_1	2_1	3_1	4_1	5_1	6_1	7_1	8_1	1_1	

The same **E** extension procedure is used for the box $P^{-1}_{32/80}$, but, due to the special numeration of box $\mathbf{P}^{-1}_{32/80}$'s control bits, Table 5.2 is transformed into Table 5.3.

The **E** procedure provides for:

- The uniformity of the participation of all 32 bits of the U vector in controlling the $\mathbf{P}_{32/80}$ box.
- The fact that there are five (according to the number of layers) different bits of U vector participating in the control for a randomly chosen commutation of one input bit with one output bit, which guarantees such a commutation with any round key values A and B, and, consequently, corresponds to the first order box determination.
- The control vector V_1 being a fixed permutation of 16 bits of the L block; in other words, transformation in the first layer of $\mathbf{P}_{32/80}$ box is performed without any time delay.

TABLE 5.3 Control Bit Values for the $P^{-1}_{32/80}$ Box

V_5	10_1	11_1	12_1	13_1	14_1	15_1	16_1	9_1	2_1	3_1	4_1	5_1	6_1	7_1	8_1	1_1	$(U \oplus A)_{lo}$ and $(U \oplus B)_{lo}$
V_4	14_2	15_2	16_2	9_2	10_2	11_2	12_2	13_2	6_2	7_2	8_2	1_2	2_2	3_2	4_2	5_2	
V_3	30_2	31_2	32_2	25_2	26_2	27_2	28_2	29_2	22_2	23_2	24_2	17_2	18_2	19_2	20_2	21_2	$(U \oplus B)_{hi}$ and $(U \oplus A)_{hi}$
V_2	26_1	27_1	28_1	29_1	30_1	31_1	32_1	25_1	18_1	19_1	20_1	21_1	22_1	23_1	24_1	17_1	
V_1	17	18	19	20	21	22	23	24	25	26	27	28	29	30	31	32	U_{hi}

Final Transformation

The ***FT*** procedure is a transformation that is the opposite of the ***IT*** procedure. This transformation looks as follows:

$$Y = \boldsymbol{FT}(X, A),$$

where $X, Y \in GF(2)^{64}$, $A \in GF(2)^{32}$.

Initially, each even bit of the input block is inverted (see Figure 5.5), and then each pair of the X input block with indices $2j-1$ and $2j$ ($j = 1, 2, \ldots, 32$) is either permuted ($a_j = 1$) or not ($a_j = 0$).

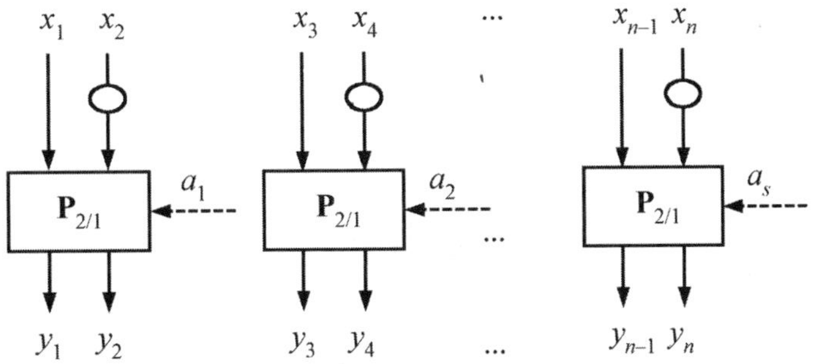

FIGURE 5.5 Final transformation ($s = n/2$).

The bit values of the Y vector are calculated with the use of the following formulas:

$$y_{2j-1} = (x_{2j-1} \oplus x_{2j} \oplus 1)a_j \oplus x_{2j-1} \text{ and } y_{2j} = (x_{2j-1} \oplus x_{2j} \oplus 1)a_j \oplus x_{2j} \oplus 1.$$

5.1.3 The Schedule for Using Round Keys

In a 12-round SPECTR-H64 block cipher, the extended key $Q^{(e)}$ is a combination of 14 subkeys; namely,

$$Q^{(e)} = (Q_{IT}^{(e)}, Q_1^{(e)}, Q_2^{(e)}, \ldots, Q_{12}^{(e)}, Q_{FT}^{(e)}),$$

where $\forall j = 1, 2, \ldots, 12$ $Q_j^{(e)} = (Q_j^{(1,e)}, Q_j^{(2,e)}, \ldots, Q_j^{(6,e)})$, when $Q_{IT}^{(e)}, Q_{FT}^{(e)}, Q_j^{(h,e)} \in GF(2)^{32}$ $\forall h = 1, 2, \ldots, 6$.

The $Q^{(e)}$ extended key is a series of 72 32-bit binary vectors, each being one of eight secret subkeys $K_1, K_2, \ldots, K_8$.

Some elements of the $Q^{(e)}$ extended key have fixed values—K_j, the rest being determined via O_i parameters, which are calculated, in turn, by the formulas:

$$O_{2i-1} = K_{2i-1+e} \text{ and } O_{2i} = K_{2i-e},$$

where $K = K_1 || K_2 || \ldots || K_8$ and $i = 1, 2, 3, 4$.

The commutation scheme between O_i and K_j is shown in Figure 5.6.

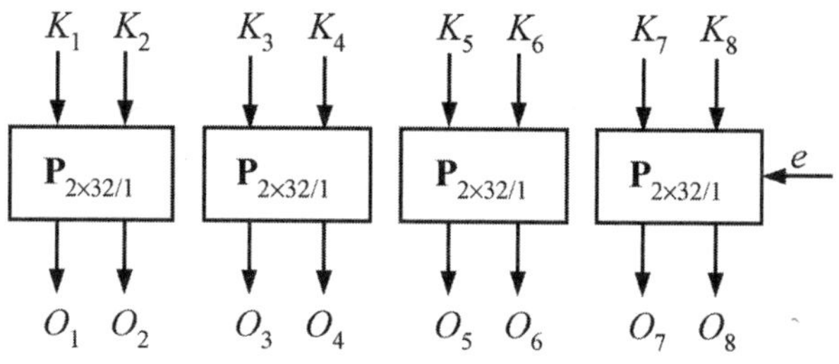

FIGURE 5.6 The subkey commutation scheme.

The correspondence of subkeys $Q_{IT}^{(e)}$, $Q_{FT}^{(e)}$, $Q_j^{(1,e)}$, $Q_j^{(2,e)}$, ..., $Q_j^{(6,e)}$ ($j = 1, 2, \ldots, 12$) is specified in Table 5.4.

TABLE 5.4 Schedule for Using Round Keys

$Q_{IT}^{(e)}$	$j =$	1	2	3	4	5	6	7	8	9	10	11	12	$Q_{FT}^{(e)}$
O_1	$Q_j^{(1,e)} =$	K_1	K_8	K_5	K_4	K_1	K_6	K_7	K_4	K_2	K_6	K_5	K_3	
	$Q_j^{(2,e)} =$	K_2	K_6	K_7	K_3	K_2	K_8	K_5	K_3	K_1	K_8	K_7	K_4	O_2
	$Q_j^{(3,e)} =$	O_6	O_1	O_2	O_5	O_7	O_3	O_4	O_8	O_6	O_1	O_2	O_5	
	$Q_j^{(4,e)} =$	O_7	O_4	O_3	O_8	O_6	O_1	O_2	O_5	O_7	O_4	O_3	O_8	
	$Q_j^{(5,e)} =$	K_3	K_5	K_6	K_2	K_4	K_7	K_6	K_1	K_4	K_5	K_8	K_1	
	$Q_j^{(6,e)} =$	K_4	K_7	K_8	K_1	K_3	K_5	K_8	K_2	K_3	K_7	K_6	K_2	

For example, for the fifth round ($j = 5$), the subkey sequence $K_1||K_2||O_7||O_6||K_4||K_3$ corresponds to the formal parameters $A^{(1)}$, $A^{(2)}$, ..., $A^{(6)}$ of the ***Crypt*** procedure; namely,

$$Q_5^{(e)} = (Q_5^{(1,e)}, Q_5^{(2,e)}, Q_5^{(3,e)}, Q_5^{(4,e)}, Q_5^{(5,e)}, Q_5^{(6,e)}) = (K_1, K_2, O_7, O_6, K_4, K_3).$$

That is, $Q_5^{(e)} = (K_1, K_2, K_{7+e}, K_{6-e}, K_4, K_3)$.

For the encryption mode—$Q_5^{(0)} = (K_1, K_2, K_7, K_6, K_4, K_3)$, and for the decryption mode—$Q_5^{(e)} = (K_1, K_2, K_8, K_5, K_4, K_3)$.

For the initial and final transformations, the keys $Q_{IT}^{(e)}$ and $Q_{FT}^{(e)}$ look as follows:

$$Q_{IT}^{(e)} = O_1 \text{ and } Q_{FT}^{(e)} = O_2.$$

That is,

$$Q_{IT}^{(e)} = K_{1+e} \text{ and } Q_{FT}^{(e)} = K_{2-e}.$$

For the encryption mode,

$$Q_{IT}^{(0)} = K_1 \text{ and } Q_{FT}^{(0)} = K_2,$$

and for the decryption mode

$$Q_{IT}^{(1)} = K_2 \text{ and } Q_{FT}^{(1)} = K_1.$$

5.2 THE SPECTR-128 CIPHER (ALGORITHM)

This algorithm is a practical implementation of the main ideas for synthesis of a fast block cipher based on controlled operations and considered in previous chapters, and it is aimed at high-speed information processing with a 64-bit data exchange bus.

5.2.1 A General Scheme of Block Encryption

For the SPECTR-128 algorithm, a general encryption scheme (encryption and decryption) is determined by the formula:

$$Y = \mathbf{F}(X, Q^{(e)}),$$

where $Q^{(e)} = \mathbf{H}(K, e)$ is an *extended key* that is a function of a 256-bit secret key K and the encryption mode e (e = 0—encryption, e = 1—decryption), while in the encryption mode X is the initial block of binary data (plaintext), and in the decryption mode it is a transformed block of binary data (ciphertext). In encryption mode, the resulting value Y is ciphertext, and in decryption mode, it is plaintext.

The secret key K is represented as a combination of four 64-bit subkeys; namely, $K = K_1||K_2||K_3||K_4$, where $K_1, K_2, K_3, K_4 \in GF(2)^{64}$.

The encryption algorithm (the **F** function) is described in Section. 5.2.2, and the procedure for building the $Q^{(e)} = \mathbf{H}(K, e)$ working key is in Section 5.2.3.

5.2.2 The Encryption Algorithm

The **F** function (Figure 5.1) is implemented using the following procedures:

- The initial transformation—***IT***
- 12 rounds (loops) of transformations using the ***Crypt*** procedure
- The final transformation—***FT***

First, the ***IT*** procedure is performed: $Y = \boldsymbol{IT}(X, Q_{IT}^{(e)})$.

Block Y is divided into two subblocks of the same length—L_0 and R_0; in other words, $(L_0, R_0) = Y$, where $L_0, R_0 \in GF(2)^{64}$. Then, 12 rounds of transformation are performed using the ***Crypt*** procedure according to the formulas:

$$L_j = \boldsymbol{Crypt}(R_{j-1}, L_{j-1}, Q_j^{(e)});$$
$$R_j = L_{j-1} \quad (j = 1, 2, \ldots, 12).$$

After the 12th round, the final transformation ***FT*** is performed over the block $X = (R_{12}, L_{12})$ according to the formula:

$$Y = \boldsymbol{FT}(X, Q_{FT}^{(e)}).$$

Initial Transformation

The initial transformation ***IT*** looks as follows:

$$Y = \boldsymbol{IT}(X, A),$$

where $X, Y \in GF(2)^{128}$, $A \in GF(2)^{64}$.

The implementation scheme of this transformation is shown in Figure 5.2, in which each pair of bits of the input block X with the indices $2j-1$ and $2j$ $(j = 1, 2, ..., 64)$ is either permuted $(a_j = 1)$ or not permuted $(a_j = 0)$, after which each even bit is inverted. The bit values of vector Y are calculated by the following formulas:

$$y_{2j-1} = (x_{2j-1} \oplus x_{2j})a_j \oplus x_{2j-1} \text{ and } y_{2j} = (x_{2j-1} \oplus x_{2j})a_j \oplus x_{2j} \oplus 1.$$

The *Crypt* Procedure

Formally, the ***Crypt*** procedure looks as follows:

$$R = \boldsymbol{Crypt}(R, L, (A^{(1)}, A^{(2)}, A^{(3)}, A^{(4)})),$$

where $L, R \in GF(2)^{64}$ and $A^{(1)}, A^{(2)}, A^{(3)}, A^{(4)} \in GF(2)^{64}$.

The elements $A^{(1)}$, $A^{(2)}$, $A^{(3)}$, and $A^{(4)}$ are formal parameters of the key information; in other words, $Q_j^{(i,e)}$ is an element of the round key $Q_j^{(e)} = (Q_j^{(1,e)}, Q_j^{(2,e)}, Q_j^{(3,e)}, Q_j^{(4,e)})$, and corresponds to parameter $A^{(i)}$. Accordingly, R and L are the formal parameters for the left and right parts of the input data block.

One feature of such an implementation of the ***Crypt*** procedure is the use of four subkeys with a length of 64 in one round—all the bits of 256-bit secret key K are used. In addition, a more complicated vector boolean function G is used.

The procedure employs:

- The *rotation operation* ">>>" by a fixed number of bits
- *Bit-wise addition modulo 2*—"⊕"
- A nonlinear vector boolean function **G**
- *Controlled permutations boxes* $\mathbf{P}_{64/192}$ and $\mathbf{P}^{-1}_{64/192}$ of the first order
- The control vector **E** extension procedure (expansion box)

A two-stage Clos network $\mathbf{C}_{<8,\,8>}$ is used as $\mathbf{P}_{64/192}$ and $\mathbf{P}^{-1}_{64/192}$ boxes (Figure 5.7) when the first layer is made up of $\mathbf{R}_3$ boxes, and the second is made up of $\mathbf{R}_3^{-1}$ boxes. Since the structure of the $\mathbf{P}_{64/192}$ and $\mathbf{P}^{-1}_{64/192}$ boxes are the same, in Figure 5.7, column (I) corresponds to a control vector for the direct transformation, and column (II) to a reverse transformation.

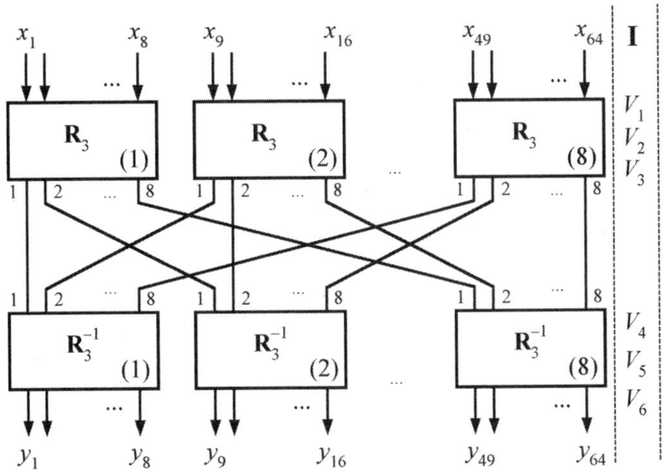

FIGURE 5.7 Controlled permutations box $\mathbf{P}_{64/192}$.

The sequence of transformations and their interaction are shown in Figure 5.8. The time base of operations in the ***Crypt*** procedure is presented in Table 5.5.

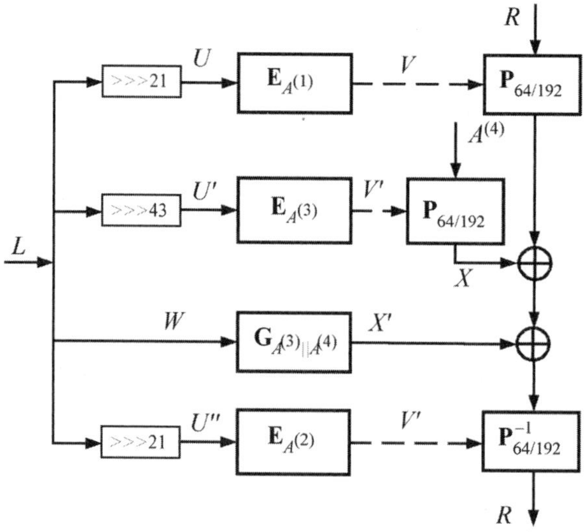

FIGURE 5.8 The ***Crypt*** procedure scheme.

TABLE 5.5 The Time Base for Operations in the ***Crypt*** Procedure

	Time base ($\tau_\oplus$)	Operations
1	0	$U = L^{>>>21}$ $\quad U' = L^{>>>43}$ $\quad U'' = L^{>>>21}$
2	0 ÷ 1	$V = \mathbf{E}_{A^{(1)}}(U)$ $\quad V' = \mathbf{E}_{A^{(3)}}(U')$ $\quad V'' = \mathbf{E}_{A^{(2)}}(U'')$
3	0 ÷ 6	$R = \mathbf{P}_{64/192(V)}(R)$ $\quad X = \mathbf{P}_{64/192(V')}(A^{(4)})$
4	0 ÷ 5	$X' = \mathbf{G}_{A^{(3)}\|\|A^{(4)}}(L)$
5	6 ÷ 7	$R = R \oplus X$
6	7 ÷ 8	$R = R \oplus X'$
7	8 ÷ 14	$\mathbf{R} = \mathbf{P}^{-1}_{64/192(V'')}(\mathbf{R})$

As it follows from Table 5.5, most of the operations are performed concurrently, and the total time required for the performance of the procedure is equal to the consecutive performance of 14 operations of the XOR type.

Vector Boolean Function *G*

A controlled substitution operation—which is one of the implementations of a sequential bijective model—is used as a vector boolean function **G**. Formally, the **G** function looks as follows:

$$X' = \mathbf{G}(L, A, B), \text{ where } X', L, A, B \in \mathrm{GF}(2)^{64}.$$

The formal parameters A and B correspond to the formal parameters $A^{(3)}$ and $A^{(4)}$ of the ***Crypt*** procedure. In vector form, the **G** function is determined by the formula:

$$X' = L^{(0)} \oplus A^{(0)} \oplus (L^{(1)} \otimes B^{(2)}) \oplus (L^{(6)} \otimes L^{(8)}) \oplus (A^{(2)} \otimes L^{(7)}) \oplus$$
$$\oplus (A^{(1)} \otimes B^{(1)}) \oplus (L^{(3)} \otimes L^{(9)}) \oplus (L^{(1)} \otimes L^{(9)} \otimes A^{(2)}) \oplus (L^{(1)} \otimes L^{(6)} \otimes L^{(9)} \otimes B^{(1)}),$$

where vectors L_j ($j = 0, 1, 2, \ldots, 9$) are expressed recursively via L; namely,

$$L^{(0)} = (l_1^{(0)}, l_2^{(0)}, l_3^{(0)}, \ldots, l_{63}^{(0)}, l_{64}^{(0)}) = L = (l_1, l_2, l_3, \ldots, l_{63}, l_{64})$$

and $\forall j = 0, 1, \ldots, 5,$

$$L^{(j)} = (l_1^{(j)}, l_2^{(j)}, l_3^{(j)}, \ldots, l_{63}^{(j)}, l_{64}^{(j)}) = (1, l_1^{(j-1)}, l_2^{(j-1)}, l_3^{(j-1)}, \ldots, l_{63}^{(j-1)}).$$

Vectors $A^{(j)}$ and $B^{(j)}$ for $j = 0, 1, 2$ are determined in a similar manner.

Taking into account the option of concurrently performing some operations, it is easy to establish that the **G** function is implemented during five time delay units ($5\tau_{\oplus}$).

Grounds for Selecting a Nonlinear *G* Function

We'll define the mapping of **G**—$\mathrm{GF}(2)^{64} \times \mathrm{GF}(2)^{64} \times \mathrm{GF}(2)^{64} \rightarrow \mathrm{GF}(2)^{64}$—as a boolean vector function $Y = \mathbf{G}(X, A, B)$ with the following appearance:

$$(y_1, y_2, \ldots, y_{64}) = (\mathbf{g}_1(X, A, B), \mathbf{g}_2(X, A, B), \ldots, \mathbf{g}_{64}(X, A, B)),$$

where $\mathbf{g}_i$ represents certain generator boolean functions. If $\mathbf{g}_i(X, A, B) = = \mathbf{g}_i(x_1, x_2, \ldots, x_i, A, B)$ is true for each i condition, then such a mapping is a sequential model of a controlled substitution operation. If the function $\mathbf{g}_i(X, A, B) = x_i \oplus \mathbf{g}_i'(x_1, x_2, \ldots, x_{i-1}, A, B)$ is selected as a generator function in the considered model, then the vector Boolean **G** function implements bijective mapping by X. A single unified boolean function of 12 variables is used as a *generator functions prototype* in the **G** function. It looks as follows:

$$\mathbf{g} = \mathbf{g}(z_1, z_2, \ldots, z_{12}) = z_{11} \oplus z_{12} \oplus \varphi(z_1, z_2, \ldots, z_{10}),$$

where $\varphi(z_1, z_2, \ldots, z_{10}) = z_1z_2 \oplus z_3z_4 \oplus z_5z_6 \oplus z_7z_8 \oplus z_9z_{10} \oplus z_1z_5z_9 \oplus z_1z_3z_7z_9$ is a bent function (see Definition 5.1. A Walsh-Hadamard transformation (see Definition 5.2) of the **g** function consists of 1024 elements possessing the value $|\mathbf{U}^*_\alpha(\mathbf{g})| = 128$ for all vectors $\boldsymbol{\alpha} = (\alpha_1, \alpha_2, \ldots, \alpha_{10}, 0, 0)$, and for the rest of the 3072 elements, they have the value $\mathbf{U}^*_\alpha(\mathbf{g}) = 0$. With respect to the selected structure and properties of bent functions, we have the following characteristics of the **g** function:

- The nonlinearity of the **g** function is equal to $\mathbf{N}(\mathbf{g}) = 2^{m-1} - 2^{((m+2)/2)-1} = 1984$ (with $m = 12$), which is quite close to the maximum possible nonlinearity of boolean functions of 12 variables ($\mathbf{N}_{\max} = 2^{m-1} - 2^{(m/2)-1} = 2016$).
- **g** is a correlation immune function on a set of vectors $\{(z_1, z_2, \ldots, z_{12})\} \subset GF(2)^{12}$, where $z_{11} \neq 0$ or $z_{12} \neq 0$, which makes up 75% of the whole $GF(2)^{12}$ set.
- **g** possesses good autocorrelation properties because for all nonvanishing avalanche vectors $(\Delta z_1, \Delta z_2, \ldots, \Delta z_{12}) \in GF(2)^{12}$ except for three—((0, …, 0, 0, 1), (0, …, 0, 1, 0), and (0, …, 0, 1, 1))—the *propagation criteria of the 12th order* is fulfilled; that is, the function $\Delta\mathbf{g} = \mathbf{g}(z_1, z_2, \ldots, z_{12}) \oplus \mathbf{g}(z_1 \oplus \Delta z_1, \ldots, z_{12} \oplus \Delta z_{12})$ is a balanced one.
- The degree of the algebraic normal form of function **g** is equal to 4 ($\mathbf{deg}(\mathbf{g}) = 4$).

A transition from the general form of the **g** function to certain generator functions of a sequential model of a controlled substitution operation is performed by the following substitution of variables:

$$\begin{pmatrix} z_1 & z_2 & z_3 & z_4 & z_5 & z_6 & z_7 & z_8 & z_9 & z_{10} & z_{11} & z_{12} \\ l_{i-1} & b_{i-2} & l_{i-6} & l_{i-8} & a_{i-2} & l_{i-7} & b_{i-1} & a_{i-1} & l_{i-9} & l_{i-3} & l_i & a_i \end{pmatrix},$$

where $\forall i \in \{1, 2, \ldots, n\}$ and $n = 64$.

Thus, generator functions look like:

$$y_i = \mathbf{g}_i = l_i \oplus a_i \oplus l_{i-1}b_{i-2} \oplus l_{i-6}l_{i-8} \oplus a_{i-2}l_{i-7} \oplus a_{i-1}b_{i-1} \oplus l_{i-3}l_{i-9} \oplus l_{i-3}a_{i-2}l_{i-9} \oplus l_{i-1}b_{i-1}l_{i-6}l_{i-9},$$

where l_j, a_j, b_j are the components of vectors $L, A, B \in GF(2)^{64}$, and the initial conditions correspond to the vector $(x_{-4}, x_{-3}, x_{-2}, x_{-1}, x_0) = (1, 1, 1, 1, 1)$.

The Procedure for Extending Control Vector *E* (Extension Box)

This procedure is intended for building a 192-bit control vector from a 64-bit one. Formally, the **E** procedure looks as follows:

$$V = (V_1||V_2||V_3||V_4||V_5||V_6) = \mathbf{E}(U, A) = \mathbf{E}_A(U),$$

where $V \in \mathrm{GF}(2)^{192}$, $V_1, V_2, V_3, V_4, V_5, V_6 \in \mathrm{GF}(2)^{32}$, $U, A \in \mathrm{GF}(2)^{64}$.

The V vector is calculated according to the formulas:

$$V_1 = U_{hi}\ V_2 = \mathbf{P}_{\pi(1)}((U \oplus A)_{hi})\ V_3 = \mathbf{P}_{\pi(11)}(U_{hi}) \oplus \mathbf{P}_{\pi(8)}(A_{hi})$$
$$V_6 = U_{lo} \oplus (A_{lo})^{>>>28}\ V_5 = \mathbf{P}_{\pi(1)}((U \oplus A)_{lo})\ V_4 = \mathbf{P}_{\pi(11)}(U_{lo}) \oplus \mathbf{P}_{\pi(8)}(A_{lo}),$$

where the $\mathbf{P}_{\pi(s)}$ transformation looks like $\mathbf{P}_{\pi(s)}\ (Z) = (Z_{hi})^{>>>s}||(Z_{lo})^{>>>s}$.

For the $\mathbf{P}_{64/192}$ box, you see the correspondence of the V and U vectors' bit-numbers, which is shown in Table 5.6. For example, 19 in the fourth line, corresponding to vector V_4, means that the value u_{19} is used as the control bit $v_{10}^{(4)}$; in other words, v_{102} of V. 22 corresponds to the value u_{22}, and 7 to the value u_7.

Table 5.6 The Correspondence between the U and V Vector Bits for the $\mathbf{P}_{64/192}$ Box

V_1	33	34	35	36	37	38	39	40	41	42	43	44	45	46	47	48	49	50	51	52	53	54	55	56	57	58	59	60	61	62	63	64
V_2	50	51	52	53	54	55	56	57	58	59	60	61	62	63	64	49	34	35	36	37	38	39	40	41	42	43	44	45	46	47	48	33
V_3	58	59	60	61	62	63	64	49	50	51	52	53	54	55	56	57	42	43	44	45	46	47	48	33	34	35	36	37	38	39	40	41
V_4	26	27	28	29	30	31	32	17	18	19	20	21	22	23	24	25	10	11	12	13	14	15	16	1	2	3	4	5	6	7	8	9
V_5	18	19	20	21	22	23	24	25	26	27	28	29	30	31	32	17	2	3	4	5	6	7	8	9	10	11	12	13	14	15	16	1
V_6	1	2	3	4	5	6	7	8	9	10	11	12	13	14	15	16	17	18	19	20	21	22	23	24	25	26	27	28	29	30	31	32

Similarly, Table 5.7 shows the correspondence of bit numbers for vectors V and A; the table's analysis proves that V_1 does not depend on A.

Table 5.7 The Correspondence between the A and V Vector Bits for the $\mathbf{P}_{64/192}$ Box

V_1																																
V_2	50	51	52	53	54	55	56	57	58	59	60	61	62	63	64	49	34	35	36	37	38	39	40	41	42	43	44	45	46	47	48	33
V_3	57	58	59	60	61	62	63	64	49	50	51	52	53	54	55	56	41	42	43	44	45	46	47	48	33	34	35	36	37	38	39	40
V_4	25	26	27	28	29	30	31	32	17	18	19	20	21	22	23	24	9	10	11	12	13	14	15	16	1	2	3	4	5	6	7	8
V_5	18	19	20	21	22	23	24	25	26	27	28	29	30	31	32	17	2	3	4	5	6	7	8	9	10	11	12	13	14	15	16	1
V_6	1	2	3	4	5	6	7	8	9	10	11	12	13	14	15	16	17	18	19	20	21	22	23	24	25	26	27	28	29	30	31	32

The extension is done in such a way that the 32 high order bits of vector A control only $\mathbf{R}_3$ boxes, and those of the lower order control only boxes $\mathbf{R}_3^{-1}$, whereas in each box $\mathbf{R}_3$ and $\mathbf{R}_3^{-1}$ all bit numbers of vectors U and A are different. Moreover, there are no two $\mathbf{P}_{2/1}$ boxes with control bits of the same expression of the $u_i \oplus a_j$ type.

The **E** procedure provides for:

- The uniformity of the participation of all 64 bits of the U vector in controlling the $\mathbf{P}_{64/128}$ box.
- The fact that, for a randomly chosen commutation of one input bit with one output bit, there are six different bits of the U vector and five different bits of the A key participating in the control, which guarantees the implementation of all commutation variants.
- The control vector V_1 being a fixed substitution of 32 bits of the U vector; in other words, transformation in the first layer of the $\mathbf{P}_{64/192}$ box is performed without a time delay.

Final Transformation

The ***FT*** procedure is a transformation that is the reverse of the ***IT*** procedure. This transformation looks as follows:

$$Y = \boldsymbol{FT}(X, A),$$

where $X, Y \in \mathrm{GF}(2)^{128}$, $A \in \mathrm{GF}(2)^{64}$.

Initially, each even bit of the input block is inverted (see Figure 5.7), and then each pair of the X input block with indices $2j–1$ and $2j$ ($j = 1, 2, \ldots, 64$) is either permuted ($a_j = 1$) or not ($a_j = 0$).

The bit values of the Y vector are calculated using the following formulas:

$$y_{2j-1} = (x_{2j-1} \oplus x_{2j} \oplus 1)a_j \oplus x_{2j-1} \quad \text{and} \quad y_{2j} = (x_{2j-1} \oplus x_{2j} \oplus 1)a_j \oplus x_{2j} \oplus 1.$$

5.2.3 The Schedule for Using Round Keys

In a 12-round SPECTR-128 block cipher, the extended key $Q^{(e)}$ is a combination of 14 subkeys; namely,

$$Q^{(e)} = (Q_{IT}^{(e)}, Q_1^{(e)}, Q_2^{(e)}, \ldots, Q_{12}^{(e)}, Q_{FT}^{(e)}),$$

where $Q_j^{(e)} = (Q_j^{(1,e)}, Q_j^{(2,e)}, Q_j^{(3,e)}, Q_j^{(4,e)})\ \forall j = 1, 2, \ldots, 12$,
when $Q_{IT}^{(e)}, Q_{FT}^{(e)}, Q_j^{(h,e)} \in \mathrm{GF}(2)^{64},\ \forall h = 1, 2, 3, 4$.

The extended key $Q^{(e)}$ is a series of 50 64-bit binary vectors, each being one of four secret subkeys—K_1, K_2, K_3, K_4.

The elements of the extended key $Q^{(e)}$ are determined via O_i parameters, which are calculated, in turn, by the formulas:

$$O_{2i-1} = K_{2i-1+e} \text{ and } O_{2i} = K_{2i-e},$$

where $K = K_1||K_2||K_3||K_4$ and $i = 1, 2$.

The commutation scheme between O_i and K_j is shown in Figure 5.9.

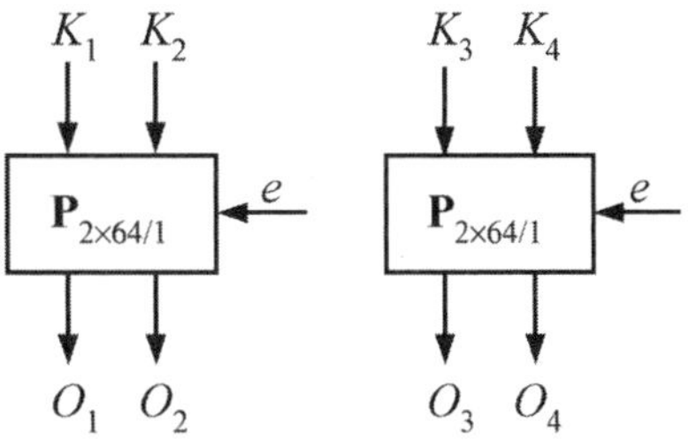

FIGURE 5.9 The subkey commutation scheme.

The subkey correspondence $Q_{IT}^{(e)}, Q_{FT}^{(e)}, Q_j^{(1,e)}, Q_j^{(2,e)}, Q_j^{(3,e)}, Q_j^{(4,e)}$ ($\forall j = 1, 2, \ldots, 12$) is given in Table 5.8.

TABLE 5.8 Schedule for Using Round Keys

$Q_{IT}^{(e)}$	$j =$	1	2	3	4	5	6	7	8	9	10	11	12	$Q_{FT}^{(e)}$
O_4	$Q_j^{(1,e)} =$	O_1	O_3	O_2	O_4	O_3	O_1	O_4	O_2	O_1	O_3	O_2	O_4	O_3
	$Q_j^{(2,e)} =$	O_3	O_1	O_4	O_2	O_1	O_3	O_2	O_4	O_3	O_1	O_4	O_2	
	$Q_j^{(3,e)} =$	O_4	O_2	O_1	O_3	O_2	O_4	O_3	O_1	O_4	O_2	O_1	O_3	
	$Q_j^{(4,e)} =$	O_2	O_4	O_3	O_1	O_4	O_2	O_1	O_3	O_2	O_4	O_3	O_1	

For example, for the fifth round ($j = 5$), the subkey sequence O_3, O_1, O_2, O_4 corresponds to formal parameters $A^{(1)}, A^{(2)}, A^{(3)}, A^{(4)}$ of the ***Crypt*** procedure; namely,

$$Q_5^{(e)} = (Q_5^{(1,e)}, Q_5^{(2,e)}, Q_5^{(3,e)}, Q_5^{(4,e)}) = (O_3, O_1, O_2, O_4).$$

That is,

$$Q_5^{(e)} = (K_{3+e}, K_{1+e}, K_{2-e}, K_{4-e}).$$

For the encryption mode

$$Q_5^{(0)} = (K_3, K_1, K_2, K_4),$$

and for the decryption mode

$$Q_5^{(1)} = (K_4, K_2, K_1, K_3).$$

For the initial and final transformations, the keys $Q_{IT}^{(e)}$ and $Q_{FT}^{(e)}$ look like:

$$Q_{IT}^{(e)} = O_4 \text{ and } Q_{FT}^{(e)} = O_3.$$

That is,

$$Q_{IT}^{(e)} = K_{4-e} \text{ and } Q_{FT}^{(e)} = K_{3+e}.$$

For the encryption mode,

$$Q_{IT}^{(0)} = K_4 \text{ and } Q_{FT}^{(0)} = K_3,$$

and for the decryption mode,

$$Q_{IT}^{(1)} = K_3 \text{ and } Q_{FT}^{(1)} = K_4.$$

5.3 THE CIKS-128 CIPHER (ALGORITHM)

The CIKS-128 algorithm is a type of iterated block cipher that uses the scheme of Russian patent No. 2140714 as the basic scheme for one round. Compared to SPECTR-128, the round structure function is changed. In particular, instead of a controlled $\mathbf{P}_{64/192}$ permutation box and a nonlinear vector boolean **G** function, two identical nonlinear vector boolean **G** functions are used.

Like SPECTR-128, the CIKS-128 algorithm is a practical implementation of basic ideas of synthesizing a fast block cipher based on controlled operations, which we considered in the previous chapters. It is aimed at high-speed information processing with a 64-bit data exchange bus.

5.3.1 A General Scheme of Block Encryption

For the CIKS-128 algorithm, a general encryption scheme (encryption and decryption) is determined by the formula:

$$Y = \mathbf{F}(X, Q^{(e)}),$$

where $Q^{(e)} = \mathbf{H}(K, e)$ is an *extended key*, which is a function of a 256-bit secret key K and encryption mode e ($e = 0$—encryption, $e = 1$—decryption). In encryption mode, X is the initial block of binary data (plaintext), and in decryption mode, it is a transformed block of binary data (ciphertext). In encryption mode, the resulting value Y is ciphertext, and in decryption mode it is plaintext.

The secret key K is represented as a combination of four 64-bit subkeys; namely, $K = K_1||K_2||K_3||K_4$, where $K_1, K_2, K_3, K_4 \in GF(2)^{64}$.

The encryption algorithm (**F** function) is described in Section 5.3.2, and the building procedure for the $Q^{(e)} = \mathbf{H}(K, e)$ working key can be found in Section 5.3.3.

5.3.2 The Encryption Algorithm

The **F** function (Figure 5.1) is implemented using the following procedures:

- Initial transformation—***IT***
- 12 rounds (loops) of *transformations* using the ***Crypt*** procedure
- Final transformation—***FT***

First, the ***IT*** procedure is performed: $Y = \boldsymbol{IT}(X, Q_{IT}^{(e)})$.

Block Y is divided into two subblocks of the same length—L_0 and R_0; in other words, $(L_0, R_0) = Y$, where $L_0, R_0 \in GF(2)^{64}$. Then, 12 rounds of transformation are done using the ***Crypt*** procedure according to the formulas:

$$L_j = \boldsymbol{Crypt}(R_{j-1}, L_{j-1}, Q_j^{(e)}),\ R_j = L_{j-1}\ \ (j = 1, 2, \ldots, 12).$$

After the 12th round, the final transformation ***FT*** is performed over the block $X = (R_{12}, L_{12})$ according to the formula:

$$Y = \boldsymbol{FT}(X, Q_{FT}^{(e)}).$$

Initial and Final Transformations

The simplest operation of bitwise addition with the key is used here; namely,

$$Y = \boldsymbol{IT}(X, A) = X \oplus A$$

and

$$Y = \boldsymbol{FT}(X, B) = X \oplus B,$$

where $X, Y, A, B \in GF(2)^{128}$.

The formal A parameter corresponds to the $Q_{IT}^{(e)}$ key, and the B parameter corresponds to the $Q_{FT}^{(e)}$ key.

The *Crypt* Procedure

Formally, the ***Crypt*** procedure looks like this:

$$R = \boldsymbol{Crypt}(R, L, (A^{(1)}, A^{(2)}, A^{(3)}, A^{(4)})),$$

where $L, R \in GF(2)^{64}$ and $A^{(1)}, A^{(2)}, A^{(3)}, A^{(4)} \in GF(2)^{64}$.

The elements $A^{(1)}, A^{(2)}, A^{(3)}$, and $A^{(4)}$ are formal parameters of key information; in other words, $Q_j^{(i,e)}$ is an element of the round key $Q_j^{(e)} = (Q_j^{(1,e)}, Q_j^{(2,e)}, Q_j^{(3,e)}, Q_j^{(4,e)})$ corresponding to the $A^{(i)}$ parameter. R and L are formal parameters for the left and right parts of the input data block.

A feature of such an implementation of the ***Crypt*** procedure is the use of two vector boolean **G** functions, four subkeys with a length of 64 in one round; in other words, all bits of the 256-bit secret key K are used, and an involution between the $\mathbf{P}_{64/192}$ and $\mathbf{P}^{-1}_{64/192}$ boxes when the right part of the input data is transformed.

The procedure employs:

- *The rotation operation* ">>>" by a fixed value of bits
- *Bit-wise modulo 2 addition* "⊕"
- *Two nonlinear vector boolean* **G** *functions* with the same structure
- $\mathbf{P}_{64/192}$ and $\mathbf{P}^{-1}_{64/192}$ *controlled permutation* boxes of the first order
- *A one-layer box of controlled permutations* $\mathbf{P}_{2\times 64/1}$ (to provide universality for a scheme with a noncommutative structure for information transformation)
- Fixed 64-bit commutators set by the permutation $\boldsymbol{\pi}$ and the involution **I**
- The extension procedure for control vector **E** (extension box)

A two-stage Clos network $\mathbf{C}_{<8,8>}$ is used as $\mathbf{P}_{64/192}$ and $\mathbf{P}^{-1}_{64/192}$ boxes (Figure 5.7), where the first layer is compiled of $\mathbf{R}_3$ boxes, and the second is made up of $\mathbf{R}_3^{-1}$ boxes. Since the structure of boxes $\mathbf{P}_{64/192}$ and $\mathbf{P}^{-1}_{64/192}$ is the same, in Figure 5.7, column (I) corresponds to a control vector for direct transformation, and column (II) corresponds to one for a reverse transformation.

The sequence of the transformations and their interaction is shown in Figure 5.10.

The time base for performing operations in the ***Crypt*** procedure is presented in Table 5.9.

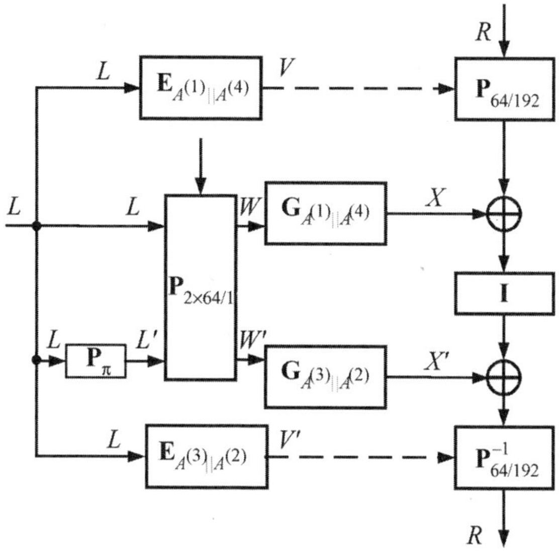

FIGURE 5.10 The ***Crypt*** procedure scheme.

TABLE 5.9 The Time Base for Performing Operations in the ***Crypt*** Procedure

	Time base ($\tau_\oplus$)	Operations
1	0	$L' = \mathbf{P}_\pi(L)$
2	0 — 1	$V = \mathbf{E}_{A^{(1)}\|A^{(4)}}(L)$ $(W\|W') = \mathbf{P}_{2\times 64/1(e)}(L\|L')$ $V' = \mathbf{E}_{A^{(3)}\|A^{(2)}}(L)$
3	0 — 6	$R = \mathbf{P}_{64/192(V)}(R)$
4	1 — 6	$X = \mathbf{G}_{A^{(1)}\|A^{(4)}}(W)$ $X' = \mathbf{G}_{A^{(3)}\|A^{(2)}}(W')$
5	6 — 7	$R = \mathbf{I}(R \oplus X)$
6	7 — 8	$R = R \oplus X'$
7	8 — 14	$\mathbf{R} = \mathbf{P}^{-1}_{64/192(V'')}(\mathbf{R})$

It follows from Table 5.9 that most operations are performed concurrently, and the total time required for the procedure's performance is equal to the consecutive performance of 14 operations of the XOR type.

Fixed Commutators P_π and I

The main purpose of the π permutation is in changing the mutual bit position of a data block simultaneously fed to the input of two nonlinear boolean **G** functions that have an identical appearance but use different round keys. The permutation consists of four loops with a length of 16, and looks as follows:

$$\pi = (1, 50, 9, 42, 17, 34, 25, 26, 33, 18, 41, 10, 49, 2, 57, 57)$$
$$(3, 64, 43, 24, 19, 48, 59, 8, 35, 32, 11, 56, 51, 16, 27, 40)$$
$$(4, 7, 28, 47, 52, 23, 12, 63, 36, 39, 60, 15, 20, 55, 44, 31)$$
$$(5, 14, 13, 6, 21, 62, 29, 54, 37, 46, 45, 38, 53, 30, 61, 22)$$

Correspondingly, the $\mathbf{P}_\pi$ substitution transformation implemented by this permutation is specified by the formula $Y = \mathbf{P}_\pi(X)$, where $X, Y \in \mathrm{GF}(2)^{64}$; namely,

$$y_{\pi(i)} = x_i, \forall i = 1, 2, \ldots, 64.$$

For example, $y_{50} = x_1$, $y_9 = x_{50}$, $y_1 = x_{57}$, and so on.

The **I** involution looks like:

$$Y = \mathbf{I}(X) = (X_6^{>>>4}||X_5^{>>>4}||X_4^{>>>4}||X_3^{>>>4}||X_2^{>>>4}||X_1^{>>>4}||X_8^{>>>4}||X_7^{>>>4}),$$

where $X = (X_1, X_2, X_3, X_4, X_5, X_6, X_7, X_8)$ and $X_1, X_2, \ldots, X_8 \in \mathrm{GF}(2)^8$. In other words, there is a byte permutation, and each byte shifts by 4.

To make sure involution is specified, it is sufficient to perform the $\mathbf{I}^2$ transformation; namely,

$$\mathbf{I}^2(X) = \mathbf{I}((X_6)^{>>>4}||(X_5)^{>>>4}||(X_4)^{>>>4}||(X_3)^{>>>4}||(X_2)^{>>>4}||(X_1)^{>>>4}||(X_8)^{>>>4}|| (X_7)^{>>>4}) = \mathbf{I}(((X_1)^{>>>4})^{>>>4}||((X_2)^{>>>4})^{>>>4}||((X_3)^{>>>4})^{>>>4}||((X_4)^{>>>4})^{>>>4}|| ||((X_5)^{>>>4})^{>>>4}||((X_6)^{>>>4})^{>>>4}||((X_7)^{>>>4})^{>>>4}||((X_8)^{>>>4})^{>>>4}) = (X_1, X_2, X_3, X_4, X_5, X_6, X_7, X_8) = X.$$

A $P_{2\times64/1}$ One-Layer Box of Controlled Permutations

A mapping implemented by the $\mathbf{P}_{2\times\omega/1}$ box looks like this:

$$(W||W') = \mathbf{P}_{2\times64/1}(L||L', e),$$

when the values of jth bits of vectors W and W' ($j = 1, 2, \ldots, 64$) are calculated by the following formulas:

$$w_j = (l_j \oplus l'_j)e \oplus l_j \text{ and } w'_j = (l_j \oplus l'_j)e \oplus l'_j.$$

Vector Boolean *G* Function

A controlled substitution operation is used as a vector boolean **G** function. It is one of the implementations of a sequential model. Formally, the **G** function looks like this:

$$X = \mathbf{G}(W, A, B), \text{ where } X, W, A, B \in \mathrm{GF}(2)^{64}.$$

In vector form, the **G** function is determined by the formula:

$$X = U^{(0)} \oplus A^{(0)} \oplus (U^{(1)} \otimes B^{(0)}) \oplus (U^{(2)} \otimes U^{(5)}) \oplus (U^{(6)} \otimes A^{(1)}) \oplus (A^{(2)} \otimes B^{(1)}) \oplus$$
$$\oplus (U^{(3)} \otimes U^{(4)}) \oplus (U^{(1)} \otimes U^{(4)} \otimes U^{(6)}) \oplus (U^{(2)} \otimes U^{(6)} \otimes B^{(1)}) \oplus$$
$$\oplus (U^{(1)} \otimes U^{(2)} \otimes U^{(4)} \otimes B^{(1)}),$$

where the vectors U_j ($j = 0, 1, 2, \ldots, 6$) are expressed recursively via W; namely,

$$U^{(0)} = (u_1^{(0)}, u_2^{(0)}, u_3^{(0)}, \ldots, u_{63}^{(0)}, u_{64}^{(0)}) = W = (w_1, w_2, w_3, \ldots, w_{63}, w_{64}),$$

$$U^{(j)} = (u_1^{(j)}, u_2^{(j)}, u_3^{(j)}, \ldots, u_{63}^{(j)}, u_{64}^{(j)}) = (1, u_1^{(j-1)}, u_2^{(j-1)}, u_3^{(j-1)}, \ldots, u_{63}^{(j-1)}).$$

Vectors $A^{(j)}$ and $B^{(j)}$ for $j = 0, 1, 2$ are determined in a similar manner.

Taking into account the option of concurrently performing certain operations, it is easy to establish that the **G** function is implemented in five delay time units ($5\tau_{\oplus}$).

Grounds for Selecting a Nonlinear *G* Function

Define the mapping of **G**: $\mathrm{GF}(2)^{64} \times \mathrm{GF}(2)^{64} \times \mathrm{GF}(2)^{64} \to \mathrm{GF}(2)^{64}$ as the boolean vector function $Y = \mathbf{G}(X, A, B)$ having the following appearance:

$$(y_1, y_2, \ldots, y_{64}) = (\mathbf{g}_1(X, A, B), \mathbf{g}_2(X, A, B), \ldots, \mathbf{g}_{64}(X, A, B)),$$

where $\mathbf{g}_i$ are certain generator boolean functions. A single unified boolean function of 12 variables will be considered a *generator functions prototype.* It looks as follows:

$$\mathbf{g} = \mathbf{g}(z_1, z_2, \ldots, z_{12}) = z_{11} \oplus z_{12} \oplus \varphi(z_1, z_2, \ldots, z_{10}),$$

where $\varphi(z_1, z_2, \ldots, z_{10}) = z_1z_2 \oplus z_3z_4 \oplus z_5z_6 \oplus z_7z_8 \oplus z_9z_{10} \oplus z_1z_5z_9 \oplus z_3z_5z_7 \oplus z_1z_3z_7z_9$ is a bent function (see Definition 5.1). A Walsh-Hadamard transformation (see Definition 5.2) of the **g** function consists of 1024 elements possessing the value of $|\mathbf{U}^*_{\alpha}(\mathbf{g})| = 128$ for all vectors $\boldsymbol{\alpha} = (\alpha_1, \alpha_2, \ldots, \alpha_{10}, 0, 0)$, and for the rest of the 3072 elements it has a value of $\mathbf{U}^{\#}_{\alpha}(\mathbf{g}) = 0$. With respect to the selected structure and properties of bent functions, we have the following characteristics of the **g** function:

- The nonlinearity of the **g** function is equal to $\mathbf{N}(\mathbf{g}) = 2^{m-1} - 2^{((m+2)/2)-1} = 1984$ (with $m = 12$), which is quite close to the maximum possible nonlinearity of boolean functions of 12 variables ($\mathbf{N}_{max} = 2^{m-1} - 2^{(m/2)-1} = 2016$).
- **g** is a correlation immune function on a set of $z^* = \{(z_1, z_2, \ldots, z_{12})\} \subset GF(2)^{12}$ vectors, where $z_{11} \neq 0$ or $z_{12} \neq 0$, which makes up 75% of the whole $GF(2)^{12}$ set.
- **g** possesses good autocorrelation properties, since for all nonvanishing avalanche vectors $(\Delta z_1, \Delta z_2, \ldots, \Delta z_{12}) \in GF(2)^{12}$ except for three—$(0, \ldots, 0, 0, 1)$, $(0, \ldots, 0, 1, 0)$, and $(0, \ldots, 0, 1, 1)$—*propagation criteria of the 12th order* are implemented; that is, the function $\Delta\mathbf{g} = \mathbf{g}(z_1, z_2, \ldots, z_{12}) \oplus \mathbf{g}(z_1 \oplus \Delta z_1, z_2 \oplus \Delta z_2, \ldots, z_{12} \oplus \Delta z_{12})$ is balanced.
- The degree of the algebraic normal form of the **g** function is equal to 4 ($\mathbf{deg}(\mathbf{g}) = 4$).

A transition from the general form of the **g** function to certain generator functions of the sequential model of the controlled substitution operation is done using the following substitution of variables:

$$\begin{pmatrix} z_1 & z_2 & z_3 & z_4 & z_5 & z_6 & z_7 & z_8 & z_9 & z_{10} & z_{11} & z_{12} \\ u_{i-1} & b_i & u_{i-2} & u_{i-5} & u_{i-6} & a_{i-1} & b_{i-1} & a_{i-2} & u_{i-4} & u_{i-3} & u_i & a_i \end{pmatrix},$$

where $\forall i \in \{1, 2, \ldots, n\}$ and $n = 64$.

Thus, we have a generator function set that looks like this:

$$y_i = g_i = u_i \oplus a_i \oplus u_{i-1}b_i \oplus u_{i-2}u_{i-5} \oplus a_{i-1}u_{i-6} \oplus b_{i-1}a_{i-2} \oplus \\ \oplus u_{i-4}u_{i-3} \oplus u_{i-1}u_{i-4}u_{i-6} \oplus u_{i-2}b_{i-1}u_{i-6} \oplus u_{i-1}u_{i-2}b_{i-1}u_{i-4},$$

where l_j, a_j, and b_j are the components of vectors $L, A, B \in GF(2)^{64}$, and the initial conditions correspond to the vector $(x_{-4}, x_{-3}, x_{-2}, x_{-1}, x_0) = (1, 1, 1, 1, 1)$.

The Extension Procedure for Control Vector E

This procedure is intended for building a 192-bit control vector from a 64-bit one using the following formal **E** procedure:

$$V = (V_1||V_2||V_3||V_4||V_5||V_6) = \mathbf{E}(U, A, B) = \mathbf{E}_{A||B}(U),$$

where $V \in GF(2)^{192}$, $V_1, V_2, V_3, V_4, V_5, V_6 \in GF(2)^{32}$, $U, A, B \in GF(2)^{64}$.

The V vector is calculated according to the formulas:

$$V_1 = \mathbf{P}_{\pi_1}(U_{lo});\ V_2 = \mathbf{P}_{\pi_2}((U \oplus A)_{lo});\ V_3 = \mathbf{P}_{\pi_3}((U \oplus B)_{lo}); \\ V_4 = \mathbf{P}_{\pi_4}(U_{hi}) = U_{hi};\quad V_5 = \mathbf{P}_{\pi_5}((U \oplus A)_{hi});\ V_6 = \mathbf{P}_{\pi_6}((U \oplus A)_{hi}),$$

where for the $\mathbf{P}_{64/192}$ box, the transformations $\mathbf{P}_{\pi_1}, \mathbf{P}_{\pi_2}, \ldots, \mathbf{P}_{\pi_6}$ implement the fixed permutations of bits specified in Table 5.10.

TABLE 5.10 Control Bit Values for the $\mathbf{P}_{64/192}$ Box

V_1	31	32	3	4	5	6	7	8	9	10	11	12	13	14	15	16	17	18	19	20	21	22	23	24	25	26	27	28	29	30	1	2
V_2	10	24	25	26	29	13	27	16	1	2	31	32	3	4	19	6	7	8	9	23	11	12	28	15	14	30	17	18	5	20	21	22
V_3	13	14	15	16	17	18	19	20	21	22	23	24	25	26	27	28	29	30	31	32	1	2	3	4	5	6	7	8	12	10	11	9
V_4	33	34	35	36	37	38	39	40	41	42	43	44	45	46	47	48	49	50	51	52	53	54	55	56	57	58	59	60	61	62	63	64
V_5	55	56	57	58	59	60	61	62	63	64	33	34	35	36	37	38	39	40	41	42	43	44	45	46	47	48	49	50	51	52	53	54
V_6	45	46	47	48	49	50	51	52	53	54	55	56	57	58	59	60	61	62	63	64	33	34	35	36	37	38	39	40	41	42	43	44

For example, 32 in the first line, corresponding to vector V_1, means the value u_{32} is used as the control bit $v_2^{(1)}$ of V_1; in other words, v_2 of V. 22 in the second line corresponds to the control bit $v_{32}^{(2)} = u_{22} \oplus a_{22}$, and 53 in the sixth line corresponds to the control bit $v_9^{(6)} = u_{53} \oplus b_{53}$.

The **E** extension procedure is done in such a way that the 32 higher order bits of the U vector participate in controlling only $\mathbf{R}_3^{-1}$ boxes, whereas the lower order bits control only $\mathbf{R}_3$ boxes, all bit numbers of vectors U, A, and B being different in each $\mathbf{R}_3^{-1}$ and $\mathbf{R}_3$ box.

The control vector extension procedure provides for:

- The uniformity of the participation of all 64 bits of U, A, and B vectors in controlling the $\mathbf{P}_{64/128}$ box.
- The fact that, for a randomly chosen commutation of one input bit with one output bit, there are six different bits of the U vector and two different bits of keys A and B participating in the control, which guarantees the implementation of all commutation variants.
- Control vector V_1 being a fixed substitution of 32 bits of the U vector; in other words, transformation in the first layer of the $\mathbf{P}_{64/192}$ box is performed without any time delay.

5.3.3 The Schedule for Using Round Keys

As in the 12-round SPECTR-128 block cipher, the $Q^{(e)}$ extended key in a CIKS-128 block cipher is a combination of 14 subkeys; namely,

$$Q^{(e)} = (Q_{IT}^{(e)}, Q_1^{(e)}, Q_2^{(e)}, \ldots, Q_{12}^{(e)}, Q_{FT}^{(e)}),$$

where $Q_j^{(e)} = (Q_j^{(1,e)}, Q_j^{(2,e)}, Q_j^{(3,e)}, Q_j^{(4,e)})$, $\forall j = 1, 2, \ldots, 12$,
when $Q_{IT}^{(e)}, Q_{FT}^{(e)} \in \mathrm{GF}(2)^{128}$, but $Q_j^{(h,e)} \in \mathrm{GF}(2)^{64}$, $\forall h = 1,2,3,4$.

The $Q^{(e)}$ extended key is a series of 52 64-bit binary vectors, each being one of four secret subkeys—K_1, K_2, K_3, K_4.

The elements of the $Q^{(e)}$ extended key are determined via the O_i parameters, which are calculated, in turn, by the formulas:

$$O_{2i-1} = K_{2i-1+e} \text{ and } O_{2i} = K_{2i-e},$$

where $K = K_1||K_2||K_3||K_4$ and $i = 1, 2$.

The commutation scheme between O_i and K_j is shown in Figure 5.11.

The key correspondence $Q_{IT}^{(e)}, Q_{FT}^{(e)}, Q_j^{(1,e)}, Q_j^{(2,e)}, Q_j^{(3,e)}, Q_j^{(4,e)}$ ($\forall j = 1, 2, \ldots, 12$) is specified in Table 5.11.

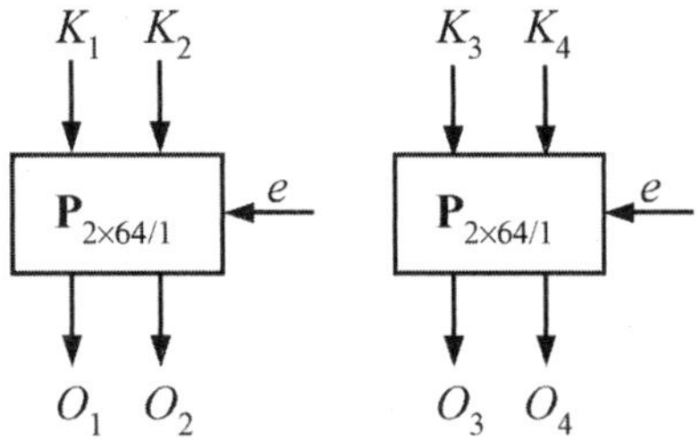

FIGURE 5.11 Subkey commutation scheme.

TABLE 5.11 Schedule for Using Round Keys

$Q_{IT}^{(e)}$	$j =$	1	2	3	4	5	6	7	8	9	10	11	12	$Q_{FT}^{(e)}$
$O_1\|\|O_3$	$Q_j^{(1,e)} =$	O_2	O_3	O_1	O_4	O_2	O_1	O_2	O_1	O_3	O_2	O_4	O_1	$O_2\|\|O_4$
	$Q_j^{(2,e)} =$	O_4	O_1	O_3	O_2	O_4	O_3	O_4	O_3	O_1	O_4	O_2	O_3	
	$Q_j^{(3,e)} =$	O_1	O_4	O_2	O_3	O_1	O_2	O_1	O_2	O_4	O_1	O_3	O_2	
	$Q_j^{(4,e)} =$	O_3	O_2	O_4	O_1	O_3	O_4	O_3	O_4	O_2	O_3	O_1	O_4	

For example, for the fifth round ($j = 5$), the subkey sequence O_2, O_4, O_1, O_3 corresponds to the formal parameters $A^{(1)}$, $A^{(2)}$, $A^{(3)}$, $A^{(4)}$ of the ***Crypt*** procedure; namely,

$$Q_5^{(e)} = (Q_5^{(1,e)}, Q_5^{(2,e)}, Q_5^{(3,e)}, Q_5^{(4,e)}) = (O_2, O_4, O_1, O_3).$$

That is,

$$Q_5^{(e)} = (K_{2-e}, K_{4-e}, K_{1+e}, K_{3+e}).$$

For the encryption mode $Q_5^{(0)} = (K_2, K_4, K_1, K_3)$, and for the decryption mode $Q_5^{(1)} = (K_1, K_3, K_2, K_4)$.

For the initial and final transformations, the keys $Q_{IT}^{(e)}$ and $Q_{FT}^{(e)}$ look as follows:

$$Q_{IT}^{(e)} = (O_1 || O_3) \text{ and } Q_{FT}^{(e)} = (O_2 || O_4).$$

That is,

$$Q_{IT}^{(e)} = (K_{1+e} || K_{3+e}) \text{ and } Q_{FT}^{(e)} = (K_{2-e} || K_{4-e}).$$

For the encryption mode,

$$Q_{IT}^{(0)} = (K_1 || K_3) \text{ and } Q_{FT}^{(0)} = (K_2 || K_4),$$

and for the decryption mode,

$$Q_{IT}^{(1)} = (K_2 || K_4) \text{ and } Q_{FT}^{(1)} = (K_1 || K_3).$$

Scheme Universality

To prove the universality of the scheme, it is sufficient to demonstrate the universality (reversibility) of one round scheme, or rather, the universality of the transformation highlighted in gray in Figure 5.10. Here are the formulas for $e = 0$ and $e = 1$:

$$\mathbf{e} = 0 \Rightarrow R' = \mathbf{I}(R) \oplus \mathbf{I}(\mathbf{G}(L, A^{(1)}||A^{(4)})) \oplus \mathbf{G}(\mathbf{P}_\pi(L), A^{(3)}||A^{(2)}).$$
$$\mathbf{e} = 1 \Rightarrow U' = \mathbf{I}(U) \oplus \mathbf{I}(\mathbf{G}(\mathbf{P}_\pi(L), A^{(3)}||A^{(2)})) \oplus \mathbf{G}(L, A^{(1)}||A^{(4)}).$$

By sequentially performing the ($U = R'$) encryption and decryption, we get:

$$U' = \mathbf{I}(U) \oplus \mathbf{I}(\mathbf{G}(\mathbf{P}_\pi(L), A^{(3)}||A^{(2)})) \oplus \mathbf{G}(L, A^{(1)}||A^{(4)}) =$$
$$= \mathbf{I}^2(R) \oplus \mathbf{I}^2(\mathbf{G}(L, A^{(1)}||A^{(4)})) \oplus \mathbf{I}(\mathbf{G}(\mathbf{P}_\pi(L), A^{(3)}||A^{(2)})) \oplus$$
$$\oplus \mathbf{I}(\mathbf{G}(\mathbf{P}_\pi(L), A^{(3)}||A^{(2)})) \oplus \mathbf{G}(L, A^{(1)}||A^{(4)}) = R.$$

By sequentially performing the ($R = U'$) decryption and encryption, we get:

$$R' = \mathbf{I}(R) \oplus \mathbf{I}(\mathbf{G}(L, A^{(1)}||A^{(4)})) \oplus \mathbf{G}(\mathbf{P}_{\pi}(L), A^{(3)}||A^{(2)}) =$$
$$\mathbf{I}^2(U) \oplus \mathbf{I}^2(\mathbf{G}(\mathbf{P}_{\pi}(L), A^{(3)}||A^{(2)})) \oplus$$
$$\oplus\, \mathbf{I}(\mathbf{G}(L, A^{(1)}||A^{(4)})) \oplus \mathbf{I}(\mathbf{G}(L, A^{(1)}||A^{(4)})) \oplus \mathbf{G}(\mathbf{P}_{\pi}(L), A^{(3)}||A^{(2)}) = U.$$

In other words, a truly universal scheme is implemented.

5.4 PROSPECTIVE PROGRAM CIPHERS BASED ON CONTROLLED PERMUTATIONS

Since fiber-optic channels provide for data transfer with very high speed, processor developers consider the issue of integration (on a hardware level) of a cryptographic means of information transformation into the processors, one that implements one of the universally accepted algorithms meeting modern requirements of stability and speed. One drawback of this trend is that the transformation algorithm is forced on customers, limiting the user's freedom of choice, and regardless of whether the user trusts the particular algorithm.

An alternative trend in solving this problem is the extension of the list of commands implementing cryptographic-like transformations with a high speed, and created as special instructions. In particular, the implementation of *controlled bit permutation operations* is rather interesting. The dimension of controlled permutation boxes that implement such operations should correspond to the bit capacity of the processor used.

For example, for processors operating with 32-bit binary vectors (figures, words), bit permutations are effectively implemented using a $\mathbf{P}_{32/96}$ box of the second order of controlled permutations (Figure 5.12).

In this chapter, we consider the description of this command and how to efficiently use it in software block ciphers.

5.4.1 Description of the Hypothetical DDP32 Command

Enter the $\mathbf{P}_{32/32}^{(U,e)}$ conditional symbol for the new command, and the identifier DDP32 (Data Dependent Permutation 32 bit).

The input parameters of this command are:

- *X:* 32-bit transformed binary vector
- *U:* 32-bit control vector forming a permutation modification
- *e:* 1-bit control vector with a value that determines the data transformation mode ($e = 0$—direct permutation, $e = 1$—reverse permutation)

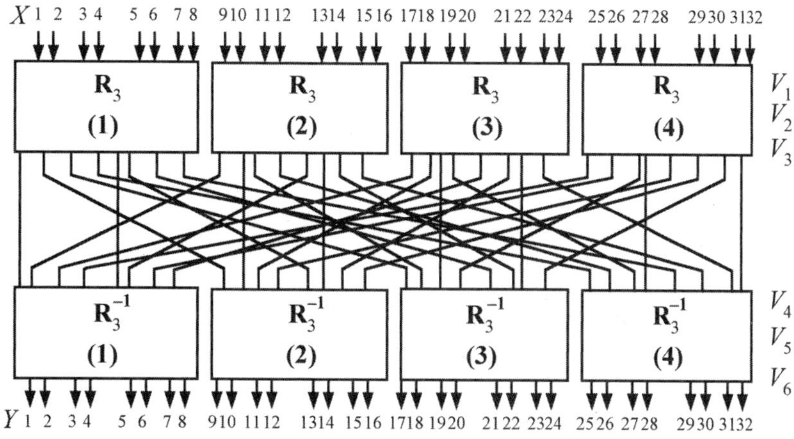

FIGURE 5.12 The $\mathbf{P}_{32/96}$ controlled permutations box.

The result of applying the $\mathbf{P}^{(U,e)}_{32/32}$ command is the permutation of the 32-bit binary vector X. In other words, the command *DDP32* implements the mapping of $GF(2)^{32} \times GF(2)^{32} \times GF(2) \rightarrow GF(2)^{32}$; namely,

$$Y = \mathbf{P}_{32/32}(X, U, e).$$

Since the second order box $\mathbf{P}_{32/96(V)}$ is used as the operation prototype, in which the bit capacity of the control vector is equal to 96, in a new command, you must implement the control vector $V = E(U)$ expansion procedure, and the $\mathbf{P}_{32/96(V)}$ box; namely,

$$\mathbf{E}\text{: } GF(2)^{32} \rightarrow GF(2)^{96}),$$

which provides the commutation of each bit of the U binary vector with three different bits of the 96-bit binary vector V.

To perform a reverse transformation $\mathbf{P}^{-1}_{32/96(V)}$ in box $\mathbf{P}_{32/96}$, you have to reverse the order of vectors $V_1, V_2, \ldots, V_6$; in other words, $\mathbf{P}^{-1}_{32/96(V)} = \mathbf{P}_{32/96(V')}$, where $V = (V_1, V_2, \ldots, V_6)$ and $V' = (V_6, V_5, \ldots, V_1)$. This reversal is effectively implemented using the one-layer $\mathbf{P}^{(e)}_{96/1}$ box, shown in Figure 5.13.

Thus, the operational box implementing the $\mathbf{P}^{(U,e)}_{32/32}$ command looks like the one shown in Figure 5.14.

Thanks to such a structure, the $\mathbf{P}^{(U,e)}_{32/32}$ box performs either a direct controlled permutation operation ($e = 0$), or a reverse permutation operation ($e = 1$).

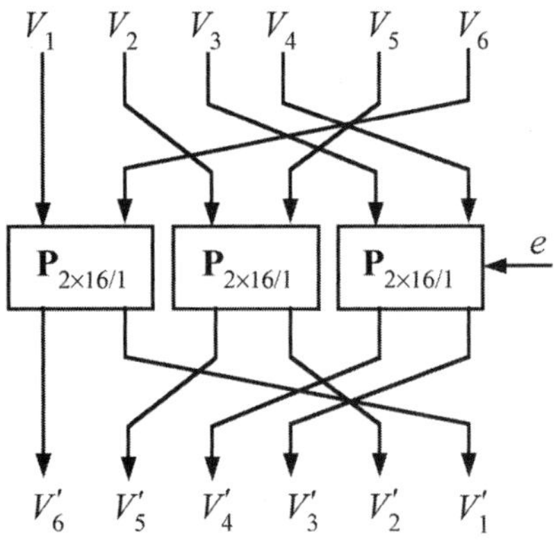

FIGURE 5.13 The $\mathbf{P}^{(e)}_{96/1}$ box for controlling the data transformation mode in the $\mathbf{P}^{(U,e)}_{32/32}$ command.

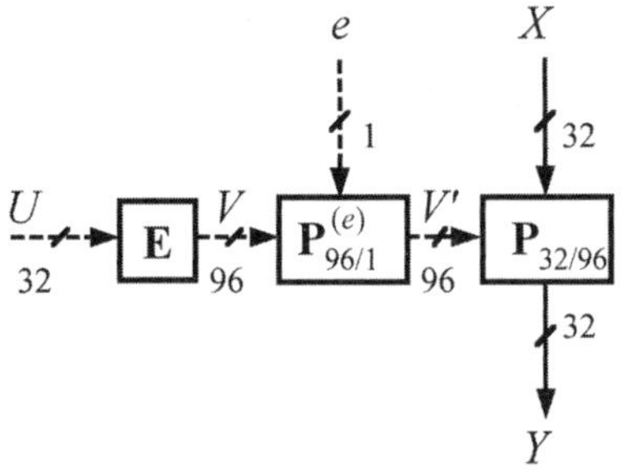

FIGURE 5.14 The $\mathbf{P}^{(U,e)}_{32/32}$ controlled permutations box.

When program ciphers are developed based on controlled permutations, it is assumed that the value of the $U = (u_1, u_2, ..., u_{32})$ vector is a block of transformed data where each bit of vector U determines three different bits of the binary vector V. We need to mention that the $\mathbf{P}_{32/96}$ box is a second order box, and therefore there are just two variants of commutation between random input and random output bits, and there are six elementary $\mathbf{P}_{2/1}$ switches controlled by the V vector in each such commutation. Consequently, to provide any such commutation by the U vector when a mapping is formed between the bits of the U and V vectors in the **E** procedure, it is best to be governed by the following criterion: six various bits of the U vector should participate in the control of six $\mathbf{P}_{2/1}$ boxes, implementing a commutation between randomly chosen input and output bits.

In particular, Table 5.12 shows an example of the correspondence between the U and V vectors that meets such a criterion, and can be used in building an **E** extension procedure.

TABLE 5.12 Correspondence between the Bits of Vectors U and V for the $\mathbf{P}_{32/96}$ Box

V_1	9	10	11	12	1	2	3	4	5	6	7	8	13	14	15	16
V_2	16	15	14	13	6	5	8	7	1	2	3	4	12	11	10	9
V_3	4	3	2	1	11	12	15	16	14	13	9	10	8	7	6	5
V_4	27	28	19	20	31	32	23	24	17	18	21	22	25	26	29	30
V_5	31	32	17	18	29	30	21	22	25	26	27	28	23	24	19	20
V_6	24	23	22	21	28	27	26	25	32	31	30	29	20	19	18	17

For example, in the first row corresponding to vector V_1, 10 means that the value u_{10} is fed to the input $v_2^{(1)}$ controlling the second box $\mathbf{P}_{2/1}$, whereas 10 in the second row corresponds to the value $v_{15}^{(2)} = u_{10}$, and 26 in the sixth row corresponds to the value $v_7^{(6)} = u_{26}$.

In a hardware implementation, an elementary switch that uses no more than 12 transistors is implemented. Accordingly, to implement a $\mathbf{P}_{32/32}^{(U,e)}$ operational box, no more than 1800 transistors will be needed. Therefore, if you include the DDP32 command into the set of the standard operations of a contemporary processor, it will not considerably complicate the circuit implementation of such processors. The availability of such a command will help to enhance the speed of software ciphers using this operation (up to 1 Gbit/s and more). This will make it possible to solve many urgent problems in developing computer security systems that provide real-time information security in contemporary, highly efficient automation systems.

5.4.2 The SPECTR-SZ Software Cipher

Let's look at the SPECTR-SZ program cipher, in which a new command of controlled permutations, ***DDP32***, is used. Initially, this cipher was called DDP-S, but the name has been changed due to the following circumstances.

- In its structure, the cipher being considered is an updated variant of the SPECTR-Z software cipher, in which a looped shift operation is replaced by the new ***DDP32*** command.
- The algorithm description has been amended, which was necessary to correctly use the ***DDP32*** command, and to simplify the understanding of the algorithm's operation.

This chapter also deals with two block ciphers (DDP-S64 and DDP-S128), which significantly differ from the SPECTR-Z software cipher in their structure, and thus, using the name *DDP-S* for the cipher being considered is not quite correct.

Designations and Input Data

The following additional designations were used in the description of the SPECTR-SZ cipher:

- Bytes (binary vectors with lengths of 8) will be designated by lowercase letters without italics. For example:

$$\mathrm{u} = (u_0, u_1, \ldots, u_7), \text{ where } \forall i = 0, 1, \ldots, 7,\ u_i \in \{0,1\}.$$

- The designation **B** will be used for a set of all bytes; namely,

$$\mathbf{B} \equiv \{0,1\}^8 \text{ and } \mathrm{u} \in \mathbf{B}.$$

- The term "word" designates 32-bit binary vectors marked by uppercase letters in italics. For example, $U = (u_0, u_1, \ldots, u_{31})$, where $\forall i = 0, 1, \ldots, 31,\ u_i \in \{0,1\}$. It is obvious that $U = (\mathrm{u}_0, \mathrm{u}_1, \mathrm{u}_2, \mathrm{u}_3)$, where $\forall j = 0, 1 \ldots, 3$, $\mathbf{u}_j \in \mathbf{B}$, and $U \in \mathbf{B}^4$.
- To designate byte sequences larger than 4, uppercase letters in bold italics will be used; for example, $\boldsymbol{Q} \in \mathbf{B}^{2051}$, where $\boldsymbol{Q} = (q_0, q_1, \ldots, q_{2050})$.
- The operations "$+_m$" and "$-_m$" are designated, respectively, as "2^m congruence addition" and "2^m congruence subtraction."
- The operation "$W \leftrightarrow V$" designates a value exchange operation for words W and V.

Note: *As a rule, discrete mathematics considers numbers represented by binary vectors of a specified size (e.g., m). For example, regular addition with the transfer of two numbers X and Y ($X \geq 2^{m-1}$ and $Y \geq 2^{m-1}$) ceases to make sense because it is impossible to represent the resulting value as one binary vector with a size of m. Therefore, we usually speak of the "2^m congruence addition" operation, and $(X + Y) \bmod 2^m$ is used. When composite formulas are written, it entails an increase in the number of brackets, and as a result, it is very difficult to quickly understand such formulas. It is often predetermined in articles that X + Y means "2^m congruence addition," and the "mod 2^m" designation is not used. This, however, is done only if m is a fixed value. If operations with several different values ($m_1, m_1, \ldots, m_k$) are performed, difficulties in the visual representation of formulas and expressions emerge. So, instead of the conventional $(X + Y) \bmod 2^m$, we ask that you use $X +_m Y$; that is:*

$$X +_m Y \stackrel{def}{=} (X + Y) \bmod 2^m.$$

The designations "$+_m$" and "$-_m$" have not yet been generally adopted, but we think that such expressions are a natural development of index symbols for sets of variables, and so forth. There is no doubt that the expressions "$+_{2m}$" and "$-_{2m}$" are more common, since they allow you to consider any p module, and not only a power of 2 (e.g., "$+_p$" and "$-_p$"). This difference, however, is less important than the representations of the expressions $(X + Y) mod\ 2^m$ and $X +_m Y$.

The following hexadecimal constants a, b, g, d are used in the algorithm:

- $\alpha = 0D_x$, $\alpha \in \mathbf{B}$
- $\beta = FFFF07FF_x$, $\beta \in \mathbf{B}^4$
- $\gamma = B25D28A7\ 1A62D775_x$, $\gamma \in \mathbf{B}^8$
- $\delta = 98915E7E\ C8265EDF\ CDA31E88\ F24809DD$
- $B064BDC7\ 285DD50D\ 7289F0AC\ 6F49DD2D_x$, $\delta \in \mathbf{B}^{32}$

The index "$_x$" means that the hexadecimal number representation is used, and the lower order bit is to the right. For example, the byte $\alpha = 0D_x$ can be represented in the vector form as:

$$\alpha = (\alpha_0, \alpha_1, \ldots, \alpha_7), 1, 1, 0, 0, 0, 0).$$

Such a feature of number representation is a consequence of an ancient dispute between mathematicians and programmers as to the side whether the lower order significant bit is on (right or left).

When several sequential bytes $\{u_0, u_1, \ldots, u_{s-1}\}$ are represented by a binary number, the u_{s-1} byte in all cases is related to the higher order bits of the number. If, for example, the 64-bit constant $\gamma = B25D28A7\ 1A62D775_x$ is represented as a sequence of bytes $u_0, u_1, \ldots, u_7$, then $u_0 = 75_x$, $u_1 = D7_x$, ..., $u_7 = B2_x$.

The SPECTR-SZ cipher is aimed at use in computers with a 32-bit processor, and is a *block stream cipher* in its structure. This peculiarity of the cipher structure stems from the fact that in the ***Encrypt*** and ***Decrypt*** procedures of data transformation, the first and last rounds implement the stream cipher scheme, and the rest of the rounds (internal ones) implement the iterative scheme of a block cipher.

Cipher Structure

The SPECT-SZ software cipher is usually implemented as two modules (Figure 5.15):

- The *initialization module* (used for program settings and the formation of all necessary parameters, including the **Q** extended key)

- The *resident module*, which serves other applications' requests for data encryption and decryption

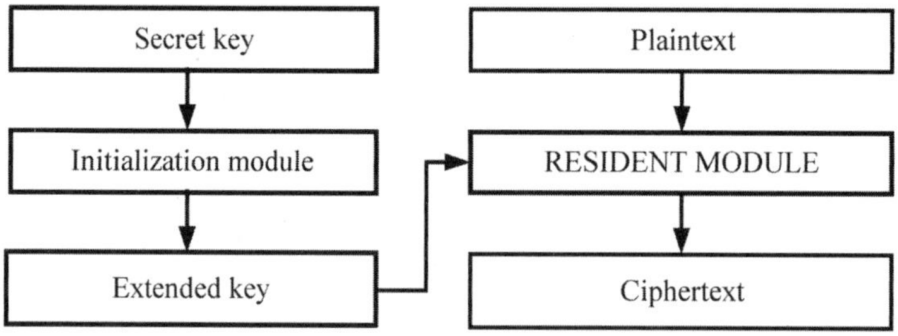

FIGURE 5.15 The SPECTR-Z software cipher scheme.

The $\boldsymbol{Q}$ ($\boldsymbol{Q} \in \mathbf{B}^{2051}$) extended key, designed using the secret key $\boldsymbol{K}$, is formed by the initialization module in two cases:

- In the application initialization stage
- When the secret key is changed

The resident module consists of two *Encrypt* and *Decrypt* subprograms, which are intended for the encryption and decryption of information represented as data blocks with m 32-bit words in each, respectively.

The Extended Key Generation Procedure

Initially, the sequence $\boldsymbol{Q}' = (q_0', q_1', \ldots, q'_{2050})$ ($\boldsymbol{Q}' \in \mathbf{B}^{2051}$) is formed by repeating the secret key $\boldsymbol{K} = (k_0, k_1, \ldots, k_s)$ the necessary number of times, where $8 \le s \le 2050$.

Such a "strange" length of sequence $\boldsymbol{Q}'$ *is stipulated by the necessity of working with 2048 32-bit words. Indeed, the byte sequence* $u_0, u_1, \ldots, u_{n-1}$ *can be used for forming 32-bit* $U_j = \{u_j, u_{j+1}, u_{j+2}, u_{j+3}\}$ *words, where* $j = 0, 1, \ldots, n-4$*. Therefore, if 2048* (2^{11}) *32-bit words formed by this method are used, the length of the initial sequence should be equal to 2051 bytes* ($n = 2051$)*.*

The next step is the use of the ***Table_H***($\boldsymbol{Q}'$) procedure to form the $\boldsymbol{H}$ ($\boldsymbol{H} \in \mathbf{B}^{2051}$) auxiliary key.

The *Table_H* Procedure

The algorithm of the *Table_H*(Q') procedure is as follows:

1. Set the counter value $i := 0$.
2. Calculate the 32-bit number $\boldsymbol{H}_i' := (\alpha^{23+i} \bmod \gamma)^{17} \bmod \delta$, $(\boldsymbol{H}_i' \in \mathbf{B}^{32})$.
3. Increase the counter value $i := i + 1$. If $i \neq 64$, then go to step 2.
4. Create a sequence $\boldsymbol{H} := ||\boldsymbol{H}_0'||\boldsymbol{H}_1'||\ldots||\boldsymbol{H}_{63}'||h_0'||h_1'||h_2'$, where $(h_0'||h_1'||h_2')$ are the first three bytes of the $\boldsymbol{H}_0' = (h_0', h_1', h_2', \ldots, h_{63}')$ number.
5. Perform the transformation $\boldsymbol{H} := \boldsymbol{Q}' \oplus \boldsymbol{H}$.
6. Represent $\boldsymbol{H}$ as the byte sequence $\boldsymbol{H} = (h_0, h_1, \ldots, h_{2050})$.
7. STOP.

The extended key $\boldsymbol{Q}$ is finally formed with the use of the *Form_Key* procedure; namely, $Q = Form\_Key(Q', H)$, when the sequence $\boldsymbol{Q}'$ is interpreted as a combination of four 512-byte sequences (data blocks)—$\boldsymbol{Q}'^{(1)}$, $\boldsymbol{Q}'^{(2)}$, $\boldsymbol{Q}'^{(3)}$, $\boldsymbol{Q}'^{(4)}$—and three bytes; namely,

$$\boldsymbol{Q}' = \boldsymbol{Q}'^{(1)}||\boldsymbol{Q}'^{(2)}||\boldsymbol{Q}'^{(3)}||\boldsymbol{Q}'^{(4)}||q'_{2048}||q'_{2049}||q'_{2050}.$$

One of two programs of the resident module is used in the *FormKey* procedure; namely, the *Encrypt* procedure. The latter depends on three parameters, the first one determining the length of the data block being transformed (expressed in 32-bit words), the second determining the transformed data block itself, and the third determining the extended key.

The *FormKey* Procedure

The algorithm of the *FormKey* procedure looks as follows:

For the *Encrypt* procedure, specify the parameter value $m := 128$, and use the $\boldsymbol{H}$ sequence as an encryption key.

1. Transform $\boldsymbol{Q}'^{(1)}$: $\boldsymbol{Q}'^{(1)} := \boldsymbol{Encrypt}(m, \boldsymbol{Q}'^{(1)}, \boldsymbol{H})$.
2. Transform $\boldsymbol{Q}'^{(2)}$: $\boldsymbol{Q}'^{(2)} := \boldsymbol{Encrypt}(m, \boldsymbol{Q}'^{(2)} \oplus \boldsymbol{Q}'^{(1)}, \boldsymbol{H})$.
3. Transform $\boldsymbol{Q}'^{(3)}$: $\boldsymbol{Q}'^{(3)} := \boldsymbol{Encrypt}(m, \boldsymbol{Q}'^{(3)} \oplus \boldsymbol{Q}'^{(2)}, \boldsymbol{H})$.
4. Transform $\boldsymbol{Q}'^{(4)}$: $\boldsymbol{Q}'^{(4)} := \boldsymbol{Encrypt}(m, \boldsymbol{Q}'^{(4)} \oplus \boldsymbol{Q}'^{(3)}, \boldsymbol{H})$.
5. Form an extended key: $\boldsymbol{Q} := \{\boldsymbol{Q}'^{(1)}, \boldsymbol{Q}'^{(2)}, \boldsymbol{Q}'^{(3)}, \boldsymbol{Q}'^{(4)}, q'_{2048}, q'_{2049}, q'_{2050}\}$.
6. STOP.

Thus, the expanded encryption key $\boldsymbol{Q}$ is a sequence of 2051 bytes: $\boldsymbol{Q} = \{q_0, q_1, q_2, \ldots, q_{2047}, q_{2048}, q_{2049}, q_{2050}\}$.

The *Encrypt* Procedure

The *Encrypt* (m, T, Q) procedure is one of two programs of the resident module used for data transformation (encryption). The *Encrypt* procedure depends on three parameters, the first determining the length of the data block being transformed (expressed in 32-bit words), the second determining the transformed data block itself, and the third determining the extended key.

So, the length of the data block subject to transformation is determined by the m parameter ($m \geq 4$). The value of m is chosen depending on the area in which it is used. For example, this value may be determined by the hard disk sector size, or the size of the clipboard. In particular, for $m = 128$, the length of the transformed data block (in bytes) is equal to $4m$; in other words, 512 bytes.

32-bit words (subkeys) with the following appearance are used during encryption:

$$Q_j = q_j || q_{j+1} || q_{j+2} || q_{j+3},$$

where $j = 0, 1, \ldots, 2047$.

The *Encrypt* procedure includes two full and four reduced transformation rounds (Figure 5.16). If $m = 4$, the full and reduced rounds are identical.

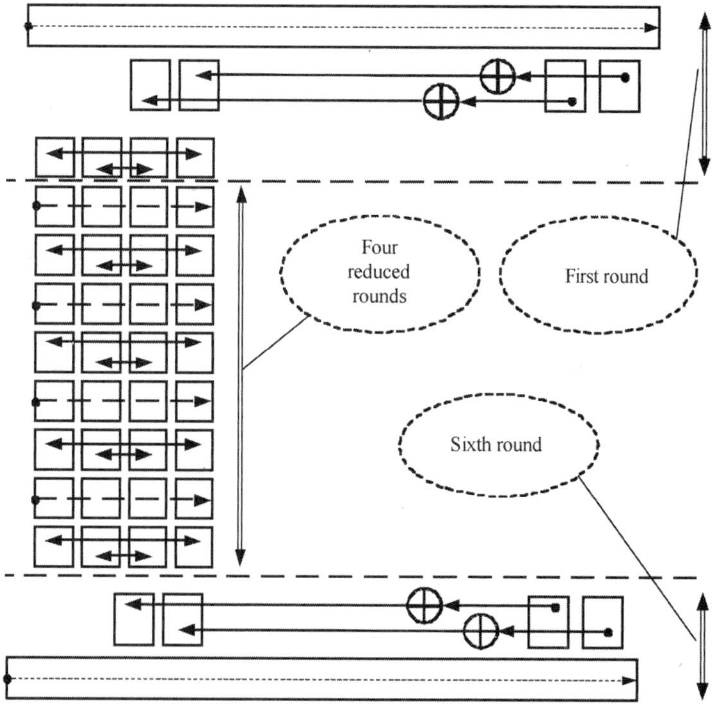

FIGURE 5.16 Order of the transformation of 32-bit words in the SPECTR-SZ cipher.

For a specified m, the data block being transformed is a sequence m of 32-bit words; namely,

$$T = \{T_0, T_1, T_2, \ldots, T_{m-1}\},$$

where $m \geq 4$ and $\mathbf{T} \in \mathbf{B}^{4m}$.

The consecutive transformation of the words T_0, T_1, ..., T_{m-1} is performed in each round. After each round, except for the last, two operations are performed: $T_0 \leftrightarrow T_3$ and $T_1 \leftrightarrow T_2$.

The two following standard procedures are performed in round transformations:

Initialize procedure: {Set $i := 0$; $R := Q_9$; $V := Q_{17}$; $N := Q_{31}$}.

Change NV procedure: {$N := \mathbf{P}^{(R,0)}_{32/32}(N) \oplus R$;

$n := N +_{11} 0$;

$V := \mathbf{P}^{(N,1)}_{32/32}(V) +_{32} Q_n$ }.

The First (Full) Encryption Round

The algorithm of the first (full) encryption round looks like this:

1. Perform the *Initialize* procedure.
2. Perform the *Change NV* procedure.
3. Transform: $T_i := \mathbf{P}^{(R,0)}_{32/32}(T_i -_{32} V)$.
4. Transform variable R: $R := \mathbf{P}^{(V,1)}_{32/32}(R +_{32} T_i)$.
5. Transform: $T_i := T_i +_{32} N$.
6. Increase the counter value: $i := i + 1$.
7. If $i \neq m$, go to step 2.
8. If $m > 4$, transform words T_2 and T_3 by one another: $T_2 := T_2 \oplus T_{m-2}$; $T_3 := T_3 \oplus T_{m-1}$.
9. Perform the operations $T_0 \leftrightarrow T_3$ and $T_1 \leftrightarrow T_2$.
10. STOP.

The Four Reduced Rounds

The algorithm for the four reduced rounds looks like this:

1. Set the initial value for reduced rounds' number counter $j := 0$.
2. Perform the *Initialize* procedure.
3. Perform the *Change NV* procedure.
4. Transform: $T_i := \mathbf{P}^{(R,0)}_{32/32}(T_i -_{32} V)$.
5. Transform variable R: $R := \mathbf{P}^{(V,1)}_{32/32}(R +_{32} T_i)$.

6. Transform $T_i := T_i +_{32} N$.
7. Increase the counter value: $i := i + 1$. If $i \neq 4$, go to step 3.
8. Perform operations $T_0 \leftrightarrow T_3$ and $T_1 \leftrightarrow T_2$. Increase the counter value: $j := j + 1$.
9. If $j \neq 4$, go to step 2.
10. STOP.

The Sixth (Full) Encryption Round

The algorithm of the sixth (full) encryption round looks like this:

1. Perform the ***Initialize*** procedure.
2. If m > 4, transform the words T_3 and T_2 by one another: $T_3 := T_3 \oplus T_{m-1}$ and $T_2 := T_2 \oplus T_{m-2}$.
3. Perform the ***Change NV*** procedure.
4. Transform: $T_i := \mathbf{P}^{(R,0)}_{32/32}(T_i -_{32} V)$.
5. Transform variable R: $R := \mathbf{P}^{(V,1)}_{32/32}(R +_{32} T_i)$.
6. Transform word T_i: $T_i := T_{i+32} N$.
7. Increase the counter value: $i := i + 1$.
8. If $i \neq m$, go to Step 2.
9. STOP.

The *Decrypt* Procedure

The ***Decrypt*** (m, T, Q) procedure is the second program of the resident module, used for decryption of the transformed data. This procedure performs a transformation that is the reverse of the ***Encrypt*** procedure. The procedure is not described, but an interested reader can form such a procedure on his own, taking into account the fact that the word transformation sequence is the same as for encryption (see Figure 5.16).

Speed Parameters and the Cryptographic Security of a Cipher

Since generally, only part of the input data block is transformed in two full rounds, the encryption speed depends on the size of the input block. If $m = 4$, it is minimal—about 200 Mbit/s (for a processor of Celeron 500 type, assuming that the *DDP32* command is implemented inside as a special instruction). As the block size is increased, the speed increases as well, up to 600 Mbit/s, if $m \geq 32$.

The SPECTR-SZ cipher possesses a higher encryption speed than the program algorithms considered in Chapter 2, because of the smaller number of operations performed, and due to a fewer number of times accessing the memory (from 5 to 3).

The necessary practical security of the algorithm is gained thanks to the following features:

- A long extended key $\mathbf{Q}$ ($\mathbf{Q} \in \mathbf{B}^{2051}$).
- Using T_i words of 32 bits at every step for three 32-bit variables N, V, and R, each of them depending on both the extended key $\mathbf{Q}$ and on the already transformed input data.
- Meeting the criterion of a strict avalanche effect, both by performing operations selecting Q_j subkeys and by using the input data (data to be transformed) to form the control vectors for the new ***DDP32*** command.

The second item needs a little explanation. The *Encrypt* procedure is such that for two data blocks $\mathbf{T}$ and $\mathbf{T}'$ that differ in the ith word ($T_i \neq T'_i$) the values of the R and R' variables are different in the first round already, during the transformation of the words T_i and T'_i. In the next step, the difference between the R and R' variables generates a difference between the variables N and N' and between V and V', and consequently, between T_{i+1} and T'_{i+1}. Accordingly, all subsequent values of the 32-bit words T_j and T'_j are different, and such a difference has an avalanche-like character when moving on to the next words to be transformed. Transformations of subsequent rounds propagate differences at each 32-bit word of the data being transformed.

Thanks to the many transformation steps performed in one round, a strong avalanche effect can be gained by performing only two full encryption rounds.

Reduced encryption rounds are aimed at implementing a strong avalanche effect when differences occur only in the last word T_{m-1}.

The ***DDP32*** operation, controlling the vector depending on the data block being transformed, contributes much to the avalanche effect's propagation when the words T_i and variable V are transformed.

According to the estimations for the combinatory probabilistic model considered in Chapter 2, the security of the SPECTR-SZ cipher is no less than 2^{190} (2^{95}) operations, on the condition that the attacker has a specially chosen input text with a volume of no less than 2^{100} (2^{50}) bytes and corresponding ciphertext.

The option of parametrically specifying the transformed data block size enhances the range of practical uses of the SPECTR-SZ block cipher and makes its universality clear.

When speaking about the prospects of the new ***DDP32*** command, we must mention that it can be used to create high-speed software hashing functions. The hashing speed becomes much higher than that of the SPECTR-SZ cipher because the hashing algorithms can be created in such a way that you need only access the memory once. Using the ***DDP32*** operation, you can provide a hashing speed of 1–2 Gbit/s. Just to compare: there are three memory access operations used for one 32-bit transformed word in SPECTR-SZ:

- Reading the current transformed word
- Reading one subkey
- Recording the transformed word

Since the ***DDP32*** operation is for use in cryptographic applications, there are objective conditions for the creation of high-speed encryption and hashing algorithms that possess the necessary practical security.

5.4.3 The COBRA-F64a and COBRA-F64b Block Ciphers

Let's consider the variants of building firmware block ciphers with a small input data block. Such ciphers can be used, for example, in microcontrollers and intellectual electronic cards, where it is necessary to maximize the ratio of encryption efficiency to the number of active electronic circuit elements used.

Following is a description of two iterated block ciphers, COBRA-F64a and COBRA-F64b, with a 64-bit input and a 128-bit secret key, both aimed at firmware implementation. The algorithms are described according to the designations accepted for block ciphers.

The General Encryption Scheme

In the COBRA-F64a and COBRA-F64b block ciphers, an encryption scheme is used that is not universal according to the previously accepted terms. Remember that a scheme is universal when changing the encryption mode (encryption and decryption) entails only changing the order of round keys. However, the encryption scheme of the COBRA-F64a and COBRA-F64b algorithms can be called semi-universal, since the only difference is the use of a new command—$\mathbf{P}_{32/32}^{(U,e)}$—which depends on the e parameter. Using the superscript "(e)," the general encryption scheme can be expressed by the following formula:

$$Y = \mathbf{F}^{(e)}(X, Q^{(e)}),$$

where $Q^{(e)} = \mathbf{H}(K, e)$ is an *extended key*, and a function of the 128-bit K key and the encryption mode e ($\mathbf{F}^{(0)}$—encryption, $\mathbf{F}^{(1)}$—decryption), when in encryption mode X ($X \in GF(2)^{32}$) is the incoming block of binary data (plaintext), and in decryption mode it is the transformed block of binary data (ciphertext). In encryption mode, the resulting value Y ($Y \in GF(2)^{32}$) is a ciphertext, and in decryption mode, it is plaintext.

Taking into account contemporary principles of developing block ciphers, an extended key, $Q^{(e)} = \mathbf{H}(K, e)$, should be formed using a cryptographically secure extended key generation procedure. Actually, it is sufficient simply to create a pseudorandom sequence $S = Q^{(0)} = \mathbf{H}(K, 0)$ with a length that depends on the number of rounds and the total length of one round key.

The extended key $Q^{(1)}$ is a permutation of the $Q^{(0)}$ extended key's elements, the permutation determined by the constructive features of the scheme, including the initial and final transformations.

A generalized scheme of transformations is shown in Figure 5.17, and a one-round scheme for the COBRA-F64a and COBRA-F64b algorithms is shown in Figure 5.18.

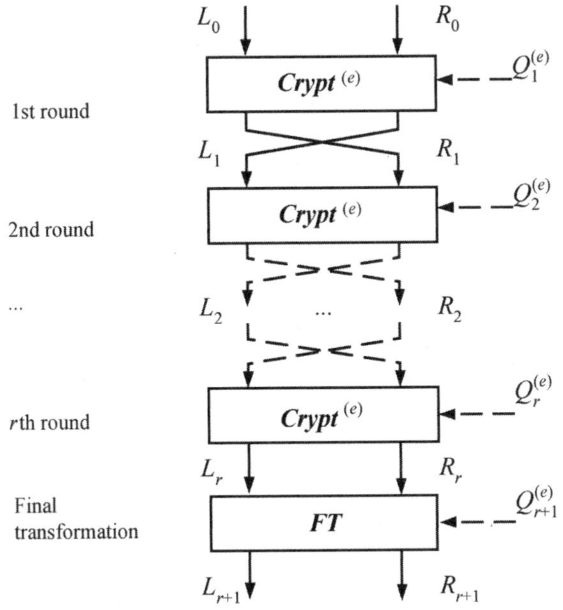

FIGURE 5.17 A general encryption scheme in the COBRA-F64 (a and b algorithms).

The absence of an initial transformation is a feature of the general encryption scheme. Encryption and decryption, however, are performed using the same algorithm, since the structure of each round is such that the final transformation is one of its components.

The Schedule for Using Round Keys

In the COBRA-F64a and COBRA-F64b algorithms, both in one round and in the final transformation, two 32-bit subkeys are used; namely,

$$Q_j^{(e)} = (Q_j^{(1,e)}, Q_j^{(2,e)}),$$

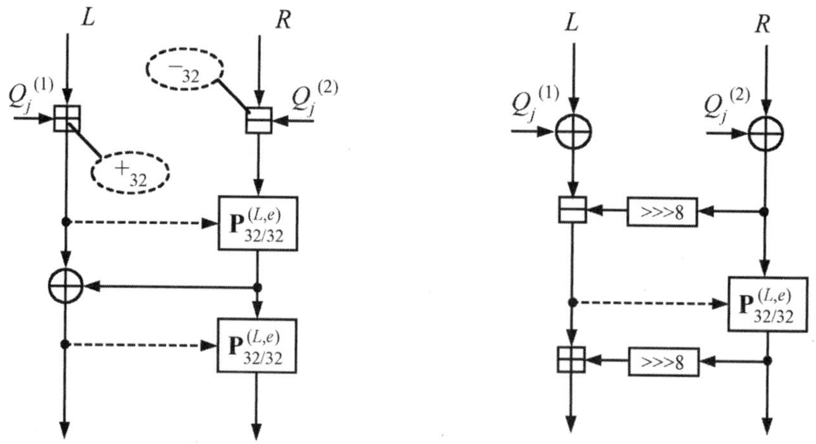

FIGURE 5.18 The ***Crypt***$^{(e)}$ procedure in: *a*—COBRA-F64a and *b*—COBRA-F64b.

where $1 \le j \le r + 1$ and r is the number of encryption rounds.

Taking into account where the algorithms will be applied—microcontrollers and intellectual electronic cards where the occupied memory size is a critical parameter—using a secure extended key generation procedure is hardly justified. A more efficient variant would be to use a key schedule.

For example, let secret key K be represented as a combination of four 32-bit words—$K = K_0||K_1||K_2||K_3$—where $K_0, K_1, K_2, K_3 \in GF(2)^{32}$. Let the extended key Q(0) = S be represented in Table 5.13.

Then, the values of the round keys $Q_j^{(e)} = (Q_j^{(1,e)}, Q_j^{(2,e)})$, for both encryption and decryption modes, are determined by Table 5.13 and the following formula:

$$(Q_j^{(i,e)}, Q_{r+1-j}^{(i,e)}) = \mathbf{P}^{(e)}_{2\times 32/1}(S_j^{(1)}, S_{r+1-j}^{(2)})$$

where $i = 1, 2$ and $j = 1, 2, \ldots, r$.

TABLE 5.13 Schedule for Using Round Keys

$j =$	1	2	3	4	5	6	7	8	9	10	11	12
$S_j^{(1)} =$	K_1	K_2	K_3	K_4	K_2	K_1	K_4	K_3	K_1	K_2	K_4	K_3
$S_j^{(2)} =$	K_4	K_3	K_1	K_2	K_3	K_2	K_1	K_4	K_2	K_3	K_1	K_2
$j =$	13	14	15	16	17	18	19	20	21	22	23	24
$S_j^{(1)} =$	K_1	K_4	K_2	K_3	K_1	K_4	K_3	K_1	K_2			
$S_j^{(2)} =$	K_3	K_1	K_3	K_4	K_2	K_1	K_4	K_2	K_3			

Taking into account the cryptographic properties of the operations performed and the constructive features of one round, 16 encryption rounds is the optimal number for the COBRA-F64a algorithm, whereas for COBRA-F64b it is 20. Nevertheless, you can increase the number of encryption rounds if you need to raise the lower border of cryptographic security of a cipher.

The Encryption Algorithm

The **F** function (see Figure 5.1) is implemented as a series of the following procedures:

- r rounds (loops) of *transformations* using the $\boldsymbol{Crypt}^{(e)}$ procedure
- Final transformation—$\boldsymbol{FT}$

Initially, the block X is divided into two subblocks of the same length—L_0 and R_0; in other words, $(L_0, R_0) = X$, where $L_0, R_0 \in GF(2)^{32}$. Then, r rounds of transformations are performed using the $\boldsymbol{Crypt}^{(e)}$ procedure according to the formulas:

$$L_j = \boldsymbol{Crypt}(R_{j-1}, L_{j-1}, Q_j^{(e)});\ R_j = L_{j-1},\ (j = 1, 2, \ldots, r).$$

After the rth round, the final transformation $\boldsymbol{FT}$ is performed over block $X = (R_r, L_r)$ according to the formula:

$$Y = \boldsymbol{FT}(X, Q_{FT}^{(e)}).$$

The final transformation $\boldsymbol{FT}$ for the algorithm COBRA-F64a looks like this:

$$Y = (L_{r+1}, R_{r+1}) = (R_r -_{32} Q_{r+1}^{(1,e)}, L_r +_{32} Q_{r+1}^{(2,e)}).$$

And for the COBRA-F64b algorithm, the $\boldsymbol{FT}$ transformation looks like this:

$$Y = (L_{r+1}, R_{r+1}) = (R_r \oplus Q_{r+1}^{(1,e)}, L_r \oplus Q_{r+1}^{(2,e)}).$$

Speed Parameters and the Cryptographic Security of Ciphers

The advantage of the COBRA-F64a and COBRA-F64b algorithms is the small length of binary code if they are software-implemented, which is very important in designing cryptosystems integrated into the secure initialization procedure of a computer. The microprogrammatic implementation of these algorithms using microcontrollers working at a clock speed of 33 MHz provides for an efficiency exceeding 20 Mbit/s.

With a software implementation of the COBRA-F64a and COBRA-F64b algorithms (for a processor of Celeron 500 MHz type, assuming that the ***DDP32*** command is implemented inside it as a special instruction), the estimated speed of encryption will be approximately 400 and 300 Mbit/s, respectively.

These examples prove that software ciphers, which use controlled permutations executed depending on data, when compared to the fastest known ciphers, may potentially increase the speed by several times.

Estimating a cipher's cryptographic security against all known cryptanalysis methods is a complex and expensive procedure. Therefore, investigations are also performed to find the most efficient methods of cryptanalysis. The differential cryptanalysis method is considered one of these.

In the differential cryptanalysis method (which is considered in detail in Section 5.6), the differences in the pairs of transformed data blocks X and X',—$\Delta(X, X')$—are studied, and so are the corresponding differences in the transformed blocks $\delta(Y, Y')$. Usually, a case is chosen when $\Delta(X, X') = X \oplus X' = \Delta =$ const. The value Δ is called the input difference. Nonzero bits of the considered Δ difference are called active bits. The task of differential cryptanalysis is to find Δ and d values for which the inequality $p(\delta/\Delta) > 2^{-n}$ holds, where n is the length of the input block in bits, and $p(\delta/\Delta) = \Pr(\delta/\Delta)$ is a conditional probability. Usually, "significant probabilities" $p(\delta/\Delta)$—those differing from the average values as much as possible—are the differences with a small number of active bits for the considered differential cryptanalysis. In Section 5.6, the differential cryptanalysis of the COBRA-F64a, COBRA-F64b, DDP-S64, and DDP-S128 ciphers is described in more detail.

As a result of a cryptographic security investigation for the COBRA-F64a and COBRA-F64b ciphers, it was added to the differential cryptanalysis method that the most significant probabilities correspond to differential characteristics with differences containing only one "active bit." Remember that the term "active bit" is used in the sense that the Hamming weight of the difference of two considered vectors is equal to one. So, for the COBRA-F64a algorithm, the best characteristic among those found is a three-round characteristic, for which a 1-bit output difference δ_1 with a probability of $p_a(3) = 2^{-21}$ best corresponds to a 1-bit input difference of Δ_1. Accordingly, for the COBRA-F64b algorithm, the best among the characteristics found is a two-round one, for which, after two transformation rounds, a 1-bit output difference of δ_1 with a probability of $p_b(2) = 2^{-12}$ corresponds to an input difference of Δ_1 with one active bit in the right (or left) data block. However, the iterative application of these characteristics for 15 rounds in the first case and for 20 rounds in the second does not allow us to form efficient 15- and 20-round characteristics, since the values of the probabilities $p_a(15) = 2^{-105}$ and $p_b(20) = 2^{-120}$ do not exceed the value of the corresponding probability in an arbitrary 64-bit block cipher. The development of differential characteristics with a large number of active bits does not give the desired result of efficient characteristics, which proved the high cryptographic security of these ciphers against differential cryptanalysis.

High indices for the speed and cryptographic security of ciphers, where the ***DDP32*** command is used, allow us to hope that microprocessor developers will include this command in the set of standard operations of multipurpose processors.

The advantages of program ciphers were already considered in previous chapters. Therefore, here we will just mention the feasibility of the procedure of program cipher creation. Indeed, integration of an encryption algorithm (even a generally recognized one) into a processor on the circuit level actually gives users no choice. Such unification additionally stimulates potential violators to develop effective methods of cracking the cipher, since, in case of success, unauthorized access to information stored in computer systems and secured by this cipher would then be possible on a wide scale. It is more profitable to analyze one cipher instead of ten or a hundred, right?

A software implementation of a new command (cryptographic primitive) requires only minimal circuit costs and does not lead to a rise in the cost of modernized processors. However, the possibility of creating a whole series of high-speed algorithms is thus heightened. However, if an algorithm is discredited, it is very easy to change it for another one, which is impossible with a hardware implementation.

We already mentioned that controlled bit permutations of a general type can be used for solving other urgent information security tasks, such as developing high-speed integrity algorithms and hashing functions. Another promising trend in the area of applied bit permutations is their integration on a microprogramming level, which provides minimum use of circuit resources, but retains a high speed for the cryptographic transformations performed both for data integrity control and for information security (hashing and encryption).

5.4.4 The DDP-S64 and DDP-S128 Algorithms

The COBRA-F64a and COBRA-F64b ciphers considered previously are aimed both at a software and at a microprogramming implementation, which is achieved using a simple transformation structure. If the purpose is only software implementation, it is possible to apply more complex transformations.

Let's look the at 64-bit and 128-bit program ciphers DDP-S64 and DDP-S128, where the DDP32 command of controlled permutation is also used.

General Encryption Scheme

Just as the COBRA-F64, a and b block ciphers, the DDP-S64 and DDP-S128 software ciphers also use a semi-universal encryption scheme, whose difference from a universal scheme is in the use of the new $\mathbf{P}^{(U,e)}_{32/32}$ command.

The general encryption scheme can be expressed by the following formula:

$$Y = \mathbf{F}^{(e)}(X, Q^{(e)}),$$

where $Q^{(e)} = \mathbf{H}(K, e)$ is an *extended key* that is a function of the 256-bit K key and the encryption mode e ($\mathbf{F}^{(0)}$—encryption, $\mathbf{F}^{(1)}$—decryption). In encryption mode, X is the incoming block of binary data (plaintext), and in decryption mode, it is the transformed block of binary data (ciphertext). In encryption mode, the resulting value Y is ciphertext, and in decryption mode, it is plaintext.

Everything that was said previously relating to the necessity of using a cryptographically secure extended key generation procedure is applicable to the ciphers considered in this section. We just need to create a pseudorandom sequence $S = Q^{(0)} = \mathbf{H}(K, 0)$ with a length depending on the number of rounds and the total length of one round key, and the extended key $Q^{(1)}$ will turn out to be a permutation of the $Q^{(0)}$ extended key elements. This permutation is determined by the constructive features of the scheme, including the initial and final transformations. You can also use the algorithms built based on controlled permutations for the extended key generation procedure.

When describing the algorithms, a case of using a key schedule that is especially efficient for the frequent key change mode is considered.

The DDP-S64 64-Bit Cipher

The general encryption scheme is shown in Figure 5.19.

The $\mathbf{F}^{(e)}$ function (Figure 5.19b) is implemented with the following procedures:

- Initial transformation—***IT***
- r rounds (loops) of *transformations* using the ***Crypt***$^{(e)}$ procedure
- Final transformation—***FT***

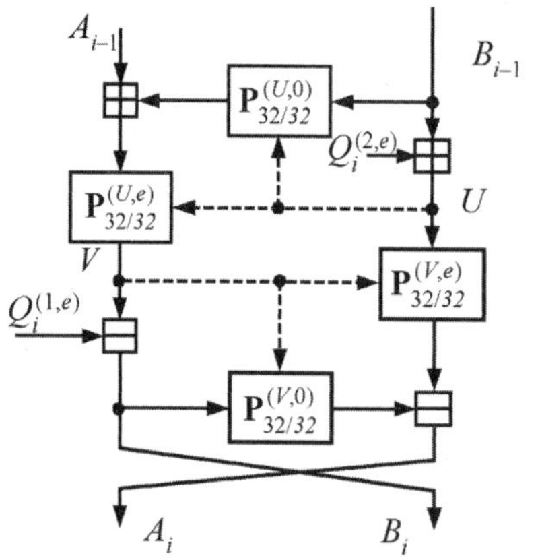

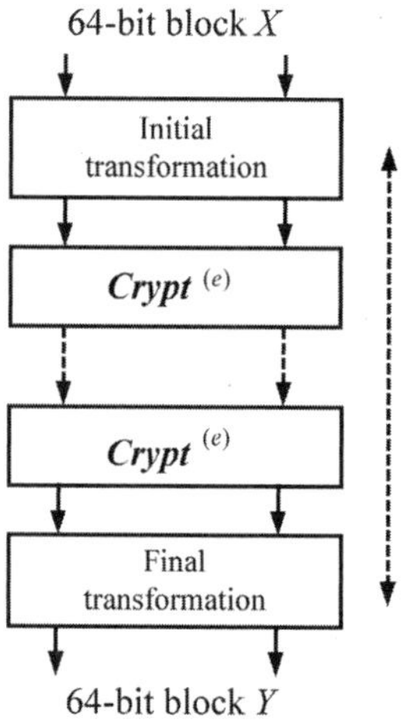

FIGURE 5.19 The general encryption scheme (b) and one transformation round (a) in the DDP-S64 algorithm.

Initially, block X is divided into two subblocks of the same length—X_{lo} and X_{hi}; in other words, $(X_{lo}, X_{hi}) = X$, where $X_{lo}, X_{hi} \in \mathrm{GF}(2)^{32}$, and the ***IT*** procedure is performed:

$$(A_0, B_0) = \boldsymbol{IT}(X, Q_0^{(e)}) = (X_{lo} \oplus Q_0^{(1,e)}, X_{hi} \oplus Q_0^{(2,e)}).$$

Then, $r = 10$ rounds of transformations are performed using the $\boldsymbol{Crypt}^{(e)}$ procedure, according to the formulas:

$$A_j = \boldsymbol{Crypt}^{(e)}(B_{j-1}, A_{j-1}, Q_j^{(e)});\ B_j = A_{j-1},\ (j = 1, 2, \ldots, r).$$

After the rth round, the final transformation ***FT*** is performed over block $X = (B_r, A_r)$ according to the formula:

$$Y = \boldsymbol{FT}(X, Q_{r+1}^{(e)}) = (B_r \oplus Q_{r+1}^{(1,e)}, A_r \oplus Q_{r+1}^{(2,e)}).$$

One transformation round is shown in Figure 5.19a.

In the $\boldsymbol{Crypt}^{(e)}$ procedure, a controlled permutation operation $\mathbf{P}_{32/32}^{(U,e)}$ is designated as $\mathbf{P}^{(U,e)}$, the algorithm itself having the following appearance:

$$U := B +_{32} Q_i^{(2,e)}.$$

$$A := A +_{32} \mathbf{P}^{(U,0)}(B).$$

$$V := \mathbf{P}^{(U,e)}(A).$$

$$B := \mathbf{P}^{(V,e)}(U).$$

$$A := V -_{32} Q_i^{(1,e)}.$$

$$B := B -_{32} \mathbf{P}^{(V,0)}(A).$$

$(A, B) := (B, A)$.

STOP.

The schedule of using subkeys in the DDP-S64 cipher is shown in Table 5.14.

TABLE 5.14 Schedule for Using Subkeys in the DDP-S64 Cipher

$i =$	0	1	2	3	4	5	6	7	8	9	10	11
$Q_i^{(1,1)} =$	K_6	K_1	K_2	K_3	K_4	K_8	K_7	K_5	K_6	K_7	K_8	K_7
$Q_i^{(2,1)} =$	K_4	K_5	K_6	K_7	K_8	K_3	K_5	K_2	K_1	K_4	K_3	K_5
$Q_i^{(1,0)} =$	K_7	K_3	K_4	K_1	K_2	K_5	K_3	K_8	K_7	K_6	K_5	K_6
$Q_i^{(2,0)} =$	K_5	K_8	K_7	K_6	K_5	K_7	K_8	K_4	K_3	K_2	K_1	K_4

Estimating the Security of the DDP-S64 Cipher

In differential cryptanalysis for this model, the most efficient characteristics are those related to the input differences Δ_1 (with one active bit in the left data subblock) in two rounds. After two rounds, these differences transform into the difference δ_1 (where the active bit also belongs to the left subblock) with a probability of 2^{-23}. At the output of the first round, the δ_2' difference is formed (each of the subblocks containing one active bit), which at the second round turns into the 1-bit difference δ_1. Considering the structure of a round transformation for DDP-S64, we estimate the probability for the first round as $p_1(\delta_2'/\Delta_1) \approx 2^{-9}$, and for the second round as $p_2(\delta_1/\delta_2') \approx 2^{-14}$. Accordingly, for two rounds, the probability is $p(2) = p(\delta_1/\Delta_1) = p_1 p_2 \approx 2^{-23}$. However, continuing by building six- and eight-round characteristics will not lead to the desired result, since the probabilities $p(6) = p(\delta_1/\Delta_1) \approx 2^{-69}$ and $p(8) = p(\delta_1/\Delta_1) \approx 2^{-92}$ do not exceed the value of the corresponding probability in random 64-bit block cipher. Developing differential characteristics with a large number of active bits did not give the desired result of efficient characteristics, which proved the high cryptographic security of the DDP-S64 block cipher against differential cryptanalysis.

The DDP-S128 128-Bit Cipher

The general encryption scheme is shown in Figure 5.20b.

There are 12 encryption rounds ($r = 12$) provided in the DDP-S128 128-bit cipher, and, for a software implementation, the 128-bit data block is split into four 32-bit subblocks—*A, B, C,* and *D*—which are subject to further transformation.

The increase in the number of encryption rounds (compared to DDP-S64) is due to the larger size of data subblocks. One distinctive feature of the DDP-S128 algorithm is that in the ***Crypt***$^{(e)}$ procedure (Figure 5.20, *a*), two controlled permutations are performed over subblocks *A* and *D*, one of such permutations depending on subblock *B*, and the other on subblock *C*. This structure provides for the implementation of a large number (about 264) of permutations to be performed

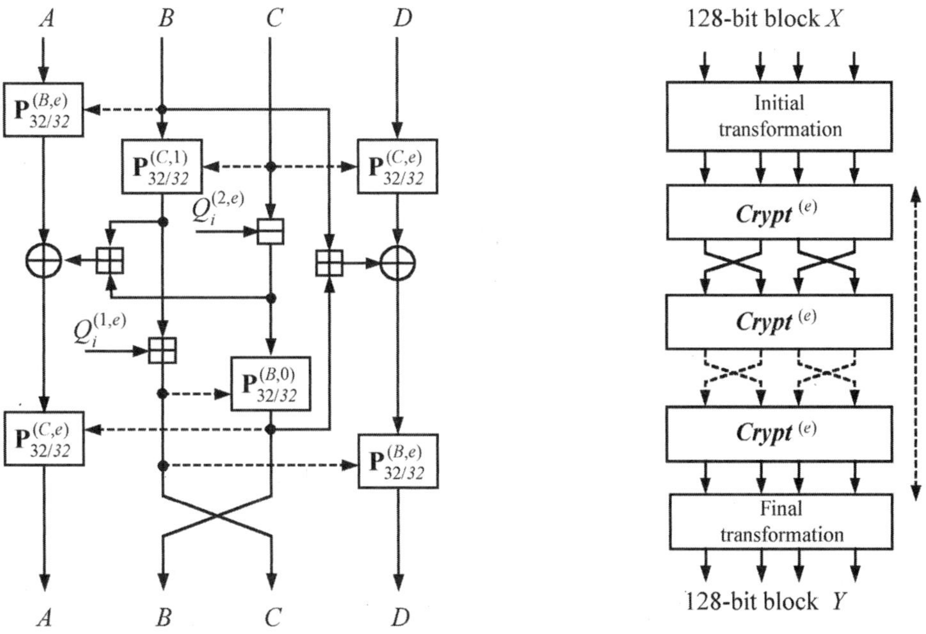

FIGURE 5.20 The general encryption scheme (b) and one transformation round (a) in the DDP-S128 algorithm.

over the subblocks A and D within one round. The superposition of controlled permutations $\mathbf{P}^{(B,e)}_{32/32}$ and $\mathbf{P}^{(C,e)}_{32/32}$ is a block of maximum order.

The DDP-S128 block cipher algorithm (Figure 5.20b) is implemented using the following procedures:

- Initial transformation—***IT***
- *r* rounds (loops) of *transformations* with the use of $\boldsymbol{Crypt}^{(e)}$ procedure
- Final transformation—***FT***

In the $\boldsymbol{Crypt}^{(e)}$ procedure, the controlled permutation operation $\mathbf{P}^{(U,e)}_{32/32}$ is designated as $P(^{U,e})$.

Initially, block X is divided into four subblocks of the same length—A, B, C, and D; in other words, $(A, B, C, D) = X$, where $A, B, C\ D \in GF(2)^{32}$, and the ***IT*** procedure is performed:

$$(A_0, B_0, C_0, D_0) = \boldsymbol{IT}(A \| B \| C \| D, Q_{IT}^{(e)}) =$$
$$(A \oplus Q_1^{(1,e)}, B \oplus Q_2^{(1,e)}, C \oplus Q_3^{(1,e)}, D \oplus Q_4^{(1,e)}).$$

Then, $r = 12$ rounds of transformations are performed using the $\boldsymbol{Crypt}^{(e)}$ procedure, according to the formulas:

$$(A, B, C, D) = \boldsymbol{Crypt}^{(e)}(A_{j-1}, B_{j-1}, C_{j-1}, D_{j-1}, Q_j^{(1,e)}, Q_j^{(2,e)})\ ;$$

$$(A_j, B_j, C_j, D_j) = (B, A, D, C)\ (j = 1, 2, \ldots, r).$$

After the rth round, the final transformation $\boldsymbol{FT}$ is performed over block $X = (B_r, A_r)$ according to the formula:

$$Y = \boldsymbol{FT}(B_r, A_r, D_r, C_r, Q_{FT}^{(e)}) = (B_r \oplus Q_r^{(2,e)}, A_r \oplus Q_{r-1}^{(2,e)}, D_r \oplus Q_{r-2}^{(2,e)}, C_r \oplus Q_{r-3}^{(2,e)}).$$

The $\boldsymbol{Crypt}^{(e)}$ procedure is shown in Figure 5.20a:

$V := B.$

$A := \mathbf{P}^{(B,0)}(A);\ B := \mathbf{P}^{(C,1)}(B);\ D := \mathbf{P}^{(C,0)}(D).$

$C := C -_{32} Q_i^{(2,e)}.$

$A := A \oplus (B +_{32} C).$

$B := B +_{32} Q_i^{(1,e)}.$

$C := \mathbf{P}^{(B,0)}(C).$

$D := D \oplus (V +_{32} C).$

$A := \mathbf{P}^{(C,0)}(A);\ D := \mathbf{P}^{(C,1)}(D).$

$(B, C) := (C, B).$

STOP.

As in the previous algorithms, the key use schedule is employed. In the jth round $(1 \le j \le r)$ two 32-bit subkeys are used; namely,

$$Q_j^{(e)} = (Q_j^{(1,e)}, Q_j^{(2,e)}).$$

The extended key $Q^{(0)} = S$ is shown in Table 5.15, where the 32-bit keys K_0, $K_1, \ldots, K_7$ are the subsettings of the secret key K ($K = K_0 || K_1 || \ldots || K_7$), and the values of round keys $Q_j^{(e)} = (Q_j^{(1,e)}, Q_j^{(2,e)})$ for the encryption and decryption modes are determined according to the following formula:

$$(Q_j^{(1+e,e)}, Q_{r+1-j}^{(2-e,e)}) = \mathbf{P}_{2\times 32/1}^{(e)}(S_j^{(1)}, S_{r+1-j}^{(2)}).$$

TABLE 5.15 Schedule for Using Subkeys in the DDP-S128 Cipher

$j =$	1	2	3	4	5	6	7	8	9	10	11	12
$S_j^{(1)} =$	K_0	K_1	K_2	K_3	K_4	K_5	K_6	K_7	K_0	K_2	K_4	K_6
$S_j^{(2)} =$	K_7	K_5	K_6	K_4	K_2	K_3	K_0	K_1	K_5	K_7	K_3	K_1

In the initial and final transformations of the DDP-S128 algorithm, four 32-bit subkeys are used in each; namely,

$$Q_{IT}^{(e)} = (Q_1^{(1,e)}, Q_2^{(1,e)}, Q_3^{(1,e)}, Q_4^{(1,e)}),\ Q_{FT}^{(e)} = (Q_r^{(2,e)}, Q_{r-1}^{(2,e)}, Q_{r-2}^{(2,e)}, Q_{r-3}^{(2,e)}),$$

where r is the number of encryption rounds.

It is necessary to mention that ***Crypt***$^{(e)}$ is characterized by the following features:

- Controlled permutations over each A and D subblock are performed depending on the B and C subblocks.
- The B subblock is transformed using operations that are the reverse of those performed over subblock C.
- The sums of the values of subblocks B and C used in bitwise addition with subblocks A and D are different.
- The value exchange operation on subblocks B and C is an element of the ***Crypt***$^{(e)}$ procedure.

The structure of the DDP-S128 cipher round transformation successfully combines the ideas of building iterative cryptoschemes.

Estimating the Security of the DDP-S128 Cipher

For the DDP-S128 cipher, the best differences in the differential cryptanalysis are Δ_2's that have two active bits going in turn along the outermost and middle branches of a cryptoscheme. The unit differences go along the outermost branches without duplication, with a probability of $p_1 = 1$. Two unit differences may also go along the middle branches without a difference occurring in the outermost branches when, at the moment of each sum calculation, $(B +_{32} C)$ (see the algorithms for the ***Crypt***$^{(e)}$ procedure) unit differences will appear in the same bits of blocks B and C. In this case, when calculating each sum with a probability of 0.5, the differences for blocks B and C are mutually eliminated. If the probability of this event is designated as p_2, then justifying the value $p_2 \approx 2^{-32}$ can be easily done. The difference indicated passes two rounds with a probability of $p(2) = p_1p_2 \approx 2^{-32}$, and eight rounds with a probability of $p(8) = p_1p_2 \approx 2^{-128}$.

For 10 and 12 rounds, such probabilities have values of $p(10) \approx 2^{-160}$ and $p(12) \approx 2^{-192}$, respectively. Thus, if the number of rounds is $r \geq 8$, it is possible to state that the DDP-S128 block cipher is secure against differential cryptanalysis.

5.5. STATISTICAL PROPERTIES OF ALGORITHMS

To check the statistic properties of block algorithms, it is advised that you test them according to the method offered by the New European Project for creating base primitives with the purpose of future standardization (NESSIE, New European Schemes for Signature, Integrity, and Encryption).

5.5.1 Criteria for Estimating the Properties of the "Avalanche Effect"

For each developed algorithm, it is necessary to analyze the results of statistical processing according to the following criteria:

- The average number of output bits changed when changing input bit—1
- The degree of completeness—2
- The degree of avalanche effect—3
- The degree of strict avalanche criterion—4

Let $U^{(i)} = U \oplus E_i$; in other words, a binary vector obtained by inversion of the ith bit in vector U. Then, binary vector $Y^{(i)} = \mathbf{F}(U^{(i)}) \oplus \mathbf{F}(U))$ is called an *avalanche vector* for the ith component. For a block cipher, $U = X||K$. Let the dimension of vector U be equal to n, and vector Y equal to m.

In criteria 2 and 4, a dependency matrix of $||a_{ij}||_{n \times m}$ is used; namely,

$$a_{ij} = \#\{Y^{(i)}, y_j^{(i)} = 1\}.$$

The $||a_{ij}||_{n \times m}$ matrix reflects the dependence of the jth bit of the output vector on the ith bit of the input vector. The degree of completeness (criterion 2) is estimated by the formula:

$$d_c = 1 - \frac{\#\{(i,j) \mid a_{ij} = 0\}}{nm}$$

and the degree of strict avalanche criterion (Criterion 4) can be estimated using the formula:

$$d_{sa} = 1 - \frac{\sum_{i=1}^{n} \sum_{j=1}^{m} \left| \frac{2a_{ij}}{N} - 1 \right|}{nm},$$

where $N = \#\mathbf{U} = \#\{U\}$.

To obtain an accurate estimation, a complete set of samples of all U vector values is needed. However, taking into account the integral character of these estimations, in order to obtain approximated values, you need just use the Monte Carlo method; in other words, a rather small set of samples of input values.

Criteria 1 and 3 use the $||b_{ij}||_{n\times m}$ distance matrix; namely,

$$b_{ij} = \#\{Y^{(i)} | \, w(Y^{(i)}) = j\},$$

which is a marking of the Hamming weight of the avalanche vectors.

The average number of output bits changed when changing 1 input bit (criterion 1) is estimated by the formula:

$$d_1 = \frac{1}{n} \sum_{i=1}^{n} \frac{\sum_{j=1}^{m} jb_{ij}}{N}$$

and the degree of avalanche effect (criterion 3) can be estimated by the formula:

$$d_a = 1 - \frac{\sum_{i=1}^{n} \left| \frac{1}{N} \sum_{j=1}^{m} 2jb_{ij} - m \right|}{nm}.$$

The next two sections contain the results of testing the SPECTR-128 block cipher. The results of the rest of the testing algorithms are obtained in a similar manner.

5.5.2 Estimating the Influence of Incoming Text Bits on the Transformed Text

The criteria for estimating the influence of the plaintext text bits on the transformed text are intended for detecting possible weak sides of an algorithm that might be used in cryptanalysis based on a chosen plaintext, or by using the differential cryptanalysis method. For the criteria described in Section 5.5.1, we consider the case when *avalanche vector* $Y^{(i)}$ is formed by the input vectors $U = X||K$ and $U = X^{(i)}||K$, where $X^{(i)} = X \oplus E_i$.

The following values are specified as parameters: q for keys, t for incoming texts. $N = qt$. The values of q and t depend on the values of n and m and the computational resources available. The $||a_{ij}||_{n \times m}$ *dependence matrix* and the $||b_{ij}||_{n \times m}$ *distance matrix* look like this:

$$a_{ij} = \#\{X \in \mathbf{X}, K \in \mathbf{K} \mid (\mathbf{F}(X^{(i)}, K))_j \neq (\mathbf{F}(X, K))_j\},$$

$$b_{ij} = \#\{X \in \mathbf{X}, K \in \mathbf{K} \mid w(\mathbf{F}(X^{(i)}, K) \oplus \mathbf{F}(X, K)) = j\}.$$

Keys and incoming texts are built using a random number monitor.

For the SPECTR-128 algorithm, integral estimates both for a declared number of rounds and for a reduced number of rounds were obtained. Similar to the test results of the five finalists of the contest for New American Standard of block encryption held by the USA National Institute of Standards and Technologies—the "one key and 10,000 texts" variant was implemented, as well as "100 keys and 100 texts" (Table 5.16).

The results of testing the SPECTR-128 algorithm correspond to the test results for the contest finalists. They prove that the given transformation algorithm possesses good scattering properties, even with a small number of rounds, and may be treated as a good generator of pseudorandom substitutions, even with a small number of rounds. In particular, the *completeness criterion*, according to which "each input bit should influence each output bit," is implemented already after two encryption rounds. For example, in the DES and GOST algorithms, this criterion is implemented in no less than four encryption rounds, which is determined only by the Feistel scheme used.

5.5.3 Estimating the Influence of Key Bits on the Transformed Text

In this case, the *avalanche vector* $Y^{(i)}$ is formed by the input vectors $U = X||K$ and $U = X||K^{(i)}$, where $K^{(i)} = K \oplus E_i$. In the criteria, the $||a_{ij}||_{n \times m}$ dependence matrix and the $||b_{ij}||_{n \times m}$ distance matrix look like this:

$$a_{ij} = \#\{X \in \mathbf{X}, K \in \mathbf{K} \mid (\mathbf{F}(X, K^{(i)}))_j \neq (\mathbf{F}(X, K))_j\},$$

$$b_{ij} = \#\{X \in \mathbf{X}, K \in \mathbf{K} \mid w(\mathbf{F}(X, K^{(i)}) \oplus \mathbf{F}(X, K)) = j\}.$$

The test data for the SPECTR-128 algorithm (Table 5.17) prove that a rather strong diffusion influence of each key bit upon all bits of the transformed text is provided for, even without a secure procedure for generating an extended key.

We must mention that these criteria are efficient tools for detecting weak sides in separately developed procedures and transformations, in making up the schedule for using round keys, and when an optimal number of rounds are chosen.

TABLE 5.16 Values of Influence Criteria 1–4 of the Incoming Text on the Transformed Text (for Various Numbers of Rounds)

Number of rounds	#K=1, #X=10000				#K=100, #X=100			
	(1)	(2)=d_c	(3)=d_a	(4)=d_{sa}	(1)	(2)=d_c	(3)=d_a	(4)=d_{sa}
12	64.00145	1.00000	0.99922	0.99208	64.00385	1.00000	0.99937	0.99198
11	63.99543	1.00000	0.99922	0.99206	64.00783	1.00000	0.99929	0.99214
10	64.00466	1.00000	0.99933	0.99204	64.00295	1.00000	0.99930	0.99197
9	63.98921	1.00000	0.99932	0.99205	64.00405	1.00000	0.99921	0.99205
8	63.99262	1.00000	0.99935	0.99200	63.99932	1.00000	0.99928	0.99194
7	64.00420	1.00000	0.99927	0.99206	64.00502	1.00000	0.99926	0.99203
6	64.00168	1.00000	0.99929	0.99205	63.99895	1.00000	0.99937	0.99203
5	63.99244	1.00000	0.99931	0.99208	63.99628	1.00000	0.99930	0.99206
4	63.64805	1.00000	0.99421	0.98838	63.62012	1.00000	0.99369	0.98805
3	52.35455	1.00000	0.81804	0.81594	52.45568	1.00000	0.81962	0.81759
2	26.45824	0.98535	0.41341	0.41330	26.55646	1.00000	0.41494	0.41490
1	6.24359	0.48852	0.09755	0.08970	6.22903	0.50781	0.09732	0.09663

TABLE 5.17 The Values for Criteria 1–4 on the Influence of Key Bits on Transformed Text (for Various Numbers of Rounds)

Number of rounds	#K=400, #X=25				#K=100, #X=100			
	(1)	(2)=d_c	(3)=d_a	(4)=d_{sa}	(1)	(2)=d_c	(3)=d_a	(4)=d_{sa}
12	63.99562	1.00000	0.99931	0.99202	64.00289	1.00000	0.99931	0.99206
11	63.99997	1.00000	0.99923	0.99202	64.00450	1.00000	0.99928	0.99203
10	64.00301	1.00000	0.99932	0.99204	63.99632	1.00000	0.99930	0.99202
9	63.99707	1.00000	0.99930	0.99204	63.99466	1.00000	0.99923	0.99202
8	64.00112	1.00000	0.99930	0.99200	64.00076	1.00000	0.99926	0.99195
7	63.99715	1.00000	0.99932	0.99200	63.99873	1.00000	0.99932	0.99201
6	64.00123	1.00000	0.99928	0.99200	64.00549	1.00000	0.99927	0.99201
5	63.94757	1.00000	0.99885	0.99195	63.95256	1.00000	0.99891	0.99202
4	63.94757	1.00000	0.99070	0.98590	63.41481	1.00000	0.99072	0.98592
3	54.33583	1.00000	0.84899	0.84733	54.36625	1.00000	0.84947	0.84783
2	27.21150	1.00000	0.42518	0.42510	27.22301	1.00000	0.42536	0.42528
1	4.59536	0.50390	0.07180	0.07173	4.59477	0.50390	0.07179	0.07171

With respect to contemporary recommendations, the number of rounds in block encryption algorithms should be greater than the minimum secure level by two, which is implemented; for example, in the SPECTR-H64 and SPECTR-128 algorithms.

Main Results

The following can be considered the main results of our discussion on designing fast ciphers based on controlled operations.

- We presented basic schemes for building universal iterated block ciphers based on controlled operations.
- We gave concrete models of block ciphers, both for a hardware and a software implementation.
- We considered the prospects of using controlled permutational and substitutional operations as cryptographic primitives. In particular, we offered a new command to processor developers, implementing a controlled permutation operation that can be efficiently used in developing program ciphers if implemented as a special instruction.
- We presented specific schemes and constructions of applying one-stage controlled permutation blocks not only for round key selection control, but also in forming control vectors for inverse transformation implementation in controlled permutation blocks of a special type.
- Since block ciphers might possess only practical security (and not theoretical), it is necessary to strictly observe their contemporary development principles. The statistical tests described in this chapter are a well-tested tool, allowing you to detect obvious weak sides of an algorithm.

5.6 ELEMENTS OF THE CRYPTANALYSIS OF CIPHERS BASED ON CONTROLLED OPERATIONS

5.6.1 Estimating Flexible Ciphers

As a rule, cryptanalysis is based on the use of algebraic and/or statistical mechanisms of ciphers. If mechanisms are found that enable you to distinguish a determinate transformation implemented by a cipher controlled by a secret key from a random one, then actual prerequisites for cipher breakability appear. Therefore, the general task of cryptanalysis is the detection of such mechanisms and the development of methods of using them in breaking the whole cipher or its elements.

The best known universal statistical method of cryptanalysis is *frequency cryptanalysis*. It is based on using the irregularity of the occurrence of different alphabetic symbols or their combinations in the plaintext, which is leveled out (though not completely) by applying an encryption transformation. For example, if a simple substitution cipher is used (each alphabetical symbol of the plaintext corresponds to a unique symbol of the ciphertext alphabet), then the transformed text (ciphertext) fully retains the structure of the occurrence of the source text symbols. Provided that a cipher text of a size sufficient for detecting considerable differences in the occurrence of various symbols is available, such a mechanism helps to decrypt the cipher because you have the option of establishing a correspondence between the symbols of the ciphertext and those of the plaintext.

It is common knowledge that one of the main modes of using block ciphers is the simple substitution mode (e-code book). Contemporary block ciphers, however, are practically invulnerable to the frequency cryptanalysis method, due to a very large number of possible data blocks (2^{64} or 2^{128}). In other words, it is practically impossible to find the actual frequency of the occurrence of the input data blocks, and especially to find a significant sampling for the transformed texts. Therefore, cryptanalysis methods being developed for contemporary block ciphers take into account the mechanisms for the detection of which you need not only use transformed texts, but also incoming ones, including those that are specially collated. These ways of attacking allow you to create more varied statistical methods of analysis.

There are two main tasks of cipher cryptanalysis. The first task is the computation of the secret key, or finding a way to keylessly read ciphertexts, which is solved by a violator (decipherer, cryptanalyst) with the purpose of accessing information. This is the so-called decryption problem. Note that in the process of solving the first task, in order to determine the prospects of a cipher's development, a cryptanalyst should obtain a high level of cipher security for each cryptanalysis method he or she knows, with respect to conditions of practically applying them, and then choose the most efficient method of decryption. Therefore, for each particular method, the cryptanalyst should determine, for example, the maximum number of elementary operations (if such an estimation is determined by the number of elementary operations) that must be performed to solve a cryptanalysis task.

The cryptanalyst can obtain this estimation with respect to the labor expenditures needed to differentiate the encryption algorithm from a random transformation, and the labor spent for computing the key using the detected statistical mechanisms. When security is estimated, apart from the labor spent to solve a cryptanalysis task, the memory necessary for implementation of the assault method is often determined as well. As a rule, when a large amount of memory is used, the number of operations necessary is considerably reduced. A general requirement for contemporary ciphers is the high computational complexity of the cryptanalysis (for example, 10^{40} operations) when a large amount of memory is used (for example, 10^{20} bytes).

The second task, cipher security estimation, is usually done by the developer. As a rule, the conditions for solving the first task are less pleasant than those of the second task. The latter, however, is no less complicated, since the cipher developer has to find the lowest security level for the cipher being developed for each cryptanalysis method he knows, including methods that are currently impossible to implement but that are theoretically justified. The cryptosystem developer tries to obtain an estimation corresponding to the minimal number of operations needed to solve a cryptanalysis task using the best cryptanalysis algorithm. Since it is not always possible to determine the best cryptanalysis algorithm, a minimum estimation is given to the best of the known cryptanalysis algorithms. The developer can also estimate the cipher's security as the labor expenditure needed to determine how it is different from a random cipher.

Thus, the estimations gained in the course of solving the first task should be higher than those gained in the course of solving the second task. In practice, however, this condition is not always observed, since much depends on the subjective conditions of solving each task.

During cryptanalysis, it is usually assumed that the integrity of the encryption device is sufficient when the algorithm is not modified during the encryption process, and the violator has no way to read the key information from any kind of leakage (feed circuit inducing, side electromagnetic radiations, computation time measurement, machine errors, etc.). Lately, however, attacks on encryption device integrity are considered more often. This is due to the expanding application of encryption, in which these devices are used to solve various tasks in various operating conditions. Be aware that the cryptographic analysis of special purpose ciphers always used to include the study of the violation of the encryption device's integrity. The active study of such forms of attack started when encryption began to be widely used as an element of information security in computer-aided systems.

Estimating the security of *flexible* ciphers—those where the use of a concrete cryptalgorithm is determined by the secret key—is of special interest. Note that in this type of cipher, the Kerckhoff principle, according to which the only unknown element is the secret key, can be implemented by using pre-computations that include a building procedure for the encryption algorithm that depends on the user's secret key. In this case, a concrete encryption algorithm is an easily changeable element. It is automatically changed when the secret key is changed. If the number of possible modifications of the cryptalgorithm is large (e.g., 10^{20}), then it is rather difficult to analyze each of them. Therefore, when flexible ciphers are built, a base mechanism is developed in which certain principles that determine the general properties of all modifications are fixed. As a rule, the developer estimates the level of security for a limited set of algorithms by assuming that the cryptanalyst knows the particular modification. To obtain the lowest security level of a cipher, it is advisable to find the same estimate for the "weakest" modification. Another important way to analyze flexible algorithms assumes that the encryption key is known, with only the cryptalgorithm modification remaining unknown. It makes sense to only use flexible ciphers with high security against all variants of cryptanalysis mentioned previously.

The confidentiality of the cryptalgorithm modification in flexible ciphers should not be treated as the main factor of high security, but rather as a mechanism to determine the additional security reserve. Indeed, if a cryptanalyst does not know the modification of the cryptalgorithm, the cryptographic task will be considerably more complex.

The universal method of cryptanalyzing flexible ciphers is by keyless reading and trying the entire possible key space. These methods do not require knowledge of the concrete modification of a cryptalgorithm, but the first one is efficient only when decrypting relatively weak ciphers, and the second one when using small keys.

For the flexible program ciphers described in Chapter 2, using these universal methods does not allow you to actually decrypt a cryptoscheme. Using more efficient methods based on the availability of statistical mechanisms in the samplings gained during studies of certain transformations requires much more labor expenditure if the modification of a cryptalgorithm is unknown, compared to the labor needed to decrypt well known transformation procedures.

To gain the minimal security estimation for ciphers based on the data-dependent subkey selection, the *combinatory-probabilistic model* was introduced. This model and methods of its use were described in Chapter 2 when estimating the security of some software-oriented 512-byte algorithms. The reason for using this model to get the minimal security estimation is that one encryption round includes a large number of operations ($128k$, where $k = 2, 4, 6$), where at least half are performed in complex dependence on each bit of the plaintext and each bit of the secret key. The selected keys are not used directly in the transformation of the current data subblock, but rather are elements of the procedure for forming accumulating key variables.

These variables are transformed within one round in concatenation mode, which determines the influence of the current (including the initial) value of each of these variables upon all its subsequent values. The concatenation method explains the inclusion of each accumulating variable in the transformation and, consequently, in the transformation of each data subblock—long chains of subkeys selected pseudorandomly. Trying to compute such chains based on source and transformed texts using algebraic relationships leads to the formation of a nonlinear boolean equation system with many unknowns, which is very hard to solve.

Generating equations that can be solved using reasonable computing resources necessitates the inclusion of some pseudorandom values of accumulating variables in such equations. Assuming some pseudorandom parameters in the relationships used for cryptanalysis is generally done for many statistical types of attacks, including both linear and differential methods recognized as the most general and efficient methods used in block cryptosystem analysis. Currently, except for the combinatory-probabilistic model, no other methods of 512-byte algorithm security estimation have been introduced, although they have been discussed for about 10 years in various scientific papers.

5.6.2 Differential Characteristics of Controlled Permutation Boxes

One of the universal methods of block cipher cryptanalysis used for estimating security is differential cryptanalysis (DC).

Following is a brief explanation of differential cryptanalysis.

Let's say there is a rather complex one-to-one mapping $Y = \mathbf{F}(X)$ depending on the key, where the cardinal number X is a large number (e.g., 2^{64}). As a rule, it is impossible to predict the value of Y for a randomly chosen X. Let's say there is already a rather large number of nonrecurrent pairs (X_1, Y_1), (X_2, Y_2), ..., (X_r, Y_r). If, for any X not belonging to a set $\{X_1, X_2, ..., X_r\}$, it is impossible to predict Y with a probability exceeding $(2^n - r)^{-1}$; in other words, if values of Y that have not yet occurred are equiprobable, this proves the pseudorandom character of this mapping. Otherwise, the mapping is not pseudorandom.

Now let's consider two vectors simultaneously—X_1 and X_2. Using a binary operation, a third vector can be made to correspond to each pair of binary vectors, and this vector will be called the *difference*. Usually, an XOR $(X_1 \oplus X_2)$ operation is used as such a binary operation, and the difference is commonly designated with the symbol Δ^X. Thus, the incoming difference Δ^X looks like $\Delta^X = X_1 \oplus X_2$. Accordingly, the difference in the values of the **F** function, called the *output difference*, looks like $\Delta^Y = Y_1 \oplus Y_2$. Usually, the same binary operation is used when input and output differences are determined, although such a coincidence is not mandatory. In the considered example, even with the absence of a statistical dependence between the samplings of the transformed texts and those being transformed, a statistical dependence may exist between the sampling differences of the transformed texts and those being transformed. That is, there may be an irregularity of output difference Δ^Y values as a result of the transformation of a set of binary vector pairs interconnected by a certain difference.

The idea of differential cryptanalysis lies in the task of finding a difference that, after the entire encryption transformation, would generate a difference with a frequency of occurrence that considerably differs from the average value. Finding such input and output differences is the main task of DC. If such differences are found, this means that the conditions under which an encryption transformation is recognized as a nonrandom one have been found. After this, a way of using this circumstance to compute a secret key must be found. Since DC deals with the encryption of specially selected pairs of texts, this type of cryptanalysis is related to attacks based on specially chosen texts.

Thus, in using the DC method, we consider the propagation of differences of certain type through separate operations, a round, or the entire encryption transformation. When it is implemented, the encryption of a large number of data block pairs is required, with the fixed difference.

In other words, the DC method searches for an efficient differential characteristic that can be used to decrypt a cipher. Remember that the differential characteristic is a triad of values (Δ^X, Δ^Y, $p(\Delta^X \to \Delta^Y)$), where $p(\Delta^X \to \Delta^Y) = p(\Delta^Y/\Delta^X)$ —the probability of the occurrence of the Δ^Y difference if the input difference Δ^X is available. That characteristic for which the probability value $p(\Delta^X \to \Delta^Y)$ for a full number of encryption rounds considerably exceeds 2^{-n}, where n is the length of vectors X and Y, is known as efficient.

Let's say that an efficient characteristic (Δ^X, Δ^Y, $p(\Delta^X \to \Delta^Y)$) is found, where $2^{-n+20} \approx p(\Delta^Y/\Delta^X) >> 2^{-n}$. For key computation, however, the encryption of a very large number of data block pairs is required. As a rule, for such a number N, the inequality $N \geq 1/p^2(\Delta^Y/\Delta^X)$ exists. In the example considered, to prove that the encryption transformation is not pseudorandom—it is indistinguishable from a random one—it is sufficient to encrypt about 2^{n-20} pairs of data blocks. To compute the key, however, 2^{2n-40} incoming data blocks will be required, which is problematic at $n = 64$, and practically unrealizable at $n = 128$.

Thus, it is possible to show that some block ciphers implement an encryption transformation that is different from a random one, but that the key computation is a very difficult task. If such a situation is revealed at the stage of a cipher design, the developer needs to modernize the current version of the cipher in such a way to make it a pseudorandom substitution (keeping in mind that every block cipher is a substitution). The DC performed by the developer may not include the key computation stage or an estimation of the labor expenditures needed to implement its variants. It is sufficient to build a cipher that is undistinguishable from a random transformation for all possible differential characteristics.

Important differential characteristics are iterative characteristics with identical input and output differences. For ciphers based on permutations that depend on the data being transformed, differential characteristics with input and output differences that belong to the same class and have the same (usually small) Hamming weight are also important.

At first, *operations of controlled permutations* seem too complicated for DC. However, with a gradual transition from the analysis of the differential characteristics of an elementary switch to more complicated blocks of controlled permutations, it is possible to find rather simple general dependencies connected with the most important cases of DC. Such cases are related to determining the probability of the propagation of differences with a small number of active bits. It is these differences that have the greatest probabilities for cryptoschemes based on using controlled permutation blocks. Indeed, it was shown in the description of specific ciphers in this chapter that two permutation operations are normally used in one encryption round, these operations depending on the data being transformed and their superposition forming a permutation of the maximal order. The active then bits become arbitrary. This is the reason why increasing the number of active bits leads to a considerable reduction in the probability of obtaining the expected difference at the outcome of one round. This is shown in the DC of specific ciphers earlier in this chapter.

It is rather easy to establish the main differential characteristics of an elementary box $\mathbf{P}_{2/1}$, which have nonzero probabilities. These characteristics are shown in Figure 5.21, where the superscript of a difference Δ indicates its correspondence to input (x), output (y), or control input (v), and the subscript indicates the number of nonzero bits in the difference. Using these properties of an elementary switch that is the base element of more complex boxes of controlled permutations, and taking into account the bit distribution of the control data subblock, it is easy to compute the probabilities of differential characteristics for the most important types of controlled permutation boxes.

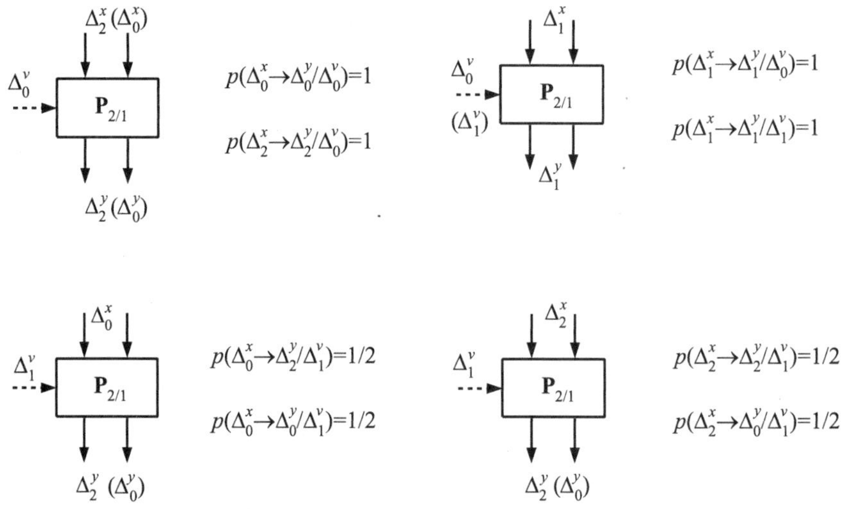

FIGURE 5.21 Probabilities of passing differences through elementary switch $\mathbf{P}_{2/1}$.

Let's consider a case of using expansion box **E**, which provides for the influence of each bit of control data subblock L on q ($q = 2, 3$) different bits at output **E**, and the strictly one-time influence of each control bit on all input bits of the controlled permutations box.

The general scheme shown in Figure 5.22 can contain boxes $\mathbf{P}_{16/32}$ ($q = 2$), $\mathbf{P}_{32/96}$ ($q = 3$), or $\mathbf{P}_{64/192}$ ($q = 3$) as box $\mathbf{P}_{n/m}$. Designate the number of nonzero bits of the difference going through the control data subblock L as z, and the number of elementary events related to the generation of a pair of active bits in an elementary box $\mathbf{P}_{2/1}$, whose control input is fed with a nonzero difference (Figure 5.22c), as w. These $\mathbf{P}_{2/1}$ boxes will be called *active*.

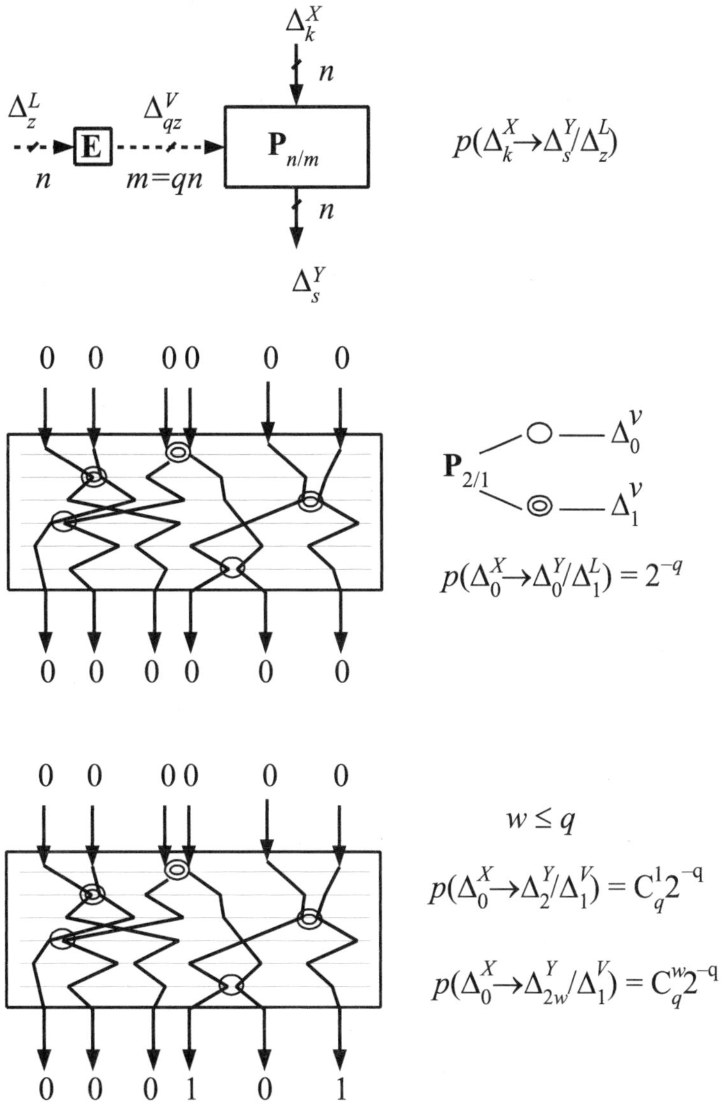

FIGURE 5.22 The general scheme of the passing of differences through a controlled permutations box (a), zero difference passing through the $\mathbf{P}_{2/1}$ active boxes without active bit generation (b), and with active bit generation (c).

If the input of an expansion box is fed with the difference Δ_1^L with one active bit, then the difference Δ_q^V with q active bits appears at the control input of the controlled permutations box. If a zero difference Δ_0^X is fed to the input of the controlled permutations box, then—depending on the specific bit values entering the inputs of the elementary switches corresponding to active bits of difference Δ_q^V—a zero difference Δ_0^Y or a nonzero difference Δ_{2w}^Y $(w \le q)$ with an even number of active bits may occur at the output of the controlled permutations box. Taking into account the probability of a zero difference transformation while passing through an active elementary switch $\mathbf{P}_{2/1}$, it is easy to get the following formula:

$$p(\Delta_0^X \rightarrow \Delta_{2w}^Y / \Delta_z^L) \approx 2^{-qz} C_{qz}^w$$

If $z = 1$, then this formula is exact, and if $z \ge 2$, it provides a good approximation. When $q = 3, 4, 5$, the formula provides a rather exact probability value. You can also use it at higher q values, but differences with a large number of active bits do not contribute much to differential characteristics with maximum probabilities.

Another important case is related to the passing of difference Δ_1^X with one active bit through the controlled permutations box in the presence of a nonzero difference Δ_z^L, where $z \ne 0$ at the control input. The active bit of the input difference may pass all active elementary switches with the probability $p' \approx (n - 2qz)/n$, and pass through one of the last active elementary switches $\mathbf{P}_{2/1}$ with the probability $p'' \approx 2qz/n$. Then, for $z = 1$, the indicated expressions of the probabilities are exact, and for $z = 2, 3, 4$, they provide a rather good approximation. Taking into account the fact that each active elementary switch $\mathbf{P}_{2/1}$ can generate two active bits of output difference with a probability of 0.5, it is easy to derive the following approximation for the probability value of the considered event:

$$p(\Delta_1^X \rightarrow \Delta_{1+2w}^Y / \Delta_z^L) \approx 2^{-qz} C_{qz}^w \frac{(n-2qz)}{n} + 2^{1-qz} C_{qz-1}^w \frac{2qz}{n}$$

When a difference with two or more active bits passes through the controlled permutations box, there is the possibility of the "annihilation" of the even number of active bits. The maximum probability corresponds to the zeroing of two active bits. Consider how this happens for the differences Δ_2^X and Δ_z^L. With a probability close to $2qz/n$, one of the active bits of the Δ_2^X difference goes to the input of one of the active elementary switches. With a probability of $1/(n - 1)$, the second active bit moves to the input of the same box $\mathbf{P}_{2/1}$. With a probability of 0.5, these active bits are simultaneously zeroed. The remaining $qz - 1$ of the $\mathbf{P}_{2/1}$ active elementary switches with a probability of 2^{-qz+1} will not generate new pairs of active bits in the output difference.

After multiplying the probabilities of all these independent events, we derive:

$$p(\Delta_2^X \rightarrow \Delta_0^Y / \Delta_z^L) \approx 2^{1-qz} \frac{qz}{n(n-1)}$$

This formula is derived for the case of averaging all possible values of the number of active bits i and j of the input difference $\Delta_{2|i,j}^X$ (assuming that both i and j are random equiprobable values). The considered mechanism of active bit "annihilation" proves that the simultaneous zeroing of two and more pairs of active bits has a considerably smaller probability. Some values of the probability $p(\Delta^X \rightarrow \Delta^Y / \Delta_z^L)$ are shown in Tables 5.18 and 5.19.

TABLE 5.18 Probability Values $p(\Delta^X \rightarrow \Delta^Y / \Delta_1^L)$ for the $\mathbf{P}_{64/192}$ Box

$z = 1$	Δ_0^Y	Δ_2^Y	Δ_4^Y	Δ_6^Y
Δ_0^X	2^{-3}	$1.5 \cdot 2^{-2}$	$1.5 \cdot 2^{-2}$	2^{-3}
Δ_2^X	$1.52 \cdot 2^{-13}$	$1.11 \cdot 2^{-3}$	$1.42 \cdot 2^{-2}$	$1.27 \cdot 2^{-2}$

$z = 1$	Δ_1^Y	Δ_3^Y	Δ_5^Y	Δ_7^Y
Δ_1^X	$1.1 \cdot 2^{-3}$	$1.55 \cdot 2^{-2}$	$1.45 \cdot 2^{-2}$	$0.91 \cdot 2^{-3}$

TABLE 5.19 Probability Values $p(\Delta^X \rightarrow \Delta^Y / \Delta_2^L)$ for the $\mathbf{P}_{64/192}$ Box

$z = 2$	Δ_0^Y	Δ_2^Y	Δ_4^Y	Δ_6^Y
Δ_0^X	2^{-6}	$1.5 \cdot 2^{-4}$	$1.88 \cdot 2^{-3}$	$1.25 \cdot 2^{-2}$
Δ_2^X	$1.52 \cdot 2^{-15}$	$1.1 \cdot 2^{-6}$	$1.51 \cdot 2^{-4}$	$1.72 \cdot 2^{-3}$

$z = 2$	Δ_1^Y	Δ_3^Y	Δ_5^Y	Δ_7^Y
Δ_1^X	$1.19 \cdot 2^{-6}$	$1.69 \cdot 2^{-4}$	2^{-2}	$1.25 \cdot 2^{-2}$

It is worth mentioning that the preceding formulas for computing the probability for events related to either class of differences and that are characterized mainly by different Hamming weights provide integral estimations within a rather large class of differences. If additional active bits are generated, then there is no binding of active bits to specific numbers of bits. However "annihilation" includes the binding of the second bit to a specific position because it is the fact of two active bits going to the input of the same active elementary switch that is considered. Assuming that the previous estimations are correct for both direct and inverse layered boxes of controlled permutations, the "annihilation" events can be examined by changing the bit movement from output to input, which leads to a case similar to active bit generation in a reverse box of controlled permutations. Therefore, it is easy to understand why "annihilation" probabilities have considerably smaller values. It is because the generation of an active bit pair does not require that two specific bits move to the input of the same active elementary switch—such a case deals with much more numerous classes of events. The "annihilation" event has probability values that correspond to a case of active bit generation in the specified output classes. We will encounter this circumstance later on, during the DC of specific ciphers that use controlled permutations as a base cryptographic primitive.

Studying the differential properties of cryptosystems based on controlled operations also includes the preliminary consideration of the probabilities of passing various differences through a **G** operation. Probability values can be easily derived from formulas describing the boolean functions corresponding to this operation. Since different operations of such type are used in different ciphers, their properties will be considered directly during the DC of the specific cryptosystems.

5.6.3 Analysis of the SPECTR-H64 Cryptosystem

Using multilayer boxes of controlled permutations in the SPECTR-H64 block cipher leads to the fact that the largest probabilities have differential characteristics with a small number of active bits.

In the considered scheme, the difference with one active bit in the right branch (with a zero difference in the left branch) passes through one transformation round with a probability equal to 1. In the same scheme, if one active bit is available in the left branch and a zero difference is available in the right branch, there is a rather large probability of obtaining a zero difference in the right branch. That is, in this case, the general output difference will be the same as the input difference. Let's consider this case in more detail, which, with respect to the previous one, will allow us to form 2-, 4-, and 2*k*-round characteristics.

However, in the considered case, the difference in the right arm is equal to the difference at the output of one round, and within the round, the active bit passing through the left branch of the cryptoscheme considerably influences the generation of new active bits in the right branch. In the controlled permutations box, active bits are generated at random, and during the performance of the **G** operation, by both the probability law and the deterministic one. If there is one active bit at the input of the **G** operation, there are from two to six active bits generated at its output (two active bits are generated according to the deterministic law). Generation of an even number of active bits (0, 2, 4, 6) is also implemented in each **P**' or **P**'' box. After the XOR operation is performed (before the $\mathbf{P}^{-1}_{32/80}$ controlled permutation is implemented), the total number of active bits can increase (up to 18), and can decrease (to 0).

Because we are interested in a situation where a zero difference (the absence of the active bits' "propagation") is implemented at the output of box $\mathbf{P}^{-1}_{32/80}$, a case in which the number of such active bits after the XOR operation is performed is equal either to zero or two is of the greatest interest for us. It is for these probability values that the probabilities of obtaining a zero difference at the output of box $\mathbf{P}^{-1}_{32/80}$ are especially important.

These arguments enable us to form the two-round differential characteristic shown in Figure 5.23 *with the use of the following designations*:

- Δ^L and Δ^R—the difference in the left (L) and right (R) subblock
- $\Delta^{\mathbf{F}}$ and $\Delta^{(\mathbf{F})}$—the input and output differences that correspond to the **F** operation
- $\Delta^{(\mathbf{G})}_{2|i,i+1}$—the difference with a subscript indicating: the total number of active bits first and, after the vertical line, the numbers of active bits

With such a designation, the $\Delta_{2|i,j}$ and Δ_2 entries have the following meaning: the first one designates a specific difference with two active bits, and the second indicates only one of the differences with two active bits.

Taking into account the design philosophy of the $\mathbf{P}_{32/80}$ box, used in one round of the SPECTR-H64 cipher, the l_i active bits of data subblock L control a different number of $\mathbf{P}_{2/1}$ boxes, depending on the i ordinal number and on the L data subblock's cycle shift value before the expansion procedure is performed. The number of $\mathbf{P}_{2/1}$ boxes controlled by one bit l_i will be designated as q.

Figure 5.23 shows the main variants of one active bit passing in the ith order of the left arm without generating active bits at the output of box **P''**.

Event A1

1. The difference $\Delta^{(\mathbf{G})}_{2|i,i+1}$ is formed at the output of operation **G** with a probability of $p_2^{(i)}$.
2. The difference $\Delta^{(\mathbf{P'})}_{2|i,i+1}$ is formed at the output of box **P'** with a probability of $p_3^{(i,i+1)}$.
3. The difference $\Delta^{(\mathbf{P''})}_{0}$ is formed at the output of box **P''** with a probability of $p_1^{(i)} = 2^{-q}$.
4. After two XOR operations are performed, a zero difference is formed at the input of box $\mathbf{P}^{-1}$, passing through this box with a probability of $p_4^{(i)} = 2^{-q}$.

Event A2

1. The difference $\Delta^{(\mathbf{G})}_{2|i,i+1}$ is formed at the output of operation **G** with a probability of $p_2^{(i)}$.

2. The difference $\Delta_0^{(\mathbf{P}')}$ is formed at the output of box **P'** with a probability of $p_3^{(i)} = 2^{-q}$.
3. The difference $\Delta_{2|i,i+1}^{(\mathbf{P}'')}$ is formed at the output of box **P"** with a probability of $p_1^{(i,i+1)}$.
4. After two XOR operations are performed, a zero difference is formed at the input of box $\mathbf{P}^{-1}$, passing through this box with a probability of $p_4^{(i)} = 2^{-q}$.

Event A3

1. The difference $\Delta_{2|i,i+1}^{(\mathbf{G})}$ is formed at the output of operation G with a probability of $p_2^{(i)}$.
2. The difference $\Delta_0^{(\mathbf{P}')}$ is formed at the output of box **P'** with a probability of $p_3^{(i)}$.
3. The difference $\Delta_0^{(\mathbf{P}')}$ is formed at the output of box **P"** with a probability of $p_1^{(i)}$.
4. After two XOR operations are performed, the D2|i,i+1 difference is formed at the input of box $\mathbf{P}^{-1}$ that is zeroed in this box with a probability of $p_4^{(i,i+1)}$.

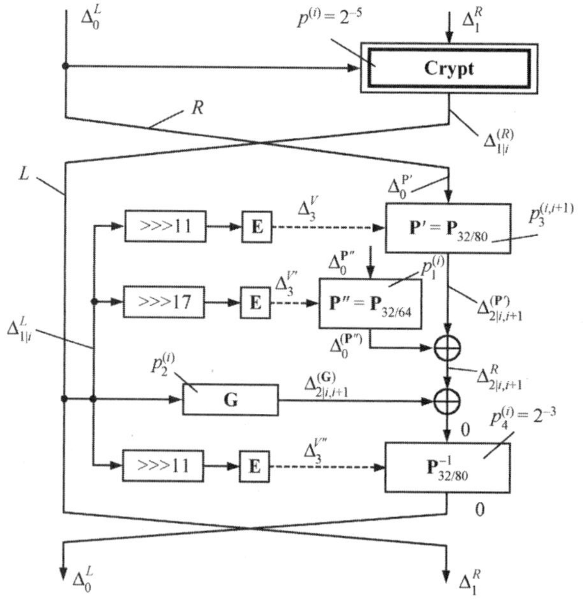

FIGURE 5.23 A two-round characteristic formation scheme in the SPECTR-H64 cipher for event A1.

Following is a brief explanation of the computation of the probability $p_2^{(i)}$. In it, we will write a general formula for bit computation in the ith order at the output of the **G** function specifying the $Y = \mathbf{G}(X, A, B)$ transformation, where A and B are subkeys used during the implementation of this transformation:

$$y_i = .x_i \oplus x_{i-1} \oplus x_{i-2}a_i \oplus x_{i-2}x_{i-5}b_i \oplus x_{i-3}x_{i-5} \oplus x_{i-4}b_i,$$

where a_i and b_i are subkey bits. From this last relationship, it is easy to derive the following formulas that characterize the changes in the y_i, y_{i+1}, y_{i+2}, y_{i+3}, y_{i+4}, y_{i+5} output bits, stipulated by changing the single input bit x_i ($\Delta x_i = 1$); namely,

$$\Delta y_i = \Delta x_i; \ \Delta y_i + 1 = \Delta x_i;$$

$$\Delta y_i + 2 = \Delta x_i(a_{i+2}); \ \Delta y_i + 3 = \Delta x_i(x_{i-2});$$

$$\Delta y_i + 4 = \Delta x_i(b_{i+4}); \ \Delta y_i + 5 = \Delta x_i(x_{i+2} \oplus x_{i+3} \oplus b_{i+5}).$$

Based on these formulas, it is easy to compute the following probability values:

$$p(\Delta y_i = 1/\Delta x_i = 1) = p(\Delta y_{i+1} = 1/\Delta x_i = 1) = 1.$$

and for $k = 2, 3, 4, 5$:

$$p(\Delta y_{i+k} = 0/\Delta x_i = 1) = 1/2.$$

Then, assuming that subkeys A and B are random equiprobable values, the value of $p_2^{(i)}$ is determined by the formula:

$$p^i_2 = p(\Delta y_i = 1/\Delta x_i = 1)\ p(\Delta y_{i+1} = 1/\Delta x_i = 1)\ p(\Delta y_{i+2} = 0/\Delta x_i = 1) \ ... \ p(\Delta y_{i+5} = 0/\Delta x_i = 1).$$

In the formula, you must take into account the limits on the maximum possible values of the indices i and i + k of the co-factors with Δy_{i+k}, which should not exceed 32.

The $p_2^{(i)}$ probabilities for various values of the i index are set forth here:

- $p_2^{(i)} = 0$ for $i = 1, 2$ because in these cases no less than three active bits are formed in the output difference.
- $p_2^{(i)} = 2^{-4}$ for $3 \le i \le 27$; this value, derived by the multiplication of all six co-factors, is present in the preceding formula.

With respect to the remark for values $i \geq 28$, we have:

- $i = 28$—$p_2^{(i)} = 2^{-3}$
- $i = 29$—$p_2^{(i)} = 2^{-2}$
- $i = 30$—$p_2^{(i)} = 2^{-1}$
- $i = 31$—$p_2^{(i)} = 1$
- $i = 32$—$p_2^{(i)} = 0$

To compute the probability of event A1, we can use the table of the influence distribution of the L subblock's bits on the elementary switches of box **P**'. Such a table can be easily created from the description of the SPECTR-H64 algorithm (Table 5.20), where cells mean $\mathbf{P}_{2/1}$ boxes, and the numbers in them (i) mean the numbers of the corresponding bits in subblock L.

TABLE 5.20 The Distribution of the Influence of Control Subblock L Bits in the P' Box

28	29	30	31	32	1	2	3	4	5	6	7	8	9	10	11
5	6	7	8	9	10	11	4	29	30	31	32	1	2	3	28
9	10	11	4	5	6	7	8	1	2	3	28	29	30	31	32
25	26	27	20	21	22	23	24	17	18	19	12	13	14	15	16
21	22	23	24	25	26	27	20	13	14	15	16	17	18	19	12

Using this table, you can determine all values of i for which the difference $\Delta_{2|i,i+1}^{(\mathbf{P}')}$ can appear at the output of box **P**', and also determine the value of the probability of this event; namely,

$$p(\Delta_0^{\mathbf{P}'} \rightarrow \Delta_{2|i,i+1}^{(\mathbf{P}')} / \Delta_{1|i}^{L}) = p_3^{(i,i+1)}$$

For example, at $i = 28$, the elementary boxes $\mathbf{P}_{2/1}^{(1)}$, $\mathbf{P}_{2/1}^{(32)}$, *and* $\mathbf{P}_{2/1}^{(44)}$ are active, and at the output of each of them with a probability of 0.5 a pair of active bits can appear (the superscript in designation $\mathbf{P}_{2/1}^{(j)}$ corresponds to the elementary box number). Only for box $\mathbf{P}_{2/1}^{(1)}$ can an output pair of active bits simultaneously enter into orders i and $i + 1$.

We are interested in the case of active bits appearing at the output of $\mathbf{P}_{2/1}^{(1)}$, with the simultaneous absence of active bits at the outputs of $\mathbf{P}_{2/1}^{(32)}$ and $\mathbf{P}_{2/1}^{(44)}$. The probability of this event is equal to $p_3^{(i,i+1)} = 2^{-3}2^{-4}2^{-4} = 2^{-11}$, since the left and the right output bits of box $\mathbf{P}_{2/1}^{(1)}$ will fall at the 28th and 29th bits, respectively, at the output of box **P**' with a probability of 2^{-4}.

Altogether, four bits of the left subblock (numbers 4, 8, 18, and 28) satisfy the situation described previously. For i = 4, 8, and 28, we have the probabilities $p_3^{(4,5)} = p_3^{(8,9)} = p_3^{(28,29)} = 2^{-11}$, and for i = 18, we have a probability of $p_3^{(18,19)} = 2^{-4}$. Note that the order i = 18 contributes the most in forming the value of the probability of the A1 event.

The probability of the difference Δ_1^R falling at the specified ith bit at the output of the first round is equal to $p^{(i)} = 2^{-5}$. The probability that no active bits in digits $i+2, i+3, i+4, i+5$ will be formed at the output of the **G** function (for $3 \leq i \leq 27$ and averaging by random round keys) is equal to $p_2^{(i)} = 2^{-4}$. Accordingly, for i = 28, $p_2^{(28,29)} = 2^{-3}$.Thus, we have the following integrated probability for the A1 event:

$$P' = \sum_{i=1}^{i=32} p^{(i)} p_1^{(i)} p_2^{(i)} p_3^{(i,i+1)} p_4^{(i)} = \sum_{i=4,8,18,28} p^{(i)} p_1^{(i)} p_2^{(i)} p_3^{(i,i+1)} p_4^{(i)} \approx 2^{-17}.$$

The predominant contribution to the value of P' is made by the 18th bit in the left subblock, for which the probability values are higher—$p_1^{(18)}$, $p_4^{(18)}$, and $p_3^{(18,19)}$ ($p_1^{(18)} = p_4^{(18)} = 2^{-2}$, and $p_3^{(18,19)} = 2^{-4}$).

In the A1 event, for all values of i, we have $p_1^{(i)} = 2^{-3}$, and for events A1 and A2, we have $p^{(i)} = 2^{-5}$ and $p_4^{(i)} = 2^{-3}$.

With respect to the full symmetry of the direct (**P**') and inverse ($\mathbf{P}^{-1}$) controlled permutations transforming the right data subblock in one round of the SPECTR-H64 cipher, the probabilities of the A1 and A3 events are the same; that is:

$$P''' = P' \approx 2^{-17}.$$

Assuming that the key element at the input of box **P**'' is an equiprobable random value, it is easy to compute the probability of the A2 event using the following formula, which is similar to the previous one:

$$P'' = \sum_{i=1}^{i=32} p^{(i)} p_1^{(i,i+1)} p_2^{(i)} p_3^{(i)} p_4^{(i)} = \sum_{i=4,8,12,16,21} p^{(i)} p_1^{(i,i+1)} p_2^{(i)} p_3^{(i)} p_4^{(i)} \approx 2^{-15}.$$

In the A2 event, for all values of i, we have $p_3^{(i)} = 2^{-3}$. However, when $p_1^{(i,i+1)}$ values are computed, Table 6.4 should be used instead of Table 5.21. Because before the left subblock enters the **E** expansion box, it is subject to transformation by a cycle shift operation not by 11, but by 17 bits. The predominant contribution to the value of the probability of P'' is made by the 21st order, for which $p_1^{(21,22)} = 2^{-2}$ and $p_3^{(21)} = p_4^{(21)} = 2^{-2}$.

Thus, the probability of the difference $(0, \Delta_1^R)$ passing through two rounds is equal to $P(2) \approx P' + P'' + P''' \approx 1.5 \cdot 2^{-15}$.

TABLE 5.21 The Distribution of the Influence of Control Subblock L Bits in the P" Box

2	3	4	5	6	7	8	9	10	11	12	13	14	15	16	17
11	12	13	14	15	16	17	10	3	4	5	6	7	8	9	2
15	16	17	10	11	12	13	14	7	8	9	2	3	4	5	6
31	32	1	26	27	28	29	30	23	24	25	18	19	20	21	22
27	28	29	30	31	32	1	26	19	20	21	22	23	24	25	18

In this value of $P(2)$, the contribution of the events corresponding to the appearance of four or six active bits in the output difference of the **G** function is not taken into account, nor are the events with two active bits leading to the simultaneous formation of three differences $\Delta^{(\mathbf{G})}_{2|i,i+1}$, $\Delta^{(\mathbf{P}')}_{2|i,z}$, and $\Delta^{(\mathbf{P}'')}_{2|i+1,z}$ that meet the condition:

$$\Delta^{(\mathbf{G})}_{2|i,i+1} \oplus \Delta^{(\mathbf{P}')}_{2|i,z} \oplus \Delta^{(\mathbf{P}'')}_{2|i+1,z} = 0.$$

These events may be neglected, since their integral probability is considerably less than 1.5×2^{-15}.

With respect to the mechanisms revealed during the computation of the probabilities of the events being considered (A1 and A2), we can conclude that a cipher's security against differential cryptanalysis depends considerably on the distribution of control bits in expansion box **E**. In addition, the value of the probability of a two-round differential characteristic can be reduced if expansion box **E** is optimized. For example, if you swap the numbers 21 and 20 in the lower line of Table 5.20, and swap 18 and 19 in Table 5.21, this permutation enables you to reduce the probability values; namely, $P' \approx 2^{-23}$, $P'' \approx 2^{-21}$, and $P(2) \approx 1.5 \times 2^{-21}$. That is, this permutation leads to the reduction of the probability of the two-round characteristic by approximately 2^6 times.

After such a change, the most efficient differential characteristic is a three-round one, considered here.

Indeed, there is another differential characteristic available for the SPECTR-H64 cipher that corresponds to differences with a small number of active bits. This characteristic corresponds to the difference $(0, \Delta^R_1)$ passing through three rounds. Its formation is described by the following mechanism. After the first round, the active bit enters the 32nd order with a probability of 2^{-5}. In the second round, the active bit passing through the **G** operation with a probability of 1 generates an active bit in the difference going through the right branch that, with a probability of 2^{-5}, turns out to be in the 32nd bit at the output of the right branch of the second round. The probability that no additional active bits will appear in the right branch during the performance of three controlled permutation operations is equal to $(2^{-3})^3 = 2^{-9}$. The differences $\Delta^L_{1|32}$ and $\Delta^R_{1|32}$ are distributed through the third round. With a probability of 2^{-5}, the active bit of the right difference turns out to be in the 32nd order, after the **P'** operation is performed, and is zeroed after the XOR operation with an output difference of $\Delta^{G}_{1|32}$ is performed. In the third round, also with a probability of 2^{-9}, three controlled permutation operations will not generate new active bits. Taking into account the given scheme of the (Δ_0^L, Δ_1^R) difference's distribution in three rounds, we have the following probability value for it: $P(3) \approx 2^{-28}$ (the "approximately equal" symbol takes into account the fact that we neglect the contribution of events where intermediary differences with several active bits in the right subblock are formed). Accordingly, for six rounds, the probability of the (Δ_0^L, Δ_1^R) difference passing with the given three-round characteristic is equal to $P''(6) \approx (2^{-28})^2 = 2^{-56}$, and with the two-round characteristic, it is $P'(6) \approx (1.5 \times 2^{-15})^3 \approx 1.7 \times 2^{-44} >> P''(6)$. Thus, when a six-round characteristic with one active bit is formed, a two-round characteristic is more efficient for analyzing the SPECTR-H64 encryption algorithm.

It is possible to derive the following probability values using a two-round characteristic for building differential characteristics with an even number of rounds:

$$P(8) \approx (1.5 \times 2^{-15})^4 \approx 5 \times 2^{-60} > 2^{-64}$$

$$P(10) \approx (1.5 \times 2^{-15})^5 \approx 2^{-72} << 2^{-64}$$

$$P(12) \approx (1.5 \times 2^{-15})^6 \approx 2^{-87} << 2^{-64}$$

These last relationships prove that if 10 or 12 encryption rounds are used by SPECTR-H64 encryption algorithms, the use of corresponding characteristics based on a two-round characteristic with one active bit is not applicable for cipher decryption, since these characteristics do not allow us to distinguish the SPECTR-H64 cipher from a random cipher. That is, we can say that the SPECTR-H64 algorithm is secure against the considered variant of differential analysis.

Basically, a variant with eight encryption rounds can be decrypted after about 2^{60} pairs of specially selected 64-bit input data blocks are encrypted, although such an attack most likely cannot be practically implemented.

As we mentioned previously, the corresponding probability for a two-round characteristic of the SPECTR-H64 cipher can be considerably reduced by optimizing an **E** expansion box **E**. For a three-round characteristic, however, the analogous probability is weakly dependent on the type of control bit distribution specified by the **E** expansion. Therefore, after the SPECTR-H64 cipher is modernized, its security against differential cryptanalysis will be determined by the three-round characteristic. To reduce the probability in the three-round characteristic, it is additionally required that you change the boolean functions specifying a specific type of **G** operation.

5.6.4 Differential Cryptanalysis of the SPECTR-128 Cipher

The structure of the SPECTR-128 iterative cryptosystem is analogous to that of the SPECTR-H64 algorithm, which determines the similarity of the differential properties of both ciphers. For SPECTR-128 algorithms, differential characteristics with a small number of active bits also have the largest probabilities. The largest probability has a characteristic corresponding to the difference (Δ_0^L, Δ_1^R) passing through two rounds. The mechanism of its distribution is analogous to that of SPECTR-H64. However, due to the peculiarities of the **G** operation and the bigger size of the subblocks being transformed, computations are more intricate. When differential cryptanalysis is performed, you must take account of the fact that, if only one input bit of the **G** operation is changed, one bit will be surely changed at its output, corresponding to the same order as the changed input bit. Besides which, six more bits can be changed with a probability of 0.5. The main variants of a two-round characteristic formation are connected with the appearance of the differences $\Delta^{(G)}_{2|i,i+1}$, $\Delta^{(G)}_{2|i,i+3}$, $\Delta^{(G)}_{2|i,i+6}$, $\Delta^{(G)}_{2|i,i+7}$, $\Delta^{(G)}_{2|i,i+8}$, and $\Delta^{(G)}_{2|i,i+9}$ at the output of the **G** operation. Each of these differences contributes to the value of the probability of the two-round characteristic. This contribution is computed in a manner similar to that used in the SPECTR-H64 algorithm for the specified i, and when an output difference $\Delta^{(G)}_{2|i,i+1}$ with two active bits is considered. The possibility of the appearance of different differences at the output of the **G** operation can be taken into account in events A1, A2, and A3, which is done here. Using the dependence of the output bits values expressed as a boolean function, it is easy to derive formulas expressing the changes in the output bits having numbers $i + k$, where $k = 0, 1, 2, \ldots, 9$ (Table 5.22).

Let's consider events A1, A2, and A3 (Figure 5.24) for SPECTR-128.

TABLE 5.22 The Probability of Active Bit Generation at the Output of the G Operation in the $(i + k)$th Order, When the ith Input Bit Is Changed

Formula	Probability
$\Delta y_i = \Delta l_i$	$p(\Delta y_i=1) = 1$
$\Delta y_{i+1} = \Delta l_i(a^{(4)}_{i-1} \oplus a^{(3)}_{i-1} l_{i-8} \oplus a^{(4)}_{i} l_{i-5} l_{i-8})$	$p(\Delta y_{i+1}=1) = ½½$
$\Delta y_{i+2} = 0$	$p(\Delta y_{i+2}=1) = 0$
$\Delta y_{i+3} = \Delta l_i\, l_{i-6}$	$p(\Delta y_{i+3}=1) = ½½$
$\Delta y_{i+4} = 0$	$p(\Delta y_{i+4}=1) = 0$
$\Delta y_{i+5} = 0$	$p(\Delta y_{i+5}=1) = 0$
$\Delta y_{i+6} = \Delta l_i(l_{i-2} \oplus l_{i-3} l_{i+5} a^{(4)}_{i+5})$	$p(\Delta y_{i+6}=1) = ½½$
$\Delta y_{i+7} = \Delta l_i a^{(3)}_{i+5})$	$p(\Delta y_{i+7}=1) = ½½$
$\Delta y_{i+8} = \Delta l_i l_{i+2}$	$p(\Delta y_{i+8}=1) = ½½$
$\Delta y_{i+9} = \Delta l_i(l_{i+6} \oplus l_{i+8} a^{(3)}_{i+7} \oplus l_{i+3} l_{i+8} a^{(4)}_{i+8})$	$p(\Delta y_{i+9}=1) = ½½$

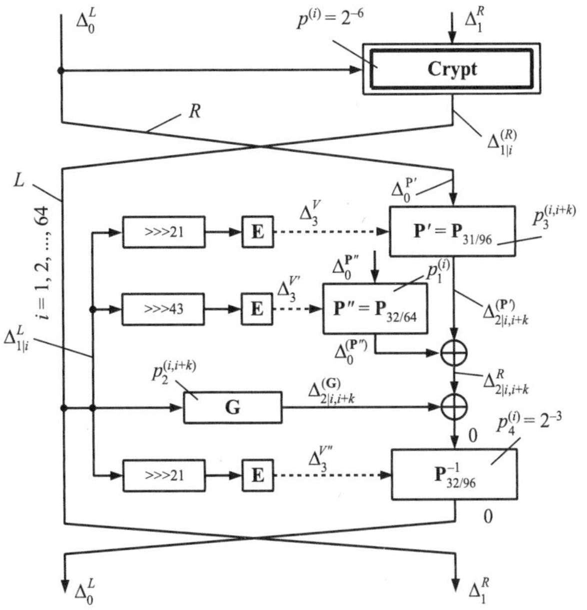

FIGURE 5.24 The two-round characteristic formation scheme in the SPECTR-128 cipher for event A1.

Event A1

1. The difference $\Delta^{(\mathbf{G})}_{2|i,i+k}$ is formed at the output of operation G with a probability of $p_2^{(i,i+k)}$, where $k \in \{1, 3, 6, 7, 8, 9\}$.
2. The difference $\Delta^{(\mathbf{P}')}_{2|i,i+k}$ is formed at the output of box **P'** with a probability of $p_3^{(i,i+k)}$.
3. The difference $\Delta_0^{(\mathbf{P}'')}$ is formed at the output of box **P''** with a probability of $p_1^{(i)} = 2^{-3}$.
4. After two XOR operations are performed, a zero difference is formed at the input of box $\mathbf{P}^{-1}_{64/192}$, passing through this box with a probability of $p_4^{(i)} = 2^{-3}$.

Event A2

1. The difference $\Delta^{(\mathbf{G})}_{2|i,i+k}$ is formed at the output of operation G with a probability of $p_2^{(i,i+k)}$.
2. The difference $\Delta_0^{(\mathbf{P}')}$ is formed at the output of box **P'** with a probability of $p_3^{(i)} = 2^{-3}$.
3. The difference $\Delta^{(\mathbf{P}'')}_{2|i,i+k}$ is formed at the output of box **P''** with a probability of $p_1^{(i,i+k)}$.

4. After two XOR operations are performed, a zero difference is formed at the input of box $\mathbf{P}^{-1}_{64/192}$, passing through this box with a probability of $p_4^{(i)} = 2^{-3}$.

Event A3

1. The difference $\Delta^{(\mathbf{G})}_{2|i,i+k}$ is formed at the output of operation G with a probability of $p_2^{(i,i+k)}$.
2. The difference $\Delta_0^{(\mathbf{P'})}$ is formed at the output of box **P'** with a probability of $p_3^{(i)} = 2^{-3}$.
3. The difference $\Delta_0^{(\mathbf{P''})}$ is formed at the output of box **P"** with a probability of $p_1^{(i)} = 2^{-3}$.
4. After two XOR operations are performed, the $\Delta_{2|i,i+k}$ difference is formed at the input of box $\mathbf{P}^{-1}$, which is zeroed in this box with a probability of $p_4^{(i,i+k)}$.

As in the case with the SPECTR-H64 algorithm, due to the symmetry of events A1 and A3, they have the same probabilities. Therefore, it will suffice to determine probabilities of events A1 and A2.

Using the description of the SPECTR-128 algorithm to compute events A1 and A2, we will compile the tables of the distribution of the left subblock bits in control of the elementary switches of boxes **P'** and **P"** (Tables 5.23 and 5.24).

TABLE 5.23 Distribution of Subblock L Bits in the P' Box of the SPECTR-128 Cipher

Left part of P′ (corresponds to input bits with numbers from 1 to 32)															
54	55	56	57	58	59	60	61	62	63	64	1	2	3	4	5
7	8	9	10	11	12	13	14	15	16	17	18	19	20	21	6
15	16	17	18	19	20	21	6	7	8	9	10	11	12	13	14
47	48	49	50	51	52	53	38	39	40	41	42	43	44	45	46
39	40	41	42	43	44	45	46	47	48	49	50	51	52	53	38
22	23	24	25	26	27	28	29	30	31	32	33	34	35	36	37
Right part of P′ (corresponds to input bits with numbers from 33 to 64)															
6	7	8	9	10	11	12	13	14	15	16	17	18	19	20	21
55	56	57	58	59	60	61	62	63	64	1	2	3	4	5	54
63	64	1	2	3	4	5	54	55	56	57	58	59	60	61	62
31	32	33	34	35	36	37	22	23	24	25	26	27	28	29	30
23	24	25	26	27	28	29	30	31	32	33	34	35	36	37	22
38	39	40	41	42	43	44	45	46	47	48	49	50	51	52	53

TABLE 5.24 Distribution of Subblock L Bits in the P'' Box of the SPECTR-128 Cipher

Left part of P''															
12	13	14	15	16	17	18	19	20	21	22	23	24	25	26	27
29	30	31	32	33	34	35	36	37	38	39	40	41	42	43	28
37	38	39	40	41	42	43	28	29	30	31	32	33	34	35	36
5	6	7	8	9	10	11	60	61	62	63	64	1	2	3	4
61	62	63	64	1	2	3	4	5	6	7	8	9	10	11	60
44	45	46	47	48	49	50	51	52	53	54	55	56	57	58	59
Right part of P''															
28	29	30	31	32	33	34	35	36	37	38	39	40	41	42	43
13	14	15	16	17	18	19	20	21	22	23	24	25	26	27	12
21	22	23	24	25	26	27	12	13	14	15	16	17	18	19	20
53	54	55	56	57	58	59	44	45	46	47	48	49	50	51	52
45	46	47	48	49	50	51	52	53	54	55	56	57	58	59	44
60	61	62	63	64	1	2	3	4	5	6	7	8	9	10	11

The probability of event A1 is computed by the formula:

$$P' = \sum_{i=1}^{64}\sum_{k=1}^{9} p^{(i)} p_1^{(i)} p_2^{(i,i+k)} p_3^{(i,i+k)} p_4^{(i)} \approx 1.5\times 2^{-21},$$

where $p^{(i)} = 2^{-6}$ is the probability of the transition of the active bit of the difference into the ith order after the first round. Using the structure of box $\mathbf{P}_{64/192}^{-1}$ and Tables 5.23 and 5.24, it is easy to determine the probability values included in this sum. In addition, the variant corresponding to the active bit in the 43rd order of the left subblock, for which the probability is $p_3^{(43,44)} = 2^{-3}$ (about 70 percent of the value of P') contributes the most to the probability value. About 15 percent fall on numbers $i = 33$ and 34, for which $p_3^{(33,39)} = p_3^{(33,40)}$. The remaining share falls on values where $i = 3, 7, 8, 11, 12, 15, 16, 20$, and 54.

The probability of event A2 is computed by the formula:

$$P'' = \sum_{i=1}^{64}\sum_{k=1}^{9} p^{(i)} p_1^{(i,i+k)} p_2^{(i,i+k)} p_3^{(i)} p_4^{(i)} \approx 1.3\cdot 2^{-21}.$$

The cases where $i = 54$ and 57 ($p_1^{(54,55)} = p_1^{(57,60)} = 2^{-5}$), and $i = 9, 10, 11, 44$ ($p_1^{(9,15)} = p_1^{(9,16)} = p_1^{(10,13)} = p_1^{(10,16)} = p_1^{(11,14)} = p_1^{(44,45)} = p_1^{(44,47)} = 2^{-7}$), are the main contributors to the probability of P''. The probability of the difference (Δ_0^L, Δ_1^R) passing through two rounds is $P(2) \approx P' + P'' + P''' \approx 1.1 \times 2^{-19}$.

We should mention that, as with the differential property analysis of the SPECTR-H64 cipher, certain features of the distribution of the influence of the left subblock bits exert a considerable influence upon controlled permutation operations. It is possible to easily reduce the probability of $P(2)$ by introducing insignificant changes in expansion box **E**.

There is also a three-round characteristic available for the SPECTR-128 cipher that corresponds to the difference (Δ_0^L, Δ_1^R) passing through three rounds. Unlike the SPECTR-H64 algorithm, the passing of the (Δ_0^L, Δ_1^R) difference is not related to the active bit of the left subblock's number $i = 32$. Each bit makes its contribution, since, due to the use of a **G** operation that is different from the one used in the SPECTR-H64 cipher, the availability of the active bit in the L subblock changes only one bit at the output of this operation in a predefined manner. The scheme of a three-round characteristic formation is shown in Figure 5.25.

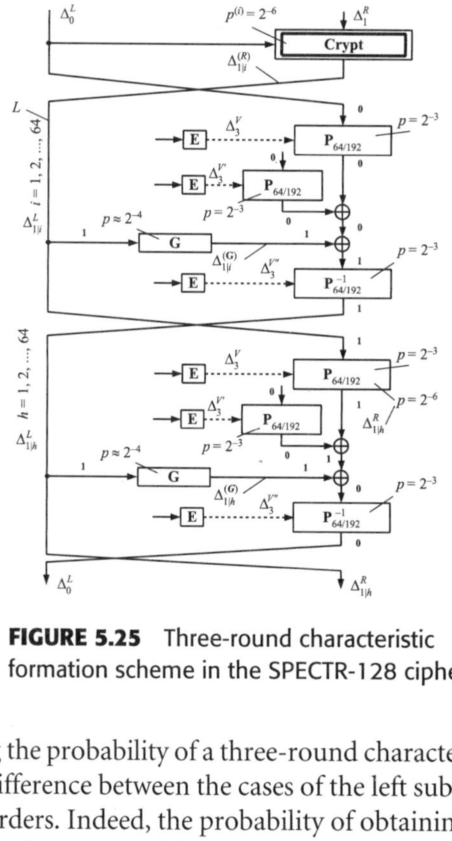

FIGURE 5.25 Three-round characteristic formation scheme in the SPECTR-128 cipher.

When computing the probability of a three-round characteristic, $P(3)$, you need to be able to tell the difference between the cases of the left subblock's active bit distribution in various orders. Indeed, the probability of obtaining the difference $\Delta_{1|i}^{(\mathbf{G})}$ for different i values at the output of the **G** operation is equal to:

- $p = 2^{-6}$ for $i = 1, 2, \ldots, 55$
- $p = 2^{-5}$ for $i = 56$
- $p = 2^{-4}$ for $i = 57$
- $p = 2^{-3}$ for $i = 58$
- $p = 2^{-2}$ for $i = 59, 60, 61$
- $p = 2^{-1}$ for $i = 62, 63$
- $p = 1$ for $i = 64$

If i is a uniformly distributed random variable, it is easy to derive the average probability of the occurrence of difference $\Delta_1^{(\mathbf{G})}$ with one active bit at the output of the **G** operation; namely,

$$p(\Delta_1^{(\mathbf{G})}) = 0.97 \cdot 2^{-4} \approx 2^{-4}$$

In the second and third rounds, one active bit is distributed in the left arm. In each of these rounds, the probability of nongeneration of the active bit pairs at the outputs of three controlled permutation boxes is 2^{-9}. In addition, in the second round, an active bit in the right subblock is generated because of the **G** operation. In the third round, the active bit of the right branch is zeroed by the active bit of the difference $\Delta_{1|h}^{(\mathbf{G})}$ with a probability of 2^{-6} (this is the probability of shifting the right subblock's active bit to the specified hth order by the operation $\mathbf{P}_{64/192}$). With respect to these remarks, it easy to have $P(3) \approx 2^{-32}$.

The contribution of the three-round characteristic to the probability of the difference (Δ_0^L, Δ_1^R) passing through six rounds is $P''(6) < (2^{-32})^2 = 2^{-64}$. The two-round characteristic contribution is $P'(6) \approx (1.1 \cdot 2^{-19})^3 \approx 1.3 \cdot 2^{-57} >> P''(6)$. Thus, when the security of the SPECTR-128 cipher is determined, a two-round characteristic is more efficient.

It is possible to derive the following probabilities using the value of the probability $P(2)$:

- $P(8) \approx (1.1 \times 2^{-19})^4 \approx 1.5 \times 2^{-76}$
- $P(10) \approx (1.1 \times 2^{-19})^5 \approx 1.7 \times 2^{-95}$
- $P(12) \approx (1.1 \times 2^{-19})^6 \approx 2^{-113}$

If you compare the probabilities of the two-round characteristics of SPECTR-H64 and SPECTR-128, you are likely to notice that the value of $P(2)$ for SPECTR-H64 is higher than the value of $P(2)$ for SPECTR-128. The first one, however, is undistinguishable from a random cipher with the help of differential cryptanalysis, and the second is distinguishable due to the large size of the input block.

Indeed, for a random 128-bit cipher, the probability of the occurrence of a random output difference is 2^{-128}, whereas for SPECTR-128, the probability $P(12)$

of the (Δ_0^L, Δ_1^R) output difference is approximately equal to 2^{-113}. Therefore, with the use of the (Δ_0^L, Δ_1^R) difference considered here, it is possible to distinguish the SPECTR-128 cipher from a random one. However, you will have to perform an unrealizable number of encryption operations with 128-bit data blocks. For example, for the 10-round variant of the SPECTR-128 cipher, it would be necessary to perform more than 2^{94} encryption operations with 128-bit data blocks.

This cipher can be reinforced either by adding two supplementary encryption rounds, or by optimizing the **E** expansion box and the **G** operation. The second variant enables you to reduce the value of $P(2)$ down to a value of 2^{-25}.

Differential cryptanalysis of the SPECTR-H64 and SPECTR-128 ciphers is one of the steps in designing ciphers based on controlled operations. Depending on the differential characteristic values obtained and the peculiarities of difference distribution revealed, this step requires amendments aimed at improving the considered characteristics, after which a differential cryptanalysis should be performed again.

The Security of the SPECTR-128 Cryptosystem with a Modified Expansion Box

We mentioned in the previous section that the probability of a two-round characteristic of SPECTR-128 considerably depends on the bit distribution of the control data subblock along the elementary switches of the controlled permutation box. Such a distribution for the **P'** box is additionally determined by a rotation operation by 21 bits, and for box **P''** by 43 bits, and by extension box **E**.

Leaving the rotation values unchanged, you can reduce the probability of the two-round characteristic by modifying the table that describes extension box **E**. When such a modification is performed, it is best to follow the criterion according to which, with any value of the control subblock, each bit of a controlled permutation box is only influenced by a arbitrary control bit once.

Table 5.25 is a modified expansion box **E** with amendments that reduce the probabilities of events A1, A2, and A3 to zero.

The last circumstance leads to the fact that other events, which before modification contributed much less to the probability of the two-round characteristic and could be neglected, are now deciding factors. Let's consider these events and their contribution.

Event B. This event includes the following events:

1. The difference $\Delta_{2|i,i+k}^{(\mathbf{G})}$ is formed at the output of the G operation with a probability of $p_2^{(i,i+k)}$.
2. The difference $\Delta_{2|i,t}^{(\mathbf{P'})}$ is formed at the output of box **P'** with a probability of $p_3^{(i,t)}$ and the difference $\Delta_{2|i+k,t}^{(\mathbf{P''})}$ is formed at the output of box **P''** with a probability of $p_1^{(i+k,t)}$, or, the difference $\Delta_{2|i+k,t}^{(\mathbf{P'})}$ is formed at the output of box **P'** with a probability of $p_3^{(i+k,t)}$ and the difference $\Delta_{2|i,t}^{(\mathbf{P''})}$ is formed at the output of box **P''** with a probability of $p_1^{(i,t)}$.

TABLE 5.25 Bit Distribution at the Output of the Expansion Box (the Numbers of Bits and of the Binary Vector Entering Expansion Box E's Input Are Indicated)

Left part of E (corresponds to input bits with numbers from 1 to 32)															
33	34	35	36	37	38	39	40	41	42	43	44	62	63	34	60
50	41	52	53	42	61	56	57	61	38	48	55	45	46	47	49
58	59	45	58	62	49	64	63	33	51	52	53	54	55	39	54
26	27	28	29	1	19	10	17	18	31	20	21	22	23	24	25
18	19	20	21	14	23	24	25	26	27	28	29	30	31	32	17
1	2	3	4	5	6	7	8	9	10	11	12	13	14	15	16
Right part of E (corresponds to input bits with numbers from 33 to 64)															
35	36	37	43	44	54	55	56	57	58	59	60	61	62	63	64
64	49	50	51	38	39	40	41	42	48	53	45	46	47	52	33
57	46	44	60	43	47	48	50	34	35	36	37	59	56	40	51
32	11	8	9	22	15	16	30	2	3	4	5	6	7	12	13
2	3	4	5	6	7	8	9	10	1	12	13	22	15	16	11
17	18	19	20	21	28	23	24	25	26	27	22	29	30	31	32

3. A zero difference that appears as a result of Events B1 and B2, as well as after the performance of two XOR operations, passes through the controlled permutation box $\mathbf{P}^{-1}$ with a probability of 2^{-3}.

The probability of Event B2 is equal to $p_{1,3}^{(i,i+k)} = p_3^{(i,t)} p_1^{(i+k,t)} + p_3^{(i+k,t)} p_1^{(i,t)}$. On the whole, the contribution of Event B to the probability of the two-round characteristic is $P' \approx 1.5 \times 2^{-30}$.

Event C. This event includes the following events:

1. The difference $\Delta_{2|i,i+k}^{(\mathbf{G})}$ is formed at the output of the G operation with a probability of $p_2^{(i,i+k)}$.
2. The difference $\Delta_0^{(\mathbf{P}')}$ is formed at the output of box P' with a probability of $p_3^{(i)} = 2^{-3}$.
3. The difference $\Delta_{2|i+k,t}^{(\mathbf{P}'')}$ is formed at the output of box P" with a probability of $p_1^{(i+k,t)}$, or difference $\Delta_{2|i,t}^{(\mathbf{P}'')}$ is formed with a probability of $p_1^{(i,t)}$.
4. After two XOR operations are performed, the differences $\Delta'_{2|i,t} = \Delta_0^{(\mathbf{P}')} \oplus \Delta_{2|i,i+k}^{(\mathbf{G})} \oplus \Delta_{2|i+k,t}^{(\mathbf{P}'')}$ and $\Delta'_{2|i+k,t} = \Delta_0^{(\mathbf{P}')} \oplus \Delta_{2|i,i+k}^{(\mathbf{G})} \oplus \Delta_{2|i,t}^{(\mathbf{P}'')}$ are "transformed" by box $\mathbf{P}^{-1}$ into a zero difference with probabilities of $p_4^{(i,t)}$ and $p_4^{(i+k,t)}$, respectively.

Event **C** includes the occurrence of two active bits with numbers i and t (or $i + k$ and t) at the input of box $\mathbf{P}^{-1}$, and the "annihilation" of this pair of active bits in one of three active elementary $\mathbf{P}_{2/1}$ boxes within box $\mathbf{P}^{-1}$.

Since Event **C** is "symmetric" to Event **B**, then $P' = P(\mathbf{C}) = P(\mathbf{B}) = P''$. That is, the contribution of Events **B** and **C** to the probability of the two-round characteristic $P(2)$ is the same.

Event D. This event includes the following events:

1. The difference $\Delta^{(\mathbf{G})}_{2|i,i+k}$ is formed at the output of the G operation with a probability of $p_2^{(i,i+k)}$.
2. The difference $\Delta_0^{(\mathbf{P}'')}$ is formed at the output of box P" with a probability of $p_1^{(i)} = 2^{-3}$.
3. The difference $\Delta^{(\mathbf{P}')}_{2|i+k,t}$ is formed at the output of box **P**' with a probability of $p_3^{(i+k,t)}$, or the difference $\Delta^{(\mathbf{P}')}_{2|i,t}$ is formed with a probability of $p_3^{(i,t)}$.
4. After two XOR operations are performed, the differences $\Delta'_{2|i,t} = \Delta_0^{(\mathbf{P}'')} \oplus \Delta^{(\mathbf{G})}_{2|i,i+k} \oplus \Delta^{(\mathbf{P}')}_{2|i+k,t}$ and $\Delta'_{2|i+k,t} = \Delta_0^{(\mathbf{P}'')} \oplus \Delta^{(\mathbf{G})}_{2|i,i+k} \oplus \Delta^{(\mathbf{P}')}_{2|i,t}$ are "transformed" by box $\mathbf{P}^{-1}$ into a zero difference with probabilities of $p_4^{(i,t)}$ and $p_4^{(i+k,t)}$, respectively.

Event **D** is analogous to Event **C**. One feature of Event **D** is that two controlled permutation boxes with symmetric structure are considered, and the active elementary switches positioned symmetrically are as well. The contribution of Event **D** to the probability $P(2)$, computed assuming that round subkeys are uniformly distributed random variables, is $P''' \approx 1.1 \times 2^{-28}$.

Taking into account the contribution of Events **B**, **C**, and **D** to the probability $P(2)$, the value of the probability $P(2)$ for the two-round characteristic, after expansion box **E** is modified, looks like this:

$$P(2) = P' + P'' + P''' \approx 1.85 \cdot 2^{-28} \approx 2^{-27}.$$

Thus, modification of expansion box **E** enables us to reduce the probability of the two-round characteristic by approximately 2^8 times. Correspondingly, the security of the modified SPECTR-128 cipher against differential cryptanalysis is now determined by a three-round characteristic, for which such a modification of the **E** expansion box is not crucial.

That is, using the three-round characteristic probability value $P(3) \approx 2^{-32}$ for the source model of the SPECTR-128 cipher, the probability $P(12)$ of difference $(\Delta^L{}_0, \Delta^R{}_1)$ passing through all twelve rounds is the following:

$$P(12) \approx (2^{-32})^4 = 2^{-128}.$$

The derived value does not exceed the probability value of the specified occurrence of the difference for a random cipher, and so the application of the considered differential characteristics does not allow us to use differential cryptanalysis to decrypt the modified variant of SPECTR-128.

The considered example, which includes the initial and modified version of the SPECTR-128 algorithm, demonstrates a certain step in cipher design based on controlled permutations, where the structure of expansion box **E** is of crucial importance. The structure of expansion box **E** is initially selected with respect to a general criterion, after which the probabilities are computed for the most significant differential characteristics. Then, based on the revealed features of the control data subblock bit distribution, a modification of expansion box **E** is performed, which leads to the reduction of the probabilities of the indicated characteristics, after which differential cryptanalysis should be performed once again.

5.6.5 Main Differential Characteristics of the DDP-S64 and DDP-S128 Ciphers

The DDP-S64 and DDP-S128 ciphers have a structure of round transformation that is different from that of the SPECTR-H64 and SPECTR-128 cryptosystems. However, due to use of the controlled permutation box $\mathbf{P}^{(L,e)}_{32/32}$ as a base primitive for all four ciphers, when variants of differential characteristics are considered, it is possible to establish that characteristics with a small number of bits have the greatest probability. The mechanism for forming such characteristics for the first pair of ciphers differs from that of the second pair, because no **G** operations with two active bit differences formed at the output are used in DDP-S64 and DDP-S128. These ciphers also differ in the mechanism of passing differences through two rounds, although in both ciphers the most efficient characteristics are connected with the permutation of one of the active bits in the necessary digit after the difference has passed the controlled permutation box.

Analysis of the DDP-S64 Cipher

This cipher has a one-round characteristic with a difference (Δ_0^A, Δ_1^B), where Δ_0^A and Δ_1^B are the left and right subblocks of input difference. This difference passes through one round in the following way (Figure 5.26). The right subblock that passed through one of the controlled permutation operations is superposed over the left subblock using a modulo 2^{32} addition operation, introducing at least one active bit into it.

We are interested in the case of the formation of one active bit in the left subblock. Before the round is completed, the left subblock Δ_1^A that passed through operation $\mathbf{P}^{(A,0)}_{32/32}$ participates in the transformation of the right subblock using a modulo 2^{32} subtraction operation. Thanks to the controlled permutation operation over both subblocks, the active bits turn out to have the same number with a probability of 2^{-5}. As a result, after the subtraction operation is completed, the active bit in the right subblock is zeroed with an averaged probability close to 0.5. The round

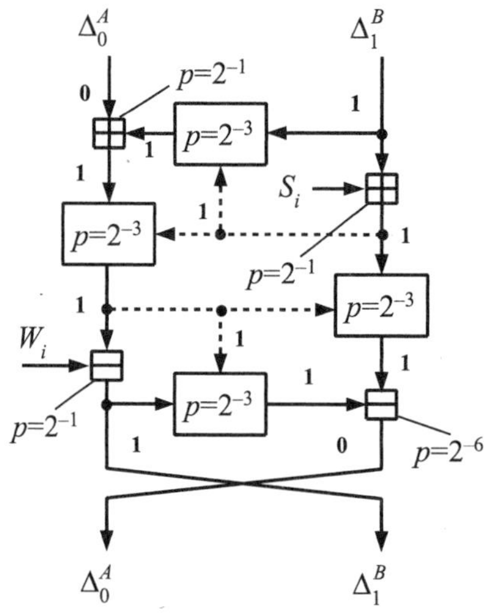

FIGURE 5.26 A one-round characteristic formation scheme in the DDP-S64 cipher.

is completed with the permutation of subblocks Δ_1^A and Δ_1^B that form an output difference that coincides with the input one.

In this mechanism, one of the active bits is subjected to arithmetic operations four times. The active bit passes through each of these operations without forming a carry bit with a probability $\approx 2^{-1}$. When four controlled permutation operations are performed, the control input of the corresponding controlled permutation box is fed with one active bit. The probability that no active bits are generated during the performance of one controlled permutation operation is approximately equal to 2^{-3} (the fact that a nonzero difference passes through the controlled permutation box is considered). In addition, taking into account the probabilities of all these events related to passing the difference through one round, we compute the probability of the one-round characteristic:

$$P(1) \approx (2^{-1})^4 \cdot (2^{-3})^4 \cdot 2^{-5} = 2^{-21}.$$

The two-round characteristic (Δ_1^A, Δ_0^B) is more efficient, and this should be remembered when the number of encryption rounds is selected in order to obtain a pseudorandom transformation. The scheme of this difference passing through two rounds is shown in Figure 5.27.

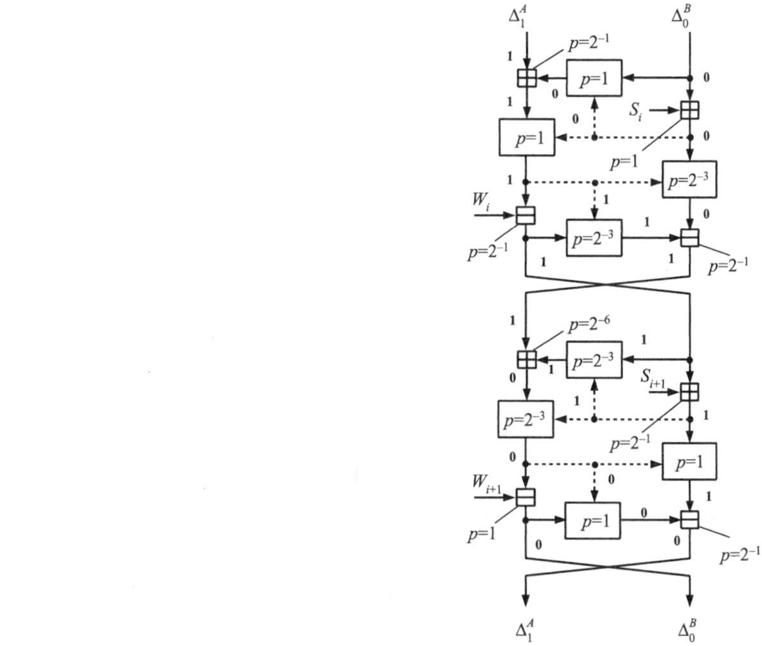

FIGURE 5.27 The scheme for forming a two-round characteristic in the DDP-S64 cipher.

The algorithm of this difference passing through two rounds goes like this:

1. An active bit of the left subblock generates an active bit in the right one in the end of the first round when a modulo 2^{32} subtraction operation is performed.
2. Then, the difference (Δ_1^A, Δ_1^B) enters the input of the second round.
3. At the start of the second round, the active bit of the left subblock is zeroed after the modulo 2^{32} addition operation is performed.
4. A zero difference is distributed around the left branch of the second round.

In the first round, the active bit is subjected to three arithmetic operations, and influences the performance of two controlled permutation operations, which determines the formation of the probability of the difference (Δ_1^A, Δ_1^B) at the output of the first round as equal to $P' \approx (2^{-1})^3 \cdot (2^{-3})^2 = 2^{-9}$. In the second round, three arithmetic operations are performed with the participation of the active bits. In addition, two controlled permutation operations are performed with one active bit available at the control input. This determines the probability P'' of the formation of difference (Δ_1^A, Δ_0^B) at the output of the second round:

$$P'' \approx (2^{-1})^3 \cdot (2^{-3})^2 \cdot 2^{-5} = 2^{-14}.$$

Thus, the probability of the two-round characteristic is equal to

$$P(2) \approx P' \cdot P'' \approx 2^{-9} \cdot 2^{-14} = 2^{-23}.$$

The contribution of the one-round characteristic may be neglected, since it is equal to $(P(1))^2 \approx 2^{-42} << 2^{-23}$. The number of rounds r for which the DDP-S64 cipher is indistinguishable from a random transformation can be determined during a differential analysis from the relationship $2^{-64} \geq P^{r/2}(2) \approx 2^{-23r/2}$, from which it is easy to obtain that $r \geq 6$. To have a certain margin of security, it is possible to add another two rounds and recommend values of $r \geq 8$.

Analysis of the DDP-S128 Cipher

For this cipher, the two-round characteristic with the difference $(\Delta_1^A, \Delta_0^B, \Delta_0^C, \Delta_1^D)$ is the most efficient. This difference passes through two rounds according to Figure 5.28.

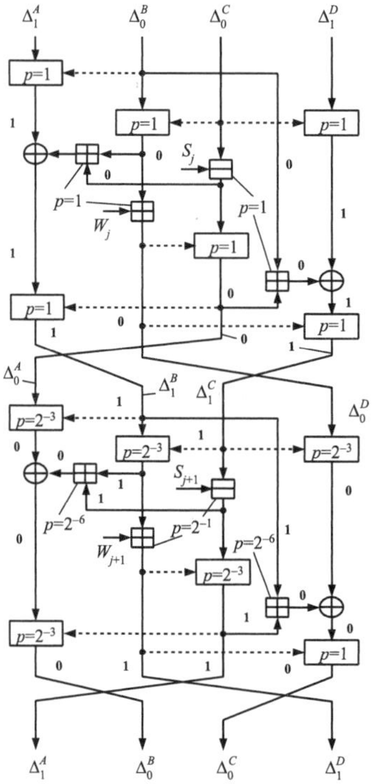

FIGURE 5.28 The two-round characteristic formation mechanism in the DDP-S128 cipher.

With a probability equal to 1, the differences Δ_1^A and Δ_1^D pass through the first round and, after the subblocks are permuted, turn to the differences Δ_1^B and Δ_1^C, respectively. Thus, the input difference of the first round, $(\Delta_1^A, \Delta_0^B, \Delta_0^C, \Delta_1^D)$, with a probability equal to 1 is transformed into the input difference $(\Delta_0^A, \Delta_1^B, \Delta_1^C, \Delta_0^D)$ of the second round. In the second round, two internal subblocks with one active bit are summed up twice by module 2^{-32} at different stages in the transformation of subblocks *B* and *C*.

When each addition operation is performed, an output difference with a probability of 2^{-6} will not contain active bits, since with a probability of 2^{-5}, the active bits in different subblocks turn out to have the same number, and no carry bit is generated with a probability of 2^{-1}. In this case, XOR operations performed over subblocks *A* and *D* do not add active bits in the differences Δ^A and Δ^D.

In addition, each of the active bits participates in the performance of three different controlled permutation operations. In other words, you must consider six independent events, each consisting of the fact that no pair of active bits with an approximate probability of 2^{-3} is generated in the corresponding controlled permutation boxes. It is also necessary to take into account the fact that each of two operations of summing the internal sub boxes with round subkeys with a probability close to 2^{-1} generates no additional active bit (due to the carry bit).

Taking into account all these elementary events related to the mechanism of two-round characteristic formation, we can derive the following value for its probability:

$$P(2) \approx (2^{-6})^2 \cdot (2^{-3})^6 \cdot (2^{-1})^2 = 2^{-32}.$$

Determine the number of rounds for which the DDP-S128 cipher is indistinguishable from a random transformation during differential analysis. To do this, use the relationship $2^{-128} \geq P^{r/2}(2) \approx 2^{-16r}$, from which it follows that $r \geq 8$.

Summing up the results of the differential cryptanalysis of several ciphers based on controlled permutation, the following common property becomes evident. An active bit entering the input of the controlled permutation operation does not contribute to the avalanche effect. The property of the avalanche effect being introduced by a controlled permutation operation is related to the availability of active bits in the subblocks used for forming control vectors. At the same time, if you consider not the bits of the differences, but rather the data bits, it is easy to see that each bit at the input of controlled permutation box influences all the input bits of this operation.

5.6.6 Estimating the Security of the COBRA-F64a and COBRA-F64b Ciphers

As in all previously considered ciphers, in COBRA-F64a and COBRA-F64b, the active bits make the biggest contribution to the avalanche effect when they appear at the control input of the controlled permutation box. This leads to the phenomenon that differential characteristics with a small number of active bits have the greatest probability.

It is necessary to find such characteristics when intermediary differences also have the minimal number of active bits in their formation schemes. Indeed, the availability of one active bit at the control input of a controlled permutation box gives a multiplier of 2^{-3} in an expression for the probability, while the availability of one active bit at the input of the controlled permutation box gives a multiplier of 2^{-5} when an event related to its transition into the specified digit is expected (this is needed to zero a pair of active bits when addition operations are performed; otherwise, the number of active bits will be increased avalanche-like). You can build characteristics for the COBRA-F64a and COBRA-F64b algorithms in which all intermediary differences contain no more than one active bit in the left and right subblock. Obviously, such characteristics possess a maximum probability.

The formation schemes for the differential characteristics of the COBRA-F64a and COBRA-F64b ciphers are shown in Figure 5.29. In both ciphers, the most efficient characteristics are related to the difference (Δ_0^L, Δ_1^R) passing through two or three rounds. In one round of the COBRA-F64a cipher, the active bit of difference is carried once from the right branch into the left one when the XOR operation is performed. Therefore, to return to the initial difference in the COBRA-F64a cryptoscheme, you must perform three rounds, where the second round is related to the event of the right and left subblocks' active bits entering into the same digit.

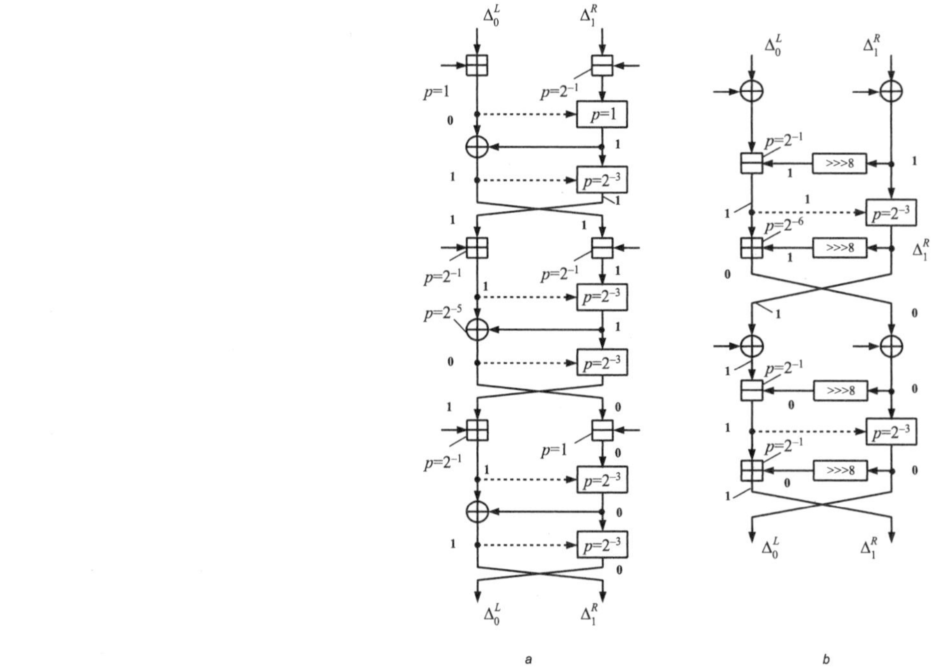

FIGURE 5.29 A three-round characteristic formation scheme in the COBRA-F64a cipher (a) and a two-round characteristic in COBRA-F64b (b).

The feature distinguishing the COBRA-F64b cipher from COBRA-F64a is that in one round, the active bit of difference Δ_1^R is carried from the right branch into the left one twice, which provides for the retention of the difference (Δ_0^L, Δ_1^R) at the output of the first round. A permutation, however, takes place after the first round, transforming difference (Δ_0^L, Δ_1^R) into difference (Δ_1^L, Δ_0^R), and so the second round is included in the differential characteristic formation scheme, where with a probability of 2^{-3}, difference Δ_1^L passes through the left arm without generating additional active bits in the right and left subblocks. The permutation of subblocks after the second round leads to the formation of the initial difference (Δ_0^L, Δ_1^R).

Considering the probabilities of the events related to the three-round characteristic formation for COBRA-F64a for the input difference (Δ_0^L, Δ_1^R), it is easy to say that the probability of the formation of difference (Δ_1^L, Δ_1^R) at the output of the second round is equal to $P' = P\{(\Delta_0^L, \Delta_1^R) \to (\Delta_1^L, \Delta_1^R)\} = 2^{-4}$.

This probability is determined by the event of the active bit passing through a subtraction operation in the right branch, generation of an active bit in the left subblock after an XOR operation, and the performance of one controlled permutation operation with the active bit available at the control input. The difference (Δ_1^L, Δ_1^R) after the second round (and permutation operation) is carried into the difference (Δ_1^L, Δ_0^R), with a probability of $P'' = P\{(\Delta_1^L, \Delta_1^R) \to (\Delta_1^L, \Delta_0^R)\} = 2^{-1} \cdot 2^{-1} \cdot 2^{-3} \cdot 2^{-5} = 2^{-10}$.

After the third round is performed, including modulo 2^{32} addition and two controlled permutation operations, the difference (Δ_1^L, Δ_0^R) is transformed into the difference (Δ_0^L, Δ_1^R), with a probability of $P''' = P\{(\Delta_1^L, \Delta_0^R) \to (\Delta_0^L, \Delta_1^R)\} = 2^{-1} \cdot 2^{-3} \cdot 2^{-3} = 2^{-7}$.

Now for the three-round characteristic's probability, we have $P(3) = P'P''P''' = 2^{-21}$. Using this value, it is possible to establish that, with a round number $r \geq 10$, the COBRA-F64a cipher is indistinguishable from a random transformation with differential cryptanalysis using the preceding characteristic. Thus, the 16-round COBRA-F64a algorithm provides a sufficient security margin against differential analysis. Note that a three-round characteristic for this cryptosystem may also use (Δ_1^L, Δ_1^R) and (Δ_1^L, Δ_0^R) as input differences. These variants of the three-round characteristic have the same probability as the characteristic considered previously. The use of three variants, however, is not fully equivalent. For example, with a round number not divisible by 3, the difference passing through the last or the last and next to last rounds correspond to it passing through an incomplete scheme of differential characteristic formation. Depending on the input difference variant, from the latter is excluded one or two of the last rounds, characterized by different probability values. If one round is excluded, it may relate to a probability of 2^{-7}, 2^{-10}, or 2^{-4}. If two rounds are excluded, then pairs corresponding to probabilities of $p_1 = 2^{-7} \cdot 2^{-10}$, $p_2 = 2^{-10} \cdot 2^{-4}$, or $p_3 = 2^{-4} \cdot 2^{-7}$ can be excluded.

These examples demonstrate that, for different variants, the ratio of the resultant probability values for the whole cipher may be 2^6. This circumstance is worth noting when the minimal number of rounds is selected with the purpose of accelerating the encryption procedure.

From the COBRA-F64b two-round characteristic formation scheme where the input difference (Δ_0^L, Δ_1^R) is used, it is easy to see that probability of the formation of the difference (Δ_1^L, Δ_0^R) at the second round input is equal to:

$$P' = P\{(\Delta_0^L, \Delta_1^R) \to (\Delta_1^L, \Delta_0^R)\} = 2^{-7}$$

This probability is determined by the active bit passing through the subtraction operation of the first round and the generation of one active bit in the left branch (co-factor $\approx 2^{-1}$), the coincidence of the order numbers corresponding to the active bits of the right and left subblocks (co-factor 2^{-5}), and the active bits passing through the addition operation in the left branch leading to the zeroing of the active bit in the left subblock (co-factor 2^{-1}).

When the difference (Δ_1^L, Δ_0^R) passes through the second round (including the swapping data subblocks), it is transformed into the difference (Δ_0^L, Δ_1^R), with a probability of $P'' = P\{(\Delta_1^L, \Delta_0^R) \to (\Delta_0^L, \Delta_1^R)\} = 2^{-5}$. The probability of the two-round characteristic is equal to:

$$P(2) = P'P'' = 2^{-12}.$$

Another variant of the two-round characteristic is connected with the difference (Δ_1^L, Δ_0^R) passing through two rounds. In reality, both variants employ the same mechanisms within separate rounds. A certain discrepancy in the selection of the input difference matters for the case of an odd number of encryption rounds. The ratio of the probability values obtained for an odd number of encryption rounds, depending on the selection of one of these two difference variants, is 2^2. A similar remark can also be made for the SPECTR-H64 and SPECTR-128 ciphers, and others.

For some ciphers, the probability of viewing a certain expected difference at the output of an encryption algorithm can be enhanced by selecting a certain input difference that differs from those corresponding to the most efficient characteristics. Enhancing the probability is done by forced specification of the necessary difference with active bits in the specified digits when the first round is performed. For example, this can be implemented in the case of the COBRA-F64b cipher, where the input difference $(\Delta_{1|32}^L, \Delta_{1|32}^R)$ at the output of the first round is transformed into the difference (Δ_1^L, Δ_0^R), with a probability equal to 1. Its further passing is considered in accordance with a two-round characteristic.

It is easy to derive the following formulas for the probability of the occurrence of the difference (Δ_1^L, Δ_0^R) at the output of the algorithm:

- $P(r) = P\{(\Delta^L_{1|32}, \Delta^R_{1|32}) \to (\Delta^L_1, \Delta^R_0)\} = 2^{-6r+5}$ for an even r
- $P(r) = P\{(\Delta^L_{1|32}, \Delta^R_{1|32}) \to (\Delta^L_1, \Delta^R_0)\} = 2^{-6(r-1)}$ for an odd r

From the condition $P(r) \leq 2^{-64}$, the minimal recommended number of encryption rounds for the COBRA-F64b algorithm is: $r_{\min} = 12$. If $r \geq r_{\min}$, the transformation specified by this algorithm is indistinguishable from a random one.

Table 5.26 is the summary table of the differential properties of the considered algorithms.

The differential cryptanalysis performed is part of the complex investigations carried out during cipher design with the purpose of optimizing certain primitives, and substantiating its cryptographic security.

TABLE 5.26 Comparative Data for Differential Characteristics of Block Ciphers Based on Controlled Operations

Cipher	r	Characteristic		$P(r)$ **
		Difference	Probability	
SPECTR-H64	12	(Δ^L_0, Δ^R_1)	$P(2) \approx 1.5 \cdot 2^{-15}$	2^{-87}
SPECTR-H64	12	(Δ^L_0, Δ^R_1)	$P(3) \approx 2^{-28}$	2^{-112}
SPECTR-128	12	(Δ^L_0, Δ^R_1)	$P(2) \approx 1.1 \cdot 2^{-19}$	2^{-113}
SPECTR-128*	12	(Δ^L_0, Δ^R_1)	$P(3) \approx 2^{-32}$	2^{-128}
SPECTR-128*	12	(Δ^L_0, Δ^R_1)	$P(2) \approx 2^{-27}$	2^{-162}
COBRA-F64a	16	(Δ^L_1, Δ^R_1)	$P(3) = 2^{-21}$	$< 2^{-105}$
COBRA-F64b	20	(Δ^L_0, Δ^R_1)	$P(2) = 2^{-12}$	2^{-120}
DDP-S64	10	(Δ^A_1, Δ^B_0)	$P(2) \approx 2^{-23}$	2^{-115}
DDP-S128	12	$(\Delta^A_1, \Delta^B_0, \Delta^C_0, \Delta^D_1)$	$P(2) \approx 2^{-32}$	2^{-192}

* Modified variant.

** Contribution of the characteristic to the probability of the difference passing through r rounds.

In particular, it was demonstrated that the **E** control bits distribution table is critical, and is compiled in several steps:

1. First, the general criteria for the table's compilation are formulated.
2. The differential characteristics are computed, and as a result, the numbers of the most contributing bits are determined.

3. The table is modified by changing the position of the appearing bits.
4. Differential cryptanalysis is repeated.
5. Experiments are performed to determine the probabilities of differential characteristics that correspond to one or more encryption rounds.
6. The theoretical results are compared with the experimental data.
7. If theory and experiment agree, a conclusion is drawn to the effect that the main mechanisms of difference formation are taken into account in the theoretical model, and the resulting estimates of cryptanalysis are trustworthy.

Thus, to complete the differential analysis of the considered ciphers, the last three items should be performed. It may turn out, however, that the experimental probability values considerably exceed the theoretical values. This would mean that certain mechanisms that make a considerable contribution are not taken into account in the characteristic formation models.

There is no doubt that an enterprising reader will be able to complete on his own the differential analysis cycle and find the necessary refinements of the previous models used to estimate the security of the SPECTR-H64, SPECTR-128, COBRA-F64a, COBRA-F64, DDP-S64, and DDP-S128 ciphers.

5.6.7 Attacks Based on Hardware Faults

When various encryption algorithms are compared in order to select a cryptosystem for a particular application, it is interesting to consider the attacks that provide the cryptanalyst with more options than just pure knowledge of the encryption algorithm and a large number of ciphertext and plaintext pairs corresponding to each other, including specially selected texts.

One type of attack that provides the cryptanalyst with additional options is based on the encryption device (or microprocessor, in the case of program ciphers) generating errors caused by some external action. This type of assault features a high efficiency against many known and used cryptosystems.

The type of attacks related to the expectation or purposeful generation of hardware errors of an encryption device is rather specific, but, due to the mass use of intelligent electronic cards, their study has taken on important practical significance. It is evident that the expectation of errors differs from their generation only in the fact that spontaneous errors are extremely rare, and those that occur during the cryptographic transformation of the specified input blocks are even rarer. We will dwell on the case in which the cryptanalyst is able to purposefully generate random errors in the encryption device during the transformation of the selected data blocks.

Thus, we will consider a model in which the cryptanalyst is provided with the additional option of externally acting on the encryption device with the entered key in order to cause hardware faults, and compare the resulting output data with those we obtained without faults. The cryptanalyst may feed the input specially selected texts. It is assumed that access to the memory area containing the key parameters and the encryption algorithm cannot be realized without their being erased. This assumption is based on the fact that modern technology enables us to produce microelectronic devices with a secure memory. Thus, the cryptanalyst may have an encryption device with the entered secret key, but cannot decrypt it. Neither can he make intentional amendments to the encryption algorithm.

The intensity level of the external action (e.g., heating, high frequency, or ionizing radiation) the cryptanalyst uses with the encryption device is such that it causes one or more individual errors in the microprocessor registers during the encryption of one data block. It is impossible to specify the place where the error will be generated beforehand, but after many experiments, errors of specified types will occur in some of them; for example, the inversion of one of the register's binary digits after the ith encryption round is completed and before the $(i + 1)$th one. Therefore, an expected error is characterized by both spatial and physical localization. For many known ciphers, there is the option of recognizing the experiments where the expected event occurred, which consists of trying input blocks with a special structure and analyzing the differences in the output block structure caused by errors. The computational complexity of this recognition may vary within a wide range, and depends on the specific encryption mechanism. In some ciphers, many errors are recognized trivially.

Hardware faults during encryption may be divided into two main types:

- Data area errors
- Command area errors

Actually, errors of the second type may lead to the formation of the encryption key at the encryption device output, but the probability of events occurring in which the executable code after a random modification corresponds to an application useful for the cryptanalyst is very low. We will consider cases of error generation in the data area. (The results of the experiments in which error generation of the second type took place may be neglected.) For example, random errors in the 8-bit areas of registers containing values of 32-bit subblocks being transformed may be used, and the errors are expected during a certain stage of the encryption procedure (usually during the execution of one or more commands of the microprocessor).

Let's assume that experiments have helped you choose an external action intensity in which, on average, one error is generated for the full encryption time of one block. Make an approximate estimate of the average number of experiments necessary to generate one expected error; in other words, the one occurring in the specified register containing a data subblock, in the specified transformation stage.

Let's also assume that the probability of error generation is proportional to the time of exposure of the corresponding registers that are in a state favorable for error occurrence and have the number of binary digits within the range of which the error is expected. With such an assumption, it is easy to estimate the probability of the expected error generation p within one experiment; in other words, during the encryption of one block —$p_{512} \approx p_d/RZ$—where p_d is the probability of error generation in the data area during one data block encryption procedure, R is the number of transformation rounds, and Z is the number of elementary transformation steps within one round. Because an error is expected during the time it takes to perform an encryption step, the probability of the occurrence of the necessary error is inversely proportional to the total number of encryption steps. (That is why, for 512-bit ciphers, the value of p is considerably lower than with 64- and 128-bit ciphers.) The cryptanalyst can use pulse radiation synchronized with the encryption procedure. In this case, it is possible to use a higher radiation intensity and a length of pulse excitation equal to the time for which the transformed data subblocks are in a state favorable to the cryptanalyst.

When impulse excitation and synchronization with the encryption process are used, the indicated probabilities may be enhanced significantly. The expected labor expenditure employed to form a sufficient number of necessary errors does not seem high in any of the cases. There is no basic difference among cases in which impulse and stationary action are used upon the encryption device. The main thing is that the possibility of the purposeful generation of random hardware errors in the data registers is real. From now on, we will assume that stationary action is used on the encryption device.

For a software implementation of a cipher as a set of standard cycle repetitions, you must use the encryption rounds counter. This requires taking into account the possibility of the generation of an error in the register containing the current number of performed cycles. To prevent the completion of encryption after a small number of encryption rounds is performed (e.g., one round), the condition of exiting from the cycle should be properly arranged for. The most reliable method of preventing the pre-term completion of the encryption procedure is the repetition of round encryption R times, even if this increases the size of the encryption application. Let's consider the security of some fast ciphers against this type of assault.

Cryptanalysis of the RC5 Cipher

The RC5 cipher provides a high rate of data encryption, and if 12 or more rounds are used, is secure against known methods of cryptanalysis, on the condition that the integrity of the encryption algorithm is provided for. However, when the cryptanalyst has the option of forming random hardware errors, the RC5 cryptosystem turns out to be sensitive. Let's look at the security of the RC5 cipher against this type of assault.

Provided in the RC5 cipher is the option of selecting the input block length ($2n$) and a different number of encryption rounds (R). There are precomputations used in this cryptosystem that provide for the formation of an extended key by the secret key as a series of n-bit subkeys $S_0, S_1, S_2, \ldots, S_{2r+1}$.

The RC5 cipher is described by the following pseudocode:

$$A := A + S_0 \pmod{2^n},$$

$$B := B + S_1 \pmod{2^n},$$

for $i = 1$ to R do

$$A := (A \oplus B)^{<B<} + S_{2i} \pmod{2^n}$$

$$B := [(B \oplus A)^{<A<}] + S_{2i+1} \pmod{2^n}$$

where A and B are the left and the right n-bit data subblocks, and "$W^{<b<}$" indicates a cycle shift to the left of word W by b bits. Assume that an external action's intensity is experimentally selected, which generates one error on average for the full time of one data block's encryption. After a comparatively small number of experiments, it is possible to generate an error in the register containing subblock A after performing the transformation using $A := (A \oplus B)^{<B<} + S_{2i} \pmod{2^n}$at $i = R$. The fact that an error occurred on this step is easily recognized by the block structure of the ciphertext obtained from the given input block without entering errors ($C = A||B$) and with entering errors ($\tilde{C} = \tilde{A} \,||\, \tilde{B}$).

It is very easy to derive the following relationship from $B := [(B \oplus A)^{<A<}] + S_{2i+1} \pmod{2^n}$:

$$A \oplus \tilde{A} = \{(\tilde{B} - S_{2R+1})^{>\tilde{A}>} \oplus (B - S_{2R+1})^{>A>}\} \bmod 2^n$$

In the latter formula, the only unknown quantity is S_{2R+1}. With a high probability, it is possible to derive $A \bmod 2^5 = \tilde{A} \bmod 2^5$. In this case, expression $A \oplus \tilde{A} = \{(\tilde{B} - S_{2R+1})^{>\tilde{A}>} \oplus (B - S_{2R+1})^{>A>}\} \bmod 2^n$ is transformed to have the following appearance:

$$(A \oplus \tilde{A})^{<A<} = \{(\tilde{B} - S_{2R+1}) \oplus (B - S_{2R+1})\} \bmod 2^n$$

It is easy to compute the part of the subkey S_{2R+1} using the last relationship. You can determine the full value of the S_{2R+1} subkey by forming various errors. Then, by forming the errors in subblock B, it is possible to compute the S_{2R} subkey after the transformations specified by $B := [(B \oplus A)^{<A<}] + S_{2i+1} \pmod{2^n}$ and corresponding to round $i = R - 1$ are performed. The formation of these errors is easily recognized with the known subkey S_{2R+1}, which provides the cryptanalyst with the option of restoring the value of subblock B after the $(R-1)$th round. If you act sequentially, this is a very good method for easily computing subkeys S_{2R-1}, S_{2R-2}, ..., S_0. For $R = 10 \div 30$, the labor expenditure for the computation of all subkeys does not exceed 10^8 operations. Also of interest is that an attack based on the generation of hardware errors is rather efficient for the decryption of flexible ciphers in which an encryption algorithm is formed depending on the secret key—in other words, it is unknown to the cryptanalyst.

Cryptanalysis of Flexible Ciphers

A flexible R-round 64-bit algorithm is described where, depending on the encryption key, about 10^{16R} nonequivalent modifications of the cryptalgorithm are formed. Each potentially implemented modification of the cryptalgorithm uses the selection of a data-dependent subkey. To reflect this fact, we will call this algorithm DDSS-1. This cipher includes precomputations used to transform the initial secret key into the expanded encryption key, represented as a set of 32-bit subkeys Q_i, where $i = 0, 1, \ldots, 255$. Figure 5.30 shows the structure of one encryption round in the DDSS-1 cryptosystem.

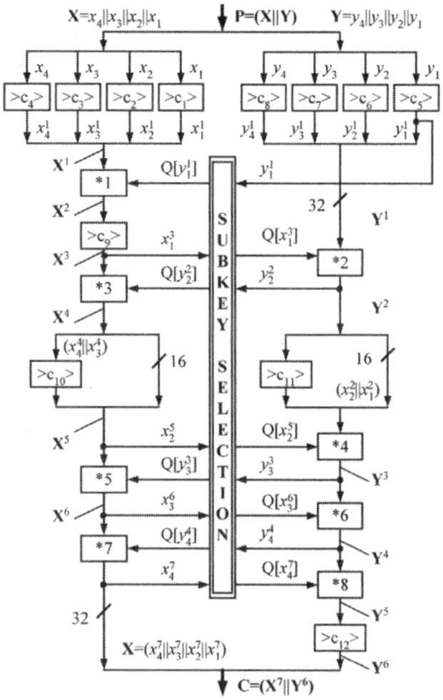

FIGURE 5.30 One round in the DDSS-1 cipher.

The following designations are used in the illustration:

- "$>c_i>$"—the operation of a cycle shift to the right by c_i bits
- "$*_j$"—one of three possible operations:

- XOR
- Modulo 2^{32} addition
- Modulo 2^{32} subtraction

In the precomputations stage, depending on the secret key in various encryption rounds, the independent values c_i and "$*_j$" are specified in identical positions, which creates a large number of various modifications of the cryptalgorithm. The abbreviation SS denotes the subkey selection procedure. The output of the SS function is the value of the 32-bit subkey that is currently selected.

Designate the intermediate values of the data subblocks being transformed as Xi, Yj. Assume that an external action on the encryption device is selected where, on average, a single error is generated during the time of one data block encryption. To obtain an error in subblocks Xi and Yj at the specified steps of transformation, the encryption of a certain number of input blocks will be needed. Some of these blocks may be the same. First, encrypt plaintext P1 and obtain ciphertext C10. Then, providing that there is an external action forming single errors, perform a multiple encryption of block P1. In these experiments, ciphertexts will be recorded in which, with permanent values of subblocks (x_3^7, x_2^7, x_1^7), the value in subblock x_4^7 is erroneous. Designate as C_{11}, C_{12}, ..., C_{1n} the ciphertexts corresponding to the first plaintext P1 and the occurrence of a single error only in subblock x_4^7. Now, subkey differences can be computed $\delta_{x_4^7 \tilde{x}_4^7} = Q_{x_4^7} \bar{*}_8 Q_{\tilde{x}_4^7}$, where x_4^7 is a subblock without errors, $\tilde{x}_4^7$ are subblocks containing errors (subblocks $\tilde{x}_4^7$ are part of ciphertexts C_{11}, C_{12}, ..., C_{1n}, subblock x_4^7 is a part of C_{10}), and $\bar{*}_8$ is a group operation that is the reverse of operation $*_8$).

According to our attack scheme, all the x_4^7 and $\tilde{x}_4^7$ subblocks correspond to the same plaintext P_1.

Designate differences where $i = x_4^7$ and $j = \tilde{x}_4^7$ as δ_{ij}. If i is a fixed value, the total number of such differences is equal to $n = 255$. There is no need to expect the occurrence of all possible values of j for a given i. To determine all the possible subkey differences, you can use other plaintexts P_2, P_3, ..., P_n, and observe the ciphertexts C_{20}, C_{30}, ..., C_{n0} that correspond to them. Since the encryption algorithm specifies pseudorandom values of x_4^7 in these ciphertexts, we should take on average $256(1 + \frac{1}{2} + \frac{1}{3} + ... + \frac{1}{256}) \approx 1618$ plaintexts to obtain all the possible values (there are 256 of them) for subblock x_4^7. Now, designate the plaintexts corresponding to various values of x_4^7 as P_1, P_2, ..., P_{256}. Encrypt each plaintext P_1, P_2, ..., P_{256} under the conditions of the generation of n hardware errors, and obtain the sets of ciphertexts C_{11}, C_{12}, ..., C_{1n}, where $l = 2, 3, ..., 256$, that contain errors only in subblock x_4^7.

The computed differences $\delta_{i,j} = Q_{x_4^7} \bar{*}_8 Q_{\tilde{x}_4^7}$ that correspond to plaintexts P_2, P_3, ..., P_{256} will contain arbitrary pairs of index values. This enables you to use a group property of operation "$*_8$" and compute 256 various differences corresponding to the same value of index i. For this purpose, use the formula $\delta_{ij} = \delta_{ik} *_8 \delta_{kj}$.

It is easy to see that with a full set of values of subblock x_4^7, the $\delta_{ij} = \delta_{ik} *_8 \delta_{kj}$ relationship enables us to find an i_0 that provides a full set of differences $\delta_{i_0 j}$, $j = 0, 1,$

2, ..., 255. This gives us the option of computing all subkeys by trying the values of the Q_{i_0} subkey. There are only 2^{32} variants, which can be quickly tried. However, directly trying variants by known values of the plaintext and ciphertext is impeded by the fact that the "$*_1$" ... "$*_8$" and "$> c_1 >$" ..."$> c_{12} >$" operations are unknown, and it is necessary to find them first. This can be done in parts, using the fact that, while guessing the correct combination of operations, the differences of the computed δ_{ij} subkey will depend only on the indices (i, j), and not on the incoming text. There are 93 various combinations of operations "$*_8$" and "$> c_{12} >$," and so it is easy to find the correct values of both operations that meet the previous condition.

After operations "$*_8$" and "$> c_{12} >$" are determined, we can move on to determining the extended key. Select a value Q_{i_0}. This specifies all subkeys (Q_0, Q_1, ..., Q_{255}), since the differences $\delta_{i_0 j}$, $j = 0, 1, 2, ..., 255$ are already determined. When the extended key is computed, and the operations "$*_8$" and "$> c_{12} >$" are known, it is possible to compute Y^4 (as well as subblock y_4^4) for any given plaintext P, and determine subkey $Q_{y_4^4}$. Then, encrypt plaintext P for conditions of hardware error generation, and observe ciphertext ($\tilde{X}^7 \| \tilde{Y}^6$). If the Q_{i_0} subkey has been guessed correctly, we will find a single error in subblock y_4^4, with a rather high probability. If the current value Q_{i_0} is false, there is a low probability of a single error occurrence in subblock Y^4, since the latter will be computed using a false value of subkey $Q_{x_4^7}$. This fact may be used as a criterion for selecting the correct Q_{i_0} value.

Knowing the true extended key, it is easy to determine the rest of the unknown operations. To determine operation "$*_7$," generate an error in subblock y_4^4 under the condition of error-free (y_3^4, y_2^4, y_1^4). Such an event can be selected, since subblock Y^4 can be computed with a known Y^6. If "$*_7$" is guessed correctly, then the value X^6 computed with a known X^7 and $Q_{y_4^4}$ is the same both with error availability, and the absence of it for the same plaintext P. This is the criterion for recognizing the true " "$*_7$" operation independently of the value of the operations in the previous steps of encryption. Using an analogous method, we can sequentially determine operations "$*_6$," "$*_5$", and so forth, until all operations in all rounds have been determined (for a multiround DDSS-1 cryptoscheme, the attack described is connected with the last round). Note that we do not need to perform an encryption operation with simultaneous error generation, since the required cases can already be found in the available set of experimental data. These are cases that were unnecessary for the previous steps of assault. Now they can be used because we have the option of computing previous values of subblocks X^i and Y^j. It is easily noticed that the most difficult computational step of the attack is finding the right value of the Q_{i_0} subkey, which requires, on average, consideration of 2^{31} variants. This step requires the implementation of about $\approx 2^{32} l_0$ operations, where l_0 is the number of attempts necessary to obtain an error in the required place. Considerably enhancing the security (e.g., up to 10^{30} times) against this type of assault by increasing the value l_0, means a special implementation of the DDSS-1 algorithm. Therefore, this cipher cannot be treated as secure against an assault based on the generation of hardware errors.

Security of the GOST 28147-89 Algorithm

The GOST 28147-89 Russian encryption standard is an example of a widely used block cryptosystem with its security determined by both key secrecy and substitution tables. In its structure, this cryptosystem is similar to DES, and uses a 256-bit secret key and 4×4 secret substitution boxes. The full transformation includes 32 encryption rounds. An assault on the GOST 28147-89 algorithm using hardware error generation presumes the computation of 32-bit keys in every round, and that of secret substitution tables in the last round. The total number of substitution table variants is $(16!)^8$, but they are easily computed, despite the large number of them. The weakness of this algorithm against assaults based on hardware errors lies in using an operation of addition by modulo 2^{32}, and in the small size of the substitution boxes. This makes an assault based on using the avalanche effect stipulated by a carry bit rather efficient. To perform such an assault, you just need to have two encrypted messages (one with errors, and the other without) worked out from the same initial message with a size of about 10^5 bytes. The initial message may be unknown to the violator. The work effort for such an assault does not exceed 10^{10} operations.

Cipher Security Based on Pseudorandom Subkey Selection

The option of generating random errors enables the violator to make use of the following method. Instead of studying complicated encryption procedures with many unknown subkeys, the difference in the transformation results of some unknown intermediary subblock, obtained both before and after the error was introduced, is studied. This error is introduced into another data subblock, influencing the transformation procedure of the first one. Comparing the transformation results before and after the error was introduced enables the violator to create the necessary statistics that he can use to identify all unknown transformation parameters of the selected step of encryption. Since the number of various values of unknown parameters in separate transformation steps is rather small, they can be computed by simply trial and error, and this can be done both for numerical values of subkeys and to determine unknown operations and procedures.

In this scheme, cryptanalysis starts from the last encryption step. The errors introduced before the second to last and the last encryption steps were performed are dispersed in great degree by the time the encryption is completed, so they cannot be directly used to determine the key parameters corresponding to these steps. Taking this circumstance into account, it is possible to offer an easy method of reinforcing the encryption algorithm against the considered types of assault, which consists of using additional transformation algorithms in the last step; for example, substitution operations on large subblocks (8, 16, or 32 bit) performed using secret tables (i.e., by those formed at the precomputations step, depending on the secret key).

The examples of the cryptanalysis of the RC5, DDSS-1, and GOST ciphers show that the use of secret substitution tables, key-dependent and data-dependent operations, cannot in itself provide high security against an attack based on the generation of random hardware errors. To provide high security against such an attack, you must use algorithms with a special transformation structure. Taking into account the peculiarities of such an assault, we can assume that the 512-byte algorithms described in Chapter 2 that use a more efficient mechanism of the data-dependent subkey selection has a high security against assaults based on random hardware error generation. This is connected with the following features of the transformation mechanism:

- The indices of the selected subkeys are not specified directly by the data subblocks being transformed.
- The subkeys are not directly used during the transformation of the data subblocks, but serve only to modify accumulating variables.
- Nondeterministic 512-byte algorithms do not allow you to perform computation of the components of individual unknown operations used in one encryption round.

Therefore, high security against assaults based on hardware errors is obtained by using a special structure of the round transformation function, and not due to the use of additional encryption rounds. One of the methods for providing security against assaults based on hardware error generation is the use of probabilistic encryption, but this leads to an increase in the size of the encrypted data. Using algorithms that are themselves secure against assaults based on error generation is preferable.

5.7. FAST CIPHERS WITH SIMPLE KEY SCHEDULE

This section covers a range of ciphers based on controlled operations, including variable substitutions and permutations. The main advantages of these cryptosystems are high security and encryption speed. At the same time, the complexity of their hardware implementation is relatively low. Materials provided in further sections include differential analysis of fast ciphers with simple key schedule. Also covered are some other types of cryptanalytic attacks.

5.7.1 Cryptoschemes and Ciphers Based on Controlled and Switched Operations

One specific feature of the development of block ciphers based on controlled operations is that all bits of the data subgroup being transformed are used when executing a single operation. At the same time, the nature of their use depends on the type of the data subgroup they relate; namely, to the controlling subgroup or to the data subgroup being transformed. When using this type of cryptographic primitives, the specific features of the development of block ciphers are closely related to this issue.

Variants of Ciphers Implementation based on Variable Permutations

For the moment, the use of data-dependent permutations as the main primitive of the entire range of block ciphers has been well tried. The SPECTR-H64 block cryptosystem is an example of the efficient use of permutations networks as a cryptographic primitive. The structure of the round transformation can be considered an improved Feistel cryptoscheme, where the right data subgroup is transformed using $\mathbf{P}_{32/80}$ controlled permutations block executed simultaneously with the computation of the round function by the left subgroup. In this case, the following transformation takes place:

$$L \leftarrow L;$$
$$R \leftarrow \mathrm{F}(L) \oplus \mathbf{P}^{(V)}{}_{32/80}(R),$$

where "←" stands for the assignment operation, R and L are right and left data subgroups, F is the round function, and V is the controlling vector formed depending on the left subgroup.

The advantage of the improved cryptographic scheme is increase of the parallelism level of the encrypting transformations. To preserve the possibility of decrypting a block of ciphertext using the same algorithm that carries out the encryption (the universality property), it is necessary to carry out an inverse controlled permutation $\mathbf{P}^{-1}{}_{32/80}$ after superimposing the round function over the transformed right block. Both aforementioned operations, $\mathbf{P}_{32/80}$ and $\mathbf{P}^{-1}{}_{32/80}$, are carried out in dependence of the left data subgroup, which determines its participation in each operation carried out within the encryption round. Despite active use of the left data subgroup, this subgroup as such is not subject to transformation in the course of the execution of the encryption round. Because of this, there arises the problem of forming different values of controlling vectors for the $\mathbf{P}_{32/80}$ and $\mathbf{P}^{-1}{}_{32/80}$ operations. This problem consists in that in case of equality of controlling vectors, the execution of two $\mathbf{P}_{32/80}$ and one $\mathbf{P}^{-1}{}_{32/80}$ operations is reduced to the execution of one $\mathbf{P}^{-1}{}_{32/80}$ operation carried out over the computed value of the round function. In the SPECTR-H64 cipher, this problem is solved by using different subkeys in addition to L when forming controlling vectors for $\mathbf{P}_{32/80}$ and $\mathbf{P}^{-1}{}_{32/80}$. The complete round of the transformation appears as follows:

$$L \leftarrow L;$$
$$R \leftarrow \mathrm{F}(L) \oplus \mathbf{P}^{(V)}{}_{32/80}(R);$$
$$R \leftarrow (\mathbf{P}^{-1})^{(V')}{}_{32/80}(R).$$

The cryptoscheme considered here is of general interest when designing ciphers based on variable operations. Because of this, it is necessary to detect the drawbacks, if there are any, and consider the possibility of their elimination. The use of relatively large number of subkeys—six 32-bit ones—is a certain drawback of the SPECTR-H64 cryptosystem. This implies the requirement of using key extension procedures or relatively long secret keys—for example, the SPECTR-H64 algorithm uses 256-bit secret key. Thus, when building ciphers based on mutually inverse blocks of controlled permutations, the developer must face the specific problem of implementing an efficient mechanism of forming various control vectors corresponding to mutually inverse blocks of controlled permutations. At the same time, it is necessary to ensure the properties of universality and high transformation parallelism.

To solve this problem, a method was suggested that doesn't require the use of auxiliary subkeys. This method consists of the use of fixed permutations carried out over the left and/or the right subgroup of the data. The perseverance of the universality property of the encryption algorithm is achieved because two identical round functions are used for such a transformation. In addition to this, the following elements are used:

- Permutation involutions (over the left and/or the right subgroup)
- Switched fixed permutations (over the left and/or the right subgroup)
- Transformation of the left subgroup by superimposing the subkey over it

Consider several variants of cryptoschemes implemented according to this method of solving the problem of forming controlling vectors for executing mutually inverse variable operations. The use of a switched operation over the right subgroup is shown in Figure 5.31, where **G** denotes some operation built the same way as the similar operation in the SPECTR-H64 cipher, and **Crypt**$^{(e)}$ designates the round transformation procedure as a whole.

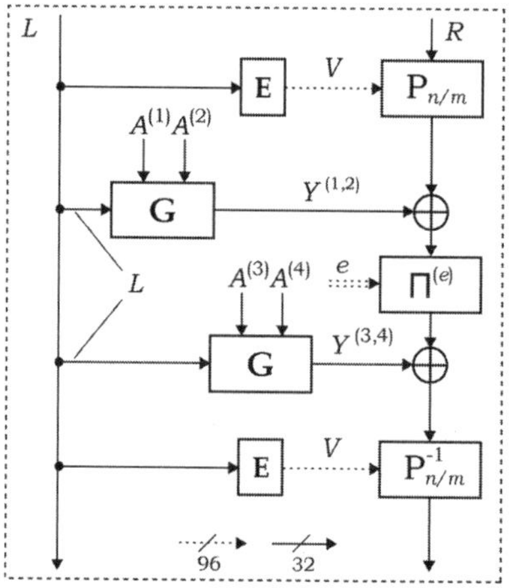

FIGURE 5.31 General scheme of the **Crypt**$^{(e)}$ procedure with a switched operation.

This mechanism is based on that the transformation of the right branch is the $\mathbf{P}^{(V)}_{n/m} \bullet \mathbf{\Pi}^{(e)} \bullet (\mathbf{P}^{-1}_{n/m})^{(V)}$ superposition, which actually is an operating block controlled by vector V and carrying out variable permutations having the structure of the cyclic permutation $\mathbf{\Pi}^{(e)}$.

Obviously, in this superposition intended for implementing only permutations with the cyclic structure $\mathbf{\Pi}^{(e)}$, the natural requirement is the equality of controlling vectors corresponding to direct $\mathbf{P}_{n/m}$ block or to inverse block $\mathbf{P}^{-1}_{n/m}$. In the general case, for different values of the left subgroup (different values of the controlling data subgroup L), different modifications of permutations with the specified cyclic structure are implemented. The advantage of this variant of the cryptoscheme design is the possibility of using the extension block, which is implemented as a simple branching of conductors. This allows us to economize on the hardware resources. In addition, there is no need to use additional keys for forming various controlling vectors. The possibilities of encryption and decryption using the same algorithm is ensured because both operations **G** are identical, and for the inverted fixed permutation the following condition is satisfied: $\Pi^{(e=1)}=(\Pi^{(e=0)})^{-1}$. Both in the course of encryption and decryption, the aforementioned superposition implements permutations with the specified cycle structure; for example, one-cycle permutations.

In the particular case of one-cycle permutation $\Pi^{(e)}$, the mechanism of optimization consists in that the bit from the j-th position at the input of the $\mathbf{P}_{n/m}$ block with approximately the same probability falls into all positions at the output of the $\mathbf{P}^{-1}_{n/m}$ block, except for the j-th bit, into which it won't fall with any value of the controlling vector. The similar property is ensured by any permutation that doesn't contain loops of the length 1. To ensure approximately uniform influence of each input bit of the **P**32/96 operational block to the values of all output bits of block $\mathbf{P}^{-1}_{32/96}$, it is possible to use the invertible permutation containing only one cycle of length 1.

For example, an invertible permutation can be implemented using a single-layered controlled permutations block containing 32 elementary switches. The same bit e is supplied to the controlling input of all elementary switches. The structure of permutation $\Pi^{(e)}$, implementing the classical cyclic right (e = 1) or left (e = 0) shift is shown in Figure 5.32. The delay time corresponding to the execution of this operation is determined by the time required to the signal to pass through one active layer. This time is approximately equal to the delay time of the operation of modulo-2 bit-by-bit summation ($t_\oplus$). The delay time corresponding to the operations of bit permutations provided that $\mathbf{P}_{32/96}$ and $\mathbf{P}^{-1}_{32/96}$ controlled permutations blocks are used, makes $6t_\oplus$. The execution time of one round then makes $15t_\oplus$.

This variant of solving the problem of forming control vectors can be applied for controlled permutations, and for the pairs of mutually inverse variable operations of other types built on the basis of controlled SP-networks (that is, for the case of using $\mathbf{F}_{n/m}$ and $\mathbf{F}^{-1}_{n/m}$ blocks).

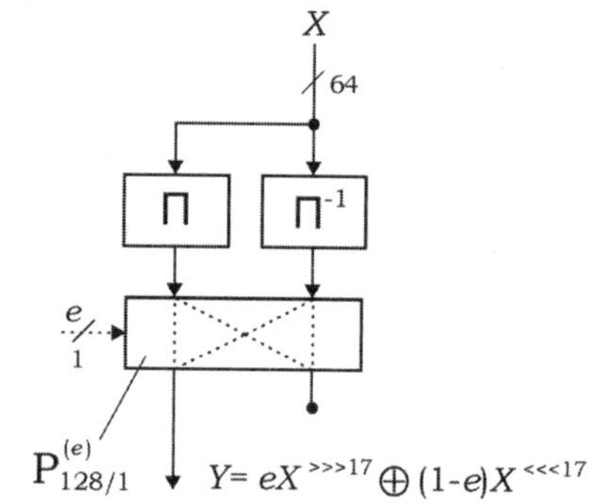

FIGURE 5.32 The structure of invertible one-cycle permutation.

Specific Features of Using Two G operations of the Same Type

The advantage of controlled permutations is that the influence of one input bit on all output bits is ensured with the minimum delay time. However, this transformation preserves the value of the Hamming weight. For this reason, when building ciphers, it is expedient to use transformations of other types that change the weight and parity of the binary vectors being transformed in addition to permutations. To achieve this goal, it seems expedient to use an operation similar to the controlled binary operation **G**, which was tried as a cryptographic primitive in the SPECTR-H64 cipher and made a good show of it. This operation can also be applied in case of use of the pairs of mutually inverse operations of other types (built on the basis of controlled SP-networks) for the transformation of the right subgroup.

The previously considered scheme of the round transformation when using two similar **G** operations is characterized by the following specific feature: in contrast to the SPECTR-H64 cipher, it uses two similar **G** operations instead of one in the round transformation shown in Figure 5.31. Each of these operations "mixes" the left data subgroup with different pairs of subkeys. From the description of the structure of this operation provided here, it can be easily seen that changing the i-th bit of L results in the deterministic change of the i-th bit and in the probabilistic change of several bits following it at the output of the **G** operation. In the case of direct addition of the output values of two **G** operations, the avalanche effect is weakened. The use of the substitution operation (in particular, cyclic shift by the number of bytes exceeding the value d), carried out over the output value of one of the **G** operations allows us to weaken such a suppression of the avalanche effect. For this purpose, it is possible to use one-cycle permutation $\Pi^{(e)}$, which corresponds to a cyclic shift by, say, 17 bits (right shift if $e = 0$, and left shift if $e = 1$). In the cryptoscheme shown in Figure 5.31 the extinguishing of the avalanche effect is eliminated by means of executing a fixed permutation operation over the right data subgroup after executing the first **G** operation, but before executing the second one. Thus, the fixed permutation used for the right branch of the cryptoscheme plays the double role. It coordinates the two similar **G** operations in a certain way, and ensures optimization of the mechanism of forming controlling vectors for the controlled permutations block.

Nevertheless, there is another important feature related to the mechanism represented in Figure 5.31 and including two identical operations **G**. This feature consists in that each bit of the left subgroup both in the first and in the second **G** operations influences the output bits belonging to the same positions. These bits are divided by the fixed bit permutation in the right branch; however, the probabilities of generation of the active difference bits in identical positions of both **G** operations are dependent, because the keys are fixed elements. This feature results in a certain increase of the probability of encryption according to the scheme of encrypting differences with a small weight. To eliminate this drawback, it is possible to execute the fixed permutation involution **I** over the left data subgroup. The use of such an operation also implements the second goal—improvement of the mechanism of forming controlling vectors.

Permutation involution **I** is chosen with the account of the structure of operation **G**. Let this operation have such a property that the i-th input bit x_i influences four output bits y_i, y_{i+1}, y_{i+2}, and y_{i+3}. This means that the i-th output bit is influenced by input bits with the numbers $i-1$, $i-2$, $i-3$ (for **G** operational with initial conditions the values $i = 1, 2$, and 3 are exceptions). For such operation **G**, it is natural to choose such a permutation involution, which for each i would shift bits l_{i-1}, l_{i-2}, l_{i-3} of the left data subgroup to the distance no less than four steps from the shifted bit l_i. This criterion ensures the dependency of the pair of output bits of the upper and lower operation **G**, belonging to the same predefined bit; for example, to the j-th bit, on seven different bits of the left data subgroup for the maximum number of different values j (in case of operations **G** without initial conditions, this is true for all values of j). For the case of 32-bit subgroups, this condition is satisfied, for example, by the following permutation:

$$\mathbf{I} = (1,17)(2,21)(3,25)(4,29)(5,18)(6,22)(7,26)(8,30)(9,19)$$
$$(10,23)(11,27)(12,31)(13,20)(14,24)(15,28)(16,32).$$

If general-type permutation instead of involution **I** is used in the left branch of the cryptoscheme, this will simplify the development of the required permutation. However, to ensure the possibility of using the same algorithm for encryption and decryption it will be necessary to use the operational block implementing an invertible fixed permutation similar to $\Pi^{(e)}$. In the right branch of the cryptoscheme, instead of invertible permutation $\Pi^{(e)}$ it is possible to use the respective permutation involution **I'**, different from **I**. Note that the use of fixed permutations in the left and in the right branches of the cryptoscheme requires their coordination.

Other Mechanisms of Coordinating Control Vectors

Consider other variants of building round transformations assuming they are used as a basis for building an iterative cipher with the structure shown in Figure 5.33. To avoid using additional active elements in the circuit implementation as intermediate fixed permutation, it is possible to use permutation involution containing only loops of length 2. In this case, as in the case of single-loop permutation, for all values of j in one round, the influence or the j-th input bit on the j-th output bit isn't ensured within one round. This nonuniformity is equalized in the next round, which allows us to abandon superposition of different round subkeys when forming control vectors corresponding to direct and inverse blocks of controlled permutations. This simplifies hardware implementation of cryptosystems with the round structure similar to the encryption round used in the SPECTR-H64 cryptosystem. Thus, adding a fixed permutation between $\mathbf{P}_{n/m}$ and $\mathbf{P}^{-1}_{n/m}$ blocks is an efficient method of optimizing a mechanism of controlling mutually inverse data-dependent permutations.

In the round transformation shown in Figure 5.34, the transformation of the left subgroup is used, at the expense of which different control vectors are built for controlling mutually inverse substitution blocks.

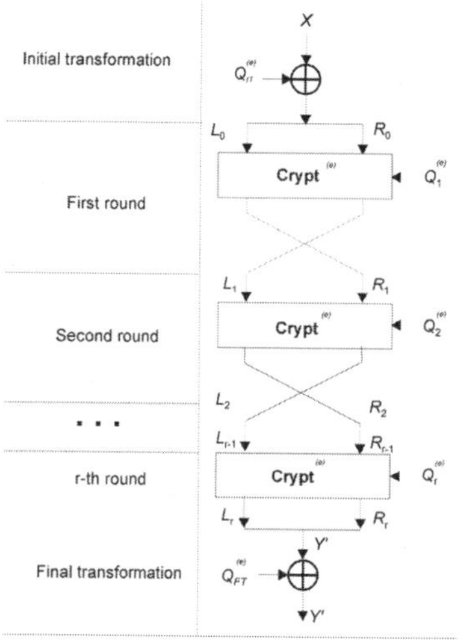

FIGURE 5.33 The generalized scheme of an iterative cipher.

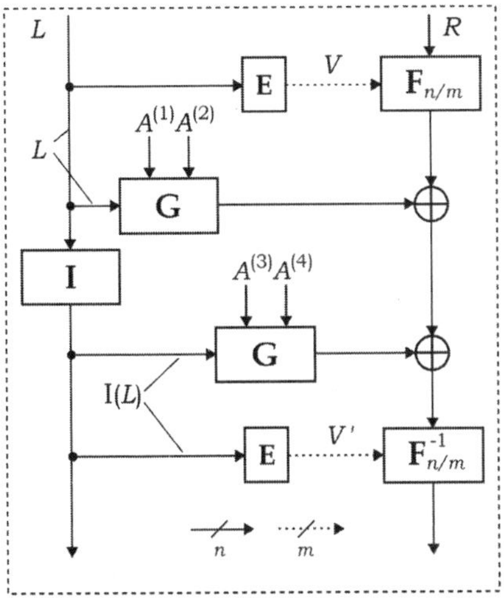

FIGURE 5.34A Encryption round using transformation of the left data subgroup using fixed permutation involutions.

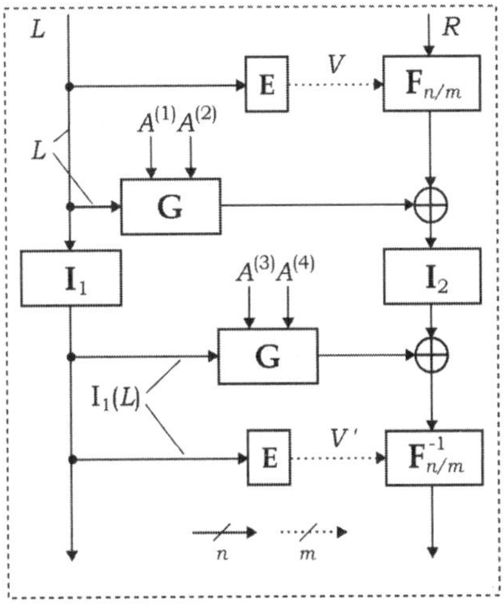

FIGURE 5.34B Encryption round using left and right data subgroups using fixed permutation involutions.

Statistical studies of the influence of the input bits of the $\mathbf{F}_{n/m}$ block on the output bits of the $\mathbf{F}^{-1}{}_{n/m}$ lock has shown that even for the simple mechanism shown in Figure 5.34a, it is possible to find a permutation involution simple enough to ensure the uniform influence.

Similar investigations of the scheme shown in Figure 5.34b have demonstrated that the simultaneous use of permutation involutions carried out over the left and the right subgroups also can be used, because the effects introduced by these two mechanisms do not neutralize one another.

A similar mechanism is shown in Figure 5.35, where in the left branch a switched permutation is used instead of the fixed one, which allows for using general-type permutations. At the same time, this switched operation doesn't introduce any time delays, because after execution of the upper **G** operation the XOR operation is executed, thanks to which the output value of the lower **G** operation is formed simultaneously with the forming of the output value of permutation **I**.

To decrease the amount of key material used within a round, it is possible to apply the scheme shown in Figure 5.36, where two controlled operations $\mathbf{S}_{32/32}$ are used for forming the round function. Instead of $\mathbf{S}_{32/32}$ blocks, in this scheme it is possible to use $\mathbf{S}_{32/96}$ blocks, which, when implementing programmable LICs, will be coordinated by the delay time with the $\mathbf{R}_{32/96}$ block that carries out transformation of the right data subgroup. Such a structure of the round transformation allows for easy evaluation of differential characteristics with differences of small

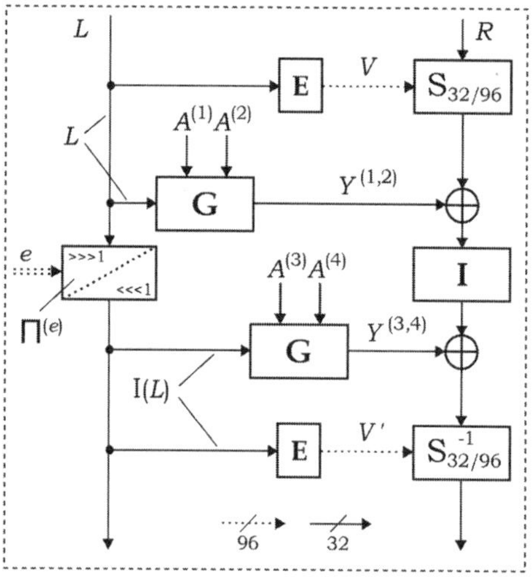

FIGURE 5.35 Structure of the ***Crypt***$^{(e)}$ procedure with switched permutation in the left branch of the cryptoscheme.

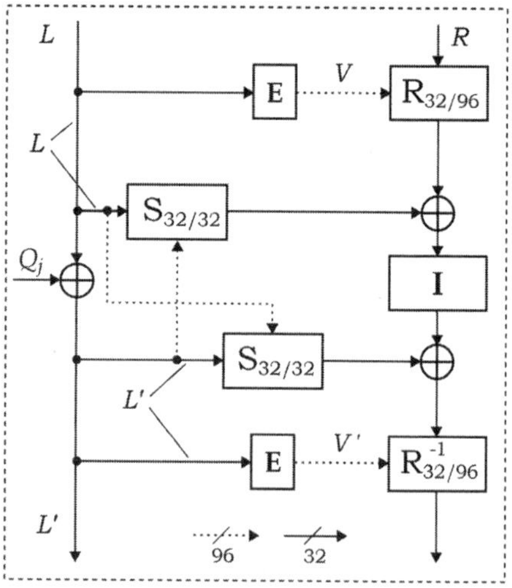

FIGURE 5.36 The structure of the ***Crypt***$^{(e)}$ procedure with the transformation of the cryptoscheme by means of superposition of the subkey over it.

weight, which are the most efficient when implementing a differential attack. This variant demonstrates the possibility of using minimal key material within a single encryption round.

In the previously considered examples of internal optimization of the distribution of control bits over elementary controlled units of controlled operational blocks $\mathbf{F}_{n/m}$ and $\mathbf{F}^{-1}_{n/m}$, an intermediate reversible transformation was carried out over the left subgroup, which either didn't introduce any delay at all, or introduced the delay approximately equal to the time required to execute a XOR operation. Principally, it was possible to apply more complicated transformations of the left subgroup. However, such transformations result in the increase of the critical path of the combinational scheme carrying out the round transformation. In addition to increased hardware requirements for manufacturing the encrypting devices, this also reduces the encryption speed. Obviously, more sophisticated transformations carried out over the left subgroup allow for efficient elimination of the problem of forming control vectors, and provide the possibility of reducing the number of rounds. Potentially, this might result in the performance gain and reduction of the implementation cost. The possibility of reducing the number of rounds is due to the fact that two subgroups will be transformed within the same round (in other words, the entire data block is going to be transformed). However, to implement this idea, it is necessary to develop other building procedures with high parallelism of transformations execution.

Because of the nature of data-dependent operations as such, transformations parallelism is included automatically. Therefore, it is possible to apply two schemes of building round transformations, which are shown in Figures 5.37a and 5.37b. The first scheme uses controlled 2-bit operations and requires a considerable amount of the key material within one encryption round. Specific feature of the second scheme is coordination between direct and inverse operations $\mathbf{R}_{n/m}$ and $\mathbf{R}^{-1}_{n/m}$ executed in parallel before execution of the first (top) XOR operation. One of these operations is carried out over the right subgroup, which then is exchanged with the left subgroup. Coordination is necessary here, because operations are carried out using the same values of control vectors. Two sequentially executed $\mathbf{R}_{n/m}$ operations, between which the second XOR operation is carried out are also coordinated. A specific feature of employing two internal $\mathbf{R}_{n/m}$ operations is that they are carried out over round subkeys (one of these operations is executed simultaneously with the transformation of the right subgroup). The problem of coordination is eliminated if different extension blocks are used for operations executed over subkeys and over the right subgroup. In addition, this problem is eliminated by applying operations of different types, carried out over the right subgroup and over subkeys. Note that in the scheme presented in Figure 5.37b, it isn't expedient to replace two $\mathbf{R}_{n/m}$ operations carried out over subkeys by $\mathbf{R}^{-1}_{n/m}$ operations.

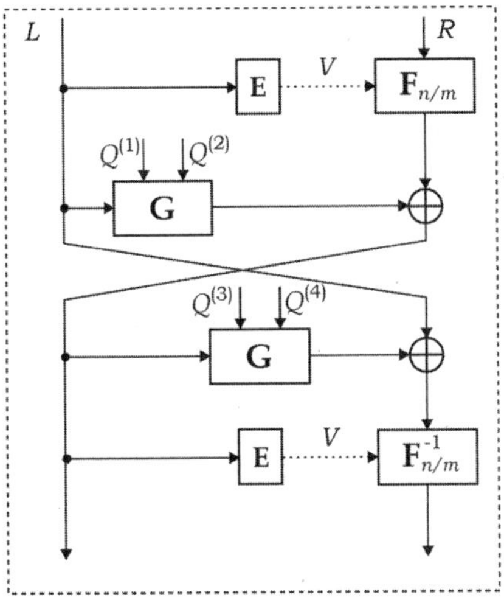

FIGURE 5.37A The round encryption mechanism with transformation of both data subgroups using two identical operations **G**.

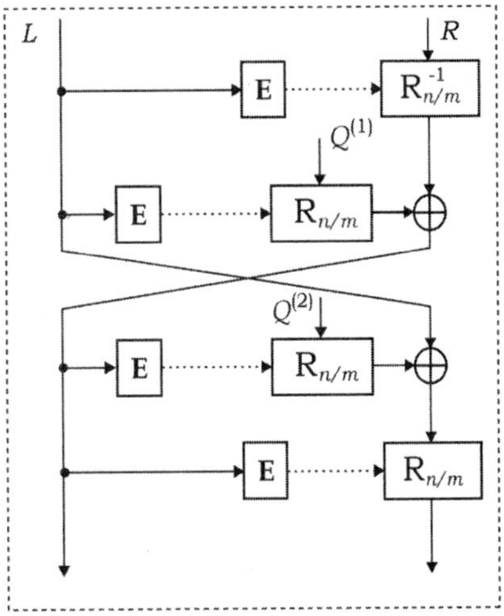

FIGURE 5.37B The round encryption mechanism with transformation of both data subgroups using three identical operations $\mathbf{R}_{n/m}$.

Although these two apparently elegant schemes ensure building strong ciphers with the number of rounds from 6 to 12 for different variants of operational blocks, their critical path is approximately 1.5 times longer than critical paths of earlier considered cryptoschemes, because the first of the two sequentially executed operations cannot be executed simultaneously with the pair of operations executed in parallel. As a result, the execution time of the encryption round is approximately equal to $6mt_{\oplus}/n + 2$. In the previously considered cryptoschemes, the parallelism level can be evaluated by the value 2 (on average, two operations are executed in parallel—first, three operations are executed in parallel, after which the fourth operation is executed), and in the latter two cryptoschemes the parallelism is evaluated by the value 4/3 (two operations are executed in parallel, then the third and the fourth operations are executed sequentially). In the next section, more efficiently designed schemes of the round transformation will be covered. They transform both data subgroups and are characterized by the parallelism level 2.

It should be mentioned that after building efficient mechanisms of forming control vectors that do not require using round subkeys, it is possible to return to using rounds subkeys, as it becomes necessary due to some design considerations. In this case, some statistical nonuniformities of the influence of the bits from the right subgroup can be eliminated. Such nonuniformities might take place when executing one round of the SPECTR-H64 encryption algorithm even when using different subkeys for forming $\mathbf{P}_{32/80}$ and $\mathbf{P}^{-1}_{32/80}$ controlled operations. Note that for the previously considered mechanisms, such nonuniformities are smoothed even without using different subkeys for forming control vectors.

Cryptoschemes Combining Transformation of Both Subblocks with High Parallelism Level

To implement the transformation of the entire data block within the same round, while preserving high enough parallelism level, the cryptoscheme shown in Figure 5.38 was developed.

This cryptoscheme is based on the following ideas:

- Two identical data-dependent transformation operations are used, which depend on the left subgroup and are placed in bilaterally symmetric positions in the structure of the encryption round. Output values of these operations are added to the right data subgroup as in the Feistel cryptoscheme.
- One of the aforementioned operations is computed simultaneously with the transformation of the left data subgroup, and the right operation is carried out simultaneously with the transformation of the right data subgroup using the operation depending on the left data subgroup. Thus, this scheme has parallelism level equal to 2.

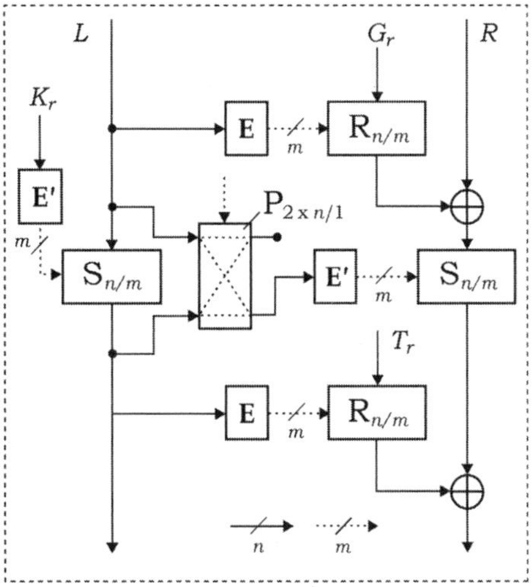

FIGURE 5.38 The structure of round encryption with transformation of both data subgroups while preserving high parallelism level of the computations.

- To ensure the universality of the cryptoscheme, the left data subgroup is transformed using an operation representing an involution or switched controlled operation. For the same purpose, the control vector used when executing the controlled operation over the right data subgroup is formed by the initial value of the left data subgroup in the course of encryption, and by the transformed value of the left data subgroup in the course of decryption.

In this cryptoscheme, there are two pairs of operations $\mathbf{S}_{n/m}$ and $\mathbf{R}_{n/m}$. Operations of the first pair are executed over the left data subgroup ($\mathbf{S}_{n/m}$) and subkey G_r ($\mathbf{R}_{n/m}$), and operations of the second pair are carried out over the right data subgroup ($\mathbf{S}_{n/m}$) and subkey T_r ($\mathbf{R}_{n/m}$). At the same time, only the operation carried out over the left subgroup is fixed after establishing the key. All the other controlled operations are variable, because they depend on the left data subgroup. In this cryptoscheme, it is assumed that the extension blocks are built so that no bit of the left data subgroup influences any bit of the binary vector being transformed (subkey or data subgroup) more than once. Operations depending on the left data subgroup specify nonlinear transformation, and the operation executed over the left subgroup is linear, if operation $\mathbf{S}_{n/m}$ is built using controlled elements of the $\mathbf{F}_{2/1}$ type (when using controlled elements with the size $\mathbf{F}_{3/1}$ or more, this operation also becomes nonlinear). Operation $\mathbf{S}_{n/m}$ ensures good avalanche effect, and three nonlinear operations ensure a high degree of the round transformation nonlinearity (algebraic degree of nonlinearity is 7). Further on, different variants of nonlinear transformation of the left subgroup will be considered, which are built on the basis of minimal controlled elements and ensure algebraic nonlinearity degree of the round transformation over 20. The variant of the left subgroup transformation using 4×4 S-boxes executing in parallel also appears a good solution.

It is necessary to mention that to ensure universality of such a cryptoscheme, it is necessary to imply certain limitations on the controlled operations used for transforming left and right data subgroups. Two types of such operations are possible:

- Controlled involutions
- Switched controlled operations of the general type

Thanks to modification of the bit specifying a direct operation or its corresponding inverse operation, it is possible to ensure the possibility of executing encryption and decryption using the same algorithm. Economic variants of building controlled operations make their use within the framework of the cryptoscheme considered here very promising for developing fast and easily implemented block ciphers.

Building controlled involutions based on a controlled substitution-permutation network is easily implemented in comparison to controlled permutation involutions. To achieve this, it is possible to use the following variants: sequential (Figure 5.39a) and parallel (Figure 5.39b). The advantage of the first scheme is that it specifies the transformation of the input vector as a single whole; however, it is necessary to execute two mutually inverse operations $\mathbf{F}_{n/m}$ and $\mathbf{F}^{-1}{}_{n/m}$. The advantage of the second variant is the parallelism of the operations being executed, which reduces the delay time. However, in the second case, the binary input vector is split and transformed as two independent values. In the first case, the resulting block $\mathbf{F}_{n/2m}$ is formed, and in the second case, the $\mathbf{F}_{2n/m}$ block. Despite the difference in the way of specifying involutions, both schemes ensure approximately equal design possibilities for synthesizing ciphers for the given number of active layers.

It can be easily shown that these schemes result in building controlled involutions. Actually, transform the output vector Y using the $\mathbf{F}_{n/2m}$ operation while preserving the value of the control vector. For a sequential scheme, this transformation appears as follows:

$$
\begin{aligned}
Y' = \mathbf{F}_{n/2m}(Y) &= (\mathbf{F}^{-1}{}_{n/m})^{(V)}(\mathbf{I}(\mathbf{F}^{(V)}{}_{n/m}(Y))) = (Y)\mathbf{F}^{(V)}{}_{n/m} \bullet \mathbf{I} \bullet (\mathbf{F}^{-1}{}_{n/m})^{(V)} = \\
&= ((X)\mathbf{F}^{(V)}{}_{n/m} \bullet \mathbf{I} \bullet (\mathbf{F}^{-1}{}_{n/m})^{(V)})\mathbf{F}^{(V)}{}_{n/m} \bullet \mathbf{I} \bullet (\mathbf{F}^{-1}{}_{n/m})^{(V)} = \\
&= (X)\mathbf{F}^{(V)}{}_{n/m} \bullet \mathbf{I} \bullet (\mathbf{F}^{-1}{}_{n/m})^{(V)} \bullet \mathbf{F}^{(V)}{}_{n/m} \bullet \mathbf{I} \bullet (\mathbf{F}^{-1}{}_{n/m})^{(V)} = \\
&= (X)\mathbf{F}^{(V)}{}_{n/m} \bullet \mathbf{I} \bullet \mathbf{I} \bullet (\mathbf{F}^{-1}{}_{n/m})^{(V)} = (X)\mathbf{F}^{(V)}{}_{n/m} \bullet (\mathbf{F}^{-1}{}_{n/m})^{(V)} = X.
\end{aligned}
$$

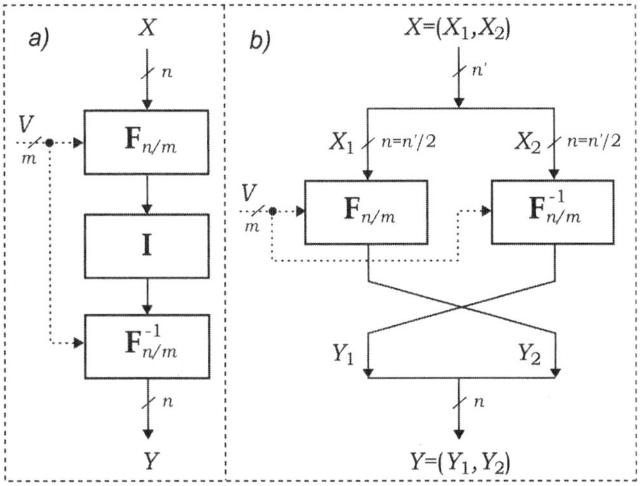

FIGURE 5.39 Sequential (a) and parallel (b) scheme of building a controlled involutions block implemented based on a controlled substitution-permutation network.

Thus, the first scheme implements the controlled operation that represents an involution. For the second scheme, the transformation appears as follows:

$$Y' = \mathbf{F}_{2n/m}(Y) = \mathbf{F}_{2n/m}(Y_1, Y_2) = (\mathbf{F}^{-1}{}_{n/m})^{(V)}(Y_2), \mathbf{F}^{(V)}{}_{n/m}(Y_1)) =$$
$$= ((\mathbf{F}^{-1}{}_{n/m})^{(V)}(\mathbf{F}^{(V)}{}_{n/m}(X_1)), \mathbf{F}^{(V)}{}_{n/m}((\mathbf{F}^{-1}{}_{n/m})^{(V)}(X_2))) = (X_1, X_2).$$

This means that in the second case, we also are dealing with controlled involution having an arbitrary $\mathbf{F}_{n/m}$ block.

Another variant of cryptoscheme with high parallelism level is obtained by means of replacing operations used for round keys transformation by **G** operations. Modification of the operation carried out over the left subgroup also presents a great interest. For this operation, it is possible to enforce the nonlinearity property by means of using the transformation shown in Figure 5.40 instead of using larger controlled elements. This transformation consists of splitting the left subgroup L into two subgroups L_1 and L_2, of the half size, and sequential transformation of these subgroups using mutually inverse controlled operations followed by permutation of subgroups L_1 and L_2. Since the control vector is formed based on one of the data subgroups when executing each controlled operation, each specifies nonlinear transformation. Consequently, the resulting transformation as a whole also is nonlinear. In addition, this $\mathbf{H}_{n/m}$ transformation is an involution, which can be shown by transforming the output value $L'=(L'_1, L'_2)$:

$$L'' = \mathbf{H}_{n/m}(L'_1, L'_2) = \mathbf{H}_{n/m}(\mathbf{H}_{n/m}(L_1, L_2)) = \mathbf{H}_{n/m}(\mathbf{F}^{(V')}{}_{n'/m'}(L_2), (\mathbf{F}^{-1})^{(V)}{}_{n'/m'}(L_1)) =$$
$$= (\mathbf{F}^{(V'')}{}_{n'/m'}((\mathbf{F}^{-1})^{(V)}{}_{n'/m'}(L_1)), (\mathbf{F}^{-1})^{(V')}{}_{n'/m'}(\mathbf{F}^{(V')}{}_{n'/m'}(L_2))) = (X_1, X_2),$$

because $V'' = V$. Concatenation of the input and output values of the $\mathbf{F}_{n'/m'}$ operation in the course of the transformation of block L is $L^* = (L'_2, L_2)$, and when transforming block L' the same concatenation is equal to $L^{**} = (L_2, L'_2)$. Thus, the resulting nonlinear operational block based on two variable operations also forms the binary vector, where components L_2 and L'_2 are transposed in the course of repeated transformation of the same output value using the same block.

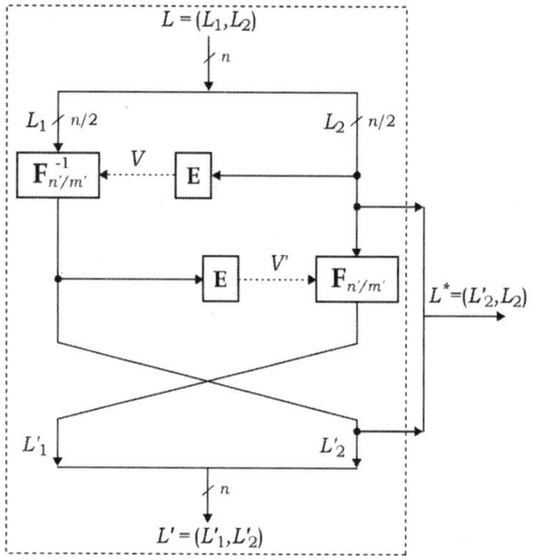

FIGURE 5.40 The structure of nonlinear controlled operation for transformation of the left data subgroup (the $\mathbf{H}_{n/m}$ operation).

As was shown in Chapter 4, in an economic variant of the switched operation implementation, these functions are carried out by a single-layer block carrying out transposition of two halves of the control vector. Thus, using the just designed operational block and using vector $L^* = (L'_2, L_2)$ as the control value for executing switched operation $\mathbf{S}^{(e)}{}_{n/m}$, carried out in economic variant, it is possible to avoid using the transposition block of the control vector, because its functions are automatically implemented by the previously considered operational block in relation to vector L^*. This allows for further economy on the hardware resources when using switched operation $\mathbf{S}^{(e)}{}_{n/m}$.

As the result of the provided analysis, it is possible to suggest another variant of the encryption round implementation shown in Figure 5.41. When developing a specific cipher and aiming at achieving the greatest performance, it is necessary to coordinate the delay time of the operations executed in parallel. This is due to the limitation of the number of active layers that can be used in $\mathbf{F}_{n'/m'}$ and $\mathbf{F}^{-1}{}_{n'/m'}$ operations on the basis of which the $\mathbf{H}_{n/m}$ block is formed. This demonstrates that nonlinearity is achieved at the expense of reducing the number of active layers, because both direct and inverse operations are carried out sequentially over subgroups L_1 and L_2. Depending on specific type of the $\mathbf{F}_{n'/m'}$ operation, this might result in reduction of the contribution of the operation carried out over subgroup L into the avalanche effect. Consequently, when choosing the transformation operation to be carried out over the left data subgroup, it is necessary to account for the compromise between nonlinearity and avalanche effect.

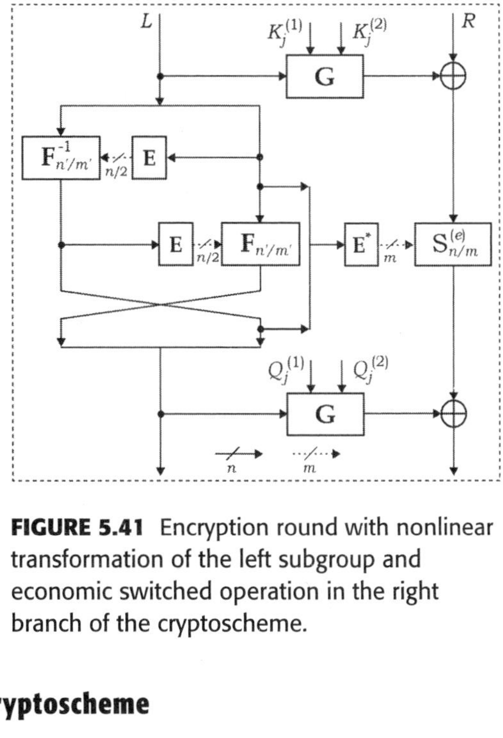

FIGURE 5.41 Encryption round with nonlinear transformation of the left subgroup and economic switched operation in the right branch of the cryptoscheme.

5.7.2 The COBRA-H64 Cryptoscheme

The COBRA-H64 block cipher is designed with the account of the results of linear and differential cryptanalysis of the SPECTR-H64 cipher. The latter turned out strong enough against suggested variants of attacks. However, from the investigation of its strength, it follows that by improving the extension block that forms control vectors used for executing variable permutations and by using nonlinear operation **G**, the number of rounds can be reduced. This allows for increasing the encryption speed in case of iterative implementation or reducing the implementation complexity in case of the pipelined implementation. Another task that had to be solved when designing the COBRA-H64 system was simplification of the key use schedule and reduction of the key length.

The General Encryption Scheme

Main features of this cipher are as follows:

- The round transformation of the COBRA-H64 cipher uses two second-order $\mathbf{P}_{32/96}$ and $\mathbf{P}^{-1}_{32/96}$ controlled permutations blocks, while SPECTR-H64 uses three first-order controlled permutations blocks: two $\mathbf{P}_{32/80}$ blocks and one $\mathbf{P}^{-1}_{32/80}$ block. This allows for achieving more uniform distribution of the influence of the control data subgroup on the execution of variable bit permutations over the data subgroup being transformed.
- Round transformation of COBRA-H64 uses two identical nonlinear **G** operations, while SPECTR-H64 uses only one such operation.
- Thanks to the previous feature, it is possible to execute permutation involution over the controlling data subgroup in the COBRA-H64 round transformation. This allowed for abandoning the use of keys when forming control vectors corresponding to mutually inverse controlled permutations blocks.
- COBRA-H64 uses a new cryptographic primitive—switched operation—although in its simplest variant. The use of switched operations allowed for eliminating weak and semi-weak keys.

The general scheme of encryption and decryption in the COBRA-H64 cipher is defined by the following transformations:

$$Y = \mathbf{T}^{(0)}(X, K) \text{ and } X = \mathbf{T}^{(1)}(Y, K),$$

where $X \in \{0, 1\}^{64}$ – is the plaintext (input block), $Y \in \{0, 1\}^{64}$ is the ciphertext (output block); $K \in \{0, 1\}^{128}$ is the secret key; $\mathbf{T}^{(e)}$ is the data block transformation function; $e \in \{0, 1\}$ is the parameter defining the modes of encryption ($e = 0$) and decryption ($e = 1$).

The secret key is considered as the concatenation of four subkeys $K = (K_1, K_2, K_3, K_4)$, where $K_i \in \{0, 1\}^{32}$ for all $i = 1, 2, 3, 4$. The general scheme of encryption represents the 10-round iterative structure with easy initial and final transformations (see Figure 5.42). When executing each j-th round ($j = 1, 2, \ldots, 10$), the round key $Q_j^{(e)}$ is used. This key is formed on the basis of direct use of all four subkeys K_1, K_2, K_3, K_4 without using any special transformations (extension) of the secret key.

This means that each $Q_j^{(e)}$ key is formed as a sequence of secret keys K_i, used according to the order specified by relatively simple key schedule.

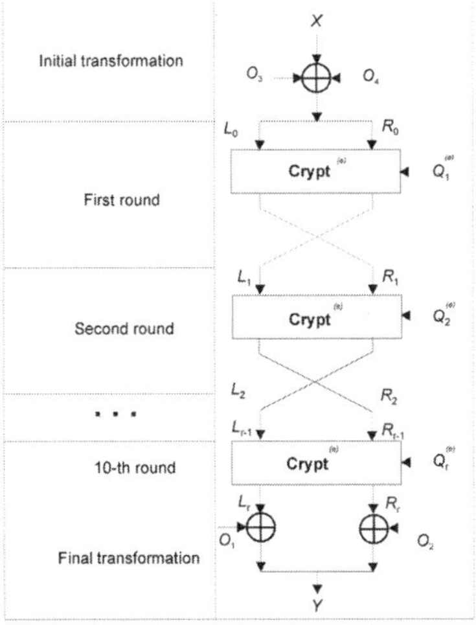

FIGURE 5.42 The general scheme of encryption in COBRA-H64 ($r = 10$) and COBRA-H128 ($r = 12$).

The encryption procedure starts with relatively simple **IT** transformation. Then 10 rounds of encryption are carried out according to the ***Crypt***$^{(e)}$ procedure, followed by the final transformation **FT**. Formally, encrypting transformations are written in the form of the following algorithm.

1. The input block X is split into two 32-bit subgroups of equal size, L and R: $X = (L, R)$.
2. Initial transformation IT is carried out according to the following formulae: $L0 = L \oplus O_3$ and $R_0 = R \oplus O4$.
3. For $j = 1, 2, \ldots, 9$, the following procedure is executed sequentially: $\{ (L_j, R_j) := \boldsymbol{Crypt}^{(e)}(L_j - 1, R_j - 1, Q_j^{(e)}),\ M := R_j, R_j := L_j, L_j := M; \}$.
4. The last encryption round is executed: $(L_{10}, R_{10}) := \boldsymbol{Crypt}^{(e)}(L_9, R_9, Q_{10}^{(e)})$.
5. The final transformation FT is carried out according to the following formulae: $L' = L_r \oplus O_1$ and $R' = R_r \oplus O_2$.

The output block of ciphertext appears as follows $Y = (L', R')$.

The scheme of the ***Crypt***$^{(e)}$ procedure of the COBRA-H64 block cipher is shown in Figure 5.43.

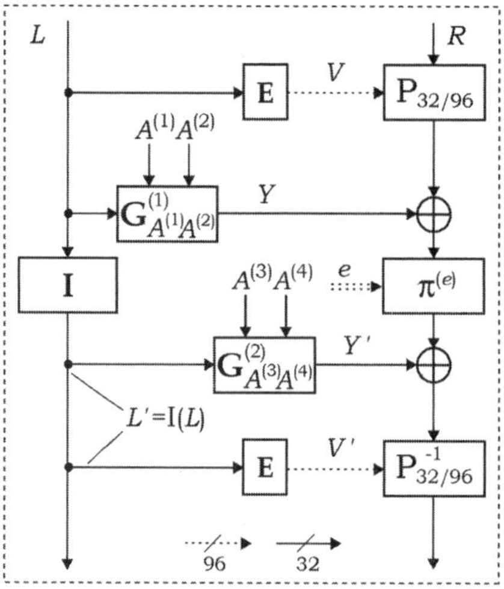

FIGURE 5.43 The ***Crypt***$^{(e)}$ procedure of the COBRA-H64 block cipher.

Forming the Key Use Schedule

Each round key $Q_j^{(e)}$ is made up of four round subkeys depending on the e parameter: $A^{(i)} \in \{0, 1\}^{32}$, where $i = 1, 2, 3, 4$. These round keys are written in the form $Q_j^{(e)} = (A^{(1)}, A^{(2)}, A^{(3)}, A^{(4)})_j^{(e)}$, where $j = 1, \ldots, 10$. Specification of the round keys of the COBRA-H64 cipher is defined by Table 5.27 and Figure 5.44.

TABLE 5.27 Key Schedule in the COBRA-H64 Cipher

j	1	2	3	4	5	6	7	8	9	10
$A_j^{(1)}$	O_1	O_4	O_3	O_2	O_1	O_1	O_2	O_3	O_4	O_1
$A_j^{(2)}$	O_2	O_1	O_4	O_3	O_4	O_4	O_3	O_4	O_1	O_2
$A_j^{(3)}$	O_3	O_2	O_1	O_4	O_3	O_3	O_4	O_1	O_2	O_3
$A_j^{(4)}$	O_4	O_3	O_2	O_1	O_2	O_2	O_1	O_2	O_3	O_4

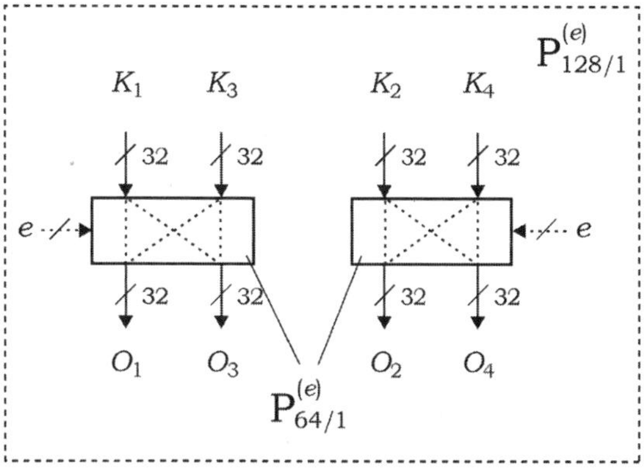

FIGURE 5.44 Implementation scheme of the key transposition when switching from encryption (e = 0) to decryption (e = 1).

Switching between encryption and decryption modes is carried out by simple modification of the parameter *e*, which controls a single-layer controlled permutation block $\mathbf{P}^{(e)}_{128/1}$, carrying out an appropriate permutation of subkeys K_1, K_2, K_3, K_4. The $\mathbf{P}^{(e)}_{128/1}$ block is a cascade of two $\mathbf{P}^{(e)}_{64/1}$ blocks shown in Figure 5.44. At the output of the first $\mathbf{P}^{(e)}_{64/1}$ block the pair of subkeys O_1 and O_3 is formed, while the pair O_2 and O_4 appears at the output of the second block. For $e = 0$ the condition $O_i = K_i$ for all $i = 1, 2, 3, 4$ is satisfied, and for $e = 1$ we have $O_1 = K_3$, $O_3 = K_1$, $O_2 = K_4$ and $O_4 = K_2$.

Subkeys O_1, O_2, O_3, O_4, which are dependent on bit *e*, are used in each encryption round according to Table 5.27 instead of formal subkeys $A^{(1)}$, $A^{(2)}$, $A^{(3)}$, $A^{(4)}$. Encryption universality (the possibility of using the same algorithm for encryption and for decryption) is ensured because the fixed permutation $\boldsymbol{\pi}^{(0)}$ is replaced by the inverse one provided that bit *e* is inverted: $\boldsymbol{\pi}^{(1)} = (\boldsymbol{\pi}^{(0)})^{-1}$, and by means of appropriate modification of the K_1, K_2, K_3, K_4 subkeys schedule. Encryption round is not an involution; however, in case of inversion of bit *e* and permutation of subkeys $A^{(1)}$ to $A^{(3)}$ and $A^{(2)}$ to $A^{(4)}$, the round transformation is inverted:

$$\mathbf{\mathit{Crypt}}^{(0)}_{A^{(1)},A^{(2)},A^{(3)},A^{(4)}} = (\mathbf{\mathit{Crypt}}^{(1)}_{A^{(3)},A^{(4)},A^{(1)},A^{(2)}})-1.$$

In the course of encryption, round keys $Q_j^{(0)} = (A^{(1)}, A^{(2)}, A^{(3)}, A^{(4)})_j^{(0)}$ are used, where $j = 1, \ldots, 10$, and in the case of decryption, the keys in use are $Q_j^{(1)} = (A^{(1)}, A^{(2)}, A^{(3)}, A^{(4)})_j^{(1)}$. For correct encryption for $j = 1, \ldots, 10$ the following conditions must be satisfied:

$$(A^{(1)})_j^{(1)} = (A^{(3)})_{11-j}^{(0)},\ (A^{(2)})_j^{(1)} = (A^{(4)})_{11-j}^{(0)},$$
$$(A^{(3)})_j^{(1)} = (A^{(1)})_{11-j}^{(0)},\ (A^{(4)})_j^{(1)} = (A^{(2)})_{11-j}^{(0)}.$$

Using Figure 5.44 and Table 5.27, it is easy to write the schedule of keys K_1, K_2, K_3, K_4 in explicit form for the cases of encryption (Table. 5.28) and decryption (Table 5.29). It can be easily seen that the provided conditions have been satisfied.

TABLE 5.28 Schedule of Subkeys K_1, K_2, K_3, K_4 in Case of Encryption ($e = 0$)

j	1	2	3	4	5	6	7	8	9	10
$A_j^{(1)}$	K_1	K_4	K_3	K_2	K_1	K_1	K_2	K_3	K_4	K_1
$A_j^{(2)}$	K_2	K_1	K_4	K_3	K_4	K_4	K_3	K_4	K_1	K_2
$A_j^{(3)}$	K_3	K_2	K_1	K_4	K_3	K_3	K_4	K_1	K_2	K_3
$A_j^{(4)}$	K_4	K_3	K_2	K_1	K_2	K_2	K_1	K_2	K_3	K_4

TABLE 5.29 Schedule of Subkeys K_1, K_2, K_3, K_4 in Case of Decryption ($e = 1$)

j	1	2	3	4	5	6	7	8	9	10
$A_j^{(1)}$	K_3	K_2	K_1	K_4	K_3	K_3	K_4	K_1	K_2	K_3
$A_j^{(2)}$	K_4	K_3	K_2	K_1	K_2	K_2	K_1	K_2	K_3	K_4
$A_j^{(3)}$	K_1	K_4	K_3	K_2	K_1	K_1	K_2	K_3	K_4	K_1
$A_j^{(4)}$	K_2	K_1	K_4	K_3	K_4	K_4	K_3	K_4	K_1	K_2

Variable Permutations

Data-dependent permutations are carried out using blocks of controlled permutations $\mathbf{P}_{32/96}$ and $\mathbf{P}^{-1}_{32/96}$. The current permutation carried out over the right 32-bit data subgroup depends on the 96-bit control vector $V \in \{0, 1\}^{96}$. Vector V is formed on the basis of the left data subgroup using extension block **E**, representing a simple circuit branching. The control vector can be represented as $V = (V_1, V_2, V_3, V_4, V_5, V_6)$, where each component controls one of the six active layers of controlled permutations blocks. Transformation in block **E** is carried out according to the following formulae:

$$V_1 = L_{lo}\ V_2 = L_{lo}^{>>>6},\ V_3 = L_{lo}^{>>>12},\ V_4 = L_{hi}\ V_5 = L_{hi}^{>>>6},$$
$$V_6 = L_{hi}^{>>>12},$$

where $L_{lo} = (l_1, l_2, \ldots, l_{16}) \in \{0, 1\}^{16}$, $L_{hi} = (l_{17}, l_{n/2+2}, \ldots, l_{32}) \in \{0, 1\}^{16}$ and "$>>> k$" stands for the cyclic shift by k bits (for the bit representation of binary vectors being used this is the left shift). This rule of forming control vectors corresponds to criteria of forming control vectors, and permutation of each input bit in the $\mathbf{P}_{32/96}$ controlled permutation depends on six different bits from L. At the same time, under any conditions none of the bits of the controlling subgroup influences any bit of the data being transformed more than once.

Switched Permutation $\pi^{(e)}$

The $\boldsymbol{\pi}^{(e)}$ operation is a fixed switched permutation. Its use eliminates weak and semi-weak keys. Depending on the value of bit e this switched operation implements either direct fixed bit permutation $\boldsymbol{\pi}^{(0)}$, or inverse bit permutation $\boldsymbol{\pi}^{(1)}$. Fixed permutations $\boldsymbol{\pi}^{(0)}$ and $\boldsymbol{\pi}^{(1)}$ have the following representation:

$$\boldsymbol{\pi}^{(0)}(x_1, x_2, \ldots, x_{32}) = ((x_1, x_2, \ldots, x_{31})^{>>>5}, x_{32})$$
$$\boldsymbol{\pi}^{(1)}(x_1, x_2, \ldots, x_{32}) = ((x_1, x_2, \ldots, x_{31})^{>>>26}, x_{32}).$$

Switching between these permutations is carried out using a single-layer controlled permutations block $\mathbf{P}^{(e)}_{64/1}$ according to the scheme shown in Figure 5.45.

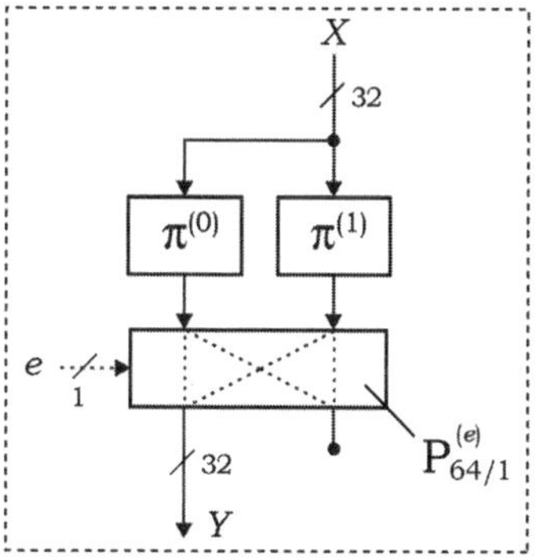

FIGURE 5.45 Switched permutation $\pi^{(e)}$.

Switched permutation $\boldsymbol{\pi}^{(e)}$ ensures the influence of each input bit of the $\mathbf{P}_{32/96}$ controlled permutations block on each output bit of the $\mathbf{P}^{-1}_{32/96}$ controlled permutations block even in case when there is no permutation involution $\mathbf{I}$ in the left branch; that is, even when the values of control vectors corresponding to blocks $\mathbf{P}_{32/96}$ and $\mathbf{P}^{-1}_{32/96}$ of the same round are equal. Thus, the goal of switched permutation consists of:

- Elimination of weak and semi-weak keys
- Elimination of the need in using subkeys when forming control vectors.

Fixed Permutation I

Bit permutation **I**, executed over the left data subgroup, is an involution. It is intended for increasing the avalanche effect propagating the modifications of the bits of the data subgroup L while simultaneously executing two nonlinear transformations $\mathbf{G}^{(1)}$ and $\mathbf{G}^{(2)}$. Permutation **I** has the following cyclic structure:

$$\mathbf{I} = (1, 17)(2, 21)(3, 25)(4, 29)(5, 18)(6, 22)(7, 26)(8, 30)(9, 19)$$
$$(10, 23)(11, 27)(12, 31)(13, 20)(14, 24)(15, 28)(16, 32).$$

Criteria for building involution **I** are related to specific structure of the **G** operation. Assume that the output bits y_k and y_l of the **I** operation correspond to input bits x_i and x_j. When choosing the permutation involution **I** the following principles were used:

- For each i and j from condition $|j - i| \leq 3$, it follows that $|l - k| \geq 4$.
- For each i, the following condition is satisfied: $|i - k| \geq 6$.

Applying involution **I** and inversion of one bit in subgroup L results in the inversion of several bits (from 2 to 8) at the output of the block R after the output blocks $\mathbf{G}^{(1)}(L)$ and $\mathbf{G}^{(2)}(\mathbf{I}(L))$ are summed with the initial block R using the "⊕" operation.

Nonlinear Operation G

Nonlinear operations $\mathbf{G}^{(1)}$ and $\mathbf{G}^{(2)}$ have the same structure and are defined according to the following formula:

$$\mathbf{G}_{AB}(X) = X \oplus A \oplus X_3X_2 \oplus X_2X_1 \oplus X_3X_1 \oplus B_1X_2 \oplus A_1X_3 \oplus BX_2X_1,$$

where:

- $X, A, B \in \{0, 1\}^{32}$
- AX denotes bit-by-bit modulo-2 multiplication of vectors A and X
- For all $i = 1, 2, 3$ vector X_i is defined as $X_i = X^{\to i} \oplus X^{(0)\leftarrow(3-i)}$, where $X^{(0)} = (1, 1, 1, 0, \ldots, 0) \in \{0, 1\}^{32}$ is a fixed block of initial conditions, "$\to k$" and "$\leftarrow k$" are logical shifts of the vector operand by k positions left or right (the released positions are filled with zeros)

- $A_1 = A^{\to 1} \oplus A^{(0)}$, where $A^{(0)} = (1, 0, \ldots, 0) \in \{0, 1\}^{32}$ is a fixed block of initial conditions
- $B_1 = B^{\to 1} \oplus B^{(0)}$, where $B^{(0)} = (1, 0, \ldots, 0) \in \{0, 1\}^{32}$ is a fixed block of initial conditions

Operations $\mathbf{G}^{(1)}$ and $\mathbf{G}^{(2)}$ are intended for increasing the nonlinearity of the ***Crypt***$^{(e)}$ procedure and strengthening the avalanche effect propagating modifications of the input data bits at the output of the procedure. When considering the influence of one bit of the input vector X of the operation $\mathbf{G}$ on the bits of its output vector $Y = \mathbf{G}(X)$, the following formula describing the influence of individual output bits on the input bits is useful:

$$y_i = x_i \oplus a_i \oplus x_{i-3}x_{i-2} \oplus x_{i-2}x_{i-1} \oplus x_{i-3}x_{i-1} \oplus b_{i-1}x_{i-2} \oplus a_{i-1}x_{i-3} \oplus b_i x_{i-2}x_{i-1},$$

where $(x_{-2}, x_{-1}, x_0) = (1, 1, 1)$; $a_0 = b_0 = 1$.

5.7.3 The COBRA-H128 Block Cipher

The COBRA-H128 block cipher that has a 128-bit variant of input is in many respects similar to the CIKS-128 cryptosystem. The difference between them consists of a minor modification of the operation **G**, which contributes to the avalanche effect that takes place within on encryption round the same for all bits of the left data subgroup. In this section, only a brief description of the COBRA-H128 cipher will be provided. More detailed description of this cipher and substantiation of the primitives used when designing it can be found in publications listed in the References section of this book. Nevertheless, the description provided here is complete enough to understand the differential cryptanalysis of this system that will be provided further in this chapter.

The general encryption scheme of the COBRA-H128 algorithm corresponds to the scheme presented in Figure 5.42, except that 12 transformation rounds take place instead of 10. The secret key K is 256 bits in length, and is split into four subkeys $K_i \in \{0, 1\}^{64}$: $K = (K_1, K_2, K_3, K_4)$. Round subkeys $Q_j^{(e)}$, where $j = 1, 2, \ldots, 12$ are formed as concatenations of secret subkeys without using any special procedures for transforming the secret key. Initial transformation **IT** corresponds to formulae $L_0 = L \oplus O_3$ and $R_0 = R \oplus O_4$, and the final transformation (**FT**) is carried out according to the following formulae: $L' = L_{12} \oplus O_1$ and $R' = R_{12} \oplus O_2$. The scheme of the ***Crypt***$^{(e)}$ procedure of the COBRA-H128 algorithm is presented in Figure 5.46.

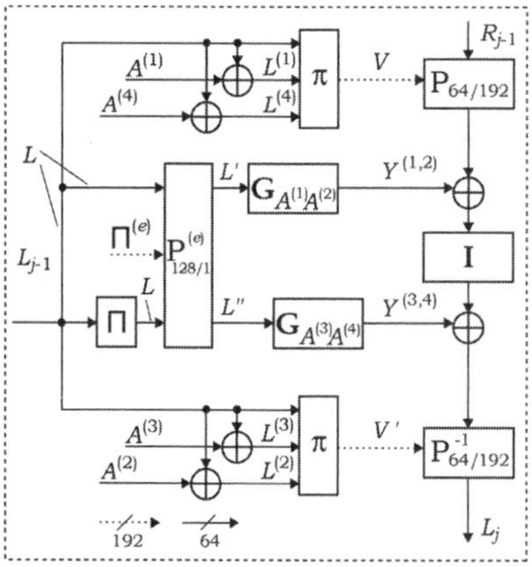

FIGURE 5.46 The ***Crypt***$^{(e)}$ procedure of the COBRA-H128 block cipher.

Forming the Round Key

Each round key used in the ***Crypt***$^{(e)}$ procedure is made up of four subkeys $(A^{(i)})_j^{(e)}$, which depend on parameter e and the round number $j = 1, \ldots, 12$. They can be written as $Q_j^{(e)} = (A^{(1)}, A^{(2)}, A^{(3)}, A^{(4)})_j^{(e)}$. Specification of round keys $Q_j^{(e)}$ is presented in Tables 5.30 and 5.31.

TABLE 5.30 Schedule of the Round Keys of the COBRA-H128 Cipher in Encryption Mode (e = 0)

j	1	2	3	4	5	6	7	8	9	10	11	12
$A_j^{(1)}$	K_1	K_4	K_3	K_2	K_1	K_3	K_3	K_1	K_2	K_3	K_4	K_1
$A_j^{(2)}$	K_2	K_3	K_4	K_1	K_2	K_4	K_4	K_2	K_1	K_4	K_3	K_2
$A_j^{(3)}$	K_3	K_2	K_1	K_4	K_3	K_1	K_1	K_3	K_4	K_1	K_2	K_3
$A_j^{(4)}$	K_4	K_1	K_2	K_3	K_4	K_2	K_2	K_4	K_3	K_2	K_1	K_4

TABLE 5.31 Schedule of the R Keys of the COBRA-H128 Cipher in Decryption Mode

j	1	2	3	4	5	6	7	8	9	10	11	12
$A_j^{(1)}$	K_3	K_2	K_1	K_4	K_3	K_1	K_1	K_3	K_4	K_1	K_2	K_3
$A_j^{(2)}$	K_4	K_1	K_2	K_3	K_4	K_2	K_2	K_4	K_3	K_2	K_1	K_4
$A_j^{(3)}$	K_1	K_4	K_3	K_2	K_1	K_3	K_3	K_1	K_2	K_3	K_4	K_1
$A_j^{(4)}$	K_2	K_3	K_4	K_1	K_2	K_4	K_4	K_2	K_1	K_4	K_3	K_2

Controlled Permutations

Variable permutations in COBRA-H128 are implemented using first-order $\mathbf{P}_{64/192}$ and $\mathbf{P}^{-1}{}_{64/192}$ blocks, shown in Figure 5.47.

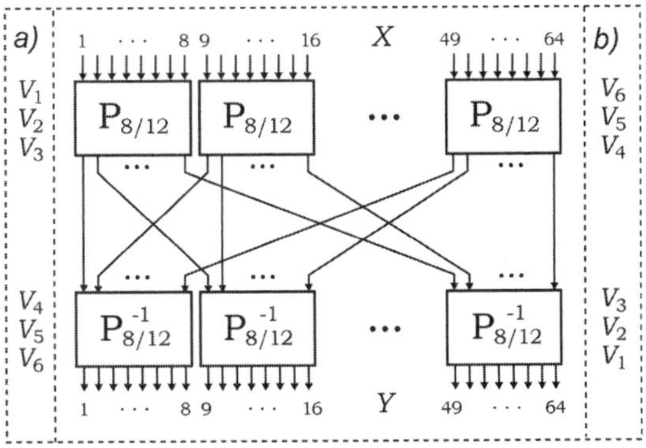

FIGURE 5.47 Operational blocks of variable permutations controlled by vector $V = (V_1, V_2, V_3, V_4, V_5, V_6)$: a) $\mathbf{P}_{64/192}$ and b) $\mathbf{P}^{-1}{}_{64/192}$.

Formation of control vectors V and V' is described by Table 5.32, which demonstrates that (see Figure 5.47) in case of vector V (V'), the rows corresponding to vectors V_1 and V_6 (V_1' and V_6') contain numbers of bits of vector L (L); rows corresponding to vectors V_2 and V_5 (V_2' and V_5') contain numbers of bits of vector $L^{(1)}$ ($L^{(3)}$); and rows corresponding to vectors V_3 and V_4 (V_3' and V_4') contain numbers of bits of vector $L^{(4)}$ ($L^{(2)}$).

Fixed Permutations

Permutation **I** is an involution described by the following formula:

$$Y = (Y_1, Y_2, \dots, Y_8) = \mathbf{I}(X_1, X_2, \dots, X_8),$$

where $X_i, Y_i \in \{0, 1\}^8$; $Y_1 = X_6^{>>>4}$; $Y_2 = X_5^{>>>4}$; $Y_3 = X_4^{>>>4}$; $Y_4 = X_3^{>>>4}$; $Y_5 = X_2^{>>>4}$; $Y_6 = X_1^{>>>4}$; $Y_7 = X_8^{>>>4}$; and $Y_8 = X_7^{>>>4}$.

Permutation Π is intended for strengthening the avalanche effect due to execution of two identical nonlinear operations $\mathbf{G}^{(1)}$ and $\mathbf{G}^{(2)}$. It includes for cycles of length 16:

$$(1, 50, 9, 42, 17, 34, 25, 26, 33, 18, 41, 10, 49, 2, 57, 58)$$

$$(3, 32, 11, 56, 51, 16, 27, 40)$$

$$(4, 7, 28, 47, 52, 23, 12, 63, 36, 39, 60, 15, 20, 55, 44, 31)$$

$$(5, 14, 13, 6, 21, 62, 29, 54, 37, 46, 45, 38, 53, 30, 61, 22).$$

Permutation π distributes the influence of bits of the control subgroup L specified in Table 5.32.

TABLE 5.32 Distribution of the Influence of the Bits of Control Subgroup L in the $\mathbf{P}_{64/192}$ Block

V_1	31	32	3	4	5	6	7	8	9	10	11	12	13	14	15	16
V_2	10	24	25	26	29	13	27	16	1	2	31	32	3	4	19	6
V_3	13	14	15	16	17	18	19	20	21	22	23	24	25	26	27	28
V_4	33	34	35	36	37	38	39	40	41	42	43	44	45	46	47	48
V_5	55	56	57	58	59	60	61	62	63	64	33	34	35	36	37	38
V_6	45	46	47	48	49	50	51	52	53	54	55	56	57	58	59	60
17	18	19	20	21	22	23	24	25	26	27	28	29	30	1	2	V_1
7	8	9	23	11	12	28	15	14	30	17	18	5	20	21	22	V_2
29	30	31	32	1	2	3	4	5	6	7	8	12	10	11	9	V_3
49	50	51	52	53	54	55	56	57	58	59	60	61	62	63	64	V_4
39	40	41	42	43	44	45	46	47	48	49	50	51	52	53	54	V_5
61	62	63	64	33	34	35	36	37	38	39	40	41	42	43	44	V_6

Switched Transposition Block

Block $\mathbf{P}^{(e)}_{128/1}$ implements transposition of vectors L and $\Pi(L)$ having $e = 1$, which ensures correctness of the decryption.

Nonlinear Operation G

Nonlinear operations $\mathbf{G}^{(1)}$ and $\mathbf{G}^{(2)}$ have the same structure and are defined according to the following formula:

$G_{AB}(X) = X \oplus A \oplus BX_1 \oplus X_2X_5 \oplus A_1X_6 \oplus B_1A_2 \oplus X_4X_3 \oplus X_1X_6X_4 \oplus B_1X_2X_6 \oplus B_1X_1X_2X_4$, where:

- $X, A, B \in \{0, 1\}^{64}$
- AB denotes bit-by-bit modulo-e multiplication of vectors A, B
- For $i = 1, 2, 3, 4, 5, 60$, we have $X_i = X^{>>>64-i}$.
- For $i = 1, 2$, we have $A_i = A^{\to i} \oplus A^{(0)\leftarrow(2-i)}$, where $A^{(0)} = (1, 1, 0, \ldots, 0) \in \{0, 1\}^{64}$ is a fixed block of initial conditions, "$\to k$" and "$\leftarrow k$" are logical shifts of the vector by k positions right or left (the released positions are filled with zeros) .
- $B_1 = B^{\to 1} \oplus B^{(0)}$, where $B^{(0)} = (1, 0, \ldots, 0) \in \{0, 1\}^{64}$ is a fixed block of initial conditions.

In the differential analysis of CIKS-128, which will be described later in this chapter, the following expression is used for computing the i-th output bit:

$$y_i = x_i \oplus a_i \oplus b_i x_{i-1} \oplus x_{i-2}x_{i-5} \oplus a_{i-1}x_{i-6} \oplus a_{i-2}b_{i-1} \oplus x_{i-3}x_{i-4} \oplus x_{i-1}x_{i-4}x_{i-6} \oplus b_{i-1}x_{i-2}x_{i-6} \oplus b_{i-1}x_{i-1}x_{i-2}x_{i-4},$$

where $(x_{-5}, x_{-4}, x_{-3}, x_{-2}, x_{-1}, x_0) = (x_{59}, x_{60}, x_{61}, x_{62}, x_{63}, x_{64})$; $a_0 = a_{-1} = b_0 = 1$.

Investigation of statistical properties of the COBRA-H128 cipher was carried out according to the standard tests earlier used for evaluation of the influence of the bits of the source text of the AES contest finalists and bits of the key on the ciphertext in such ciphers as SPECTR-H64 and SPECTR-128. The obtained results have shown that COBRA-H128 has statistical properties similar to AES candidates, SPECTR-H64, and SPECTR-128. Experimental results are provided in Tables 5.33 and 5.34, where the "*" sign denotes the "1 key and 40,000 texts" experiment, the "**" sign stands for "200 keys and 200 texts" experiment, and the «+» sign corresponds to the case «4,000 keys and one text». From the results of experiments it is clearly seen that after six rounds of the COBRA–H128 algorithm, statistical criteria are satisfied completely both for the influence of the bits of the source text, and for the influence of the key bits. Investigation of statistical properties of the influence of the key bits for this cipher is of high importance, because this cipher uses very simple key schedule.

5.7.4 Block Ciphers based on Controlled Substitution-Permutation Networks

In this section, the variants of algorithms for encrypting 128-bit data blocks will be covered. The general structure of these algorithms is a combination of the classes of balanced Feistel networks and substitution-permutation networks (Figure 5.48).

TABLE 5.33 The Influence of the Source Text Bits

R	*	*	*	*	**	**	**	**
	(1)	(2)	(3)	(4)	(1)	(2)	(3)	(4)
12	64,002	1.0000	0.9997	0.9960	64,001	1.0000	0.9996	0.9961
10	64,001	1.0000	0.9996	0.9960	64,002	1.0000	0.9997	0.9960
8	63,995	1.0000	0.9997	0.9960	64,000	1.0000	0.9996	0.9960
7	64,001	1.0000	0.9996	0.9960	64,002	1.0000	0.9997	0.9960
6	63,996	1.0000	0.9996	0.9960	63,999	1.0000	0.9996	0.9960
5	63,999	1.0000	0.9996	0.9960	63,996	1.0000	0.9996	0.9960
4	63,899	1.0000	0.9982	0.9953	63,895	1.0000	0.9982	0.9953
3	53,732	1.0000	0.8396	0.8382	53,726	1.0000	0.8395	0.8382
2	28,367	0.9983	0.4432	0.4430	28,270	1.0000	0.4417	0.4415
1	6,940	0.5005	0.1084	0.1006	6,934	0.5039	0.1083	0.1005

TABLE 5.34 The Influence of the Key Bits

R	+	+	+	+	**	**	**	**
	(1)	(2)	(3)	(4)	(1)	(2)	(3)	(4)
12	63,997	1.0000	0.9997	0.9960	64,005	1.0000	0.9994	0.9921
10	64,002	1.0000	0.9996	0.9960	64,001	1.0000	0.9996	0.9960
8	64,003	1.0000	0.9997	0.9960	64,001	1.0000	0.9997	0.9960
7	64,001	1.0000	0.9996	0.9960	64,001	1.0000	0.9997	0.9960
6	63,996	1.0000	0.9996	0.9960	64,004	1.0000	0.9996	0.9960
5	63,928	1.0000	0.9986	0.9954	63,929	1.0000	0.9986	0.9954
4	63,405	1.0000	0.9906	0.9879	63,418	1.0000	0.9908	0.9881
3	55,604	1.0000	0.8688	0.8660	55,596	1.0000	0.8687	0.8660
2	29,417	0.9040	0.4596	0.4541	29,439	1.0000	0.4600	0.4545
1	5,803	0.4099	0.0907	0.0792	5,799	0.5040	0.0906	0.0792

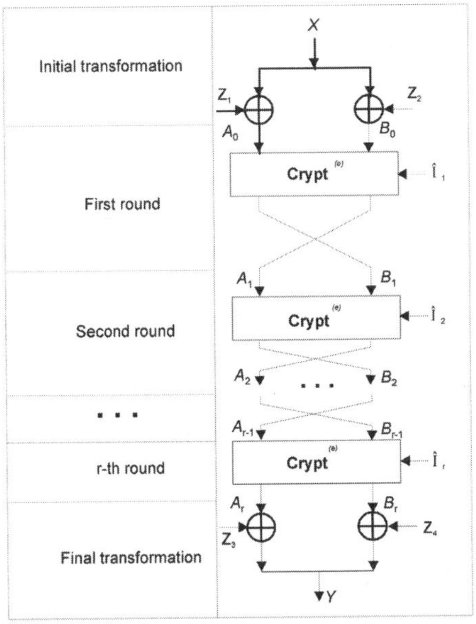

FIGURE 5.48 The general scheme of the encryption algorithm.

The encryption is carried out on the basis of sequential transformation of two 64-bit subblocks A and B:

1. Assign i:=1 and carry out the initial transformation: $A := A \oplus Z_4$, $B : = B \oplus Z_3$.
2. Execute the round transformation and, if $i < R$, transpose A and B subblocks.
3. Assign $i := i + 1$ and, if $i \leq R$, go to step 2.
4. Execute the final transformation: $A := A \oplus Z_2$, $B := B \oplus Z_1$.

The basis of these algorithms is formed by blocks of controlled substitution-permutation networks $\mathbf{F}_{64/192}$ and $\mathbf{F}^{-1}{}_{64/192}$, where blocks shown in Table 5.35 are used as elementary $\mathbf{F}_{2/1}$ blocks. In particular, in the course of the strength analysis, $\mathbf{F}_{2/1}$ blocks are used, which are synthesized on the basis of boolean functions of the following form: $f_1 = x_2x_3 \oplus x_1$, $f_2 = x_1x_3 \oplus x_1 \oplus x_2$, (the first row in Table 5.35).

5.7.5 Analysis of Cryptographic Strength and Statistical Testing of Ciphers Built on the Basis of Controlled and Switched Operations

Evaluation of the efficiency of the use of any cryptographic primitives is necessary when determining the achieved level of performance or complexity of the hardware

TABLE 5.35 Pairs of Boolean functions Used as Elementary $\mathbf{F}_{2/1}$ Blocks for Building Algorithms Intended for Encrypting 128-bit Data Blocks

$f_1(x_1, x_2, x_3)$	$f_2(x_1, x_2, x_3)$
$x_2x_3 \oplus x_1$	$x_1x_3 \oplus x_1 \oplus x_2$
$x_2x_3 \oplus x_1 \oplus x_2$	$x_1x_3 \oplus x_2$
$x_2x_3 \oplus x_1 \oplus x_3$	$x_1x_3 \oplus x_1 \oplus x_2$
$x_2x_3 \oplus x_1 \oplus x_2 \oplus x_3 \oplus 1$	$x_1x_3 \oplus x_2$
$x_2x_3 \oplus x_1 \oplus x_2$	$x_1x_3 \oplus x_2 \oplus x_3$
$x_2x_3 \oplus x_1$	$x_1x_3 \oplus x_1 \oplus x_2 \oplus x_3 \oplus 1$
$x_2x_3 \oplus x_1 \oplus x_3$	$x_1x_3 \oplus x_1 \oplus x_2 \oplus x_3 \oplus 1$
$x_2x_3 \oplus x_1 \oplus x_2 \oplus x_3 \oplus 1$	$x_1x_3 \oplus x_2 \oplus x_3$

implementation, and for evaluation of the cryptographic strength. At the same time, cryptanalysis is the most resource- and labor-intensive stage of development new cryptographic algorithms and bringing them into operation.

One of the main methods of the cryptanalysis of the block iterative encryption algorithms is the differential method. It is based on the nonuniformity of the distribution of the output differences and consists of searching for some specially chosen metric, for which the probability of the output difference is the highest.

The differential method is applicable for cryptanalysis of Markovian cryptoalgorithms. Cryptographic algorithms are called Markovian if the round encryption equation satisfies the following condition: the probability of the occurrence of the difference does not depend on the choice of plaintext messages. In this case, the sequence of differences on each round makes up a Markovian chain, in which the next state depends only on the previous one. The probabilistic characteristics of the encryption algorithm form the basis of this method.

Let some pair (X, X') of plaintexts correspond to the input difference $\Delta X = X - X' = X \oplus X'$ and generate the following sequence of output differences in the course of sequential execution of the $Y = F_{k_r} F_{k_{r-1}} \ldots F_{k_1}(X)$ transformation:

$$\Delta Y(1) = Y(1) \oplus Y'(1), \Delta Y(2) = Y(2) \oplus Y'(2), \ldots, \Delta Y(r) = Y(r) \oplus Y'(r),$$

where $Y(i)$, $Y'(i)$ are the results of execution of i transformation rounds over X and X', respectively. For the sequence of s differences, consider the probability of the s-round characteristic

$$\Pr\{\Delta Y(1) = \beta(1), \ldots, \Delta Y(s) = \beta(s) \mid \Delta X = \alpha\},$$

$1 \le s \le r$, assuming that X, X' are random elements with even distribution over the entire set of plaintexts, and $k_1, k_2, \ldots, k_r$ are random round keys uniformly distributed over the entire set of keys. For Markovian encryption algorithms, the probability of s-round differential is determined by the following equality:

$$\Pr\{\Delta Y(s) = \beta(s) \mid \Delta X = \alpha\} =$$

$$\sum_{\beta(1)} \sum_{\beta(2)} \cdots \sum_{\beta(s-1)} \prod_{i=1}^{s} \Pr\{\Delta Y(i) = \beta(i) \mid \Delta Y(i-1) = \beta(i-1)\}$$

The goal of attack is reconstruction of the round key k_r. Before doing this, it is necessary to discover $(r-1)$ – round characteristic $(\alpha, \beta(r-1))$ with the maximum probability p. Then, by carrying out N experiments, the cryptanalyst generates random plaintexts X_j, computes $X_j' = X_j \approx \alpha$ and determines Y_j, Y_j', where $j = 1, \ldots, N$. The assessment $\widehat{k}$ of the unknown round key k_r is chosen to be equal to the following value:

$$\widehat{k} = \arg\max_{k \in \mathbf{K}} \sum_{j=1}^{N} I\left\{ F_k^{-1}(Y_j) \oplus F_k^{-1}(Y_j') = \beta(r-1) \right\}$$

where $I\{\bullet\}$ is the indicator of a random event. $I\{\Theta\} = 1$, if event Θ takes place; otherwise, $I\{\Theta\} = 0$. The preceding operations are repeated the required number of times, until the actual round key is discovered as the most probable one.

The computational complexity of the attack using differential analysis is no less than $W_{\min} \ge \frac{1}{p}$ of $Y = F_{k_r} F_{k_{r-1}} \ldots F_{k_1}(X)$ transformation operations.

Analysis of the Cryptographic Strength of the DDP-64 Cipher Against Differential and Linear Cryptanalysis

The DDP-64 cipher is an example of block cipher based only on data-dependent permutations (that is, data-dependent permutations are the only nonlinear cryptographic primitive used). Variable permutations are used for solving the following problems:

- Transformation of the right data subblock using $\mathbf{P}_{32/96}$, $\mathbf{P}^{-1}_{32/96}$ operational blocks ensuring the possibility of inverse transformation
- Execution of nonlinear transformation using **F** blocks, which doesn't allow for unambiguous inverse transformation
- Transposition of the corresponding pairs of subkeys when switching from encryption to decryption
- Implementation of a switched permutation $\Pi^{(e')}$

Similarly to SPECTR-H64, the DDP-64 cryptoscheme is characterized by high performance in case of frequent change of keys, because it doesn't use key precomputations. Another common feature is that for variable permutations carried out by operational blocks **F**, $\mathbf{P}_{32/96}$,and $\mathbf{P}^{-1}{}_{32/96}$, it is possible to easily compute differential characteristics corresponding to the differences with small number of active bits; with all that being so, such characteristics have the highest probabilities. In comparison to SPECTR-H64, the DDP-64 has the following specific features:

- DDP-64 uses the entire secret key in each round.
- DDP-64 uses two **F**-boxes carried out simultaneously with the $\mathbf{P}_{32/96}$ operation. Each of the two **F**-boxes represents a controlled permutations block of a special type.
- Round transformation includes special permutation involutions carried out over the left and over the right data subgroups.
- The avalanche effect propagates because the bits being changed are used as control bits. When transforming binary vectors containing modified bits, the number of modified bits remains unchanged; this means there is no avalanche effect. (A certain exception takes place in case of an **F**-block, where 8 input bits are used as an internal control vector earlier designated as W_6).

When considering the strength of the DDP-64 cipher against differential cryptanalysis the result was obtained, which is typical for ciphers based on data-dependent permutations. This result is that the differential characteristics with the differences having the smallest weight have the highest probabilities. Let's use the following notation. Let $\Delta^W{}_h$ be the difference containing h active (that is, nonzero) bits and corresponding to vector W. Let $\Delta_{h|i_1,\ldots,i_n}$ be the difference with active bits in positions $i_1, \ldots, i_n$. In contrast to the previous designation, the second one fixes the positions, to which active bits belong. In the first case the sets of differences with specified number of active bits are considered (in individual variants of differences $\Delta^W{}_h$ active bits belong to different positions in the general case). Let $p(\Delta \rightarrow \Delta'/\mathbf{P})$ be the probability of the case when the input difference Δ, having passed through operation **P**, is transformed into the output difference Δ'.

The avalanche effect corresponding to operations $\mathbf{P}_{32/96}$ and $\mathbf{P}^{-1}{}_{32/96}$ is due to the use of the data subgroup L for specifying values V and V'. Each bit of the left data subgroup influences three bits of each of these control vectors. Each control bit influences two bits of the right data subgroup. Thus, thanks to controlled permutations carried out over the right data subgroup R using $\mathbf{P}_{32/96}$ and $\mathbf{P}^{-1}{}_{32/96}$ blocks, one bit of L influences approximately 12 bits of R. In the case when a certain difference with one active bit $\Delta'' = \Delta_{1/i}$ passes through the left branch of the cryptoscheme, it influences three elementary switching elements that transpose six different bits of the right data subgroup. For example, if the input difference of the $\mathbf{P}_{32/96}$ block controlled permutations block doesn't contain active bits (this is the case of zero difference), then the difference $\Delta^L_{1/i}$ can cause the following events depending on the right data subgroup:

- Active bits in controlled permutation block are not formed (that is, the output difference Δ'_0 is formed) with the probability equal to 2^{-3}.
- The output difference Δ'_2 is formed at the output of the controlled permutations block with the probability of $3 \cdot 2^{-3}$.
- The output difference Δ'_4 is formed with the probability of $3 \cdot 2^{-3}$.
- The output difference Δ'_6 is formed with the probability of 2^{-3}.

Average probabilities $p(\Delta_q \rightarrow \Delta'_g/\mathbf{P}_{32/96})$ corresponding to input and output differences of block $\mathbf{P}_{32/96}$ with several active bits ($q = 0, 1, 2$ and $g = q + a$, where $a = -2,0,2,4$ passing through the left branch of the encryption round. Probabilities $p(\Delta_{q|i_1,\ldots i_q} \rightarrow \Delta'_g)$ are computed assuming that the values of numbers $i_1, \ldots, i_q$, corresponding to the positions of active bits are equiprobable. In this case, the computation is carried out because the positions of active bits considered in Table 5.36 are not fixed. It can be easily shown that for the arbitrary input difference Δ_q and its corresponding output difference Δ'_g the sum $q + g$ is always even.

TABLE 5.36 Probability Values of Certain Characteristics of the $\mathbf{P}_{32/96}$ Controlled Permutations Block

Δ''	$\Delta_0 \rightarrow \Delta'_0$	$\Delta_0 \rightarrow \Delta'_2$	$\Delta_0 \rightarrow \Delta'_4$	$\Delta_1 \rightarrow \Delta'_1$	$\Delta_1 \rightarrow \Delta'_3$
Δ^L_0	1	0	0	1	0
Δ^L_1	2^{-3}	$1.5 \cdot 2^{-2}$	$1.5 \cdot 2^{-2}$	$1.17 \cdot 2^{-3}$	$1.59 \cdot 2^{-2}$
Δ^L_2	2^{-6}	$1.5 \cdot 2^{-4}$	$1.88 \cdot 2^{-3}$	$1.38 \cdot 2^{-6}$	$1.88 \cdot 2^{-4}$
Δ''	$\Delta_1 \rightarrow \Delta'_5$	$\Delta_2 \rightarrow \Delta'_0$	$\Delta_2 \rightarrow \Delta'_2$	$\Delta_2 \rightarrow \Delta'_4$	$\Delta_2 \rightarrow \Delta'_6$
Δ^L_0	0	0	1	0	0
Δ^L_1	$1.41 \cdot 2^{-2}$	$1.55 \cdot 2^{-9}$	$1.08 \cdot 2^{-3}$	$1.36 \cdot 2^{-2}$	$1.15 \cdot 2^{-2}$
Δ^L_2	$1.06 \cdot 2^{-2}$	$1.55 \cdot 2^{-8}$	$1.38 \cdot 2^{-6}$	$1.69 \cdot 2^{-4}$	$1.72 \cdot 2^{-3}$

The contribution of the **F** operation into the avalanche effect is determined mainly thanks to the use of the left subgroup for specifying control vectors W and W'. Additional contribution is introduced at the expense of the dependence of the output vector W_6, formed by the "Ext" extension block (see Figure 3.6 in Chapter 3) on L. Consider vector $L = (L_l, L_h)$ before the "<<< 16" operation. Each bit l_i from L_l, where $1 \leq i \leq 16$, influences three elementary $\mathbf{P}_{2/1}$ blocks of the $\mathbf{P}_{32/48}$ block in the bottom **F** block, and two $\mathbf{P}_{2/1}$ blocks of the $\mathbf{P}^{-1}_{32/48}$ block in the top **F**-block (after execution of the "<<< 16" operation, bit l_i moves to the most significant half of the bits of block L). In addition, with the probability of 2^{-2} (this is the probability of the case when l_i will be moved to one of the positions corresponding to vector H_5), bit l_i influences two $\mathbf{P}_{2/1}$ blocks belonging to the first active layer of the $\mathbf{P}^{-1}_{32/48}$ controlled permutation block in the top **F**-block, and with the same probability l_i influences two similar $\mathbf{P}_{2/1}$ blocks in the bottom **F**-block. All bits of L_h have the same properties, because after the "<<<16" operation components of the input vector L_l and vector L_h exchange positions, and the transformations in the top and bottom **F** blocks are symmetric.

Consider the mechanism that forms the iterative two-round characteristic function with the difference $(\Delta^L{}_1, \Delta^R{}_0)$. The difference with one active bit $\Delta^L{}_1$, passing through the left branch of the cryptoscheme, can generate zero difference at the output of both **F** blocks. This might happen in two most probable cases described here. Case 1 corresponds to implementation of all elementary events listed here:

- In both **F** blocks, the active bit is moved into one of the eight bits of vector H_5 at the output of permutation Π' (the probability of this event is $p_1 = 2^{-2} \cdot 2^{-2} = 2^{-4}$).
- In both **F** blocks, the active bit doesn't generate any pairs of active bits in the $\mathbf{P}_{32/48}$ and $\mathbf{P}^{-1}_{32/48}$ operational blocks (the probability of this event is $p_2 = 2^{-2} \cdot 2^{-3} \cdot (2^{-2})^2 = 2^{-9}$).
- In the $\mathbf{P}_{32/96}$ block, the active bit of the left data subgroup doesn't generate any additional active bits in the right data subgroup (the probability of this event is $p_3 = 2^{-3}$).
- In the $\mathbf{P}^{-1}_{32/96}$ block, the active bit doesn't generate active bits (the probability of this event is $p_4 = 2^{-3}$).

In Case 2, we have the following events:

- In both **F** blocks, the active bit is moved at the output of the permutation Π' into one of the 32 bits of vector (H_1, H_2, H_3, H_4) (the probability of this event is $p'_1 = (1 - 2^{-2})^2 \approx 1.12 \cdot 2^{-1}$).
- In both **F** blocks, the active bit of the left branch doesn't result in generation of the pairs of active bits in blocks $\mathbf{P}_{32/48}$ and $\mathbf{P}^{-1}_{32/48}$ (the probability of this event is $p'_2 = 2^{-2} \cdot 2^{-3} = 2^{-5}$).

- In block $\mathbf{P}_{32/96,}$ the active bit of the left data subgroup doesn't generate additional active bits in the right subgroup (the probability of this event is $p'_3 = 2^{-3}$).
- In block $\mathbf{P}^{-1}_{32/96}$, the active bit of the left data subgroup doesn't generate active bits (the probability of this event is $p'_4 = 2^{-3}$).
- At the output of the top and bottom **F** blocks, the difference $\Delta'_{1|i}$ and $\Delta'_{1|j}$, respectively, are generated, where $i = \mathbf{I}_2(j)$ (the probability of this event is $p'_5 = 2^{-5}$).

Designate the probabilities of Cases 1 and 2 as P' and P'', respectively. By considering the probabilities of elementary events, it is easy to obtain the following result:

$$P' = p_1 p_2 p_3 p_4 = 2^{-4} \cdot 2^{-9} \cdot 2^{-3} \cdot 2^{-3} = 2^{-19}\ ?$$

$$P'' = p'_1 p'_2 p'_3 p'_4 p'_5 = 2^{-1} \cdot 2^{-5} \cdot 2^{-3} \cdot 2^{-3} \cdot 2^{-5} = 1.12 \cdot 2^{-17}.$$

There are several other possible mechanisms of obtaining zero difference at the output of the right branch of the cryptoscheme; however, their contribution into the probability of iterative two-round characteristics is considerably smaller than that of Cases 1 and 2—therefore, this contribution can be neglected. Thus, the most significant cases produce the probability $P(2) = P' + P'' = 1.37 \cdot 2^{-17}$. The difference (Δ^L_1, Δ^R_0) passes one round with the probability $P(2) = 1.37 \cdot 2^{-17}$. After transposition of the data blocks at the input of the second round, we'll have the difference (Δ^L_0, Δ^R_1), which passes it with the probability 1 and after transposition of the data subgroups produces the initial difference (Δ^L_1, Δ^R_0). As the result, for the two-round characteristic function the following probability is obtained: $P(2) \approx P = 1.37 \cdot 2^{-17}$.

Characteristics with differences (Δ^L_0, Δ^R_1) and (Δ^L_1, Δ^R_0) appear to be the best. Consideration of other differential characteristics with different numbers of active bits in corresponding differences allows us to discover that adding active bits considerably reduces the probability of characteristics. The difference (Δ^L_1, Δ^R_0) passes eight or ten rounds of the DDP-64 cipher with the following probability:

$$P(8) = P^4(2) \approx 1.76 \cdot 2^{-67}\ ?\ P(10) = P^5(2) \approx 1.2 \cdot 2^{-83}.$$

For random ciphers, we have $P((\Delta^L_1, \Delta^R_0) \rightarrow (\Delta^L_1, \Delta^R_0)') = 2^{-64} \cdot 2^5 = 2^{-59} > P(8) > P(10)$. Thus, the DDP-64 cipher with eight and ten rounds is undistinguishable from the random cipher in the case of a differential attack using the most efficient iterative characteristics.

The use of linear cryptanalysis for detecting the difference of the DDP-64 cipher from a random one is less efficient in comparison to differential attack. Investigations have shown that linear characteristics with small number of active bits have the greatest offset, and maximum offset is typical for linear characteristics with two active bits, which are built with the account of events that take into account the facts of replacement of the bits of data being transformed by the bits of the $C = (10101010)$ constant. Let $A = (A^L, A^R)$ and $B = (B^L, B^R)$ be the input and output masks, respectively. The L and R superscripts designate the left and right parts of the mask, respectively. Because of the idea implemented when designing the DDP-64 cipher, linear characteristics with masks $A = B = (111\ldots1)$ have very low offset, because **F**-blocks implement the transformation with high nonlinearity.

Using the formulae for computing linear characteristics provided in "Cryptography: Fast Ciphers" by A. A. Moldovyan, N. A. Moldovyan, N. D. Goots, and B. V. Izotov, it is easy to compute that the offset of the linear characteristic with the number of active bits $z \leq 31$ has the value $b \leq 2^{-6}$ for each of the blocks $P_{32/96}$, $P^{-1}_{32/96}$, and F. Maximum value $b = 2^{-6}$ corresponds to the case $z = 1$. Computation of linear characteristics of controlled permutations blocks can be conveniently carried out by means of considering "physical" movement of data by the permutations network. Because the DDP-64 cipher is mainly built based on permutation operations, this approach also can be applied for its analysis. Let's introduce subscript indices in designation of masks, which, by analogy with designation of differential characteristics, will specify the number of active (nonzero) bits and positions to which active bits belong. For example, A_2 and $A_{2|5,7}$ designate an arbitrary mask with two active bits, and the mask with two active bits located in the fifth and seventh positions counted from left to right, respectively.

Consider a single-round linear characteristic with masks $A = (A^L{}_{1|i}, A^R{}_{1|j})$ and $B = (B^L{}_{1|i'}, B^R{}_{1|g})$, where the value i' is determined by the value i (i' is the number of the position into which the i-th bit of the left subgroup is moved at the input of the first round). The offset of the aforementioned linear characteristic is determined by the fact that there exists the probability of the event when the active bit of the left subgroup will be used twice with the active bit of the right subgroup when carrying out the XOR operation. For this to occur, this bit must be moved by the top **F**-block into the same position, into which the active bit of the right data subgroup falls at the output of the $\mathbf{P}_{32/96}$ operation (the probability of this event is $p_1 = 2^{-5}$). The active bit of the left subgroup also must be moved by the bottom **F**-block into the position, into which the active bit of the right subgroup falls at the output of the operation **I** (the probability of this event is $p_2 \approx 0.75 \cdot 2^{-5}$). After that, the active bit in the right branch must fall into position g at the output of the $\mathbf{P}^{-1}{}_{32/96}$ block (probability of this elementary event is $p_3 = 2^{-5}$). Thus, two bits separated at the input of the first round fall into the known positions at the output with the probability

$P(1) = p_1 p_2 p_3 \approx 0.75 \cdot 2^{-15}$. Knowing this probability, it is easy to compute the offset $b(1)$ of the single-round characteristic $((A^L{}_{1|i}, A^R{}_{1|j}); (B^L{}_{1|i'}, B^R{}_{1|g}); b(1))$:

$$b(1) = 0.5(1 - P(1)) + P(1) = 0.5P(1) = 0.75 \cdot 2^{-16}.$$

For r-round characteristic $((A^L{}_{1|i}, A^R{}_{1|j}); (B^L{}_{1|i'}, B^R{}_{1|g}); b(r))$, proceeding in a similar way, it is possible to obtain the following evaluation:

$$b(r) = 0.5P(r) < 2^{-15r-1}.$$

From the obtained evaluations, it follows that three encryption rounds of the DDP-64 cipher are enough for preventing linear cryptanalysis.

It is necessary to mention that the value of the constant $C = (10101010)$ is chosen so that its weight $\phi(C)$ is equal to 4. This value was chosen because for any other weight, another mechanism of forming linear characteristic $((A^L{}_0, A^R{}_{1|j}); (B^L{}_{0'}, B^R{}_{1|g}); b(2))$ takes the prevailing role. This mechanism is due to the different probability of the replacement of the active bit passing from the left branch of the round transformation into the right branch by zero and one values. This mechanism determines the following value of the offset of the aforementioned two-round linear characteristic:

$$b(2) = 2^{-2r-6} (|\phi(C)-4|/4)^{r/2} = 2^{-3r-6}|\phi(C)-4|^{r/2}.$$

From this formula, it can be clearly seen that having $\phi(C) \neq 4$ linear cryptanalysis becomes considerably more efficient. Thanks to the aforementioned choice of the weight $\phi(C)$, it is possible to ensure high strength of the DDP-64 cipher against linear cryptanalysis.

Now it is time to consider several other types of attacks. Algebraic attacks at the DDP-64 algorithm are impossible because of high degree of the algebraic normal form. The complexity of boolean functions (containing more than 100,000 terms) describing the round transformation of the DDP-64 algorithm further complicate such attacks. Despite a very simple key schedule, DDP-64 is strong against slide attacks on ciphers that do not use key precomputation procedures. This is achieved because the cipher under consideration uses the following:

- Aperiodic subkey schedule
- Round transformation that doesn't represent an involution and contains switched operation with aperiodic schedule of modes

In particular, the latter factor prevents slide attacks in the case when all subkeys have the same values. Despite the simplicity of the key schedule, "symmetric" keys $K'' = (X, Y, Y, X)$ and $K'' = (X, X, X, X)$ are neither weak, nor semi-weak, because decryption requires appropriate switching of the $\Pi^{(e')}$ operation. For example, by considering the round transformation, it is easy to notice that $T^{(e=0)}(C, K')\ M$, where $C = T^{(e=0)}(M, K'')$. Finding semi-weak pairs of keys for DDP-64 is difficult, if ever possible.

The latter notes allow for drawing the following important conclusion: permutations dependent on e play an important role in DDP-64, which doesn't include the procedure of key precomputation. For comparison, note that for the SPECTR-H64 cipher, where there are no switched operations, for every value X the 256-bit key $K = (X, X, X, X, X, X, X, X)$ is weak. In addition, using such a key creates prerequisites for successful implementation of slide attacks.

Evaluation of DDP-64 Hardware Implementation

The interest in evaluation of different variants of hardware implementation of the DDP-64 cipher is because this cipher in its "pure" form demonstrates high efficiency of variable permutations as a cryptographic primitive. Consequently, hardware resources used for implementation, and efficiency parameters, depend only on the implementation of variable permutations. On the example of this cipher, it is possible to obtain typical evaluations of hardware implementations. Time delay corresponding to one active layer of multilayer controlled permutations blocks is approximately equal to τ, where τ is the delay time of the XOR ($\oplus$) operation. The delay time (T) of the $\mathbf{P}_{m/n}$ block can be evaluated as $T \approx 2m\tau/n$. The critical path of combinational schemes implementing different cipher elements are hard to evaluate in terms of τ, because in this case there is no binding to specific microelectronic technology. In chosen units the critical path of one round of DDP-64 is equal to 16τ. Critical path of 10-round DDP-64 cipher makes 162τ (two units are related to the execution of initial and final transformations).

Complexity of the hardware implementation of the $\mathbf{P}_{n/m}$ block is $6m$ AND—NOT gates. Implementation of 10 DDP-64 rounds requires less than 30,000 AND—NOT gates. To this set, it is necessary to add a certain number of gates corresponding to the 160-bit key register and two 64-bit registers for input and output data, which makes approximately 4500 gates. According to these evaluations, the total complexity of implementing 10 (8) rounds of DDP-64, including overhead for the registers for storing keys and data is less than 35,000 (29,000) AND—NOT gates when using the implementation variant consisting of the execution of the combinational scheme including full number of encryption rounds. Table 5.37 presents comparative evaluation of the complexity of circuit implementation for different ciphers (numbers marked by the * sign relate to the results provided in "Hardware Evaluation of the AES Finalists" by T. Kasua, T. Ichikawa, and M. Matsui). The convenient way to express the cipher performance is to present it in the number of bits transformed during the time τ.

TABLE 5.37 Comparative Evaluation of the DDP-64 Hardware Implementation

Cipher	Number of gates		Critical path, τ	
	Key computation	Encryption	Key computation	Encryption
DDP-64 (10 rounds)	320	34,500	–	162
DDP-64 (8 rounds)	320	28,500	–	130
DES	12,000*	42,000*	–	80
Triple-DES	23,000*	120,000*	–	220
Rijndael	94,000*	520,000*	83	95
RC6	900,000*	740,000*	3,000	880
TwoFish	230,000*	200,000*	23	470

From the data provided in Table 5.37, it can be clearly seen that the fastest implementation corresponds to the 128-bit Rijndael cipher (the performance is approximately $f \approx 1.35$ bit/τ), which is achieved by relatively high implementation cost. The cheapest implementation corresponds to DDP-64 (453 – 547 gates/bit). The DDP-64 cipher has the performance $f \approx 0.42 - 0.52$ bit/τ, which exceeds the performance values of most widely used cryptoschemes, such as RC6 ($f \approx 0.15$ bit/τ), Triple-DES ($f \approx 0.29$ bit/τ), and TwoFish ($f \approx 0.27$ bit/τ). It is remarkable that implementation of DDP-64 requires considerably fewer circuit resources in comparison to DES. These results show that the DDP-64 cryptoscheme is well suited for building into intellectual chips and microcontrollers of different types. Thanks to the low cost of circuit implementation, efficiency of the cryptographic primitive, and general importance of various operations of bit permutations, the controlled permutation operation is a good candidate for implementation in the form of a new fast command for building into the standard command set of general-purpose processors.

For obtaining more general patterns of the parameters of hardware implementations of different ciphers, special research was conducted for designing encrypting devices on the basis of various algorithms based on data-dependent permutations. The following two variants of implementation have been chosen:

- Using programmable logical matrices of the FPGA type from **Xilinx Vitrex**
- Using custom chips designed and implemented using the 0.33-mkm technology

This research was carried out in cooperation with the Patras University (Greece). Implementation parameters of the DDP-64, CIKS-1, and SPECTR-H64 were studied. Implementation was carried out for the following two architectures:

- Circuit implementation of one round and its use for carrying out all encryption rounds with changing round keys (iterative architecture—IA).
- Pipelined implementation with the number of levels equal to the number of encryption rounds, implementing full number of encryption rounds at the circuit level (pipelined architecture—PA).

Pipelined architecture ensures considerably higher performance; however, it also requires higher expenses for the hardware resources. Iterative architecture ensures minimum cost of implementation; however, the performance drop is significant. Nevertheless, IA has one significant advantage consisting of the possibility of using block ciphers in the mode of concatenation of the cipher blocks while preserving the same level of performance that is ensured in the electronic code book mode (independent encryption of data blocks).

Implementation results are outlined in Table 5.38. Comparison to the similar implementation of other ciphers (Table 5.39) shows that DDP-64, COBRA-H64 and SPECTR-H64 ensure higher speed with smaller hardware expenses in comparison to AES and IDEA cryptosystems. Their implementation cost slightly exceeds the implementation cost of the DES algorithm; however, they raise the encryption speed multiple times.

TABLE 5.38 Parameters of Hardware Implementation of DDP-64, COBRA-H64, and SPECTR-H64 Ciphers Using Programmable and Custom VLSI Circuits

Cipher	Architecture	Programmable VLSI circuit (Xilinx Vitrex)			Custom VLSI circuit (0.33 mkm)		
		Number of CLBs*	Frequency, Mbps	Encryption speed, Gbps	Area, sqmil**	Frequency, Mbps	Encryption speed, Gbps
DDP-64	IA	615	85	0.544	2 620	92	0.589
DDP-64	PA	3,440	95	6.100	14 050	101	6.500
CIKS-1	IA	907	81	0.648	3456	93	0.744
CIKS-1	PA	6,346	81	5.184	21036	95	5.824
SPECTR-H64	IA	713	83	0.443	3194	91	0.485
SPECTR-H64	PA	7,021	83	5.312	32123	94	6.016

*Configurable Logic Blocks (CLB) are standard logical elements of this type of VLSI circuits.

**The area of the used surface of the semiconductor chip is specified in sqmil units;1 sqmil = $7.45\ 10^{-4}$ mm^2.

TABLE 5.39 Comparison of the Results of Hardware Implementation of Different Ciphers Using Programmable VLSI Circuits

Cipher	Implementation architecture	Programmable VLSI circuit (Xilinx Vitrex)		
		Number of CLBs	Frequency Mbps	Encryption speed Gbps
DDP-64	Iterative	615	85	0.544
DDP-64	Pipelined	3,440	95	6.100
CIKS-1	Iterative	907	81	0.648
CIKS-1	Pipelined	6,346	81	5.184
SPECTR-H64	Iterative	713	83	0.443
SPECTR-H64	Pipelined	7,021	83	5.312
AES	Iterative	2,358	22	0.259
AES	Pipelined	17,314	28.5	3.650
IDEA	Iterative	2,878	150	0.600
DES	Iterative	722	11	0.181

The DDP-64 and COBRA-64 ciphers are characterized by smaller hardware expenses in comparison to the SPECTR-H64 cryptosystems for all variants of implementation, which is ensured by individual features of building of the encryption round. By performance, they exceed the SPECTR-H64 cryptoscheme in any case. Nevertheless, all three ciphers based on variable permutations have very close parameters and give an estimate of the efficiency of hardware implementation of such ciphers.

Thus, it is possible to draw the following conclusions in relation to the DDP-64 cipher:

- DDP-64 ensures high performance and inexpensive hardware implementation.
- The DDP-64 structure is well suited for carrying out detailed differential analysis, in particular for computing differential characteristics with low number of active bits that have the highest probability values.
- This cipher is strong against differential, linear, and other attacks.
- The DDP-64 cryptosystem is an example of ciphers based only on controlled permutations and illustrating high efficiency of controlled permutations as a cryptographic primitive.

Differential Cryptanalysis of the COBRA-H64 Cipher

Similar to some other ciphers based on data-dependent permutations, in the COBRA-H64 cryptosystem variable bit permutations carried out over the right data subgroup result in that the differential characteristics with differences having low weight have the highest probability. The probability of characteristic significantly decreases with the growth of the difference weight, because active bits fall into random positions when the difference passes through the right branch. Differential analysis provided in this section is an empiric one. It is based on the study of various differences having the weight ranging from 1 to 6. Although the probability tends to considerably decrease with the growth of the difference weight, to accomplish the differential analysis it is necessary to carry out a generalized theoretical investigation. Such an investigation will allow us to obtain a formal proof of the fact that there are no characteristics with the probability exceeding some predefined value. In general, this task seems too labor-intensive even for a small number of rounds. Empiric analysis is meaningful as one of the stages of the strength analysis. This note also relates to the analysis carried out for other ciphers.

Differences corresponding to the left and to the right data subgroups are denoted as Δ^L and Δ^R. The difference of an iterative differential characteristic appears as (Δ^L, Δ^R). When considering some individual operation **F**, input and output differences related to it are denoted as Δ^{F} and $\Delta^{(\mathrm{F})}$, respectively. The number of active bits of the difference and positions to which they belong are specified in lowercase characters. Bit values will be written after the vertical line (|) character. At the same time, it will be assumed that notations $\Delta_{2|i,j}$ and Δ_2 are essentially different: the first designation stands for specific difference with two active bits, while the second stands for one of the differences with two active bits.

The mechanism of forming the differential characteristic is determined by the properties of operations carried out within the round transformation and by the structure of that transformation. Using these operations, it is easy to compute characteristics of the $\mathrm{P}_{32/96}$ and $\mathrm{P}^{-1}{}_{32/96}$ controlled permutations blocks that correspond to small values of z in difference Δ^L_z, which determines the difference at the control input of the controlled permutations block. Probability values of different characteristics are presented in Tables 5.40 and 5.41, where Δ^X and Δ^Y are input and output differences of the controlled permutations block.

Table 5.40 Values of Probabilities $p(\Delta^X \rightarrow \Delta^Y / \Delta^L_1)$ for Block $\mathbf{P}_{32/64}$

$z=1$	Δ^Y_0	Δ^Y_2	Δ^Y_4	Δ^Y_6
Δ^X_0	2^{-3}	$1.5 \cdot 2^{-2}$	$1.5 \cdot 2^{-2}$	2^{-3}
Δ^X_2	$1.5 \cdot 2^{-11}$	$1.1 \cdot 2^{-3}$	$1.4 \cdot 2^{-2}$	$1.1 \cdot 2^{-2}$

TABLE 5.41 Values of Probabilities $p(\Delta^X \to \Delta^Y / \Delta_2^L)$ for Block $\mathbf{P}_{32/64}$

$z=2$	Δ_0^Y	Δ_2^Y	Δ_4^Y	Δ_6^Y
Δ_0^X	2^{-6}	$1.5{\cdot}2^{-4}$	$1.9{\cdot}2^{-3}$	$1.2{\cdot}2^{-2}$
Δ_2^X	$1.5{\cdot}2^{-13}$	$1.4{\cdot}2^{-6}$	$1.7{\cdot}2^{-4}$	$1.7{\cdot}2^{-3}$

When executing operation **G**, bits in positions 1, 2, …, 29 influence four output bits. In this case, modification of the input bit in position i results in deterministic modification of the output bit belonging to this position, and probabilistic change of the output bits in positions $i + k$, where $k = 1, 2, 3$. Formulae describing the dependency of modification of the output bits in case of modification of the input bit x_i are provided in Table 5.42. As can be easily noticed, difference $\Delta_{1\|i}$ passes operation **G** without modification with probability values equal to 2^{-3} if $1 \le i \le 29$, 2^{-2} if $i = 30$, 2^{-1} if $i = 31$, and 1 if $i = 32$.

TABLE 5.42 Probabilities of Active Bit Generation in Different Positions of the Output of Function G in Case of Modification of the Input Bit i

Formula	**Probability**	**Note**
$\Delta y_i = \Delta l_i$	$p(\Delta y_i=1)=1$	$1 \le i \le 32$
$\Delta y_{i+1} = \Delta l_i(l_{i-1} \oplus l_{i-2} \oplus l_{i-1}b_{i+1})$	$p(\Delta y_{i+1}=1)=1/2$	$1 \le i \le 31$
$\Delta y_{i+2} = \Delta l_i(l_{i-1} \oplus l_{i+1} \oplus b_{i+1} \oplus l_{i+1}b_{i+1})$	$p(\Delta y_{i+2}=1)=1/2$	$1 \le i \le 30$
$\Delta y_{i+3} = \Delta l_i(l_{i+1} \oplus l_{i+2} \oplus a_{i+2})$	$p(\Delta y_{i+3}=1)=1/2$	$1 \le i \le 29$

Thus, we have discovered that two-round iterative differential characteristics with differences $(0,\Delta_1^R)$ or $(\Delta_1^L,0)$ are the most efficient. Mechanisms used for forming them are identical; therefore, it is reasonable to consider only the passing of the first difference through two rounds. Because we do not specify the number of specific rounds to which the active bit belongs, only one of the existing single-bit differences in the right data subgroup is meant.

Assume that in the first round the difference Δ_1^R propagates through the right branch. Then, with the probability $p(i) = 2^{-5}$, the difference $\Delta_{1\|i}^R$ will appear at the output of the $\mathbf{P}^{-1}_{32/96}$ block, which after transposition of subgroups will be transformed into difference $\Delta_{1\|i}^L$. The latter difference introduces no less than two active bits into the right branch as it propagates through the left branch of the cryptoscheme at the expense of executing two **G** operations and superimposing their output values on the right subgroup using the modulo-e summation operation. Each with the probability 2^{-3} introduces only one bit, and the probability of introducing only two active bits into the right branch is 2^{-6}. The main contribution into the forming of two-round characteristic is due to the following two cases.

Event A

- Top operation **G** generates only one active bit at its output with the probability $p_1 = 2^{-3}$.
- Bottom operation **G** generates only one active bit at its output with the probability $p_1 = 2^{-3}$.
- Because of the presence of the difference of the control vector generated by difference $\Delta^L_{1|i}$, the $\mathbf{P}_{32/96}$ block forms difference $\Delta^R_{2|i,j'}$, where $j' = \pi^{(e \oplus 1)}(\mathbf{I}(i))$, with the probability p_3 depending on i.
- Difference $\Delta^R_{2|i,j'}$ after summation with active bits formed at the output of operations **G** is transformed into zero difference that passes the $\mathbf{P}^{-1}_{32/96}$ block without modification with the probability $p_4 = 2^{-3}$.

Event B

- Difference Δ^R_0 passes the $\mathbf{P}_{32/96}$ controlled permutations block without modification with the probability $p_3 = 2^{-3}$.
- Top operation **G** generates only one active bit at its output with the probability $p_1 = 2^{-3}$.
- Bottom operation **G** generates only one active bit at its output with the probability $p_2 = 2^{-3}$.
- Because of the presence of the difference at the control input of block $\mathbf{P}^{-1}_{32/96}$, the latter resets to zero both active bits of the difference $\Delta^R_{2|i',j}$, where $i' = \pi^{(e)}(i)$, supplied at its input, with the probability p_3 dependent on i.

The contribution of other mechanisms into the probability of two-round characteristic $P(2)$ can be neglected because it is significantly lower than the contribution of events A and B. The probability contributions of these two events will be designated as P' and P'', respectively. Thus, the result appears as follows: $P(2) \approx P' + P''$. To compute probabilities P' and P'', it is necessary to take into account the distribution of control bits over both controlled permutations blocks present in the right branch. Contributions of different bits of the left subgroup, to which the active bit of the difference $\Delta^L_{1|i}$ belongs, are different. Both events are considered similarly, with the only difference that consists in the following. When studying Event A, the probability of the situation when two active bits generated by the active switching element (that is, the element to which the active bit of the control vector difference is applied) of the $\mathbf{P}_{32/96}$ block fall into positions j' and i is considered. When studying Event B, we consider the probability of two active bits present in positions j and $i' = \pi^{(e)}(i)$ at the output of the bottom controlled permutations block falling to the input of the same active switching element of block $\mathbf{P}^{-1}_{32/96}$. Because of the topological symmetry of blocks $\mathbf{P}_{32/96}$ and $\mathbf{P}^{-1}_{32/96}$, consideration of Event B can be reduced to consideration of Event A, in which the operational block $\mathbf{P}_{32/96}$ forms the difference $\Delta^{R}_{2|i',j}$ at its output provided that the difference $\Delta^{L}_{1|j}$ is present in the left branch.

Consider the computation of the probability P' using the scheme of forming two-round characteristic shown in Figure 5.49. The difference of the left subgroup $\Delta^{L}_{1|i}$, which at the same time is the input difference of the permutation involution **I**, after the operation **I** is transformed into difference $\Delta^{L}_{1|j}$. Because of this, the top operation **G** introduces the active bit belonging to i-th position into the right branch, and the bottom operation **G** introduces the active bit belonging to position j.

The probability of the event in which the top (bottom) operation **G** forms only one active bit of the difference at its output is equal to the value p_1 (p_2), which is dependent on i (j). One of the three active switches of the top controlled permutations block can generate a pair of active bits, which can fall into positions i and j as they propagate to the output.

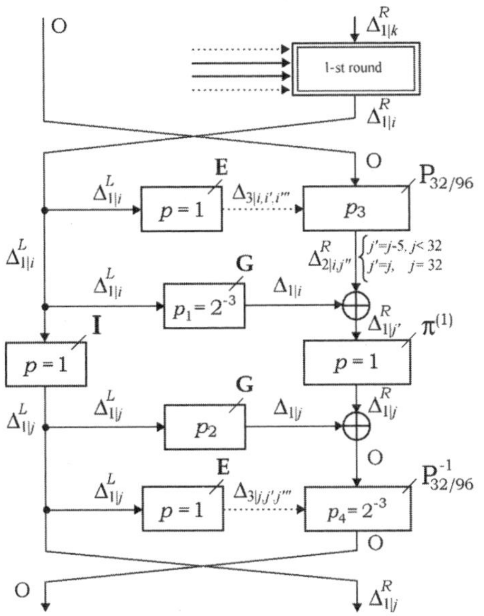

FIGURE 5.49 Two-round differential characteristic $0||\Delta_{1|k}$ of the COBRA-H64 cipher.

Probability of this event (p_3) depends on i. As the result of summation with the active bit introduced by the top operation **G**, only j'-th active bit remains at the input of the switched permutation $\pi^{(e)}$. This bit, after execution of operation $\pi^{(e)}$, falls into position with the number equal to $\pi^{(e)}(j') = \pi^{(e)}(\pi^{(e \oplus 1)}(j)) = j$, where it annihilates with the active bit introduced by the bottom operation **G**. As the result, zero difference is formed at the input of the bottom controlled permutations block, which passes it with the probability $p_4 = 2^{-3}$. Values of probabilities p_1, p_2, p_3, and p_4 are listed in Table 5.42. Note the specific feature of the case $i = 13$, for which active bits generated by both operations **G** can cancel each other. Because of the latter circumstance, in case $i = 13$ the following output differences of the top controlled permutations block bring a considerable contribution into the probability P': $\Delta^R_{2|13,15}$, $\Delta^R_{2|13,16}$, $\Delta^R_{2|13,17}$ and $\Delta^R_{2|13,18}$. For this case, Table 5.42 provides several averaged integral values of p_1, p_2, and p_3. Probability P' can be computed according to the following formula:

$$P' \approx \sum_{i=1}^{i=32} p(i) p_1 p_2 p_3 p_4 = p(i) p_4 \sum_{i=1}^{i=32} p_1 p_2 p_3 \approx 1.33 \cdot 2^{-20},$$

where the first sign of approximate equality accounts for neglecting of the weak dependency between events to which probabilities p_3 and p_4 are related. Values of probability p_3 are computed with the account of the distribution of bits of the control left data subgroup over elementary switches of the top block of controlled permutations; that is, with the account of the structure of extension block E. For example, in case $i = 5$ we have $j = 18$ and $j' = 15$; in which case, switching elements with numbers 5, 31, and 41 are active.

Also, it is necessary to account for the following three cases when the top block of controlled permutations generates difference $\Delta^R_{2|5,13}$:

1. Depending on the value of the right data subgroup R, the fifth switching element forms at its output a pair of active bits with the probability (this happens in the case when two of its input bits are different). Element 31 forms zero difference at its output with the probability 0.5, and the probability of zero difference appearing at the output of element 41 is also 0.5 (this takes place when both input bits of the corresponding element are equal).
2. Switches 5 and 41 form zero difference at their outputs with the probability 0.5, and switch 31 produces two active bits with the probability 0.5.
3. Switching elements with numbers 5 and 31 with the probability 0.5 form zero difference at their outputs, and element 41 produces two active bits.

Taking into account the structure of block **E**, each bit of the L subgroup controls permutation of six different bits of the R subgroup. Because of this, the probability of each of the preceding listed three events is exactly equal to 2^{-3}. One of the output bits of element 5 with the probability 2^{-5} (it passes five active layers of block $\mathbf{P}_{32/96}$) falls into position five at the output of the $\mathbf{P}_{32/96}$ operation. The second output bit of element 5 falls into position 13 with the same probability. As the result, the first event forms the difference $\Delta^{R}_{2|5,13}$ with the probability $p^{(1)} = 2^{-3}(2^{-5})^2 = 2^{-13}$.

The second even cannot result in forming such a difference at the output of the $\mathbf{P}_{32/96}$ block, which means that $p^{(2)} = 0$. For the third even, the result appears as follows: $p^{(3)} = 2^{-3}(2^{-3})2 = 2^{-9}$. Thus, for $i = 5$ the probability will be $p_3 = p^{(1)} + p^{(2)} +$ $+ p^{(3)} \approx 1.06 \cdot 2^{-9}$. Proceeding the same way, it is possible to compute the probability values of all the other values of i. Note that cases with values $17 \leq i \leq 32$ introduce zero contribution into probability P2.

For Event B, it is possible to obtain the probability value P22 H 2 20, proceeding the similar way, and then compute the value P(2):

$$P(2) \approx P' + P'' \approx 1.33 \cdot 2^{-20} + 2^{-20} \approx 1.16 \cdot 2^{-19}.$$

For the cases of 8 and 10 encryption rounds of the COBRA-H64 cipher, the following values are obtained: $P(8) = \mathrm{P}^4(2) \approx 1.82 \cdot 2^{-76}$ and $\mathrm{P}(10) = \mathrm{P}^5(2) \approx 1.05 \cdot 2^{-94}$.

Taking into account that for random transformation a single-bit difference $(0, \Delta_1^R)$ is formed at the output, with the probability $P = 32 \cdot 2^{-64} = 2^{-59} > P(8) > P(10)$, it is possible to conclude that COBRA-H64 is strong against differential cryptanalysis, because it is undistinguishable from a random transformation using characteristics with the greatest probabilities.

The use of switched operation $\pi^{(e)}$ eliminates weak and semi-weak keys. This makes the use of simple key schedule more secure. The use of different values of parameter e in different encryption rounds ensures elimination of the periodicity of the encryption procedure. Consequently, it ensures protection against slide attacks even in the case of using the same round keys in all rounds, which can take place in the case of secret keys having structures like $K = (X, X, \ldots, X)$.

Differential Cryptanalysis of the COBRA-H128 Cipher

The COBRA-H128 cipher is similar in structure to the COBRA-H64 algorithm. This similarity can be traced even in the differential properties of these ciphers. For the COBRA-H128 cipher, differential characteristics with a small number of active bits also have higher probabilities in comparison to characteristics including differences of greater weights. The characteristic corresponding to the passing of the difference $(0, \Delta_1^R)$ through two rounds has the greatest probability. The mechanism of its passing through the encryption procedure is similar to that of the COBRA-H64 cipher. The difference is that dimensions of the used controlled permutations blocks and G operations are different.

Active bit passes the first round with the probability 1. In this case, it is moved into another position; however, for the case when positions are not specified when denoting the difference, any output difference with the specified number of active bits will present interest (no matter what the numbers of the positions of active bits might be). This means that in this case, we will consider sets of all differences with the specified number of active bits instead of individual differences. When only one input bit of the G operation is modified, only one bit will change at its output, which corresponds to the same position as the modified input bit. In addition, six more output bits can change with the probability 0.5. Main variants of forming different variants of two-round characteristic are related to consideration of occurrence of differences $\Delta^{(G)}_{2|i,i+1}$, $\Delta^{(G)}_{2|i,i+2}$, $\Delta^{(G)}_{2|i,i+3}$, $\Delta^{(G)}_{2|i,i+4}$, $\Delta^{(G)}_{2|i,i+5}$, and $\Delta^{(G)}_{2|i,i+6}$ at the output of operation G (for $i > 58$ indices $i + k$ have values that exceed 64; for such indices it is necessary to adopt the value $i + k - 64$). By specifying operation G through boolean functions, it is easy to write the formulae describing modification of the output bits in position $i + k$, where $k = 0, 1, \ldots, 6$ (see Table 5.43).

TABLE 5.43 Probabilities of Generation of the Active Bit at the Output of Function G in the Case of Modification of the i-th Input Bit

Formula	Probability
$\Delta y_i = \Delta l_i$	$p(\Delta y_i = 1) = 1$
$\Delta y_{i+1} = \Delta l_i(a''_{i+1} \oplus l_{i-3}(l_{i-5} \oplus l_{i-1}a''_1))$	$p(\Delta y_{i+1} = 1) = 1/2$
$\Delta y_{i+2} = \Delta l_i(l_{i-3} \oplus a''_{i+1}(l_{i+1}l_{i-2} \oplus l_{i-4}))$	$p(\Delta y_{i+2} = 1) = 1/2$
$\Delta y_{i+3} = \Delta l_i\, l_{i-1}$	$p(\Delta y_{i+3} = 1) = 1/2$
$\Delta y_{i+4} = \Delta l_i(l_{i+1} \oplus l_{i+3}(l_{i-2} \oplus l_{i+2}a''_{i+3}))$	$p(\Delta y_{i+4} = 1) = 1/2$
$\Delta y_{i+5} = \Delta l_i\, l_{i+3}$	$p(\Delta y_{i+5} = 1) = 1/2$
$\Delta y_{i+6} = \Delta l_i(a'_{i+5} \oplus l_{i+5}l_{i+2} \oplus l_{i+4}a''_{i+5}))$	$p(\Delta y_{i+6} = 1) = 1/2$

Described here are events A1 and A2, the contribution of which into the probability of two-round characteristic of the COBRA-H128 cipher is the most significant. Consider the mechanism of forming two-round characteristic with the difference $(0, \Delta^R_1)$ shown in Figure 5.50. The difference Δ^R_1 after the execution of the first round will transform into difference $\Delta^R_{1|i}$ with the probability $p' = 2^{-6}$, and after transposition of data subblocks the difference will transform to $\Delta^L_{1|i}$; that is, the difference $(\Delta^L_{1|i}, 0)$ is supplied to the input of the second round with the probability $p = 2^{-6}$. The active bit from the left branch passes through the top operation **G** with probability 2^{-6}, generating difference $\Delta_{1|i}^{G}$ at the output of this operation. The active bit from the left branch also passes through the bottom operation **G**; however, before doing this it passes through the fixed permutation Π and transforms into difference $\Delta_{1|j}$, where $j = \Pi(i)$. Difference $\Delta_{1|j}$ passes through bottom operation **G** with the probability 2^{-6}. In this case, thanks to permutation Π, in the course of execution of operations **G** different bits of the left data subgroup influence the generation of new active bits in positions $i + k$ (for the top operation **G**) and positions $j + k$ (for the bottom operation **G**), where $k = 0, 1, \ldots, 6$. Thus, the two events just considered are independent. Differences $\Delta_{1|i}^{G}$ and $\Delta_{1|j}^{G}$ are superimposed of the right subgroup. If a pair of active bits is generated in the top controlled permutations block, and these bits fall into positions i and j, they will be superimposed over one bits introduced from the left branch of the cryptoscheme and reset them to zero, thus forming zero difference at the input of the bottom controlled permutations block. Generation of active bits in controlled permutation block can take place, because the active bit from the left subgroup generates three unit differences of the control vector V; that is, the difference Δ_3^V will appear at the control input of the controlled permutations block. If the zero difference of the right subgroup passes the top controlled permutations block, then two active bits introduced from the left branch can annihilate in the bottom controlled permutations block provided they simultaneously are moved to the same elementary switch, to whose control input unit bit from the control vector is supplied.

There also are other mechanisms of forming two-round characteristic with difference $(0, \Delta_1^R)$; however, their contribution into the probability of the characteristic is considerably smaller. There are only two events with significant contribution.

Event A1 (see Figure 5.50):

- Difference $\Delta_{1|i}^{G}$ is formed at the output of the top operation **G** with the probability $p_1 = 2^{-6}$.
- Difference $\Delta_{1|j}^{G}$ is formed at the output of the bottom operation with the probability $p_2 = 2^{-6}$.
- Difference $\Delta_{2|i,j'}^{P'}$, where $j' = \mathbf{I}(j)$ is formed at the output of the top controlled permutations block ($\mathbf{P}_{64/192}$) with the probability $p_3^{(i,j')}$.
- Difference $\Delta_{1|i}^{G} \oplus \Delta_{2|i,j'}^{P'} \oplus \Delta_{1|i}^{G} = \Delta_0$ is formed at the input of the bottom controlled permutations block ($\mathbf{P}^{-1}_{64/192}$).
- Zero difference passes the bottom controlled permutations block with the probability $p_4 = 2^{-3}$.

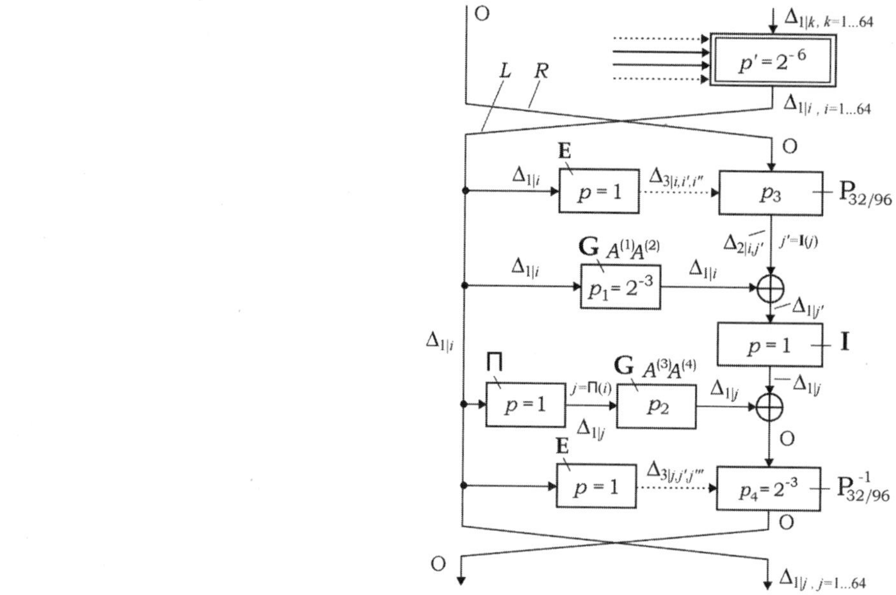

FIGURE 5.50 Two-round differential characteristic $0||\Delta_{1|k}$ of the COBRA-H128 cipher.

Event A2:

- With the probability $p_1 = 2^{-6}$, difference is formed at the output of the top operation **G**, which, after passing operation **I**, turns into difference $\Delta^{G}_{1|i}$, where $i' = \mathbf{I}(i)$.
- Zero difference passes the top controlled permutations block with the probability $p_3 = 2^{-3}$.
- Difference $\Delta^{G}_{1|i}$ is formed at the output of the bottom operation **G** with the probability $p_2 = 2^{-6}$.
- Difference $\Delta^{R}_{2|i',j}$ is reset to zero when passing the lower controlled permutations block with the probability $p_4^{(i',j)}$.

Computation of probabilities $p_3^{(i,j')}$ and $p_4^{(i',j)}$ requires consideration of the extension block structure and the topology of controlled permutations block. The obtained data are presented in Table 5.44.

TABLE 5.44 Probabilities of Elementary Events of the Case A1

i	p_1	p_2	$p_3^{(i,j')}$	p_4	$P^{(i)}$	p'
$i = i^* \in \{1,\ldots,5,10,\ldots,14,$ $20,21,22,23,29,\ldots,32$	2^{-6}	2^{-6}	2^{-13}	2^{-3}	2^{-28}	2^{-6}
$\forall i \neq i^*$	2^{-6}	2^{-6}	0	2^{-3}	0	2^{-6}

The probability of event A1, in the case if the active bit of the left subblock belongs to position i, is designated as $P^{(i)} = p_1 p_2 p_3^{(i,j')} p_4$. Accounting for the dependency of the probability $P^{(i)}$ on the value i, the contribution of event A1 into the probability of two-round characteristic can be written as follows:

$$P' = p' \sum_{i=1}^{i=64} P^{(i)} = p' p_1 \, p_2 p_4 \sum_{i=1}^{i=64} p_3^{(i,j')} \approx 1.125 \cdot 2^{-30},$$

where $p_2 = 2^{-6}$ is the probability of the event in case of which the active bit of the difference falls into position i after the first round. Events A1 and A2 are symmetric. Computation of the contribution of the second event into the probability of two-round characteristic $P'' = 1.125 \approx 2^{-30}$ is carried out in a similar way. Thus, the probability of the two-round characteristic takes the following value:

$$P(2) \approx P' + P'' \approx 1.125 \cdot 2^{-29}.$$

Probability of the event when differences with one active bit pass the complete number of rounds is equal to $P(12) = P^6(2) \approx 2^{-173}$. For 10 rounds of the COBRA-H128 cipher, the result will be as follows: $P(10) = P^5(2) \approx 2^{-144}$. Accounting that for a random transformation 1-bit difference $(0, \Delta_1^R)$ is formed at the output with the probability $P = 64 \cdot 2^{-128} = 2^{-122} > P(10) > P(12)$, it is possible to conclude that COBRA-H128 is strong against the attack under consideration, because in relation to this attack, the cipher is not distinguishable from a random transformation.

The use of switched operation $\Pi^{(e)}$ eliminates weak and semi-weak keys. This makes the use of simple key schedule more secure. Employing different values of parameter e in different rounds of encryption (and decryption) ensures elimination of periodicity and protection against slide attacks in the case when the same round keys are used in all rounds; consequently, the protection is also ensured for the case of secret keys having the structure like $K = (X, X, \ldots, X)$.

SUMMARY

To conclude, consider comparative characteristics of the cryptographic strength of the ciphers discussed here against differential cryptanalysis. These characteristics are outlined in Table 5.45.

TABLE 5.45 Comparison of Cryptographic Strength of the Various Fast Ciphers Against Differential Cryptanalysis

Cipher	*r*	Characteristic Value		*P(r)**
		Difference	**Probability**	
COBRA-H64	10	$(0, \Delta_1^R)$	$P(2) \approx 1.13 \times 2^{-19}$	2^{-75}
COBRA-H64	8	$(0, \Delta_1^R)$	$P(2) \approx 1.13 \times 2^{-19}$	2^{-94}
COBRA-H128	12	$(0, \Delta_1^R)$	$P(2) \approx 1.125 \times 2^{-29}$	2^{-173}
COBRA-H128	10	$(0, \Delta_1^R)$	$P(2) \approx 1.125 \times 2^{-29}$	2^{-144}
DDP-64	10	$(\Delta_1^L, 0)$	$P(2) \approx 1.37 \times 2^{-17}$	1.2×2^{-83}
DDP-64	8	$(\Delta_1^L, 0)$	$P(2) \approx 2^{-32}$	1.7×2^{-67}

*The contribution of the characteristic parameter into the probability after passing through r rounds.

Recommended Reading

PROBLEMS OF CONTEMPORARY CRYPTOGRAPHY

Shannon, C. E., "Communication Theory of Secrecy Systems." Bell Systems Technical Journal, vol. 28, 1949, pp. 656–715.

Diffie W., and M. E. Hellman, "New Directions in Cryptography." IEEE Transactions on Information Theory, 1976, vol. IT-22. pp. 644–654.

Rabin, M. O., "Digitalized Signatures and Public Key Functions as Intractable as Factorization." Technical Report MIT/LCS/TR-212, Mit Laboratory for Computer Science, 1979.

Fiat A., and A. Shamir, "How To Prove Yourself: Practical Solutions to Identification and Signature Problems." Advances in Cryptology—CRYPTO'86, Springer-Verlag, 1987, vol. 263, pp. 186–194.

Elgamal, T., A Public Key Cryptosystem and a Signature Scheme Based on Discrete Logarithms." IEEE Transactions on Information Theory, 1985, vol. IT-31, No. 4, pp. 469–472.

Schnorr, C. P., "Efficient Signature Generation by Smart Cards." J. Cryptology, 1991, vol. 4., pp. 161–174.

Schnorr, C. P., "Efficient Identification and Signatures for Smart Cards." Advances in Cryptology—CRYPTO'89, Springer-Verlag, 1990, vol. 435, pp. 239–252.

Chaum, D., "Blind Signatures for Untraceable Payments." Advances in Cryptology: Proc. of CRYPTO'82, Plenum Press, 1983, pp. 199–203.

Chaum, D., "Security Without Identification: Transaction Systems to Make Big Brother Obsolete." Communication of the ACM, 1985, vol. 28, No. 10., pp. 1030–1044.

Wenbo, Mao, *Modern Cryptography. Theory and Practice.* Prentice Hall PTR, New Jersey, 2004.

Pieprzyk, J., T. Hardjono, and J. Seberry, *Fundamentals of Computer Security.* Springer-Verlag. Berlin, 2003.

Menezes, A. J., and S. A. Vanstone, *Handbook of Applied Cryptography*. CRC Press, 1996.

Schneier, B., *Applied Cryptography: Protocols, Algorithms, and Source Code* (Second Edition). New York: John Wiley & Sons, 1996.

PERMUTATIONS NETWORKS AND CIPHERS ON THEIR BASIS

Benes, V. E., "Algebraic and Topological Properties of Connecting Networks." Bell Systems Technical Journal, 1962, vol. 41, pp. 1249–1274.

Benes, V. E., *Mathematical Theory of Connecting Networks and Telephone Traffic*. New York: Academic Press, 1965.

Waksman, A., "A Permutation Network." Journal of the ACM. 1968, vol. 15, No. 1, pp. 159–163.

Parker, S., "Notes on Shuffle/Exchange-Type Switching Networks." IEEE Transactions on Computers, 1980, vol. C-29, No. 5, pp. 213–222.

Portz, M. A., "Generalized Description of DES-Based and Benes-Based Permutation Generators." Advanced in Cryptology–AUSCRYPT'92 // Lecture Notes in Computer Science, Springer-Verlag, 1992, vol. 718, pp. 397–409.

Van Rompay, B., L. Knudsen, and V. Rijmen, "Differential Cryptanalysis of the ICE Encryption Algorithm." Proceedings of the 6th International Workshop, Fast Software Encryption—Fse'98, LNCS, Springer-Verlag, vol. 1372, 1998, pp. 270–283.

Rivest, R. L., "The RC5 Encryption Algorithm." 2nd Int. Workshop "Fast Software Encryption," Proc./Springer-Verlag LNCS, 1995, vol. 1008, pp. 86–96.

Rivest, R. L., M. J. B. Robshaw, R. Sidney, and Y. L. Yin, "The RC6 Block Cipher." Proc. of 1st Advanced Encryption Standard Candidate Conference, Ventura, CA, August 20–22, 1998, (*http://www.nist.gov/aes*).

Moldovyan, A. A., and N. A. Moldovyan, "A Cipher Based on Data-Dependent Permutations." Journal of Cryptology, 2002, vol. 15, pp. 61–72.

Moldovyan, A. A., "Fast Block Ciphers Based on Controlled Permutations." Computer Science Journal of Moldova, 2000, vol. 8, No. 3, pp. 270–283.

Goots, N. D., A. A. Moldovyan, and N. A. Moldovyan, "Fast Encryption Algorithm Spectr-H64." Proceedings of the International Workshop, Methods, Models, and Architectures for Network Security/LNCS, Springer-Verlag, 2001, vol. 2052, pp. 275–286.

Moldovyan, N. A., A. A. Moldovyan, and N. D. Goots, "Variable Bit Permutations: Linear Characteristics and Pure VBP-Based Cipher." Computer Science Journal of Moldova, 2005, vol. 13, No. 1(37), pp. 84–109.

Izotov, B. V., N. D. Goots, A. A. Moldovyan, and N. A. Moldovyan, "Fast Ciphers For Cheap Hardware: Differential Analysis of SPECTR-H64." Proceedings of the International Workshop, Methods, Models, and Architectures for Network Security (MMM-ANCS'03). LNCS, Springer-Verlag, vol. 2776, 2003, pp. 449–452.

Lee, Changhoon, Deukjo Hong, Sungjae Lee, Sanjin Lee, Hyungjin Yang, and Jongin Lim, "A Chosen Plaintext Linear Attack on Block Cipher CIKS-1." Springer-Verlag LNCS, vol. 2513, pp. 456–468.

Izotov, B., A. Moldovyan, and N. Moldovyan, "Controlled Operations as a Cryptographic Primitive." Proceedings of the International Workshop, Methods, Models, and Architectures for Network Security, Lecture Notes in Computer Science, Berlin: Springer-Verlag, vol. 2052. 2001, pp. 230–241.

Ko, Y., D. Hong, S. Hong, S. Lee, and J. Lim, "Linear Cryptanalysis on SPECTR-H64 With Higher Order Differential Property." Proceedings of the International Workshop, Methods, Models, and Architectures for Network Security, Lecture Notes in Computer Science, Springer-Verlag, Berlin: 2003, vol. 2776, pp. 298–307.

Moldovyan N. A., "Fast DDP-Based Ciphers: Design and Differential Analysis of Cobra-H64." Computer Science Journal of Moldova, 2003, vol. 11, No. 3 (33), pp. 292–315.

SUBSTITUTION-PERMUTATIONS NETWORKS AND CIPHERS ON THEIR BASIS

Kam, J. B., and G. I. Davida, "Structured Design of Substitution-Permutation Encryption Networks." IEEE Transactions on Computers, 1979. vol. 28, No. 10, pp. 747–753.

Moldovyan, N. A., A. A. Moldovyan, and M. A. Eremeev, "A Class of Data-Dependent Operations." Int. Journal of Network Security, 2006, vol. 2, No 3, pp. 187–204 (*http://isrc.nchu.edu.tw/ijns/*).

Moldovyan, N. A, A. A. Moldovyan, M. A. Eremeev, and N. Sklavos, "New Class of Cryptographic Primitives and Cipher Design for Networks Security." Int. Journal of Network Security, 2006, vol. 2, No. 2, pp. 114–125 (*http://isrc.nchu.edu.tw/ijns/*).

Moldovyan, N. A., A. A. Moldovyan, M. A. Eremeev, and D. H. Summerville, "Wireless Networks Security and Cipher Design Based on Data-Dependent Operations: Classification of the FPGA Suitable Controlled Elements." Int. Conf. on Computing, Communications and Control Technologies, August 14–17, 2004, Austin, TX, CCCT2004 Proc., vol. vii, pp. 123–128.

Moldovyan, N. A., N. Sklavos, A. A. Moldovyan, and O. Koufopavlou, "CHESS-64, A Block Cipher Based On Data-Dependent Operations: Design Variants and Hardware Implementation Efficiency." Asian Journal of Information Technology, 2005, No. 4(4), pp. 323–334.

Moldovyan, A. A., N. A. Moldovyan, and N. Sklavos, "Minimum Size Primitives For Efficient VLSI Implementation of DDO-Based Ciphers." Proceedings of the 12th IEEE Mediterranean Electrotechnical Conference–Melecon 2004, May 12–15, Dubrovnik, Croat.

Moldovyan, N. A., M.A. Eremeev, N. Sklavos, and A. Kristiansen, "Encryption Hardware Optimization Via Designing New Primitives." Int. Conference on Computing, Communications and Control Technologies, August 14–17, 2004, Austin, TX, CCCT2004 Proc., vol. vi, pp. 464–469.

Moldovyan, N. A., M.A. Eremeev Sklavos, and O. Koufopavlou, "New Class of the FPGA Efficient Cryptographic Primitives." Proceedings of the ISCAS, 2004.

BIT PERMUTATION INSTRUCTION

Moldovyan, N. A., N. D. Goots, P. A. Moldovyan, and D. H. Summerville, "Fast DDP-Based Ciphers: From Hardware to Software." Proceedings of the 46th IEEE Midwest Symposium on Circuits and Systems, Cairo, Egypt, December 27–30, 2003.

Shi, Z. J., and R. B. Lee, "Bit Permutation Instructions for Fast Software Cryptography." Proceedings of the IEEE International Conference on Application-pecific Systems, Architecture and Processors, Boston, MA, July 10–12, 2000, p. 138–148.

Lee, R. B., Z. J. Shi, and X. Yang, "Efficient Permutation Instructions for Fast Software Cryptography." *IEEE Micro*, 2001, vol. 21 (6), pp. 56–69.

Lee, R. B., Z. J. Shi, R. L. Rivest, and M. J. B. Robshaw, "On Permutation Operations in Cipher Design." Proceedings of the International Conference on Information Technology: Coding and Computing (ITCC'04), Las Vegas, NV, April 5–7, 2004, vol. 2, pp. 569–579.

SOFTWARE CIPHERS

Moldovyan, A. A., and N. A. Moldovyan, "Fast Software Encryption Systems for Secure and Private Communication." 12th International Conf. on Computer Communication. Seoul, Korea, August 21–24, 1995, Proceedings, vol. 1, pp. 415–420.

Moldovyan, A. A., and N. A. Moldovyan, "Software Encryption Algorithms for Transparent Protection Technology." Cryptologia, January 1998, vol. xxii, No. 1, pp. 56–68.

Moldovyan, A. A., N. A. Moldovyan, and B. Ya Sovetov, "Software-Oriented Ciphers for Computer Communication Protection." Int. Conf. Applications of Computer Systems, ACS'97 Proceedings, November 13–14, 1997, Szczecin, Poland, pp. 443–450.

Moldovyan, N. A. "Provably Indeterminate 128-Bit Cipher," Computer Science Journal of Moldova, 1997, vol. 5, No. 2(14), pp. 185–197.

Eremeev, M. A., V. I. Korjik, N. A Moldovyan, and A. Mukherjii, "Fault-Based Analysis of Flexible Ciphers." Computer Science Journal of Moldova, 2002, V. 10, No. 29, pp. 46–52.

HARDWARE IMPLEMENTATION OF BLOCK CIPHERS

Sklavos, N. and O. Koufopavlou, "Architectures and VLSI Implementations of the AES-Proposal Rijndael." IEEE Transactions on Computers, vol. 51, Issue 12, 2002, pp. 1454–1459.

Sklavos, N. and O. Koufopavlou, "Architectures and FPGA Implementations of the SCO (-1,-2,-3) Ciphers Family." Proceedings of the 12th International Conference on Very Large Scale Integration, (IFIP VLSI SOC '03), Darmstadt, Germany, December 1–3, 2003.

Sklavos, N., N. A. Moldovyan, and O. Koufopavlou, "Pure DDP-Base Cipher: Architecture Analysis, Hardware Implementation Cost and Performance Up to 6.5 Gbps." International Arab Journal of Information Technology, 2005, vol. 2, No. 1, January 2005, pp. 24–32.

Sklavos, N., A. A. Moldovyan, and O. Koufopavlou, "Encryption and Data Dependent Permutations: Implementation Cost and Performance Evaluation Workshop MMM-ANCS'2003 Proc." LNCS, Springer-Verlag, Berlin, 2003, vol. 2776, pp. 343–354.

Sklavos, N., A. A. Moldovyan, and O. Koufopavlou, "High Speed Networking Security: Design and Implementation of Two New DDP-Based Ciphers." Mobile Networks and Applications, Special Issue on Algorithmic Solutions for Wireless, Mobile, Ad Hoc and Sensor Networks, MONET Journal, Kluwer, 2004.

Elbirt, A. J., W. Yip, B. Ghetwynd, and C. Paar (2000), "An FPGA Implementation and Performance Evaluation of the AES Block Cipher Candidate Algorithm Finalists." 3rd Advanced Encryption Standard Conference Proceedings. April 13–14, 2000. New York, NY, (*http://www.nist.gov/aes*).

Cheung, O. Y. H, K. H. Tsoi, P. H. W. Leong, and M. P. Leong, "Tradeoffs in Parallel and Serial Implementations of The International Data Encryption Algorithm." Proceedings of CHES 2001, LNCS 2162, pp. 333–337, Springer-Verlag, 2001.

Chitu, C., and M. Glesner, "An FPGA Implementation of the AES-Rijndael in OCB/ECB Modes of Operation." Microelectronics Journal, Elsevier Science, vol. 36, pp. 139–146, 2005.

Rudra Atri , Pradeep K. Dubey, Charanjit S. Jutla, Vijay Rumar, Josyula R. Rao, and Pankaj Rohatgi, "Efficient Rijndael Encryption Implementation with Composite Field Arithmetic." Proceedings of the 3rd International Workshop Cryptographic Hardware and Embedded Systems—CHES 2001, Lecture Notes in Computer Science, Springer-Verlag LCNS 2162, pp. 171–180, 2001.

Albirt, A. J., W. Yip, B. Ghetwynd, and C. Paar, "FPGA Implementation and Performance Evaluation of the AES Block Cipher Candidate Algorithm Finalists." 3rd Advanced Encryption Standard Conference Proceedings. April 13–14, 2000. New York, NY, (*http://www.nist.gov/aes*).

Preneel, B., Et Al., "Performance of Optimized Implementations of the Nessie Primitives." Project IST-1999-12324, 2003, (See p. 36; *http://www.cryptonessie.org*).

Index